Inside Social Life

Readings in Sociological Psychology and Microsociology

Seventh Edition

Spencer E. Cahill
University of South Florida

Kent Sandstrom
North Dakota State University

Carissa Froyum
University of Northern Iowa

New York Oxford
OXFORD UNIVERSITY PRESS

Oxford University Press is a department of the University of Oxford.
It furthers the University's objective of excellence in research,
scholarship, and education by publishing worldwide.

Oxford New York
Auckland Cape Town Dar es Salaam Hong Kong Karachi
Kuala Lumpur Madrid Melbourne Mexico City Nairobi
New Delhi Shanghai Taipei Toronto

With offices in
Argentina Austria Brazil Chile Czech Republic France Greece
Guatemala Hungary Italy Japan Poland Portugal Singapore
South Korea Switzerland Thailand Turkey Ukraine Vietnam

For titles covered by Section 112 of the US Higher Education Opportunity Act, please visit www.oup.com/us/he for the latest information about pricing and alternate formats.

Published by Oxford University Press
198 Madison Avenue, New York, New York 10016
http://www.oup.com

ISBN 978-0-19-997811-3

Printing number: 9 8 7 6 5 4 3 2 1

Printed in the United States of America
on acid-free paper

CONTENTS

*Denotes chapters and introductions new to the Seventh Edition.

INTRODUCTION

Sociology examines a broad and diverse range of topics. Sociologists study everything from the operation of the global social system to how people manage emotions and identities in their everyday interactions. Given this topical range, many sociologists draw a distinction between macrosociology, or the study of broad patterns of social life, and microsociology.

Macrosociological studies provide a kind of aerial view of social life. They enable us to identify the distinguishing features of the social landscape. Yet, to understand the actual social processes responsible for such patterns of social life, we need to get closer to the ground—to the actual places where everyday social life is lived.

The study of everyday social processes and interactions falls within the purview of microsociology. Microsociology focuses on the daily details of how people create and sustain the social worlds they inhabit. These social worlds include preschools, classrooms, neighborhoods, hospitals, street corners, and Facebook sites. Microsociologists go to such places to observe and sometimes participate in the activities that occur there so that they can identify the social patterns that characterize them. Microsociologists also interview participants in depth to learn about the meanings that guide their conduct. Some even examine conversations in detail to investigate how particular social identities and situations are talked into being. In doing so, microsociologists strive to understand the processes that serve to produce and reproduce the social relationships, organizations, and systems that macrosociology studies in the abstract.

Many sociologists do not stop there but also look inside the hearts and minds of individuals who inhabit different social worlds. They examine relationships between people's social and subjective experience—their thoughts, feelings, and private views of themselves. Sociologists share this field of study with psychologists, and it is commonly referred to as *social psychology*. However, sociologists and psychologists generally approach the study of interrelations between social life and individuals' inner lives from different directions. Psychologists tend to look for the operation of universal principles of human psychology in social life, while sociologists consider the social variability of subjective experience to be more significant and informative. This difference in emphasis has led to the cumbersome expressions *sociological social psychology* and *psychological social psychology.* But there is a more economical way of distinguishing between these two approaches. Psychologists can retain the title of *social psychology* if sociologists claim the title of *sociological psychology* as their own. This latter expression clearly refers to a psychology based on a distinctively sociological understanding of the human condition in all of its varied forms.

The concerns of microsociology and sociological psychology are not unrelated to those of macrosociology. Both types of study are essential for a comprehensive understanding of human social life. Although we, as individuals and groups, produce and reproduce the social worlds that we inhabit, we do not do so under conditions of our own choosing. Recurring patterns of interaction result in relatively stable features or structures of social life. For example, we routinely place one another into different gender, ethnic, age, and other categories, treating one another differently based on such identifications. Organized patterns of social life result in unequal distributions of resources and power among us. These distributions influence where we live and with whom we are likely to interact. Such social divisions and hierarchies or social structures influence interaction in ways that tend to lead to their perpetuation. As previously suggested, microsociology examines how we interactionally produce and reproduce the social divisions, organizations, institutions, and systems that macrosociology studies in the abstract. Microsociology and sociological psychology also address how social structures influence our social lives and subjective experiences differently. They thereby complement macrosociology and bring alive the study of human social life.

The readings collected in this volume provide an introduction to sociological psychology and microsociology. College students are often introduced to these fields of study in courses with titles such as Social Psychology or The Individual and Society. This volume is intended for them and for other readers who are interested in the inner workings of social life and how each of us influences and is influenced by it. The volume includes both statements of theoretical positions and empirical studies that draw and elaborate upon those positions.

Some of the selections included herein are classics of sociological psychology and microsociology. Others are more recent and have yet to weather the test of time. The combination of classic and more current readings is intended to give readers a sense of the intellectual roots of sociological psychology and microsociology, as well as their continuing vitality. The selections can be read in any order, although we have tried to arrange them so that they build on the ideas and empirical findings that have preceded each. In whatever order the articles may be read, our hope is that they convey an appreciation of the intricate artfulness of daily social action and the fascinating variety of human social experience.

Microsociologists have long maintained that language is central to the social shaping of human experiences, so we would like to add a note about some of the language in this anthology. Because a few of the selections were published many years ago, they use the masculine generic and contain other references to gender that may seem insensitive to the contemporary reader. Rather than change that language, we have left most of it intact in part because there is a microsociological lesson in our reactions to such gender usage. It indicates just how much our thinking about gender has socially changed since those selections were written. Other language in this volume may offend ethnic and racial sensibilities. This language is found in empirical studies that report, as accurately as possible, what was actually observed, including the language that was actually used. If we are to understand human social life, it is essential that we confront such everyday language, however uncomfortable it may make us.

NEW TO THIS EDITION

This Seventh Edition of *Inside Social Life* is much changed from the Sixth Edition. We have included ten new selections that have not been used in previous editions. These selections address such topics as the following:

- The emotion norms that shape the experience and expression of romantic love among adolescent girls
- The emotion work engaged in by Mixed Martial Arts fighters, especially to provoke fear, manage anxiety, and display their sense of "manhood"
- The bodily labor and discipline expected of fashion models
- The staging of the self in everyday life
- Online presentations of self, particularly in the virtual social world known as Second Life
- The dramaturgical teamwork and rituals performed by young heterosexual men as they take part in "girl hunts"
- Young women's negotiation and enactment of "the code of the street" in urban neighborhoods
- Mobile home residents' use of stigma management strategies that salvage a sense of personal decency but perpetuate class inequalities
- The norms and practices that reinforce racial hierarchies in an organization designed to serve black youth
- The strategies that conservative Christian women use to justify divorce and sustain their Christian identity
- The process through which disruptions become defined as serious family "troubles" that warrant medical or therapeutic intervention

We have also added two other new features to the Seventh Edition. *Inside Social Life* now includes extended introductions to each of its nine parts. These introductions identify the core themes, concepts, and insights that characterize the group of selections found in each part of the book. Along with making this change in the Seventh Edition, we have added almost 200 sets of reflective questions for students to consider. Four or more of these sets of questions are included at the end of each selection. We have designed the reflective questions to help students identify the key ideas addressed in specific readings and to think about how these ideas could be applied to understand other arenas of social life.

This volume is clearly not a product of the editors' efforts alone. We were greatly aided in this revision by the comments and evaluations shared by colleagues and by instructors who have used previous editions. We are most grateful to the following reviewers for their thoughtful and constructive comments on the Sixth Edition:

William Marsiglio, University of Florida
Elaine McDuff, Truman State University
Emily McKendry-Smith, University of North Carolina at Chapel Hill
Ryan A. Wilke, Florida State University
Robert Wonser, Moorpark College
Alison Alkon, University of the Pacific
Elfriede Wedam, Loyola University Chicago

We would also like to thank Vicki Kessler, Donilee Loseke, Sherith Pankratz, and Adam Roisse for the support and encouragement they have provided in completing the current edition of this volume. In this edition, we have again tried to emulate the passion, curiosity, and insight that characterized the work of Spencer Cahill, who died in 2006. We have also tried to be guided by Spencer's uniquely perceptive sociological eye.

USES OF THE SELECTIONS

Inside Social Life can be used effectively as a single assigned text. However, for instructors who wish to use this anthology to supplement another text, the following chart may be helpful. It groups the chapters in this volume by topics conventionally used to organize courses in social psychology and microsociology. Primary and secondary emphases are listed separately. (Parentheses indicate an alternative primary use for a chapter.)

Topic	Primary Emphasis	Secondary Emphasis
Cognition and Perception	2, 3, 4, 6, (5)	7, 17, 24, 42
Emotions	7, 8, 9, 10, 20, (27), (31), (32), (35)	5, 19, 38, 40
Bodies and Embodiment	11, 12, 13, 14, 15	6, 9, 10, 24, 26, (27)
Self and Identity	16, 17, 18, 20, 22, 23, 24, 25, 40, (19)	11, 33, 34, 38
Socialization	11, 41, (8), (10), (13), (14), (19)	16, 17, 30, 33
Social Interaction	21, 25, 26, 27, 28	22, 23, 24, 33, 35
Power, Inequality, and Social Reproduction	18, 27, 33, 34, 35, 36, 37, (13)	11, 14, 39, 40, 41, (19), (22)
Culture	4, 5, (7), (8)	6, 15, (2), (3), (28), (29)
Social Structures and Institutions	29, 30, 31, 32	10, 11, 28, 35, 37, (38)
Gender	8, 9, 11, 12, 22, 33, 37, (36)	10, 13, 14
Class and Ethnicity	18, 27, 30, 34, 35, (37), (40)	13, 14
Deviance and Social Control	38, 39, 40, (10)	6, 13, 27, 30, 34, 36, 41, (31)
Social Problems and Identity Politics	1, 36, 41, (38), (40)	10, 19, 28, (14), (27)
Social Change	1, 5, 20, 42	40, 41, (24), (32), (39)

ABOUT THE CONTRIBUTORS

Patricia Adler is Professor of Sociology at the University of Colorado. She is the author of *Wheeling and Dealing* (1985) and coauthor (with Peter Adler) of *Paradise Laborers* (2004) and *The Tender Cut* (2011).

Peter Adler is Professor of Sociology at the University of Denver. He is the coauthor (with Patricia Adler) of *Backboards and Blackboards* (1991), *Paradise Laborers* (2004), and *The Tender Cut* (2011).

Arnold Arluke is Professor of Sociology at New York University. He is a coauthor of the award-winning *Regarding Animals* (1996) and author of *Just a Dog* (2006) and *Beauty and the Beast* (2010).

Peter Berger is Professor of Sociology and Theology at Boston University. His many authored and coauthored books include *An Invitation to Sociology* (1963), *The Sacred Canopy* (1963), and *Modernity, Pluralism, and the Crises of Meaning* (1995).

Herbert Blumer (1900–1987) was a prominent advocate for the sociological perspective of symbolic interactionism and Professor of Sociology at the University of California, Berkeley. Among his many articles and books, the most widely read is *Symbolic Interactionism: Perspective and Method* (1969).

Spencer E. Cahill (1949–2006) was Professor of Sociology at the University of South Florida and editor of the first five editions of this volume. He was also the author of *Children and Society* (2006) and co-editor of *The Praeger Handbook of American High Schools* (2006). In addition to publishing these books and dozens of journal articles, Dr. Cahill served as editor of *Social Psychology Quarterly,* as co-editor of the *Journal of Contemporary Ethnography,* and as a leader in the Society for the Study of Symbolic Interaction.

Daniel Chambliss is the Eugene M. Tobin Distinguished Professor of Sociology at Hamilton College in New York. He is the author of *Beyond Caring: Hospitals, Nurses and the Social Organization of Ethics* (1996), which won the Eliot Freidson Prize in 1998 for the best book in medical sociology from the American Sociological Association. He is also the author of *Champions: The Making of Olympic Swimmers* (1988).

Charles Horton Cooley (1864–1929), an economist turned sociologist, had a long teaching career at the University of Michigan. His major works are *Human Nature and Social Order* (1902), *Social Organization* (1909), and *Social Process* (1919).

Amanda Czerniawski is an Assistant Professor of Sociology at Temple University. Her current research focuses on the body as a site of disembodied feminist protest by examining popular discourse over reproductive rights, sexuality, and gendered violence.

Donna Eder is Professor of Sociology at Indiana University. She is the author of *School Talk: Gender and Adolescent Culture*, which examines middle-school peer cultures and how they maintain and resist gender stereotypes. Her current research involves in-depth interviews with storytellers from different cultures to better understand the role of storytelling in teaching about social differences and social dynamics.

Joe R. Feagin is the Ella C. McFadden Professor of Liberal Arts at Texas A&M University. He is the author and coauthor of many books, including *White Racism* (1995), *Double Burden* (1998), and *Black and Blue* (2004).

Jessica Fields is an Associate Professor of Sociology at San Francisco State University. She is the author of *Risky Lessons: Sex Education and Social Inequality* (2008), which received the Distinguished Contribution to Scholarship Book Award from the American Sociological Association.

Ara A. Francis is an Assistant Professor of Sociology at College of the Holy Cross. Guided by her interests in deviance and disorganization in everyday life, she studies how people manage and make sense of troubling life circumstances.

Carissa Froyum is an Associate Professor of Sociology at the University of Northern Iowa and co-editor of this volume. Her research examines the reproduction of inequalities through emotion and identity work at programs for low-income black youth. Her work appears in *Ethnic and Racial Studies*, *Qualitative Sociology*, *Sexualities*, and *Culture, Health & Sexuality*.

Patricia Gagné is an Associate Professor of Sociology at the University of Louisville. She is the author of *Battered Women's Justice* (1998) and coauthor of *Social Problems* (2001).

Kenneth J. Gergen is Professor of Psychology at Swarthmore College. He is the author of several books, including *The Saturated Self* (1991) and *An Invitation to Social Construction* (1999).

Erving Goffman (1922–1982) was the Benjamin Franklin Professor of Anthropology and Sociology at the University of Pennsylvania and president of the American Sociological Association at the time of his death. His many highly influential books include *The Presentation of Self in Everyday Life* (1959), *Asylums* (1961), *Relations in Public* (1971), and *Frame Analysis* (1974).

Simon Gottschalk is Professor of Sociology at the University of Nevada, Las Vegas. He is the coauthor of *Authenticity in Culture, Self, and Society* (2009). He also served as the editor of *Symbolic Interaction* from 2003 to 2007.

David Grazian is an Associate Professor of Sociology at the University of Pennsylvania. He is the author of *Blue Chicago: The Search for Authenticity in Urban Blues Clubs* (2003), *On the Make: The Hustle of Urban Nightlife* (2008), and *Mix It Up: Popular Culture, Mass Media, and Society* (2010).

Arlie Russell Hochschild is Professor of Sociology at the University of California, Berkeley. She is the author of *The Second Shift* (1989), *The Time Bind* (1997), and *The Commercialization of Intimate Life* (2003).

Nikki Jones is an Associate Professor of Sociology at the University of California, Santa Barbara. She is the author of *Between Good and Ghetto: African American Girls and Inner-City Violence* (2010). She is also a co-editor of *Fighting for Girls: New Perspectives on Gender and Violence* (2010) and *Sociologists Backstage* (2011).

Margarethe Kusenbach is an Associate Professor and Graduate Director in the Department of Sociology at the University of South Florida. Her research interests include urban and community sociology, emotions, and qualitative methods, and she has published numerous articles and book chapters in these areas. She is working on a monograph based on her study of mobile home communities in Florida, and she is editing a book on issues of home and belonging.

Robert Jay Lifton is Distinguished Professor of Psychiatry and psychology at the John Jay College of the City University of New York. He is the author of several books, including *The Broken Connection* (1979), *The Nazi Doctors* (1986), and *Superpower Syndrome* (2003).

Thomas Luckmann was Professor of Sociology at the University of Konstanz in Germany. Since 1994 he has been professor emeritus, and he lectures internationally. He is a coauthor of *The Social Construction of Reality* (1966) and *The Structures of the Life-World* (1974).

Daniel D. Martin is an Associate Professor of Sociology at the University of Minnesota, Duluth. He is a coauthor of *Symbols, Selves, and Social Reality* (2010).

Karin A. Martin is an Associate Professor of Sociology at the University of Michigan. She is the author of *Puberty, Sexuality, and the Self: Boys and Girls at Adolescence* (1996).

Amir Marvasti is an Associate Professor of Sociology at Pennsylvania State University, Altoona. He is the author of *Being Homeless: Textual and Narrative Constructions* (2003), *Middle Eastern Lives in America* (2004), and *Doing Qualitative Research* (2008).

Janice McCabe is an Assistant Professor of Sociology at Dartmouth. She studies gender, race/ethnicity, sexuality, education, and childhood. Her current projects include investigations of inequalities in college culture, same-sex behavior during young adulthood, and media representations of children.

George Herbert Mead (1863–1931) profoundly influenced early generations of American sociologists while he was Professor of Philosophy at the University of Chicago. His published lectures and other work provided the basis for a distinctively sociological psychology and include *Mind, Self and Society* (1934) and *The Philosophy of the Act* (1938).

Angela Orend is an adjunct lecturer in sociology at the University of Louisville. She teaches classes in theory, diversity, inequality, social problems, and the sociology of families. Her research focuses on issues of commodificaton with respect to the body and popular culture.

Mark R. Pogrebrin is Professor and Director of Criminal Justice at the University of Colorado, Denver. He is the coauthor of *The Invisible Justice System* (1982) and *Guns, Violence, and Criminal Behavior* (2009).

Kent Sandstrom is Professor of Sociology and Dean of the College of Arts, Humanities, and Social Sciences at North Dakota State University. He is the co-editor of this volume and the coauthor of *Knowing Children* (1988) and *Symbols, Selves, and Social Reality* (2013). He is also the co-editor of the *Journal of Contemporary Ethnography.*

Douglas Schrock is an Associate Professor of Sociology at Florida State University. His recent publications have focused on how emotion, identity, narrative, and the body are implicated in gender construction and the reproduction of inequalities.

Michael Schwalbe is Professor of Sociology at North Carolina State University. He is the author of *Rigging the Game* (2007), *The Sociologically Examined Life* (2007), and *Remembering Reet and Shine* (2004).

Barry Schwartz is Professor Emeritus of Sociology at the University of Georgia. His books include *Vertical Classification* (1981), *Abraham Lincoln and the Forge of National Memory* (2000), and *Abraham Lincoln in the Post-Heroic Era* (2008).

Shane Sharp is an Assistant Professor of Sociology at Northern Illinois University. He investigates religious phenomena through the lens of social psychological theory. His work has appeared in *Social Problems*, *Social Forces*, *Social Psychology Quarterly*, and the *Journal for the Scientific Study of Religion.*

Robin W. Simon is Professor of Sociology at Florida State University. She is the author of several articles that examine gender and other status variations in the experience and expression of emotion.

Paul B. Stretesky is an Associate Professor of Sociology at Colorado State University. He is the coauthor of *Environmental Law, Crime, and Justice* (2008).

Barrie Thorne is Professor of Sociology and Women's Studies at the University of California, Berkeley. She is a coauthor of *She Said/He Said* (1976) and the author of *Gender Play* (1993).

Chauntelle Anne Tibbals holds a Visiting Scholar position at the University of Southern California.

Christian Vaccaro is an Assistant Professor and Research Associate at MARTI (Mid-Atlantic Addiction Research and Training Institute). He is a symbolic interactionist interested in the study of gender, emotions, identity, and embodiment.

Debra Van Ausdale is Professor of Sociology at Syracuse University and the coauthor of *The First R* (2000).

Phillip Vannini is Professor in the School of Communications and Culture at Royal Roads University and the Canada Research Chair in Innovative Learning and Public Ethnography. He is the author or coauthor of several books, including *Understanding Society through Popular Music* (2006), *Authenticity in Culture, Self, and Society* (2009), *Ferry Tales* (2011), and *The Senses in Self, Society, and Culture* (2012).

Dennis D. Waskul is Professor of Sociology at Minnesota State University, Mankato. He is the author of *Self Games and Body Play* (2003), editor of *net.seXXX: Readings on Sex, Pornography and the Internet* (2004), and coauthor of *Authenticity in Culture, Self, and Society* (2009) and *The Senses in Self, Society, and Culture* (2012).

Desiree Wiesen (now Wiesen-Martin) is a Ph.D. student at the University of New Hampshire. Her specific areas of research interest include issues pertaining to victimization, gender and crime, and women and the criminal justice system.

Amy C. Wilkins is an Assistant Professor of Sociology at the University of Colorado–Boulder. Her research on gender, race, sexuality, and emotions among young adults has been published in various articles and in *Wannabes, Goths, and Christians: The Boundaries of Sex, Styles, and Status* (2008).

Eviatar Zerubavel is Professor of Sociology at Rutgers University. He is the author of several books, including *Hidden Rhythms* (1981), *Social Mindscapes* (1997), and *Time Maps* (2003).

PART I

Human Being and Social Reality

The study and understanding of any subject must start with something—with some general ideas about that subject. The subject of sociological psychology and microsociology is human experience, in both its shared and its private forms. Thus, sociological psychology and microsociology must start with some general ideas about human nature, human experience, and social existence. The five selections in this section advance some ideas about these fundamental questions. Taken together, they provide the conceptual foundations on which a study of human social life and experience can be built. In doing so they highlight the following themes:

- *The sociological perspective provides us with a unique understanding of ourselves and the social world.* It enables us to understand how we create the realities that shape our everyday lives, how we acquire culture and connect with others, how we fashion and realize identities, how we exercise power, and how we construct and perpetuate social patterns and inequalities. Perhaps most crucially, the sociological perspective helps us to gain an in-depth understanding of how and why we think, feel, and act in the ways we do, particularly by enabling us to see how our thoughts, feelings, and actions are influenced by our social positions and relationships. Through acquiring this understanding, we can become more thoughtful and responsible members of our communities, as Michael Schwalbe points out in his discussion of "sociological mindfulness." When we are sociologically mindful, we can make more conscious choices about when, how, and why we should comply with or resist social expectations.

- *Human nature is relatively "plastic" and open-ended.* Some scholars assert that almost all human characteristics are products of genetic inheritance. Others argue that people are almost totally products of their experience. This disagreement is often described as the "nature versus nurture" debate, as if human biology and experience were easily separable. Although some scholars still embrace either biological or environmental determinism, a growing number of biological and social scientists recognize that most human characteristics result from complex interactions between biological processes and experience. Probably the most telling research in this regard is that which focuses on human neural plasticity, or how the human brain responds to its social environment and experiences.

  The authors of the selections in Part I recognize the plasticity and "world-openness" of our human biological makeup. That is, they recognize that we are not born with genetic or instinctual hard wiring that dictates how we will act in our social and physical environments. Instead, we have a relatively open-ended biological constitution characterized by highly unspecialized and undirected drives. For instance, even our drives to eat and reproduce are guided by our culture. We must learn when, where, how, and what we should eat. We must also learn when, where, how, and why we should have sex. Because of our biological openness, human nature can manifest itself in an incredibly diverse number of ways. Indeed, as Berger and Luckmann note in Selection 2, "the ways of becoming and being human are as numerous as [human] cultures." Most important, due to the plasticity of our human biological constitutions, we must learn how we fit into the world and how we should respond to the natural and social realities that make up this world. In doing so we must rely on the meanings and guidelines we acquire from the society into which we are born. In essence, then, we can learn our place in the world, and how to act in it, only through interacting with others who expose us to culture, or a widely shared system of social meanings, standards, and guidelines.

- *Reality is socially constructed and human behavior is guided by social meanings.* All of the selections in Part I advance ideas that are consistent with the arguments of Herbert Blumer, the founder of the sociological perspective known as *symbolic interactionism.* Blumer emphasized that if social scientists want to understand human behavior, they must understand how people construct and define reality. More specifically, they must consider how we define the things we encounter in our environment. These things do not have a fixed or intrinsic meaning. Rather, their meanings differ depending on how we interpret and respond to them. For example, the thing we call a "tree" will have a different meaning depending upon whether we identify it as something to chop, climb, decorate, prune, or turn into lumber. If you cut down a tree, chop it into smaller pieces, and burn it in a fireplace, it becomes "fuel." On the other hand, if you take it into your house, put it in a stand, and trim it with lights and ornaments, it becomes a holiday "decoration." A tree has different meanings depending on how we define and respond to it. In the same way, a person will mean different things to us and call out different responses depending upon whether we define him or her as a teacher, parent, lover, terrorist, or friend. The crucial factor, then, is how we name, or give meaning to, the things we encounter, because that will shape our actions toward them.

In pointing out how our behavior is directed by the meanings we give to things, Blumer also emphasized that these meanings derive from and emerge through our social interaction. Put simply, we learn what things mean through interacting with others. In this process we rely heavily on language and the shared system of symbols it provides. Guided by language and the processes of communication and role taking it facilitates, we learn how to define and act toward the objects, events, and experiences that constitute our environment. We thus learn to see and respond to symbolically mediated realities—realities that we name, such as friend, party, college, dorm, car, and football game. These realities are socially constructed. In other words, they are jointly created and sustained by us, especially as we use language and engage in ongoing conversations with others. Through these conversations, we establish a correspondence between the shared and seemingly "objective" reality of society and our subjective experience as individuals.

- *Language both constrains and enables human perceptions and actions.* On the one hand, language profoundly conditions how we see, interpret, and respond to the world, particularly by providing us with a *social lens*—a shared system of meanings and classifications—through which we organize our perceptions of reality. Guided by this lens, we learn how to shape the world into distinct islands of meaning, thereby giving order to our experiences and our relations to the environment. Yet, while language organizes our experience and thus constrains our perceptions and actions in some ways, it also provides us with a vital resource—a system of symbols—that enables us to have agency, or the capacity to act freely. Through acquiring and using symbols, we can think, remember, make plans, imagine alternatives, transcend the here and now, communicate with others, and most crucially, exercise a notable element of choice in crafting our actions.

- *The nature of social reality has changed significantly in recent years.* Some scholars argue that we live in a new and distinctly different social world—a world they describe as "postmodern." In using this term, they emphasize that we live in an era marked by unprecedented social, economic, and technological change. Western societies are characterized by the explosive growth of information technologies, the transformation of images into commodities, the emergence of increasingly diverse communities, the fragmentation of personal selves, and the crumbling of previously dominant outlooks, such as beliefs in progress or absolute truth. In addition, many of our interactions are becoming characterized by a profound change in their temporal rhythms, marked by an increasing emphasis on speed. In many respects, those of us who live in the West now find ourselves immersed in a "speed culture"—a culture that places a premium on change and accentuates the value and importance of speed. Indeed, as Simon Gottschalk observes in the fifth selection in Part I, speed has now become a central feature of Western culture. That is, speed has become a cultural milieu—"an environment and a social psychological force which fundamentally transforms what we do, how we do it, how we think and feel, and thus, what we become." Our lives have become marked by the value of speed—fast food, fast communication, fast travel, fast computers, fast changes, and sometimes even fast relationships. Through the growing impact of electronically mediated interactions, such as email, cell phones, social networking sites, and TV commercials, we have learned to regard speed as a necessity of everyday life and, in some cases, as a key ingredient of happiness.

Overall, the selections in Part I offer conceptual pillars and analytic insights that securely support sociological psychology and microsociology. They also remind us that more popular ways of thinking about human beings and social reality may not do justice to their fascinating complexity.

I

Sociological Mindfulness

MICHAEL SCHWALBE

In the late 1950s, C. Wright Mills championed the promise and virtues of what he called the sociological imagination. According to Mills, this unique form of imagination enables its possessors to grasp the intersections of history, society, and personal biography. Those who possess the sociological imagination can better understand how their thoughts, feelings, and actions are shaped by larger social and historical forces. They can also recognize how their seemingly personal troubles—unemployment, divorce, depression—are linked to larger public issues, such as economic crisis, increased mobility, the dispersion of families, and rapid social change.

In the following selection, Michael Schwalbe updates and extends some of the key points that Mills proposed when discussing the merits of the sociological imagination. In doing so Schwalbe highlights the nature and benefits of what he describes as sociological mindfulness. As noted by Schwalbe, this form of consciousness enables us to see and appreciate the unique qualities that characterize our social worlds, particularly by being attuned to the patterns, conditions, processes, and relationships that constitute it. Sociological mindfulness also enables us to realize both social and personal benefits, including the benefits of seeing how we are connected to others, how we can change social patterns and arrangements, and how we can live more just, compassionate, and rewarding lives.

In the end, Schwalbe demonstrates how and why sociological mindfulness provides us with a distinctive and especially valuable way of looking at the world. Through practicing this form of consciousness, we can gain useful insights into aspects of social life that we may have previously overlooked or taken for granted. We can also acquire a deeper understanding of who we are, how we developed into that person, how we might change in the future, and how we can better respond to the social and historical forces that are shaping our identities, interactions, and everyday lives.

Sociological mindfulness is the practice of tuning-in to how the social world works. We are all tuned-in to some extent, of course, just by being members of society. But to be truly mindful of the social world we must learn to see it for what it is. We must learn, in other words, the ideas necessary to see what makes the social world a unique phenomenon. These are ideas about *how to pay attention* to the social world. Sociological mindfulness is the practice of paying attention in these ways.

What do we see if we practice sociological mindfulness? We see, for example, how the social world is created by people; how infants become functional human beings; how we are interdependent with others; how people's behavior is a response to the conditions under which they live; how social life

Reprinted from: Michael Schwalbe, *The Sociologically Examined Life: Pieces of the Conversation,* 3rd ed., pp. 3–7.

consists of patterns within patterns; how contingencies shape our fates; how appearances are strategically crafted; how power is exercised; how inequalities are created and maintained; and how we can create valid and reliable knowledge about the social world.

A Justification for Sociological Mindfulness

Why bother to be sociologically mindful? What is the point of all this analytic thinking about social life? . . .

Mindfulness is useful because it helps us see *how* our lives are intertwined and how our words and deeds help or harm others in nonobvious ways. Being sociologically mindful is especially important for helping us see that the consequences of our words and deeds often escape our intentions.

For example, a person who tells a racist joke may intend only to be funny. Yet what this person does is to reinforce beliefs that some kinds of people are stupid, vain, immoral, or inferior. Even if no one is offended when the joke is told, in the long run people can be hurt. The sentiments expressed in the joke might decrease sensitivity to others' feelings and to their needs for help. Or it might be that the joke makes others seem unworthy of friendship, thus cutting people off from each other. The harm, in other words, can be indirect, subtle, and delayed. It doesn't matter that no harm was intended. It can happen nonetheless.

Harm can arise even when our actions seem honorable. For example, working hard at one's job is usually a good thing to do. But when people work for companies that make weapons, cigarettes, or pornography, or when they work for companies that advertise, sell, or defend such products, violence, death, disease, and misery are the ultimate results. No one may intend others to be hurt, yet that is what happens, and those who make it happen are responsible. The harm could not happen if not for their hard work.

The kind of awareness that sociological mindfulness produces can be unsettling because it sometimes forces us to see things we would prefer not to. But by failing to be mindful, we can inadvertently damage or destroy what we would like to preserve. Or we might, through short-sighted action, diminish our own and others' chances of living good lives. By helping us see beyond our intentions to the consequences of our actions, sociological mindfulness can help us avoid traps like these, though it does not make them easy to escape.

Being sociologically mindful also means paying attention to the hardships and options other people face. If we understand how others' circumstances differ from ours, we are more likely to show compassion for them and to grant them the respect they deserve as human beings. We are also less likely to condemn them unfairly for doing things we dislike. By helping us appreciate the conditions under which others act, sociological mindfulness can help decrease the amount of hatred and conflict in the world.

Being caught up in our daily concerns, we often fail to see and appreciate all of our connections to others—to those who make our clothes, grow our food, clean up our messes, pay for the schools we use, use the schools we pay for, benefit or suffer from actions by politicians we elect; look to us as examples, and so on. Sociological mindfulness helps us see these threads of social life and how they sustain and obligate us. The main benefit of this awareness is that it can make us more responsible members of a human community. That seems to be as good a reason as any for learning a new intellectual practice.

The Rarity of Sociological Mindfulness

If sociological mindfulness were common, I wouldn't need to argue for it. You would simply take it for granted that we all need to be aware of and to think carefully about how the social world works. You would probably think it strange for anyone to make a big deal about doing so. But it seems that sociological mindfulness is actually quite rare in our society.

One reason might be that sociological mindfulness doesn't seem like much fun. Who wants more rules for how to think? As soon as there are rules, then we must worry about getting it right or wrong. So we might feel like saying, "Enough with fancy intellectual schemes! I'm doing just fine with common sense, thank you. Besides, I would prefer to *live* life rather than analyze it to death." This sentiment is not unreasonable in a society where we are constantly being offered ideas of dubious merit.

Another reason that sociological mindfulness is rare might be a belief that it won't matter. Why bother thinking analytically about social life if doing so won't make a difference? Some smart and caring people withdraw from the world because they do not believe they can do anything to change it. They feel powerless, as do many people in our society. I think this is what really impedes sociological mindfulness. We tend to be mindful of things that we feel responsible for and have some control over. But if we feel powerless to change a situation, we probably won't try to analyze it deeply. We might feel lucky just to avoid trouble.

American individualism also inhibits sociological mindfulness. As Americans we learn that it is good to be self-reliant, to achieve on our own, and to look out for ourselves. Under some conditions these are helpful ideas. But they can also blind us to our interdependence with others, and keep us from seeing how our ties to others lead us to think, feel, and behave in certain ways. Ideas that lead us to think of ourselves solely as competing individuals, free to do anything we want at any time, can keep us from being mindful of the social world in which we are immersed.

It is also possible that a desire for money and status may so preoccupy us that we fail to think much about how society works or how other people experience it. Or we might fear the loss of security that can come from questioning the beliefs we grew up with. Or we might be so angry at those who abuse us that we lose all sympathy for others who are worse off. Or perhaps we prefer not to reflect on how we participate in oppressing others, because it would make us feel guilty or sad.

People resist being sociologically mindful for many reasons, but not because they are naturally selfish, competitive, or cowardly. If such feelings arise and inhibit sociological mindfulness, it is because of how people have grown up. In a less competitive society where good jobs were available for everyone, people could feel more secure and would probably be willing to spend more time reflecting on how society works. When it seems like life is a race, few people may want to stop to analyze what all the racing is about or where it is leading, lest they fall behind.

Being sociologically mindful goes against the grain in Western society. It may also go against many of the impulses that have been instilled in us as Americans. How can these resistances be overcome? With ideas, first of all, since people must think it is worthwhile to practice sociological mindfulness. I hope that the ideas I have offered so far have persuaded you, at least partly, if you needed persuading.

Here is one more idea that might nudge you toward more mindfulness: Even if you are young now, you will probably die in forty to sixty years; if you are older, you have fewer years remaining. The time will pass quickly. How do you want to use it? You could try to acquire as much wealth and fame as possible. That seems to be the main ambition for many people in our culture; there are, however, other goals for a human life. You could try to enrich the lives of others by teaching, creating art, restoring a piece of the earth, promoting health, resisting violence, or organizing for change. The question is, What kind of mark do you want to leave on the earth for having lived? If you would like to leave the earth a better place than you found it, sociological mindfulness will help you see what needs to be done.

Reflective Questions

1. What are the key characteristics of sociological mindfulness? Why are these characteristics so rare in our society?
2. What kind of world do you want to leave behind for the next two generations? Think about your everyday routine, ranging from how you get ready for work or school, to how you get places, to how you greet others, to how you deal with routine conflicts, to what you eat. If you approach your

everyday routine while thinking about the next generations, what aspects of your routine would you change? How would you change them?

3. Schwalbe argues that our actions have unintended consequences for others, even if we cannot see them in the moment. Dave Chappelle, a famous black comedian, had a provocative sketch show on Comedy Central. The sketches parodied political and social life, including race. During season three, Chappelle abruptly quit the successful production and went to South Africa. During an interview with Oprah Winfrey about his show, Chappelle recalled how he questioned the racial implications of his work when a white person on set laughed at a sketch on the "visual personification of the n-word." "I know the difference of people laughing with me and people laughing at me," he told Winfrey. "And it was the first time I had ever gotten a laugh that I was uncomfortable with" (http://www.oprah.com/oprahshow/Chappelles-Story/5). What implications did sociological mindfulness have for Dave Chappelle, and how did he deal with his new awareness? Why would sociological mindfulness have such a profound effect on Dave Chappelle and others? What implications might it have for you?
4. Recall the most recent comedy movie you viewed, its main characters, and the moments you found most humorous. Did the humor derive from portraying some people in stereotypical ways or from others breaking stereotypes? What makes these episodes so funny? Was the humor built on laughing at or with people? Does consuming humor have unintended implications for the groups depicted?

2

The Social Foundations of Human Experience

PETER BERGER AND THOMAS LUCKMANN

Most people today are at least vaguely aware of the wide variety of human cultures or ways of life that populate the globe. Although they may consider their own way of life superior to that of others, they recognize that other people hold radically different beliefs and observe wildly different customs than they do. It is as if such people inhabit different worlds than they do, and, in an important sense, this is true. Humans at all times and in all places do not experience the same reality. Rather, they experience a socially constructed reality that their predecessors have bequeathed to them and that they routinely reproduce. In this selection, sociologists Peter Berger and Thomas Luckmann briefly explain why humans must construct their own reality, how that reality is transmitted from one generation to the next and routinely confirmed, and some implications for understanding the relation of the individual to society.

As Berger and Luckmann argue, people's biological constitution does not adequately order their relationship to their environment. Instead, they must interpret, define, and endow their environment with meanings to respond to it effectively. Human meanings provide the regulation and order to human conduct that human biology does not. However, individual humans construct these meanings together rather than alone. They endow their environment with shared meanings that promote the coordination of action. Moreover, because those meanings are shared or intersubjective, they assume an objective status, as existing apart from any particular individual's experience.

The seeming objectivity of socially constructed realities is further enhanced by the fact that human infants are born into a world already interpreted and organized by others. The significant others who care for the infant transmit the prevailing definitions and interpretations of reality in their society to him or her. To the naïve child, this construction of reality is simply given and inevitable. In addition, the significant others who care for infants and children also transmit messages to them concerning their own socially defined identities. They might tell a child that she is and treat her as a girl, an African American, pretty, a tomboy, and the like. Eventually, the child comes to define herself similarly and acquires a self, a process that will be discussed in far more detail later in this volume.

As Berger and Luckmann note, the term socialization is commonly used to refer to this process whereby children are inducted into a society and its shared or objective reality. One goal of socialization is to establish a correspondence between that shared or objective reality and the individual's own subjective experience. This is initially accomplished during primary or childhood socialization by the seeming inevitability of the significant others' definitions of reality. These definitions provide the child with his or her most basic nomic structure, or ways of meaningfully ordering

---

experience. Subsequent or secondary socialization into particular roles builds on this primary reality.

Yet correspondence between socially shared or objective reality and subjective experience is never established once and for all. It must be constantly confirmed and maintained. According to Berger and Luckmann, the most important means of reality maintenance is conversation. Conversation with others continually reaffirms social definitions of reality, not so much by what is said but by what is taken for granted and undeserving of comment. Conversation also maintains the shared reality through the language in which it is conducted. Language classifies, typifies, and defines experience. Because it is shared, it gives the reality it constructs the accent of objectivity.

But the organization of individuals' experience does change. Sometimes individuals undergo radical transformations of subjective experience or alternations, involving a kind of resocialization. More commonly, individuals' subjective experience and selves are gradually transformed through secondary socialization and gradual changes in social experience. In societies in which such change is common, socially standard explanations are available that minimize inconsistency between the individuals' past and present, helping to maintain a correspondence between the socially objective reality and individual experience.

Social definitions of reality also include definitions of the types of people who populate society and of how they think, feel, and act. Berger and Luckmann refer to these as theories of identity, but they might better be called psychologies. These "psychologies" are always embedded in more comprehensive definitions of reality and cannot be fully understood apart from those broader constructions of reality. This implies that assessments of psychological functioning are always relative to particular definitions of reality. What may seem quite insane in one society may be quite normal in another. Hence, in an important sense, there is no such thing as human psychology, except in the vaguest sense. There are only human psychologies, psychologies as numerous as the human societies, cultures, and realities that populate and have populated the earth.

. . . [People's] relationship to [their] environment is characterized by world-openness. Not only [have people] succeeded in establishing [themselves] over the greater part of the earth's surface, [their] relationship to the surrounding environment is everywhere very imperfectly structured by [their] own biological constitution. The latter, to be sure, permits [humans] to engage in different activities. But the fact that [they] continued to live a nomadic existence in one place and turned to agriculture in another cannot be explained in terms of biological processes. This does not mean, of course, that there are no biologically determined limitations to [people's] relations with [their] environment; [their] species-specific sensory and motor equipment poses obvious limitations on [their] range of possibilities. The peculiarity of [people's] biological constitution lies rather in its instinctual component.

[People's] instinctual organization may be described as underdeveloped, compared with that of the other higher mammals. [People do] have drives, of course. But these drives are highly unspecialized and undirected. This means that the human organism is capable of applying its constitutionally given equipment in a very wide and, in addition, constantly variable and varying range of activities. This peculiarity of the human organism is grounded in its [individual] development. . . . [T]he developing human being not only interrelates with a particular natural environment, but with a specific cultural and social order, which is mediated to him [or her] by the significant others who have charge of him [or her]. Not only is the survival of the human infant dependent upon certain social arrangements, the direction of his [or her] organismic development, and indeed a large part of his [or her] biological being as such, are subjected to continuing socially determined interference.

Despite the obvious physiological limits to the range of possible and different ways of becoming [human] in this double environmental interrelationship, the human organism manifests an immense plasticity in its response to the environmental forces at work on it. This is particularly clear when one observes the flexibility of [people's] biological constitution as it is subjected to a variety of socio-cultural determinations . . . [T]he ways of becoming and being human are as numerous as [humans'] cultures. Humanness is socio-culturally variable. In other words, there is no human nature in the sense of a biologically fixed substratum. There is only human nature in the sense of anthropological constants (for example, world-openness and plasticity of instinctual structure) that delimit and permit [humans'] socio-cultural formations. But the specific shape into which this humanness is molded is determined by those socio-cultural formations and is relative to their numerous variations. While it is possible to say that [humans have] a nature, it is more significant to say that [humans construct] their own nature, or more simply, that [humans produce themselves]. . . .

[S]ocial order is a human product, or more precisely an ongoing human production. Social order is not biologically given or derived from any biological *data* in its empirical manifestations. Social order, needless to add, is also not given in [people's] natural environment, though particular features of this may be factors in determining certain features of social order (for example, its economic or technological arrangements). Social order is not part of the "nature of things," and it cannot be derived from the "laws of nature." Social order exists *only* as a product of human activity. No other ontological status may be ascribed to it without hopelessly obfuscating its empirical manifestations. Both in its genesis (social order is the result of past human activity) and its existence in any instant of time (social order exists only and insofar as human activity continues to produce it), it is a human product.

***

The individual . . . is not born a member of society. He [or she] is born with a predisposition toward sociality, and he [or she] becomes a member of society. In the life of every individual, therefore, there *is* a temporal sequence, in the course of which he [or she] is inducted into participation [in society]. . . . The [crucial] process by which this is brought about is socialization, which may be . . . defined as the comprehensive and consistent induction of an individual into the objective world of a society or sector of it. Primary socialization is the first socialization an individual undergoes in childhood, through which he [or she] becomes a member of society. Secondary socialization is any subsequent process that inducts an already socialized individual into new sectors of the objective world of his [or her] society. . . .

It is at once evident that primary socialization is usually the most important for an individual, and that the basic structure of all secondary socialization has to resemble that of primary socialization. Every individual is born into an objective social structure within which he [or she] encounters the significant others who are in charge of his [or her] socialization. These significant others are imposed upon him [or her]. Their definitions of his [or her] situation are posited for him [or her] as objective reality. He [or she] is thus born into not only an objective social structure but also an objective social world. The significant others who mediate this world to him [or her] modify it in the course of mediating it. They select aspects of it in accordance with their own location in the social structure, and also by virtue of their individual, biographically rooted idiosyncrasies. The social world is "filtered" to the individual through this double selectivity. Thus, the lower-class child not only absorbs a lower-class perspective on the social world, he [or she] absorbs it in the idiosyncratic coloration given it by his [or her] parents (or whatever other individuals are in charge of his [or her] primary socialization). The same lower-class perspective may induce a mood of contentment, resignation, bitter resentment, or seething rebelliousness. Consequently, the lower-class child will not only come to inhabit a world greatly different from that of an upper-class child, but may do so in a manner quite different from the lower-class boy next door. . . .

In primary socialization, then, the individual's first world is constructed. Its peculiar quality of firmness is to be accounted for, at least in part, by the inevitability of the individual's relationship to his [or her] first significant others. The world of childhood, in its luminous reality, is thus conducive to confidence not only in the persons of the significant others but in their definitions of the situation. The world of childhood is massively and indubitably real. Probably this could not be otherwise at this stage of the development of consciousness. Only later can the individual afford the luxury of at least a modicum of doubt. . . . [T]he world of childhood is so constituted as to instill in the individual a nomic structure in which he [or she] may have confidence that "everything is all right"—to repeat what is possibly the most frequent sentence mothers say to their crying offspring. The later discovery that some things are far from "all right" may be more or less shocking, depending on biographical circumstances, but in either case the world of childhood is likely to retain its peculiar reality in retrospection. It remains the "home world," however far one may travel from it in later life into regions where one does not feel at home at all. . . .

Secondary socialization is the [induction into] institutional or institution-based "sub-worlds". . . . Forgetting for a moment its other dimensions, we may say that secondary socialization is the acquisition of role-specific knowledge, the roles being directly or indirectly rooted in the division of labor. There is some justification for such a narrow definition, but this is by no means the whole story. Secondary socialization requires the acquisition of role-specific vocabularies, which means, for one thing [systems of meaning] structuring routine interpretations and conduct within the institutional area. At the same time "tacit understandings," evaluations and affective colorations of these [systems of meaning] are also acquired. The "subworlds" internalized in secondary socialization are generally partial realities in contrast to the "base-world" of primary socialization. Yet they too are more or less cohesive realities. . . .

The formal processes of secondary socialization are determined by its fundamental problem: it always presupposes a preceding process of primary socialization; that is, that it must deal with an already formed self and an already internalized world. It cannot construct subjective reality [out of nothing]. This presents a problem because the already internalized reality has a tendency to persist. Whatever new contents are now to be internalized must somehow be superimposed upon this already present reality. There is, therefore, a problem of consistency between the original and the new internalizations. The problem may be more or less difficult to solve in different cases. Having learned that cleanliness is a virtue in one's own person it is not difficult to transfer the same virtue to one's horse. But having learned that certain obscenities are reprehensible as a pedestrian child, it may need some explanation that they are now [required] as a member of the cavalry. To establish and maintain consistency secondary socialization presupposes conceptual procedures to integrate different bodies of knowledge. . . .

Since socialization is never complete and the contents it internalizes face continuing threats to their subjective reality, every viable society must develop procedures of reality maintenance to safeguard a measure of symmetry between objective [shared] and subjective [individual] reality. . . . [T]he reality of everyday life [generally] maintains itself by being embodied in routines. . . . Beyond this, however, the reality of everyday life is ongoingly reaffirmed in the individual's interaction with others. Just as reality is originally internalized by a social process, so it is maintained in consciousness by social processes. . . .

The most important vehicle of reality-maintenance is conversation. One may view the individual's everyday life in terms of the working away of conversational apparatus that ongoingly maintains, modifies and reconstructs his [or her] subjective reality. Conversation means mainly, of course, that people speak with one another. This does not deny the rich aura of non-verbal communication that surrounds speech. Nevertheless speech retains a privileged position in the total conversational apparatus. It is important to stress, however, that the greater part of reality-maintenance in conversation is implicit, not explicit. Most conversation does not in so many words define the nature of the world.

Rather, it takes place against the background of a world that is silently taken for granted. Thus an exchange such as, "Well, it's time for me to get to the station," and "Fine, darling, have a good day at the office" implies an entire world *within which* these apparently simple propositions make sense. By virtue of this implication the exchange confirms the subjective reality of this world.

If this is understood, one will readily see that the great part, if not all, of everyday conversation maintains subjective reality. Indeed, its massivity is achieved by the accumulation and consistency of casual conversation—conversation that can *afford to be casual* precisely because it refers to the routines of a taken-for-granted world. The loss of casualness signals a break in the routines and, at least potentially, a threat to the taken-for-granted reality. Thus one may imagine the effect on casualness of an exchange like this: "Well, it's time for me to get to the station," "Fine, darling, don't forget to take along your gun."

At the same time that the conversational apparatus ongoingly maintains reality, it ongoingly modifies it. Items are dropped and added, weakening some sectors of what is still being taken for granted and reinforcing others. Thus the subjective reality of something that is never talked about comes to be shaky. It is one thing to engage in an embarrassing sexual act. It is quite another to talk about it beforehand or afterwards. Conversely, conversation gives firm contours to items previously apprehended in a fleeting and unclear manner. One may have doubts about one's religion; these doubts become real in a quite different way as one discusses them. One then "talks oneself into" these doubts; they are objectified as reality within one's consciousness. Generally speaking, the conversational apparatus maintains reality by "talking through" various elements of experience and allocating them a definite place in the real world.

This reality-generating potency of conversation is already given in the fact of linguistic objectification. . . . Language objectifies the world, transforming the [ragged cloth] of experience into a cohesive order. In the establishment of this order, language *realizes* a world, in the double sense of apprehending and producing it. Conversation is the actualization of this realizing efficacy of language in the face-to-face situations of individual existence. In conversation the objectifications of language become objects of individual consciousness. Thus the fundamental reality-maintaining fact is the continuing use of the same language to objectify unfolding biographical experience. In a sense, all who employ this same language are reality-maintaining others. The significance of this can be further differentiated in terms of what is meant by a "common language"—from the group—idiosyncratic language of the primary groups to regional or class dialects to the national community that defines itself in terms of language. There are corresponding "returns to reality" for the individual who goes back to the few individuals who understand his [or her] in-group allusions, to the section to which his [or her] accent belongs, or to the larger collectivity that has identified itself with a particular linguistic tradition—in reverse order, say, a return to the United States, to Brooklyn, and to the people who went to the same public school.

In order to maintain subjective reality effectively, the conversational apparatus must be continual and consistent. Disruptions of continuity and consistency [necessarily] posit a threat to the subjective reality in question. . . . Subjective reality is thus always dependent upon specific plausibility structures, that is, the specific social base and social processes required for its maintenance. One can maintain one's self-identification as a man [or woman] of importance only in a milieu that confirms that identity; one can maintain one's Catholic faith only if one retains one's significant relationship with the Catholic community; and so forth. Disruption of significant conversation with the mediators of the respective plausibility structures threatens the subjective realities in question. . . . The individual may resort to various techniques of reality-maintenance even in the absence of actual conversation, but the reality-generating potency of these techniques is greatly inferior to the face-to-face conversations they are designed to replicate.

The longer these techniques are isolated from face-to-face confirmation, the less likely they will be to retain the accent of reality. The individual living for many years among people of a different faith and cut off from the community of those sharing his [or her] own may continue to identify himself [or herself] as say, a Catholic. Through prayer, religious exercises, and similar techniques his [or her] old Catholic reality may continue to be subjectively relevant to him [or her]. At the very least the techniques may sustain his [or her] continued self-identification as a Catholic. They will, however, become subjectively empty of "living" reality unless they are "revitalized" by social contact with other Catholics. To be sure, an individual usually remembers the realities of his [or her] past. But the way to "refresh" those memories is to converse with those who share their relevance. . . .

Everything that has been said so far on socialization implies the possibility that subjective reality can be transformed. To be in society already entails an ongoing process of modification of subjective reality. To talk about transformation, then, involves a discussion of different degrees of modification. [The extreme case is that of] near-total transformation; that is, in which the individual "switches worlds." . . . Such transformations we . . . call alternations.

Alternation requires processes of re-socialization. These processes resemble primary socialization, because they have to radically reassign reality accents and, consequently, must replicate to a considerable degree the strongly affective identification with the socializing personnel that was characteristic of childhood. They are different from primary socialization because they do not start [from nothing], and as a result must cope with [the] problems of dismantling, disintegrating the preceding nomic structure of subjective reality. . . . The historical prototype of alternation is religious conversion [but other] examples are in the areas of political indoctrination and psychotherapy. . . .

There are in practice . . . many intermediate types between resocialization . . . and secondary socialization that continue to build on the primary internalizations. In these there are partial transformations of subjective reality or designated sectors of it. Such partial transformations are common in contemporary society in connection with the individual's social mobility and occupational training. Here the transformation of subjective reality can be considerable, as the individual is made into an acceptable upper-middle-class type or an acceptable physician, and as he [or she] internalizes the appropriate reality-appendages. But these transformations typically fall short of resocialization. They build on the basis of primary internalizations and generally avoid abrupt discontinuities within the subjective biography of the individual. As a result, they face the problem of maintaining consistency between the earlier and later elements of subjective reality. This problem, not present in th[e] form of resocialization, which ruptures the subjective biography and reinterprets the past rather than correlating the present with it, becomes more acute the closer secondary socialization gets to resocialization without actually becoming it. . . .

The procedures for maintaining consistency also involve a tinkering with the past, but in a less radical manner—an approach dictated by the fact that in such cases there is usually association with persons and groups who were significant before. They continue to be around, are likely to protest too fanciful reinterpretations, and must themselves be convinced that such transformations as have taken place are plausible. For example, in the case of transformations occurring in conjunction with social mobility, there are ready-made interpretive schemes that explain what has happened to all concerned *without* positing a total metamorphosis of the individual concerned. Thus the parents of such an upwardly mobile individual will accept certain changes in the latter's demeanor and attitudes as necessary, possibly even desirable, accompaniment[s] of this new station in life. "Of course," they will agree, Irving has had to de-emphasize his Jewishness now that he has become a successful doctor in suburbia; "of course" he dresses and speaks differently; "of course" he now votes Republican; "of course" he married a Vassar girl—and perhaps it will also become a matter of course that he only rarely comes to visit his parents. Such interpretative schemes, which are ready-made in a society with high . . . mobility and already internalized by the individual before he himself is actually mobile, guarantee biographical continuity and smooth inconsistencies as they arise. . . .

* * *

Identity is, of course, a key element of subjective reality . . . and is formed by social processes. Once crystallized, it is maintained, modified, or even reshaped by social relations. The social processes involved in both the formation and the maintenance of identity are determined by the social structure. Conversely, the identities produced by the interplay of organism, individual consciousness, and social structure react upon the given social structure, maintaining it, modifying it, or even reshaping it. Societies have histories in the course of which specific identities emerge; these histories are, however, made by [humans] with specific identities. . . .

Identity is a phenomenon that emerges from the [interrelationship] between the individual and society. Identity *types*, on the other hand, are social products [through and through], relatively stable elements of objective social reality (the degree of stability being, of course, socially determined in its turn). As such, they are the topic of some form of theorizing in any society, even if they are stable and the formation of individual identities is relatively unproblematic. Theories about identity are always embedded in a more general interpretation of reality. . . . Identity remains unintelligible unless it is located in a world. Any theorizing about identity—about specific identity types—must therefore occur within the framework of the theoretical interpretation within which it and they are located. . . .

If theories about identity are always embedded in the more comprehensive theories about reality, this must be understood in terms of the logic underlying the latter. [It should be stressed . . . that we are here referring to theories of identity as a social phenomenon, that is, without prejudice as to their acceptability to modern science.] For example, a psychology interpreting certain empirical phenomena as a possession by demoniacal beings has as its matrix a mythological theory of the cosmos, and it is inappropriate to interpret it in a non-mythological framework. Similarly, a psychology interpreting the same phenomena in terms of electrical disturbances of the brain has as its background an overall scientific theory of reality, both human and non-human, and derives its consistency from the logic underlying this theory. Put simply, psychology always presupposes cosmology.

This point can be well illustrated by reference to the much used psychiatric term "reality-oriented." A psychiatrist trying to diagnose an individual whose psychological status is in question asks him [or her] questions to determine the degree of his [or her] "reality-orientedness." This is quite logical; from a psychiatric viewpoint there is obviously something problematic about an individual who does not know what day of the week it is or who readily admits he [or she] has talked with departed spirits. Indeed, the term "reality-oriented" itself can be useful in such a context. The sociologist, however, has to ask the additional question, "*Which*" reality? Incidentally, this addition is not irrelevant psychiatrically. The psychiatrist will certainly take it into account, when an individual does not know the day of the week, if he [or she] has just arrived on a jet plane from another continent. He [or she] may not know the day of the week simply because he [or she] is still "on another time"—Calcutta time, say, instead of Eastern Standard Time. If the psychiatrist has any sensitivity to the socio-cultural context of psychological conditions he [or she] will also arrive at different diagnoses of the individual who converses with the dead, depending on whether such an individual comes from, say, New York City or from rural Haiti. The individual could be "on another reality" in the same socially objective sense that the previous one was "on another time." In other words, questions of psychological status cannot be decided without recognizing the reality-definitions that are taken for granted in the social situation of the individual. To put it more sharply, psychological status is relative to the social definitions of reality in general and is itself socially defined. . . .

Reflective Questions

1. Berger and Luckmann argue that people are not driven by biological instincts or constitutions. Why not? What does drive people? In what ways are we social? How is our sociality related to biology and nature?
2. How do we become members of a society? What is the difference between primary and secondary socialization?
3. What role does conversation play? Why is conversation so important? Where does identity come from? How is it sustained?
4. Many women consider hot flashes to be a normal and bothersome experience during menopause. But not all women in all places experience them similarly. In the United States, white, educated, and higher-income women experience hot flashes more frequently than other women. People in sub-Saharan Africa view menopause as a positive life transformation for women. The Japanese had no word for "hot flashes" or menopause at all until Western pharmaceutical companies began advertising hormone replacement therapy there in 1995. How can there be this much variation in how women experience menopause? Isn't menopause a biological reality? If not, what is it? Where do symptoms come from? Does this mean that women's menopausal symptoms are somehow not real or should not be treated? How is menopause a blend of both biological and social realities?
5. Research shows that children who grow up in gender-neutral households still develop gendered ideologies as they get older. Why does this happen? Where do these children learn gender differences? What happens when different people socialize children in contradictory ways?

3

Symbols and the Creation of Reality

KENT SANDSTROM

Many thinkers who are influenced by evolutionary theory emphasize similarities between humans and other species. In recent years, a growing number of thinkers, including a few sociological psychologists, have argued that humans and their companion animals share a number of common features, including the ability to take the role of the other and to have preverbal experiences of selfhood. Yet, when we compare humans and other species, we cannot help but conclude that we are relatively unique within the animal kingdom. For good or ill, we brought heat to frigid climates, illuminated the darkness, erected huge and magnificent cities, and invented terrifying devices that could destroy them. The accomplishments of other animals do not even compare. In adapting to the environments that we inhabit, we have adapted those environments to our needs, desires, and dreams to an extent unparalleled by any other species. There is clearly something different about us.

In this selection, Kent Sandstrom contends that what makes us different from other creatures is our ability to make and use symbols. In highlighting this point, Sandstrom draws upon the sociological perspective known as symbolic interactionism, which serves as a foundation for many of the readings in this book. Guided by the insights of Herbert Blumer, the symbolic interactionist perspective emphasizes that because we use and rely upon symbols, we do not respond to stimuli in a direct or automatic way. Rather, through drawing on symbols we give meaning to stimuli and act toward them based on that meaning. For instance, if a person throws a ball in our direction, we will not know how to act until we interpret and give meaning to this stimulus. If we define it as a baseball pitch that we are supposed to hit, we will respond by swinging a bat at it. By contrast, if we define it as a weapon that is designed to hurt us, we will probably respond by trying to avoid it. Most crucially, we will act toward the stimulus of the ball thrown toward us based on the meaning we give to it.

The symbolic interactionist perspective also stresses that the meanings we give to things derive from and arise out of social interaction. We learn the meaning of things, such as baseballs, books, cars, and beer, as we interact with others. In doing so, we rely heavily on symbols and language. Indeed, as Sandstrom illustrates in this selection, symbols organize our perceptions and shape our experiences of "reality." Symbols allow us to categorize and make sense of what is happening around and inside of us, particularly by enabling us to give names to the objects, events, people, and experiences we encounter. Through naming these things, we transform them into social objects, or objects that have shared meanings. These shared meanings, in turn, call out a common response in us. For instance, when we name something a textbook, we give it the shared meaning of "something to read, reflect upon, and study." We thus know how to act toward it.

Reprinted from: Kent Sandstrom, Daniel Martin, and Gary Alan Fine, *Symbols, Selves and Social Reality: A Symbolic Interactionist Approach to Sociology and Social Psychology*. Copyright © 2013 by Oxford University Press. Reprinted by permission of the author.

Above all, the symbolic interactionist perspective emphasizes that our ability to use symbols allows us to transcend our immediate environments and to represent to ourselves and others things that are not otherwise available to our senses, such as feelings, ideas, and products of the imagination. Unlike other species, we humans are not confined simply to the world of perceptions and perceptual images. We also reside in a world of symbols, meanings, and values that we impose upon the perceptual world.

As Sandstrom implies, it is not the individual human being who creates these uniquely human environments. Symbols and their meanings must have a separate existence in order to have the same power over the individual's experiences as her or his perceptions. The only possible source of that separate existence is other humans. Symbols are necessarily shared. And, if what is uniquely human is uniquely social, then understanding human experience necessarily requires an understanding of social life.

> All human behavior consists of, or is dependent upon, the use of symbols. Human behavior is symbolic behavior; symbolic behavior is human behavior. The symbol is the universe of humanity.
>
> Leslie A. White

Compared with other animals, we find ourselves in a unique situation as human beings. We do not live directly in a state of nature, nor do we see "reality" nakedly. As the philosopher Suzanne Langer (1948) observed, human perception consists of the continuous creation and re-creation of images and symbols. Our only means of taking in the world of objects and people around us is through continually re-creating them. In other words, we convert our experiences into images and symbols. Our brains do not simply record or relay what is going on "outside" or "inside" of us. Instead, when processing information or sensations, our brains act like giant, symbolic transformers, changing virtually everything that passes through them into a stream of symbols.

According to Langer, this tendency for our brains to act like symbolic transformers is a crucial feature of our experience as human beings. It allows us to have a "constructive" rather than passive relationship to our environment. We do not simply react to things that exist in the world around us. Nor do we see these things "in the raw." Instead, we transform and interpret them through a symbolizing process. Thus, as we participate in the process of perception—the process of making sense of stimuli in our environment—we rely on our capacity to create and use symbols. Through this capacity we transform the stimuli that bombard us, such as a cluster of stars on a clear night, into a coherent and meaningful pattern—in this case, a pattern we call the Big Dipper.

Sensation

Throughout our lives we are barraged by a flood of sensory experiences. We swim in a sea of sensation. Consider this very moment. Your attention is (I hope) focused on this chapter and the words you are reading in this sentence. But pause for a moment and think of all the other things you are experiencing. For instance, what else are you seeing besides this page and sentence? Are you seeing what's above, below, and to the sides of the page? Are you periodically glancing up to see what else is around you? Are you being affected by anything besides visual images? For instance, are you hearing any noises or smelling any odors? Do you feel any pressures on your body, such as the touch of your fingers on the book, your back on a chair, your elbows on a table, or your feet on the floor? After briefly paying attention to what's going on around you, you can recognize that you are being bombarded with stimuli.

If we remained at the level of sensation, we would soon be overwhelmed. Our world would lack continuity or coherence. Life would be a booming, buzzing confusion of lights, sounds, smells, colors, and movements. We would bounce from one experience to another with little if any direction or purpose. We would not be able to organize our sensory experiences into broader patterns or configurations. Our perceptions, then, are not merely a matter of sensation; they also involve interpretation. Our senses provide us with the raw data to arrive at meaning.

As commonly recognized, we rely on five major senses as we interact with and gather information from our environment: sight, hearing, taste, smell, and touch. When any of these senses are stimulated, as when the receptors in our ears respond to sound waves emitted by a roaring engine, they transmit a message to the brain, which processes this input. Each sense can be aroused by external stimuli, as when we are moved by a beautiful sunset, refreshed by a cool breeze or, less pleasantly, repulsed by the smell of manure. Our senses can also be aroused by stimuli that come from sources within us, as when we feel a pang of hunger, a flash of pain, or a surge of sexual desire.

Most important, we do not react passively to our environment. We actively seek out stimuli through our bodily senses. For instance, we move our head, eyes, hands, and body to explore the sensations of light, sound, and contact that surround us. In this process, we extract information about our sensations and select what is relevant. We turn toward or away from shades of light. We turn toward or away from various noises, such as a whispering voice or an exploding firecracker. We sniff for pleasant odors and hold our nose at unpleasant odors in the air around us. We feel physical objects, enjoying their texture, evaluating how we can use them, and gauging their potential dangers. Our senses, then, do not merely receive stimuli; they actively seek out stimuli until they achieve a clearer understanding of their nature.

Conceptualization and Categorization

We understand our sensory experiences through grouping them into units, categories, or concepts, based on their similarities. We thereby engage in the process of *conceptualization*. That is, we experience the world in terms of concepts—regularized ways of thinking about real or imagined objects and events. These concepts enable us to picture "things" in our world, to describe or represent these things to ourselves and one another, and to grasp their meaning. We use concepts because we are "cognitive misers" and we want to find relatively simple ways to deal with the stimuli picked up by our senses. By sorting these stimuli into related and manageable units and giving them labels, we recode their contents into summary categories—categories such as *red, tall, dark, beer, roommate, professor,* and *dorm room.* By using these and other categories, we simplify and generalize the world—we chunk and cluster its elements into meaningful concepts. For example, we look into the sky and register a collection of light waves striking our retinas as "blue"; we bite into a candy bar and interpret thousands of transmissions from our taste buds as "sweet"; we walk up to a person in a store and recode the range of sensations she emits into "friendly-looking clerk." Through condensing and transforming our perceptions into these categories, we simplify the abundance of stimuli and information available to us. We organize our experiences.

At the same time, we bring order, continuity, and predictability into our perceptual world. Through plugging various stimuli into categories, we can link our present sensations to past sets of experience and perceptual organization. We can view an object or event as the same object or event despite the fact that it changes during each moment and from various perspectives. For example, we can recognize an event that shifts back and forth from one person lecturing to several people exchanging ideas as a "social psychology course." We can also treat a number of objects that differ in a few ways, such as cars, vans, and trucks, as essentially similar "vehicles." Through this ability to categorize objects, we can reduce the anxiety we would feel in an otherwise disordered and ambiguous world of stimuli.

Conceptualization allows us to sort and organize stimuli in a meaningful and orderly way. Through this process we actively attune ourselves to certain stimuli while ignoring others. We lump or group stimuli together and then respond to these groups as if they were objects. The key point is that we do not respond to the world "as it is." It does not have an inherent meaning. Instead, as human beings we actively slice up the world and organize it into concepts—plants and animals, fruits and vegetables, cities and villages—that allow us to give it meaning and see it as orderly. Although this is an intricate process, it seems fairly simple because many of the concepts we rely on are supplied by the groups to which we belong. We learn these concepts as we learn the language and culture of our society (Lindesmith, Strauss, and Denzin 1993).

Symbols, Signs, and Meanings

Human experience takes on distinctive characteristics because people respond not only to signs but also to symbols. A sign is directly connected to an object or event and calls forth a fixed or habitual response. Its meaning is associated with its physical form and can be grasped through the senses. For instance, dark clouds are a sign of rain and smoke is a sign of fire. Both animals and people can make sense of and respond to these signs. Symbols, however, are a uniquely human phenomenon. Roughly speaking, symbols are something that people create and use to stand for something else. A powerful example is a flag. People use a colored rectangle of cloth to stand for a nation and its guiding principles. This cloth evokes passionate sentiments—pride, loyalty, patriotism, and, for some, disgust or animosity. Another example of a symbol is a hug. In our society a hug is widely regarded as a symbol of affection; thus, the willingness of one person to hug another is seen as an expression of his or her caring for that person. Among the various sets of symbols, the most important are linguistic symbols, those combinations of spoken sounds or written marks that are used for all meanings. A symbol, then, is any object, gesture, or word that becomes an abstract representation of something else. Whatever it represents constitutes its meaning.

In most cases, the association between a symbol and the meanings it represents are arbitrary. The meanings designated by a symbol have no intrinsic relationship to the object it describes; the meanings are generally a matter of convention. Therefore, the meaning of a symbol cannot be discerned by examining the nature of the symbol itself. Think, for example, of the word *rose*. There is nothing inherent in this combination of four letters that would necessitate or even suggest it as a representation for a particular plant. The word has no color, smell, or thorns. Nor does it have anything in its spoken or printed form that would lead one to automatically think of the flower it describes. We conjure up an image of a velvety and sweet-smelling flower when hearing the word "rose" only because we have learned to make this association since childhood. We could just as easily have learned to call a rose "by any other name." Of course, if we had been born in a non-English speaking country, such as Romania, a rose would not be a rose to us—it would be a *trandafir*.

The Importance of Symbols

Our ability to use symbols has several important implications for our experience and activity. First, because symbols are abstractions, their use allows us to transcend our immediate environments and to have experiences that are not rooted in the here and now. We do not simply respond to the stimuli that arouse our senses in our current situation. We interpret these stimuli and respond to them in terms of our images of the past, present, and future, as well as our images of what is good, right, or important. In essence, we respond to stimuli of our own creation—that is, stimuli provided by the shadowy world of symbols. Thus we act within and toward a world that we have a major part in creating, a world that is inherently abstract rather than concrete, a world of symbols that in some senses is imaginary (Hewitt 1994).

To understand this point, think of the abstract concepts that guide people's outlooks and actions, such as equality, justice, freedom, love, and honesty. At bottom, these are humanly created symbols. They do not exist "in nature" or have a material reality. But most of us tend to respond to them as if they are representations of essential truths about the world that should guide our actions.

Even in situations that have a physical character, such as sporting events, people are guided by and respond to symbolic realities. For example, athletes know that coaches stress the concepts of hustle, sportsmanship, and teamwork. These concepts are real only in terms of the representations that players and coaches make of them. Coaches presume that they can gauge "hustle" through observing the behavior and demeanor of their players. If a player displays a high level of effort, he or she is hustling. "Sportsmanship" is behavior that accords with certain moral standards of fair play and thoughtfulness. When a player behaves "properly" in an instance when improper behavior is possible, we have witnessed sportsmanship. If his or her team, having just lost a hard-fought game, graciously congratulates their opponents, they are seen as demonstrating sportsmanship. Likewise, "teamwork" is not the act of a single player but depends on the relationship among players. A single action doesn't demonstrate teamwork, but two or more coordinated actions (such as a throw, a catch, and a tag) do. Hustle, sportsmanship, and teamwork are not objective behaviors but rather depend on symbolic interpretations within the context of a sports event.

In addition to allowing us to transcend our immediate environment, symbols allow us to remember, imagine, plan, and have vicarious experiences (O'Brien 2005). Whenever we remember things, imagine things, or make plans to do things, we rely on and manipulate symbols. We also use symbols to have vicarious experiences. These experiences allow us to learn about the world and understand others' experiences through observation; we do not have to experience everything ourselves in order to understand it. This ability is important not only for our individual and collective survival but also for another distinctive human characteristic: the transmission of culture.

Symbols provide the mechanism by which we create and acquire culture, or the ways of thinking, feeling, and acting that characterize our society. Interactionists believe that it is through communication, or symbolic interaction, that we learn, create, and pass on culture. The boundaries of the spread of culture are linked to the boundaries of effective communication (Shibutani 1955). This point is important in that groups develop their own symbol systems, which come to exemplify how people are expected to think, feel, and behave. Every group develops its own idioculture (Fine 1987), or system of shared knowledge, beliefs, sentiments, and behaviors that serves as a frame of reference and basis of interaction for group members. Nicknames serve as a case in point. Often they characterize members of the group to each other and demonstrate that the individuals truly belong. Further, these nicknames are frequently connected to a particular group itself. In Gary Alan Fine's (1987) research on Little League baseball, many of the players had team nicknames that reflected their position on the team. One boy, for instance, was called "Maniac," both a linguistic play on his last name and an indicator that he often threw the ball wildly. The next year this same boy became the starting third baseman, his throwing skills improved, and his teammates started calling him "Main Eye."

Finally, the most crucial implication of symbols is that they provide us with templates for categorizing our experiences and placing them within a larger frame of reference. Without symbols, we cannot give meaningful form to what is happening around us, and our understandings of the world have a hit-or-miss quality. We combine and cluster symbols to form concepts that we use to sort our sensory experiences into orderly social categories. These categories often take the form of *names*—names that have shared meanings for the members of a culture. Through using these names, we come to "know" the world around us.

Naming "Reality" and Creating Meaningful Objects

As Anselm Strauss (1959) has observed, people act toward objects in light of the names they give to these objects. Naming is an integral part of human cognition. In naming an object, we classify and give meaning to it, thereby evaluating it and calling forth action toward it. The name organizes our perceptions and serves as a basis for our subsequent behavior; that is, it intervenes between the "stimulus" provided by the object and our "response" to it. In other words, we respond to the name that we give to the object and not to the essence of the object itself.

Take the example of a green, 2½″ × 6″ rectangular piece of paper with Andrew Jackson's picture on it. Call it "money" or, more specifically, a "twenty-dollar bill." Based on this name, you immediately know how to act toward it. You know that you can use it at a store or business to purchase goods or services, such as groceries, clothing, or a haircut. And you know this because you have learned the meaning that the name "money" calls forth in our society. This meaning is not inherent to green, 2½″ × 6″ rectangular pieces of paper, as demonstrated by the fact that it is also granted to silver and copper circular-shaped pieces of metal. Instead, it emerges out of a shared agreement about what the objects we call "money" represent and how we should act toward them.

As another example of how we respond to things based on the names we give them, imagine a situation that involves you interacting with an unnamed person. It's late at night and you're walking across campus on your own. After you walk through a passageway between two buildings, you suddenly hear footsteps about 50 feet behind you. Feeling somewhat nervous, you glance backward and see a large male figure in the shadows. You pick up your pace. The man behind you matches your speed and even starts to gain on you. You tentatively name (or categorize) this man as a potential "mugger" or "rapist," and panic wells up within you. In turn, as he draws steadily closer to you, you prepare to run, yell, or defend yourself. Just as you're about to take defensive action, the man behind you calls out your name and says, "Hey, I've been trying to catch up with you since you walked between those buildings back there! I was going to yell 'wait up' but I wasn't sure it was you until now. Anyway, I was wondering if you'd like to walk back to the dorm together." As you hear these words, you quickly recognize that it is one of your friends who has been walking behind you. In that moment he is transformed from "mugger" or "rapist" into "thoughtful friend." Your response to him shifts accordingly. Your feelings of anxiety dissipate and you feel relaxed and reassured. You respond warmly rather than with a scream or a punch.

What these examples illustrate is that we formulate lines of action within and through the symbolic processes of naming and categorization. We use these processes to give meanings to things around us and to our actions as well as those of others. In other words, when we engage in the processes of naming and categorization, we transform things, events, and actions into *social objects,* or objects that have shared meaning. These objects call out a common mode of response in us.

According to interactionists, meaning is a socially created phenomenon. As such, it has three key features. First, it is extrinsic; that is, it is not a quality innate to particular objects. Instead, it is conferred on those objects "from the outside" based on how they are named and their intended use. Second, the meaning of objects is not fixed but varies with time, culture, situation, and the people acting toward them. For example, a bank is a different social object to student loan-seekers, to its managers and employees, and to potential bank robbers. Each acts differently toward the bank, and, consequently, to each it is a different object with a different meaning. This point leads us to the third important feature of meaning: It emerges and gets transformed through our communication with others as we learn from them how to define the meaning of an object and as we offer our own meaningful view of that object. Think, for instance, of how we learn the meaning of an upright middle finger in the United States. We observe the anger or upset feelings that others convey when they raise this finger or have it displayed toward them. In turn, we quickly learn that raising one's middle finger toward others, or "flipping them off," is not a kind gesture nor is it meant to tell them to look up in the air. Instead, we learn that this is a lewd and hostile gesture that conveys feelings of anger and tells others that we wish them harm (ironically, through engaging in sexual activity). Most important, what this example demonstrates is that meaning emerges and becomes established through the process of social interaction. The establishment of meaning through this process is essential because human action requires symbolization. Without meaning, we do not know how to act toward the "things" around us—including others and ourselves. To name "things" is not only to know them but also to know how to *respond* to them. The names, or symbolic categories, we attribute to things represent knowledge, communication, and action.

Language, Naming, and the Construction of Reality

Given the emphasis that interactionists place on symbols and the process of communication, they accord a special place to language. Language is the key medium through which people share meanings and construct "reality." It is a system of symbols that members of a culture use for representation and communication. Hence, language is the source of the symbols we use to give meanings to objects, events, or people and to convey these meanings to ourselves and others.

Language serves as the foundation for the development of the most important kind of symbols: words. Words have a unique and almost magical quality—they not only have meaning on their own but also when joined with others. In addition, words serve as the basis for other symbols (Charon 1992). While people often use other modes of communication, such as gestures, facial expressions, and postures, these expressions become meaningful to us through words. For instance, in our culture a red light at an intersection means "Stop!"; a side-to-side turning of the head means "No!"; a waved hand toward an arriving friend means "Hi!"; and a police siren means "Pull over to the side of the road!"

Words facilitate our ability to communicate and share meanings. To understand this fact, try the following exercise. Approach several friends and tell them something about yourself without using any spoken or written words. Try to let them know what you are going to do this weekend. If this task seems too difficult, try letting them know what day it is. Obviously, without using words you face a challenging task. That is part of the amusement of the game of charades. Even if you are adept at using nonverbal gestures, you could probably communicate much more easily and accurately with your friends through relying on spoken or written words.

Overall, words are important because they offer shared names or categories through which we give meanings to our experiences and share these meanings. Words have their fullest impact and significance in relationship to other words within a language. As a part of the structure of language, words frame our conceptions and understandings of the world and guide our actions toward it.

Although words facilitate our ability to communicate and act, they do not necessarily make it *easy* for us to interact with others. The words we use are often ambiguous, and they may lead us to experience gaps or difficulties in our conversations with others. As an example, consider the following exchanges between a mother and her teenage daughter:

DAUGHTER: Mom, can I take the car for a while to see my friends?

MOTHER: Okay, but don't be out too late—it's a school night and I need to use the car sometime to go to the grocery store.

DAUGHTER: Okay, that's no problem. I'll see you later. *The daughter returns four hours later, at 10:30 p.m.*

DAUGHTER: Hi, Mom, I just wanted to let you know I'm home and the car is back.

MOTHER: [Angrily] Where the heck have you been? I told you not to be out too late!

DAUGHTER: [Defensively] I wasn't out late—it's only 10:30! I don't go to bed until midnight!

MOTHER: But it's a school night; you should be in earlier than that!

DAUGHTER: Well, you didn't tell me a time. You just said that I shouldn't be out too late. 10:30 is not late!

MOTHER: Well, I did tell you that I needed the car sometime tonight to go grocery shopping.

DAUGHTER: Yeah, and I brought it back for you. You can go shopping now. The grocery store is open until midnight.

MOTHER: It's too late for me to go grocery shopping now! It's 10:30 and I'm tired.

DAUGHTER: Well, I don't see how that's my fault.

MOTHER: Oh, go to your room! I don't know why you can't listen to me better!

As this dialogue illustrates, the words we use do not always have a straightforward meaning; nor are they always interpreted in the way we intend them. Instead of leading to shared understanding and effective interaction, a number of the words we use, such as "a while," "later," and "sometime," have imprecise meanings and can lead to misinterpretations that result in frustrating or ineffective interaction. Thus, even when we use the same words as others, we do not necessarily "speak the same language" (and interact smoothly with them), as most parents and teenagers can attest.

References

Charon, Joel. 1992. *Symbolic Interactionism: An Introduction, an Interpretation, an Integration,* 4th ed. Englewood Cliffs, NJ: Prentice-Hall.

Fine, Gary Alan. 1987. *With the Boys: Little League Baseball and Preadolescent Culture.* Chicago: University of Chicago Press.

Hewitt, John P. 1994. *Self and Society,* 6th ed. Boston: Allyn and Bacon.

Langer, Suzanne. 1948. *Philosophy in a New Key.* New York: Mentor Books.

Lindesmith, Alfred R., Anselm L. Strauss, and Norman K. Denzin. 1993. *Social Psychology,* 7th ed. Englewood Cliffs, NJ: Prentice-Hall.

O'Brien, Jodi. 2005. *The Production of Reality,* 4th ed. Thousand Oaks, CA: Pine Forge Press.

Shibutani, Tamotsu. 1955. "Reference Groups as Perspectives," *American Journal of Sociology* 60: 962–965.

Strauss, Anselm. 1959. *Mirrors and Masks.* San Francisco: Sociology Press.

Reflective Questions

1. What is perception? How is perception selective? For instance, how are our perceptions influenced and directed by social categories?
2. What is a symbol? What is the difference between a sign and a symbol? What makes symbols such an important aspect of human behavior and interaction?
3. What makes an object into a "social object"? How and why are the names we give to people or things important?
4. Ask your friends or classmates to form two or more groups with an equal number of members in each group. Next, have the groups order themselves by birthday (from youngest to oldest) *without speaking a single word.* After the groups finish this task, analyze what happened. How did people in each group communicate what they needed to with one another? Did they use symbols? If so, what kinds of symbols did they use? What characteristics do these symbols have? Do they have the same characteristics and consequences as verbal symbols? What are the key consequences of symbols?
5. Analyze the speech of a local or national politician. What kind of language and symbols does he or she use when speaking? What does this language emphasize? What does it conceal? How does it frame the "issues" the speaker addresses? How and why is language an important aspect of exercising power?

Islands of Meaning

EVIATAR ZERUBAVEL

The second selection implied that human infants are born with a predisposition to distinguish human faces, and probably voices, from other sensory stimuli. However, apart from that, initially human perception is a kaleidoscope of smells, sounds, sights, and tactile sensations. We are confronted with a dizzying array of unique objects and events. If we are to order our relations with our environment, we must organize our perceptual experience. Regulating our responses to the environment requires that we regularize our experience. We must treat certain groups of objects and events as similar to one another and other groups of objects and events as distinctly different. Hence, classification and typification are basic building blocks for ordering humans' relation to their environments. They are the most fundamental means through which humans define, interpret, and endow their world with meaning—through which they construct their own realities. And, as Berger and Luckmann suggest in the second reading, humans do not do so alone but in concert with one another. The systems they use to classify and typify their experience are shared or intersubjective and, consequently, are experienced as objective. Moreover, as previously noted, humans are born into a world already interpreted and organized by others. They learn socially prevailing systems of classification and typification in the course of their socialization and thereby come to experience the organized worlds that other members of their society do.

In this selection, Eviatar Zerubavel examines how humans sort their experiences into distinct categories, or what he describes as "islands of meaning." We lump together things we consider similar, ignoring their differences, and separate them from other things, ignoring similarities and exaggerating differences. The world we experience does not come prepackaged in such categories. We pack it into them, and, as Zerubavel observes, our packaging of experience into discrete categories of meaning is an "inevitably arbitrary act." There are an indefinite variety of ways to break up reality into such discrete islands of meaning, as the cultural and historical variety of human classification systems attests.

Zerubavel notes that language largely guides our classification of our experience. We learn a logic of classification when we learn a language and other symbol systems. In this way society teaches us how to perceive our world, shape it into discrete islands of meaning, and construct reality. This is one of the ways in which socialization completes our unfinished human nature. It provides social lenses through which we can see meaningful shapes in our largely shapeless experience. And individuals who acquire the social lenses of different societies see, and therefore live, in different realities. We must understand what others are seeing in order to understand how they think, feel, and act, and that requires inspection of the social lenses—the systems of classification and typification—through which they are looking.

Although classification and typification are necessary if humans are to relate to their environment effectively, they also have their dark side. For example, every human society classifies and typifies its own members, at least in regard to sex category—male or female—and to age or general stage of life. Some societies, like our own, also classify their members into races on the basis of visible physical characteristics and typify one or another race as superior to others. Of course, these and other systems of classification and typification are subject to dispute and historical change. Indeed, they are often sources of protracted human conflict. What is at stake in such conflicts is the very construction of social reality. Classification and typification are, then, very serious business.

We transform the natural world into a social one by carving out of it mental chunks we then treat as if they were discrete, totally detached from their surroundings. The way we mark off islands of property is but one example of the general process by which we create meaningful social entities.

In order to endow the things we perceive with meaning, we normally ignore their uniqueness and regard them as typical members of a particular class of objects (a relative, a present), acts (an apology, a crime), or events (a game, a conference). After all, "If each of the many things in the world were taken as distinct, unique, a thing in itself unrelated to any other thing, perception of the world would disintegrate into complete meaninglessness."[1] Indeed, things become meaningful only when placed in some category. A clinical symptom, for instance, is quite meaningless until we find some diagnostic niche (a cold, an allergic reaction) within which to situate and thus make sense of it. Our need to arrange the world around us in categories is so great that, even when we encounter mental odds and ends that do not seem to belong in any conventional category, we nonetheless "bend" them so as to fit them into one anyway, as we usually do with the sexually ambiguous or the truly novel work of art. When such adjustment does not suffice, we even create special categories (avant-garde, others, miscellaneous) for these mental pariahs. . . .

Creating islands of meaning entails two rather different mental processes—lumping and splitting. On the one hand, it involves grouping "similar" items together in a single mental cluster—sculptors and filmmakers ("artists"), murder and arson ("felonies"), foxes and camels ("animals"). At the same time, it also involves separating in our mind "different" mental clusters from one another—artists from scientists, felonies from misdemeanors, animals from humans. In order to carve out of the flux surrounding us meaningful entities with distinctive identities, we must experience them as separate from one another.

Separating one island of meaning from another entails the introduction of some mental void between them. As we carve discrete mental chunks out of continuous streams of experience, we normally visualize substantial gaps separating them from one another. Such mental versions of the great divides that split continuous stretches of land following geological upheavals underlie our basic experience of mental entities as situated amid blank stretches of emptiness. It is our perception of the void among these islands of meaning that makes them separate in our mind, and its magnitude reflects the degree of separateness we perceive among them.

Gaps are critical to our ability to experience insular entities. The experiential separateness of the self, for example, is clearly enhanced by the actual gap of "personal space" that normally envelops it. By literally insulating the self from contact with others, such a gap certainly promotes its experience as an insular entity. A similar experience of an island situated in a vacuum often leads us to confine our horizons to, and never venture beyond, our neighborhood, hometown, or country. The great divides we visualize between women and men, children and adults, and blacks and whites likewise promote our perception of such entities as discrete. . . .

I have thus far drawn a deliberately one-sided picture of reality as an array of insular entities neatly separated from one another by great divides. Such discontinuity, however, is not as inevitable as we normally take it to be. It is a pronouncedly mental scalpel that helps us carve discrete mental slices out of reality. . . . The scalpel, of course, is a *social* scalpel. It is society that underlies the way we generate meaningful mental entities.

Reality is not made up of insular chunks unambiguously separated from one another by sharp divides, but rather, of vague, blurred-edge essences that often "spill over" into one another. It normally presents itself not in black and white, but, rather, in subtle shades of gray, with mental twilight zones as well as intermediate essences connecting entities. Segmenting it into discrete islands of meaning usually rests on some social convention, and most boundaries are, therefore, mere social artifacts. As such, they often vary from one society to another as well as across historical periods within each society. Moreover, the precise location—not to mention the very existence—of such mental partitions is often disputed even within any given society. . . .

Breaking up reality into discrete islands of meaning is, thus, an inevitably arbitrary act. The very existence of dividing lines (not to mention their location) is a matter of convention. It is by pure convention, for example, that we regard Danish and Norwegian as two separate languages yet Galician as a mere dialect of Portuguese. It is likewise by sheer convention that we draw a line between heroin and other lethal substances such as alcohol and tobacco (not to mention its own chemical cousins, which we use as pain-killers or as controlled substitutes for heroin itself). It is mere convention that similarly leads us to regard cooking or laundering as "service" occupations and fishermen or raftsmen as less skilled than assembly-line workers or parking-lot attendants. Just as arbitrary is the way in which we carve supposedly discrete species out of the continuum of living forms, separate the masculine from the feminine, cut up continuous stretches of land into separate continents (Europe and Asia, North and Central America), or divide the world into time zones. Nor are there any natural divides separating childhood from adulthood, winter from spring, or one day from the next (both my children, indeed, used to refer to the morning before their last afternoon nap as "yesterday"), and if we attribute distinctive qualities to decades ("the Roaring Twenties") or centuries ("nineteenth-century architecture"), it is only because we happen to count by tens. Had we used nine, instead, as the basis of our counting system, we would have undoubtedly discovered the historical significance of 9-, 81-, and 729-year cycles and generated fin-de-siècle and millenary frenzy around the years 1944 and 2187. We probably would also have experienced our midlife crisis at the age of thirty-six!

It is we ourselves who create categories and force reality into supposedly insular compartments. Mental divides as well as the "things" they delineate are pure artifacts that have no basis whatsoever in reality. A category, after all, is "a group of things [yet] things do not present themselves . . . grouped in such a way. . . . [Nor is their resemblance] enough to explain how we are led to group . . . them together in a sort of ideal sphere, enclosed by definite limits."[2] Classification is an artificial process of concept formation rather than of discovering clusters that already exist. Entities such as "vitamins," "politicians," "art," and "crime" certainly do not exist "out there." The way we construct them resembles the way painters and photographers create pictures by mentally isolating supposedly discrete slices of reality from their immediate surroundings. In the real world, there are no divides separating one insular "thing" from another. . . .

And yet, while boundaries and mental fields may not exist "out there," neither are they generated solely by our own mind. The discontinuities we experience are neither natural nor universal, yet they are not entirely personal either. We may not all classify reality in a precisely identical manner, yet we certainly do cut it up into rather similar mental chunks with pretty similar outlines. It is indeed a mind that organizes reality in accordance with a specific logic, yet it is usually a group mind using an unmistakably social logic (and therefore also producing an unmistakably social order). When we cut up the world, we usually do it not as humans or as individuals but rather as members of societies.

The logic of classification is something we must learn. Socialization involves learning not only society's norms but also its distinctive classificatory schemes. Being socialized or acculturated entails knowing not only how to behave, but also how to perceive reality in a socially appropriate way. An anthropologist who studies another culture, for example, must learn "to see the world as it is constituted for the people themselves, to assimilate their distinctive categories. . . . [H]e may have to abandon the distinction between the natural and the supernatural, relocate the line between life and death, accept a common nature in mankind and animals."[3] Along similar lines, by the time she is three, a child has already internalized the conventional outlines of the category "birthday present" enough to know that if someone suggests that she bring lima beans as a present, he must be kidding.

Whenever we classify things, we always attend some of their distinctive features in order to note similarities and contrasts among them while ignoring all the rest as irrelevant. The length of a film, for example, or whether it is in color or black and white is quite irrelevant to the way is rated, whereas the color of a dress is totally irrelevant to where it is displayed in a department store. What to stress among what is typically a "plethora of viable alternatives" is largely a social decision,[4] and being socialized entails knowing which features are salient for differentiating items from one another and which ones ought to be ignored as irrelevant. It involves learning, for example, that, whereas adding cheese makes a hamburger a "cheeseburger," adding lettuce does not make it a "lettuce-burger," and that it is the kind of meat and not the condiment that goes with it that gives a sandwich its distinctive identity. It likewise involves learning that the sex of the person for whom they are designed is probably the most distinctive feature of clothes (in department stores men's shirts are more likely to be displayed alongside men's pajamas than alongside women's blouses), and that the way it is spelled may help us locate an eggplant in a dictionary but not in a supermarket. Similarly, we learn that in order to find a book in a bookstore we must attend its substantive focus and the first letters of its author's last name (and ignore, for example, the color of its cover), yet that in order to find it in a book exhibit we must first know who published it. (We also learn that bookstores regard readers' ages as a critical feature of books, thus displaying children's books on dogs alongside children's books on boats rather than alongside general books on dogs.) We likewise learn that, in supermarkets, low-sodium soup is located near the low-sugar pineapple slices ("diet food"), marzipan near the anchovy paste ("gourmet food"), and canned corn near the canned pears (rather than by the fresh or frozen corn). And so we learn that, for the purpose of applying the incest taboo, brotherhood "counts" as a measure of proximity to oneself, whereas having the same blood type is irrelevant.

Separating the relevant (figure) from the irrelevant (ground) is not a spontaneous act. Classifying is a normative process, and it is society that leads us to perceive things as similar to or different from one another through unmistakably social "*rules* of irrelevance"[5] that specify which differences are salient for differentiating entities from one another and which ones are only negligible differences among variants of a single entity. Ignoring differences which "make no difference" involves some social pressure to disregard them. Though we often notice them, we learn to ignore them as irrelevant, just as we inhibit our perception of its ground in order to perceive the figure. Along the same lines, ignoring the stutter or deformity of another is not a spontaneous act but rather a social display of tact. It is rules of irrelevance that likewise lead judges, professors, and doctors to display "affective neutrality"[6] and acquit innocent defendants, reward good students, and do their best to save patients' lives even when they personally despise them. They also lead bureaucrats who screen applications to exclude applicants' sex or race from their official considerations even if they are personally attentive to it.

The social construction of discontinuity is accomplished largely through language:

> We dissect nature along lines laid down by our native languages. The categories . . . we isolate from the world of phenomena we do not find there because they stare every observer in the face. . . . [T]he world is presented in a kaleidoscopic flux of impressions which has to be organized by our minds. We cut nature up . . . as we do, largely because we are parties to an agreement to organize it in this way—an agreement that . . . is codified in the patterns of our language. . . . [W]e cannot talk at all except by subscribing to the organization and classification of data which the agreement decrees.[7]

Not only does language allow us to detach mental entities from their surroundings and assign them fixed, decontextualized meanings, it also enables us to transform experiential continuums into discontinuous categories ("long" and "short," "hot" and "cold"). As we assign them separate labels, we come to perceive mental essences such as "professionals," "criminals," or "the poor" as if they were indeed discrete. It is language that allows us to carve out of a continuous voice range the discrete categories "alto" and "soprano," distinguish "herbs" (basil, dill) from leaves we would never allow on our table, define vague discomfort in seemingly sharp categories such as "headache" or "nausea," and perceive aftershave lotion as actually different from eau de toilette or cologne. At the same time, it is our ability to assign them a common label that also allows us to lump things together in our mind. Only the concept "classical," for example, makes Ravel's music similar to Vivaldi's, and only the concept "alcoholic" makes wine seem "closer" to vodka than to grape juice.

Since it is the very basis of social reality, we often forget that language rests on mere convention and regard such mental entities, which are our own creation, as if they were real. . . .

By the same token, as we divide a single continuous process into several conceptual parts ("cause" and "effect," "life" and "death") we often commit the fallacy of misplaced concreteness and regard such purely mental constructs as if they were actually separate. We likewise reify the mental divide separating "white-collar" from "manual" labor as well as the purely mental outlines of such entities as races, classes, families, and nations. Like the dwellers of Plato's proverbial cave, we are prisoners of our own minds, mistaking mere social conceptions for actual experiential perceptions.

It is society that helps us carve discrete islands of meaning out of our experience. Only English speakers, for example, can "hear" the gaps between the separate words in "perhapstheyshouldhave-trieditearlier," which everyone else hears as a single chain of sound. Along similar lines, while people who hear jazz for the first time can never understand why a seemingly continuous stretch of music is occasionally interrupted by bursts of applause, jazz connoisseurs can actually "hear" the purely mental divides separating piano, bass, or drum "solos" from mere "accompaniment." Being a member of society entails "seeing" the world through special mental lenses. It is these lenses, which we acquire only through socialization, that allow us to "perceive things." The proverbial Martian cannot see the mental partitions separating Catholics from Protestants, classical from popular music, or the funny from the crude. Like the contours of constellations, we "see" such fine lines only when we learn that we should expect them there. As real as they may feel to us, boundaries are mere figments of our minds. Only the socialized can "see" them. To all cultural outsiders they are totally invisible.

Only through such "glasses" can entities be "seen." As soon as we remove them, boundaries practically disappear and the "things" they delineate fade away. What we then experience is as continuous as is Europe or the Middle East when seen from space or in ancient maps, or our own neighborhood when fog or heavy snow covers curbs and property lines, practically transforming familiar milieu into a visually undifferentiated flux. This is the way reality must appear to the unsocialized—a boundless, unbroken world with no lines. That is the world we would have inhabited were it not for society.

Notes

1. George C. Simpson, *Principles of Animal Taxonomy* (New York: Columbia University Press, 1961), p. 2.
2. Emile Durkheim and Marcel Mauss, *Primitive Classification* (Chicago: University of Chicago Press, 1973), pp. 7–8.
3. Rodney Needham, "Introduction" to Durkheim and Mauss, *Primitive Classification,* p. viii.
4. Steven J. Gould, "Taxonomy as Politics: The Harm of False Classification," *Dissent,* Winter 1990, p. 73.
5. Erving Goffman, *Encounters* (Indianapolis: Bobbs-Merrill, 1961), pp. 19–26.
6. Talcott Parsons, *The Social System* (New York: Free Press, 1964), pp. 60, 435, 458–62.
7. Benjamin Whorf, "Science and Linguistics," in *Language, Thought, and Reality* (Cambridge: MIT Press, 1956), pp. 213–14.

Reflective Questions

1. What does Zerubavel mean when saying classifications are a "social scalpel"? Where do our classifications come from? How are they different from typifications?
2. What constitutes "family"? What makes someone family rather than a close friend? How and where did you learn that definition? How do we collectively reinforce these social constructs? You may have joined someone else's family or had someone join yours. Did you have the same definition of family as the new member? What happens when someone doesn't fit in? Did your family make this connection legal? Why or why not? How do we treat "family" differently from "close friends" in terms of taxes and hospital visitation? What happens if you consider someone to be family but he or she is not recognized by others as such? Whose definition wins out? Whose should?
3. What is a chef, and what differentiates a chef from a cook? Generate a list of what you see as the defining features of each as well as their differences. Now, go ask five of your friends. Did they come up with the same list? How do you explain the variability or consistency? Do you notice any correlation to the food preparer's social class or gender? What are the consequences of being considered a "chef" versus a "cook" in terms of respect, pay, and hours worked?
4. Classifications have personal, legal, moral, and even health-related implications. The fifth edition of the *Diagnostic and Statistical Manual of Mental Disorders* (DSM), the book published by the American Psychiatric Association (APA) that catalogues the symptoms of mental illnesses, is being published in May 2013. Not only do practitioners use the DSM to diagnose disorders, but insurance companies use the definitions to establish guidelines for funding treatment. With each new edition, some mental disorders are introduced to the manual while others are dropped. The definitions or symptoms for still others change, expand, or retract. Several changes proposed in the fifth edition have raised considerable controversy, including narrowing the definition of Autism Spectrum Disorder and dropping the exemption for bereavement from the definition of Major Depressive Disorder. How do these changes matter for people's identities, how others view them, and their access to medical care? The APA listed a draft of the manual on its website to elicit public comment, and task forces have responded to criticism by issuing press releases, writing rationales, and modifying diagnostic criteria. Who should decide the diagnostic criteria for mental illness? Should the APA have elicited public comment, and should it change criteria in response to it? Does it matter who the respondent is? How do definitions of mental disorders found in an oversized technical reference book work their way into popular culture? How do everyday people reinforce and challenge them?

5

Speed Culture

SIMON GOTTSCHALK

Some students of social life argue that we have entered a new epoch of human history. Current modes of transportation and electronic means of communication have profoundly altered social life. We may now watch television programs on Iraq in the morning, telephone someone in Japan that afternoon, send an email message to someone in Australia later, and fly to the Bahamas for the weekend that evening. Such travel and communication expand and multiply our networks of social interaction and relationships, exposing us to numerous and often clashing versions of reality. Moreover, the wide array of goods and services sold in the marketplace enable us to create collages of such diverse realities. We may dress like a New England woodsman, courtesy of L.L. Bean, while sitting in our Chicago apartment with Southwestern decor, listening to rap music, and feasting on Thai food. We see a kaleidoscope of realities on television, on city streets, and during our travels. Under these conditions, it is difficult to believe that any human reality is inevitable. Even supposedly authoritative experts are suspect. They often disagree and quickly change their minds. Nothing seems certain. This is what many students of social life call the "postmodern condition." Some welcome it while others condemn it, but they all agree that human social life and experience are profoundly changing right before our eyes. They also agree that sociologists and other students of social life who ignore those changes will be left behind.

The following selection by Simon Gottschalk is one attempt to understand postmodern social experience and its implications for our everyday outlooks and actions. Gottschalk illustrates how postmodern culture has become characterized by a dizzying pace of life and a regime of speed. We are bombarded by popular discourses that emphasize the value and primacy of speed, portraying it as essential, empowering, and even irresistible. TV commercials serve as one of the key vehicles through which these discourses become disseminated to us. Through systematically analyzing dozens of commercials, Gottschalk highlights the strategies that advertisers employ to "inscribe speed as a normal and desirable quality" of our everyday lives and selves. These strategies include a diverse array of visual effects, narrative structures, linguistic devices, and paralinguistic communications that promote and reinforce a speed logic. According to this logic, speed is a key ingredient of fun, pleasure, leisure, and contentment and thus is an essential element of our everyday lives. Perhaps most crucially, Gottschalk demonstrates how the meanings we give to things, such as speed, are profoundly influenced by our mediated interactions—interactions we have through electronic formats—as well as by our face-to-face interactions. Indeed, in postmodern society mediated interactions are becoming an increasingly important means through which we learn, produce, and perpetuate the meanings by which we live.

Reprinted from: Simon Gottschalk, Speed Culture: Fast Strategies in Televised Commercial Ads. *Qualitative Sociology* 22(4): 311–329.

*Quick*lube, *Quick* Cash, *Minute* Maid, American *Express*, Federal *Express*, *Mach 3*, Slim*fast*, *Speedo*, *Speed*stick, *Speed* dial, *Instant* credit. Delivery *in twenty minutes* or you don't pay. You must act *NOW*, You will be approved *in less than 2 minutes. Hurry! Only a few days remaining. They'll be gone soon!* Where Guy Debord saw the "society of the spectacle" (1983), Virilio (1996, 1990, 1986) exposes the new regime of speed. In his approach, speed is a "milieu," an environment, and a social psychological force which fundamentally transforms what we do, how we do it, how we think and feel, and thus, what we become. . . .

With the increasing speed of locomotion, we have less space to move about, with the accelerating speed of information and telepresence, we have less mental-emotional distance—less time to reflect, less delay between interpellation, interpretation, selection, and consummation (see Ansay 1994). As phones replace letters and face-to-face contacts, computer screens displace books, images supplant language, and news substitutes for history (Bertman 1998:26). As the commercial ad for my local FOX station news program claims, "If at 10 o'clock it's news, at 11 it's History" (with a vocal stress on *History*). Under the speed regime, Foucault's "Great Confinement" no longer refers to coercive practices which control and constrain individuals behind the brick walls of total institutions. Rather, the accelerating speed of everyday life ends up confining us in what Rifkin (1987:165) calls "a temporal ghetto"—a physical, social, and mental space which is becoming increasingly *narrower* in terms of its spatial boundaries, *immediate* in terms of its temporal requirements, and exhausting in terms of the emotional and mental energy it exacts. Under conditions of acceleration, the great refusal, the great NO, has surrendered to the great NOW! Every desire and urge must be fulfilled right now as real time and space limitations become increasingly experienced as unwarranted and intolerable. As a commercial slogan produced by *Sprint* (and the company name is already significant) puts it: "Be There Now!"—but it is rather difficult to establish whether this slogan is a promise or an order. . . .

The constant linking of speed to a variety of commodities both promote the desirability of these commodities and simultaneously celebrate and normalize speed. As an example, even though breakfast cereals have nothing to do with speed, really, when a commercial ad repeatedly juxtaposes images of cereals to images of children happily running around the kitchen, a connection is created between these signifiers (cereals, happiness, speed), and this connection simultaneously reinforces and normalizes both their interrelatedness and desirability. When countless commercials deploy the same strategy and link speed to an infinite array of commodities (from laxatives to liposuction), the desirability of speed becomes taken-for-granted, self-evident, and restructuring our very *commonsense*. . . . Simultaneously, these commodities and the practices surrounding their use also become vehicles of certain meanings about speed, certain expectations, and certain criteria for evaluating self and others. Permeating images of fun, adventure, leisure, performance, and pleasure, speed insinuates itself as an essential necessity of everyday life.

Methodology

I chose to focus on TV commercial ads for a number of reasons. First, these texts constitute probably the lion's share of the growing number of commercial impressions we (un)consciously attend to on a daily basis. As Harvey (1989), Pfohl (1992), Gottschalk (1997), and other analysts of the postmodern scene suggest, televised commercials have become a most important site of the contemporary cultural landscape. Second, they are readily accessible, free, easy to collect, allowing for various levels of analysis and repeated viewing. Third, as complexly structured texts, it seems that TV ads might communicate (about) speed more effectively than static pictures, written descriptions, or audio messages. While each of these three media can doubtlessly communicate about speed, TV ads can probably do so more effectively since they often combine moving pictures, written words, and audio messages into one single and often mesmerizing text. The ads discussed here were recorded on the four major TV channels (ABC, CBS, NBC, FOX) during the months of January and February of 1999. Ads were collected every day of the week and—with the exception of the 1 am to 7 am time slot—at every hour of the day. Having recorded and viewed a total of 270 commercials, I rejected 148 of them because they did not communicate about speed in any discernible way. Since speed was present in some fashion in the remaining 122, I retained those for further analysis. After watching these ads a number of times, focusing first on the visual, then on the verbal and the aural, I started extracting various themes—communication strategies— that seemed significant. These emerging themes constituting analytical categories, I continued the iterative process between those emerging categories and data in order to refine, combine or split them, eliminate those that did not seem useful, and enrich the remaining ones with illustrations and examples. Throughout the analysis, I sought to answer three questions (see Goldman and Dickens 1983:593–594): First, *what* do ads communicate about speed? In other words, what are the meanings they associate with it? Second, *how* do ads communicate these meanings or what are the strategies they deploy to inscribe speed in particular ways? Third, in what ways are the meanings generated by these ads consequential?

Right Now! Speed in the Commercial World

> Time-space compression always exacts its toll on our capacity to grapple with the realities unfolding around us (Harvey 1989:306).

In a large number of commercials I examined, it seems that the oral obsession of "bigger is better" is increasingly being displaced by the Oedipal compulsion of "faster is better." In the world of televised commercial ads, speed rather than size is now represented as an essential source of pleasure, and everyday life is orchestrated by a speed logic which seems inherently satisfying, empowering, and *irresistible*—both in the sense of being seductive and in the sense of withstanding any resistance against it. In this pleasurable fantasyland, there's never a line at the supermarket check-out counter, cars shooting along empty freeways produce an instant sense of freedom, a mother's anxious look immediately transforms raw vegetables into a delicious meal, hair thickens and grows under your very eyes, logging onto the net brings an immediate response, dozens of extra pounds disappear overnight, a ketchup smudge on a favorite shirt decomposes as soon as a drop of detergent touches it, lime on bathroom tiles liquefies and vanishes after just one spray, toothpaste whitens yellow teeth on contact, every medication cures instantly, a totally new YOU is only a phone call away, and an ear-shattering female orgasm can be reached in about 15 seconds—or the time it takes her to shampoo, lather, and rinse her hair.

But speed is presented as *irresistible* also in terms of overcoming all resistance against it. Thus, while most commercials inscribe speed as pure pleasure, others acknowledge that the everyday does indeed, and even unfortunately, unfold at an increasingly dizzying pace. Yet, while sometimes deploring this acceleration, commercials also tacitly communicate that this new condition is unavoidable. Rarely suggesting that we *could* resist speed or perhaps even slow down a bit, they call upon us to adapt to this new regime, to go with the flow, and to remain grateful for those commodities which assist us in performing at full capacity. Whether by pleasure or necessity, in the speed regime, fast is good, the good are fast, and you better be fast, for your own good. As they also say on Wall Street, in the 1990s there are only two kinds of people: The quick and the dead (Schor 1993).

Televised ads deploy various strategies to inscribe speed as desirable and normal, as well as to promote commodities and selves as vehicles of this desirability. While some verbalize the normalcy and desirability of speed openly, others communicate this meaning indirectly—by metaphor, contrast, narrative structure, juxtaposition, and implication. Approaching these ads as combining both a written/spoken textual level and a pictorial one, I first separate between them, analyze their various components in details, and examine how speed is inscribed in each. At the same time, it is important to remember that separating written/spoken text from picture is accomplished for analytical purposes only as the effectivity of televised ads requires the artful combination of both. For example, reading the brand names *MACH 3*, *DIET FUEL* or *NISSAN* on a piece of paper will convey different meanings than when seeing these words rapidly flashing in big red zooming letters on a screen, flying against a background of rapidly changing images which visually propel us—the spectators—in a mad pursuit after a speeding car, while an aggressive male voice-over is barking a slogan against a fast-paced heavy metal soundtrack.

Finally, although a comprehensive understanding of the visceral impact these ads produce can only be properly accomplished by reproducing them as film clips, since this chapter is a printed medium, I will have to re-present these multilayered and dynamic texts as mute and static letters on sheets of paper. In spite of these limitations, I still hope that this chapter will make these speed strategies sufficiently visible and encourage readers to watch TV ads differently, to develop new ways of reading them, to uncover additional strategies, and to ask new questions about this seemingly benign glorification and normalization of speed in TV ads, in other media texts, and in everyday interaction.

(A) The Pictorial Level

Any analysis of speed in TV ads (as compared to, for example, printed ones) must first acknowledge the constraints imposed on them by the very medium in which they appear, and by the economic considerations which shape their format. More specifically, since TV ads cost quite a bit of money, they must communicate a great deal of information within the rigid time limits of about 10 to 30 seconds—a most unusual feature when compared to most everyday face-to-face communication. As such, and regardless of what they sell, the ad's very format will already communicate the speed imperative or a certain sense of urgency. On the other hand, if these temporal parameters constrain these ads' format, they do not necessarily determine their content.

(1) Visual Strategies as Metaphors

At the pictorial level, commercial ads deploy several film strategies and visual effects which effectively present speed as normal and desirable. These include the showing of: (1) rapidly moving objects, humans, and other entities which we "naturally" associate with speed (joggers, train, cars, planes, running tigers, boats, wild horses); (2) film segments of objects, landscapes, humans, and other organisms moving at faster than normal speed; (3) rapid shot changes which force the viewer to quickly and mentally switch between various spatial positions; (4) rapid panning of areas, people, landscapes evoking rapid ocular and physical motion; (5) rapid-motion blur, tracers, flying graphics, and other visual effects which connote speed; (6) characters' facial gestures and body language denoting pleasure, satisfaction, and well-being when experiencing speed as opposed to discomfort, frustration, and anxiety when experiencing slowness.

The frequent use of these techniques to depict commodities, social transactions, and physiological processes thus normalizes and celebrates the experience of a fast-paced everyday life. Such techniques might also tacitly legitimize the idea that we are not all that unreasonable when we expect everyday objects, transactions, and processes to proceed at a speed comparable to the one propelling the world of TV ads (see Postman 1985 and Rifkin 1987).

(2) Narrative Structure

Ads also communicate the desirability and normalcy of speed *directly* through their narrative structure (person is unhappy when experiencing slowness, things speed up, person becomes happy) as well as *indirectly*, through the very *pace* at which this structure unfolds. As the commercial for *Phazyme* (an intestinal gas-relief medication) below illustrates, the rapid juxtaposition of particular film segments invites us to "close the circuit" to imagine or mentally "insert" the presence of speed even if (and especially when) speed itself has not been explicitly mentioned (see Williamson 1992). Looking at the narrative structure of the *Phazyme* ad, we see the following: The first segment centers on a pleasant-looking white woman in her sixties. It is night, and she is standing on a balcony or a front porch, in front of an open door where a good number of people interact in a friendly atmosphere (you can hear soft music, soft voices, and relaxed laughter). Looking visibly uncomfortable and anxious, she looks at us and secretly confides: "the party is in there, so why am I out here?" She then becomes silent, and, both frustrated and embarrassed, admits: "Gas. Again." This segment then leads to a short second "medical" one showing a liquid rapidly flowing through plastic tubes (a metaphor for our intestines, I assume). The confident, peppy male voice-over states: "Maximum strength *Phazyme*. Has 30% more medicine doctors recommend." The third segment then brings us back to the woman. In contrast to the first segment, she is now happily smiling and seems magically relieved of all discomfort. "One little pill, and I'm back!" she tells us as she gracefully hurries back to the room where the party is still going on, raising a few approving young male gazes in the process. The male voice-over then concludes "Serious medicine for serious gas. *Phazyme*."

While on a first level, this ad reproduces the familiar and quasi-mythical chain of: lack → consumption → satisfaction so prevalent in the advertising logic, its *structure* also communicates the desirability of speed even though the word "speed" is never mentioned. Here, the *very pace* at which this story unfolds through these three segments by itself already signifies speed, since it implies that relief has actually occurred as rapidly as the progression from the first segment (lack/pain) to the last one (satisfaction). This particular message which is communicated simply through the very pace at which the story moves from one segment to another is replicated in countless other "realist" commercials selling everything from wrinkle removal to detoxification, from education to transatlantic travel, [and] from a remodeled kitchen to a happy family life. In all these cases, the actual minutes, hours, days, weeks, months or years which such transformations often realistically necessitate are condensed to a few seconds.

(3) Meaningful Contrasts: Slowness

Ads also communicate the desirability and normalcy of speed by depicting slowness—its opposite—as problematic, abnormal, and otherwise symptomatic of a condition which is neither desirable nor welcome. Here again, even though speed is nowhere directly present, it is nevertheless *implied* by depicting its opposite— slowness—as undesirable. A commercial ad for *Halls' Vitamin C* tablets is a good example of this strategy. The first segment depicts blurry silhouettes of people dressed in similar grayish clothes. Carrying open umbrellas, hunched over, and keeping their heads down, they all walk past each other in slow motion on a rainy street, to the sound of a slow and eerie musical score (as a contrast perhaps to the mental images we may "naturally" associate with *Singing in the Rain*?). These visual scenes are in black and white, [are] out of focus, and connote a state of bleakness, discomfort, disorientation, and crowding—the sensations one might experience when suffering from a cold. The main character is a young white man who we follow as he walks in slow motion away from the street crowd, finds shelter from the rain under a balcony, and coughs violently. He then extracts from his pocket a green package of *Halls' Vitamin C* tablets—the only entity in this ad which is shown in bright colors. He swallows the tablet which provides immediate relief because, in the next segment, we are now watching him from up close as he looks up, smiling, his face bright and relaxed. Magically fortified, he returns to the street, but walking at a faster pace than everybody else and than he himself did in the first segment. As the male voice-over assures us: "*Halls' Vitamin C*. It will help you keep going when it feels like the whole world is slowing down."

While this ad tells a story similar to the one of the woman in the throes of gastro-intestinal pain described above, it simultaneously (and even in the absence of the voice-over) associates slowness with illness, with a disordered state, and provides a meaningful contrast between, on one hand, slow = ill = undesirable = everybody else, against on the other, fast = healthy = desirable = me. The key to this transformation, the intervening term, is *Halls' Vitamin C* tablets. Like the first two visual strategies described above, the present one is also deployed with minor variations in countless others which repeatedly depict "slow" (read: naturally occurring) processes and interactions as undesirable, unwarranted, and necessitating acceleration.

(B) The Textual Level

The textual level is of course central to the construction of meanings in many televised ads, and is an integral part of their effective communication. Here, I distinguish between (1) language (what is being said) from (2) paralanguage (*how* is something said) and sound effects (music scores, flying planes, etc.). As stated above, a comprehensive appreciation of the strategies used in these ads necessitates a simultaneous reading of all these levels together with the pictorial one. For purposes of description and interpretation, however, they must first be separated.

(1) Language: What Is Being Said

(a) Naming. One first and obvious linguistic device consists in the verbalization of products' names—names which both denote and connote speed. When chanted like a mantra, repeated like a political slogan, and enunciated with a tone of approval, relief and enthusiasm, these names simultaneously convey the desirability of speed and of the products they designate. Familiar examples include: *Slim Fast, Boost, Raid, Federal Express, Minute Maid, Minute Rice, Mach 3, Sprint, QuickLube, Rapid Refund, Speedo, Speed Stick,* etc. Thus, without having to launch into lengthy explanations about the desirability of speed, the brand names by themselves celebrate speed and the companies which deliver these commodities.

(b) Promising Links. A second textual strategy consists of simple statements which simultaneously (1) inscribe speed as an important quality and a valuable resource, (2) associate speed with other valued qualities (efficiency, popularity, a competitive edge, performance, competence, respect), and (3) promise that by consuming a certain product, we'll have access to speed and the qualities associated with it. Some typical examples include: "Fastest way to cure symptoms," "Fastest way to fall asleep," "Fastest gas relief," "Remove your wrinkles in only 12 weeks. That's a promise," "You can get a degree in less time than you think," "Chicken Voila: 10 minutes. This good this fast," "Approved in less than 2 minutes," "Be the person you always wanted to be: Right Now," "Fast results with Weight Watchers," "One step and you're done," "Instant Winner," "Absolutely nothing works faster," "Relief of constipation overnight," "Dinner in just 5 minutes." In all these cases, the statements imply that the designated products will gratify a need speedily, and that this gratification in turn "naturally" translates into desirable qualities—popularity, beauty, approval, youth, peace of mind, excitement, etc. Although seemingly un-problematic, statements such as these increasingly establish the curious idea that the quickest solutions to a wide array of problems are necessarily the best ones. Rarely heard is the idea that some problems simply cannot be resolved quickly, and that attempts to use speed might in fact increase their severity.

(c) Commanding. *"Join now!", "Call right now!", "Hurry!", "Don't be late!", "Call today!", "Don't miss it", "Don't wait."* A third textual strategy consists simply in injunctions or direct orders. Such statements do not seek to explain, promise or justify. They simply order us to act fast, faster, or rather right now. Of course, these orders are communicated through various paralinguistic forms: from the soft, sensuous, seductive feminine voice whispering "Hurry to *Victoria's Secret's* semi-annual sale" to the roaring "Call Now!" bark ordering us to hurry without delay to a particular car lot or store. In contrast to the previous strategy which seeks to convince us that a commodity will give us access to speed and to other desired qualities speed connotes, here it is the very absence of justifications or explanations which effectively normalizes the desirability and importance of speed. By routinely ordering viewers to produce a fast response, such statements thus indirectly imply that time is a valued resource and that speed is an important quality of everyday life. Such statements also position the viewer as a certain kind of subject (see Williamson 1992). After all, in what other kinds of everyday life situations do we find ourselves ordered to move fast?

(d) Rewarding. *"Call now and get a free estimate," "Call right now and get two free CDs," "Call right now and get a 15% discount on your first visit," "Join now and get the first month free."* A fourth strategy combines injunctions to respond rapidly with the use of incentives. Here also, this mode of address does not explain to viewers why they should indeed act fast or what is so urgent about consuming a certain commodity or service. Yet, by promising that a fast response will be generously rewarded, through this simple juxtaposition, it is not only the commodity which is celebrated but speed itself. In this case also, such statements position the viewer as a certain kind of subject—a person who will perform at full speed when properly rewarded. In fast capitalism, the logic of rewarding speedy performance in the sphere of *production* now naturally crosses over into the spheres of *consumption* and *leisure*. In both, speed becomes commodified and commands an augmenting exchange value (see also Harvey 1989:284).

(e) Threatening. If the previous strategies fail to generate a rapid response, then a fifth one uses dirtier means. Here, verbalized statements add a certain threat to the simple injunctions noted above. They impose limits on response time and warn that failure to act within these limits will be punished by the sudden disappearance of supposedly important and significant resources. For example: *"Only through Monday"* (or Tuesday, etc.), *"This week-end only," "For a limited time only," "Going fast," "The clock is ticking," "Until February," "Hurry, time is running late," "This is your last chance," "They won't last long," "Won't be around for much longer," "This could be the last time."* Such limits and threats thus naturally associate speed with importance and availability, and its opposite with failure and lack. While such statements never bother to explain why specific commodities would magically vanish after Monday, they also position viewers as certain kinds of subjects whose anxieties are routinely aroused by threats of disappearance and scarcity in the land of plenty. In what other contexts do/did we find ourselves similarly threatened? And to what effects?

(f) Contrasting. While the various verbal strategies listed above construct speed as normal, desirable and important, a sixth one communicates the same ideas, but by using slowness as a negative contrast. Slogans like *"You've waited long enough," "Every minute is a minute too long," "Get real, who has time?"* or *"Tired of waiting?"* constrict slowness as signifying boredom, anxiety, incompetence, and social undesirability. A *Wells Fargo* commercial puts it perhaps most succinctly: *"Speed. It's not about time. It's about respect"*—thereby implying that waiting or slowness is for "losers," those unworthy of respect. A *Western Union* commercial provides a good illustration of this strategy. The opening scene depicts an Oprah-like talk-show audience of mainly African-Americans witnessing a public family quarrel. Sitting on stage and under the public's amused gaze, a fortyish African-American woman is chastising her husband who is sitting next to *her* for his obvious incompetence. His crime? Having used regular mail rather than *Western Union* to send money to an old aunt who needs to fix a leaking bathtub. As the husband fails in his effort to properly justify his behavior (regular mail obviously does not count), the jeering audience endorses the wife's accusations and joins her in this ceremony of "live" public degradation. Since the money sent by regular mail never made it on time, the last segment shows an old African-American woman (presumably the aunt) submerged in her living room now transformed into a human aquarium. As the amused male voice-over claims "*Western Union.* The fastest way to send money," we suspect that the aunt will remain submerged there until the needed money finally reaches her through the proper channels.

Underneath this somewhat amusing story, this ad also inscribes the husband's use of regular mail (hence slowness) as symptomatic of being "cheap" [and] inefficient and of not caring enough. He thus deserves to be publicly humiliated. Through contrast, therefore, speed is associated with generosity, concern, care, and social approval. If the *Wells Fargo* slogan suggests an association between receiving a service speedily and being shown respect, this commercial communicates the same message but by contrast. It associates slowness with social disapproval and ridicule. Similar strategies associating slowness with undesirable social psychological conditions are also visible in countless ads promoting fast food, communication technologies, and medication, among others. The *Motrin* commercial (described below) stating that "every minute is a minute too long," for example, indicates to anxious mothers that rapidly learning the *Motrin* reflex is the necessary step to quickly end their child's suffering and reduce their own guilt.

(2) Paralanguage and Sound Effects

Paralanguage is another important dimension of the textual level in TV ads, and the meanings of the verbalized statements cannot be interpreted solely in terms of *what* is being said. These statements are not just enunciated in a flat and monotonous voice; they are delivered at a certain volume, pitch, stress, rhythm, and tone which—by themselves—communicate excitement, enjoyment, injunction, approbation, urgency, and even threat. Often also, such meanings are not only communicated through these paralinguistic features but also by the music score of commercials (hard rock, heavy metal, alternative, for example) which can act as both background to the verbal message, the pictures, or as texts in their own right. Similarly, swooshing sounds of speeding cars, trains, bikes, arrows, flying beer cans, and airplanes can signify speed by themselves. In a *Motrin* commercial, for example, the first segment opens on a white woman in her thirties who rushes through a hallway to her sick daughter's room. This first segment is completely dominated by the familiar sound of a loud and fast heartbeat which is probably hers (and our own). The sound of this fast beating heart which—given the context—can only connote anxiety and fear, is then replaced by a comfortable and soft lullaby which then recedes in the background as soon as the mother opens the medicine cabinet and grabs a bottle of *Motrin*. The lullaby soundtrack continues through the next segment which depicts the child's fever rapidly decreasing, and guides us to the last one showing the cheerful child in complete remission the next morning. In this commercial, the sounds that dominate in the various segments already communicate particular messages about slowness/waiting and hence about speed. A fast and anxious heartbeat is associated with slowness while a pleasant and comforting lullaby is associated with the relief provided by fast-acting *Motrin*. Similar and other sound effects are of course present in countless commercials and provide yet another important level of signification.

Conclusions

> Speed is the very essence of power (Virilio 1996:16).
>
> We have to face the facts: today, speed is war, the last war (Virilio 1986:137).

I have reviewed here various communication strategies commercial ads deploy to communicate certain preferred meanings about speed. Through these and other strategies, televisual ads normalize speed, celebrate it, and legitimize an everyday where [reality], natural, psychological, physiological and interactional processes unfold at a pace which would be simply delusional to expect in daily life. Although—taken separately—each one of these strategies may seem benign enough, taken together they constitute a self-referential network of messages which colonize increasing areas of everyday life.

Importantly also, televisual ads induce identification, but next to the speed propelling the processes these ads depict, we are always behind, too slow, lacking, or below standards. When pure speed becomes an essential virtue, a necessity, and a resource we increasingly feel entitled to, the normal pace of everyday interaction soon becomes frustratingly slow and intolerable. From the kitchen to the bank, from the workplace to the restaurant, from the phone to the computer, the speed imperative may very well be re-shaping the very mental structures which frame our expectations, experiences, and interpretations—this important realm of consciousness called "common sense." It is also in this sense that Virilio sees speed as profoundly anti-democratic and tyrannical.

At a micro-interactional level, one cannot help but wonder about the extent to which we also become (un)willing vehicles of the speed logic—social accelerators who enforce the speed imperative on self and others. How *do* we reproduce this imperative in the routine interactions of everyday life—on the road? in phone conversations? in face-to-face interactions? in the classroom? at work? on the net? If, as Virilio suggests, speed is a milieu, a tyranny, a new discourse, and a form of (military) occupation which must be resisted, it might perhaps be instructive to develop "breaching experiments" which would aim at a purposeful deceleration of everyday interaction. Such experiments might also yield interesting new knowledge about unexplored aspects of commonsense and consciousness in postmodern society. As Bertman reminds us, "the depth of our understanding is inversely proportionate to our velocity" (1998:84). In other words, "the faster we go, the less we truly see." And he could have added, "understand," "think," "hear," or "experience." Finally, if speed in *social psychological* phenomena follows the same logic as it does in *physical* ones, then we can also expect the former to decrease and weaken upon encountering friction and sustained resistance. In more ways than one, then, to brake down is to break down.

References

Ansay, P. (1994). *Le capitalisme dans la vie quotidienne* [Capitalism in everyday life—untranslated]. Bruxelles: Éditions Vie Ouvrière.

Bertman, P. (1998). *Hyperculture: The human cost of speed.* Westport: Praeger.

Debord, G. (1983). *The society of the spectacle.* Detroit: Black and Red.

Goldman, R. and D. R. Dickens. (1983). "The selling of rural America." *Rural Sociology* 48(4), 585–606.

Gottschalk, S. (1997). "The pains of everyday life: Between the D.S.M. and the postmodern." *Studies in Symbolic Interaction* 21, 115–146.

Harvey, D. (1989). *The condition of postmodernity.* Cambridge: Basil Blackwell.

Pfohl, S. (1992). *Death at the parasite cafe: Social science (fictions) & the postmodern.* New York: St. Martin.

Postman, N. (1985). *Amusing ourselves to death.* New York: Viking.

Rifkin, J. (1987). *Time wars: The primary conflict in human history.* New York: Henry Holt and Co.

Schor, J. B. (1993). *The overworked American: The unexpected decline of leisure.* New York: Basic Books.

Virilio, P. (1996). *Cybermonde: La politique du pire* [Cyberworld: The politics of the worst—untranslated]. Paris: Textuel.

———. (1990). *Popular defenses and ecological struggles.* New York: Semiotext(e).

———. (1986). *Speed and politics.* New York: Semiotext(e).

Williamson, J. (1992). *Decoding advertisements: Ideology and meaning in advertising.* London: Marion Boyars.

Reflective Questions

1. What are the characteristics of speed culture? How has speed become part of our expectations and common sense? What is the temporal ghetto? Should we think of speed culture in this way?
2. What strategies do ads use to promote speed? Why are these strategies so compelling to consumers? How has speed become part of the common sense of school life, work life, and politics in the United States?
3. Pay attention to how you talk, interact with others, and present yourself over the next day or two. How do you promote and embody "speed culture" in your daily actions? Do you expect speed from others? How do you resist speed, and what happens when you do? How does sociological mindfulness shape our reactions to speed culture?
4. During your next visit to a restaurant, look around and notice what technology people are using and how they use it. How is technology shaping their interactions with people, including both those in front of them and those at a distance? Think of the

last time you used technology at the table. Did anyone protest? What did they say, and how did you respond? Did technology facilitate new forms of interaction, such as passing around a picture stored on a phone? Is speed desirable and normal? Should people text while in class? On a date? On a first date?

5. Think of the stories you have heard about dating, disagreeing, and separation of lovers among your grandparents' or parents' generation. Where do you see slow culture in their stories? How has speed and access to technology changed how couples disagree? How has it changed the effects of longer-term geographic separation on romantic relationships?

PART II

The Social Shaping of Subjective Experience

Sociological psychologists stress that once we acquire language and develop a self, we have ourselves as companions. That is, we can think and converse with ourselves in the same ways we communicate with others. We can also define and interpret our own experience through inner conversations. The language, symbols, and understandings that we draw upon in conversing with ourselves are not of our own invention. We have learned them through our interactions with others. Thus, our inner reality is as much constructed as the outer reality we share with others.

The selections in Part II address the social construction of subjective experience. They examine the social shaping of our seemingly individual thoughts, feelings, and perceptions. Each selection illustrates that sociological understanding, rather than being skin deep, reaches into the depths of our individual minds, hearts, and senses. It can do so because the social life we share with others gets under our skin, creating social lives within each of us.

In examining how social life gets under our skin and shapes our inner experiences, the five selections in this section offer the following insights:

- *Our experiences of bodily senses and states are, to a significant degree, products of socially influenced interpretation and somatic work.* We make sense of our bodily sensations, or "inner worlds," through the same processes of naming and interpretation that we use to give meaning to the external world. We do not automatically react to physical or bodily sensations but define and interpret them. These definitions and interpretations are profoundly shaped by social meanings, expectations, and interactions. For instance, as we experience a sensation, such as the smell of cookies baking, we make sense of it in terms of relevant memories, associations, and relationships. If we link this smell to memories of a loving parent or a special family holiday, we will define or experience it positively. By contrast, if we associate it with working long and grueling hours at a bakery, we will interpret and experience it much less favorably.

- *Our perceptions and experiences of bodily sensations, including emotions, are structured by social rules and cultural expectations.* While we often think of emotions as biological, or as originating in our bodies, they arise out of our interactions with others and are shaped by the social definitions and feeling rules provided by the groups to which we belong. Through our interactions with others in these groups, we learn an unwritten set of expectations about how to feel and how to express those feelings in various situations. For example, as Selection 8 highlights, in the United States we learn that the feeling of romantic love is very important (especially if we are adolescent girls). We also learn that the object of our romantic attraction should be a member of the opposite sex, that we should have romantic feelings for only one person at a time, and that this person should not have a romantic relationship with anyone else. If we violate these emotional norms, we discover that others will quickly remind us that we need to get our feelings "under control."
- *To keep our emotions in line with the social expectations that prevail in a given group or setting, we engage in various forms of "emotion work" and draw upon a variety of emotion management strategies.* One of these strategies is "surface acting," or playing the part expected of us in a given context even if our mood or feelings do not match that part. Another is "deep acting," which involves suppressing inappropriate feelings and self-consciously calling forth feelings that match the demands of the situation or the emotional expressions we are conveying to others. Professionals routinely engage in these forms of emotion work as they respond to uncomfortable or anxiety-provoking situations. For instance, professionals learn to deal with uncomfortable or distressing experiences by drawing on strategies such as transforming the meaning of these experiences, using humor to

relieve their own discomfort, focusing on the rewarding elements of their work, redirecting or avoiding troubling feelings, and maintaining affective neutrality.[1]

Most crucially, through engaging in this kind of emotion work, we learn how to translate our experiences into feelings and actions that fit with the demands of a given situation. We also learn to use our emotions for dramaturgical reasons—that is, we learn to use feelings, moods, and emotional expressions to communicate information about ourselves to others and to influence how others define and act toward us. Thus, when we engage in interpersonal emotion management, we take part in the exercise of power. As Christian Vaccaro and his colleagues demonstrate in their study of Mixed Martial Arts fighters, the dramaturgical display of emotion allows the fighters not only to call forth and reshape intense feelings within themselves, but also to evoke desired sentiments in their opponents. Moreover, it enables the fighters to convey their emotions in a highly gendered manner. In other words, their emotional displays serve as means for them to express and manage their "manhood."

- Finally, *organizations, as well as individuals, define and manage bodily states and emotions.* In recent years, sociologists and sociological psychologists have focused increased attention on how organizations shape and manage bodies, feelings, and the experience of embodiment. As Daniel D. Martin demonstrates in Selection 10, weight-related organizations, such as Weight Watchers and Overeaters Anonymous, devote much of their effort to informing their members how they should define the meaning of the bodily state of obesity and how they should manage the shame this state typically evokes in North American culture. In fact, these organizations provide their members with interpretive frames that tell them how to make sense of their obese bodies, how to discuss their bodies with others, how to understand the stigma and shame they may feel, and how to avoid, manage, or confront these feelings of stigmatization and shame.

  On a broader level, Martin's study hints at the growing involvement of organizations in the business of body and emotion work. A plethora of appearance-related organizations, such as health clubs, weight loss associations, self-help groups, therapeutic clinics, athletic teams, civil rights groups, and cosmetic surgery clinics, are engaged in telling us how to manage our bodies and related feelings. In the process, these organizations offer us a broad range of resources (e.g., routines, medications, ideologies, support systems, identity narratives, and emotion work strategies) that we can use to structure our bodily states and emotional experiences. In turn, a growing number of us are relying on appearance organizations to help us understand and manage our bodies and what is going on "inside" of them. This trend demonstrates how organizations succeed in getting under our skin and how we often invite them to do so.

Note

[1] See Allen C. Smith and Sherryl Kleinman, "Managing Emotions in Medical School: Student Contacts with the Living and the Dead," *Social Psychology Quarterly* 52(1): 56–69, 1986 and Clinton Sanders, "Working Out Back: The Veterinary Technician and 'Dirty Work,'" *Journal of Contemporary Ethnography* 39(3): 243–272.

6

Smell, Odor, and Somatic Work

DENNIS D. WASKUL AND PHILLIP VANNINI

In recent years researchers have focused increased attention on the "sociology of the senses," or how human senses and perceptions are influenced by social factors. Sociological interest in this topic has a long history, as illustrated in the analyses of Georg Simmel and George Herbert Mead, who wrote in the late 1800s and early 1900s. While Simmel emphasized the important role that our senses play in facilitating social interaction, it was Mead who highlighted how our social experiences and interactions get built right into our central nervous systems, thereby having a profound impact on how we perceive the world and ourselves.

Inspired by the insights of both Simmel and Mead, the following selection by Dennis Waskul and Phillip Vannini presents an innovative study of sociosomatics, or how the social world shapes our bodily sensations and processes. Drawing on data derived from journals kept by 23 graduate students, Waskul and Vannini demonstrate how one of our most powerful senses—smell—is informed and influenced by social meanings and expectations. They point out that to sense a smell, whether it is the smell of freshly baked cookies, a scented candle, or a pile of cow manure, is to make sense of it. That is, the act of smelling is marked by somatic work, or the process of interpreting bodily sensation and perception. Our interpretation of a particular smell, such as the odor of a turkey baking, is shaped by a variety of social factors, including our interactions, relationships, experiences, and memories of those experiences.

Waskul and Vannini also reveal how our sense of smell, like other perceptions, is structured by somatic rules grounded in cultural norms and linked to a larger moral order. In essence, the meanings we give to smells are commonly linked to value judgments. These value judgments are rooted in cultural expectations regarding the proper intensity of odors, the appropriate context for these odors, and the character assessments associated with "bad" or offensive odors, such as the smells that are emitted by either end of the human digestive system or by unwashed armpits. We attach moral judgments to these smells, and we tend to regard those who emit these bad odors as "bad" people. Because of these judgments, the management of odor is a core feature of our everyday interactions and identity work. As Waskul and Vannini observe, we carefully and strategically manipulate the odors on our bodies and in our environments to get others to view us favorably. Like most of us, the respondents in their study took great care to regulate their bodily odors and to remedy any undesirable scents, including bathroom odors, when they occurred. Thus, they became centrally concerned with odor management, or "smelling nice," as they presented themselves to others. They recognized that managing odors was an essential feature of managing the impressions of others.

Reprinted from: Dennis D. Waskul and Phillip Vannini, "Smell, Odor, and Somatic Work: Sense-Making and Sensory Management." *Social Psychology Quarterly* 71(1): 53–71.

Waskul and Vannini's analysis of how we experience and respond to odors has broad implications. It illustrates how we do not react automatically to physical sensations but define and interpret them. We cannot do anything we please with either the external environment or our bodies, but we can interpret our perceptions of them in an infinite variety of ways. Our social experience is the source of those possible interpretations. It shapes our bodily sensations and experiences, including our experiences of pain, illness, excitement, and sexual pleasure, to name but a few. Physiological sensations, then, are only the raw materials out of which our bodily experiences are socially constructed.

Few social norms are clearer than those which stipulate against foul odors (see Tuzin 2006). As Corbin (1986) has pointed out, rules against the excessive presence of odors have been strictly and invariantly enforced throughout successive historical waves of the sanitization movement. . . .

Indeed, olfactory somatic rules are largely legitimized by discourses of "health" and "cleanliness" (Largey and Watson 1972)—discourses that, among many things, equate cleanliness with godliness and that which is healthy and clean with a pleasant smell—a cultural motif frequently exploited by the advertising industry. For example, "laundry not only has to be clean, but it has to *smell* clean" (Synnott 1993:193, emphasis in original).

As stated by Largey and Watson (1972:1022), "particular odors, whether real or alleged, are sometimes used as indicants of the moral purity of particular individuals and groups within the social order, the consequences of which are indeed real." The bitter stench of stigma clearly reveals moral judgment (see Tuzin 2006). During the middle ages, it was believed that sorcerers and heretics could be detected by their foul odor (Summers 1956:44). In medieval Europe, one of the most widely accepted theories of causes of the plague was the pathogenic odor of putrefaction (Classen, Howes, and Synnott 1994). Even Martin Luther agreed that contagion "poisoned the air or otherwise infected the poor people by their breath and injected the moral poison into their bodies" (Norton 1975:20). Just as "evil stinks" (Synnott 1993:191), the aroma of sanctity is pleasing. In the book of Exodus (30:22–4), the Lord gave Moses a formula and instructions to create perfume. In the New Testament, Jesus was anointed with perfume from an alabaster vase—a treatment suitable for the most worldly great and, according to Matthew (26:6–13), much appreciated by at least this living deity.

The fundamentally public nature of odor partly explains why olfaction so directly intersects with morality and moral discourse. In direct opposition to the fundamentally private nature of taste (see Fine 1995), odor is shared by all within olfactory sensual proximity. For this reason Dewey (1887:222) deemed taste the most "personal in the narrowest of sense" and smell more communal due to its "objective and universal" quality:

> It must be noticed that the organic sensations and taste are personal in the narrowest of sense . . . a substance must be actually taken into the organism through the mouth before it can be tasted. Such feelings tend to divide one individual from another, for their enjoyment by one is either not shared with another, or is actually incompatible with such sharing. In smell, feeling becomes a whit more objective and universal. The odorous object, as a whole, is not dissolved in the organism. A number may get and enjoy similar feelings from one object.

In short, olfaction is a rich arena for sociological investigation, especially in terms of morality, because odor is fundamentally public and shared. Like dust (Fine and Hallett 2003:12), odor "once recognized, becomes a cultural marker and is used to create social order . . . [olfaction] is not simply something that happens. It is something with which groups must deal. As groups deal with [odor], they reproduce the larger cultures in which they are embedded, they demonstrate processes of contention and control, and they negotiate meanings through similar processes that occur in larger units."

Because olfaction and odor are constructions of normative aesthetic and moral code, olfactory rules are enforced and odor is faithfully managed. The management of odor is common and widespread, observable in almost every body, everywhere. In Anglo-phone North America, odor is traditionally something to be eliminated or produced—on (and in) the body, the home, at work, automobiles, our communities—by use of air fresheners, deodorants, breath mints, fans, ventilation, air purification systems, and pollution laws. Even the mere mention of odors in conversation, especially body odors, is a delicate subject and it is not uncommon to find ourselves occasionally ignoring or denying the presence of uncontrollable, bad odors out of both a sense of tactfulness and taboo (cf. Zerubavel 2006). Adherence to the olfaction rules of moral odor/moral order represent more than the folkways of a culture and more than a matter of manners, politeness, and etiquette. As testified by recent "scent free" work and public space regulations, violations of olfaction rules are of potential legal concern and the production of inappropriate odor can be cause for civil litigation (although, given its gaseous consequences, one might wonder if the same logic might result in a bean prohibition—at least for human consumption, and possibly, our companion animals). . . .

Methods and Data

We collected data through the use of research journals (Alaszewski 2006). We asked two cohorts of graduate students enrolled in an applied communication program at Royal Roads Western Canadian University to record their experiences with smell over a period of two weeks. We approached the students with an email explaining our interest in the role of non-verbal communication and solicited volunteers to participate. We did not promise extra credit or other incentives. Those who volunteered were provided with instructions and the research journal via email as an electronic file. We also invited the students to solicit the participation of acquaintances of theirs whom they thought might be interested in the study. We guaranteed anonymity by creating a research email account, which participants could use to send us their completed journals in the form of email attachments. A total of twenty-three journals were completed, fifteen by women and eight by men. Ages ranged from twenty-four to fifty-nine, with a mean of almost thirty-eight years of age. The sample was ethnically diverse, including fifteen Caucasians, two East Indians, two East Asians, two South Americans, one Middle Easterner, and one African.

The journals contained questions that asked participants to describe their favorite and least favorite odors, to identify memories associated with odors, to document daily body-odor management efforts, to describe moments when during the course of daily life they became explicitly aware of smell, and to disclose and describe a situation in which they felt they smelled bad. In response to seven questions, respondents answered with as few as 181 words and as many as 1,303. Average response was just under 700 words (roughly two and one-half pages of double-spaced typed text).

Sensations of smell, like sensations of taste, are not easy to express (Fine 1995) and for this reason we felt that the use of the written word, and the reflective possibilities that writing provides, would help our research endeavors. Whereas the collection of data via the use of research journals offers the researcher no opportunity to observe interaction, it offers a wealth of reflective, thought-out, richly descriptive self-reported verbal data that allows the researcher to focus on the semiotic and linguistic components of olfactory experiences. . . .

Making Sense of Odors

Olfaction is commonly marked by what we call *somatic work*: a process whereby a somatic perception undergoes a reflexive interpretation. Such interpretation is marked by activities such as active reminiscing, forming chains of associations, evaluating, interpreting the significance of unique biographical particulars and/or social norms, and attributing meanings. Thus somatic work yields evaluations that fall in line with interpersonal and/or normative expectations. Consider, for example, the somatic work that accounts for Kate's (age 29, ellipses in original) dislike of the smell of baby powder.

> I despise the smell of baby powder. I went out with a guy who put it down his pants and to this day it makes me a bit sick. We went out for a couple of years and he was pretty tortured, negative, smoked too much pot, wanted to live in a cabin away from all people—he hated people for some reason. We had some kind of crazy chemistry and I did love him, but that part is hard to remember. He would wear jeans that were waaay [sic] too baggy, weighed down with a big belt, wallet chain, and smelling like baby powder mixed with pot and cigarettes. That is my strongest memory of him . . . maybe it was that the smell permeated the air of a relationship that was thoroughly bad for me. It makes me shudder when I think of it.

Kate's narrative displays what we refer to as the sense-making component of somatic work, a type of negotiating activity that constitutes work even in the absense of highly expressive language. For example, in the excerpt below Frank (age 45) described one of his favorite odors—vividly evaluating the sense that he makes of it—all of this without describing its essence. Frank explains, "One of my favorite smells is that of fresh baked bread. It reminds me of many things including my grandmother, my mother, my brother and I making numerous loaves to get ready for winter in Alberta. It has associated with it thoughts of a warm kitchen, important people in my life."

As Synnott (1993:187) has argued, "odor, memory and meaning are . . . intimately linked and reach deep into our personal lives, all day, every day." . . . A *somatic career* is the historical dimension of somatic work: a living history of the somatic self and of the social organization of the labor of perception, as well as a received orientation to future somatic work. Somatic careers are built of habits of sensing.

Habits of Sensing

Our data analysis shows that, rather than elaborating on the essential qualities of the odors themselves alone, participants were more likely to distinguish between enjoyable and disagreeable odors in terms of the habits of sensing that olfaction evokes. For example, Frank's sense-making reported above is informed by meaningful biographical resources—family memories that date back to his childhood in Alberta—which bear on his olfactory evaluation. These "involuntary memories" (cf. Proust 2001) are semiotic resources that inform his interpretation. We refer to these biographical resources as *habits of sensing*, i.e., sense-making patterns that express, articulate, and are the result of individual and collective sensorial biographies and histories.

By taking into account an individual or a group's somatic career, it is easy to understand the evaluative outcomes of perception. Consider, for example, Ashley's (age 48) account in the excerpt below; even the occasionally questionable smell of Lake Ontario (and lake water in general) gives rise to positive evaluations that are understandable by virtue of her reported nostalgic feelings.

> [I enjoy of the smell of t]he shore of a fresh water lake! Because I grew up close to Lake Ontario (long enough ago that it smelled ok most days). I went down to the lake in all stages of my life. With my family as a young child, with my friends when we went off on our bikes, as a teenager for quiet, and as a young adult on runs and refuge . . . to look out over the water, listen and breathe. It all goes together under the smell.

Nostalgia shapes the meaning of odor by dwelling at the core of individual biography and "at the very heart of a generation's identity" (Davis 1979:111). Nostalgia is a form of attachment to habits, in this case habits of perception, which play a powerful role in sense-making. As each of the following illustrate, nostalgia informs the interpretive act as a cluster of habits and perspectives, as a form of sentimental selective attention (James 1890; Mead 1938) toward certain characters of the sensory fields—an attention "which answers both to [the perceiver's] immediate sensitivities and to his [sic] experience" (Mead 1938:7).

> I remember a kid's book called Pat the Bunny which has different textures for kids to touch; daddy's rough beard (sandpaper), a shiny mirror, etc.

> At the end, you got to pat the bunny's belly, which was soft cottony fur and has a very unique smell. I bought the book again several years ago when a friend had a baby and found that it still smells the same—a little bit like baby soap or something, but very distinct. It brings me right back to my childhood. I think it's a combination of a nice, clean, fragrance combined with happy childhood memories (I loved that book and remember reading it with unidentifiable but very nice adults) that makes it so special (Kate, 29).

> One of the most pleasurable odors I recall is from my childhood—it was during the fall in Edmonton when my parents would make mustard pickle. This would take an entire weekend and involved the chopping and cutting of cauliflower, peppers, onions, etc. and the very strong scent of vinegar and mustard would take over our house. It was a happy memory of my parents together in the kitchen, engaging in a ritualistic activity as the coziness of fall and autumn surrounded us (Rose, 39).

. . . "Habits are acquired" functions—wrote Dewey (1922:14)—which manifest "skill of sensory and motor organs, cunning or craft, and objective materials. They assimilate objective energies, and eventuate in command of environment" (Dewey 1922:15). Habits are not synonymous with sensing, yet for Dewey (1922:32) it is "habitual attitudes which govern concrete sensory materials." Thus we intend our concept of habits of sensing as "filters [of] all the material that reaches our perception and thought." It is precisely these habits of sensing that account for Peter's (age 57) attachment to the scent of face powder; his habituation with the fragrance his grandmother used to exude and as wistful disposition toward earlier times.

> My mother's mother, my Nana, used a face powder. She was a poor widow-lady so her choice of product was probably the cheapest available in Moncton, New Brunswick in the 1950s. But it was her smell. Throughout my life I've had fleeting sniffs, usually of old ladies, that take me back like Proust's Madeleine, to being 5 years old and meeting my Nana at the bus station after her shift at the airplane engine factory (she was a "Rosie the Riveter" who wasn't laid off after WW2). Her unfailing gift of a stick of Juicy Fruit gum was the highlight of my day. It was pure unadulterated pleasure to be hugged and kissed by my powdery Nana.

As we have illustrated, participants told of nostalgic feelings for moments in time—they also expressed nostalgic feelings for special places, which are often informed by feelings of "displacement" or the "involuntary disruption of place attachment" (Milligan 2003:381). As Milligan argued, displacement from a beloved place is marked by discontinuity in one's biographical identity and in this fashion "nostalgia provides one way of maintaining or regaining identity continuity" (380). Examples of this relation have been noted by researchers of smell (e.g. Hirsch 2006) and also abound in our data. For example, Susan (age 25, ellipses in original) identifies her liking of the smell of Coppertone sun block lotion with vacationing in Spain:

> This is such a funny thing to have as a favorite smell, but I just love it. I used to say that if I could find it in a perfume I would wear it everyday! When I was little, my family used to go to Spain for vacations. Every year we would pack up and ship out for three weeks. This was the only time when I actually saw my father, as he was often away half the year traveling for work (and the other half he spent at the office) so I associate a sense of wellbeing and peace with that smell. It was great to be so carefree—no school, no chores . . . nothing to do but swim and run around in the sun! I smell it sometimes on other people, usually in the summer, and I get immediately transported to the beach. I feel warm, I can hear the waves . . . it's quite the experience!

Similarly, Allison (age 32) is delighted by the smell of jasmine because it evokes blissful memories of her experiences in Thailand:

> The most pleasurable odor I recall is the smell of jasmine flowers opening on a warm evening. On a trip back to Bangkok from Changmai, Thailand I

> remember sitting on the train car surrounded by my backpack and all my personal possessions. I had spent the morning at the market shopping for food items for a Thai cooking class that I was taking. My instructor bought each of her students a necklace of jasmine flowers at the market that were tightly closed. It wasn't until the warmth of the day had taken effect and the flowers began to open on the evening train trip that I noticed that I still had the necklace on. The smell was wonderfully sweet and musty and encompassed all the good things I had experienced in Thailand. I rarely smell the same smell anymore but when I do it reminds me of my independence traveling alone in foreign lands and the beauty of Thailand.

On the other hand, even an odor generally deemed pleasant or neutral can be interpreted as noxious when linked to negative memories. Consider, for example, Beth's (age 31) "gag reflex" at the smell of the fabric stain-remover Spray and Wash:

> Right now I would say [I dislike the smell of] Spray and Wash because I recently had a very bad and sickly night that involved imbibing large quantities of red wine. By "accident," I spilled a glass of red wine on the white carpet in the office of my parent's house. They were away on vacation at the time and so I drunkenly panicked [and] tried my best to clean it up. I didn't know where they kept their carpet cleaner, so instead I used Spray and Wash, the stain remover for clothing. I used half the bottle on the stain. I reasoned at the time that more was better and the more it soaked into the carpet the more the stain would magically disappear. To make a long story short, my brain has linked the two smells (red wine & Spray and Wash), and my sickly drunken state together to create an instant gag reflex at the smell of Spray and Wash.

Beth's evaluation of Spray and Wash has nothing to do with the essential qualities of the odor itself—it can only be understood in light of her unique somatic career, that is, in light of a sensorial reservoir of "memories that contains versatile, resourceful interpretive models and cultural schemes" (Rapoport, Lomsky-Feder, and Heider 2002:176). This is not to suggest that all odors are associated with biographical particulars or that odors' essential qualities are inconsequential. Rather, we suggest that perceptions associated with "symbolic images and allusions from the past . . . by virtue of their resource in a particular person's biography tend to be more idiosyncratic, individualized, and particularistic in their reference" (Davis 1979:222) and thus tend to matter greatly within individual acts of perception. Habits shape sense-making by functioning as interpretive resources rooted in past sensation and conduct, but at the same time in the very course of their operation in the process of perception habits have the potential of adding "new qualities and rearrang[ing] what is received" (Dewey 1922:32). This aspect of the process is magnified in the case of *somatic escalation*, the second component of somatic career. . . .

Somatic Rules and Somatic Escalation

Ashley's (age 48) statement:

> I think smell immediately communicates to guests if a home is hygienic, or well cared for, and consequently, if the family cares well for itself. Civilized I suppose. Status. A foul smelling home is totally low class—same with an individual. The consequences of not paying attention to odors in the home could be hygienic/illness and stigma.

For Ashley certain odors "immediately" connote hygiene (or lack thereof). Hygiene is associated with care for the self and others, class, status, health, and civilization. Ashley is not alone in these sentiments. For example, linking bad smell of her children with the code of motherly labor of love, Karla (age 32) writes,"[My least favorite smell is] the smell of my children when I tuck them in at night and they should have had a bath—the way their hair smells—it makes me feel as though I have neglected my motherly duties." Ashley (age 48) echoes Karla's sentiments by linking the odor of feces with a call to motherly duty to keep up with hygienic control of the house and children:

> [My least favorite is the smell of] poo. For a while there my daughter was in diapers, I had two cats with their litter tray, and was house training a very

> large (45 lb) puppy. I got terribly tired of looking after their potty habits! It was also worrisome that if things got the slightest bit ahead of me, the house would smell, or my daughter might get some on her hands. Hygiene and self-respect go together.

Perception is often associated with cultural values (Fine 1995; Zerubavel 1997). As Fine (1995:246) writes, "sensory judgments are grounded in social relationships, face-to-face negotiations, social structures, and organizations." These are value judgments that have seemingly "immediate" and potent somatic significance: odor is perceived, with great ease, as essentially bad, foul, ill, thus conflating what emanates a particular odor with how that object smells. It is, indeed, *common sense*—an expression that refers to a widely shared way of making sense of sensory perceptions—to suggest that a certain olfactory condition has seemingly "natural" or "essential" qualities which make it good or bad or even uncivilized, sick, and low in social status. Yet—regardless of the prevailing beliefs that these immediate associations are "natural"—they are inevitably learned (Herz 2006), and thus cultural, even ideological. Thus are the conditions of *somatic escalation*—conditions in which the denotation and connotation of an odor are blurred into one immediate "common-sense perception," so that an odor immediately and simultaneously both denotes and connotes an abstract evaluative concept (like civilized hygiene or status)....

A somatic escalation is, in sum, a process of naturalization: of turning multiple abstract interpretations, deeply entrenched within a culture and highly idiosyncratic, into an illusion that perception is natural and free of interpretive work; into an illusion that the object and the sense that is made of it are immediate, "common-sense," identical, and transparent. As Volosinov (1973:105) has rightly pointed out, "meaning is molded by evaluation ... meaning is always permeated with value judgment."

The fact that some odors are judged offensive and others are deemed pleasing clearly implies a system of order that is bound by somatic rules that are normatively aesthetic and moral. Borrowing from Douglas (1970:48), we suggest that disagreeable odors are those that offend against order; they are "the by-product of a systematic ordering and classification of matter, in so far as ordering involves rejecting inappropriate elements." Offensive odors are those that deviate from olfactory somatic rules. Somatic escalation functions on the basis of somatic rules for sense-making. Somatic rules are contextual and diverse; their application is consistent but variable. Our data show the functioning of basic olfactory somatic rules disciplining somatic work in relation to variables such as the intensity of odor, its context, and its moral/aesthetic character.

The olfaction order of prevailing somatic rules entails a negotiated structure of intensity. Odor is sometimes perceived as too pungent or perhaps not fragrant enough. Several participants in this study wrote about the desire to be aromatic—but also expressed concerns about overpowering scent. Nichole (age 40) wrote: "I like to wear a fragrance that is appealing, yet not overpowering." Kate (age 29) recollects her near *faux pas*—a close rush with olfactory intensity deviance—how a friend reminded her of the applicable somatic rule, and her prompt conformity: "I tried some perfume (from a sample my sister-in-law gave me) this evening before going out for dinner with a friend. She said it was too strong, so I washed it off." More than just a personal preference, for some participants in this study, olfactory somatic rules of intensity are regulated and enforced by contemporary "fragrance free" mandates that demand olfactory political correctness.

> In my field of work, and generally in public service, there has been a push toward scent free environments. So, aftershaves, cologne, and perfumes are not politically correct. There also seems to be a higher prevalence of environmental allergies. Those allergies can be debilitating. Finding a good deodorant without a scent is difficult (Frank, 45).

Olfaction order also concerns a negotiated structure of contexts: we are more or less sensitive to odor depending on whether we perceive the aroma as appropriate to the context. As Michelle (age 30) suggests, the smell of garlic may be appealing in a Caesar salad but, once consumed, the same aroma evoked a very different response in her friend's car:

> There was a day (way back when) that I went to Earl's for lunch and had a Caesar salad. I was probably 17 or 18 years old. I enjoyed the salad at the time. It wasn't until I sat in an enclosed space (my friend's car) that I noticed that the smell of garlic was radiating from my pores. The garlic smell was even more apparent to me when my friend commented. I felt awful. We both agreed that stopping to get some gum or mints was a very good idea.

Even a normally disagreeable odor might be deemed pleasing when appropriately contextualized. Unpleasant odors can be made tolerable if the circumstances are appropriate. For example, Ashley (age 48) admits to enjoying the smell of her dog—"even though he smells rather awful"—and explains, "[I enjoy the smell of m]y dog when we cuddle. Frankly even though he smells rather awful, the scent is associated with our 'friendship.' It smells like home, and oddly enough, peace."

Finally, olfaction order is also structured by somatic rules regarding assessments of moral/aesthetic character. As previously suggested, many odors are immediately evaluated as positive or negative, good or bad, and these evaluations are not neutral: what smells good is good, what smells bad is bad (Herz 2006; Synnott 1993). For example, Jackie (age 36) wrote, "It is important to control or manipulate odor on your body when you will be in social situations so that you are not judged based on poor body odor. Strong or bad body odor could be taken as a sign of being unclean or sloppy."

Among the most morally and aesthetically offensive are odors that originate in the body, odiously upset public space, and assault the olfaction of others. As Simmel suggests, "that we can smell the atmosphere of somebody is the most intimate perception of him [or her]"—and some atmospheres are apparently too intimate, obliging "a selection and a taking of distance" (1907:658). Particularly offensive is the moral and aesthetic character of odors that originate and waft from either end of the digestive system: halitosis, vomit, flatulence, urine, and feces. There is a cultural expectation as to what belongs inside and outside the body and odors that violate these expectations are considered polluting or contaminating (Turner 2003; Weinberg and Williams 2005). Thus, for example, participants in this study were commonly concerned about bad breath. Kate (29) said, "I'm always slightly paranoid about having bad breath. If I don't have gum or haven't just brushed my teeth, I'm careful not to get too close to whomever I'm talking to, and assume that any reaction/blink is them flinching at my halitosis." Because fecal products are regarded as a "universal disgust substance" (Rozin, Haidt, and McCauley 1993:579), several participants in this study suggest flatulence and the smell of feces especially contaminate moral and aesthetic character:

> As part of the long term effects of a broken back and fractured pelvis, my bowel functions can sometimes be impacted . . . literally! This can lead to flatulence. I find it most embarrassing to be at a work meeting or in a small event and to be experiencing this social challenge (Frank, 45 ellipses in original).

Allowing one's fecal smells to escape and assault the olfaction of others "suggests a momentary loss of control" (Goffman 1963:69, also see Weinberg and Williams 2005). This kind of control—and guarding against its loss—clearly implicates the expressive and impressive dimensions of olfactory impression management. In short, somatic rules of intensity, context, and moral/aesthetic character intersect with the normative dramaturgies of everyday life and rituals of face-work (Goffman 1967). "Aesthetic order"—as Fine (1995:266) has elegantly and succinctly put—is "a domain of social order." . . .

Conclusions

"That which we call a rose by any other word would smell as sweet"—or so muses Juliet in

Shakespeare's famous tragedy (Act II, Scene 2). However, not withstanding romance—in fact, quite to the contrary—our analysis suggests olfactory perception is not so simple. Olfactory perception hinges on active sense-making. Odor is made meaningful through denotative and connotative indexes, active reminiscing, the formulation of chains of associations, evaluation, interpretation, the significance of unique biographical particulars, the social norms of olfactory communities, and the indexical properties and qualities of odors themselves. Through smell, meaning is reflexively bestowed unto odor in the context of negotiated somatic rules. For this reason, odor is a "sign vehicle" (Goffman 1959) we thus manipulate and manage on bodies and in environments in an effort to convey desired impressions. Clearly, odor is a subtle but significant component of the culturally normative and aesthetic rituals of expressive and impressive everyday life.

"Smell is powerful" and yet, for the most part, "we breathe in the aromas which surround us without being consciously aware of their importance to us" (Classen, Howes, and Synnott 1994:1). Perhaps that explains the power of odor: olfactory perception seems so "natural," so unmitigated, such a raw, basic, and fundamental animal function. But this study suggests otherwise; the human animal defies such simplicities. We have empirically illustrated what Classen, Howes, and Synnott (1994:3, emphasis in original) conceptually argue—"smell is *cultural*." Yet, without pushing our social constructionist ontology too far, we have highlighted how odors themselves are signs: indexes carrying unique odoriferous qualities, a true potential for meaning. The physiological nature of odors is, in fact, the raw material of which olfactory perception is fashioned—and that fashioning is quintessentially cultural and natural at the same time. An object's meanings, including sensory perceptions, reside not in the object itself alone, but in the interaction or transaction of conduct directed toward it and the qualities emanating from it (Dewey 1934; Mead 1938; also see Halton 2004). In short, it is through forms of somatic work that sensory meaning is made. Indeed, as we suggested from the very beginning, people sense as well as make sense. Goffman (1967:44–5, emphasis added) provocatively suggests that:

> If persons have a universal human nature, they themselves are not to be looked to for an explanation of it. One must look rather to the fact that societies everywhere, if they are to be societies, must mobilize their members as self-regulating participants in social encounters. One way of mobilizing the individual for this purpose is through ritual; *he is taught to be perceptive*. . . . It is these elements that are referred to in part when one speaks of universal human nature. Universal human nature is not a very human thing. By acquiring it, the person becomes a kind of construct, built up not from inner psychic propensities but from moral rules that are impressed upon him from without.

The same may be said of the "common sense" of sense-making—olfactory or otherwise. Part of the seemingly universal "nature" of olfaction precisely owes to the fact that it is made "common sense" through ritual.

References

Alaszewski, Andy. 2006. *Using Diaries for Social Research*. Thousand Oaks, CA: Sage.

Classen, Constance, David Howes, and Anthony Synnott. 1994. *Aroma: The Cultural History of Smell*. New York: Routledge.

Corbin, Alain. 1986. *The Foul and the Fragrant: Odor and the French Social Imagination*. Boston, MA: Harvard University Press.

Davis, Fred. 1979. *Yearning for Yesterday: A Sociology of Nostalgia*. New York: Free Press.

Dewey, John. 1934. *Art as Experience*. New York: Minton.

———. [1887] 1967. *John Dewey: The Early Works* 1882–1898, Volume 2, edited by Herbert W. Schneider. Carbondale, IL: Southern Illinois University Press.

———. [1922] 2002. *Human Nature and Conduct*. Amherst, NY: Prometheus Books.

Douglas, Mary. 1970. *Purity and Danger: An Analysis of Concepts of Pollution and Taboo*. London, UK: Harmondsworth.

Fine, Gary A. 1995. "Wittgenstein's Kitchen: Sharing Meaning in Restaurant Work." *Theory and Society* 24:245–269.

Fine, Gary A., and Tim Hallett. 2003. "Dust: A Study in Sociological Miniaturism." *Sociological Quarterly* 44:1–15.

Goffman, Erving. 1959. *The Presentation of Self in Everyday Life*. Garden City, NY: Doubleday.

———. 1963. *Stigma: Notes on the Management of Spoiled Identity*. Englewood Cliffs, NJ: Prentice-Hall.

———. 1967. *Interaction Ritual: Essays in Face-to-Face Behavior.* Chicago, IL: Aldine.

Halton, Eugenee. 2004. "The Living Gesture and the Signifying Moment." *Symbolic Interaction* 27:89-114.

Herz, Rachel S. 2006. "I Know What I Like: Understanding Odor Preferences." Pp 75–94 in *The Smell Culture Reader*, edited by Jim Drobnick. New York: Berg.

Hirsch, Alan. 2006. "Nostalgia: The Odours of Childhood and Society." Pp 134–152 in *The Smell Culture Reader*, edited by Jim Drobnick. New York: Berg.

James, William. [1890] 1983. *Principles of Psychology.* Boston, MA: Harvard University Press.

Largey, Gale P., and David R. Watson. 1972. "The Sociology of Odours." *American Journal of Sociology* 77:1021–1034.

Mead, George H. 1938. *The Philosophy of the Act.* Chicago, IL: University of Chicago Press.

Milligan, Melinda. 2003. "Displacement and Identity Continuity: The Role of Nostalgia in Establishing New Identity Categories." *Symbolic Interaction* 26:381–404.

Norton, T. 1975. *Ordinal of Alchemy.* Oxford, UK: Oxford University Press.

Proust, Marcel. 2001. *In Search of Lost Time.* New York: Random House.

Rapaport, Tamar, Edna Lomsky-Feder, and Angelika Heider. 2002. "Recollection and Relocation in Immigration: Russian-Jewish Immigrants 'Normalize' Their Anti-Semitic Experiences." *Symbolic Interaction* 25:175–198.

Rozin, Paul, Jonathan Haidt, and Clark McCauley. 1993. "Disgust." Pp 575–594 in *Handbook of Emotions*, edited by Michael Lewis and Jeanette Haviland. New York: The Guilford Press.

Simmel, Georg. [1907] 1997. "Sociology of the Senses." Pp 109–120 in *Simmel on Culture*, edited by David Frisby and Mike Featherstone. Thousand Oaks, CA: Sage.

Synnott, Anthony. 1993. *The Body Social: Symbolism, Self, and Society.* London: Routledge.

Summers, Montague. 1956. *The History of Witchcraft and Demonology.* New York: University Books.

Turner, Bryan. 2003. "Social Fluids: Metaphors and Meanings of Society." *Body and Society* 9:1–10.

Tuzin, Donald. 2006. "Base Notes: Odor, Breath, and Moral Contagion in Ilahita." Pp 23–44 in *The Smell Culture Reader*, edited by Jim Drobnick. New York: Berg.

Volosinov, Valentin. 1973. *Marxism and the Philosophy of Language.* New York: Seminar Press.

Weinberg, Martin and Colin Williams. 2005. "Fecal Matters: Habitus, Embodiments, and Deviance." *Social Problems* 52:315–336.

Zerubavel, Eviatar. 1997. *Social Mindscapes: An Invitation to Cognitive Sociology.* Cambridge, MA: Harvard University Press.

———. 2006. *The Elephant in the Room: Silence and Denial in Everyday Life.* New York: Oxford University Press.

Reflective Questions

1. What is somatic work? What are some "habits of sensing"? How does smelling a particular scent translate into nostalgia or moral judgments about people?
2. What does it mean to argue that "smell is cultural"? What somatic rules and other social factors influence the somatic order? For two days, keep your own smell and sound journal. What smells and sounds catch your attention and what images, memories, evaluations, and emotions do they evoke? Which smells and sounds do you find most offensive and which do you find most pleasing? Which sensations denote high or low status? What rituals and somatic rules have influenced your ordering of somatic experiences this way? How do you manage your own smells in response to your habits of sensing?
3. Marketers and consumer consultants are often quite sociologically mindful about smells, sounds, and other sensory experiences. They know that certain music playlists, for example, compel consumers to stay longer in stores, browse, and spend more. Pay attention to the music playing in

various businesses and offices you enter. What music is playing at the grocery store? The gym? The doctor's office? While you are on hold? What interpretations and behaviors do these various playlists evoke in you? Why? Why does music often fade into the background in these settings?

4. Pain is a somatic experience that individuals experience and treat to various degrees. Because of this variability in "tolerance" to pain, medical personnel use subjective pain scales to assess individuals' pain level and determine appropriate treatment. (For instance, on a scale of one to ten, how bad is the pain? Ten is excruciating and intolerable.) But if somatic experiences are culturally inscribed, pain tolerance is socially ordered. Consider the case of childbirth, about which cultural depictions of pain abound. In the United States, where nearly all women give birth in hospitals, where do women learn what labor will feel like and how to manage pain? What common narratives address pain in childbirth? How is pain depicted in widely released Hollywood films? How do these cultural depictions affect women's interpretations of pain and pain management? How does pain management differ in other cultures? Why? Consider the same series of questions about managing pain inflicted by sports injuries.

7

Emotion Work and Feeling Rules

ARLIE RUSSELL HOCHSCHILD

Many people believe that their "true" self speaks through their emotions—emotions that are immune to social influence. Yet, many of these same people go to parties to feel good, enroll in anger management classes, and seek therapy for phobias. They implicitly recognize that feelings are more pliable than they would like to admit. There may be something innate to human emotions, but they are far from fixed. Human emotions seem to vary as much as the languages that humans speak.

For many years, students of social life ignored emotions. That changed in the late 1970s. A number of sociologists began to study and write about the social shaping and consequences of human emotionality. Arlie Russell Hochschild was one of the first to explore the subject. This selection outlines her influential approach to the sociological study and understanding of emotions.

Hochschild was admittedly not the first to recognize that emotions are subject to social regulation. She credits Erving Goffman for doing so but criticizes him for limiting attention to outward expressions of emotion. Hochschild notes that individuals attempt not only to express but also to feel what they think they should be feeling. This "emotion work" involves more than the mere surface acting of emotional expression. It also involves the deep acting of suppressing and evoking the very feelings from which emotional expression flows.

As Hochschild observes, both individuals' surface acting and deep acting of emotions are guided by "feeling rules." Although these rules are written nowhere and are seldom explicitly articulated, individuals subtly remind one another of them in a variety of ways. They inform one another of what they should, should not, and "must" be feeling. Normal feelings are socially normative feelings, and individuals work on their emotions to feel normal. Thus, variations in normal human emotions are products of variations in the feeling rules among human social groups. It is not so much the true self but social experience that speaks through our emotions.

Why is the emotive experience of normal adults in daily life as orderly as it is? Why, generally speaking, do people feel gay at parties, sad at funerals, happy at weddings? This question leads us to examine, not conventions of appearance or outward comportment, but conventions of feeling. Conventions of feeling become surprising only when we imagine, by contrast, what totally unpatterned, unpredictable emotive life might actually be like at parties, funerals, weddings, and in the family or work life of normal adults.

Erving Goffman (1961) suggests both the surprise to be explained and part of the explanation:

> . . . We find that participants will hold in check certain psychological states and attitudes, for after all, the very general rule that one enter into the prevailing mood in the encounter carries the understanding that contradictory feelings will be in

Reprinted from: Arlie Russell Hochschild, Emotion Work, Feeling Rules, and Social Structure. *American Journal of Sociology* 85: 551–575.

> abeyance. . . . So generally, in fact, does one suppress unsuitable affect, that we need to look at offenses to this rule to be reminded of its usual operation. (Goffman 1961:23)

If we take this passage seriously, as I urge we do, we may be led back to the classic question of social order from a particular vantage point—that of emotion management. From this vantage point, rules seem to govern how people try or try not to feel in ways "appropriate to the situation." Such a notion suggests how profoundly the individual is "social," and "socialized" to try to pay tribute to official definitions of situations, with no less than their feelings. . . .

The Interactive Account of Emotion and Social Psychology

If emotions and feelings can to some degree be managed, how might we get a conceptual grasp of the managing act from a social perspective? The interactive account of emotion leads us into a conceptual arena "between" the Goffmanian focus on consciously designed appearances on the one hand and the Freudian focus on unconscious intrapsychic events on the other. . . .

Goffman guides our attention to social patterns in emotive experience. He catches an irony: moment to moment, the individual is actively negotiating a course of action, but in the long run, all the action seems like passive acquiescence to social convention. The conserving of convention is not a passive business. Goffman's approach might simply be extended and deepened by showing that people not only try to conform outwardly, but do so inwardly as well. "When they issue uniforms, they issue skins" (Goffman 1974) could be extended: "and two inches of flesh."

Goffman's actors actively manage outer impressions, but they do not actively manage inner feelings. For example, a typical Goffmanian actor, Preedy at the beach (Goffman 1959), is exquisitely attuned to outward appearance, but his glances inward at subjective feeling are fleeting and blurred. The very topic, sociology of emotion, presupposes a human capacity for, if not the actual habit of, reflecting on and shaping inner feelings, a habit itself distributed variously across time, age, class, and locale. This variation would drop from sight were we to adopt an exclusive focus on the actor's attentiveness to behavioral facade and assume a uniform passivity vis-à-vis feelings.

This skew in the theoretical actor is related to what from my viewpoint is another problem: Goffman's concept of acting. Goffman suggests that we spend a good deal of effort managing impressions—that is, acting. He posits only *one* sort of acting—the direct management of behavioral expression. His illustrations, though, actually point to two types of acting—the direct management of behavioral expression (e.g., the given-off sigh, the shoulder shrug), and the management of feeling from which expression can follow (e.g., the thought of some hopeless project). An actor playing the part of King Lear might go about his task in two ways. One actor, following the English school of acting, might focus on outward demeanor, the constellation of minute expressions that correspond to Lear's sense of fear and impotent outrage. This is the sort of acting Goffman theorizes about. Another actor, adhering to the American or Stanislavsky school of acting, might guide his memories and feelings in such a way as to elicit the corresponding expressions. The first technique we might call "surface acting," the second "deep acting." Goffman fails to distinguish the first from the second, and he obscures the importance of "deep acting." Obscuring this, we are left with the impression that social factors pervade only the "social skin," the tried-for outer appearances of the individual. We are left underestimating the power of the social. . . .

Freud, of course, dealt with emotions, but for him they were always secondary to drive. He proposed a general theory of sexual and aggressive drives. Anxiety, as a derivative of aggressive and sexual drives, was of paramount importance, while a wide range of other emotions, including joy, jealousy, and depression, were given relatively little attention. He developed, and many others have since elaborated, the concept of ego defenses as generally unconscious, involuntary means of avoiding painful or unpleasant affect. Finally the notion of "inappropriate affect" is used to point to aspects of the individual's ego functioning and not used to point to the social rules according to which a feeling is or is not deemed appropriate to a situation.

The emotion-management perspective is indebted to Freud for the general notion of what resources individuals of different sorts possess for accomplishing the task of emotion work (as I have defined it) and for the notion of unconscious involuntary emotion management. The emotion-management perspective differs from the Freudian model in its focus on the full range of emotions and feelings and its focus on conscious and deliberate efforts to shape feeling. From this perspective, we note too that "inappropriate emotion" has a clearly important social as well as intrapsychic side. . . .

In sum, the emotion-management perspective fosters attention to how people try to feel, not, as for Goffman, how people try to appear and to feel. It leads us to attend to how people consciously feel and not, as for Freud, how people feel unconsciously. The interactive account of emotion points to alternate theoretical junctures—between consciousness of feeling and consciousness of feeling rules, [and] between feeling rules and emotion work. . . . In the remainder of this essay, it is these junctures we shall explore.

Emotion Work

By "emotion work," I refer to the act of trying to change in degree or quality an emotion or feeling. To "work on" an emotion or feeling is, for our purposes, the same as "to manage" an emotion or to do "deep acting." Note that "emotion work" refers to the effort—the act of trying—and not to the outcome, which may or may not be successful. Failed acts of management still indicate what ideal formulations guide the effort, and on that account are no less interesting than emotion management that works.

The very notion of an attempt suggests an active stance vis-à-vis feeling. In my exploratory study, respondents characterized their emotion work by a variety of active verb forms: "I *psyched myself up* . . . I *squashed* my anger down . . . I *tried hard* not to feel disappointed . . . I *made* myself have a good time . . . I tried to feel grateful . . . I *killed* the hope I had burning." There was also the actively passive form, as in: "I *let myself* finally feel sad."

Emotion work differs from emotion "control" or "suppression." The latter two terms suggest an effort merely to stifle or prevent feeling. "Emotion work" refers more broadly to the act of evoking or shaping, as well as suppressing, feeling in oneself. I avoid the term "manipulate" because it suggests a shallowness I do not mean to imply. We can speak, then, of two broad types of emotion work: *evocation*, in which the cognitive focus is on a desired feeling which is initially absent, and *suppression*, in which the cognitive focus is on an undesired feeling which is initially present. One respondent, going out with a priest 20 years her senior, exemplifies the problems of evocative emotion work:

> Anyway, I started to try and make myself like him. I made myself focus on the way he talked, certain things he'd done in the past. . . . When I was with him, I did like him but I would go home and write in my journal how much I couldn't stand him. I kept changing my feeling and actually thought I really liked him while I was with him, but a couple of hours after he was gone, I reverted back to different feelings. . . .[1]

Another respondent exemplifies the work, not of working feeling up, but of working feeling down:

> Last summer I was going with a guy often, and I began to feel very strongly about him. I knew though, that he had just broken up with a girl a year ago because she had gotten too serious about him, so I was afraid to show any emotion. I also was afraid of being hurt, so I attempted to change my feelings. *I talked myself into not caring about Mike* . . . but I must admit it didn't work for long. *To sustain this feeling I had to almost invent bad things about him and concentrate on them or continue to tell myself he didn't care. It was a hardening of emotions,* I'd say. It took a lot of work and was unpleasant, because I had to concentrate on anything I could find that was irritating about him.

Often emotion work is aided by setting up an emotion-work system, for example, telling friends of all the worst faults of the person one wanted to fall out of love with, and then going to those friends for reinforcement of this view of the ex-beloved. This suggests another point: emotion work can be done by the self upon the self, by the self upon others, and by others upon oneself.

In each case the individual is conscious of a moment of "pinch," or discrepancy, between what one does feel and what one wants to feel (which is, in turn, affected by what one thinks one ought to feel in such a situation). In response, the individual may try to eliminate the pinch by working on feeling. Both the sense of discrepancy and the response to it can vary in time. The managing act, for example, can be a five-minute stopgap measure, or it can be a more long-range gradual effort suggested by the term "working through."

There are various techniques of emotion work. One is cognitive: the attempt to change images, ideas, or thoughts in the service of changing the feelings associated with them. A second is *bodily*, the attempt to change somatic or other physical symptoms of emotion (e.g., trying to breathe slower, trying not to shake). Third, there is *expressive* emotion work: trying to change expressive gestures in the service of changing inner feeling (e.g., trying to smile or to cry). This differs from simple display in that it is directed toward change in feeling. It differs from bodily emotion work in that the individual tries to alter or shape one or another of the classic public channels for the expression of feeling.

These three techniques are distinct theoretically, but they often, of course, go together in practice. For example:

> I was a star halfback in high school. Before games I didn't feel the upsurge of adrenalin—in a word I wasn't "psyched up." (This was due to emotional difficulties I was experiencing and still experience—I was also an A student whose grades were dropping.) Having been in the past a fanatical, emotional, intense player, a "hitter" recognized by coaches as a very hard worker and a player with "desire," this was very upsetting. I tried to look nervous and intense before games, so at least the coaches wouldn't catch on. . . . When actually I was mostly bored, or in any event, not "up." I recall before one game wishing I was in the stands watching my cousin play for his school, rather than "out here."

Emotion work becomes an object of awareness most often, perhaps, when the individual's feelings do not fit the situation, that is, when the latter does not account for or legitimate feelings in the situation. A situation (such as a funeral) often carries with it a proper definition of itself ("this is a time of facing loss"). This official frame carries with it a sense of what it is fitting to feel (sadness). It is when this tripartite consistency among situation, conventional frame, and feeling is somehow ruptured, as when the bereaved feels an irrepressible desire to laugh delightedly at the thought of an inheritance, that rule and management come into focus. It is then that the more normal flow of deep convention—the more normal fusion of situation, frame, and feeling—seems like an accomplishment.

The smoothly warm airline hostess, the ever-cheerful secretary, the unirritated complaint clerk, the undisgusted proctologist, the teacher who likes every student equally, and Goffman's unflappable poker player may all have to engage in deep acting, an acting that goes well beyond the mere ordering of display. Work to make feeling and frame consistent with situation is work in which individuals continually and privately engage. But they do so in obeisance to rules not completely of their own making.

Feeling Rules

We feel. We try to feel. We want to try to feel. The social guidelines that direct how we want to try to feel may be describable as a set of socially shared, albeit often latent (not thought about unless probed at), rules. In what way, we may ask, are these rules themselves known and how are they developed?

To begin with, let us consider several common forms of evidence for feeling rules. In common parlance, we often talk about our feelings or those of others as if rights and duties applied directly to them. For example, we often speak of "having the right" to feel angry at someone. Or we say we "should feel more grateful" to a benefactor. We chide ourselves that a friend's misfortune or a relative's death "should have hit us harder" or that another's good luck or our own should have inspired more joy. We know feeling rules, too, from how others react to what they infer from our emotive display. Another may say to us, "You *shouldn't feel* so guilty; it wasn't your fault," or "You *don't have a right* to feel jealous, given our agreement." Another may simply declare an opinion as to the fit of feeling to situation or may cast a claim upon our managerial stance, presupposing this opinion. Others may question or call for an account of a particular feeling in a situation, whereas they do not ask for an accounting of some other situated feeling (Lyman and Scott 1970). Claims and callings for an account can be seen as *rule reminders*. At other times, a person may, in addition, chide, tease, cajole, scold, shun—in a word, sanction us for "misfeeling." Such sanctions are a clue to the rules they are meant to enforce.

Rights and duties set out the properties as to the *extent* (one can feel "too angry" or "not angry enough"), the *direction* (one can feel sad when one should feel happy), and the *duration* of a feeling, given the situation against which it is set. These rights and duties of feeling are a clue to the depth of social convention, to one final reach of social control.

There is a distinction, in theory at least, between a feeling rule as it is known by our sense of what we can *expect* to feel in a given situation, and a rule as it is known by our sense of what we *should* feel in that situation. For example, one may realistically expect (knowing oneself and one's neighbor's parties) to feel bored at a large New Year's Eve party and at the same time acknowledge that it would be more fitting to feel exuberant. However, "expect to feel" and "should ideally feel" often coincide, as below:

> Marriage, chaos, unreal, completely different in many ways than I imagined. Unfortunately, we rehearsed the morning of our wedding at eight o'clock. The wedding was to be at eleven o'clock. It wasn't like I thought (everyone would know what to do). They didn't. That made me nervous. My sister didn't help me get dressed or flatter me (nor did anyone in the dressing room until I asked them). I was depressed. I wanted to be so happy on our wedding day. I never dreamed how anyone would cry at their wedding. A wedding is "the happy day" of one's life. I couldn't believe that some of my best friends couldn't make it to my wedding and that added to a lot of little things. So I started to the church and all these things that I always thought would not happen at my wedding went through my mind. I broke down—I cried going down. "Be happy," I told myself. Think of the friends and relatives that are present. (But I finally said to myself, "Hey, people aren't getting married, you are. It's for Rich [my husband] and you.") From down the pretty long aisle we looked at each other's eyes. His love for me changed my whole being. From that point on we joined arms. I was relieved and the tension was gone. In one sense it meant misery—but in the true sense of two people in love and wanting to share life—it meant the world to me. It was beautiful. It was indescribable.

In any given situation, we often invest what we expect to feel with idealization. To a remarkable extent these idealizations vary socially. If the "old-fashioned bride" above anticipates a "right" to feel jealous at any possible future infidelity, the young "flower child" below rejects just this right.

> . . . [W]hen I was living down south, I was involved with a group of people, friends. We used to spend most evenings after work or school together. We used to do a lot of drugs, acid, coke, or just smoke dope and we had this philosophy that we were very communal and did our best to share everything—clothes, money, food, and so on. I was involved with this one man—and thought I was "in love" with him. He in turn had told me that I was very important to him. Anyway, this one woman who was a very good friend of mine at one time and this man started having a sexual relationship, supposedly without my knowledge. I knew

though and had a lot of mixed feelings about it. I thought, intellectually, that I had no claim to the man and believed in fact that no one should ever try to *own* another person. I believed also that it was none of my business and I had no reason to worry about their relationship together, for it had nothing really to do with my friendship with either of them. I also believed in sharing. But I was horribly hurt, alone and lonely, depressed, and I couldn't shake the depression and on top of those feelings I felt guilty for having those possessively jealous feelings. And so I would continue going out with these people every night, and try to suppress my feelings. My ego was shattered. I got to the point where I couldn't even laugh around them. So finally I confronted my friends and left for the summer and traveled with a new friend. I realized later what a heavy situation it was, and it took me a long time to get myself together and feel whole again.

Whether the convention calls for trying joyfully to possess or trying casually not to, the individual compares and measures experience against an expectation often idealized. It is left for motivation ("what I want to feel") to mediate between feeling rule ("what I should feel") and emotion work ("what I try to feel"). Some of the time many of us can live with a certain dissonance between "ought" and "want," or between "want" and "try to." But the attempts to reduce emotive dissonance are our periodic clues to rules of feeling.

A feeling rule shares some formal properties with other sorts of rules, such as rules of etiquette, rules of bodily comportment, and those of social interaction in general (Goffman 1961). A feeling rule is like these other kinds of rules in the following ways: it delineates a zone within which one has permission to be free of worry, guilt, or shame with regard to the situated feeling. Such zoning ordinances describe a metaphoric floor and ceiling, there being room for motion and play between the two. Like other rules, feeling rules can be obeyed halfheartedly or boldly broken, the latter at varying costs. A feeling rule can be in varying proportions external or internal. Feeling rules differ curiously from other types of rules, in that they do not apply to action but to what is often taken as a precursor to action. Therefore, they tend to be latent and resistant to formal codification.

Feeling rules reflect patterns of social membership. Some rules may be nearly universal, such as the rule that one should not enjoy killing or witnessing the killing of a human being, including oneself. Other rules are unique to particular social groups and can be used to distinguish among them as alternate governments or colonizers of individual internal events.

Conclusion

Social psychology has suffered under the tacit assumption that emotion, because it seems unbidden and uncontrollable, is not governed by social rules. Social rules, for their part, are seen as applying to behavior and thought, but rarely to emotion or feeling. If we reconsider the nature of emotion and the nature of our capacity to try shaping it, we are struck by the imperial scope of social rules.

Note

1. The illustrations of emotion work come from a content analysis of 261 protocols given to students in two classes at the University of California, Berkeley, in 1974. Many of the illustrations come from answers to the question, "Describe as fully and concretely as possible a real situation important to you, in which you experienced either changing a real situation to fit your feelings or changing your feelings to fit a situation. What did it mean to you?"

References

Goffman, Erving. 1959. *The Presentation of Self in Everyday Life*. Garden City, NY: Doubleday.

———. 1961. "Fun in Games." Pp. 17–84 in *Encounters*. Indianapolis: Bobbs-Merrill.

———. 1974. *Frame Analysis*. New York: Harper and Row.

Lyman, Stanford and Marvin Scott. 1970. *Sociology of the Absurd*. New York: Appleton Century-Crofts.

Reflective Questions

1. Sociological psychologists think of emotions as the feeling-based experiences of others and ourselves, which we shape and manage. What does emotion work look like? What is the difference between "surface acting" and "deep acting"? Which one of these forms of emotion work do you engage in more often?
2. What dimensions of emotional experience do feeling rules address? Where do we learn feeling rules from? How do people manage their internal feelings when they do not appropriately fit an occasion, for example, when they feel relief or joy at a funeral or anger at a birth? What happens when their external display of feelings does not fit the feeling rules? How do others react?
3. Waiting tables, clerking at a grocery store, selling insurance, and nursing are examples of interactive service work where employers create feeling rules for how employees should manage emotions at work. Companies may even create handbooks and train their employees in how to transform a restaurant to feel like "home" for patrons or stir feelings of fear or desperation in order to spark a sale. Many provide employees with feeling scripts that tell them to smile, be cheerful, and accommodate customers' demands. Perhaps you have worked in a workplace that dictates feeling rules. What effects do employer-prescribed feeling rules have on workers and their emotional lives? What workplace conditions lead to feelings of satisfaction and accomplishment among employees? What conditions promote feelings of burnout or inauthenticity?
4. We often approach others with the expectation that they manage emotions in their interactions with us, both to make us feel a particular way or to repress or stir particular emotions in themselves for our sake. How are our expectations shaped by gender, race, ability level, age, and social class?

8

Feeling Norms and Romantic Love

ROBIN W. SIMON, DONNA EDER, AND CATHY EVANS

In the previous selection, Arlie Russell Hochschild suggested that social exchanges of both heartfelt and surface displays of emotion create and sustain social bonds. People obviously initiate social relationships by exchanging displays of emotion, as in the case of flirting between future romantic partners. Additionally, individuals involved in a close relationship feel that they should exchange certain feelings, such as caring and loyalty, with one another. Their failure to meet this implicit emotional bargain can threaten, alter, or even destroy their relationship. That is just one of the ways that people may change the form of their relationship through the social exchange of emotions. For example, displays of heartfelt emotion can enhance the intimacy of a formally distant relationship while guilt-evoking displays of hurt or anger can alter the distribution of power in a relationship. In these and various other ways, the flow of emotions between individuals ties and reties them into complex relational networks.

Perhaps the most powerful emotion that links people together in Western societies is romantic love, at least for individuals involved in marital or erotic relationships. People often think of this emotion as natural, unregulated, and uncontrollable. But, as the following selection reveals, romantic love is powerfully shaped by social expectations. For instance, through their interactions with others individuals learn what romantic love means and why it is important. They also learn who should be the object of this sentiment, how and when they should convey this feeling, and why they should not direct it toward more than one person at a time. In essence, people undergo a process of emotional socialization that profoundly influences their experience and expression of what they regard as a natural feeling. This process is infused with emotions that serve as compelling mechanisms of social control. These emotions include trust, anger, loyalty, shame, guilt, and attachment.

Robin Simon, Donna Eder, and Cathy Evans reveal how the process of emotional socialization unfolds among white adolescent girls in school settings. In so doing, they highlight the key emotion norms these girls learn with respect to the feeling of romantic love. They also demonstrate how adolescent girls enact, enforce, and sometimes resist these norms. While the authors focus their attention on adolescent girls, the processes of emotional socialization they depict are not limited to these girls or even to the emotion of romantic love. These same processes are involved in the development, diffusion, and expression of feeling rules in many groups. Emotions are continually experienced and managed in the context of relationships governed by feeling rules, and this reality is just as true for romantic love as for any other sentiment. While these feeling rules are negotiated and occasionally challenged, they serve as a crucial form of

Reprinted From: Robin W. Simon, Donna Eder and Cathy Evans, "The Development of Feeling Norms Underlying Romantic Love Among Adolescent Females," *Social Psychology Quarterly*, 55(1): 29–46.

social cement—that is, they link people together in groups and relationships based on reciprocal feelings.

In American society, love is an important emotion (Cancian 1985, 1987; Cancian and Gordon 1988; Hochschild 1983a; Swidler 1980). Like other feelings, romantic love is a social sentiment, for which a cultural label and a set of ideological beliefs exist (Gordon 1981). Embodied in ideological beliefs about love are "feeling norms" which guide individuals' romantic feelings and behaviors (Hochschild 1979, 1983a). Feeling norms that underlie romantic love not only influence whether we should or should not love (Hochschild 1983a), but also help us identify the appropriate object of romantic feelings. Yet in spite of the importance attached to love in American culture, we know little about the content of the feeling norms that govern romantic love and the ways in which cultural knowledge about love is acquired socially. . . .

In this paper we discuss the content of feeling and expression norms underlying romantic love as they emerge in adolescent girls' peer culture. We also discuss the various ways in which feeling norms are communicated to group members. Although adolescent girls may obtain normative information about romantic feelings in other social relationships and in other social contexts—as well as through media such as romance novels, music, television, and films—the focus of this paper is limited to affective socialization processes among peers in school contexts because we do not have data on those other socialization agents. Peer groups, however, are an important source of emotional socialization because of the primacy of these groups to youths. In interaction with peers, young people draw on norms and beliefs that are available in the broader culture and make them meaningful by applying them to their everyday concerns and activities (Corsaro and Rizzo 1988; Mead 1934). By focusing on peer group socialization, we show that while adolescent girls are acquiring cultural knowledge about love, they also are creating and continuously negotiating feeling norms which pertain to the emergent concerns of their peer culture.

Data and Methods

We collected the data for this paper as part of an ethnographic study of adolescent socialization and peer interaction in a middle school. The school that was selected for the study was located in a medium-sized midwestern community. The school enrolls sixth-, seventh-, and eighth-grade students from a range of socioeconomic backgrounds, including youths from upper middle-class and lower working-class families. Most of the students were white, but a small number of black youths were enrolled at the school. The school was large, with approximately 250 students in each grade.

Data on peer interaction and relations were collected over a three-year period and involved a variety of methods, including participant observation, audio and audiovisual recording, and in-depth group interviews. Three female researchers observed a total of 10 female peer groups during lunch periods twice a week, over periods ranging from five to nine months. Three of these groups were studied for two years. The groups were representative of groups at different status levels within the school as well as of different-sized cliques. Data were obtained on high- through low-status peer groups and on peer groups that ranged in size from dyads to groups of 12 members. . . .

Although data from all of the groups were analyzed for this paper, some groups of girls were more interested in romance and had more contact with boys than others. Among the girls who had romantic interests, relationships with boys varied considerably. In fact, at this school, the term "going together" was used widely by both girls and boys to refer to a variety of romantic relationships, ranging from those which lasted several months to those which lasted one or two days. In some cases, the girl and the boy spent their lunch period together; in others, the couple had minimal contact at school. In most cases, the relationships were brief (less than two weeks) and were limited to some social contact at school, which sometimes included expressions of affection such as hand holding and kissing. Interestingly, even though many of the high-status girls were going with boys, they engaged in fewer conversations about romance than girls in the medium high- and medium low-status peer groups. Most conversations about romance took place when boys were absent, so these girls may have discussed romance less frequently because boys were regular members of their lunch group. The group that discussed romance the least was the low-status group of special education students, none of whom had a boyfriend. Thus, although the feeling norms and the affective socialization processes discussed in this paper are likely to be generalizable to other groups of white adolescent females who are interested in romance and in male-female relationships, they are not meant to reflect the experiences of all girls of this age.

Feeling Norms Underlying Romantic Love in Adolescent Female Peer Culture

We begin with the observation that romantic love was a frequent topic of conversation among the female students. By the seventh grade, most of the girls at the school had become concerned with romance and had begun to form relationships with boys. While the girls were obtaining normative information about romantic love, the feelings and behavior that group members considered appropriate were still in the process of negotiation. Some feeling norms were generally accepted; others were not shared by all group members. An examination of the girls' talk about romantic love revealed that they used a variety of discourse strategies to communicate normative information and clarify feeling norms. . . .

The Object of Romantic Love

According to Gordon (1981, p. 567), "sentiments," such as romantic love, are feelings that are "organized around a relationship to a social object, usually another person." While the girls were developing a norm about the relative importance of romance, they also were acquiring cultural knowledge about the object of romance. In fact, by the eighth grade, three norms concerning the object of romantic feelings had emerged.

Norm 1: One should have romantic feelings only for someone of the opposite sex.

The most basic feeling norm concerning the object of romance was that one should have romantic feelings only for someone of the opposite sex. By the time they had become actively interested in romance, a norm of heterosexuality had developed in these groups of girls. . . . [In light] of the general negative view of homosexuality at the school and the label attached to alleged norm violators, it is not surprising that this norm was widely accepted. We found that the girls used a variety of discourse strategies to clarify and reinforce the norm of heterosexuality to friends. How this norm was communicated depended upon whether alleged norm violators were non-group or group members.

One way the norm of heterosexuality was communicated was through gossip about nongroup members' deviant affect and behavior. Girls who did not express romantic interest in boys or who had gender-atypical interests often were the targets of gossip. For example, Sandy and Paula were discussing Sandy's sister in the sixth grade, who did not share their romantic interest in boys and who was interested in sports and in becoming a mechanic.

> Sandy said her sister is extremely different from her and has absolutely no interest in boys—she considers boys pests. Sandy referred to her sister as a tomboy. She said that since her sister is a tomboy, if she liked boys then she would be queer, but on the other hand, if she liked girls then she would really be queer. Then Paula added jokingly that if she didn't like anyone at all she would still be queer. I [researcher] said, "It sounds like she doesn't have a chance" (field notes, seventh grade, May 24).

This example shows that Sandy and Paula were reinforcing a feeling norm of which they had only limited understanding. Girls at this school were establishing violations of the norm of heterosexuality on the basis of gender-inappropriate behavior.

Sandy's sister's outward disinterest in boys as well as her nontraditional interests and behaviors were considered by these group members to be deviant with regard to the norm of heterosexuality. Yet, by establishing violations of this norm on the basis of non-stereotypical gender-role behavior, the girls were reinforcing and reproducing existing gender norms that ultimately constrain their own behavior.

In general, it was not uncommon for girls and boys who were not actively pursuing romantic relationships or who routinely engaged in gender-inappropriate behavior to be labeled homosexual. In fact, children at the school who were perceived to be deviant in other ways were the objects of these allegations as well (Evans and Eder 1989). Unpopular students who were viewed as unattractive and/or unintelligent also were singled out for group discussions in which they were accused indirectly of being homosexual.

> Annie said, "I'm gonna beat that girl up someday," referring to twins and a little chubby girl in a green sweater who were sitting at the middle of the table pretty far down. So we all turned to look at her and Marsha agreed that she was really disgusting, that "they're gay" (field notes, seventh grade, February 3).

Rather than relying on the display of romantic feelings toward someone of the same sex as an indication of affective deviance, Annie and Marsha accused these girls of being "gay" solely on the basis of physical appearance.

A second way the norm of heterosexuality was communicated was by teasing group members. Humor often was used when the girls confronted their friends about norm violations. Group members frequently teased one another about behaviors that could be interpreted as homosexual, such as close physical contact between friends. Although many girls still viewed close physical contact between friends as acceptable, others were beginning to redefine such expressions of affection as inappropriate.

> The little girl with glasses came over and actually sat on Andrea's lap. She's so tiny that she can do this easily, and Andrea laughed and said, "You're really not my type" (field notes, sixth grade, May 20).

Not only did the girls tease one another about overt expressions of affection; they also chided one another about their actual feelings. Statements concerning both positive and negative affect for females were a frequent source of group humor.

> . . . they were talking about why would somebody like this particular girl. Debby said, "I wouldn't like her!" Melinda said, "Well, I should hope not" (field notes, eighth grade, April 20).

In addition to teasing one another about their feelings and behaviors, group members also chided each other about their best-friend relationships. In fact, adolescence is a period in which female friendships are faced with a dilemma. Even while intimate feelings between close friends usually deepen, girls routinely tease one another about the romantic implications of these relationships.

> Julie said something about how Bonnie and somebody were considered her best mates. Right away Mia said, "Ooooh . . . " as this sort of implied that they were gay. Hillary picked up on that and went "Ooooh!" (field notes, eighth grade, April 9).

The final way in which the norm of heterosexuality was communicated was through self-denial. Self-denials often were used to clarify the nature of intimate female friendships. Although many girls at the school continued to have strong positive feelings for their female friends, verbal and behavioral expressions of affection frequently were followed by a disclaimer.

In light of the pressures for heterosexuality from peers and the seriousness of norm violations, it is not surprising that many girls at the school became quite concerned that their own feelings and behaviors towards their close friends might be perceived by others as homosexual.

> Sally was really talkative today, and it was interesting to see her being so talkative. She was going on

> and on about how somebody would sign her letters "love you queerly." She said, "I always sign my letters 'love you dearly, but not queerly.'" But then she was joking, saying, "I didn't know what that meant," until Mary explained it to her. Then they were joking about how innocent she was and didn't even know what "queer" meant (field notes, seventh grade, March 3).

Whereas self-denials often were humorous, denials of affective deviance with respect to the norm of heterosexuality sometimes were quite serious. The girls were especially self-conscious about expressions of affection that were overt and therefore readily observable. They were concerned that nongroup members would misinterpret these visible signs of affection as romantic.

> Alice told me that she had taken a bunch of photographs recently. She said it was embarrassing because most of the pictures were taken when people happened to be hugging and kissing each other, and that she hoped she got hold of the pictures before her mother did when they got back from being developed. She said, for example, "Natalie and another girl were hugging each other in friendship" (which meant that she wanted me to know that that was differentiated from a romantic hug) (field notes, eighth grade, February 7).

Not only was Alice embarrassed by the hugging and kissing in the photographs, but she also was concerned that if her mother saw the pictures, she might interpret these actions as homosexual. By distinguishing between a "friendship" hug and a "romantic" hug, however, Alice clarified both to herself and to the researcher that this behavior was within the realm of acceptable conduct.

Overall, the norm of heterosexuality was communicated among adolescent females through gossip, teasing, and self-denials. In these discussions, group members collectively explored what does and does not constitute homosexual feeling and behavior in order to develop an understanding of this feeling norm and of norm violations. Through these discussions, however, the girls not only expressed their own homophobic concerns but also supported and maintained the broader cultural norm of heterosexuality. Many girls at the school continued to value intimate relationships with females; nevertheless they upheld and reproduced what Rich (1980) called "the norm of compulsory heterosexuality."

Norm 2: One should not have romantic feelings for a boy who is already attached.

Another feeling norm that had emerged in regard to the object of romance was that one should not have romantic feelings for a boy who is already attached. A corollary of this norm was that if one had such feelings, they should not be expressed. In most groups, the development of this norm was a direct response to changes in group members' romantic activities. The norm of exclusivity had only minimal relevance during an earlier phase, when the girls were first becoming interested in romance, but this norm had become highly salient by the time they began to form relationships with boys. Early in the seventh grade, most of the girls talked about the boys they liked, but often were shy about letting boys know their feelings. As long as romantic activities consisted of only talking about the objects of their affection, the norm of exclusivity had little significance. In fact, during this stage in the development of their romantic activities, it was not uncommon for many group members to like the same boy. Just as they might have other interests in common, sharing a romantic interest in a particular boy was considered to be acceptable, if not appropriate.

> Interestingly enough, Marsha and Josephine talked about how they both liked this guy Jack. They pointed him out to me, and I [researcher] said, "Oh, oh, you both like the same guy?" They said, "Oh yeah, it's okay. We can do that. We always like the same people, but we don't get mad at each other" (field notes, seventh grade, March 30).

In an interview with another group of seventh-grade girls, it became clear that the distinction between liking and going with the same boy is important. The former is permissible; the latter is not.

1 Carrie: They can like, like, like as much as they want, but they
2 don't// (go)
3 Marla: They don't two-time!
4 Researcher: But what?
5 Carrie: They can like a person as much as they want.
6 Researcher: Can two friends go together // with the same boy?
7 (Alice): Oh, they don't have any choice // (they)
8 Carrie: No.
9 Bonnie: No (interview, seventh grade, May 24).

Throughout this year, many girls began to pursue boys openly and to make their feelings more public, often through a friend who served as an intermediary. Once a group member had acted openly on her feelings and formed a relationship with a boy, it was no longer acceptable for other girls either to have or to express romantic feelings for him. At this point in the development of their romantic activities, the norm of exclusivity had become highly salient, and violations began to be perceived as a serious threat. Most of the girls became concerned about violations; they were resentful and jealous of those who did not abide by the norm of exclusivity.

Gossip was one way in which the girls clarified and reinforced this norm. In the following example from a seventh-grade interview, Natalie is accusing Rhoda, an attractive group member, of flirting with her and Tricia's boyfriends.

1 Natalie: Rhoda, every time I get a boyfriend or Tricia gets a boyfriend
2 # or or we like somebody, she starts # y'know messing around
3 with him and everything and # y'know-and everything, she
4 shows her ass off and so, they start likin' her, right? And she
5 did that, she was trying to do that to Sammy Jones #
6 Tricia's boyfriend # ya know, the one that broke up with her
7 after four months (interview, seventh grade, May 24).

Although gossip episodes such as this do not inform norm violators about the deviant nature of their behavior, they communicate normative information to other group members (Eder and Enke 1988; Fine 1986; Goodwin 1980). The girls considered it inappropriate to have or express romantic feelings not only for a boy who was involved with someone else, but also for a boy whom a group member was in the process of pursuing. Group members sometimes engaged in confrontations with alleged norm violators in order to communicate their inappropriate behavior and affect. In the next exchange, several members of a seventh-grade group directly accuse Carol of flirting with Ted, a boy Betty is pursuing but not currently going with. Although Carol argues initially that she has not done anything wrong, later she agrees to be an intermediary for Betty in order to resolve the dispute.

1 Mary: Ted came up to Carol and said she—that he loved her.
2 Linda: Who?
3 Betty: Carol!
4 Carol: What?
5 Betty: I don't like you no more.
6 Carol: What'd I do?
7 Linda: Taking Betty's boyfriend.
8 Carol: I didn't either! ((pounds table as she half laughs))
9 Mary: It wasn't Carol's fault, though.
10 Betty: Yes it was! She flirts!
11 Carol: I was just walking there //
12 Betty: You flirt, You flirt. Yes, you //
13 Carol: I didn't even do nothing. ((laughter))
14 Betty: You flirt, Carol! You're mean! I don't like you no more.
15 Carol: You won't (mind me) after I get done talking # if you still
16 want me to.
17 Betty: Huh?
18 Carol: If you – do you want me to still talk to him? // ((Betty
19 nods)) Alright, shut up. God.

20 NANCY: Hell, she called me up, she goes, "Nancy, call Ted and talk to
21 him."
22 BETTY: (I sank you) ((silly voice)) (taped conversation, seventh grade, May 5).

This example is interesting because it shows that these girls expect their friends to know not only with whom they are going, but also their intentions to become romantically involved with certain boys. Acceptable contact with these boys is limited to behavior that will promote their friends' romantic interests (e.g., serving as intermediaries), and excludes any friendly behavior that might encourage romantic feelings to develop. As shown in the previous example, such behavior makes a girl subject to the negative label "flirt." It is also noteworthy that group members use confrontations such as this to sanction inappropriate behavior and affect. Because violations of the norm of exclusivity have serious consequences for group members, including the possibility of being in competition with friends over boys, it is not surprising that confrontations sometimes are used to clarify and reinforce this norm.

Although most group members increasingly saw the need for the norm of exclusivity to protect themselves from unpleasant feelings of jealousy, some girls were reluctant to give up the freedom to have or express romantic feelings whenever they desired. Because norm violations were viewed as serious, girls who continued to defy this norm occasionally engaged in playful modes of interaction whereby they could express their "deviant" feelings while acknowledging the norm of exclusivity.

For example, several seventh-grade girls were teasing Mary about "liking" Wally and dragged her over to the ball diamond, where Wally was playing softball. The teasing consisted of trying to get Mary to talk with him and telling Wally that Mary wanted to "go in the stairwell" with him. Mary refused to talk to Wally. This reaction led to some joking exchanges among the other group members, several of whom also had romantic feelings for Wally.

1 CAROL: I'll take him if you don't.
2 ELAINE: Whoo! You hear that one, Wally?
3 CAROL: Well, I don't care.
4 ELAINE: Wally, Wally, Wally, Wally. She says she'll take
5 ya if Mary don't want ya. ((Unrelated talk for 6 five turns.))
7 ELAINE: She said she'd take ya if Mary don't want ya.
8 MARY: What'd you tell him Elaine? Elaine 11 ( )
9 LINDA: Hey you! If Mary don't want ya and Carol don't 10 want ya, I'll take ya!
11 CAROL: Uh uh, I will. I'll take him if Mary don't and
12 then if I don't, you do (taped conversation, seventh grade, April 7).

Here the girls use playful teasing to inform Wally of their romantic feelings, while acknowledging at the same time that they will wait to act on these feelings until Mary no longer "wants" him. The joking nature of this exchange provides these girls with more freedom to express their feelings for Wally and thus to violate the norm of exclusivity.

This finding suggests that feeling and expression norms do not determine adolescent girls' affect and behavior, but serve as an important cultural resource which is incorporated into their action. Through expressing their knowledge of this norm, in fact, these girls succeed in expressing their feelings for a boy who is being pursued by a friend. At the same time, their ability to transform cultural knowledge into a playful frame gives them an opportunity to violate the norm without negative sanctions.

In brief, when group members began to pursue boys and form romantic relationships, the girls developed the norm of exclusivity to deal with their new concerns. They communicated this norm through gossip and confrontations as well as in more playful modes of discourse. Yet even though norm violations were viewed negatively by most of the girls, several group members did not feel compelled to abide by this norm. Instead they responded with "resistance" by continuing to hold and express romantic feelings for boys who were already "taken." In some cases their resistance was communicated through playful teasing, which allowed them to express their normatively inappropriate feelings while simultaneously showing their awareness of the norm of exclusivity.

Norm 3: One should have romantic feelings for only one boy at a time.

The third feeling norm pertaining to the object of romance was that one should have romantic feelings for only one boy at a time. A corollary was that if one had romantic feelings for more than one boy, these feelings should not be expressed. In some groups, the development of the norm of monogamy reflected the girls' awareness of the societal norm of monogamy. In other groups, however, this norm was developed to deal with the problems created by having multiple boyfriends.

For example, when we asked one group of seventh-grade girls about the possibility of going with more than one person at a time, the reason they gave for avoiding this behavior was the likelihood of creating jealousy among boyfriends. Because jealousy and other forms of conflict among males were expressed frequently in physical fights, the consequences of creating jealousy were considered to be quite serious.

> I asked if you could only go with one person at a time and she said, "It depends on who you're talking about." She said that you should only go with one at a time but that some girls went with more than one. I asked why they shouldn't do that, and she said because "then you get a couple of jealous boyfriends on your hands" and they might end up getting into a fight, and that it was best to avoid that (field notes, seventh grade, April 27).

Some girls continued to have multiple boyfriends, but were careful to become involved only with boys who were separated geographically. As long as a boy was unaware of his girlfriend's other romantic involvements, jealousy and its negative consequences could be avoided. For some of these girls, in fact, having multiple boyfriends was a source of status—something they bragged about to their female friends.

> Effie and Laura had a long conversation. Laura told Effie that she was going with two guys, one from Royalton and another from California. She said that they were both going to be coming down this summer and she didn't know what to do. She presented this as a dilemma, but she was laughing about it. She really wanted to show that she was popular with boys (field notes, eighth grade, April 6).

Although some groups developed the norm of monogamy to deal with the practical problems associated with having multiple boyfriends, in other groups the development of this norm reflected group members' knowledge of the cultural norm of monogamy. When we asked one group of seventh-grade girls whether two people could go with the same boy, their response turned to the inappropriateness of having multiple romantic partners.

1 RESEARCHER: How come two people can't go with the same boy at the same
2 time? It seems like you could logi-
3 ELLEN: Because you're only supposed to-when you go with a person
4 like if you
5 NATALIE: It's like a bigamist.
6 ELLEN: Oh . . .
7 NATALIE: You know, when you
8 ELLEN: Like a what?
9 NATALIE: A bigamist. Like when you go with somebody. Like it's, it's
10 ELLEN: Two-timing.
11 NATALIE: When you go with each other the same-when you go with each
12 other it's kinda like gettin' married or somethin', you
13 know, and like if you're goin' with two people at the same
14 time it's like a bigamist.
15 ELLEN: Like Natalie did!
16 NATALIE: Yeah, I did that once.
17 ELLEN: Yeah, with Steve and Robert.
18 NATALIE: I did it twice. ((Natalie and Ellen burst out laughing)) (interview, seventh grade, May 24).

This example illustrates that the girls are drawing on their knowledge of the societal norm of monogamy (which pertains to marriage) in order to develop a feeling norm regarding multiple partners which is relevant to their own romantic relationships. The exchange also shows that even though these girls agreed that it was inappropriate to have romantic feelings for more than one boy at a time, violations of this norm were not perceived as serious. By the time these girls were in eighth grade, however, having romantic feelings for more than one boy was no longer viewed as acceptable. Moreover, they used different strategies to clarify this norm and to sanction deviant affect and behavior. In the following exchange, Ellen and Hanna are telling the other girls about what happened at church the night before. Because Ellen is already going with Craig, she is first accused and later reprimanded for going to church solely to meet other boys.

1 Ellen: We were sittin' there starin' at guys at church last night,
2 me and Hanna were, and-
3 Hanna: And she saw one that looked just like Craig.
4 Natalie: But # // I was-
5 Ellen: I wasn't starin' at him.
6 Hanna: That was groaty.
7 (Natalie:) You're going with Craig.
8 Ellen: I know. I stared at Steve. ((laughs))
9 Hanna: I know, but he looks like him in the face,
10 Natalie: But, um, he just-
11 Peg: You // go to church for a different reason than that, Ellen!
12 Natalie: I // get stuck on one guy.
13 Peg: Then you shouldn't have been there (interview, eighth grade, March 30).

As girls begin to take this norm seriously, they need to become more aware of their romantic feelings. They may even begin to modify their emotions on certain occasions, changing romantic attractions to nonromantic feelings in order to avoid norm violations. Sometimes the girls explicitly discussed their feelings toward boys, thus showing their close monitoring of these feelings. Awareness of romantic feelings was especially important during times of transition from one boyfriend to another. Because "going together" arrangements typically lasted less than two weeks, these transitions were frequent.

> Gwen and Ellen went "cruising" with some boys over the weekend. The boy Gwen was with asked her to go with him but he broke up with her the next morning because another boy that Gwen went with last week threatened to beat him up. So then the other boy asked her back with him Monday morning and she's going with him again now. She said that "one thing I can say for certain is that I love (the boy she's going with), but I can also say for certain that I really like (the boy she went with on Saturday)" (field notes, eighth grade, March 30).

Through Gwen's claim that she "loves" the boy she is currently going with and "likes" the boy she went with on Saturday, her feelings appear to conform with the norm of monogamy. Although it is not clear whether her current feelings are the result of emotion (or expression) work, it is clear that she pays close attention to her feelings and can discuss them with "certainty."

Other girls expressed more confusion about their emotions. In some cases, their confusion stemmed from the discrepancy between their actual feelings and the feelings they thought they ought to have. Even though they knew that they should have romantic feelings for only one boy at a time, girls sometimes found themselves feeling multiple attractions.

> I heard Karla being teased when a specific boy walked by. Her friends were saying that she had a crush on him and once they yelled it at the boy. Karla acted rather embarrassed and angry about this. When they yelled at the boy, they asked Karla if it was true that she liked him. Karla said that she did like him "for a friend." They said that they had seen her walking with him in the halls. After a long pause Karla asked Laura rather indignantly, "How could I like him when I'm already going with

somebody?" Effie said, "Two-timing." Karla was embarrassed and seemed rather mild in her denial (field notes, eighth grade, April 21).

Karla's feelings are creating some discomfort for her because they do not conform readily to this feeling norm. She claims that she likes the other boy only "for a friend," but she expresses embarrassment as well as anger toward her friends, who perceive it to be a stronger attraction. Although we do not know whether Karla subsequently modified her feelings and/or expressions toward this boy, emotion work might be necessary in situations such as this, if girls are to abide by the norm of monogamy.

Norm 4: One should always be in love.

The final feeling norm that emerged was that one should always be in love. This norm differed from those discussed previously in that it was not devised to deal with group concerns, but was developed largely to deal with the concerns of individuals. Whereas violations of most feeling norms had consequences for other group members and peers (e.g., the norms of heterosexuality, exclusivity, and monogamy), violations of this final norm had consequences only for individual girls. Because such violations did not affect others, this norm was held even less widely than those discussed previously. For many girls at the school, however, this emotion norm was a basic part of their knowledge and understanding of romantic love.

For some girls, the onset of their first romantic attraction was the beginning of a continuous state of being in love, often with frequent changes in the object of their feelings. In fact, simply having romantic feelings may have been more important than the actual boys to whom these feelings were directed. For example, a researcher noticed that a girl had "I love" written on her hand and asked her about it. Although this girl's romantic feelings had no particular target, she explained that she was ready to add the name of a boy as soon as a suitable target was found.

The importance of always being in love became particularly evident when relationships with boys ended. For instance, when girls realized that a boy they had been going with now liked someone else, they often redirected their romantic feelings toward someone new.

> She said that she was just going to go up and ask him if he had any intention of going with her again, and if he didn't, she was just "going to have to find someone else." I don't think she has the concept in her mind that she could possibly not be involved with anyone (field notes, eighth grade, March 23).

The salience of this norm was related to the duration of adolescent romantic relationships. Although it might seem that "long-term" relationships would be preferred because girls would not continually have to seek out new boyfriends, some girls reported that being in a long-term relationship was a disadvantage because it took them out of circulation.

> Apparently Alice's boyfriend broke up with her today and she was unhappy. She saw him walk by the media center and called to him several times, but he ignored her purposely. She said that the worst of it was that she had gone with him several months, and during that time had progressively cut herself off from contact with other boys so that she didn't even have any male friends left (field notes, eighth grade, March 4).

Within four days Alice had a new boyfriend, but her comments show that replacing her old boyfriend was an important concern. During the early stage in the development of their romantic activities, when the girls were beginning to have romantic feelings but did not act on them, all group members could adhere easily to this norm. Once they started to form romantic relationships, however, only the girls who were popular with boys could continually attract new boyfriends. In fact, the status associated with being popular with boys contributed to the salience of this norm among the girls at this school. At the same time, group members also had a hand in reinforcing this feeling norm.

> When Nancy came up she asked "Who do you like now, Carol?", a question which Nancy often asks Carol. Carol said, "Pete." Nancy said, "Oh yeah."

> Shortly after that Linda said, "Guess who Pete likes?" Betty said, "Carol." Nancy said, "God, you guys get everything you want" (field notes, seventh grade, April 14).

Even though less popular girls could not attract new boyfriends so easily, nevertheless they were able to abide by this norm. One strategy commonly used by these as well as by the more popular girls was to "recycle" the boys with whom they had had a previous relationship.

1 ELLEN: And then she went with George and then she went to likin' Tom
2 again.
3 NATALIE: Yeah. ((pause)) But sometimes it kinda switches on and off, like
4 s-like you'll like one boy and then you'll get tired of 'im and
5 you go with somebody else and then you'll like him again. Like
6 with Bryan and Dale. I used to do that a lot (interview, seventh grade, May 24).

Natalie's comments suggest that her and her friends' feelings for former boyfriends sometimes are recreated for the purpose of conforming to this norm. Natalie's comments also imply that conformity is likely to result in emotion work on the part of these girls, who sometimes evoke romantic feelings for boys they were previously "tired of." The advantages of conforming to this norm include appearing to be popular with boys as well as providing ongoing evidence of a heterosexual orientation; both are important concerns to girls at this age. At the same time, however, conformity carries several possible costs. One such cost is that emotion work may be necessary in order to always be in love. Although we can only speculate at this point, adolescent girls sometimes may create romantic feelings for boys to whom they are not attracted so they can conform to this norm. Hochschild (1983b) argued that when insincere feelings are created routinely, people lose touch with their actual feelings. Insofar as girls have insincere feelings, it is possible that eventually they will have difficulty in distinguishing between their "real" romantic feelings and their less authentic feelings, which they created in order to satisfy the requirements of this norm.

A second potential cost stems from the dilemma faced by adolescent females as a result of their adherence to this norm. On the one hand, girls consider being continuously in love as socially desirable because it is a way to reaffirm their popularity with boys and thus to increase their own status in relation to other females. On the other hand, group members who both attract too much attention from males and appear to be indiscriminate in their choice of romantic partners are often criticized by their friends for being "sluts," and ultimately are viewed in a negative manner.

References

Cancian, Francesca M. 1985. "Gender Politics: Love and Power in the Private and Public Spheres." Pp. 253–64 in *Gender and the Life Course*, edited by Alice S. Rossi. New York: Aldine.

———. 1987. *Love in America: Gender and Self Development*. Boston: Cambridge University Press.

Cancian, Francesca M. and Steven L. Gordon. 1988. "Changing Emotion Norms in Marriage: Love and Anger in U.S. Women's Magazines since 1900." *Gender and Society* 2(3):308–42.

Corsaro, William A. and Thomas A. Rizzo. 1988. "Discussion and Friendship: Socialization Processes in the Peer Culture of Italian Nursery School Children." *American Sociological Review* 53:879–94.

Eder, Donna and Janet Enke. 1988. "Gossip as a Means of Strengthening Social Bonds." Paper presented at the annual meeting of the American Sociological Association, Atlanta.

Evans, Cathy and Donna Eder. 1989. "'No Exit': Processes of Social Isolation in the Middle School." Paper presented at the annual meeting of the American Sociological Association, San Francisco.

Fine, Gary Alan. 1986. "The Social Organization of Adolescent Gossip: The Rhetoric of Moral Evaluation." Pp. 405–23 in *Children's Worlds and Children's Language*, edited by Jenny Cook-Gumperz, William Corsaro, and Jurgen Streeck. Berlin: Moulin.

Goodwin, Marjorie H. 1980. "He-Said-She-Said: Formal Cultural Procedures for the Construction of a Gossip Dispute Activity." *American Ethnologist* 7:674–95.

Gordon, Steven L. 1981. "The Sociology of Sentiments and Emotion." Pp. 562–92 in *Social Psychology: Sociological Perspectives*, edited by Morris Rosenberg and Ralph H. Turner. New York: Basic Books.

Hochschild, Arlie R. 1979. "Emotion Work, Feeling Rules, and Social Structure." *American Journal of Sociology* 85(3):551–75.

———. 1983a. "Attending to, Codifying and Managing Feelings: Sex Differences in Love." Pp. 250–62 in *Feminist Frontiers: Rethinking Sex, Gender, and Society*, edited by Laurel Richardson and Verta Taylor. New York: Addison-Wesley.

———. 1983b. *The Managed Heart: Commercialization of Human Feeling*. Berkeley: University of California Press.

Mead, George Herbert. 1934. *Mind, Self, and Society*. Chicago: University of Chicago Press.

Rich, Adrienne. 1980. "Compulsory Heterosexuality and Lesbian Existence." *Signs: Journal of Women in Culture and Society* 5:631–60.

Swidler, Ann. 1980. "Love and Adulthood in American Culture." Pp. 120–47 in *Themes of Work and Love in Adulthood*, edited by Neil J. Smelser and Erik H. Erickson. Cambridge: Harvard University Press.

Reflective Questions

1. In what sense are feelings biological? In what sense are they social in nature? How do we undergo a process of emotional socialization when it comes to feelings like romantic love?
2. What is a feeling norm? What are the key feeling norms that adolescent girls learn when it comes to romantic love? How do they express and reinforce these norms through their interactions with one another? How do they resist these norms? What costs do adolescent girls incur when abiding by the norm that they should "always be in love"?
3. What feeling norms do adolescent boys learn when it comes to romantic love? How do their experiences and expressions of this feeling compare to the experiences and expressions of adolescent girls?
4. Interview some of your friends or classmates about their experiences of romantic love. What do they think it means to be "in love"? How do they know they are in love? How do they express these feelings? Are they governed by the same feeling rules as adolescent girls? For instance, do they think that you should love only members of the opposite sex and that you should love only one person at a time?
5. Look up the lyrics of three or four popular songs that focus on the theme of romantic love. What feeling rules are promoted and reinforced in these lyrics? What do the lyrics suggest about what it means to be in love? What do they say about how you should feel and how you should act upon these feelings? What do they say about how you should feel or act if your lover breaks up with you?

9

Managing Emotional Manhood

CHRISTIAN VACCARO, DOUGLAS SCHROCK, AND JANICE MCCABE

For many years, students of social life ignored emotions. That changed in the 1970s when a number of sociologists began to study and write about the social shaping and consequences of human emotions. As illustrated in the previous two selections, human emotions are shaped by "feeling rules." People manage not only their outward expression of emotions but also their very feelings in order to conform to such rules. They not only express but also attempt to feel what they should be feeling. Further, feeling rules vary not just historically but also within societies, organizations, and groups.

If that is the case, then involvement in a new group or organization necessarily involves some emotional socialization. Initiates into a group or organization need to learn new feeling rules and develop new emotion management skills. This kind of emotional socialization is probably most apparent in professional schools. As Zerubavel noted in an earlier selection, professionals such as judges, professors, and doctors are expected to put personal feelings aside and display "affective neutrality" in their work. That expectation can be especially difficult for doctors, who must touch and treat the human body in ways that would evoke repulsion or notable discomfort in most of us.

This selection examines the emotional socialization of Mixed Martial Arts (MMA) fighters, who must grapple with the emotional threats posed by fear, pain, fatigue, and other forms of bodily discomfort. As the authors highlight, the education of MMA fighters includes instruction in the feeling rules that apply to their sport and to expressions of masculinity. MMA fighters learn that they must suppress their fears of pain, injury, and losing if they want to battle successfully in the cage. In their efforts to manage these fears, they draw upon strategies of emotion work used in a variety of groups and social worlds. These strategies include scripting, framing, othering, and fostering fear.

The example of MMA fighters provides a particularly clear case of how emotions are socially shaped. It also demonstrates how emotion work is a form of gendered identity work. When MMA fighters manage their emotions, they are also involved in managing and displaying their "manhood." Their concerted efforts to suppress, regulate, and call forth emotions helps us to see what we are all doing less self-consciously most of the time—managing feelings.

While fighters in the locker room prepared for combat in the cage, two men from the previous fight staggered in. Juan[1]—the victor—had shiny contusions under both eyes and made it to a folding chair where he sat staring into space. As two paramedics tried to keep him conscious, he cracked a smile with swollen lips and tried unsuccessfully to communicate meaningfully. As the

Reprinted From: "Managing Emotional Manhood: Fighting and Fostering Fear in Mixed Martial Arts," *Social Psychology Quarterly* 74(4): 414–437.

paramedics carried Juan off on a stretcher, Mike—his opponent—leaned against a wall and talked with his trainer. As blood flowed from his nose and mouth, Mike began to sob. His trainer handed him a towel, which he brought to his face with shaking hands. When asked if he was upset about Juan, he pulled away the bloodied towel and said, "I don't like losing."

Juan and Mike's post-fight experiences highlight what competitors of Mixed Martial Arts (MMA) most often say they fear: injury and losing. Competitions generally occur in a locked cage and fighters wear thin, open-fingered gloves and are allowed to punch, kick, wrestle, and use martial arts techniques. Fights are broken into rounds and end when one fighter submits or "taps out" due to pain or exhaustion, is rendered unconscious, is deemed physically unable to continue by a referee, or time runs out. Preparing for these fights entails not only perfecting "guillotine chokes" and "superman punches," it also involves fighting fear.

Although MMA fighters' emotion management may appear unique, it reflects a long-lived cultural mandate that "real men" control their fear and other emotions (Kimmel 1996). Peers (Fine 1987), parents (McGuffey 2008), and coaches (Messner 1992) often ostracize boys who express fear, pain, empathy, and sadness. Boys learn that they are supposed to exhibit emotional restraint and "quiet control" (Messner 2009:96). As adults, men often face fear, whether at work (Haas 1977), on the street (Anderson 1999), or in leisure activities (Holyfield and Fine 1997). And not letting fear get the best of you—exhibiting bravery—is a culturally revered quality of manhood (see e.g., Connell 1995). But how do men control their emotions, and what does this have to do with gender identity?

Our study . . . show[s] how men's emotion management can constitute gendered "identity work" (Snow and Anderson 1987). To emphasize the gendered and processional aspects of this emotional identity work, we refer to the MMA fighters' emotion management as managing emotional manhood. We define managing emotional manhood as emotion work that signifies a masculine self. Importantly, by the "masculine self" we are not referring to a psychological entity, how men view themselves, or the self-concept. Rather, we take the dramaturgical view that the masculine self is a virtual reality, a self that is imputed to actors based on the information given or given off (Goffman 1959). Schwalbe (2005) defines such identity work as a "manhood act" and emphasizes that signifying control is fundamental. Manhood here is not a static concept, but a malleable image that is constructed for public consumption. While there are many ways that males can put on a convincing manhood act (see Schrock and Schwalbe's [2009] review), in this study we emphasize that controlling and transforming one's own or others' emotions—especially fear—is key. Emotions here are not simply added to or subtracted from one's presumed manhood (as if manhood exists as a thing rather than a social construction); they are expressions that signify what kind of man one is. As we show, managing emotional manhood can be accomplished individually as well as interpersonally and can prime one to risk one's well-being in a quest to dominate others. . . .

Setting and Method

Data for this study derive from 24 months of fieldwork and 121 interviews. The first author gained access to a local MMA gym after calling the owner, Bruce, mentioning a long-time friendship with a professional fighter who had once been Bruce's training partner, and talking about his research interests. The ethnographer observed and openly jotted notes at about 100 evening practices at Steel Hangar Gym, which was located in a small industrial park on the outskirts of a midsized southeastern city. . . .

The first author conducted 24 formal 45- to 75-minute interviews with 15 local and 9 regional fighters and 97 brief 5- to 15-minute short interviews at competitions with 64 fighters and 15 trainers, promoters, and officials (some fighters were interviewed multiple times). . . . Of the interviewees, 70 percent were white, 16 percent were black, 11 percent were Hispanic, and 3 percent were Asian.

They ranged in age from 19 to 40 (average = 26.5). The majority (18 out of 25) of local interviewees had earned degrees from a community college or university. All interviews were recorded and transcribed.

As the first author began fieldwork, he shared copies of fieldnotes, and the coauthors became intrigued by fighters' allusions to fear. This initial interest sensitized us to pay attention to how fear permeated the field and also led us to create interview questions aimed to better understand (a) what fighters worried about and (b) how they managed it. These questions also guided the coding of fieldnotes and interview transcripts, which led to creating typologies of what they most feared (injury and losing) and how they managed their fear (scripting, framing, and othering). . . .

The Fears of Fighting

Underneath their bravado, Mixed Martial Arts fighters harbored fear. During interviews, at the local gym, and in locker rooms before competitions, the fighters often alluded to their fears by talking about "nerves," being "nervous," "worries," "pre-fight jitters," and "butterflies." For example, just before their fights, Ted said, "Oh, I'm nervous as hell!" and Buster said, "I was nervous. I was in the back about to throw up." Shortly after winning a fight, Robin said, "I was extremely nervous going into this." After losing fights, the men often blamed their poor performances on fear. For example, Ted explained, "It must have been nerves or something," and Garrett said, "I sort of felt like I kind of panicked and bitched out a little bit." As Garrett implied, uncontrollable fear was like being momentarily inhabited by womanhood, which is probably why fighters usually—but not always—avoided saying "I'm afraid/scared/fearful." Saying they were nervous or worried was arguably less damaging to their manhood acts. MMA fighters most commonly talked about fearing injury and losing. Fighters understood how painful injuries were and that serious ones could end their fighting careers, or worse. There have been two well-publicized deaths of fighters resulting from brain injuries sustained in North American MMA fights since 2007. Although interviewees agreed that, as Rocky put it, "in most cases you're going to come out of it [and] you're going to live," death lurked in the shadows of the cage. When asked what he worried about before his fights, for example, Kenneth said, "You are wondering if they are thinking of this incredible move that is really going to kill you." Dominic said, "This sport is not golf; you can't get hurt or killed playing golf." The possibility of death elevated MMA's manhood quotient. Fighters more frequently discussed worrying about injuries they could live through. Dean worried about "getting choked out or . . . getting hurt." Lou said, "I can get my arm broken [or] my nose broken, I can just get pounded." Jimmy said, "I was apprehensive about getting hurt."

Such fears were not unfounded. Local fighters suffered dislocated ribs and concussions, Louis tore his ACL, Rocky broke his foot and seriously injured his back, Lou broke his wrist and finger, and Dominic's retina became detached from his eye twice. Garrett and Dominic had elbow surgeries to remove bone fragments, and Garrett also had surgery to remove a damaged appendix. One local fighter suffered bleeding in his brain and required an induced coma and brain surgery to keep him alive. Because injuries were common, fighters could not easily escape the specter of pain.

In addition to fearing injury, cage fighters also feared losing. Casey feared looking "like a chump in front of all these people . . . if you get knocked out at your first fight in three seconds, then that's all they will remember." Mike said, "You really don't want to let your family or teammates down," and Kenneth said, "The name of the [MMA] school is kind of riding on you. You have to represent for your school." Minutes after Dean lost a fight, he said, "I feel like shit! I came out in front of my hometown and I got tapped out in like under a minute." Buster said, "The feeling of losing is the worst feeling in the world, especially when you sell 100 tickets and you have a lot of your friends and family there. . . . "

Cage fighters had much to fear. Injuries were inevitable and threatened to end their careers. Losing was also difficult to stomach, although it also seems unavoidable. Being controlled by fear, shame, or pain, however, would have undermined their manhood act, as expressing such emotions contradicted feeling rules culturally bound to manhood. But if the men could fight off their fears and foster it in their opponents, they might be victorious men.

Fighting Fear

Fighters often said that feeling fear itself was not the problem as long as they kept it under control. As Taylor put it, "Fear is an okay thing as long as you can manage it." This belief let them off the hook if they felt some fear but also oriented them toward controlling it. As we will show, their emotion work often involved transforming fear into confidence, which is more consistent with cultural ideals of manhood. One reason that feeling but managing fear is "okay" is that keeping one's poise in a dangerous situation constitutes one of our culture's most honored characteristics of manhood: bravery (see e.g., Connell 1995). As Rudyard Kipling (1976:163–64) put it in a poem often memorized by schoolboys: "If you can keep your head when all about you are losing theirs and blaming it on you . . . you'll be a Man, my son!" To avoid losing their heads, as well as their masculine status, cage fighters managed emotional manhood through scripting, framing, and othering.

Scripting

To the untrained observer, cage fighting appears to be chaotic violence. Competitors themselves understood that fights are relatively unpredictable because, as Kenneth put it, "Think of all the things you need to worry about in MMA: takedowns, knees, kicks, and elbows." To evoke a sense of control and minimize fear, fighters developed game plans. We refer to the individual as well as the collective creation, embodiment, and review of the game plan as scripting because such work involved planning out and rehearsing combat. [As] John replied, "I just think about what I want to do. What is this guy going to try to do? If I know he's a southpaw, what do I have to do to avoid that hook?" . . . [And] Rocky said,

> Me and Dominic get together and we do extensive research . . . we go to BattleBase.net—the most complete database of fighters thus far—and look at what his [the opponent's] record is. I look at what his [fight] style is. I look at how he's won his fights. I look at how he's lost his fights. And I implement that into a strict training regimen. If I'm fighting the kick boxer who wins all his fights by knock outs, you're going to be damn sure I'm practicing my striking. . . . But if I know I'm fighting a wrestler, I'm going to be working on my kick-down defenses and my knock-out punches.

Fighters regularly searched for videos and information about opponents on YouTube, MySpace, Facebook, and other Internet sites for MMA fighters and fans, such as MMAUniverse.com and Sherdog .com. In addition, if gym members had previously seen a fight involving a future opponent of a local member, they shared what they remembered. Overall, such intelligence gathering and sharing helped fighters to script game plans that bolstered confidence and manhood.

Although such scripting minimized fear as fighters prepared for competitions, fighters believed that to be successful they needed to instill the script into "bodily memory" (McCaughey 1998:290). As fight night neared, said Kenneth, "You should already have your game plan . . . in you right now. You don't have time to be thinking about that kind of stuff during a fight. . . . " When asked how he dealt with his emotions as he prepared for a fight, Ed referenced embodying the script, "It is all about putting yourself in the situation over and over again, so that nothing is new to you. [T]hat's what separates the good fighters from the mediocre fighters: [Good ones] don't panic, they are comfortable." Embodying the script thus helped manage emotional manhood by evoking confidence. . . .

Fighters also said that scripting helped them keep their fear under control during the emotionally intense minutes before their fights commenced. In the locker room, fighters often warmed up by hitting pads as their trainers went over their game plans. For example, after saying, "I was real nervous, I was sweating" before a recent fight and being asked if anything helped, Dustin said: "I had my coach and he was holding pads as well as telling me the game plan." . . .

Scripting also played a role in how the fighters made sense of both their victories and defeats in ways that preserved their commitment to enacting manhood through cage fighting. Fighters, for example, maintained the notion that scripting helped them win and control their fear by giving their game plans credit for defeating opponents. As Jimmy explained minutes after a successful bout, "I'm going to pat myself on the back and say I stuck to my game plan . . . I never really did get too frustrated or nervous." Even when their manhood acts in some ways failed (i.e., they lost), trainers and fighters used scripting to minimize the fear that they were not cut out for the cage and evoke confidence that they could come out on top in the future. One night at the local gym, for example, one trainer proclaimed to a fighter, "You lost when you didn't listen to my game plan." Keeping alive the idea that scripting propelled fighters to victory thus preserved it as a resource for managing emotional manhood.

Developing, embodying, and reviewing their scripts enabled fighters to keep their emotions in check and put on convincing manhood acts. Choreographing their violence was highly rational, taking into account their opponents' and their own perceived strengths and weaknesses to devise strategies. Such scripting thus not only signified manhood by minimizing fear but also by denoting rationality, a key cultural marker of manhood.

Framing

MMA fighters also used framing to do emotion work that signified masculine selves. Following Goffman (1974), we define a frame as a definition that answers the question, "What is going on here?" Framing shapes how one not only thinks about a situation but also how one feels. . . . Fighters' emotional framing most often involved defining cage fights as (a) just another day in the gym, (b) business, and (c) a valuable experience. They used these strategies individually and interpersonally, although they generally hid them from members of the local gym who did not compete in competitions.

Framing a fight as just another day in the gym boosted confidence and mitigated fear by defining competitions as banal. Although the audience, announcers, ring girls, medical professionals, and steel cage made competitions objectively different than training, fighters often equated fights with everyday training. Lou said that he kept "calm and composed" by thinking "in my mind that [the fight] is a sparring match. [I] think of it as another day in the gym." When asked how they dealt with their emotions prior to a competition, Scotty said, "Just be natural and do the same things that I do in the gym"; Felix answered, "I basically want the mindset that I have in practice"; and Nick said he "stay[s] cool because it's just like every other day in training." Such framing thus managed emotional manhood by mitigating fear.

Unlike scripting, framing fights as "just another day in the gym" was not part of the culture of the local gym. Because many men trained but did not participate in competitions, MMA fighters preserved their status as more dominant men by maintaining a public distinction between training and competition. Backstage, however, MMA competitors learned about this emotion management strategy from veteran fighters and trainers. When asked about how he helps fighters control their pre-fight emotions, for example, Dominic said:

> A lot of those conversations happen behind closed doors. [Or] at three in the morning. You get a phone call from a fighter and he is like, "I don't know that I can do this." And you have to be like, "Yes, you can. You do this every day in the gym."

Whereas fighters often presented themselves as invincible in the gym, they expressed more vulnerability backstage. In these hidden moments, more experienced fighters often engaged in interpersonal emotion work to ease their fears. Although such emotional support is culturally coded as "feminine," new fighters used what they learned to enact emotional manhood.

In addition to defining the fight as another day in the gym, fighters also managed fear by framing the fight as business. For example, Victor said, "Before a fight you are always a little nervous . . . but when you step into the cage . . . you just go and do your job. It is like an everyday office guy." . . . Larry said, "A true professional in this sport approaches this as a business . . . I got to put this dude down and get my money so I can put food on the table." . . .

In contradiction to framing the fight as "just another day in the gym," the fighters also mitigated fear by framing the fight as a valuable experience. Newcomers more often used this strategy than veterans. When asked what helped him deal with emotions before a recent fight, Steven said, "I just kind of looked at it as there's no pressure on me . . . it's an opportunity, obviously, to get some experience and [I should] just go out and enjoy it." Isaac managed emotional manhood by framing a fight in the wider context of his biography:

> When I showed up . . . all those doubts crept into my mind. Doubts like, "Why in the hell am I doing this?" There is obviously a risk of having your face punched in. . . . "Why am I doing this to myself? Why do I put myself in this position?" So for me what works is just to sit back . . . and say, "I'm doing something that is so important to me. And it is something that I want to do so badly. And that this is something that I am going to remember for a long time. That is why this is making me this nervous."

In this example, Isaac explains how he manages his fear by framing a fight as one of his life's most cherished moments. Doing so swept his doubts under the rug, enabling him to more convincingly display emotional manhood.

While losing matches could make fighters fear that they were no longer cut out for the cage, framing their losses as valuable learning experiences often eased their fears and gave them enough confidence to continue. Nick said, for example, that a recent "loss taught me a lot of things about being inside the cage, a lot about being calm and my nerves and just how to compose myself in the cage. So this time coming in I am ready for it." Dean emphasized that even if one loses, one gains: "And all my lessons learned from losing are the kind of lessons that stick." . . .

Othering

Fighters also mitigated fear and bolstered confidence and pride by defining themselves as superior to their opponents. Such "othering" (see e.g., Schwalbe et al. 2000)—whether it involved creating powerful virtual selves ("implicit othering") or defining their opponents as inferior ("oppressive othering")—made them feel like victory was within reach. As we will show, both the meanings of such othering and its emotional impact helped fighters signify credible masculine selves.

Managing emotional manhood via othering was often an interpersonal process and generally involved more experienced gym members easing the less experienced members' fears. "If I say, 'Oh, I feel uncomfortable with this,'" Donovan said that his trainer tells him, "You got great hands [and] can take this guy down [and] submit him." . . . Tanner said his fears were eased when "my teammate told me that there is no way in the world that this guy is going to be as tough as the guys you're training with." Felix explained that his trainer gave him the "usual pep talk" before a recent fight: "'You've trained better than this guy. You're a better fighter.'" Trainers and gym mates thus painted fighters as superior to their opponents, which mitigated fear and bolstered their confidence and pride as dominant men. . . .

Fighters individually used creative variations of these othering strategies to quell their fears and emotionally prepare themselves for battle. A few drew on cultural products such as films and racial stereotypes. When asked how he kept his fear in check, Cecil, an African American fighter, said:

> Right before my fight, I go ahead and do my prefight ritual. [Guys from] my gym call me "King Kong" because of my grappling style and [so] I awaken that inner gorilla . . . I rock back and forth and I have visions of a gorilla coming out of a cage, [like] when King Kong comes out of the cage and he pounds his chest powerfully just as lightning strikes. I hear the thunder and [see] lightning hitting the ground when I roar. You hear my roar and you look at my eyes. And I am ready to go into the cage.

Like medical students envisioning themselves as healers in order to mitigate their fear of disgust (Smith and Kleinman 1989), Cecil quelled fear and bolstered confidence by viewing himself as an animalistic monster. He thus drew on a film to symbolically align himself with dehumanizing stereotypes of violent African American men (see Collins 2004), which ironically helped him emotionally signify that he was a "real man."

Fighters' othering used not only Hollywood scripts, but also video games as resources. After Rocky asserted that he does not fear the cage, he was asked how he managed that. He said:

> I pretty much think of it as a video game. He has a little energy bar and a stamina bar above his head and everytime I hit him that bar goes down. I try to think about the fact that every second that I don't hit him that energy bar may be going back up. I think of myself the same way, except I pretend that my energy bar never goes down. It's just like I am in invincible mode.

Similar to medical students who manage emotions by, for example, "dehumanizing" a patient as a "broken toaster" (Smith and Kleinman 1989:61), Rocky muted fear by constructing his opponent as well as himself as pixelated pugilists. His othering also conveyed masculine dominance by representing his virtual self as so "invincible" that "nothing can hurt me."

In addition to defining themselves as physically superior to their opponents, fighters also regulated emotions by constructing themselves as mentally superior. [As] a veteran fighter said:

> The specific thing that I always tell myself is that I am way smarter than the other guy. And that may or may not be true obviously, but that's the thought I have because everybody trains their asses off for a fight. . . . For me, I am going to say—while I am looking across [the cage]—that, "I know you trained hard, but I trained better. I trained smarter. I know more of what I am doing than you do. I am going to be able to think faster than you and be able to deal with any situation you put me in better than you."

. . . Instead of focusing on their own mental or physical acuity, some fighters painted opponents as, emotionally speaking, insufficiently masculine. When Dominic was asked how he dealt with his nerves before entering the cage, he said,

> I like thinking about the fact that whatever the other guy is doing, you're going to beat him anyway. If the guy needs to cry like a girl in order to fight, you are still going to beat him. If he needs his parents in the stands to support him, you are still going to beat him.

Drawing on the larger culture, Dominic thus constructed competitors as fearful girls who depended on others ("parents") for emotional support. Other fighters similarly managed their own fear by imagining their opponent as fearful, which is culturally associated with women. As a veteran local fighter put it:

> What I think about . . . is not that I'm nervous, but I'm thinking about the fact that he's fucking nervous, you know what I'm saying? I know that somewhere deep down in his heart there's at least one ounce of fear or apprehensiveness or tentativeness and I just like to play on that. I imagine that he's scared shitless.

Similar to how nascent male-to-female transsexuals engage in "personal pep talks" to control fear when preparing to go out in public as women (Schrock, Boyd, and Leaf 2009), fighters' masculinist self-talk bolstered their confidence as they set forth to bash symbolic women.

Before fighters left the locker room and entered the arena, trainers often engaged in othering to emotionally prepare them. . . . Nationalism and implicit racism were occasionally used in such othering, which bolstered confidence as fighters headed to the cage. In the locker room before one contest, Larry and his trainer—both of whom were white and U.S. citizens—were waiting as Larry's opponent—a Peruvian national—entered the cage. Larry's trainer then told him that he had requested a "special song" be played for his own entrance. As Bruce Springsteen's "Born in the USA" began to play loudly over the sound system, the crowd erupted. Larry glanced at his trainer and cracked a smile, pounded his fists together, and confidently growled, "I'm taking this fucker to school" as they entered the arena.

Fighters' othering—which defined fighters as superior to their opponents—constituted managing emotional manhood. Such othering drew on cultural ideals and stereotypes, was accomplished individually and interpersonally, and not only kept fighters' fear under control but bolstered confidence as they entered an objectively fear-inducing situation. Thus, othering cultivated emotional expressions that resonated with gendered feeling rules and signified, in the dramaturgical sense, a masculine self.

Fostering Fear

Another way fighters managed emotional manhood was by fostering fear in their opponents. Inducing fear in other men essentially signified that they themselves were so powerful that they could turn other men, emotionally speaking, into women. Such emotional micropolitics not only raised one's own status (Clark 1990) but also signified masculine selves—that is, it conveyed that they were in control of not only their own but also their opponents' feelings.

Competitions provided many opportunities for the men to try to evoke fear in their opponents. The day before a match, fighters saw each other during weigh-ins and meetings with promoters and officials. Fighters sometimes strategically intimidat[ed] opponents; they walked around ' 'trying to be a badass," as one fighter put it. Local fighters sometimes donned new hairstyles at competitions that bolstered their tough image, such as getting a Mohawk, dying their hair outlandish colors, or shaving it off.

Interviewees sometimes strategically displayed their physique and, if given a chance, added some verbal innuendo intended to evoke fear. After discussing how he managed his own fear, for example, Taylor said, "Not everybody is built like me. I've had guys that have just seen me and backed out of a fight before." Asked to expound, he described what happened at a tough man contest:

> I'm walking around with my shirt off. . . . And another guy walks up to me and he says, "Hey what weight class are you fighting in?" And I said, "I'm fighting a light weight." And he looks at me and he's like, "Man, there is no way you're a light weight." And since then I ain't never seen that guy again. He was obviously in my weight class [and] was like, "Shit." And the next thing you know, all the promoters were talking, "We just lost a fighter." (mutual laughter) Intimidation is a huge, huge, huge portion of it.

Here Taylor suggests that he evoked fear in his opponent by going shirtless and displaying his considerable muscularity. Telling his opponent that he was fighting "a light weight" instead of "in the light weight division" may have also been effective. The weigh-in ritual was a key moment in which fighters attempted to intimidate each other. It generally began with fighters being called up for quick medical checkups. During this time, the room was filled with chatter and laughter as fighters, trainers, and promoters from different cities mingled. When it was time for fighters to weigh in, however, fighters and trainers coalesced into gym-based groups and—except for the announcer calling up opponents—the room was silent. When called, fighters walked up to the center of the stage, wearing nothing but boxers, and stepped on a scale. After their weight was announced, they flexed their muscles and briefly posed for pictures. Once each opponent did this, the two men posed together for "stare down" photos, in which they stood eye-to-eye in fighting stances. When asked how he tried to intimidate his opponent during the pre-fight ritual, Forrest said:

> You never let them know that you're scared of them. So you always look them dead in the eye. Never back down, never do anything to make it look like you're nervous. You know, just pretend like you're—act like you're confident the whole time.

Keeping one's own fear under control was thus key to instilling fear in opponents. Fighters typically put on one of three intimidating personas during the stare down: (a) the arrogantly confident "High School Quarterback," (b) the barely controllable angry "Wide-Eyed Madman," or (c) the unflappable "Bored Russian." The most overt attempts to induce fear were the "madmen," who often invaded opponents' personal space and made bodily contact. On the day of the fight, fighters usually had opportunities to intimidate each other backstage, as they often shared a locker room or had backstage areas that were connected. For example, Dustin said, "The way the locker rooms were set up, I could see [my opponent] watching me when I was warming up." Dustin said he looked at his trainer and said loudly, "Are you ready for me to knock this mother fucker out? I'm going to fuck him up!" He added, "I could just tell he didn't want to fight me . . . he was worried about it." When Garrett similarly saw his opponent checking him out in the locker room, he whacked the punching mitts his trainer was holding with particular vigor, hoping to intimidate his opponent. Managing emotional manhood thus involved using the body and language in [an] attempt to control others' emotions. . . .

Many fighters said they tried to intimidate opponents when entering the cage. Most often fighters said that they attempted to do this in a subtle fashion. When asked if they tried to intimidate opponents once in the ring, Tommy said, "I try to look at his face when the referee is talking to us"; another said, "I give my opponent a little stare-down and intimidate him"; and Ayden said, "I just come out and let him know that I'm not afraid. I size him up and give a little stare." Fighters' demeanor was thus part of their dramaturgical arsenal.

African American fighters sometimes presented themselves in ways that resonated with racial stereotypes, hoping to evoke fear in opponents. Dion would enter the ring doing "the gorilla stomp, just to intimidate my opponent . . . and get the crowd going." At one event he was observed running into the cage and jumping vertically about four feet into the air before stomping down on the middle of the mat with both feet, shaking the whole cage and creating a loud noise that reverberated through the arena. He then charged at his opponent, who was required to remain in his corner, and repeated the gorilla stomp, coming down a mere foot from his competitor as he yelled in unison with the roaring crowd. Immediately after this fight, the loser was asked how he felt before the opening bell: "I was terrified."

While Dion's performance constituted "passion work" (Smith 2008) because it could generate crowd excitement, it also managed emotional manhood by evoking fear in his opponent. This worked in part because the cultural stereotypes of African American men orient others to view them as dangerously animalistic and criminal (Collins 2004). If fighters sensed or caught glimpses of fear in opponents' faces, it affirmed their own manhood and motivated them to fight with confidence. In a post-victory interview, for example, Benny said he knew "the fight was mine" before it started because "I could sense that he just wasn't ready to fight me at all . . . he was nervous."

Casey offered a bit more detail in his post-fight interview: "I looked across the cage at him—his face—he seemed kind-of scared. And I thought . . . that I'm probably going to win this. So I went out and shot right away and knocked him down." If their own violence evoked fear in opponents during a fight, the men felt particularly powerful and motivated to finish them off. As Rocky said:

> Once they're all bruised up and I see the fear in their eyes and, man, I see that they realize that the fight isn't going to be as easy as they thought it was going to be—or that their game plan isn't working

like they thought it was going to—that's really what gets me going.

Evoking fear in their opponents could thus work back on fighters' own emotions, motivating them to confidently attack. Managing emotional manhood involves not only fighting one's own fear but also trying to evoke it in others. By strategically manipulating their appearance, engaging in nonverbal posturing, and engaging in discursive acts, the fighters sometimes broke through their opponents' emotional defenses. Regulating their own emotions played a role in this micropolitical emotion work—whether presenting themselves as calm and collected or on the verge of rage. In addition, some men of color strategically embodied racial stereotypes that have long been used to control minority men as a resource to exert power over others. Regardless of the strategy used, the implication of this emotion work was that they, as men, should be respected and feared.

Conclusion

. . . Putting on a convincing manhood act requires more than using language and the body; it also requires emotion work. By suppressing fear, empathy, pain, and shame and evoking confidence and pride, males signify their alleged possession of masculine selves. Such emotion work may thus create an emotional orientation that primes men to subordinate and harm others. And by signifying masculine selves through evoking fear and shame in others, such men are likely to more easily secure others' deference and accrue rewards and status. Managing emotional manhood, whether it occurs in a locker room or boardroom, at home or the Oval Office, likely plays a key role in maintaining unequal social arrangements.

Note

1. All names used are pseudonyms.

References

Anderson, Elijah. 1999. *Code of the Street: Decency, Violence, and the Moral Life of the Inner City*. New York: W.W. Norton.

Clark, Candace. 1990. "Emotions and Micropolitics in Everyday Life: Some Patterns and Paradoxes of Place." Pp. 305–33 in *Research Agendas in the Sociology of Emotions*, edited by T. Kemper. Albany, NY: State University of New York Press.

Collins, Patricia H. 2004. *Black Sexual Politics: African Americans, Gender, and the New Racism*. New York: Routledge.

Connell, Robert W. 1995. *Masculinities*. Sydney: Allen and Unwin.

Fine, Gary A. 1987. *With the Boys: Little League Baseball and Preadolescent Culture*. Chicago: University of Chicago Press.

Goffman, Erving. 1959. *The Presentation of Self in Everyday Life*. New York: Doubleday.

Goffman, Erving. 1974. *Frame Analysis*. New York: Harper.

Haas, Jack. 1977. "Learning Real Feelings: A Study of High Steel Ironworkers' Reactions to Fear and Danger." *Sociology of Work and Occupations* 4:147–70.

Holyfield, Lori and Gary A. Fine. 1997. "Adventure as Character Work: The Collective Taming of Fear." *Symbolic Interaction* 20:343–63.

Kimmel, Michael. 1996. *Manhood in America: A Cultural History*. New York: The Free Press.

Kipling, Rudyard. 1976. "If." Pp. 163–64 in *The Forty-Nine Percent Majority: The Male Sex Role*, edited by D. S. David and R. Brannon. New York: Random House.

McCaughey, Martha. 1998. "The Fighting Spirit: Women's Self-Defense Training and the Discourse of Sexed Embodiment." *Gender and Society* 12:277–300.

McGuffey, C. Shawn. 2008. "Saving Masculinity: Gender Reaffirmation, Sexuality, Race and Parental Responses to Male Child Sexual Abuse." *Social Problems* 55:216–37.

Messner, Michael. 1992. *Power at Play: Sports and the Problem of Masculinity*. Boston: Beacon Press.

Messner, Michael. 2009. *It's All for the Kids: Gender, Families, and Youth Sports*. Berkeley: University of California Press.

Schrock, Douglas P., Emily M. Boyd, and Margaret Leaf. 2009. "Emotion Work in the Public Performances of Male-to-Female Transsexuals." *Archives of Sexual Behavior* 38:702–12.

Schrock, Douglas P. and Michael Schwalbe. 2009. "Men, Masculinity, and Manhood Acts." *Annual Review of Sociology* 35:277–95.

Schwalbe, Michael. 2005. "Identity Stakes, Manhood Acts, and the Dynamics of Accountability." Pp. 65–81 in *Studies in Symbolic Interaction*, edited by N. Denzin. New York: Elsevier.

Schwalbe, Michael, Sandra Godwin, Daphne Holden, Douglas Schrock, Shealy Thompson, and Michele Wolkomir. 2000. "Generic Processes in the Reproduction of Inequality: An Interactionist Analysis." *Social Forces* 79:419–52.

Smith, Allen and Sherryl Kleinman. 1989. "Managing Emotions in Medical School: Students' Contact with the Living and the Dead." *Social Psychology Quarterly* 52:56–69.

Smith, R. Tyson. 2008. "Passion Work: The Joint Production of Emotional Labor in Professional Wrestling," *Social Psychology Quarterly* 71:157–176.

Snow, David A. and Leon Anderson. 1987. "Identity Work among the Homeless: The Verbal Construction and Avowal of Personal Identities." *American Journal of Sociology* 92:1336–71.

Reflective Questions

1. How is emotion management a form of identity work? How is this emotional identity work gendered in nature? For example, how do men strive to express their "manhood" through emotion work? What feelings are men encouraged to express? What feelings do they learn to control or suppress?
2. What are the major fears and emotional threats faced by Mixed Martial Artists? What strategies do they use to deal with these fears and threats? How do these strategies differ from one another? How do they overlap? Which strategies seem to be most effective in enabling the fighters to manage challenging emotions?
3. What feeling rules prevail among Mixed Martial Arts fighters? How do these rules compare to the emotional norms that men abide by in other sports or in male-dominated workplaces?
4. In Selection 7, Arlie Hochschild highlighted the distinction between surface acting and deep acting. How do Mixed Martial Arts fighters engage in surface acting? How do they engage in deep acting?
5. According to the authors, the management of emotional manhood plays a major role in sustaining social inequalities, especially between women and men. Why is this the case? For instance, how do the emotion management strategies used by many men evoke fear, deference, and compliance in others?

The Organizational Management of Shame

DANIEL D. MARTIN

Some of the previous selections have illustrated how emotions are socially rooted and regulated. In doing so these selections have demonstrated how individuals learn to internalize and abide by "feeling rules," or social expectations that tell them how they should feel in a given situation and how they should convey those feelings to others. These selections also revealed how individuals draw on a range of strategies to make their emotions conform to the rules that govern their social or professional settings. Yet, like most social psychological analyses of emotion, these selections did not address an important sociological question—that is, how and why do people engage in collective strategies of emotion management?

In the following selection, Dan Martin provides a groundbreaking analysis of how organizations help people jointly manage their feelings, particularly in regard to the stigmatized attribute of obesity. Drawing on data collected through participant observation and in-depth interviews, Martin examines three organizations that deal extensively with obesity and the stigma associated with it: Weight Watchers (WW), Overeaters Anonymous (OA), and the National Association to Advance Fat Acceptance (NAAFA). Martin compares how each of these organizations defines its mission, establishes its goals, and shapes the emotions and body announcements of its members. Most important, Martin portrays how each organization not only offers its members an ideological framework that tells them what obesity means but also provides them with new strategies for managing their "fat" bodies and their related feelings and self-images. Moreover, each organization provides its members with group support for embracing its ideology and applying its recommended strategies of emotion management.

While both WW and OA try to help their members reduce their body size and conform to bodily norms, they are guided by very different belief systems, and they emphasize different strategies and rituals to help their members address body-related feelings of shame. The goal of WW is to enable members to contain and manage their shame by losing weight and transforming their bodies. By contrast, the goal of OA is to help its members understand how and why shame experiences motivate them to engage in "compulsive overeating," to acknowledge their feelings of shame to themselves and others, and to recognize how they can overcome these feelings by admitting their need for a "higher power." NAAFA is guided by a dramatically different approach. This organization argues that obesity-related feelings of shame are the result of "fat oppression" promoted and reinforced in the larger society. In turn, NAAFA tells its members that they need to deal with their feelings of shame by changing the social meanings given to obesity rather than changing themselves or their bodies.

On a broader level, Martin links the organizational characteristics of WW, OA, and NAAFA to their

Reprinted from: Daniel D. Martin, Organizational Approaches to Shame: Avowal, Management, and Contestation. *The Sociological Quarterly* 41: 125–150, January 2000.

guiding approaches for dealing with shame—that is, to whether they regard shame as something to manage, avow, or challenge. In the process he provides an insightful comparative analysis of the various types of ideologies, strategies, and self-stories promoted by differently structured groups that take part in collective emotion management. He also demonstrates how and why sociological psychologists need to focus more attention on these groups, particularly if they want to gain a deeper understanding of how emotion work and identity construction are group processes.

Both cross-cultural research and feminist studies have observed the connection between shame and gender identity, demonstrating that, while women are more susceptible to body shame, for men the emotion is associated with failure to live up to culturally prescribed norms of masculinity (Gilmore 1987; Horowitz 1983).

Feminist scholars investigating the U.S. beauty culture have observed its emergence in the 1870s (Banner 1983; Schwartz 1986) as new appearance norms were created and distributed by industries such as cinema (Featherstone 1982), advertising (Ewen 1976), and scale and corset companies (Schwartz 1986). As a result, the social formation that exists at the end of the twentieth century is a "cult of thinness" (Hesse-Biber 1996) that promotes and normalizes slenderness and its attendant anxieties (Bordo 1993). This cult has far-reaching effects. Barrie Thorne and Zella Luria's (1986) research on children's games involving cross-sex interaction reveal that girls' bodies are more sexually defined and accrue more penalties for an overweight appearance than do boys'. This pattern is consistent with findings of cross-cultural research on mate selection that demonstrate that men evaluate the social value of women more heavily in terms of appearance and that women evaluate the social value of men in terms of their occupational status and earning potential (Buss 1989). In the United States, where fat is stigmatizing (Allon 1982; Cahnman 1968), feelings of shame may result in debilitating eating disorders. Research on adolescent girls has demonstrated that the internalization of beauty norms is responsible for producing high degrees of body dissatisfaction and a profound sense of body shame (McFarland and Baker-Baumann 1990) leading to bulimia and anorexia nervosa (Rodin, Striegel-Moore, and Silberstein 1990, p. 362). Of course, the fat content of bodies, along with the degree to which it might be stigmatized and accompanied by body shame, is variable. A slightly overweight body may be experienced as an object of great shame and the focus of disordered eating, or it may be experienced as only a "minor bodily stigma" (Ellis 1998).

However, neither feminist nor sociological studies have addressed how organizations attempt to assist their members in managing shame.

Drawing upon Erving Goffman's (1986) frame analysis, I assess how shame is managed within three different "appearance organizations" through the discursive and bodily strategies that they supply their members. By appearance organizations, I mean organizations for whom the physical appearance of members is a primary concern. These organizations include Overeaters Anonymous (OA), Weight Watchers, Inc. (WW), and the National Association to Advance Fat Acceptance (NAAFA). The theoretical and substantive questions concerning these organizations are twofold. First, what kinds of organizational frames do these organizations offer their members to make sense of shame? Second, what strategies are used within the organizations in managing or contesting experiences of shame?

The Organizations

Given the sex ratio of the organizations, all three of the appearance organizations I studied might properly be recognized as "women's organizations." Therefore, the present analysis of shame is an analysis of women's shame. During interviews and participant observation, I found that men rarely talked about shame or embarrassment over the body while women seemed to be continually, acutely aware of it. Based upon information reported by the organizations, participation rates reveal significant sex differences in membership (Table 1). These differences were also revealed in the accounts that women and

Table 1 Organizational Membership

	Sex Differences in Participation		
	WW	NAAFA	OA
Women	95%	78%	86%
Men	5%	22%	14%
Total*	100%	100%	100%

*These figures represent national membership rather than participation rates in local chapters.

men constructed about joining and participating in the organizations and about the gender relations that were negotiated within them—a topic beyond the scope of the present article (Martin 1995).

At the beginning of data collection, Weight Watchers International (WW) was the leading national weight loss organization in the United States, with annual revenues of approximately $1.3 billion (Weber 1990, p. 86). Of its fifteen million members worldwide, approximately 14.3 million are women. In contrast, the exact size and composition of Overeaters Anonymous (OA), a program for compulsive overeaters, remains undetermined, even though the organization estimates that 86 percent of its U.S. members are female (OA 1992, p. 1), Because anonymity in the twelve-step program is strictly enforced, there is no comprehensive roster of OA members. Currently, the number of OA groups is estimated at over seven thousand worldwide (OA 1987, p. 10), but group site varies from five to twenty-five people, making estimates of total membership difficult.

The National Association to Advance Fat Acceptance (NAAFA) describes itself as a civil rights organization in the "size rights movement." It also defines itself as a social support organization and as a self-help group (NAAFA 1990, pp. 1–6). Unlike members of OA and WW, the NAAFA members in the local chapter I studied engaged in a variety of social and political activities. These ranged from informal parties and organized dances, to speaking at community conferences, to holding protests and conducting write-in campaigns. The national organization, founded in 1969, has headquarters in Sacramento, California, and a membership of 2,500–3,000 members. NAAFA consists of a loosely federated set of local chapters and special interest groups, including gay and lesbian groups, fat admirers groups, couples groups, singles, teen and youth groups, groups for super-sized and mid-sized individuals, and feminist groups.

Methods

Over the course of approximately two years, I conducted participant observation and in-depth interviews at Weight Watchers and NAAFA. In attempting to gain access to OA, I sought out an acquaintance and long-standing group leader in OA who was centrally located in local OA networks. She was helpful in providing me with extensive information about the organization, its program, and its local chapters. Believing that her interest in my project, her sensitivity to research needs, and the fact that we had worked together indicated an openness to facilitating entree, I directly broached the topic. My request for an introduction into the closed meetings and access to OA members was met, instead, by recalcitrance motivated by her desire to ensure the anonymity of local members. I was frozen out of the local chapters and was unable to conduct participant observation in groups other than the publicly available "open meetings." A couple of months later, I learned of a local OA audiotape library. I selectively sampled personal stories and presentations that had been taped at national and local conferences and then were produced for OA members as well as members of Alcoholics Anonymous. I utilized the strategy of "theoretical saturation" recommended by Barney G. Glaser and Anselm L. Strauss (1967), selecting audiotapes for analysis until the additional data yielded few additional insights. I was assisted by the proprietor of the service, who was instrumental in locating tapes containing life stories that were as complete as possible.[1] I conducted interviews with all of the active members of NAAFA after I had established myself with the group and had been conducting participant observation and with members of Weight Watchers who responded to ads that I had run in local newspapers. The total number of interviews for all three organizations is

Table 2 Interviews

	Women	Men
WW	20	5
NAAFA*	8	4
OA**	41	8
Total	69	17

*Defines the entire population of active chapter members during the period of my observation.
**Includes recorded personal stories of members from the OA audiotape library.

in Table 2. Because the organizations themselves constituted the sampling frames, little variation in race, class, or ethnicity was provided within the samples. All of the informants in this study were white and most were middle income.

Data Collection, Embarrassment, and Shame

Because my own bodily appearance served as a "dis-identifier" (Goffman 1967), a symbol belying a legitimate, potential, future claim for group membership in WW, OA, and NAAFA, I intentionally gained about twenty-five pounds before participation. I hoped to learn as much as I could about members' own meanings and feelings of the body and participation as well as how the organizational "frames" that were established shaped emotional experience and participation. Having gained my undergraduate degree on a wrestling scholarship attuned me to the issues of extreme dieting, binge-eating, and weigh-ins, which could similarly be found in the lived experience of Weight Watchers, NAAFA, and OA members. While my own weight gain facilitated somatic insight into the lives and meanings of members of OA and Weight Watchers, my burgeoning body size was clearly not comparable to the experience of members of NAAFA. Because I was not subjected to the stigmatization or public inconvenience suffered daily by NAAFA members (some of whom weighed in excess of three hundred pounds) my own "fat identity" never fully crystallized. Indeed, if anything, I was considered a novelty among friends, peers, and colleagues who issued positive sanctions for my "sociological commitment."

At Weight Watchers, I regularly attended weekly meetings, which entailed a logical stream of activities once members entered the meeting place. These included paying weekly dues, being weighed on physician's scales by WW personnel, receiving organizational literature concerning meal plans along with myriad other promotional materials distributed by the organization (such as the monthly newspaper), and finally selecting a seat in the meeting area. As a participating observer, I experienced the anxiety that members later recounted in interviews about "facing the scale," that is, weigh-ins. Because weigh-ins take place in semipublic space, it is possible that queuing members will learn of one's weight, increasing the anxiety that is already present for some members. Having failed weigh-in several times by gaining weight, I was struck by the capacity for the ritual to evoke, simultaneously, feelings of dependency and embarrassment. WW personnel are aware of these feelings, and they commonly query deviating members about the possible causes of weight gain. They also join in the construction of accounts and remedial work directed at either exonerating deviating members or diminishing their presumed culpability.

Organizational Frames

Experiences of shame, humiliation, and embarrassment can be found in the life stories of members of all three appearance organizations. What establishes the meaning of these experiences is the organizational "frame" (Goffman 1986) within which the experiences of members are socially and discursively organized (Table 3). A "frame," according to Goffman (1986, pp. 10–11), is a set of "definitions of situations" that are "built up in accordance with the principles of organization which govern events—at least social ones—and our subjective involvement in them." *Organizational* frames are those definitions constructed and maintained by organizational actors within which experience, interaction, and communication are structured and rendered both personally and organizationally meaningful. For the programs of organizations to be subjectively meaningful, they must facilitate a linkage of individual interpretations to organizational meanings and definitions, that is, "frame alignment" (Snow, Rochford, Worden, and Benford 1986).

In the case of these appearance organizations, the meanings, as well as the strategies that are dispensed to members for dealing with shame, reflect the structure, agenda, and ideology of the organization, its "frame." The organizational frames of Weight Watchers, OA, and NAAFA represent three unique sets of social and discursive practices developed in accordance with different historical circumstances and audiences. Thus, while the autobiographical content of participants' shame experiences seemed to bear great similarity across the organizations, the "organizational" meaning of these experiences and the strategies employed to manage or alleviate them differed vastly.

The Organizational Frame of OA: Redemption

The Overeaters Anonymous program is a redemptive model of treatment directed at developing a spiritual consciousness through a therapeutic group process. OA meetings, whether open to the public ("open meetings") or open to OA members only ("closed meetings"), are typically held in public facilities, often churches. Meetings begin with a recitation of OA's preamble and the evening's speaker

Table 3 Shame Work: A Comparison of Organizational Frames

	Overeaters Anonymous	Weight Watchers	NAAFA
Type of organization	Twelve-step program	Multinational corporation	Civil rights organization
Organizational frame	Redemption	Rationality	Activism sociality
Organizational goal	Support members in abstinence from overeating	Help clients lose weight/profit	Organize against "size discrimination"
Source of shame	Compulsive over-eating/fat body	Fat body/body image	Societal definitions of beauty, cultural appearance norms
Consequence of shame	Inhibits recovery	Leads clients to exit program	Inhibits activism
Shame strategy	Shame avowal/expiation	Shame management	Contestation of shame
Approach to shame	Self-transformation	Bodily transformation	Societal transformation
Ritual for shame removal	Shame avowal	Dieting	Identity announcement/public confrontation
Meaning of the body	Body as symptomatic display of spiritual deficit; thinner body as a symbol of regaining control over personal, spiritual, and emotional life	Body as a site of contestation over appetite; locus of self-control and self-indulgence	Body as symbol of self-acceptance; political transformation
Body as medium of communication	"Body announcement" used as evidence of program efficiency; thin bodies as part of personal testimonies	"Body announcement" via fashion shows; display and glorification of thin bodies	"Body announcement" via fashion shows; display and glorification of fat bodies
Vocabulary of motive	Overeating as disease	Overeating due to irrational management and lack of education; program as a skilling process for a total lifestyle change	Genetic accounts: large body a product of nature; program for empowerment; stories as "Oppression Tales"

testifying to the effectiveness of the OA program in her or his life. Most meetings end with members joining in the "serenity prayer."[2] OA explicitly acknowledges its reliance upon the Alcoholics Anonymous program of recovery, including the Twelve Steps and the Twelve Traditions developed by Bill W. and other AA founders. Reproduced in most literature published by the organization, the twelve-step program serves as a blueprint for achieving abstinence from compulsive overeating (OA 1990, p. 114):

The Twelve Steps of Overeaters Anonymous

1. We admitted we were powerless over food—that our lives had become unmanageable.
2. Came to believe that a power higher than ourselves could restore us to sanity.
3. Made a decision to turn our will and our lives over to the care of God *as we understood him.*
4. Made a searching and fearless moral inventory of ourselves.
5. Admitted to God, to ourselves and to another human being the exact nature of our wrongs.
6. Were entirely ready to have God remove all these defects of character.
7. Humbly ask Him to remove our shortcomings.
8. Made a list of all persons we had harmed, and became willing to make amends to them all.
9. Made direct amends to such people wherever possible, except when to do so would injure them or others.
10. Continued to take personal inventory and when we were wrong, promptly admitted it.
11. Sought through prayer and meditation to improve our conscious contact with God *as we understood him,* praying only for knowledge of his will for us and the power to carry that out.
12. Having had a spiritual awakening as the result of these steps, we tried to carry this message to compulsive overeaters and to practice these principles in all our affairs.

Essentially the organization prescribes a spiritual program of recovery for what it considers to be an "incurable disease"—compulsive overeating. The concept of disease represents OA's primary "vocabulary of motive" (Mills 1940) that alleviates members of responsibility for their unhealthy overeating: "OA believes that compulsive overeating is an illness—a progressive illness—which cannot be cured but which, like many other illnesses, can be arrested. . . . Once compulsive overeating as an illness has taken hold willpower is no longer involved because the suffering overeater has lost the power of choice over food" (OA 1988, p. 2). In defining "compulsive overeating," OA tells the prospective member that "in OA, compulsive overeaters are described as people whose eating habits have caused growing and continuing problems in their lives. It must be emphasized that only the individuals involved can say whether food has become an unmanageable problem" (OA 1988, p. 2).

The redemptive aspect of OA's program is both ideological and structural, as well as observable in relationships that members have with their sponsors. The alignment of personal with collective definitions of compulsive overeating is accomplished, in part, with the assistance of an OA sponsor, a person with substantial "program experience" who serves as the member's confessor, friend, advocate, and spiritual leader as well as a purveyor and mediator of organizational ideology. Sponsors, along with other OA members, are part of the emotion management team that members may use in expressing and policing emotions and securing social support. Redemption from compulsive overeating and an obsessive-compulsive self, according to OA members, is facilitated by sponsors and fellow group members as one "works through denial"—that is, gives up one's idiopathic justifications for compulsive overeating and the avoidance of unpleasant emotions in favor of collective definitions and meanings found in OA's twelve steps and twelve traditions.

The Organizational Frame of NAAFA: Activism

Throughout its history, NAAFA has mobilized lobbying efforts for antidiscrimination bills with state legislatures,[3] held rallies, conducted protests,[4] and brought cases of discrimination to the attention of the mass media. The objective of such action is the creation and enforcement of human rights provisions under which fat people might be identified as a protected group. Yet a bifurcation of NAAFA's primary objectives can be found in the orientation literature for new members: NAAFA refers to itself as both a "human rights organization" (NAAFA 1990, p. ii) and "a self-help group" (NAAFA 1990, p. 2). For NAAFA members both intensive involvement in social activities and activist participation constitute the dominant frame of meaning or, in the words of NAAFA members, "a way of life." Activism, as defined by the organization, includes a broad array of personal and political activities that are marked by a displayed willingness to engage in confrontation. Such activism, as described by the organization (NAAFA 1990, p. 4-3), may include:

Personal Activism: Educating people around you, not letting negative comments about your weight or preference go unchallenged, and your life as a "role model" are all forms of personal activism.

Legislative Activism: is specific activist work that leads to changes in the law. Considering the amount of time, effort, and expertise required in such undertakings, it deserves a category all its own.

Advocacy Activism: includes letter writing and other forms of communication with the "powers that be" regarding your opinions. Did you like how the fat person was portrayed on the TV show? Are you happy with the article in the magazine? Did the salesperson treat you with disrespect because of your fat? Writing letters of praise or protest to the station, the magazine, or the store owner are examples of advocacy activism.

The organizational frame of activism in NAAFA represents a way in which participants situate themselves, emotionally and practically,[5] within the ideological contours of the organization. It is a "relevance structure" through which not only social or political events but also interpersonal lines of action are developed, evaluated, and constructed.

The Organizational Frame of WW: Rationality

The weekly Weight Watchers meetings were held in weight loss centers located in shopping malls, high-rise business complexes, and basements leased from other companies. In contrast to OA, where developing a meal plan and taking inventory of daily consumption is strongly encouraged though largely voluntary, these activities are preestablished, compulsory features of WW's program. The official purpose of the program is to help clients achieve bodily reduction. Hence, emotional and spiritual "recovery" is not pertinent to WW clients as it is for OA members, and bodily reduction for clients of WW is largely a matter of technocratic administration or "technique,"[6] not spiritual practice.

The materials distributed to new clients during the first week of WW membership include a basic program guidebook (containing a multi-item questionnaire assessing eating patterns, levels of desire to succeed in Weight Watchers, and the degree of stress in one's life), a "food diary" that includes daily menus, and a list of items from various food groups. In each subsequent week, members are given additional diaries to keep along with new daily menus and comprehensive guides on various topics including exercise, eating out, socializing, tips for better eating, and dealing with obstacles to weight loss. "Portion control" (the allotment of measured meals items for which WW markets food scales, frozen entrees, and cookbooks) is the fundamental principle underlying its program.

While the topic of compulsive overeating may receive a modicum of attention within meetings, the term cannot be found within WW's literature. Instead, the term "volume eating" is used, and what is emphasized is the type rather than the amount of food consumed. "Portion control" is to be applied within those food groups that are seen as leading to the creation of fat bodies but can be ignored within food groups whose caloric content is negligible. Thus, according to WW, there are no good or bad foods, only those necessitating more or less portion control. . . .

Shame Work

In *The Managed Heart,* Arlie Russell Hochschild (1983, p. 7) described "emotion work" as labor that "requires one to induce or suppress feeling in order to sustain the outward countenance that produces the proper state of mind in others." Hochschild's definition pertains to the self-monitoring, management, and modeling of emotion as a strategy used by service personnel to evoke certain feelings. But other activities in which people engage (to elicit, constrain, and manage the emotions of others or encourage their self-management) might also be classified as emotion work, given a less restrictive definition of the term.[7] For example, confronting other people about the discrepancy between their verbal actions and nonverbal cues, such as the tone in their voice, or pointing out apparent discrepancies between seemingly frustrating situations and a lack of emotional response (as family therapists can attest) are very much work and can be emotionally exhausting. Hence, evoking emotional expression within WW's men's meetings might be considered emotion work, while displacing or channeling such expression constitutes work within women's meetings. Within OA, "working through" denial is a form of emotional labor, while for members of NAAFA, emotion work includes attempting to impassion members over issues of weight-based discrimination.

Within all three organizations, a common form of emotion work is "shame work," that is, emotional labor aimed at evoking, removing, or managing shame—though in the contemporary contexts of OA, WW, and NAAFA only the latter two objectives are sought. Within OA and WW, shame work involves activities directed at mitigating the internalized experience of shame that emanated from the personal and social practices of consuming food. Within NAAFA shame work was directed at removing shame that had been acquired through the stigmatization of a "fat identity." Like other forms of emotional labor, shame work includes communicative and expressive action that may take both discursive and bodily forms. In the following sections, I discuss the use of shame avowal (OA), shame management (WW), and shame contestation (NAAFA) and how these are accompanied by use of "body announcements" in managing and systematizing members' shame.

Shame Work in Overeaters Anonymous

For members of OA, patterns of compulsive overeating and resultant body size are seen as a source of shame. Yet this is "only secondary shame" insofar as these patterns have developed as a result of some earlier "primary shame" experience invoked by others. Both female and male members commonly located the development of primary shame experiences in early childhood, citing failures at living up to adult expectations as the reason for their present "shame-based" state. Primary sources of shame, as OA members define them, are profoundly social, most often residing in interaction episodes with significant others who have knowingly or unintentionally evoked it. One strategy used by OA members engaged in shame work might best be termed "shame avowal," an open acknowledgment of past and present shame experiences that serves to expiate the shame experience. Such avowals are commonly woven into the public testimony of OA members:

> Jason (open OA meeting): I also need to say I've never had one perfect day of abstinence, there is no such thing for me. You know there is no perfect abstinence. I've lost weight in this program, I've gained weight in this program. But I have had enough shame over my food and my weight to last me the rest of my life. I don't need to put more on me. You know my goal weight. . . . somebody asked me at a convention what my goal weight was. And I said, "My goal weight, if I'm abstinent, it's exactly what I weigh today."

The acknowledgment of shame is cited by OA members as problematic because it is premised on a self-awareness that, if not already present, must be organizationally manufactured. As indicated by one member:

> ROB (OA conference workshop): The second part [of dealing with shame] is to recognize it. To even find out that we have it. And as far as I'm concerned that is the most difficult part of it. To recognize that we have it is, is the thing that's so easy to cover up with denial. I've been in the OA program for about five years and AA about six years. And it took a long time for me to discover that I had any shame at all.

Determining whether the self exists in a deep shame-based state is a subjective evaluation, but the evaluation is also linked to a collective assessment as OA sponsors and other group members attempt to facilitate the awareness of shame-based actions on the part of nascent members. While such an awareness involves the acquisition and application of an organizational vocabulary of motive that is acquired through socialization in OA, it also necessitates the presence of viable experiences and circumstances to which it can be applied. As in other twelve-step programs (Denzin 1987; Rudy 1986), shame experiences are recognized and formulated as members of Overeaters Anonymous pragmatically invoke the organizational vocabulary for understanding and overcoming patterns of compulsive overeating. As it is applied to shame, the motive of denial is used in retrospectively interpreting compulsive overeating as behavior connected to a shame-based state. Working through denial is facilitated by "hitting bottom." Incidences of binging, stealing food, or lying about consumption, which lead to acute intra-personal states of shame, degradation, and humiliation, may all be defined subjectively as "hitting bottom," that is, reaching the lowest possible point in one's life spiritually, emotionally, and socially.[8] According to the redemptive frame of OA, salvation from a shame-based state of compulsive overeating is only possible after one acknowledges both to self and others the causes and consequences of compulsive overeating and then turns one's life over to a "higher power." As in Alcoholics Anonymous, the concept of a "higher power" is one that is idiosyncratically constructed,[9] yet members are encouraged to let it intervene in their lives and assist them in working through their denial of compulsive overeating. . . .

Shame Work in Weight Watchers

Within Weight Watchers, NAAFA, and OA, body shame is commonly discussed by women. Female members in OA also cite shame experiences in episodes of emotional, physical, or sexual abuse. By contrast, most male members of Weight Watchers and NAAFA appear to be exempt from experiences of body shame; neither did male members in OA seem to share experiences of body shame though they mentioned shame experiences rooted in a general failure to live up to a multiplicity of social expectations. Weight Watchers group leaders claim body shame as exclusive to the experience of female members:

> ROBIN: Men are not as shameful about their bodies. They don't care if they are thirty pounds overweight, they go ahead and take off their shirts at the beach anyway. Women just aren't able to do that—we're ashamed to wear bathing suits and show off our cellulite or flabby legs or varicose veins at the beach. We are overwhelmingly told we can't do that, that we must be slim.

As a former, longtime member of Weight Watchers and now group leader, Robin claims that body shame is not only central to the experience of women vis-à-vis men but that being female makes one susceptible to body shame in ways that men are not. Some men in WW, however, did discuss similar experiences:

> CARL: For phys-ed class we had to go swimming. And I always got the largest swim suit. And people would just laugh at me and call me "fatso" and, you know, names. And then if I went to lunch no one would sit with me.

Carl does not specifically identify a personal sense of shame as a residual of this experience but he cites feelings of profound differentness induced by episodes of stigmatization. While it seems reasonable to expect the presence of shame in episodes such as the one above, it remained liminal in the experience of the men I interviewed. In contrast to the OA strategy of shame avowal, the work of WW personnel consisted of shame management—that is, attempts to neither deny, contest, or specifically avow the experience but to contain it in hopes of a future, natural dissipation through dieting and weight loss. The management of shame represents a change in WW's treatment ideology over the course of its thirty-year history. Until the 1970s the organization had relied heavily upon the "shame-aversion" strategy (Serber 1970) of "card calling" in modifying the eating behaviors of clients.[10] Card calling involved placing a client's name along with the number of pounds that the client had either gained or lost during the week on an index card. The cards of all clients would then be read publicly at the beginning of each meeting. Similar instances of shaming appear to have been used in other weight loss organizations during this same period. Marcia Millman's *Such a Pretty Face* (1980) reveals that the shaming ritual used to discipline candy-sneaking "kids at fat camp" (children at summer weight loss camps) was to extract public confessions from these children on stage, humiliating them in front of their peers. Earlier research on the organization Take Off Pounds Sensibly (TOPS) reported the use of an equally drastic strategy for motivating clients to lose weight:

> There is a public announcement of each member's success or failure during the previous week. When a client has lost weight, there is applause and much vocal behavior; if she has gained weight, there is obvious disapproval with booing and derision. . . . In some groups the member who has gained the most weight is given the title of "Pig of the Week" and may be made to wear a bib with a picture of a pig on it or may have to sit in a specified area called the "pig pen." (Wagonfeld and Wolowitz 1968)

The loss of Weight Watchers revenues, which resulted when clients terminated their membership after such experiences, proved to be a compelling reason for abandoning shame aversion strategies in favor of strategies directed at its containment. One former client and now group leader of Weight Watchers recounted the outcome: "Those were the old days. Jeez, can you imagine how uncomfortable everyone was? We found that half the group had left before we even got seated." However, the absence of shame talk in WW meetings also reflects corporate concerns for liability. The training provided to group leaders does not equip them to conduct psychotherapy or deal intensively with revelations of traumatic events such as sexual, emotional, or physical abuse that might produce shame. In light of episodes where women may make such disclosures, WW developed a strategy that allows organizational personnel to maneuver efficiently through the most troublesome situations. When I asked a group leader what happens if people divulge very personal or very traumatic information that is related to weight loss, she replied:

> The line is drawn that you never touch anything that is not directly affecting the members' weight. If they can't verbalize it you move on. . . . You don't touch it, you let them tell you. And they'll take care of it. It's just amazing. I've never been as scared as when that woman remembered in the meeting having been raped. Because I didn't know what to do with her. And the question that we tell leaders and that we practice in any group—men, women, any kind of group that we're doing—is, "And how does that affect your weight control?" That's your appropriate followup, no matter what they say, if you think you're into something that you're not qualified for, you let them answer and then you let the group take care of that person. . . . You know, there's always someone that's gonna say, "Well, gee, you really need counseling for rape." So that's the point, once you've thrown it back to them, to back off . . . you don't have anything to offer them. You're not qualified. If we could just know what we're doing we could do so much more. And we do have an awful lot of psychology background given to us by the company but we can't use it, we're not really qualified.

Here, the emotion work of leaders must strike a precarious balance between the emotional resolution of members' personal problems and corporate exposure, which writes large for group leaders as "uncertified" professionals. This is accomplished by displacing the responsibility for resolving emotionally charged situations onto members themselves. Thus, group leaders do shame work as well as other kinds of emotion work but always within limits rationally guided by concerns for organizational liability.

The emotion work now done by WW personnel in women's meetings consists of assisting in the management of clients' shame experiences. Shame management in WW largely included remedial work done during weight loss meetings as well as teaching clients intra-personal strategies for minimizing body shame. Remedial work within the social context of group meetings primarily involved supplying clients with viable disclaimers or excuses (Hewitt and Stokes 1975; Lyman and Scott 1970) for program violation. An example of the latter is demonstrated in the following interaction:

> LEADER: How did everyone's week go this week?
>
> CLIENT 2: [female, approximately age 24] I almost didn't come in tonight because I was afraid to face the scale.
>
> LEADER: Ohhhh . . . what happened?
>
> CLIENT 2: I was really stressed this week and I ate everything in sight. I went off the plan, I'm afraid, I kept saying to myself [laughs] I wonder if they take your ribbon back [a red ribbon is given to clients after they lose their first ten pounds].
>
> LEADER: Okay . . . but the positive thing is that you came back this week, see . . . you could have done a lot of other unhealthy things to yourself than just eat. Does anyone have anything to say to [name]?
>
> CLIENT 3: (Woman looks at client 2) Well, tell her why you were so stressed.
>
> CLIENT 2: Well, I went to visit my mother and there was food everywhere. My future brother-in-law made it to the finals at the state wrestling tournament, and a cousin who I was very close to died this last week.
>
> CLIENT 3: I think you need to give yourself a break.
>
> CLIENT 4: I think you are being way too hard on yourself, you shouldn't worry about the program [WW] with all that you're going through.
>
> LEADER: Like I said, I think it's very positive that you *did* decide to come back this week, knowing that you may have not stuck with the program. I think that's just positive in itself. [To other clients] Don't you agree? [Everyone nods their heads yes.]

Here, the group leader enlists the support of other group members in ratifying the excuse. Because bodily monitoring means heightened awareness of body size, it evokes body shame for some members. In such cases, group leaders also recommended nondiscursive strategies for dealing with shame:

> MARGARET (group leader): I had one woman who was ashamed to find out how many inches she had lost every week and so instead of using a measuring tape would use different colored yarns to measure her bust, hips, waist, thighs, calves, and upper arms. Each week, this member would cut the tails off these pieces of yarn according to how many inches she had reduced and therein came to amass a pile of different colored yarn. She could then hold and feel the cut off yarn which represented her weight loss.

In suggesting that clients objectify their weight loss, the group leader offers a technique by which clients might manage shame and gain a sense of control over body size and weight. The tactile strategy offered above is designed to contain or manage rather than avow shame. . . .

Shame Work in NAAFA

In contrast to avowing or managing shame, NAAFA members contest it. The objective of activism as presented in NAAFA's national newsletter is to "Change the World, Not Your Body" (Wolfe 1992, p. 5). Such contestation can readily be seen in the communicative but nondiscursive practice of making a "body announcement," where the fat body is displayed as shameless. NAAFA members make a public avowal of a "fat identity" not only through these displays but also through forms of public and private confrontation. Letter-writing campaigns and confrontations with public officials, as well as proprietors of businesses and services who engage in size discrimination, comprise part of the protest activities of NAAFA members. No social context is considered exempt from "fat activism." What is formulated in these activities, according to NAAFA members, is a way of life, an organized set of attitudes, and a mode of responding to myriad situations that members face daily.

> BETH: Like one time they were making cracks in the lounge about eating, well it was at lunch time and, oh God, this one woman said, who's always dieting, "If we eat this we'll all have to shop at Women's World [clothing store for large women]." And everybody laughed. And I said, "Oh pardon me." I said. "Don't make fun of the places where I buy my clothes." I just said it in a nice, lighthearted tone. There was just dead silence. God, everybody at the table was embarrassed to death. I thought, "Hey Beth, good for you for saying that!"
>
> DEBORAH: So I was shopping and all of a sudden I found myself in front of this huge section of Slimfast products. And all of a sudden the idea came to me, [shouts] gee, I don't have to use the entire card [NAAFA business card]. So I just tore the bottom half of the card off, the part that had the NAAFA address and left the part that said, "Do something about your weight, accept it." And I just stuck it on the shelf, sort of like behind one of those little plastic place cards and said, "There."

Contestation emanates from the lived experiences of members who organize their lives around their organizational "fat" identity. The identity is viewed as relevant in all of the daily activities of NAAFA members, whether confronting fellow employees like Beth or grocery shopping like Deborah. According to NAAFA members, shame militates against the active initiation of individual and, hence, collective, political practice. NAAFA sees social stigmas as directly linked to the internalized oppression of shame. Shame contestation is thus a requisite component of identity politics where the aggrieved attempt to transform themselves by transforming both societal definitions of beauty and human value and the feeling rules that govern fat bodies. . . .

Conclusion

Sociologists studying format organizations contend that organizations are boundary maintaining social units where society and culture are both experienced by individuals and reproduced in various sets of social practices (Perrow 1986). Society, it is argued, is now absorbed by organizations that mediate culture and cultural themes for the individuals who participate within them. Rudolph Bell's (1985) analysis of "Holy Anorexia" has delineated the historic role of the Catholic Church in the creation and social reproduction of themes of shame and obesity, purity and thinness, as they came to be interwoven with the phenomenon of anorexia from the thirteenth century on. Feminist scholars (Bordo 1993; Hesse-Biber 1996; Schwartz 1986; Wolf 1991) have argued that the increasing commercialization of the body and bodily needs for the sake of expanding markets has ensured that themes of shame, slothfulness, loss of control, and embarrassment will continue to be associated with fat bodies, particularly fat female bodies. The present study indicates that the cultural meanings of shame associated with the body are not simply residues that exist as historical abstractions.[11] Rather, it is in interaction that takes into consideration organizational frames that a shame experience is formulated as a social object and given meaning. Organizational frames may be quite variable depending upon the nature, objectives, and ideology within which the organizations attempt to align members' experiences, yet they provide the template in which shame experiences may be systematized in organizational routines.

Notes

1. Many of the tapes were truncated or contained several short testimonies by members of how OA

had helped restore their lives. Yet the tapes yielded little information about the lived experience of the person or how she or he came to OA.

2. The serenity prayer of OA: "God grant me the serenity to accept the things I cannot change; the courage to change the things I can; and the wisdom to know the difference."
3. One of the more recent efforts was bill A 3484 New York State, sponsored by assemblyman Daniel Feldman. The bill was not supported by Governor Mario Cuomo. The event was reported in NAAFA's national newsletter, which commented: "Asked by his interviewer whether questions on the bill had him skating on thin ice with voters who are fat, Cuomo quipped, 'If you are overweight, you shouldn't do that—you're liable to fall through the ice'" (NAAFA 1993, p. 1).
4. On May 23, 1992, NAAFA chapters in five cities launched demonstrations against Southwest Airlines for ejecting a very large man from a half-full flight and for disallowing another large passenger to board after she had already completed one leg of her flight (NAAFA, 1992, p. 1).
5. I use the term "practically" in reference to the "investment model" of participation, discussed by Rudy and Greil (1987), observing that all organizational members mobilize personal resources to be used in and by the organizations. This is clear in the case of WW where both time and money represent "sunken costs." Yet it is also the case in OA and NAAFA where members invest time, money, and intellectual and emotional labor to keep the organization operating.
6. The collection of all shame management strategies may be labeled "technique." I have in mind Jacques Ellul's (1964, p. vi) meaning: a "complex of standardized means for attaining a predetermined result. Thus it converts spontaneous and unreflective behavior into behavior that is deliberate and rationalized." Here, the emphasis must be on the idea of a "complex"—that is, not only the measurement of food and calories but the restructuring of social relations and development of adaptive strategies for dealing with unexpected situations.
7. Goffman's notion of "cooling the mark out" (1952) would appear to be a rather pervasive form of emotion management found among all types of service personnel. Yet, curiously, in light of a rather extensive citation of Goffman's works, Hochschild (1983) does not mention it. Beyond the management of emotion, the concept of emotion work suggests a range of interactional strategies that might be used in managing the emotions of others. Lying, for example, might be used to "cool out" airline passengers who might otherwise become disruptive.
8. Rudy (1986), in his analysis of Alcoholics Anonymous, observes that "hitting bottom" is ultimately a subjective perception.
9. While some OA members refer to their higher power as "God," others adopt a Durkheimian (Durkheim 1965) conception of this power, defining it as the social force that exists outside of themselves and abides in the group.
10. Shaming appears to have been a treatment modality that was gaining limited popularity within quite diverse fields. Serber (1970), in his research on behavioral modification among transvestites, referred to the treatment as "shame aversion therapy." Braithwaite (1989) revisited the idea in the concept of "reintegrative shaming" within the context of criminal justice.
11. Pareto observed that "residues" (nonscientific belief systems) rarely mobilize people into action even though they may historically express deep collective sentiments (Coser 1977). My point is that cultural themes such as shame are socially reproduced within concrete episodes of interaction.

References

Allon, Natalie. 1982. "The Stigma of Overweight in Everyday Life" Pp. 130–174 in *Psychological*

Aspects of Obesity*, edited by Benjamin B. Wolman. New York: Van Nostrand Reinhold.

Banner, Lois W. 1983. *American Beauty.* New York: Knopf.

Bell, Rudolph. 1985. *Holy Anorexia.* Chicago: University of Chicago Press.

Bordo, Susan. 1993. *Unbearable Weight.* Berkeley: University of California University Press.

Braithwaite, John. 1989. *Crime, Shame and Reintegration.* New York: Cambridge Press.

Buss, David M. 1989. "Sex Differences in Human Mate Preferences: Evolutionary Hypotheses Tested in 37 Cultures." *Behavioral and Brain Sciences* 12:1–49.

Cahnman, Werner. 1968. "The Stigma of Obesity." *The Sociological Quarterly* 9:283–299.

Coser, Lewis A. 1977. *Masters of Sociological Thought: Ideas in Historical and Social Context.* 2d ed. New York: Harcourt, Brace, Jovanovich.

Denzin, Norman K. 1987. *The Recovering Alcoholic.* Beverly Hills, CA: Sage.

Durkheim, Emile. 1965. *The Elementary Forms of Religious Life.* New York: The Free Press.

Ellis, Carolyn 1998. "'I Hate My Voice': Coming to Terms with Minor Bodily Stigmas." *The Sociological Quarterly* 39:517–538.

Ellul, Jacques. 1964. *The Technological Society.* New York: Vintage.

Ewen, Stuart. 1976. *Captains of Consciousness: Advertising and the Roots of the Consumer Culture.* New York: McGraw-Hill.

Featherstone, Mike. 1982. "The Body in Consumer Culture." *Theory, Culture & Society* 1:18–33.

Gilmore, David B. 1987. *Honor and Shame and the Unity of the Mediterranean.* Washington, D. C.: American Anthropological Association.

Glaser, Barney G., and Anselm L. Strauss. 1967. *The Discovery of Grounded Theory.* Chicago: Aldine de Gruyter.

Goffman, Erving. 1952. "On Cooling the Mark Out: Some Aspects of Adaptation to Failure." *Psychiatry* 15:451–463.

———. 1967. *Interaction Ritual.*

———. 1986. *Frame Analysis.* Boston, MA: Northeastern University Press.

Hesse-Biber, Sharlene. 1996. *Am I Thin Enough Yet? The Cult of Thinness and the Commercialization of Beauty.* New York: Oxford University Press.

Hewitt, John P., and Randall Stokes. 1975. "Disclaimers." *American Sociological Review* 60:1–11.

Hochschild, Arlie Russell. 1983. *The Managed Heart: Commercialization of Human Feeling.* Berkeley: University of California Press.

Horowitz, Ruth. 1983. *Honor: Culture and Identity in a Chicano Community.* New Brunswick, NJ: Rutgers University Press.

Lyman, Stanford, and Marvin B. Scott. 1970. *A Sociology of the Absurd.* Pacific Palisades, CA: Goodyear.

Martin, Daniel D. 1995. "The Politics of Appearance: Managing Meanings of the Body, Organizationally." Ph.D. dissertation, University of Minnesota.

McFarland, Barbara, and Tyeis L. Baker-Baumann. 1990. *Shame and the Body: Culture and the Compulsive Eater.* Deerfield Beach, FL: Health Communications.

Millman, Marcia. 1980. *Such a Pretty Face: Being Fat in America.* New York: W. W. Norton.

Mills, C. Wright. 1940. "Situated Actions and Vocabularies of Motive." *American Sociological Review* 5:904–913.

National Association to Advance Fat Acceptance (NAAFA). 1990. *NAAFA Workbook: A Complete Study Guide.* Sacramento, CA: NAAFA.

———. 1992. "Southwest Protest: NAAFAns Demonstrate in Five Cities." *NAAFA Newsletter* XXII:1.

———. 1993. "Cuomo: One Law Too Many!" *NAAFA Newsletter* XXIII:6 (May): 1.

Overeaters Anonymous (OA). 1987. *To the Newcomer: You're Not Alone Anymore.* Torrance, CA: OA.

———. 1988. *Questions & Answers About Compulsive Overeating and the OA Program.* Torrance, CA: OA.

———. 1990. *The Twelve Steps of Overeaters Anonymous.* Torrance, CA: OA.

———. 1992. *Overeaters Anonymous: Membership Survey Summary.* Torrance, CA: OA.

Perrow, Charles. 1986. *Complex Organizations.* 3d ed. New York: McGraw-Hill.

Rodin, Judith, Ruth H. Striegel-Moore, and Lisa R. Silberstein. 1990. "Vulnerability and Resilience in the Age of Eating Disorders: Risks and Protective Factors for Bulimia Nervosa." *Risk and Protective Factors in the Development of Psychopathology*, edited by Jon Ann S. Master, Dante Cicchetti, Keith H. Nuechterlein, and Sheldon Weintraub Rolf. Cambridge, MA: Harvard University Press.

Rudy, David R. 1986. *Becoming Alcoholic: Alcoholics Anonymous and the Reality of Alcoholism.* Carbondale: Southern Illinois University Press.

Rudy, David R., and Arthur L. Greil. 1987. "Taking the Pledge: The Commitment Process in Alcoholics Anonymous." *Sociological Focus* 20:45–59.

Schwartz, Hillel. 1986. *Never Satisfied: A Cultural History of Diets, Fantasies and Fat.* New York: Free Press.

Serber, Michael. 1970. "Shame Aversion Therapy." *Experimental Psychiatry* 1:213–215.

Snow, David A., E. Burke Rochford, Jr., Steven K. Worden, and Robert D. Benford. 1986. "Frame Alignment Processes, Micromobilization, and Movement Participation." *American Sociological Review* 51:461–481.

Thorne, Barrie, and Zella Luria. 1986. "Sexuality and Gender in Children's Daily Worlds." *Social Problems* 33:176–190.

Wagonfeld, Samuel, and Howard M. Wolowitz. 1968. "Obesity and the Self-Help Group: A Look at TOPS." *American Journal of Psychiatry* 125:249–252.

Weber, Joseph. 1990. "The Diet Business Takes It on the Chin." *Business Week*, April 16, pp. 86–88.

Wolf, Naomi. 1991. *The Beauty Myth: How Images of Beauty Are Used Against Women.* New York: William Morrow.

Wolfe, Louise. 1992. "Boston 'Free' Party: The Revolution Within; The Revolution Without." *NAAFA Newsletter* 23:5.

Reflective Questions

1. How is body-related shame gendered in nature? Why is it gendered? While Martin does not analyze it as such, body shame is also racialized and classed. How so?
2. Why did the author gain 25 pounds to do the research? Would this be likely to make his research tasks easier? Why or why not?
3. What are organizational frames? What is shame work? Martin studied three different organizations. What was the purpose of each, and how did they frame shame work differently?
4. How is shame work shaped by the groups to which we belong? For instance, what provokes feelings of shame when you are with your friends or workmates? How do they expect you to manage or deal with these feelings?
5. Engage in a random act of kindness toward a stranger, or remember the last time you did. How did the target of your kindness respond? Did s/he freely accept your gesture with gratitude, insist that s/he did not need the help, or something else? What identities are at stake when someone accepts another person's generosity? Why would some Americans be reluctant to accept help from others? What thoughts, feelings, or perceptions does accepting help challenge? How do people who accept other people's help manage those feelings and thoughts?

The Social Construction of the Body and Embodiment

The selections in Part II examined how social meanings and expectations profoundly influence people's "inner" experiences, including their perceptions, emotions, and bodily sensations. While we often think of these experiences as originating in our bodies and thus as biological, they arise out of our interactions and are shaped by the groups to which we belong. Through our interactions in these groups, we learn a set of expectations about how we should think and feel, and how we should express those thoughts and feelings in various situations. We also learn what social meanings are attached to our bodies and how we should adorn, present, and control them so that they convey those meanings. These meanings are not natural outcomes of the size, shape, color, or sex of our bodies. Instead, they are results of socially created beliefs about the nature of gender, race, power, health, and sexuality.

The selections in Part III examine how these ideas become incorporated into our bodies and bodily practices, particularly through language, symbols, and socialization processes. More specifically, they illustrate the following points:

- *Culture becomes inscribed or written onto our bodies. From the moment of birth (and even while we are in the womb), our bodies are imbued with social meanings, such as age, gender, race, ethnicity, and kinship. These meanings shape the relationships we experience, the appearances we present, and the identities we enact.* Moreover, from the moment of birth, we learn how to embody social roles and expectations. For instance, we learn how we should look, feel, and act as girls or boys, particularly in the context of our family, neighborhood, and culture. As Karin Martin illustrates in Selection 11, we also learn how we should "do gender" in our bodily practices.

Martin portrays how preschool teachers subject young girls and boys to a variety of bodily "disciplines," instructing them in prevailing cultural and gender expectations about how to dress, how to use space, how to control their voices, and how to manage their bodies when in a formal setting or involved in play. As Martin points out, children do not simply or effortlessly acquire and embody these gender disciplines. Instead, they occasionally ignore, resist, or subvert them. These expressions of resistance, Martin argues, demonstrate that gendered expressions of bodily practice are not "natural," even though they take on that appearance. The gender differences we see manifested in girls' and boys' physical conduct, such as their movements, gestures, and postures, are learned through socialization and the bodily disciplines it promotes. These gender-related behavioral differences only seem natural because they are reenacted so often in everyday practices and interactions.

- *Culture also informs and influences our bodily experiences through language, both through what gets named and through what goes unnamed or unspoken.* As Selection 12 illustrates, the bodily experiences of women are powerfully "disciplined" by the fact that larger cultural discourses erase the reality of the clitoris, or at least keep it symbolically "under the hood." By failing to name or speak of the clitoris, prevailing sexual discourses foster conditions that make it more difficult for women to know their bodies, to discover a key source of sexual sensation, and to experience sexual pleasure most fully.

  In a related vein, Selection 13 portrays how the discourses and messages conveyed in sexual education courses discipline the bodily understandings and sexual self-images of students. The author of this selection, Jessica Fields, reveals how the sexual education curriculum taught in public schools has repressive effects on students, particularly by separating scientific information from their embodied experiences, by excising the clitoris from images and discussions of female sexuality, and by silencing expressions of sexuality that do not conform to prevailing heterosexual norms. At the same time, Fields shows how sex education classes have evocative effects. In some cases, these effects include calling forth and reproducing bodily images and practices that reinforce existing social inequalities. In more progressive school settings, however, these effects can include empowering students to gain knowledge and insights that enable them to experience higher levels of safety, choice, and equality as sexual beings.

- As all of the selections in Part III illustrate, *people are active agents in formulating their responses to cultural directives and bodily experiences. We do not simply internalize and abide by social expectations. Nor do we simply react to bodily sensations. Instead, we actively interpret and make sense of these sensations, drawing upon prominent social meanings and cultural discourses but also holding them up against our bodily experiences.* As the authors of Selection 12 conclude, we are not "cultural dupes" as we interpret and respond to our bodily sensations. We reflexively "make meaning of [our] body and its sensual experiences." In turn, we have the capacity to exercise some elements of choice and autonomy as we determine what these experiences mean and how they should influence our actions.

- *While we have the ability to exercise some autonomy in responding to bodily sensations and in fashioning our bodily appearances and practices, we are not necessarily exercising as much freedom as we think.* As the authors of Selections 14 and 15 highlight, in contemporary Western societies the meanings we attach to our bodies are profoundly influenced by the larger fashion and cultural industries and the rapidly expanding commodification of culture. Thus, even when we challenge dominant bodily norms or mark our bodies with what we regard as symbols of rebellion, we often draw upon bodily practices and corporate symbols that are more reflective of consumer capitalism than individual freedom. While the culture and fashion industries tell us that we can manage or adorn our bodies in ways that allow us to express unique features of ourselves, we need to be wary of their claims. For instance, when branding ourselves with their logo, we can find ourselves trapped within the logic and constraints of consumer capitalism. That is, rather than conveying our individuality through marking our body with this logo, we may actually be signifying that we have joined a corporate tribe and bought the lifestyle and identity it sells.

Taken together, the selections in Part III offer compelling empirical examples of how we learn to embody gender, culture, sex, and power. They also demonstrate the subtle, explicit, and often unrecognized ways that we regulate and manage our bodies as we negotiate what it means to be a gendered, ethnic, sexual, fashionable, and "self-expressive" person. In addressing these themes, the selections illustrate how the natural and social are co-constructed realities and how the body and society are inextricably intertwined.

11

Becoming a Gendered Body

KARIN A. MARTIN

Gender identification is one of the earliest components of children's self-definitions. Most five-year-olds routinely refer to themselves as a boy or a girl and insist that others do so as well. There are many explanations for this early acquisition of gender identity. Some assume that hormones biologically determine gender identification, while more Freudian explanations attribute it to children's psychological identification with same-sex parents or other adults. Others maintain that gender identification is a byproduct of children's cognitive development, while still others contend that it is just another learned behavior resulting from patterns of reward and punishment. Drawing on Cooley's and Mead's accounts of the social development of the self (see Selections 16 and 17), sociological psychologists suggest an alternative explanation. This selection illustrates that explanation, demonstrating the importance of social expectations, social interactions, and socially constructed personal appearances to the process of "becoming gendered."

Both Cooley and Mead propose that we acquire a sense of self, or who we are, by taking the attitudes of others toward ourselves, and we have different attitudes about males and females. At birth, infants are immediately identified as male or female. From that time forward, caretakers commonly groom, dress, and decorate infants so that their appearance clearly announces their sex to others. This is of no small importance because there is considerable evidence that we have different attitudes about male and female infants and, thus, treat them differently.

Once infants become toddlers and begin to acquire their native language, they start to learn about this sexual classification of people. They learn that people belong to discrete categories like "mommies" and "daddies," "boys" and "girls," "women" and "men." They also learn to place people into the socially appropriate categories based on perceptible differences in appearance—differences that are created through grooming, dress, posture, and other forms of behavior. When children enter what Mead called the play stage of development, they begin to play at being these different kinds of gendered people, commonly drawing on socially appropriate costumes, roles, gestures, and lines of conduct when doing so. Others' responses to this role playing and corresponding appearance inform children that no matter how they dress or act they cannot escape their socially ascribed sex. Children consequently adopt these attitudes of others toward themselves and embrace their socially bestowed gender identity as their own. In this process, children learn how to "do gender"—that is, they learn how to embody and enact it in their everyday interactions.

This selection by Karin Martin describes the routine interactional processes through which preschools not only "discipline" the bodies of children but also instruct and encourage them to do gender. These processes include regulating how preschoolers dress, use space, engage in for-

Reprinted from: Karin A. Martin, Becoming a Gendered Body: Practices of Preschools. *American Sociological Review* 63(4, August 1998): 494–511.

mal and relaxed behaviors, physically interact with others, and use their voices. Martin's research thus provides an empirical illustration of how gender, like any system of classification, is socially constructed and enacted. It also portrays how gender identity, like other dimensions of the self, arises in and through social experience.

Social science research about bodies often focuses on women's bodies, particularly the parts of women's bodies that are most explicitly different from men's—their reproductive capacities and sexuality (E. Martin 1987; K. Martin 1996; but see Connell 1987, 1995). Men and women in the United States also hold and move their bodies differently (Birdwhistell 1970; Henley 1977; Young 1990); these differences are sometimes related to sexuality (Haug 1987) and sometimes not. On the whole, men and women sit, stand, gesture, walk, and throw differently. Generally, women's bodies are confined, their movements restricted. For example, women take smaller steps than men, sit in closed positions (arms and legs crossed across the body), take up less physical space than men, do not step, twist, or throw from the shoulder when throwing a ball, and are generally tentative when using their bodies (Birdwhistell 1970; Henley 1977; Young 1990). Some of these differences, particularly differences in motor skills (e.g., jumping, running, throwing) are seen in early childhood (Thomas and French 1985). Of course, within gender, we may find individual differences, differences based on race, class, and sexuality, and differences based on size and shape of body. Yet, on average, men and women move differently.

Such differences may seem trivial in the large scheme of gender inequality. However, theoretical work by social scientists and feminists suggests that these differences may be consequential. Bodies are (unfinished) resources (Shilling 1993:103) that must be "trained, manipulated, cajoled, coaxed, organized and in general disciplined" (Turner 1992:15). We use our bodies to construct our means of living, to take care of each other, to pleasure each other. According to Turner, ". . . social life depends upon the successful presenting, monitoring and interpreting of bodies" (p. 15). Similarly, according to Foucault (1979), controlled and disciplined bodies do more than regulate the individual body. A disciplined body creates a context for social relations. Gendered (along with "raced" and "classed") bodies create particular contexts for social relations as they signal, manage, and negotiate information about power and status. Gender relations depend on the successful gender presentation, monitoring, and interpretation of bodies (West and Zimmerman 1987). Bodies that clearly delineate gender status facilitate the maintenance of the gender hierarchy.

Our bodies are also one *site* of gender. Much postmodern feminist work (Butler 1990, 1993) suggests that gender is a performance. Microsociological work (West and Zimmerman 1987) suggests that gender is something that is "done." These two concepts, "gender performance" and "doing gender," are similar—both suggest that managed, adorned, fashioned, properly comported and moving bodies establish gender and gender relations.

Other feminist theorists (Connell 1987, 1995; Young 1990) argue that gender rests not only on the surface of the body, in performance and doing, but becomes *embodied*—becomes deeply part of whom we are physically and psychologically. According to Connell, gender becomes embedded in body postures, musculature, and tensions in our bodies.

> The social definition of men as holders of power is translated not only into mental body-images and fantasies, but into muscle tensions, posture, the feel and texture of the body. This is one of the main ways in which the power of men becomes naturalized. . . . (Connell 1987:85)

Connell (1995) suggests that masculine gender is partly a feel to one's body and that bodies are often a source of power for men. Young (1990), however, argues that bodies serve the opposite purpose for women—women's bodies are often sources of anxiety and tentativeness. She suggests that women's lack of confidence and agency are embodied and stem from an inability to move confidently in space, to take up space, to use one's body to its fullest extent. Young (1990) suggests "that the general lack of confidence that we [women] frequently have about our cognitive or leadership abilities is traceable in part to an original doubt of our body's capacity" (p. 156). Thus, these theorists suggest that gender differences in minute bodily behaviors like gesture, stance, posture, step, and throwing are significant to our understanding of gendered selves and gender inequality. This feminist theory, however, focuses on adult bodies.

Theories of the body need gendering, and feminist theories of gendered bodies need "childrening" or accounts of development. How do adult gendered bodies become gendered, if they are not naturally so? Scholars run the risk of continuing to view gendered bodies as natural if they ignore the processes that produce gendered adult bodies. Gendering of the body in childhood is the foundation on which further gendering of the body occurs throughout the life course. The gendering of children's bodies makes gender differences feel and appear natural, which allows for such bodily differences to emerge throughout the life course.

I suggest that the hidden school curriculum of disciplining the body is gendered and contributes to the embodiment of gender in childhood, making gendered bodies appear and feel natural. Sociologists of education have demonstrated that schools have hidden curriculums (Giroux and Purpel 1983; Jackson 1968). Hidden curriculums are covert lessons that schools teach, and they are often a means of social control. These curriculums include teaching about work differentially by class (Anyon 1980; Bowles and Gintis 1976; Carnoy and Levin 1985), political socialization (Wasburn 1986), and training in obedience and docility (Giroux and Purpel 1983). More recently, some theorists and researchers have examined the curriculum that disciplines the body (Carere 1987; Foucault 1979; McLaren 1986). This curriculum demands the practice of bodily control in congruence with the goals of the school as an institution. It reworks the students from the outside in on the presumption that to shape the body is to shape the mind (Carere 1987). In such a curriculum teachers constantly monitor kids' bodily movements, comportment, and practices. Kids begin their day running wildly about the school grounds. Then this hidden curriculum funnels the kids into line, through the hallways, quietly into a classroom, sitting upright at their desks, focused at the front of the room, "ready to learn" (Carere 1987; McLaren 1986). According to Carere (1987), this curriculum of disciplining the body serves the curriculums that seek to shape the mind and renders children physically ready for cognitive learning.

I suggest that this hidden curriculum that controls children's bodily practices serves also to turn kids who are similar in bodily comportment, movement, and practice into girls and boys, children whose bodily practices are different. Schools are not the only producers of these differences. While the process ordinarily begins in the family, the schools' hidden curriculum further facilitates and encourages the construction of bodily differences between the genders and makes these physical differences appear and feel natural. Finally, this curriculum may be more or less hidden depending on the particular preschool and particular teachers. Some schools and teachers may see teaching children to behave like "young ladies" and "young gentlemen" as an explicit part of their curriculums.

Data and Method

The data for this study come from extensive and detailed semistructured field observations of five preschool classrooms of three to five-year-olds in a midwestern city. Four of the classrooms were part of a preschool (Preschool A) located close to the campus of a large university. A few of the kids were children of faculty members, more were children of staff and administrators, and many were not associated with the university. Many of the kids who attended Preschool A attended part-time. Although teachers at this school paid some attention to issues of race and gender equity, issues of diversity were not as large a part of the curriculum as they are at some preschools (Jordan and Cowan 1995; Van Ausdale and Feagin 1996). The fifth classroom was located at Preschool B, a preschool run by a Catholic church in the same city as Preschool A. The kids who attended Preschool B were children of young working professionals, many of whom lived in the vicinity of the preschool. These children attended preschool "full-time"—five days a week for most of the day. . . .

A total of 112 children and 14 different teachers (five head teachers and nine aides) were observed in these classrooms.[1] All teachers were female. Forty-two percent of the kids were girls and 58 percent were boys, and they made up similar proportions in each classroom. There were 12 Asian or Asian American children, 3 Latino/a children, and 4 African American children. The remaining children were white. The children primarily came from middle-class families.

A research assistant and I observed in these classrooms about three times a week for eight months. Our observations were as unobtrusive as possible and we interacted little with the kids. . . .

We focused on the children's physicality—body movement, use of space, and the physical contact among kids or between kids and teachers. Our field notes were usually not about "events" that occurred, but about everyday physical behavior and interaction and its regulation. Field notes were coded using the qualitative software program Hyper-Research. Categories that were coded emerged from the data and were not predetermined categories. Excerpts from field notes are presented throughout and are examples of representative patterns in the data. Tables presenting estimates of the numbers of times particular phenomena were observed provide a context for the field note excerpts. . . .

Results

Children's bodies are disciplined by schools. Children are physically active, and institutions like schools impose disciplinary controls that regulate children's bodies and prepare children for the larger social world. While this disciplinary control produces docile bodies (Foucault 1979), it also produces gendered bodies. As these disciplinary practices operate in different contexts, some bodies become more docile than others. I examine how the following practices contribute to a gendering of children's bodies in preschool: the effects of dressing-up or bodily adornment, the gendered nature of formal and relaxed behaviors, how the different restrictions on girls' and boys' voices limit their physicality, how teachers instruct girls' and boys' bodies, and the gendering of physical interactions between children and teachers and among the children themselves.

Bodily Adornment: Dressing Up

Perhaps the most explicit way that children's bodies become gendered is through their clothes and other bodily adornments. Here I discuss how parents gender their children through their clothes, how children's dress-up play experiments with making bodies feminine and masculine, and how this play, when it is gender normative, shapes girls' and boys' bodies differently, constraining girls' physicality.

Dressing Up (1)

The clothes that parents send kids to preschool in shape children's experiences of their bodies in gendered ways.[2] Clothes, particularly their color, signify a child's gender; gender in preschool is in fact color-coded. On average, about 61 percent of the girls wore pink clothing each day (Table 1). Boys were more likely to wear primary colors, black, fluorescent green, and orange. Boys never wore pink.

> The teacher is asking each kid during circle (the part of the day that includes formal instruction by the teacher while the children sit in a circle) what their favorite color is. Adam says black. Bill says "every color that's not pink." (Five-year-olds)

Table 1 Observations of Girls Wearing Dresses and the Color Pink; Five Preschool Classrooms

Observation	N	Percent
Girls wearing something pink	54	61
Girls wearing dresses	21	24
3-year-old girls	6	14
5-year-old girls	15	32
Number of observations	89	100
3-year-old girls	42	47
5-year-old girls	47	53

Note: In 12 observation sessions, what the children were wearing, including color of their clothing, was noted. The data in Table 1 come from coded field notes. There were no instances of boys wearing pink or dresses, and no age differences among girls in wearing the color pink.

Fourteen percent of three-year-old girls wore dresses each day compared to 32 percent of five-year-old girls (Table 1). Wearing a dress limited girls' physicality in preschool. However, it is not only the dress itself, but knowledge about how to behave in a dress that is restrictive. Many girls already knew that some behaviors were not allowed in a dress. This knowledge probably comes from the families who dress their girls in dresses.

> Vicki, wearing leggings and a dress-like shirt, is leaning over the desk to look into a "tunnel" that some other kids have built. As she leans, her dress/shirt rides up exposing her back. Jennifer (another child) walks by Vicki and as she does she pulls Vicki's shirt back over her bare skin and gives it a pat to keep it in place. It looks very much like something one's mother might do. (Five-year-olds)

> Four girls are sitting at a table—Cathy, Kim, Danielle, and Jesse. They are cutting play money out of paper. Cathy and Danielle have on overalls and Kim and Jesse have on dresses. Cathy puts her feet up on the table and crosses her legs at the ankle; she leans back in her chair and continues cutting her money. Danielle imitates her. They look at each other and laugh. They put their shoulders back, posturing, having fun with this new way of sitting. Kim and Jesse continue to cut and laugh with them, but do not put their feet up. (Five-year-olds)

Dresses are restrictive in other ways as well. They often are worn with tights that are experienced as uncomfortable and constraining. I observed girls constantly pulling at and rearranging their tights, trying to untwist them or pull them up. Because of their discomfort, girls spent much time attuned to and arranging their clothing and/or their bodies.

Dresses also can be lifted up, an embarrassing thing for five-year-olds if done purposely by another child. We witnessed this on only one occasion—a boy pulled up the hem of a girl's skirt up. The girl protested and the teacher told him to stop and that was the end of it. Teachers, however, lifted up girls' dresses frequently—to see if a child was dressed warmly enough, while reading a book about dresses, to see if a child was wet. Usually this was done without asking the child and was more management of the child rather than an interaction with her. Teachers were much more likely to manage girls and their clothing this way—rearranging their clothes, tucking in their shirts, fixing a ponytail gone astray. Such management often puts girls' bodies under the control of another and calls girls' attentions to their appearances and bodily adornments.

Dressing Up (2)

Kids like to *play* dress-up in preschool, and all the classrooms had a dress-up corner with a variety of clothes, shoes, pocketbooks, scarves, and hats for dressing up. Classrooms tended to have more women's clothes than men's, but there were some of both, as well as some gender-neutral clothes—capes, hats, and vests that were not clearly for men or women—and some items that were clearly costumes, such as masks of cats and dogs and clip-on tails. Girls tended to play dress-up more than boys—over one-half of dressing up was done by girls. Gender differences in the amount of time spent playing dress-up seemed to increase from age three to age five. We only observed the five-year-old boys dressing up or using clothes or costumes in their play three times, whereas three-year-old boys dressed up almost weekly. Five-year-old boys also did not dress up elaborately, but used one piece of clothing to animate their play. Once Phil wore large, men's winter ski gloves when he played monster. Holding up his now large, chiseled looking hands, he stomped around the classroom making monster sounds. On another occasion Brian, a child new to the classroom who attended only two days a week, walked around by himself for a long time carrying a silver pocketbook and hovering first at the edges of girls' play and then at the edges of boys' play. On the third occasion, Sam used ballet slippers to animate his play in circle.

When kids dressed up, they played at being a variety of things from kitty cats and puppies to monsters and superheroes to "fancy ladies." Some of this play was not explicitly gendered. For example, one day in November I observed three girls wearing "turkey hats" they had made. They spent a long time gobbling at each other and playing at being turkeys, but there was nothing explicitly gendered about their play. However, this kind of adornment was not the most frequent type. Children often seemed to experiment with both genders when they played dress-up. The three-year-olds tended to be more experimental in their gender dress-up than the five-year-olds, perhaps because teachers encouraged it more at this age.

> Everett and Juan are playing dress-up. Both have on "dresses" made out of material that is wrapped around them like a toga or sarong. Everett has a pocketbook and a camera over his shoulder and Juan has a pair of play binoculars on a strap over his. Everett has a scarf around his head and cape on. Juan has on big, green sunglasses. Pam (teacher) tells them, "You guys look great! Go look in the mirror." They shuffle over to the full-length mirror and look at themselves and grin, and make adjustments to their costumes. (Three-year-olds)

The five-year-old children tended to dress-up more gender normatively. Girls in particular played at being adult women.

> Frances is playing dress-up. She is walking in red shoes and carrying a pocketbook: She and two other girls, Jen and Rachel, spend between five and ten minutes looking at and talking about the guinea pigs. Then they go back to dress-up: Frances and Rachel practice walking in adult women's shoes. Their body movements are not a perfect imitation of an adult woman's walk in high heels, yet it does look like an attempt to imitate such a walk. Jen and Rachel go back to the guinea pigs, and Frances, now by herself, is turning a sheer, frilly lavender shirt around and around and around trying to figure out how to put it on. She gets it on and looks at herself in the mirror. She adds a sheer pink and lavender scarf and pink shoes. Looks in the mirror again. She walks, twisting her body—shoulders, hips, shoulders, hips—not quite a (stereotypic) feminine walk, but close. Walking in big shoes makes her take little bitty steps, like walking in heels. She shuffles in the too big shoes out into the middle of the classroom and stops by a teacher. Laura (a teacher) says, "don't you look fancy, all pink and purple." Frances smiles up at her and walks off, not twisting so much this time. She goes back to the mirror and adds a red scarf. She looks in the mirror and is holding her arms across her chest to hold the scarf on (she can't tie it) and she is holding it with her chin too. She shuffles to block area where Jen is and then takes the clothes off and puts them back in dress-up area. (Five-year-olds)

I observed not only the children who dressed up, but the reactions of those around them to their dress. This aspect proved to be one of the most interesting parts of kids' dress-up play. Children interpreted each others' bodily adornments as gendered, even when other interpretations were plausible. For instance, one day just before Halloween, Kim dressed up and was "scary" because she was dressed as a woman:

> Kim has worn a denim skirt and tights to school today. Now she is trying to pull on a ballerina costume—pink and ruffly—over her clothes. She has a hard time getting it on. It's tight and wrinkled up and twisted when she gets it on. Her own clothes are bunched up under it. Then she puts on a mask—a woman's face. The mask material itself is a clear plastic so that skin shows through, but is sculpted to have a very Anglo nose and high cheek bones. It also has thin eyebrows, blue eye shadow, blush, and lipstick painted on it. The mask is bigger than Kim's face and head. Kim looks at herself in the mirror and spends the rest of the play time with this costume on. Intermittently she picks up a plastic pumpkin since it is Halloween season and carries that around too. Kim walks around the classroom for a long time and then runs through the block area wearing this costume. Jason yells, "Ugh! There's a woman!" He and the other boys playing blocks shriek and scatter about the block area. Kim runs back to the dress-up area as they yell. Then throughout the afternoon she walks and skips through the center of the classroom, and every time she comes near the block boys one of them yells, "Ugh, there's the woman again!" The teacher even picks up on this and says to Kim twice, "Woman, slow down." (Five-year-olds)

The boys' shrieks indicated that Kim was scary, and this scariness is linked in their comments about her being a woman. It seems equally plausible that they could have interpreted her scary dress as a "trick-o-treater," given that it was close to Halloween and she was carrying a plastic pumpkin that kids collect candy in, or that they might have labeled her a dancer or ballerina because she was wearing a tutu. Rather, her scary dress-up was coded for her by others as "woman."

Other types of responses to girls dressing up also seemed to gender their bodies and to constrain them. For example, on two occasions I saw a teacher tie the arms of girls' dress-up shirts together so that the girls could not move their arms. They did this in fun, of course, and untied them as soon as the girls wanted them to, but I never witnessed this constraining of boys' bodies in play.

Thus, how parents gender children's bodies through dressing them and the ways children experiment with bodily adornments by dressing up make girls' and boys' bodies different and seem different to those around them. Adorning a body often genders it explicitly—signifies that it is a feminine or masculine body. Adornments also make girls' movements smaller, leading girls to take up less space with their bodies and disallowing some types of movements.

Formal and Relaxed Behaviors

Describing adults, Goffman (1959) defines front stage and backstage behavior:

> The backstage language consists of reciprocal first-naming, co-operative decision making, profanity, open sexual remarks, elaborate griping, smoking, rough informal dress, "sloppy" sitting and standing posture, use of dialect or substandard speech, mumbling and shouting, playful aggressivity and "kidding," inconsiderateness for the other in minor but potentially symbolic acts, minor physical self-involvements such as humming, whistling, chewing, nibbling, belching, and flatulence. The front stage behavior language can be taken as the absence (and in some sense the opposite) of this. (p. 128)

Thus, one might not expect much front stage or formal behavior in preschool, and often, especially during parents' drop-off and pick-up time, this was the case. But a given region of social life may sometimes be a backstage and sometimes a front stage. I identified several behaviors that were expected by the teachers, required by the institution, or that would be required in many institutional settings, as formal behavior. Raising one's hand, sitting "on your bottom" (not on your knees, not squatting, not lying down, not standing) during circle, covering one's nose and mouth when coughing or sneezing, or sitting upright in a chair are all formal behaviors of preschools, schools, and to some extent the larger social world. Crawling on the floor, yelling, lying down during teachers' presentations, and running through the classroom are examples of relaxed behaviors that are not allowed in preschool, schools, work settings, and many institutions of the larger social world (Henley 1977). Not all behaviors fell into one of these classifications. When kids were actively engaged in playing at the water table, for example, much of their behavior was not clearly formal or relaxed. I coded as formal and relaxed behaviors those behaviors that would be seen as such if done by adults (or children in many cases) in other social institutions for which children are being prepared.

In the classrooms in this study, boys were allowed and encouraged to pursue relaxed behaviors in a variety of ways that girls were not. Girls were more likely to be encouraged to pursue more formal behaviors. Eighty-two percent of all formal behaviors observed in these classrooms were done by girls, and only 18 percent by boys. However, 80 percent of the behaviors coded as relaxed were boys' behaviors (Table 2).

These observations do not tell us *why* boys do more relaxed behaviors and girls do more formal behaviors. Certainly many parents and others would argue that boys are more predisposed to sloppy postures, crawling on the floor, and so on. However, my observations suggest that teachers help construct this gender difference in bodily behaviors.[3] Teachers were more likely to reprimand

Table 2 Observations of Formal and Relaxed Behaviors, by Gender of Child: Five Preschool Classrooms

	Boys		Girls		Total	
Type of Behavior	**N**	**Percent**	**N**	**Percent**	**N**	**Percent**
Formal	16	18	71	82	87	100
Relaxed	86	80	21	20	107	100

Note: Structured/formal behaviors were coded from references in the field notes to formal postures, polite gestures, etc. Relaxed/informal behaviors were coded from references to informal postures, backstage demeanors, etc.

girls for relaxed bodily movements and comportment. Sadker and Sadker (1994) found a similar result with respect to hand-raising for answering teachers' questions—if hand raising is considered a formal behavior and calling out a relaxed behavior, they find that boys are more likely to call out without raising their hands and demand attention:

> Sometimes what they [boys] say has little or nothing to do with the teacher's questions. Whether male comments are insightful or irrelevant, teachers respond to them. However, when girls call out, there is a fascinating occurrence: Suddenly the teacher remembers the rule about raising your hand before you talk. (Sadker and Sadker 1994:43)

This gendered dynamic of hand-raising exists even in preschool, although our field notes do not provide enough systematic recording of hand-raising to fully assess it. However, such a dynamic applies to many bodily movements and comportment:

> The kids are sitting with their legs folded in a circle listening to Jane (the teacher) talk about dinosaurs. ("Circle" is the most formal part of their preschool education each day and is like sitting in class.) Sam has the ballet slippers on his hands and is clapping them together really loudly. He stops and does a half-somersault backward out of the circle and stays that way with his legs in the air. Jane says nothing and continues talking about dinosaurs. Sue, who is sitting next to Sam, pushes his leg out of her way. Sam sits up and is now busy trying to put the ballet shoes on over his sneakers, and he is looking at the other kids and laughing, trying to get a reaction. He is clearly not paying attention to Jane's dinosaur story and is distracting the other kids. Sam takes the shoes and claps them together again. Jane leans over and tells him to give her the shoes. Sam does, and then lies down all stretched out on the floor, arms over his head, legs apart. Adam is also lying down now, and Keith is on Sara's (the teacher's aide) lap. Rachel takes her sweater off and folds it up. The other children are focused on the teacher. After about five minutes, Jane tells Sam "I'm going to ask you to sit up." (She doesn't say anything to Adam.) But he doesn't move. Jane ignores Sam and Adam and continues with the lesson. Rachel now lies down on her back. After about ten seconds Jane says, "Sit up, Rachel." Rachel sits up and listens to what kind of painting the class will do today. (Five-year-olds)

Sam's behavior had to be more disruptive, extensive, and informal than Rachel's for the teacher to instruct him and his bodily movements to be quieter and for him to comport his body properly for circle. Note that the boys who were relaxed but not disruptive were not instructed to sit properly. It was also common for a teacher to tell a boy to stop some bodily behavior and for the boy to ignore the request and the teacher not to enforce her instructions, although she frequently repeated them.

The gendering of body movements, comportment, and acquisitions of space also happens in more subtle ways. For example, often when there was "free" time, boys spent much more time in child-structured activities than did girls. In one classroom of five-year-olds, boys' "free" time was usually spent building with blocks, climbing on blocks, or crawling on the blocks or on the floor as they worked to build with the blocks whereas girls spent much of their free time sitting at tables cutting things out of paper, drawing, sorting small pieces of blocks into categories, reading stories, and so on.

Compared to boys, girls rarely crawled on the floor (except when they played kitty cats). Girls and boys did share some activities. For example, painting and reading were frequently shared, and the three-year-olds often played at fishing from a play bridge together. Following is a list from my field notes of the most common activities boys and girls did during the child-structured activity periods of the day during two randomly picked weeks of observing:

Boys: played blocks (floor), played at the water table (standing and splashing), played superhero (running around and in play house), played with the car garage (floor), painted at the easel (standing).

Girls: played dolls (sitting in chairs and walking around), played dress-up (standing), coloring (sitting at tables), read stories (sitting on the couch), cut out pictures (sitting at tables).

Children sorted themselves into these activities and also were sorted (or not unsorted) by teachers. For example, teachers rarely told the three boys that always played with the blocks that they had to choose a different activity that day. Teachers also encouraged girls to sit at tables by suggesting table activities for them—in a sense giving them less "free" time or structuring their time more.

> It's the end of circle, and Susan (teacher) tells the kids that today they can paint their dinosaur eggs if they want to. There is a table set up with paints and brushes for those who want to do that. The kids listen and then scatter to their usual activities. Several boys are playing blocks, two boys are at the water table. Several girls are looking at the hamsters in their cage and talking about them, two girls are sitting and stringing plastic beads. Susan says across the classroom, "I need some painters, Joy, Amy, Kendall?" The girls leave the hamster cage and go to the painting table. Susan pulls out a chair so Joy can sit down. She tells them about the painting project. (Five-year-olds)

These girls spent much of the afternoon enjoying themselves painting their eggs. Simon and Jack joined them temporarily, but then went back to activities that were not teacher-structured.

Events like these that happen on a regular basis over an extended period of early childhood serve to gender children's bodies—boys come to take up more room with their bodies, to sit in more open positions, and to feel freer to do what they wish with their bodies, even in relatively formal settings. Henley (1977) finds that among adults men generally are more relaxed than women in their demeanor and women tend to have tenser postures. The looseness of body-focused functions (e.g., belching) is also more open to men than to women. In other words, men are more likely to engage in relaxed demeanors, postures, and behaviors. These data suggest that this gendering of bodies into more formal and more relaxed movements, postures, and comportment is (at least partially) constructed in early childhood by institutions like preschools.

Controlling Voice

Speaking (or yelling as is often the case with kids) is a bodily experience that involves mouth, throat, chest, diaphragm, and facial expression. Thorne (1993) writes that an elementary school teacher once told her that kids "reminded her of bumblebees, an apt image of swarms, speed, and constant motion" (p. 15). Missing from this metaphor is the buzz of the bumblebees, as a constant hum of voices comes from children's play and activities. Kids' play that is giggly, loud, or whispery makes it clear that voice is part of their bodily experiences.

Voice is an aspect of bodily experience that teachers and schools are interested in disciplining. Quiet appears to be required for learning in classrooms. Teaching appropriate levels of voice, noise, and sound disciplines children's bodies and prepares them "from the inside" to learn the school's curriculums and to participate in other social institutions.

The disciplining of children's voices is gendered. I found that girls were told to be quiet or to repeat a request in a quieter, "nicer" voice about three times more often than were boys (see Table 3). This finding is particularly interesting because boys' play was frequently much noisier. However, when boys were noisy, they were also often doing other behaviors the teacher did not allow, and perhaps the

Table 3 Observations of Teachers Telling Children to Be Quiet, by Gender of Child: Five Preschool Classrooms

Gender	N	Percent
Girls	45	73
Boys	16	26
Total	61	100

Note: Coded from references in the field notes to instances of teachers quieting children's voices.

teachers focused less on voice because they were more concerned with stopping behaviors like throwing or running.

Additionally, when boys were told to "quiet down" they were told in large groups, rarely as individuals. When they were being loud and were told to be quiet, boys were often in the process of enacting what Jordan and Cowan (1995) call warrior narratives:

> A group of three boys is playing with wooden doll figures. The dolls are jumping off block towers, crashing into each other. Kevin declares loudly, "I'm the grown up." Keith replies, "I'm the police." They knock the figures into each other and push each other away. Phil grabs a figure from Keith. Keith picks up two more and bats one with the other toward Phil. Now all three boys are crashing the figures into each other, making them dive off towers. They're having high fun. Two more boys join the group. There are now five boys playing with the wooden dolls and the blocks. They're breaking block buildings; things are crashing; they're grabbing each other's figures and yelling loudly. Some are yelling "fire, fire" as their figures jump off the block tower. The room is very noisy. (Five-year-olds)

Girls as individuals and in groups were frequently told to lower their voices. Later that same afternoon:

> During snack time the teacher asks the kids to tell her what they like best in the snack mix. Hillary says, "Marshmallows!" loudly, vigorously, and with a swing of her arm. The teacher turns to her and says, "I'm going to ask you to say that quietly," and Hillary repeats it in a softer voice. (Five-year-olds)

These two observations represent a prominent pattern in the data. The boys playing with the wooden figures were allowed to express their fun and enthusiasm loudly whereas Hillary could not loudly express her love of marshmallows. Girls' voices are disciplined to be softer and in many ways less physical—toning down their voices tones down their physicality. Hillary emphasized "marshmallows" with a large swinging gesture of her arm the first time she answered the teacher's question, but after the teacher asked her to say it quietly she made no gestures when answering. Incidents like these that are repeated often in different contexts restrict girls' physicality.

It could be argued that context rather than gender explains the difference in how much noise is allowed in these situations. Teachers may expect more formal behavior from children sitting at the snack table than they do during semistructured activities. However, even during free play girls were frequently told to quiet down:

> Nancy, Susan, and Amy are jumping in little jumps, from the balls of their feet, almost like skipping rope without the rope. Their mouths are open and they're making a humming sound, looking at each other and giggling. Two of them keep sticking their tongues out. They seem to be having great fun. The teacher's aide sitting on the floor in front of them turns around and says "Shhh, find something else to play. Why don't you play Simon Says?" All three girls stop initially. Then Amy jumps a few more times, but without making the noise. (Five-year-olds)

By limiting the girls' voices, the teacher also limits the girls' jumping and their fun. The girls learn that their bodies are supposed to be quiet, small, and physically constrained. Although the girls did not take the teacher's suggestion to play Simon Says (a game where bodies can be moved only quietly at the order of another), they turn to play that explores quietness yet tries to maintain some of the fun they were having:

> Nancy, Susan, and Amy begin sorting a pile of little-bitty pieces of puzzles, soft blocks, Legos, and so on into categories to "help" the teacher who told

them to be quiet and to clean up. The three of them and the teacher are standing around a single small desk sorting these pieces. (Meanwhile several boys are playing blocks and their play is spread all over the middle of the room.) The teacher turns her attention to some other children. The girls continue sorting and then begin giggling to each other. As they do, they cover their mouths. This becomes a game as one imitates the other. Susan says something nonsensical that is supposed to be funny, and then she "hee-hees" while covering her mouth and looks at Nancy, to whom she has said it, who covers her mouth and "hee-hees" back. They begin putting their hands/fingers cupped over their mouths and whispering in each others' ears and then giggling quietly. They are intermittently sorting the pieces and playing the whispering game. (Five-year-olds)

Thus, the girls took the instruction to be quiet and turned it into a game. This new game made their behaviors smaller, using hands and mouths rather than legs, feet, and whole bodies. Whispering became their fun, instead of jumping and humming. Besides requiring quiet, this whispering game also was gendered in another way: The girls' behavior seemed to mimic stereotypical female gossiping. They whispered in twos and looked at the third girl as they did it and then changed roles. Perhaps the instruction to be quiet, combined with the female role of "helping," led the girls to one of their understandings of female quietness—gossip—a type of feminine quietness that is perhaps most fun.

Finally, by limiting voice teachers limit one of girls' mechanisms for resisting others' mistreatment of them. Frequently, when a girl had a dispute with another child, teachers would ask the girl to quiet down and solve the problem nicely. Teachers also asked boys to solve problems by talking, but they usually did so only with intense disputes and the instruction to talk things out never carried the instruction to talk *quietly*.

Keith is persistently threatening to knock over the building that Amy built. He is running around her with a "flying" toy horse that comes dangerously close to her building each time. She finally says, "Stop it!" in a loud voice. The teacher comes over and asks, "How do we say that, Amy?" Amy looks at Keith and says more softly, "Stop trying to knock it over." The teacher tells Keith to find some place else to play. (Five-year-olds)

Cheryl and Julie are playing at the sand table. Cheryl says to the teacher loudly, "Julie took mine away!" The teacher tells her to say it more quietly. Cheryl repeats it less loudly. The teacher tells her, "Say it a little quieter." Cheryl says it quieter, and the teacher says to Julie, "Please don't take that away from her." (Three-year-olds)

We know that women are reluctant to use their voices to protect themselves from a variety of dangers. The above observations suggest that the denial of women's voices begins at least as early as preschool, and that restricting voice usually restricts movement as well.

Finally, there were occasions when the quietness requirement did not restrict girls' bodies. One class of three-year-olds included two Asian girls, Diane and Sue, who did not speak English. Teachers tended to talk about them and over them but rarely to them. Although these girls said little to other children and were generally quiet, they were what I term body instigators. They got attention and played with other children in more bodily ways than most girls. For example, Sue developed a game with another girl that was a sort of musical chairs. They'd race from one chair to another to see who could sit down first. Sue initiated this game by trying to squeeze into a chair with the other girl. Also, for example,

Diane starts peeking into the play cardboard house that is full of boys and one girl. She looks like she wants to go in, but the door is blocked and the house is crowded. She then goes around to the side of the house and stands with her back to it and starts bumping it with her butt. Because the house is cardboard, it buckles and moves as she does it. The teacher tells her, "Stop—no." Diane stops and then starts doing it again but more lightly. All the boys come out of the house and ask her what she's doing. Matt gets right in her face and the teacher tells him, "Tell her no." He does, but all the other boys have moved on to other activities, so she and Matt go in the house together. (Three-year-olds)

Thus, Diane and Sue's lack of voice in this English-speaking classroom led to greater physicality. There may be other ways that context (e.g., in one's neighborhood instead of school) and race, ethnicity, and class shape gender and voice that cannot be determined from these data (Goodwin 1990).

Bodily Instructions

Teachers give a lot of instructions to kids about what to do with their bodies. Of the explicit bodily instructions recorded 65 percent were directed to boys, 26 percent to girls, and the remaining 9 percent were directed to mixed groups (Table 4). These numbers suggest that boys' bodies are being disciplined more than girls. However, there is more to this story—the types of instructions that teachers give and children's responses to them are also gendered.

First, boys obeyed teachers' bodily instructions about one-half of the time (48 percent), while girls obeyed about 80 percent of the time (Table 4).[4] Boys may receive more instructions from teachers because they are less likely to follow instructions and thus are told repeatedly. Frequently I witnessed a teacher telling a boy or group of boys to stop doing something—usually running or throwing things—and the teacher repeated these instructions several times in the course of the session before (if ever) taking further action. Teachers usually did not have to repeat instructions to girls—girls either stopped on their own with the first instruction, or because the teacher forced them to stop right then. Serbin (1983) finds that boys receive a higher proportion of teachers' ". . . loud reprimands, audible to the entire group. Such patterns of response, intended as punishment, have been repeatedly demonstrated to reinforce aggression and other forms of disruptive behavior" (p. 29).

Second, teachers' instructions directed to boys' bodies were less substantive than those directed to girls. That is, teachers' instructions to boys were usually to stop doing something, to end a bodily behavior with little suggestion for other behaviors they might do. Teachers rarely told boys to change a bodily behavior. A list of teachers' instructions to boys includes: stop throwing, stop jumping, stop clapping, stop splashing, no pushing, don't cry, blocks are not for bopping, don't run, don't climb on that. Fifty-seven percent of the instructions that teachers gave boys about their physical behaviors were of this undirected type, compared with 15 percent of their instructions to girls (Table 4). In other words, teachers' instructions to girls generally were more substantive and more directive, telling girls to do a bodily behavior rather than to

Table 4 Observations of Teachers Giving Bodily Instructions to Children, by Gender of Child: Five Preschool Classrooms

	Boys		Girls		Mixed Groups	
Teacher's instruction/child's response	N	Percent	N	Percent	N	Percent
Bodily instructions from teachers[a]	94	65	39	26	13	9
Child obeys instructions[b]	45	48	31	80	–[c]	–[c]
Undirected bodily instructions from teachers[b]	54	57	6	15	5	55

Note: Bodily instructions are coded from references in the field notes to instances of a teacher telling a child what to do with his or her body.

[a] Percentages based on a total of 146 observations.

[b] Percentages based on a total of 94 observations for boys and 39 observations for girls.

[c] In the observations of mixed groups of girls and boys, usually some obeyed and some did not. Thus an accurate count of how the groups responded is not available.

stop one. Teachers' instructions to girls suggested that they alter their behaviors. A list of instructions to girls includes: talk to her, don't yell, sit here, pick that up, be careful, be gentle, give it to me, put it down there. Girls may have received fewer bodily instructions than did boys, but they received more directive ones. This gender difference leaves boys a larger range of possibilities of what they might choose to do with their bodies once they have stopped a behavior, whereas girls were directed toward a defined set of options. . . .

Physical Interaction Among Children

Thorne (1993) demonstrates that children participate in the construction of gender differences among themselves. The preschool brings together large groups of children who engage in interactions in which they cooperate with the hidden curriculum and discipline each other's bodies in gendered ways, but they also engage in interactions in which they resist this curriculum.

Girls and boys teach their same-sex peers about their bodies and physicality. Children in these observations were much more likely to imitate the physical behavior of a same-sex peer than a cross-sex peer. Children also encourage others to imitate them. Some gendered physicality develops in this way. For example, I observed one boy encouraging other boys to "take up more space" in the same way he was.

> James (one of the most active boys in the class) is walking all over the blocks that Joe, George, and Paul have built into a road. Then he starts spinning around with his arms stretched out on either side of him. He has a plastic toy cow in one hand and is yelling, "Moo." He spins through half of the classroom, other children ducking under his arms or walking around him when he comes near them. Suddenly he drops the cow and still spinning, starts shouting, "I'm a tomato! I'm a tomato!" The three boys who were playing blocks look at him and laugh. James says, "I'm a tomato!" again, and Joe says, "There's the tomato." Joe, George, and Paul continue working on their block road. James then picks up a block and lobs it in their direction and then keeps spinning throughout this half of the classroom saying he's a tomato. Joe and George look up when the block lands near them and then they get up and imitate James. Now three boys are spinning throughout much of the room, shouting that they are tomatoes. The other children in the class are trying to go about their play without getting hit by a tomato. (Five-year-olds)

The within-gender physicality of three-year-old girls and boys was more similar than it was among the five-year-olds. Among the three-year-old girls there was more rough and tumble play, more physical fighting and arguing among girls than there was among the five-year-old girls.

> During clean up, Emily and Sara argue over putting away some rope. They both pull on the ends of the rope until the teacher comes over and separates them. Emily walks around the classroom then, not cleaning anything up. She sings to herself, does a twirl, and gets in line for snack. Sara is behind her in line. Emily pushes Sara. Sara yells, "Aaahh," and hits Emily and pushes her. The teacher takes both of them out of line and talks to them about getting along and being nice to each other. (Three-year-olds)

From lessons like [this], this girls have learned by age five that their play with each other should not be "too rough." The physical engagement of girls with each other at age five had little rough-and-tumble play:

> Three girls leave the dress-up corner. Mary crawls on the floor as Naomi and Jennifer talk. Jennifer touches Naomi's shoulder gently as she talks to her. They are having quite a long conversation. Jennifer is explaining something to Naomi. Jennifer's gestures are adult-like except that she fiddles with Naomi's vest buttons as she talks to her. Her touching and fiddling with Naomi's clothes is very gentle, how a child might fiddle with a mom's clothing while talking to her—doing it absent-mindedly. Mary, on the floor, is pretending to be a kitty. Then Jennifer gets on the floor and is a kitty too. They are squeaking, trying to mimic a cat's meow. Naomi then puts her arm around Susan's shoulder and leads her to play

kitty too. Naomi seems to be a person still, not a kitty. She is in charge of the kitties. (Five-year-olds)

Two girls are playing with the dishes and sitting at a table. Keisha touches Alice under the chin, tickles her almost, then makes her eat something pretend, then touches the corners of her mouth, telling her to smile. (Five-year-olds)

I do not mean to suggest that girls' physical engagement with each other is the opposite of boys' or that all of boys' physical contacts were rough and tumble. Boys, especially in pairs, hugged, gently guided, or helped each other climb or jump. But often, especially in groups of three or more and especially among the five-year-olds, boys' physical engagement was highly active, "rough," and frequent. Boys experienced these contacts as great fun and not as hostile or negative in any way:

Keith and Lee are jumping on the couch, diving onto it like high jumpers, colliding with each other as they do. Alan watches them and then climbs onto the back of the couch and jumps off. Keith takes a jump onto the couch, lands on Lee, and then yells, "Ouch, ouch—I hurt my private," and he runs out of the room holding onto his crotch. The teacher tells them to stop jumping on the couch. (Five-year-olds)

The physical engagement of boys and girls *with each other* differed from same-sex physical engagement. Because girls' and boys' play is semi-segregated, collisions (literal and figurative) in play happen at the borders of these gender-segregated groups (Maccoby 1988; Thorne 1993). As Thorne (1993) demonstrates, not all borderwork is negative—40 percent of the physical interactions observed between girls and boys were positive or neutral (Table 5).

Ned runs over to Veronica, hipchecks her and says "can I be your friend?" and she says "yes." Ned walks away and kicks the blocks again three to four times. (Five-year-olds)

However, cross-gender interactions were more likely to be negative than same-sex interactions. In fact, physical interactions among children were twice as likely to be a negative interaction if they were between a girl and boy than if they were among same-gender peers. Approximately 30 percent of the interactions among girls and among boys were negative (hostile, angry, controlling, hurtful), whereas 60 percent of mixed-gender physical interactions were negative. Sixty percent of 113 boy-girl physical interactions were initiated by boys, 39 percent were initiated by girls, and only 1 percent of these interactions were mutually initiated.

Table 5 Observations of Physical Interactions among Children, by Gender of Children: Five Preschool Classrooms

	Interactions between:					
	Boys		Girls		Boys and Girls	
Type of Interaction	**N**	**Percent**	**N**	**Percent**	**N**	**Percent**
Positive	46	70	42	66	20	18
Negative	19	29	20	31	68	60
Neutral	1	2	2	3	26	23
Total	66	101	64	100	114	101

Note: Physical interaction was coded from references in the field notes to bodily interaction between children. Bodily contact that was minor and seemingly meaningless was not recorded in field notes. For example, children brushing against each other while picking up toys was not recorded if both children ignored the contact and did not alter their actions because of it. Percentages may not sum to 100 due to rounding.

At the borders of semi-segregated play there are physical interactions about turf and toy ownership:

> Sylvia throws play money on the floor from her play pocketbook. Jon grabs it up. She wrestles him for it and pries it from his hands. In doing this she forces him onto the floor so that he's hunched forward on his knees. She gets behind him and sandwiches him on the floor as she grabs his hands and gets the money loose. Then, two minutes later, she's giving money to kids, and she gives Jon some, but apparently not enough. He gets right close to her face, inches away and loudly tells her that he wants more. He scrunches up his face, puts his arms straight down by his sides and makes fists. She steps back; he steps up close again to her face. She turns away. (Five-year-olds)

Negative interactions occur when there are "invasions" or interruptions of play among children of one gender by children of another:

> Courtney is sitting on the floor with the girls who are playing "kitties." The girls have on their dress-up clothes and dress-up shoes. Phil puts on big winter gloves and then jumps in the middle of the girls on the floor. He lands on their shoes. Courtney pushes him away and then pulls her legs and clothes and stuff closer to her. She takes up less space and is sitting in a tight ball on the floor. Phil yells, "No! Aaarrhh." Julie says, "It's not nice to yell." (Five-year-olds)

As Thorne (1993) suggests, kids create, shape, and police the borders of gender. I suggest that they do so physically. In this way, they not only sustain gender segregation, but also maintain a sense that girls and boys are physically different, that their bodies are capable of doing certain kinds of things. This sense of physical differences may make all gender differences feel and appear natural.

Conclusion

Children also sometimes resist their bodies being gendered. For example, three-year-old boys dressed up in women's clothes sometimes. Five-year-old girls played with a relaxed comportment that is normatively (hegemonically) masculine when they sat with their feet up on the desk and their chairs tipped backward. In one classroom when boys were at the height of their loud activity—running and throwing toys and blocks— girls took the opportunity to be loud too as the teachers were paying less attention to them and trying to get the boys to settle down. In individual interactions as well, girls were likely to be loud and physically assertive if a boy was being unusually so:

> José is making a plastic toy horse fly around the room, and the boys playing with the blocks are quite loud and rambunctious. José flies the toy horse right in front of Jessica's face and then zooms around her and straight toward her again. Jessica holds up her hand and waves it at him yelling, "Aaaarrrh." José flies the horse in another direction. (Five-year-olds)

These instances of resistance suggest that gendered physicalities are not natural, nor are they easily and straightforwardly acquired. This research demonstrates the many ways that practices in institutions like preschools facilitate children's acquisition of gendered physicalities.

Men and women and girls and boys fill social space with their bodies in different ways. Our everyday movements, postures, and gestures are gendered. These bodily differences enhance the seeming naturalness of sexual and reproductive differences, that then construct inequality between men and women (Butler 1990). As MacKinnon (1987) notes, "Differences are inequality's post hoc excuse. . . ." (p. 8). In other words, these differences create a context for social relations in which differences confirm inequalities of power.

This research suggests one way that bodies are gendered and physical differences are constructed through social institutions and their practices. Because this gendering occurs at an early age, the seeming naturalness of such differences is further underscored. In preschool, bodies become gendered in ways that are so subtle and taken-for-granted that they come to feel and appear natural. Preschool, however, is presumably just the tip of the iceberg in the gendering of children's bodies. Families, formal schooling, and other institutions (like churches, hospitals, and workplaces) gender children's physicality as well.

Many feminist sociologists (West and Zimmerman 1987) and other feminist scholars (Butler 1990, 1993) have examined how the seeming naturalness of gender differences underlies gender inequality. They have also theorized that there are no meaningful natural differences (Butler 1990, 1993.) However, how gender differences come to feel and appear natural in the first place has been a missing piece of the puzzle.

Sociological theories of the body that describe the regulation, disciplining, and managing that social institutions do to bodies have neglected the gendered nature of these processes (Foucault 1979; Shilling 1993; Turner 1984). These data suggest that a significant part of disciplining the body consists of gendering it, even in subtle, micro, everyday ways that make gender appear natural. It is in this sense that the preschool as an institution genders children's bodies. Feminist theories about the body (Bordo 1993; Connell 1995; Young 1990), on the other hand, tend to focus on the adult gendered body and fail to consider how the body becomes gendered. This neglect may accentuate gender differences and make them seem natural. This research provides but one account of how bodies become gendered. Other accounts of how the bodies of children and adults are gendered (and raced, classed, and sexualized) are needed in various social contexts across the life course.

Notes

1. Classrooms usually contained 15 to 18 children on a given day. However, since some kids came to preschool five days a week, some three, and some two, a total of 112 different kids were observed.
2. Parents are not solely responsible for what their children wear to preschool, as they are constrained by what is available and affordable in children's clothing. More important, children, especially at ages three to five, want some say in what they wear to preschool and may insist on some outfits and object to others.
3. Throughout the paper, when I use the term "constructed," I do *not* mean that preschools create these differences or that they are the only origins of these differences. Clearly, children come to preschool with some gender differences that were created in the family or other contexts outside of preschool. My argument is that preschools reinforce these differences and build (construct) further elaborations of difference upon what children bring to preschool.
4. There were several cases for boys and girls in which the observer did not record the child's response.

References

Anyon, Jean. 1980. "Social Class and the Hidden Curriculum of Work." *Journal of Education* 162:67–92.

Birdwhistell, Ray. 1970. *Kinesics and Contexts.* Philadelphia, PA: University of Pennsylvania Press.

Bordo, Susan. 1993. *Unbearable Weight.* Berkeley, CA: University of California Press.

Bowles, Samuel and Herbert Gintis. 1976. *Schooling in Capitalist America.* New York: Basic Books.

Butler, Judith. 1990. *Gender Trouble.* New York: Routledge.

———. 1993. *Bodies That Matter.* New York: Routledge.

Carere, Sharon. 1987. "Lifeworld of Restricted Behavior." *Sociological Studies of Child Development* 2:105–38.

Carnoy, Martin and Henry Levin. 1985. *Schooling and Work in the Democratic State.* Stanford, CA: Stanford University Press.

Connell, R. W. 1987. *Gender and Power.* Stanford, CA: Stanford University Press.

———. 1995. *Masculinities.* Berkeley, CA: University of California Press.

Foucault, Michel. 1979. *Discipline and Punish: The Birth of the Prison.* New York: Vintage Books.

Giroux, Henry and David Purpel. 1983. *The Hidden Curriculum and Moral Education.* Berkeley, CA: McCutchan.

Goffman, Erving. 1959. *The Presentation of Self in Everyday Life.* Garden City, NY: Doubleday.

Goodwin, Marjorie Harness. 1990. *He-Said-She-Said: Talk as Social Organization among Black Children.* Bloomington, IN: Indiana University Press.

Haug, Frigga. 1987. *Female Sexualization: A Collective Work of Memory.* London, England: Verso.

Henley, Nancy. 1977. *Body Politics.* New York: Simon and Schuster.

Jackson, Philip W. 1968. *Life in Classrooms.* New York: Holt, Rinehart, and Winston.

Jordan, Ellen and Angela Cowan. 1995. "Warrior Narratives in the Kindergarten Classroom: Re-negotiating the Social Contract." *Gender and Society* 9:727–43.

Maccoby, Eleanor. 1988. "Gender as a Social Category." *Developmental Psychology* 24:755–65.

MacKinnon, Catharine. 1987. *Feminism Unmodified.* Cambridge, MA: Harvard University Press.

Martin, Emily. 1987. *The Woman in the Body.* Boston, MA: Beacon Press.

Martin, Karin. 1996. *Puberty, Sexuality, and the Self: Boys and Girls at Adolescence.* New York: Routledge.

McLaren, Peter. 1986. *Schooling as a Ritual Performance: Towards a Political Economy of Educational Symbols and Gestures.* London, England: Routledge and Kegan Paul.

Sadker, Myra and David Sadker. 1994. *Failing at Fairness: How America's Schools Cheat Girls.* New York: Charles Scribner and Sons.

Serbin, Lisa. 1983. "The Hidden Curriculum: Academic Consequences of Teacher Expectations." Pp. 18–41 in *Sex Differentiation and Schooling,* edited by M. Marland. London, England: Heinemann Educational Books.

Shilling, Chris. 1993. *The Body and Social Theory.* London, England: Sage.

Thorne, Barrie. 1993. *Gender Play: Girls and Boys in School.* New Brunswick, NJ: Rutgers University Press.

Thomas, Jerry and Karen French. 1985. "Gender Differences Across Age in Motor Performance: A Meta-Analysis." *Psychological Bulletin* 98: 260–82.

Turner, Bryan S. 1984. *The Body and Society: Explorations in Social Theory.* New York: Basil Blackwell.

———. 1992. *Regulating Bodies: Essays in Medical Sociology.* London, England: Routledge.

Van Ausdale, Debra and Joe R. Feagin. 1996. "Using Racial and Ethnic Concepts: The Critical Case of Very Young Children." *American Sociological Review* 61: 779–93.

Wasburn, Philo C. 1986. "The Political Role of the American School." *Theory and Research in Social Education* 14:51–65.

West, Candace and Don Zimmerman. 1987. "Doing Gender." *Gender and Society* 1:127–51.

Young, Iris. 1990. *Throwing Like a Girl.* Bloomington, IN: Indiana University Press.

Reflective Questions

1. Martin argues that socialization in preschool doesn't just lead boys and girls to develop different tastes or styles but rather inscribes gender into kids' bodies and bodily experiences. How did teachers' instructions and discipline impart gendered control of the body? When did kids resist these gendered lessons? How did they reinforce and extend them?
2. What are the long-term implications of these lessons for boys' and girls' identities and performance in schools? If gendered bodily appearances and actions are not natural and take considerable work, how do they end up feeling natural?
3. Take a few minutes and try to unlearn your own gender socialization by learning to walk like another gender. Enlist a friend to teach you. If you identify as a woman, have a man teach you to walk like a man, including body movements, comportment, and mannerisms. Try to learn to turn around and do a casual greeting of an acquaintance, too. Men, enlist a woman to teach you to walk like a woman. If you identify as transgender, you likely have experience with gender neutrality and/or gender play. Enlist a friend, and teach him/her how to walk in gender-neutral ways. How easy and comfortable was the exercise? What body movements did you struggle with the most? Were you socialized into gendered bodies like Martin's kids? What happens when people interact with someone whose sex category is not identifiable or is gender neutral?
4. After the *Toronto Star* printed a story about a Canadian family who refused to disclose their baby Storm's sex, opting instead to raise it gender neutrally, American news outlets quickly picked up the story. (Read the original here: http://

www.parentcentral.ca/parent/babiespregnancy/babies/article/995112.) ABC News's headline read: "Canadian Mother Raising 'Genderless' Baby, Storm, Defends Her Family's Decision," while CNN World ran the story under the headline: "Storm: Boy or a Girl? It's a Secret—And an International Controversy." Lisa Belkin of the *New York Times*'s *Motherlode* blog covered it under the heading "Is This Baby a Boy or Girl?" What challenges does this couple face in raising a gender-neutral child? How do others ensure categorization, even if we reject the category for ourselves? What other categories shape how people think about and use their bodies?

Women and Their Clitoris

DENNIS D. WASKUL, PHILLIP VANNINI, AND DESIREE WIESEN

In an earlier selection, Kent Sandstrom highlighted how and why the names we give to things shape our perceptions and interpretations of them, thereby guiding our actions toward them. Sandstrom thus articulated a core premise of symbolic interactionism, the social psychological perspective that emphasizes how we depend on symbols and social meanings to make sense of the realities we encounter, including the realities of our bodies and bodily sensations. But what happens when we do not have a name for a reality or experience we encounter? For instance, how do we make sense of and respond to bodily parts or sensations that have no name or that are widely regarded as unspeakable? And how do the silences and social meanings that surround these bodily parts or sensations shape our understandings and experiences of them?

This selection addresses these questions by examining how women make sense of the clitoris and its associated sensations in the face of the linguistic silences that surround it. Indeed, the authors demonstrate how many women do not even learn that they have a clitoris until their late adolescence, despite having taken sexual education classes in school. The authors also explore how women "discover" the clitoris, how they transform it into a significant symbol, and how larger cultural discourses impede these processes of discovery and signification, particularly by erasing the clitoris, or at least keeping it linguistically hidden from view. Perhaps most crucially, the authors reveal how this discursive environment promotes both symbolic clitoridectomy and symbolic purgatory, conditions that render the clitoris as mute, unspeakable, and/or as a province that others may control or occupy, even if this diminishes women's sexual pleasure.

In the end, the provocative research discussed in this selection challenges and extends the insights of symbolic interactionism and sociological psychology. The authors portray how somatic experiences can be reflexive and meaningful even when symbolic resources are relatively scarce or absent. They also show some of the key phases that characterize a somatic career, at least in regard to some women's discoveries and experiences of their clitorises. Moreover, the authors highlight how women are active agents, not passive victims, in formulating their responses to the conditions of symbolic clitoridectomy and symbolic purgatory they confront. That is, women do not simply internalize and reproduce cultural discourses that pertain to their sexual organs and sensations. Instead, they actively make meaning of their bodies, clitorises, and sensual experiences, negotiating the complex dialogues that take place between their bodily sensations and the shifting discourses and interactions that surround them.

Reprinted from: Dennis Waskul, Phillip Vannini, and Desiree Wiesen, Women and Their Clitoris: Personal Discovery, Signification, and Use. *Symbolic Interaction* 30(2): 151–174.

Symbolic Clitoridectomy and Symbolic Purgatory

> Except for the obvious, derisive "clit," I find no common slang words—no common words at all—for the clitoris, the great unmentionable, the only human organ with the single purpose of pleasure. This is an oversight almost impossible to believe, and it makes me wonder at the depth of our capacity to suppress our experience—to suppress it so deeply, even the making of language is stopped.
>
> Sally Tisdale, *Talk Dirty to Me: An Intimate Philosophy of Sex* (1994)

> I don't remember ever being told that a clitoris is a normal part of a female's body.
>
> Rebecca

Women's genitalia are generally unspeakable (Allan and Burridge 1991) and a site of considerable taboo (Braun 1999). In fact, "many people appear to consider women's genitalia to be unmentionable" (Braun and Kitzinger 2001a:146), and "language is rarely used to refer to the vagina (or women's genitalia more generally) in any detail" (Braun and Wilkinson 2001:19). The vulva is imprecisely defined, and its parts are often conspicuously absent in formal medical and dictionary definitions as well as in informal slang (Braun and Kitzinger 2001a). In place of terms that differentiate the various anatomical parts of the vulva, the word *vagina* is colloquially and popularly used to refer to the entire area "down there." Accordingly, "a language that does not enable women to talk about the different parts of the genitalia, or to conceptualize the genitalia as comprised of various parts, might perpetuate the absence of women's genitalia from their conceptualized body" (Braun and Kitzinger 2001a:155).

Vulva taboos are reflected and reinforced in a relative scarcity of language, and the clitoris may be the most muted of all. In Western culture the clitoris remains a part of women's bodies that eschews naming and mention (Bennett 1993; Ogletree and Ginsburg 2000). Throughout history the clitoris has irregularly cycled through hiding, discovery, degradation, reinvention, and destruction (Moore and Clarke 1995; Scheper-Hughes 1991). Even the history of the scientific study of anatomy shows wide-ranging variations in the technical construction of the clitoris, which have often classified the clitoris as homologous or analogous to the penis (Moore and Clarke 1995). The result is a symbolic clitoridectomy in which "it" is "kept under the hood" (Ogletree and Ginsburg 2000:917, 925) in a subdued state of symbolic purgatory—one of the many outcomes of discursive practices that have historically contributed to the hystericization of women's bodies (Foucault 1979). The conditions and consequences of symbolic clitoridectomy have provoked substantial critique: the hush reflects and perpetuates "the blank balance sheet of our society's concern for women's pleasure" (McClintock 1992:115); contributes to both silencing and control of women's sexuality (see Cornog 1986; Gartrell and Mosbacher 1984; Lerner 1976); reinforces vaginal rather than clitoral constructions of feminine sexual pleasure (see Bennett 1993); and contributes to a partial absence of genitalia from women's conceptualized bodies (see Braun and Kitzinger 2001a, 2001b; Braun and Wilkinson 2001; Moore and Clarke 1995; Ogletree and Ginsburg 2000).

It might seem that symbolic clitoridectomy is an obvious case of repression, a "repression that operate[s] as a sentence to disappear" (Foucault 1984:293). However, symbolic clitoridectomy is consistent with Foucauldian arguments on bio-power and technologies of the body (see Foucault 1979, 1980). Symbolic clitoridectomy operates as a specific political anatomy strategy, a technology of the body that incites awareness, self-knowledge, and speaking the truth by way of erasing the clitoris; a mechanism by which "it" and its experiences are placed in a purgatory—where ignorance and partial knowledge ironically coexist—and abundant discourses "make possible [its] discovery" (Foucault 1979:43). There is a *relative* scarcity, but not absolute lack, of discursive resources to negotiate the meanings of women's bodies and sexualities. In fact, a Janus-faced condition exists: a dearth of symbolic meaning in the context of multiple discourses for potential discovery.[1] Thus, we characterize symbolic clitoridectomy as putting the clitoris "under erasure," allowing it to be implicitly present in discourse under conditions of its explicit absence—as we illustrate below.

Method and Data

This study was conducted at Minnesota State University, Mankato. Because data collection procedures required women to reveal personal and potentially embarrassing information, we relied on a purposive sample and an elaborate procedure to assure anonymity. Women qualified for this study if they were enrolled in or successfully completed a sexualities course taught by Dennis Waskul. We felt this population of women would be more likely to participate because of their exposure to a multiplicity of discourses on sexuality. We acknowledge the limitations of this sampling procedure—the sample is not representative, and the data likely reflect volunteer bias; we suspect that women with some of the most evocative and perhaps troubling experiences were the least likely to volunteer for this study.

By e-mail we initially contacted sixty-four women and individually invited them to participate in a research project on women's private and personal sexual experiences of their bodies. We further asked each woman to reply by e-mail if interested in participating. Forty-one women responded. Respondents subsequently received another e-mail that disclosed the research procedures, methods to guarantee relative anonymity, and all research questions. We informed women that, should they choose to participate in this study, we would provide them with a notebook and a list of questions that they would answer privately and with complete anonymity (on this and similar methods see Plummer 2001). Questions elicited basic demographic data as well as the women's earliest recollections of discovering their clitoris, earliest recollection of having been told or otherwise learned about the clitoris as a normal part of female anatomy, history with masturbation, and so on.

Women willing to participate in this study were responsible for sending an e-mail to Desiree Wiesen, who would arrange a time and place to have them sign a research consent form and would provide them with the research materials. We informed the respondents that Wiesen would collect and seal all research consent forms (in the unlikely event that they would ever be needed); she also collected and securely sealed all notebooks, which were immediately provided to Waskul. We further informed women that neither Waskul nor Phillip Vannini would have access to the research consent forms and Wiesen would not have access to the contents of their notebooks. These procedures—the strategic use of e-mail and our division of methodological and analytic labor—were designed to assure double-blind anonymity; we do not know who agreed to participate in this study and only by unsealing the research consent forms (in the possession of Wiesen) is it possible to identify those participants or match any one woman with the data she provided.

Twenty women signed consent forms and received research materials, and fifteen women returned completed notebooks. While we initially hoped for a larger sample, we also understood women's hesitation in revealing such personal information. However, in the end, a sample of fifteen proved satisfactory. The research procedures provided a private and anonymous discursive space in which women wrote exceedingly rich accounts. Women answered thirteen questions and collectively provided a total of 204 handwritten pages of text.

Our sample is overwhelmingly Caucasian; only one woman identified herself as nonwhite. The sample is equally homogeneous in other categories. Ages narrowly ranged from nineteen to twenty-two. Nine women described their upbringing as "rural"; five as a mix of "rural" and "urban" environments; one woman described her upbringing as "urban." Ten women identified themselves as either "heterosexual" or "straight"; one woman identified herself as "mostly heterosexual"; one described her sexual orientation as "straight, although I've kissed girls when I've/we've been drinking a lot"; one woman wrote "my orientation changes depending on the situation I'm in"; one woman identified herself as "bisexual"; and one woman did not identify a sexual orientation. Five women described themselves as "single"; four claimed to be "engaged"; one woman wrote that she is "soon to be engaged I hope"; the remaining five women described themselves as in "long term," "serious," or "co-habitating" relationships with men. One woman in this study described herself as a "virgin." We refer to all women in this study by pseudonyms. . . .

Clitoral Erasure and a Socialization of Genital Ignorance

> Here I am a twenty-year-old woman and I still do not know much about my genitals.
>
> Rebecca

Derived from the Greek *kleitoris,* meaning "hill" or "slope," even etymology cloaks the delectable clitoris. No mere "hill" or "slope"—semantically significant only for its shape or form—the clitoris is the most sensitive female sex organ; pleasure is its only known function. Certainly, "female sexuality, like female pleasure, is multiply sited. It presents, therefore, multiple ways in which it can be constructed—as well as experienced—by individual women" (Bennett 1993:238). Nonetheless, as all the women in this study testify, the clitoris is a corporeal epicenter of embodied female sexuality:

> Without my clitoris, I believe I'd still be an orgasm virgin. . . . clit stimulation is the only way I can be sexually orgasmic. . . . The clitoris is *the* most important part of sexual satisfaction and gratification, whether I'm solo or partnered up. (Cindy; emphasis in original)

> All the other stuff is fun, but doesn't really matter unless my clit gets attention. . . . I get some pleasure from the other things but it always goes back to my clit 100%. (Danielle)

The women in this study bestowed enormous significance on and fondness for their clitoris. As Jessica claimed, "Seriously, the clitoris was God's gift to women! (I almost pity men for all the opportunities unavailable to them)." Both Rochelle and Diana audaciously announced, "I love my clitoris!" These sentiments are understandable, but beg a question: in light of its affectionate, pleasurable, and orgasmic significance, *how* do women learn about the clitoris?

Women reported various circumstances in which they discovered and learned about their clitoris. However, one striking commonality is the frequent claim that they did not acquire this information in primary and secondary educational settings. As Jill recalled, "I don't remember ever being told about the clitoris. . . . [W]e never covered genitalia in the health classes at school. I don't remember covering human anatomy at all." Similarly, Rochelle claimed:

> [The] "Family Life" program in school (fifth grade) showed me the pictures, but did not *detail* the parts. Probably my freshman year of high school is actually when we heard the parts explained in health class. (emphasis in original)

Several women equally testified to this curricular omission that, as they recalled, was especially impoverished regarding the functions of various parts of their genitalia. This was certainly Vicki's experience: "Our teacher just explained what each part of the body and girls' anatomy was. But didn't really tell us anything about what each thing was for." Of course, adequate instruction on the clitoris would necessarily identify its function—purely pleasure. But because pleasure, especially children's pleasure, is not organized in terms of generation and reproduction, it did not "merit a hearing" (Foucault 1984:293). As several women recalled, the clitoris was "driven out, denied, and reduced to silence" (p. 293):

> In seventh grade health class we went over the anatomy of the human body. I remember learning about the vagina and the many parts of it, *but never was clitoris mentioned.* (Ann; emphasis added)

> When I went through sex ed. in fifth grade we didn't even really learn what sex really was. We just learned about the parts of our anatomy—*excluding the clitoris*—and about periods and hygiene. (Sara; emphasis added)

Children are assumed to have "no sex, which is why they were forbidden to talk about it," and this perhaps also explains why, in place of a curriculum that includes the clitoris, "a general and studied silence was imposed" (p. 293). Consequently, many women recalled entering and experiencing puberty and adolescence relatively uneducated about a significant component of their changing body, genitals, and sexuality. Indeed, despite the fact that nearly all the women in this study had been sexually active for quite some time, they commonly reported learning about the clitoris in their late teenage years—often as a college or university student—when discourses on sex have assumed the mantra of scientific propriety:

> When I found out the name, the clitoris, I was seventeen yrs old. It happened in my biology class in college. . . . I don't remember discussing the sexual function of the clitoris. Mainly I found out this part of my genitals had a name. It wasn't until other college classes that I began to fully understand the concept of a clitoris. . . . Besides professors talking about it, the clitoris was included in some textbooks, supplemental reading, and magazines. All of this information made me realize that the clitoris is for pleasure and is biologically highly sensitive because of nerve endings. (Jennifer)

Women generally reported equal silence from parents. Vicki wrote, "I was actually never told anything about it from my parents." For Jill, "it was never something that was talked about in my house, not even between my mom and I." Although some parents were more willing to talk about sex, this did not necessarily mean they told their daughters about the parts that comprise their genitalia. Sara recalled: "My parents were very open with me about sex, but they never focused on the actual parts of the vagina." Parents were not alone in their discomfort with the subject; in some cases, young girls were themselves part of a coalition of evasion and avoidance. As Rebecca explained, "I wasn't comfortable talking to my parents about it, and they weren't comfortable talking to me about it."

Foucault argued that silence and repression can only partially explain the rapport between sex, knowledge, and power. Similarly, symbolic clitoridectomy is marked as much by silence as by see-through-secrecy. In fact, discourses on sexuality and the clitoris are rather straightforwardly available in certain public arenas where sex can be safely administered (like university classrooms) or educational resources. Owing to this see-through-secrecy of a society that speaks "verbosely of its own silence" (Foucault 1984:297), some parents relied on these other means of informing girls about their body and sexuality. Books, in particular, proved useful for Rebecca and her parents—a common recollection for the women in this study:

> I remember when my sister and I were young, probably around the age of 9 or 10, our mother checked out a library book that taught young children about sex. When she showed us we were embarrassed and to make it worse, our father was there, which made us more uncomfortable. We didn't want to look at the book or talk about it. She put it under the couch and said that if we wanted to look at it we could. So, later that day I snuck it out from under the couch and took it into the bathroom and quickly looked at it. (Rebecca)

Although books may have proven helpful, they too provided a means of maintaining a vow of see-through-secrecy for parents and children alike. Books were relatively available, but girls were on their own to read them. Neither parents nor children seemingly needed to discuss the matter further. Still, the availability of books, in this case, enabled these women to learn about conceptualizations of the clitoris (although on the limitations of these books, see Moore and Clarke 1995) and thus, as we show, provided them the chance to "exit" symbolic purgatory.

While parents were not always forthcoming, many women found adequate comfort in asking them questions or in *feeling* they could talk to them—mothers, in particular—if they had questions (even if they never recalled doing so). As Cheryl explained, "I always knew that if I wanted to know I could probably ask my mom, who was a nurse. . . . I knew I could go to my parents with specific questions." And parents were sometimes quite helpful in assuring daughters who were sometimes confused about their changing bodies:

> When I was young, I was very inquisitive about my body. I asked numerous questions and they were answered to the best of my parents abilities and comfort levels. I remember discovering my pubic hair one night while I lay in bed. I quickly rushed downstairs to ask my mother what it was and why it was there. She comforted me by saying it was natural and that eventually all girls have hair there. (Rebecca)

More than a quaint story, Rebecca's mother was an important source of comforting knowledge during a time of change and apprehension. Indeed, "put[ting] sex into discourse" (Foucault 1984:299) can be important for girls who, in the absence of other information, may worry unnecessarily about their bodies and sexual subjectivity, Vicki recalled an especially evocative memory:

> I was very young, about four maybe, and I noticed it [clitoris] when I was getting dressed or something. I just remember thinking I was weird because I had bathed with my girl cousins and never remembered seeing theirs, and no one had ever told me anything about it. I got really confused about it, and eventually upset enough that I asked my mom about it. I was afraid that I must be part boy, and this was like a mini-penis or something. I remember being very concerned about what I was, if I was a boy/girl. My mom kind of giggled at me and told me I was 100% girl, and it was just a part of my vagina. And all girls had it.

Significantly, Vicki was "very concerned about what [she] was" because, even as a young girl, she was aware that boys have a penis; she was *not* aware that girls have a clitoris. Her anxiety stemmed from the fact that girls "are rarely taught the anatomical terms which differentiate parts of female genitalia (e.g., the clitoris, the inner and outer labia)—the word vagina covers the whole area" (Braun and Kitzinger 2001a:155; also see Gartrell and Mosbacher 1984; Lerner 1976). The symbolic purgatory of the clitoris compelled Vicki to seek available discourses, appropriate *known* icons—a penis—and worry that what she discovered "was like a mini-penis." Her clitoris was a part of her *corporeal* body, but not part of the body she conceptualized through language. By putting sex into discourse, her mother offered reassurances that restored order to Vicki's purgatory and eased her anxiety about being "a boy/girl."

Taking into account a genital disembodiment or alienation of children from their own bodies, as well as the relative silence, avoidance, and omissions of family and school, it is not surprising that women generally recalled growing up ignorant about their genitals. Indeed, almost none of our informants learned that their genitals were composed of various parts until well into their teenage years:

> I think I was in college before I actually knew there were different parts. As for age, I would have to say between 17 and 19. (Jill)

> My family had used "vagina" as the counterpart to "penis." "Vagina" was everything a girl had "down there." I knew it was a "third hole" (that was my only concept of what the vagina was, a hole meant to hold a penis and birth a baby). (Jessica)

Furthermore, by reproducing the existent "social regulation of the senses" (Jackson 1977: 209), ignorance persisted throughout women's somatic careers. The majority of women in this study openly admitted that they *presently* do not know or understand the various parts of the vulva. Jill wrote, "I feel like I don't know or understand the different parts of the vagina at all." Similarly, Ann wrote, "I don't feel I know the parts of female genitals very well. . . . they look a lot different in real pictures than on drawings or models. . . . I don't know what all the parts do or what all their functions are." While Cheryl claimed to "know the various parts of women's genitals," she immediately added, "I probably wouldn't get them all right on a placement test." Indeed, owing to the colloquial use of "vagina" to refer to all the parts of the vulva, Rebecca was caught off-guard when we asked the question, "How well do you feel you understand the various parts that comprise women's genitals?"

> I just reread this question and I'm unsure what it means. The vagina is composed of several different parts? I guess I never knew that. I feel a little ashamed to admit that and a little angry.

Rebecca was not alone in her embarrassment, or anger, as Sara explained:

> This is embarrassing, but I don't feel like I know the different parts of my genetalia [*sic*] at all. I was never, not that I recollect, shown a diagram of a vagina until I came to college. . . . I wish that I knew more about women's anatomy, but it is embarrassing enough to not know these things in the first place.

The women in this study reported a vagueness, lack of knowledge, and even admitted outright ignorance about their genitals—"blind spots in women's knowledge of their bodies, arousal, and desires" (Plante 2006:143). We recognize that "the implications in terms of those women's attitudes toward their own sexuality are serious" (Sanders and Robinson 1979:228) and share Plante's (2006:143) concern "that women may not know their bodies, may not have comfortable language to describe their bodies, and may not know their desires." These are the circumstances and conditions of symbolic clitoridectomy: a form of putting the clitoris under erasure not by way of sheer silencing but by a restrictive economy of discourse—among other significant forces—that confines the clitoris in a symbolic purgatory.

Discovering the Sensations of the Clitoris

> I discovered the sensations of my clitoris long before I ever properly identified the organ, the source of all the magic. I was probably about 9 or 10. I had been playing around with myself—not really masturbating, just spelunking my "down there"—and I pulled back some flesh and discovered this amazingly sensitive little knob (it almost felt a little dangerous). It was this hidden, private thing that I gazed at with some hesitancy. My first thought was something along the lines of "What the hell is *that*?!"
>
> Jessica

Women rarely acquired symbolic knowledge about the clitoris until their mid- to late teens but were seldom unaware (or innocent); many discovered "it" long before and were well acquainted with the pleasing sensations it provides. Because "children can recognize that touching their genitalia 'feels good'" (Plante 2006:106), it is not surprising that many women recalled learning, as a child, that some parts of their genitalia felt more pleasurable than others. As Jill reported,

> I discovered my clitoris when I was in third grade. So I was probably about eight. I didn't really know what was going on. I just knew that when I touched a certain spot it would feel really different than when I would touch other places. This discovery usually came along when I couldn't sleep at night.

Several women gave similar testimonials; clitoral sensations were often something they pleasingly discovered entirely for themselves in confidential, clandestine somatic explorations—often during restless nights or in the bathtub—circumstances that provided a measure of privacy, easy access to the genitals, and perhaps motivation as well. . . .

Although unaware that "it" had a name, by discovering its pleasing sensations many women "had" (Dewey [1922] 2002) some of its meanings. In this way, the body *makes sense* because, in part, the body *is sense* (Vannini and Waskul 2006). While "it" may lack symbolic meaning, it is bountiful with the iconic meaning and the "qualitative immediacy" that the body provides. Bodily awareness may be hidden or disappear from consciousness until a "sensory intensification" (Leder 1990:71) takes place, allowing body parts "waiting like tools in a box to be used by conscious resolve" (Dewey [1922] 2002:25).

This is precisely what Kari reported: "I guess I could say I was little, like ten or eleven when I discovered the good feeling of it being rubbed. . . . *I knew what 'it' was before I knew it was a clitoris*" (emphasis added). Experience cannot be understood through language alone; the body is a site of preobjective knowledge (Dewey [1934] 1958, [1922] 2002). As Frank (1995:27) suggests, "The body is not mute, but it is inarticulate; it does not use speech but it begets it." This form of linguistically "pre-reflexive experience" (Csordas 1990:6) proved equally true for women who reported discovering their clitoris by accident. Danielle recalled her discovery:

> The first time I remember having sensations, I was probably nine or ten yrs old, between fourth and fifth grade. I was climbing a pole on the playground and it felt good to climb upwards. I don't remember knowing or understanding what it meant at the time, just that it felt good. I remember not wanting anyone to know why I liked it, although I recall a girlfriend teasing me, so I figured she "knew" too. I don't recall too much from elementary and junior high [school] but I'm guessing I was about fourteen or fifteen when I was using a back massager and it fell into my lap. I suddenly realized what "that" feeling was. I knew I had a clit by then, but probably still had not been told that it was for pleasure. I put the massager away and tried to forget about what happened, but the next time I was home alone I decided to explore more. This is when I discovered that the vibrations felt the best on my clit. I liked it but I didn't want anyone to know.

As is apparent in Danielle's account, some women did not recall so freely exploring their body as a child. Both Beth and Sara did not discover the pleasures of their clitoris until a book motivated carnal exploration. As Beth explained:

> I had begun reading more mature books that had sex in them, and it made me curious. So I started to experiment touching myself. I was in my bed at night and it was a new and thrilling experience. . . . I believe I was in early junior high. . . . I couldn't believe that my body could feel like that and that I had gone so long without knowing it existed.

Beth was surprised that she "had gone so long without knowing it existed," which is understandable considering that "the possibility of pleasure is literally in [her] own hands" (Plante 2006:144), and always had been.

Symbolic Purgatory

> A sensation is only pleasurable or enjoyable, not in itself, but in the context of the meaning of the activity in which it is embedded.
>
> Robert Solomon, "Sexual Paradigms" (1997)

Women generally discovered the pleasures of the clitoris long before they knew it had a name, a circumstance we have described as *symbolic purgatory.* Like Cheryl below, several women remarked on this gap between somatic discovery and discursive knowledge:

> I didn't learn about the clitoris specifically until ninth grade (age fourteen). Before that I had learned about the female genitalia in a rather broad sense. I knew there was more to the female genitalia than just a vagina (learned from general discussion with my family/parents, not really any specific age), but I didn't know what each part was called. In ninth grade health class, my teacher passed out very detailed diagram pictures with everything labeled for both female and male genitalia. . . . In the back of my mind, I vaguely connected the clitoris to the specific part that gave me the most pleasure.

Until learning that their "special spot" is a clitoris, some women—like Sara—"just assumed that it was a part of the vagina but with no specific name." Other women, like Ann, "had no idea other people had a spot like this that felt good to touch." As we have suggested, somatic discovery is a sensual and carnal source of both meaning and information for the embodied self. However, somatic discovery is not entirely language free. For example, our informants often used the euphemism "down there"—with all its connotations of everything sexual, naughty, mysterious, unspeakable, devious, and so forth—and this clearly illustrates how the clitoris is neither confined to discursive darkness nor basking in symbolic transparency. The clitoris inhabits an intermediate state (a purgatory), awaiting linguistic conceptualization, which is evident in Cheryl's recollection: "I knew for many years that it wasn't just a vagina *but [I] never really concerned myself with more than that*" (emphasis added). A similar waiting for discursive cues is equally apparent in the accounts of Jessica and Diana:

> I always knew there was more going on "down there" than just a hole, but *until I was given names and info for the different parts I never really thought much about them.* (Jessica; emphasis added)

> I don't think I ever consciously thought about "the thing down there" *until I learned it had a name.* Once it had a name it was something ok; something more real. (Diana; emphasis added)

The relative muting of the clitoris is all the more significant because, as Rebecca claimed, "it [clitoris] does bring me great sexual pleasure, and when I think about it I usually think about the pleasure I get from it." More than mere vocabulary, language may well constitute a lexicon for experience, in this case the experience of pleasure.

Despite a certain kind of will to discursive knowledge (Foucault 1979), many women remained incapable of finding a label (see Weinberg, Williams, and Pryor 1995) for the clitoris for extended periods of time. For example, Jill wrote, "I'm not even sure I fully understood what a clitoris was until I was almost out of high school." Jill's recollection of uncertainty was consistent with the accounts of many women in this study who also reported a period of vagueness:

> Even after finding out its name (in biology class) there was still the vagueness of the concept. (Jennifer)

> The first time I ever heard the word clitoris was in my seventh grade health class. . . . [W]e got a very academic lesson of the female anatomy, but it took me a while to realize the clitoris on the diagram was the same piece of flesh that I would touch at night. (Beth)

In some cases, women reported learning of their clitoris from peers.[2] As Rochelle explained, she learned of her clitoris in the "later part of high school, from friends my age (mostly the guys talked about it, never the girls)." But her understanding was vague and confused; having heard "the guys talk about it" in reference to oral sex, Rochelle admits, "I didn't know what the clitoris had to do with 'eating out.'"

It was popular media sources that most commonly provided the knowledge that "it" is a clitoris—a telling instance of a society that disguises truth in secrecy while also generating multiple discourses through which secrets can be discovered (Foucault 1979). Jill explained, "No one really told me what it was, I just suddenly put my masturbating sensations together with these words that I kept hearing. I think *Sunday Night Sex Talk* helped me come to the realization." At least Jill recalled learning about her clitoris from a relatively accurate and reliable media source—*Sunday Night Sex Talk* is a cable broadcast featuring a registered nurse-cum-sex expert. Two women reported learning their "special spot" was called a clitoris from an episode of the cartoon *South Park*. Ann wrote:

> It is incredibly strange how I learned that my "special" spot was called the clitoris. I had been sexually active for a while and knew that when the spot was "rubbed" right I would orgasm. I was watching either an episode of or the movie *South Park* and the one character said something about how if you couldn't find a girl's clit you would be a bad boyfriend. This connected in my brain and I formally learned that this place I had been touching for so long and gave me so much pleasure had a name. . . .

Women were generally relieved to learn "it" was a clitoris. Since language is a cultural stockpile of accepted meaning and truth, simply knowing "it" has a name validates and legitimizes both the clitoris and a young woman's body, femininity, and sexuality. A word renders the clitoris a significant symbol—which is significant, indeed:

> I had spent months pleasuring myself before I learned what exactly I was using to do it. It was kind

> of nice to know my body was working properly. (Beth)

> I remember looking down there and kind of wondering about it, to find out later that it felt good, and then had a name. I think I was surprised that it had its own name. It was kind of nice to be able to label it though, and know that it was different from everything else down there. I was excited but embarrassed that I "knew." (Danielle)

Similarly, Ann wrote, "It was a relief to finally know the name." However, Ann also understandably added, "I already knew it was normal, but I thought it was strange I had never learned its function." Her clitoris had been a part of her body all her life, she had already discovered its wonderful pleasures, and yet she was denied basic anatomical knowledge. More than just "strange," some women were resentful:

> As I became aware, I also became resentful because I realized that the clitoral information/definition was kept from me on purpose. This is knowledge that everyone knows, but no one discusses—that frustrates me. (Jennifer) . . .

The Uses of Somatic Pleasure

> [As a child] I used to play with my whole genital region trying to figure out what everything was. I remember that my clitoris was played with more; probably because it felt good. I do remember feeling shameful. My knowledge of sex told me that little girls don't play with themselves. I think that moment has extended through my whole life and dictates my sexual insecurities. I always played with myself in secret cause I was afraid of the consequences of getting caught. This lent a guilty pleasure aspect to sex and the clitoris as a whole.
>
> Cindy

Considering the combined and cumulative effects of symbolic clitoridectomy and the stigma traditionally associated with masturbation—especially among children (Ajzenstadt and Cavaglion 2002)—it is small wonder the clitoris was kept in relative darkness for most of the women in this study. But, as we also illustrated, that darkness is not absolute; the whole area "down there" is shrouded in secrecy and yet subject to becoming visible through a multitude of discourses. This is why women reported—or at least recalled, which is just as significant—discovering their clitoris in circumstances of combined ignorant pleasure *and* shameful carnal knowledge:

> I always thought I was doing something bad, I thought you shouldn't touch yourself in "inappropriate places." I would touch it almost nightly for many years. I think I stopped around 14 or 15 just because I thought it was dirty and I was doing something wrong. (Ann)

> I think I started masturbating or playing with myself at age 9, roughly. I maybe did it a couple times a year if that. As I grew up it interested me more and I did it more. I remember it as my deepest most dirty secret though and I swore I would never tell anyone about what I did. My body wasn't something to be ashamed of, but what I thought about and did was. (Diana)

In view of the relative silence combined with a multitude of confessional discourses that dominate women's understandings of their genitals, it is not particularly surprising that young women who decide to try masturbation might not know what to do. As Sara recalled:

> I remember specifically the first time I masturbated. I was in tenth grade and there was all this hype surrounding this masturbation thing for girls. I asked my friend what it was so I went home and tried it that night. I had no idea what I was doing so I just kinda felt around my vagina. I didn't do any clitoral stimulation (I don't think I had an understanding of what "it" was at the time), I just put my fingers in my vagina. I really didn't get a sense of enjoyment from masturbation at that time so I didn't do it again until I was in college.[3]

Having put off masturbation until her college years, Sara effectively denied herself opportunities to learn about the organ she would *later* discover and regard as the epicenter of her sexuality. Sara wrote that, once she was in college,

> One of my friends bought me a cheap vibrator as a joke for my birthday, and it ended up being the best thing she could have done for me! I decided one night that I would give the new toy a whirl, and I had never been so sexually satisfied. I would say that I masturbate 2–3 times a week now. If I didn't rediscover masturbation I probably wouldn't have such a good sex life. I figured out what I liked and what I needed to be satisfied both alone and with my partner.

Sara's narrative is common for the women in this study; negotiating the shame and guilt associated with masturbation is a common experience, as women acquire knowledge of and about their own bodily desires and claim ownership of their clitoris and sexuality. As Smith (1987:49) notably remarked, women's daily/nightly embodied experiences are "embedded within the particular historical forms of social relations that determine that experience." Thus it is not surprising that some women overcome alienation and reclaim the meanings of their own somatic experiences by "learning the technique" (Becker 1963:46–48) or, in Foucauldian terms, by applying the right technology of care of the self to the desired use of pleasure (Foucault 1988, 1990). For example, Beth reported overcoming her shame and discovering important virtues of masturbation:

> [My] attitude has changed. Currently I masturbate almost every single day. I do not think that people should be afraid of or ashamed to masturbate. It is safe and allows people to gain a better understanding of their own bodies, which is particularly useful when teaching a partner how to pleasure you.

Certainly, some women apparently never touched their clitoris, which they discovered in the throes of a sexual encounter. Conversely, for other women in this study, the sensitivity and precise location of their clitoris allows for sensations that are not necessarily dependent on direct manipulation. For example, Jessica learned to "perceive the effects" (Becker 1963:48–53) of her clitoris on regular occasion, both "tingly reminders" during routine daily activities as well as some secrets that are perhaps best kept:

> I'd say I "encounter" my clitoris as an organ of sexual pleasure several times a day. By that, I mean not just self-stimulation but also the average day-to-day sensations of sitting in class, walking to work, taking a shower and getting tingly reminders. This often occurs when I'm bored—for example, while sitting through a long, dull lecture—and it's like my body's way of telling me that there's still some fun to be had in the world. It's quite nice actually. Kegel exercises coupled with a good fantasy takes the horror out of a 3-hour class. And no one ever knows!

Similarly, Cheryl wrote, "I'm lucky enough to have a fairly accessible clitoris, and simply wearing the right fit of jeans can almost bring me to a minor orgasm." Nonetheless, the majority of the women in this study discovered the pleasures of the clitoris primarily through clandestine exploration of their genitals and masturbation—activities that continue to carry significant stigma and taboo (Ogletree and Ginsburg 2000)—and thus require active (re)negotiations of competing somatic rules.

"Any sensory experience," Carpenter (1973:20) writes, "is partly a skill and any skill can be cultivated." Thus, for many women in this study, cultivating the uses of pleasure—or in Becker's (1963:53–58) words, "learning to enjoy the effects"—overcoming the shame of masturbation, and becoming comfortable touching their own clitoris, proved instrumental in their narrative of personal reckoning with the symbolic purgatory of the clitoris. Indeed, women who shed old somatic rules about masturbation and self-touching often cited enthusiastic benefits of masturbation, namely, the acquisition of useful carnal knowledge:

> That [shame of masturbation] changed as I grew up too. I was 19 when I bought my first vibrator, and even then I "was buying it as a joke for someone else." I had wanted one so much sooner. Now I have 2 of them—had 3 but one wore out! My attitude has changed since then. Now my attitude is very open. I'm open about the fact that I do it, that I like it, that I own vibrators, and what I think about it all. (Diana)

Considering all the ways that the clitoris is muted and potentially colonized by others, it is understandable why Jessica so ardently wrote, "Masturbation, for me, is an act of revolution, an act of defiance, and an act of ungodly enjoyment. I'd recommend it to anyone." An act of revolution and defiance, indeed; in masturbation women not only flick a defiant finger at a taboo but also directly act toward and interact with their clitoris—in defiance of prevailing somatic rules, symbolic purgatory, and symbolic clitoridectomy. In short, women masturbate because it feels good. Yet in masturbation women also interact with their clitoris *on their own terms* and, in the process, potentially evoke important components of their body, sexuality, femininity, and self. It is in this sense that women's somatic work is a "technique of the body" (Mauss [1934] 1973:75). Body techniques, Mauss suggests, share three basic characteristics: they are techniques, in that they rely on the operation of certain movements or forms of experience; they are traditional, in that they are acquired through practice or socialization; and they are efficient, in that they are oriented toward fulfilling a goal or function.

Conclusion

> It is interesting, but somewhat disturbing, to note the strong tendency for women to report they remain silent and do not refer to their own genitals.
>
> Janet S. Sanders and William L. Robinson, "Talking and Not Talking about Sex: Male and Female Vocabularies" (1979)

> Exploring the hidden complexities of being female is a damn edgy thing to do, and it takes a certain amount of guts and determination.
>
> Jessica

Broadly reflecting on our findings, we note two key conclusions. On the one hand, the women in this study illustrated the consequences of symbolic clitoridectomy and the validity of its many critics and criticisms (see Bennett 1993; Braun and Kitzinger 2001a, 2001b; Braun and Wilkinson 2001; Moore and Clarke 1995; Ogletree and Ginsburg 2000; Scheper-Hughes 1991). Symbolic clitoridectomy creates conditions in which the clitoris is a part of a woman's *corporeal* body while simultaneously excised from her *conceptual* body. If we define the "conceptual body" as an abstraction that subsists of significant symbols (primarily language and discourse), then it is also a social structure of knowledge and stock cultural schemas that inform, organize, and configure carnal and sensual experiences. Indeed, as the women in this study candidly reported, the erasure of the clitoris from their conceptual body did not necessarily prevent the carnal discovery of clitoral pleasures, but it did render the clitoris mute, inarticulate, a symbolic terrain that others may occupy—or some combination thereof. On the other hand, the women in this study equally illustrated that the body may be inscribed by discourse—*but it is also made meaningful in action, transaction, and practice* even when the symbolic resources to do so are scarce or contradictory. Sensation is, by definition, emergent from acts of sense making. Thus, as the women in this study illustrated, subjectivity—in this case, sensual embodiment—does not exist prior to experience but flows from it. Further, an object's meanings—including a body part and sensations associated with it—reside not in the object itself but in the interaction or transaction of conduct directed toward it and the qualities emanating from it (Dewey [1934] 1958; Mead 1934; also see McCarthy 1984). Indeed, the women in this study are neither "cultural dupes" nor passive victims of symbolic clitoridectomy but active agents who reflexively made and make meaning of their body and its sensual experiences.

Thus the central dynamic that characterized women's recollections of the discovery of their clitoris is a negotiation between the potential *to sense* the qualitative immediacy of the body and the ability to *make sense* of the see-through-secrecies of symbolic purgatory. Both immediate carnal knowledge *and* emergent and shifting discourses characterize this negotiation. Perceiving the clitoris, using it, naming it, and understanding the significance of the discourses surrounding it is a complex and emergent biographical process: a *career,* if you will, of somatic discovery.

Notes

1. A clear and pertinent example of what we mean by symbolic clitoridectomy and related conditions of symbolic purgatory is expressed in Foucault's four "great strategic unities" of power/knowledge on and about sexuality. According to Foucault, tactics deployed in the political struggle against children's masturbation resulted in a "pedagogization" of children's sexuality and therefore in its productive constitution as a subject of knowledge and discourse. Pedagogization is thus not a case of repression; "what this actually entail[s], throughout this whole secular campaign that mobilized the adult world around the sex of children, [is] using these tenuous pleasures as a drop, *constituting them as secrets* (that is, forcing them into hiding *so as to make possible their discovery*)" (Foucault 1979:43; emphasis added).
2. Other women also reported a similar silence among peers. Even after learning "it" is a clitoris, many women in this study do not recall ever mentioning it again; they were already acculturated to a norm of silence and committed to maintaining it. Indeed, as Diana (age twenty-two) reflects: "[After learning it is called a clitoris,] I still never referred to it openly to anyone—even as I grew up and my girl friends and I would talk about boys and things we did with our boyfriends. I don't think I remember any of us referring to it by name."
3. Sara's account vividly illustrates how sensory skill acquisition is achieved via a process that Leder (1990:351) coined "incorporation," a "bring[ing] within a body": "A skill [that] is finally and fully learned when something that once was extrinsic, grasped only though explicit rules of example, now comes to pervade . . . corporeality." Similarly, in Dewey's ([1922] 2002:126) words, we can understand incorporation as the process whereby acquired habits are reorganized and "modified . . . by redirection of impulses."

References

Ajzenstadt, Mimi and Gabriel Cavaglion. 2002. "The Sexual Body of the Young Jew as an Arena of Ideological Struggle, 1821–1948." *Symbolic Interaction* 25:93–116.

Allan, Keith and Kate Burridge. 1991. *Euphemism and Dysphemism: Language as a Shield and Weapon.* New York: Oxford University Press.

Becker, Howard S. 1963. *Outsiders.* New York: Free Press.

Bennett, Paula. 1993. "Critical Clitoridectomy: Female Sexual Imagery and Feminist Psychoanalytic Theory." *Signs: Journal of Women in Culture and Society* 18:235–59.

Braun, Virginia. 1999. "Breaking a Taboo? Talking (and Laughing) about the Vagina." *Feminism & Psychology* 9:367–72.

Braun, Virginia and Celia Kitzinger. 2001a. "'Snatch,' 'Hole,' or 'Honey-Pot'? Semantic Categories and the Problem of Nonspecificity in Female Genital Slang." *Journal of Sex Research* 38:146–58.

———. 2001b. "Telling It Straight? Dictionary Definitions of Women's Genitals." *Journal of Sociolinguistics* 5(2):214–32.

Braun, Virginia and Sue Wilkinson. 2001. "Socio-Cultural Representations of the Vagina." *Journal of Reproductive and Infant Psychology* 12:17–32.

Carpenter, Edmund. 1973. *Oh What a Blow That Phantom Gave Me!* New York: Holt, Rinehart, and Winston.

Cornog, Martha. 1986. "Naming Sexual Body Parts: Preliminary Patterns and Implications." *Journal of Sex Research* 22:393–98.

Csordas, Thomas, ed. 1990. *Embodiment and Experience: The Existential Ground of Culture and the Self.* Cambridge: Cambridge University Press.

Dewey, John. [1934] 1958. *Art as Experience.* New York: Capricorn.

———. [1922] 2002. *Human Nature and Conduct.* Amherst, NY: Prometheus.

Foucault, Michel. 1979. *The History of Sexuality, Volume One: An Introduction.* Translated by Robert Hurley. New York: Vintage/Random House.

———. 1980. *Power/Knowledge: Selected Interviews and Other Writings, 1972–1977.* Edited and translated by Colin Gordon. New York: Prometheus Books.

———. 1984. "We Other Victorians," Pp. 292–300 in *The Foucault Reader,* edited by P. Rabinow. New York: Pantheon.

———. 1988. *The History of Sexuality, Volume Three: The Care of the Self.* Translated by Robert Hurley. New York: Vintage.

———. 1990. *The History of Sexuality, Volume Two: The Use of Pleasure.* Translated by Robert Hurley. New York: Vintage.

Frank, Arthur. 1995. *The Wounded Storyteller: Body, Illness, and Ethics.* Chicago: University of Chicago Press.

Gartrell, Nanette and Diane Mosbacher. 1984. "Sex Differences in the Naming of Children's Genitalia." *Sex Roles* 10:869–76.

Jackson, Michael. 1977. *The Kuranko: Dimensions of Social Reality in a West African Society.* London: Hurst.

Leder, Drew. 1990. *The Absent Body.* Chicago: University of Chicago Press.

Lerner, H. E. 1976. "Parental Mislabeling of Female Genitals as a Determinant of Penis Envy and Learning Inhibitions in Women." *Journal of the American Psychoanalytic Association* 24:269–83.

Mauss, Marcel. [1934] 1973. "Techniques of the Body." *Economy and Society* 70–88.

McCarthy, Doyle. 1984. "Toward a Sociology of the Physical World." *Studies in Symbolic Interaction* 5:105–21.

McClintock, A. 1992. "Gonad the Barbarian and the Venus Flytrap." Pp. 111–31 in *Sex Exposed: Sexuality and the Pornography Debate,* edited by L. Segal and M. McIntosh. London: Virago.

Mead, George Herbert. 1934. *Mind, Self, and Society.* Edited by C. Morris. Chicago: University of Chicago Press.

Moore, Lisa and Adele Clarke. 1995. "Clitoral Conventions and Transgressions: Graphic Representations in Anatomy Texts." *Feminist Studies* 21:255–302.

Ogletree, Shirley M. and Harvey J. Ginsburg. 2000. "Keep Under the Hood: Neglect of the Clitoris in Common Vernacular." *Sex Roles* 43:917–26.

Plante, Rebecca. 2006. *Sexualities in Context: A Social Perspective.* Boulder, CO: Westview.

Plummer, Ken. 2001. *Documents of Life: An Invitation to a Critical Humanism.* London: Sage.

Sanders, Janet S. and William L. Robinson. 1979. "Talking and Not Talking About Sex: Male and Female Vocabularies." *Journal of Communication* 29:222–30.

Scheper-Hughes, Nancy. 1991. "The Male Discovery of the Clitoris." *Medical Anthropology* 5:25–28.

Smith, Dorothy E. 1987. *The Everyday World as Problematic.* Boston: Northeastern University Press.

Solomon, Robert. [1974] 1997. "Sexual Paradigms." Pp. 21–29 in *The Philosophy of Sex: Contemporary Readings,* edited by A. Soble. 3rd ed. New York: Rowman and Littlefield.

Tisdale, Sallie. 1994. *Talk Dirty to Me: An Intimate Philosophy of Sex.* New York: Anchor.

Vannini, Phillip and Dennis Waskul. 2006. "Body Image Beyond Dualism." Pp. 183–200 in *Body/Embodiment: Symbolic Interaction and the Sociology of the Body,* edited by D. Waskul and P. Vannini. Aldershot, U.K.: Ashgate.

Weinberg, Martin, Colin Williams, and Douglas Pryor. 1995. *Dual Attraction: Understanding Bisexuality.* New York: Oxford University Press.

Reflective Questions

1. How did the authors recruit participants, get consent, and collect data for their study? Why did they engage in such elaborate procedures?
2. In what ways is the clitoris in symbolic purgatory? How is the corporeal body different from the conceptual body? What is symbolic clitoridectomy?
3. When did women learn about their clitoris, and where did they learn it from? Generate a list of the terms you learned for male and female genitalia while growing up. Then, rank the terms according to which your family and friends preferred you use the most to those preferred the least. Was slang favored? By whom? Why? Where did clitoris, vulva, inner and outer labia appear on your list? How did that compare to penis, testicles, and vas deferens? How did your upbringing affect your comfort with reading this article? Would you have been more comfortable reading about male genitalia and sexuality? Why or why not? Why do the authors consider fully naming female genitalia to be important? How did girls'/women's lack of terminology for the clitoris shape their sexual experiences?
4. Perhaps you have read or seen Eve Ensler's play *Vagina Monologues.* If not, take twenty minutes to view some Internet clips of performances at http://www.ted.com/talks/eve_ensler_on_happiness_in_body_and_soul.html, where Ensler reflects on the

Vagina Monologues and V-Day, a social movement to stop violence against women. Which of Ensler's comments draw laughter and why? What role does humor play in symbolic clitoridectomy? What cultural factors influence women's interpretations of sexuality as pleasurable or painful? Now watch Sarah Jones's performance of "Your Revolution" at http://www.youtube.com/watch?v=xRgIGMwZd2o&feature=related. Where did Jones get her lyrics from and how did she remix them? How does popular culture shape women's understandings of their bodies? What cultural materials do women appropriate, reshape, or cultivate to create new ones?

Risky Lessons

JESSICA FIELDS

The previous two selections highlighted how we internalize and negotiate the cultural meanings that become attached to our bodies or bodily organs. Both selections also revealed the social and personal consequences of these cultural meanings, and how these consequences vary profoundly based on our gender. In this selection Jessica Fields explores these themes in more depth, illustrating how sex education classes serve as powerful mechanisms of socialization through which adolescent boys and girls learn, challenge, and reproduce the cultural meanings of sex and sexuality.

Fields draws on data gathered through participation-observation of sex education classes at three middle schools. Two of these schools, Southern and Dogwood, are public institutions. Southern's student body is predominantly African American, while Dogwood's is predominantly white. The third middle school, Fox Academy, is a private Quaker school, and its student body is predominantly white. "Mrs. Wilkie" is the sex education teacher at Dogwood. She teaches sexual education for four days as part of a physical education course. "Ms. Gianni" is the sex education teacher at Southern. She teaches sexual education for two to three weeks as part of a health education class.

Based on her observations of Southern and Dogwood, Fields reveals the hidden and not-so-hidden lessons that boys and girls learn through their sex education classes in public schools. These lessons include the notions that sex is primarily a procreative concern; that it consists of heterosexual pairings; that sexual bodies are thin, modest, and pink-skinned; that sexual pleasure is largely the purview of men; that sex is best discussed in clinical terms that emphasize facts rather than sexual feelings or bodily experiences; and that the key role of the sex educator is to communicate these facts to students in an "objective" manner.

Yet Fields demonstrates how student reactions to depictions of sexual organs and discussions of sexual matters undermine the efforts of public school teachers to present sex education in a neutral and disembodied way. Students are not passive participants in the socialization that takes place in sex education classrooms. Instead, they challenge and often undermine their teachers' attempts to divorce sex education from bodily experiences, strongly felt emotions, and a sense of sexual agency. For instance, students challenge their teachers' definitions of sex education as an objective process by breaking into laughter, expressing embarrassment or disgust, making sarcastic comments, or asking pointed questions about their teachers' sexual activities or contraceptive practices.

In the end, while illustrating how the reality of sex is contested and negotiated in sex education classrooms, Fields also portrays how the messages students receive in these contexts "discipline" their bodily understandings and sexual self-definitions, not only by privileging dominant forms of sexual desire and behavior, but also by silencing alternative forms of sexuality and providing messages that reinforce prevailing social inequalities. At the same time, through comparing the very different form of sex education taught at Fox Academy, Fields demonstrates how sex education can promote greater empowerment and justice, especially by enabling girls, as well as boys, to recognize and embrace their rights to make choices and to experience bodily safety, respect, and pleasure.

Sexual subjectivity is fundamental to young people's sense of agency in all aspects of their lives. As young people learn that they and others can—or cannot—experience, assert, and satisfy sexual desires and boundaries, they also gain a sense of their own and others' abilities to act and effect a range of changes they want to make in their worlds. Adolescence is a period of significant emotional, physical, and social growth for girls and boys in our society. Visceral experiences of puberty, desire, sexual behaviors, and violence make the body of particular importance to girls' and boys' sense that they can make change and have influence. The lessons that both boys and girls learn about what they should expect and seek in bodily sensations, pleasures, and vulnerabilities also contribute to their sense of sexual subjectivity. Sex education classes that obscure bodily experiences and pleasures by offering only disembodied or clinical depictions of the physicality hinder students' development of an agentic sexual subjectivity.

Sexism in our society renders girls' sexual subjectivity and agency particularly vulnerable. Girls in the United States enter puberty earlier than boys and earlier than girls in previous decades (Brooks-Gunn, Petersen, and Eichorn 1985; Herman-Giddens 2006; Herman-Giddens, Slora, Wasserman, Bourdony, Bhapkar, Koch, and Hasemeir 1997). They are young when they confront feminine norms of beauty and behavior that are "more unattainable, more enforced, and more oppressive than those for men" (Martin 1996, 12). The visible changes that girls experience—breast development and widening hips, for example—make them newly vulnerable to unwanted and unsolicited public attention from their peers, older men, and other adults.

Boys' increasing social autonomy and the visible changes of male puberty—for example, hair growth, muscle development, and deepening voices—are markers of strength and power for many. Boys, like girls, contend with norms of heterosexuality that constrain their sexual options and leave gay, bisexual, and feminine boys—any boys who do not conform to the conventions of masculine gender and sexuality—vulnerable to violence and oppression (Russell 2002; Russell and Consolacion 2003; Savin-Williams 1997). Even within this heteronormative context, hegemonic masculinity grants boys status and power; and social scripts allow boys a sense of pride in heterosexual desire and activity, while for many girls—whether straight, lesbian, bisexual, feminine, or masculine—heterosexual desire and activity foster shame (Connell 1987; Tolman 1994a, 1994b, 2002).

Such social concerns slip out of the formal curriculum when sex educators divorce sexual agency and subjectivity from the physiological experiences of puberty and sexuality. In classes on "the plumbing," Mrs. Wilkie asked her Dogwood Middle School students to focus their attention on textbook and video views of internal reproductive organs, seemingly generic anatomical depictions, and challenging terms and definitions to memorize and recall. Similarly, at Southern Middle School, Ms. Gianni had students sit quietly at their desks, copying definitions from overhead transparencies into their notebooks in preparation for weekly vocabulary quizzes. She projected on the screen at the front of the room images of pubescent female and male bodies as generic silhouettes and reproductive organs with precise, thin lines leading from the bodies to descriptions of changes in "primary and secondary sex characteristics." With these gestures, Mrs. Wilkie and Ms. Gianni signaled that students would best understand their embodied experiences of sex and sexuality through rational thought and that adults would be trusted sources of that thought. Within this classroom curriculum, bodily experiences of sex and puberty became issues of fact, no more scintillating than any other middle school health or science class on nutrition, respiratory systems, and dental health.

But those issues that Dogwood and Southern county sex education teachers and administrators regularly called "natural"—pubertal change and sexual desire and activity—are inextricably linked with other bodily issues that the teachers evaded—including socially constructed ideas about power, desire, vulnerability, gender, race, and sexual identities and behaviors. The natural and the social may best be considered *coconstructed*—each helping to create and maintain the other (Haraway 1991). As Lisa Jean Moore and Adele Clark describe, the natural and the social offer each other "particular constraints, opportunities, and resources" (Moore and Clarke 1995, 257). Physical and social capacities and expectations inform each other, make experiences seem more or less possible, and disallow and facilitate relationships and sensations. Recognizing sexuality and bodies as social *and* natural discourages the search for the moment in which sexuality is purely natural or purely social, before the polluting influence of the other. There is no such moment; instead, sexualities are always social and natural. Even apparent "facts" about body parts are infused with social meaning. Images of "natural" bodies reinforce and build on social ideals about thin, white, able-bodied women and men. The consistent pairing of female and male affirms heterosexuality at the expense of other sexual expression. And sex educators' focus on reproduction posits sexuality as a predominantly procreative concern, contributing to an overall muting of sexual pleasure in the ways young people learn about, discuss, and experience their sexual lives. . . .

The Challenges of Embodiment

Anatomical images, sex education videos, and flipcharts are familiar teaching tools that help students and teachers to navigate a range of difficult topics. Claims to science and neutrality help to defuse community concerns about the possibility that discussions of bodies, puberty, and sexuality threaten to corrupt young people. These depictions contribute to a classroom curriculum that makes several assertions: there are facts about sexuality; the teachers' role is to communicate those facts; and it is students' responsibility to learn the facts. The contentious process of talking to young people about pubescent bodies and sexual activity becomes more palatable as anatomical depictions render otherwise dynamic and varying pubescent bodies static and uniform.

At the same time, anatomical images present sex educators with significant challenges. While these bodily images ironically deny much of embodied experience, they also provide incontrovertible evidence that sex education is to a significant extent about bodies. Pictures and discussions of body parts and organs make visible and tangible what may otherwise feel like abstract ideas: "pleasure" becomes erections and orgasms; "pregnancy prevention" becomes condoms slipped over erect penises and diaphragms inserted in vaginas; "puberty" becomes pubic hair, breasts, testicles, perspiration, and menstruation. Talk and images of bodies invite students to locate otherwise abstracted risks and pleasures in their own, their classmates,' and their teachers' bodies. Sexuality becomes something they can experience and recognize in their everyday lives.

With this potential for recognition and identification came yet another challenge for Mrs. Wilkie and Ms. Gianni. Sex educators occupy an especially fraught position in the classroom as they stand before the flipcharts, air the videos, and read aloud the texts that feature the derided "scientific" accounts of female sexuality. Ironically, even as apparently neutral information about sex and reproductive organs was a resource for sex educators trying to maintain control over their classrooms, it was particularly volatile for students. Teachers routinely relied on anatomies and videos to communicate "just the facts" about sexuality and puberty, but, just as routinely, students collapsed into fits of laughter or choruses of groans when they confronted an image of a vulva, descriptions of pubic hair, or a definition of menstruation.

This ritual denigration of the female body made a significant impression on many girls. For example, I asked Kamii, an eleven-year-old African American sixth grader at Southern Middle School, what parts of her sex education class were difficult for her.

Kamii: The boys would see the picture of one of the girls with nothing on them.

Jessica: What did that make you feel like?

Kamii: Weird. . . . That maybe [the boys] could be picturing you, and they might pick on you about some stuff that you have and they don't.

Despite Ms. Gianni's efforts to present the female body in the context of science and rationalism, Kamii, along with many of the other girls, saw a naked girl on the screen and transposed her own body onto that image. The "picture" to which Kamii referred in this interview was any one of a number of illustrated internal views of female sex/reproductive organs; Ms. Gianni did not show pictures of naked girls in her class. Her classmates' derisive reactions to the depicted female bodies thus became reactions to Kamii's and other girls' bodies—not to abstractions. Both girls and boys expressed disgust with women's bodies, but for girls, each display was a public display of *self*-hatred. Participating in a collective scorn toward female organs and functions compelled girls to publicly disavow their own bodies.

Boys rarely expressed similar embarrassment about having to talk with girls about sex and puberty. Perhaps boys were already less accustomed than girls to being objectified, but they did not worry either that their peers would confuse their bodies with the bodies depicted and discussed in class or that the information their peers gained would become fodder for teasing. I asked Charles, an African American sixth grader in Kamii's class at Southern Middle School, how he felt about having sex education with girls. He, like many other boys, said that he sometimes wished they were not in the room, but Charles echoed the sentiments of other boys; "It is kind of neat, though, that they were there because now they know what happens to males also." The threat of bodily knowledge was differently gendered for girls and boys in Ms. Gianni's sixth-grade sex education classroom. Both experienced some embarrassment: girls found that knowledge about their bodies brought vulnerability and attack, while boys took some pleasure in others learning about their bodies.

Teachers were not immune to the denigration of female bodies. As adult women, the teachers I observed bore the female parts—and perhaps engaged in the sexual practices—at which the students laughed, and they often faced sexualizing laughter and harassing comments from their students. Valerie Walkerdine (1990) argues that, though women teachers may hold the structurally powerful position of "teacher" in the classroom, their identities as women leave them vulnerable to students' sexism. Boys—even those in nursery school, Walkerdine finds—can seize the powerful position of men by using demeaning sexist language with their female teachers. Boy students hold power in the classroom because the teacher "is not uniquely a teacher, nor are the boys *just* small boys. . . . [T]he teacher is a woman and while that itself is crucial, it is only because of the ways in which 'woman' signifies that we can understand the specific nature of the struggle. . . . Although [boys] are not physically grown men they can take the positions of men through language, and in doing so gain power which has material effects. . . . In their discourse [the teacher] is constituted as 'woman as sex object,' and as that object she is rendered the powerless object of their oppression" (1990, 5). Walkerdine recounts a scene in which boy nursery-school students harass a teacher with comments about her body, calls for her to shed her clothing, and shouts of "shit" (1990, 4). Even in their youth, the boys held male privilege that vaulted them into positions of power over their adult woman teacher.

I witnessed similar behavior in middle school sex education classes on puberty, although I found in my observations that both girls and boys demeaned women teachers by linking them to the negative connotations of adult female sexuality. On the day that Ms. Gianni discussed pregnancy prevention with the Southern Middle School eighth graders, she brought sample contraceptives to class, including female and male condoms, IUDs, and packages of birth control pills. Some items were from a teaching kit, and others she had purchased at a local pharmacy. Daphne, a white girl with a reputation among teachers for being exceptionally bright and a troublemaker, repeatedly taunted Ms. Gianni: "Are those *your* birth control pills?" Some of Daphne's classmates watched Ms. Gianni for a response; others ignored the exchange. Ms. Gianni ignored Daphne's question.

Daphne's question threw her adult schoolteacher into one of the many double binds that women face (Frye 1983). If Ms. Gianni claimed the birth control pills or condoms as her own, then she revealed herself to be a hypocrite who instructed students to abstain from sexual activity until they were married when she herself was a sexually active, unmarried woman. If she said that the pills and condoms were not hers, she risked labeling herself prudish and suggesting that contraceptive use was embarrassing. Middle school girls and boys harassed women teachers, a reflection on the vulnerability of women sex educators as the in-class embodiment of a vilified adult female sexuality. By insisting that her teacher position herself as a sexual woman, Daphne located Ms. Gianni in a place of public shame. However Ms. Gianni responded, Daphne distanced herself from a despised female sexuality. She also pointed to Ms. Gianni's potential hypocrisy in preaching abstinence though she may have been a sexually active unmarried women. As they marked women teachers as sexual, both girls and boys challenged their teachers' power and distanced themselves from the contaminating presence of female bodies and sexuality.

But Daphne's refusal to allow Ms. Gianni retreat into disembodied female sexuality achieved more than that. She also called Ms. Gianni into an embodied, agentic sexuality. For a brief moment, a woman choosing sexual activity and pleasure was possible in the Southern County sex education classroom. Daphne's question functioned as a potential "release point," one of many "ways of making potential openings in the 'assumed' and the 'common sense'" (Fine and McClelland 2007, 14). The student's transgressive, even harassing, question violated the rules about keeping sex education interpersonal and not associating one's own body with the bodies depicted or discussed in class. Daphne pointed to the lie of schoolbased sex education: none of this is personal; there are no bodies in the classroom. With her question, Daphne interrupted the disembodying formal instruction about bodies with a discourse of sexual pleasure, agency, and subjectivity (Fine 1988) that more than the "facts" of sexuality—definitions, incomplete diagrams, and depersonalized concerns—might address the patriarchal understandings of women's bodies that lay at the heart of the public school-based sex education I observed.

Ultimately, however, public school sex education teachers distanced themselves from the images and bodies they discussed. Their instructional tools—videos, flipcharts, pointers, diagrams, and definitions—emphasized science and rationality and widened the gap between the organs being discussed and any embodied or pleasurable experience of sexuality. While Lee Ann Finch relied on shiny wrapping paper and ribbons to mystify female sexuality in her presentation to the conservative Christian youth group, Ms. Gianni used a three-feet-long pointer when discussing fertilization or menstruation in her public school sex education classroom. The pointer allowed her to gesture toward organs without touching them and to trace bodily processes on the projector screen or flipchart while insisting through her posture that her own body had little to do with the processes and experiences she described. The videos and anatomical depictions on which Ms. Gianni and Mrs. Wilkie relied for most of their visual presentations of bodily concerns allowed the teachers to step out of the students' line of vision as the young people looked and laughed at female bodies. These strategies not only offered important protection from students' harassment, but these strategies also meant that teachers never modeled for students at Dogwood or Southern middle schools a prideful and pleasurable connection to female sexuality and never allowed their adult embodied female sexualities to counter the mystified pink silhouettes of their classroom illustrations. The teachers thus evaded important lessons about students' embodied experiences of sexuality, including sexual expression, desire, pleasure, harassment, and degradation.

Alternative Depictions

At Fox Academy, Jill Carter's discussion of the physiology of women's and girls' sexual pleasure countered the conventional degradation of female bodies and sexuality. Both the substance and the format of Jill's class affirmed female sexuality as pleasurable and embodied. When sharing images of women's sex organs with her white and upper-middle- and middle-class fifth-grade students at this private Quaker school, Jill sat cross-legged on the floor with a copy of the diagrams being discussed in front of her and between her legs. Jill pointed out the relevant organs and explained their functions, and when she got to the external view of a woman's sex organs she continued to hold the sheet between her legs and in front of her vulva. The effect of the worksheet's position and her posture was to allow her audience—the students and I—to transpose easily the images we saw on the worksheet onto her body.

I immediately felt uncomfortable, wondering if Jill realized what she was doing. I considered briefly how I might signal to Jill that she should move the diagram, and then I realized that I wanted Jill to protect herself, her students, and me from the embarrassment of associating the depicted female sex organs with her own body. Though I was troubled by students' embarrassed reactions to female sexuality, I seemed also to have internalized it. The picture between Jill's legs included the woman's clitoris, anus, labia, and vaginal and urethral openings. I knew these terms made many Fox students laugh in class. The terms also—with their connections to hair-to-shave, periods-to-manage, and hygiene-to-maintain—invoked shame in many women and girls. I was surprised to see Jill aligning herself with the body on the handout; her gestures differed markedly from what I had witnessed at the public Southern and Dogwood middle schools, where students and teachers consistently distanced themselves from anatomies and bodily experiences.

Jill's classroom curriculum lesson allowed an association between her body and that of the embodied female sexuality depicted in the drawing. Jill's instruction offered new grounds on which girls and boys might develop their sexual subjectivities. In much sex education, women's bodies remain absent or are present only as vulnerable, potentially pregnant, or unhygienic. By modeling an embodied sexual subjectivity, Jill suggested that girls and women could publicly experience and claim pleasure in their bodies.

Frank discussions of bodies and pleasure occupied a central position in Jill's instruction. At one class meeting, Jill distributed photocopied diagrams of female and male sex organs, internal and external views. She also handed out sheets defining the organs and asked for student volunteers to read definitions aloud. As their classmates read, the students heard about pleasure, sexual pleasure, and reproductive function. For example, according to Jill's handout, the penis "has three functions: 1) you urinate from it; 2) it gives sexual pleasure when it is rubbed, touched, or stimulated; 3) it's the passageway through which semen containing sperm leaves the body." Kendra read the definition of "clitoris": "The clitoris a small mound of skin about the size of a pea. When the clitoris is gently touched or rubbed, a woman's body feels good outside and inside." When she finished reading this definition—a far cry from the "erectile tissue" definition that Ms. Gianni offered at Southern Middle School—Kendra laughed and blushed. Her reaction was typical of students discussing sex organs and reproduction. Rarely did any students I observed at Southern, Dogwood, or Fox middle schools make it through a class on puberty or sexual behavior without some display of discomfort, embarrassment, or even revulsion. Unlike the teachers at the other schools, however, Jill insisted that the students push through their embarrassment.

As Kendra sat and squirmed, Jill stepped in. Rather than insist that Kendra stop laughing, Jill gently confirmed that, as Kendra had read, the clitoris was about the size of a pea, though it "varies from woman to woman." Jill also told the students that in her own tenth-grade sex education class, she had not learned about the clitoris. Jill's teacher had believed that, since the clitoris does not "really have anything to do with reproduction," students did not need to know about it. Jill paused, apparently offering them time to absorb the significance of the teacher's omission. The students sat quietly. They appeared attentive but cautious.

In contrast to this teacher from her childhood, Jill insisted that her students learn about the clitoris and sexual pleasure. Now that she had introduced students to the anatomy of the clitoris, Jill wanted to discuss its function in women's sexual lives. The clitoris "is really about sexual pleasure," Jill explained, "It's the equivalent to one function of the penis, right?" Jill had previously discussed the external view of men's bodies and was referring to her explanation of how boys and men experience sexual pleasure with their penises. Dante, a popular, easy-going white boy, answered "Right" as most of the other students laughed and blushed. Girls' cheeks reddened as they laughed and kept their heads down. Boys grinned widely and looked around the room at their friends. With this assertion, Jill established pleasure as a fundamental bodily function for girls, boys, women, and men.

Jill continued through the students' laughter and blushing. She pointed to the distance between the vaginal opening and the clitoris: Did the students see how they were quite a bit apart? They nodded, uncharacteristically quiet. "Why would I mention that they are separate?" asked Jill. Gabrielle offered that Jill might be talking about what would happen if a girl or woman were peeing. Jill replied that was a good point; the opening to the urethra (another word that sent the students into giggles) was not immediately next to the clitoris, and the clitoris was not part of urinating. But "in terms of intercourse—*heterosexual* intercourse—why would I mention it?" The students had no answer, so Jill went on. She said that in heterosexual intercourse, a man's penis moved in and out of the woman's vagina. "That movement in and out stimulates the man's penis, and that's how he feels pleasure." If the clitoris is the center of a woman's sexual pleasure, "some women won't feel as much pleasure" during heterosexual intercourse. The students had been giggling and blushing throughout Jill's explanation. At its close, they laughed out loud, in an apparent release of the embarrassed energy that had been building as Jill spoke.

Although Jill did not participate in the conventional muting of sexual pleasure, she did present a limited picture of female pleasure as a biological or physiological concern. In recent years feminist researchers have argued that the clitoris is a network of nerve endings and muscles that extend throughout a woman's vulva (Chalker 2000; Federation of Feminist Women's Health Centers 1991). Jill based her lesson on a 1970s feminist argument that the vaginal orgasm was a myth (Koedt 1973). In the 1960s and 1970s, women—bolstered by the work of Masters and Johnson (1966)—asserted that vaginal-penile sex is male-centered. In the last decade of the twentieth century, however, feminist women's health and sexuality activists asserted that women can and do enjoy a range of sexual acts—including vaginal penetration—because they stimulate the whole (not simply the glans) of the clitoris. Jill acknowledged quietly this ambiguity as she concluded that the clitoris is "a little bit removed," and "to feel pleasure," some women might want "more direct stimulation of the clitoris during lovemaking." However, how girls and women would achieve clitoral stimulation may have remained a mystery for some students because Jill did not directly acknowledge oral sex, digital stimulation, masturbation, and other activities. She also did not engage the social and political issues at stake. She suggested, but did not state directly, that men were not always willing to stimulate their female partners' clitorises and that women often felt inhibited about requesting such touch or touching themselves during heterosexual activity. Jill remained silent about the social conditions that afford men's sexual desires priority and that systemically mute women's desires.

Jill's story of having been denied the same information when she was in high school suggested that attitudes about women, education, and sexuality were changing. The story also highlighted that Jill, unlike her tenth-grade teacher, understood sexuality to be about more than reproduction. Though Jill continued to privilege straight sexuality in her focus on how the clitoris might not be stimulated in vaginal-penile intercourse, she took care to specify that she was discussing heterosexual—and not all—intercourse. Allowing for a range of sexual practices distinguished Jill from the public school teachers I observed, who almost always spoke of "sex" as if it referred exclusively to heterosexual, vaginal-penile intercourse. Jill also assumed that girls and women would want to experience sexual pleasure, an assumption not common in the debates and classes I observed in the public schools.

Fox students also found pleasure in learning about bodies. The models of sex organs were the crowning moment of Jill's class at Fox. The assignment was to create three-dimensional representations of female or male sex organs using brightly-colored foam, sequins, pipe cleaners, cotton balls, and other items Jill had purchased at a local store selling non-recyclable items—plastics, fabrics, wires, and more—for $5 a bag. Examples from previous semesters of Jill's sex education classes hung on her classroom walls. Students admired them throughout the semester and looked forward to the end of the term when they could make their own. Jill allowed the students to form their own groups and to decide as a group whether they would construct a model of female or male sex organs. Consistently, the students opted for single-sex groups of two or three, with girls making models of female sex organs, and boys of male organs. At no point did I see a student claim an interest in body parts that might have signaled to their peers an interest in the "opposite" sex.

The classes devoted to creating the models were fun. The students enjoyed debating what was the "perfect" material for pubic hair; steel wool worked well, as did pipe cleaners. They discovered that polished glass would make a good clitoris, and only an appropriately sized foam tube would do to represent the penis. Unlike the smooth, generic bodies routinely featured in textbooks, videos, and handouts, the Fox students' models were bright, funny, and hairy. Fox girls included tampons and labia-zippers that they could zip open and shut, laughing as they considered the possibility of offering and then denying access to their bodies. Everyone laughed when Marshall arrived in class with the model he had worked on at home the night before: Marshall had created a battery-operated penis that became erect when someone flicked the appropriate toggle switch.

Jill laughed and celebrated the students' creativity with them. At the end of the term, she issued awards, using categories derived from comments students had made on one another's models. For example, one model of female sex organs was named "most like a skittles bag," in recognition of the multi-colored yarn the girls had painstakingly wrapped around their model's fallopian tubes. The awards, affirming the students' values and perspective, echoed the students' responses to one another's work. And perhaps most important, at Fox, students authored the anatomical depictions by creating and not simply consuming images of puberty and bodies. The fanciful anatomies represented the facts: Jill insisted that students spell the terms correctly and that the students approximate the organs' size and relationship to one another. At the same time, however, the bright colors and imaginative presentations challenged the seriousness of the sex education teachers' task of presenting the facts. Fox students witnessed a proliferation of anatomical images, all student creations and all calling for an engaged and playful relationship with one's education and body.

Conclusions

At Southern and Dogwood middle schools, discussions about bodies and puberty approached sexuality as a natural and normal part of all people's lives, concerns that youth could navigate with accurate facts in hand. Fundamental to successful navigation were anatomical depictions that, on the one hand, acknowledge that sexuality is a bodily experience and, on the other, clarify the limits of that experience. Sex education classes included formal and hidden lessons that suggested a clinical and disembodied experience of sexuality. Look, but do not touch. Understand this system, but do not consider how it works with others. Know the parts, but only in particular ways. These limits are especially mystified when teachers and administrators present sex, puberty, and sexuality exclusively as matters of factual information.

As sex education teachers recognize young people as sexual, they also train students in the practices of recognition. Sex education's lessons both open and limit possibilities. Sex education is among the few classes to acknowledge students' embodied experiences of youth and to introduce desire and embodied experiences into an institution that is otherwise "delibidinizing (eros-denying)" (McLaren 1991, 191). Sex education recognizes young people and their worlds as sexual and encourages them to recognize sexuality in themselves and others. In particular, visual representations—sometimes anatomies, silhouettes, internal views, external views, and other times a shoebox wrapped in fancy ribbon—offer students images of sexual bodies and, in doing so, model particular relationships to embodied desires, choices, and behaviors. For example, how will students look at bodies? Will they see skin and pubic hair? Will they see erect or flaccid penises? Will those organs be part of a sexual system or a reproductive system? Will the organs be part of a larger body?

The disciplining implications of sex education's depictions of bodies are readily apparent in representations (and misrepresentations) of the clitoris. Female sexuality is not simply a matter of the clitoris or contraceptive choices; women and girls experience pleasure, desire, and vulnerability throughout the whole of their bodies and in a range of relationships and behaviors. However, the clitoris is especially meaningful in any discussion of women's sexuality. Excising the clitoris from images and discussions of female sexuality obscures girls' capacity for sexual pleasure, subjectivity, and agency; and the routine exclusion of fully embodied depictions of women's sexuality from sex education textbooks and videos reflects the routine silencing of women's sexual desire in school-based sex education. Sex educators omitting the clitoris from depictions of women's bodies and failing to offer students images of women using, choosing, and living with contraceptive options denies girls and boys an opportunity to recognize women's capacity for pleasure and agency. Recognizing this capacity would help girls and women recognize their potential for joy, identify the constraints on that potential, and struggle to remove them. Boys and men might also learn how to participate in women's pleasure.

Additional normalizing lessons emerge in the depictions: the absence of people of color, people with disabilities, people whose bodies do not conform to norms of thinness and modesty are absent; and an uninterrupted stream of pink-skinned anatomical images and lead characters in sex education's illustrations of pubescent and sexual bodies are ever present. As Karin Martin notes, "Adolescence is a time for making sense and self out of a newly changed body" (1996, 57). Sex education offers young people one of their few structured and informed opportunities for making sense and self. However, many students spend their time in sex education making sense of someone else's body and finding only limited potential there for making any sort of self.

Sex education classrooms contribute not only to the silencing of non-conforming sexuality but also to privileging of already dominant sexual desire and behaviors. Sex educators often recognize male sexual pleasure, albeit as biological and often involuntary concerns—wet dreams, ejaculations, and erections. In contrast, the physiology of girls' sexual pleasure—clitorises, orgasms, and lubrication—was usually absent. Like much other sex education in the United States, formal curricula in Southern and Dogwood middle schools routinely ignored female orgasms and other issues of girls' sexual pleasure and instead focused on issues of reproduction, hygiene, and modesty (Brumberg 1997; Fine 1988). These formal lessons foster hidden lessons about girls' and boys' capacities for pleasure, subjectivity, and agency. In these public schools, boys hear about their bodies as sites of pleasure and agency, while girls contend with what Michelle Fine (1988) has called a missing discourse of desire in sex education's treatment of their subjectivity.

Similarly, other students whose bodies and lives do not conform to a norm of whiteness, physical ability, and attractiveness encounter no depictions of their bodies as making choices, experiencing pleasure, and navigating the challenges of puberty and youth.

Young people's paths to agentic sexual subjectivity require a reflective engagement with the ways that their bodies feel to themselves and a critical understanding of the meanings that others attach to their bodies. Youth need to consider not only how their bodies change during puberty, but also what those changes imply for the possibilities for pleasure, vulnerability, and violence in their lives. Girls and boys require opportunities to recognize and develop their capacity to claim and assert their right to bodily safety, needs, and joy.

The students at Fox enjoyed such an opportunity as their teacher aligned herself with the bodies they discussed and encouraged the students to author images of female and male sex organs. The formal content of the Fox students' lessons did not stray markedly from that in the public schools. However, the classroom behavior of their teacher allowed the Fox students to witness an unflinching, frank female sexuality. Jill offered her students this example with the support of her school. Fox Academy faculty committed themselves to supporting their gay, lesbian, and bisexual colleagues and students. They rallied as a community in the face of homophobic graffiti and joking. They located sex education in a middle school Personal Growth curriculum. Throughout the school day, teachers and students provided one another support as sexual beings facing discrimination, forming families, and coming to a sense of self. Within such a context, Jill had the freedom to claim and assert women's and girls' right to sexual pleasure and respect. Without such a context, Mrs. Wilkie and Ms. Gianni, Jill's colleagues at Southern and Dogwood, distanced themselves from the sexuality that they embodied and discussed in their classrooms.

The lessons that sex education offers students about their bodies are neither natural nor sacred. Wrapping puberty, youth, and sexuality in mystifying [messages] or frank science only mutes—and cannot erase—political and social concerns. Even as the teachers offer students the facts about the "plumbing," anatomical images and narratives in handouts, videos, and textbooks provide students with important hidden and evaded lessons about puberty, bodily changes and functions, and sexual behaviors—ultimately, people's places in the world.

References

Brooks-Gunn, Jeanne, Anne Peterson, and Dorothy Eichorn. 1985. "Time of Maturation and Psychosocial Functioning in Adolescence," *Journal of Youth and Adolescence* 14:149–159.

Brumberg, Joan Jacobs. 1997. *The Body Project: An Intimate History of American Girls.* New York: Random House.

Chalker, Rebecca. 2000. *The Clitoral Truth: The World at Your Fingertips.* New York: Seven Stories Press.

Connell, R. W. 1987. *Gender and Power: Society, the Person, and Sexual Politics.* Stanford, CA: Stanford University Press.

Federation of Feminist Women's Health Centers. 1991. *A New View of a Woman's Body.* New York: Feminist Press.

Fine, Michelle. 1988. "Sexuality, Schooling, and Adolescent Females: The Missing Discourse of Desire," *Harvard Educational Review* 58 (1): 29–53.

Fine, Michelle and McClelland, Sara I. (2007). "The politics of teen women's sexuality: Public policy and the adolescent female body." *Emory Law Journal*, 56(4): 993–1038.

Frye, Marilyn. 1983. *The Politics of Reality.* Trumansburg, NY: The Crossing Press.

Haraway, Donna J. 1991. "Situated Knowledges: The Science Question in Feminism and the Privilege of Partial Perspective," in *Simians, Cyborgs, and Women: The Reinvention of Nature,* 183–201. New York: Routledge.

Herman-Giddens, Marcia. 2006. "Recent Data on Pubertal Milestones in United States Children: The Secular Trend Toward Earlier Development," *International Journal of Andrology* 29 (1):241.

Herman-Giddens, Marcia, Eric J. Slora, Richard C. Wasserman, Carlos J. Bourdony, Manju V. Bhapkur, Gary G. Koch, and Cynthia M. Hasemeir. 1997. "Secondary Sexual Characteristics and Menses in Young Girls Seen in Office Practice: A Study from the Pediatric Research in Office Settings Network," *Pediatrics* 99: 505–512.

Koedt, Anne. 1973. *Radical Feminism*. Quadrangle Press.

Martin, Karin A. 1996. *Puberty, Sexuality, and the Self: Boys and Girls at Adolescence*. New York: Routledge.

Masters, William H. and Virginia E. Johnson. 1966. *Human Sexual Response*. London: Little, Brown.

McLaren, Peter. 1991. "Schooling the Postmodern Body: Critical Pedagogy and the Politics of Enfleshment," in *Postmodernism, Feminism, and Cultural Politics: Redrawing Educational Boundaries*, edited by Henri A. Giroux, 144–173. Albany, NY: State University of New York Press.

Moore, Lisa Jean, and Adele Clarke. 1995. "Clitoral Conventions and Transgressions: Graphic Representations in Anatomy Texts, c. 1900–1991," *Feminist Studies* 21 (2): 255–301.

Russell, Stephen T. 2002. "Queer in America: Citizenship for Sexual Minority Youth," *Applied Developmental Science* 6 (4): 258–263.

Russell, Stephen T., and Theodora B. Consolacion. 2003. "Adolescent Romance and Emotional Health in the U.S.: Beyond Binaries," *Journal of Clinical Child and Adolescent Psychology* 32: 499–508.

Savin-Williams, Ritch C. 1997. . . . *And Then I Became Gay: Young Men's Stories*. New York: Routledge.

Tolman, Deborah L. 1994a. "Daring to Desire: Culture and the Bodies of Adolescent Girls," in *Sexual Culture and the Construction of Adolescent Identities*, edited by Janice M. Irvine, 250–284. Philadelphia: Temple University Press.

———. 1994b. "Doing Desire: Adolescent Girls' Struggles for/with Sexuality," *Gender and Society* 8 (3): 324–263.

———. 2002. *Dilemmas of Desire: Teenage Girls Talk About Sexuality*. Cambridge, MA: Harvard University Press.

Walkerdine, Valerie. 1990. *Schoolgirl Fictions*. Brooklyn, NY: Verso.

Reflective Questions

1. What is sexual subjectivity? What makes girls' sexual subjectivity particularly vulnerable? How were female bodies denigrated during sex education lessons?
2. Why did teachers at Dogwood and Southern take a sterile approach—fact-based and neutral—to sex education? How did teachers distance themselves from the bodies they were discussing?
3. What was sex education at Fox Academy like? Why was it so different? How did the teacher align the lessons with her own body and the lessons she had been taught in school?
4. What are the hidden lessons of sex education? How might the lessons children learn matter for their own sexual subjectivity?
5. Think back to your own sex education. Who taught you about sex? What did you learn about sex from family members, places of worship, the media, or school? Do the lessons reflect those described by Fields? What social factors account for the similarities or differences in what people taught you?
6. The media expose children to different lessons about sexuality, pleasure, and the body. What lessons do they teach? How do these lessons shape sexual experience? When children learn competing ideas about sexuality, how do they resolve them? Who are they most likely to believe when it comes to sex? Why?

14

Disciplining Corpulence

AMANDA CZERNIAWSKI

The body is an instrument of control, both as subject and object. We discipline bodies through regimentation, surveillance, and manipulation. We plump up or down in places through diet, weight lifting, or surgical implants. We weigh ourselves and strive to meet particular measurement benchmarks. We hold our shoulders and feet in specific ways, and we ornament ourselves through styling. All of these practices treat the body as something to be monitored and shaped through concerted, repeated effort. That is, we take ourselves as an object to be acted upon. This treatment of the physical produces what Michel Foucault termed "docile" bodies, ones that operate in the ways we want: with speed, grace, strength, suppleness, or agility.

How we experience and discipline our bodies is profoundly shaped by the symbolism we attach to particular performances of the body and physical forms. One salient meaning in Western cultures, for example, links the capacity to master—one's physical urges, nature, deficiencies—with morality or value. Being able or unable to overcome these things says something to others and to ourselves about how worthy we are of respect. Thus, the experience of chronic pain is not simply physical in nature; it also has emotional and identity-related implications. In turn, we discipline bodies in order to reinvent ourselves and what we experience as inhabitants of our bodies. We manipulate bodies to meet the expectations of others, feel sensations we learn to crave, transform ourselves into desired commodities, and become the types of people we want to be. Bodily symbolism and the creation of an embodied self, then, are social processes created through our ongoing interactions.

In Femininity and Domination, *philosopher Sandra Bartky turns our attention to the consequences of body discipline for the self. She argues that women experience a unique form of objectification of the body. Cultural prescriptions inscribe their bodies with practices that mark their subordination and deficiency. Simultaneously, their bodies come to represent their entire being, and they become instruments for others to experience and use for their own purposes. This contradictory experience of the body leads to a fragmented and constricted self. Women lose the capacity for self-expression and necessarily distance themselves from their physical self, which brings scrutiny if not disapproval. The question becomes, why do women so readily participate in narcissistic bodily practices? For Bartky, the answer lies in women's attempts to "lessen their sense of bodily deficiency" (p. 41). Women understand that others appraise them based on their looks. They come to view their bodies as others do, and they do it first because of the importance of understanding others' appraisal—they in part determine women's life prospects. As Bartky puts it, women are both the seer and seen. Women, in turn, discipline their bodies in the name of self-preservation.*

Reprinted from: Amanda Czerniawski, "Disciplining Corpulence: The Case of Plus-Size Fashion Models," *Journal of Contemporary Ethnography* 41(2): 127–153, April 2012.

In Amanda Czerniawski's study, plus-size models come to see their bodies through the eyes and demands of casting agents, fashion designers, photographers, consumers, and clothing manufacturers, what Czerniawski collectively calls the "spectacle of fashion." As Czerniawski's own experiences modeling show, the bifurcation that Bartky describes is alive and well for plus-size models. Fashion offers a unique opportunity for them to feel special and liberated from the stigma of being overweight. At the same time, it demands scrutiny and manipulation of bodies to maintain others' approval. And plus-size models do approach their bodies with vigilance: enhancing their curves with body shapers and padding, eating and exercising to maintain weight, measuring, and avoiding weight loss. They respond to the demands of agents and clients. When they do not, they risk losing work and valuable income.

But, just as Bartky argues, even successful disciplining of the body comes at a cost for the women in Czerniawski's study. Models are "haunted by a continual sense of imperfection," that their bodies—and they themselves—are not good enough. Women risk eating disorders, physical trauma, and emotional pain. Although women proudly display their curves and fat bodies, their bodies are still a commodified object, subject to preexisting ideals evident throughout the fashion industry about what makes women beautiful and valuable. The result, Czerniawski reveals, is a disembodied self.

Flash.
"Chin up and out."
Flash.
"Tilt your head a bit to your left . . . and hold it right [pause] there."
Flash.

I received another instruction from the photographer to shift my pose in some seemingly indiscriminate way. Each flash represented another frame of film. Within less than five minutes, the photographer shot a whole roll of film. Each minute the photographer peered through her camera lens translated to at least an hour of preparation in hair and makeup. But in that immortalized moment, I realized the extent to which a model needs to know her body to be able to command and control each minute muscle, as she contorts herself into positions directed by a photographer. A fashion model needs to know how her body moves, how to camouflage unsightly bits, and which camera angles best flatter the female form in order to capture a desired look.

That day in front of the camera was part of my ethnographic account of becoming a plus-size fashion model. I encountered, firsthand, the struggle to rewrite the self, wherein a woman wittingly objectifies and to a necessary degree celebrates her body—a body of curves and solid flesh that is often an object of scorn in contemporary American society. With society regarding models as walking mannequins or passive hangers for clothes, I examined how it felt to be "just a body," a body that was average in society but "plus-size" in fashion.

The basic definition of "plus-size" in modeling does not match the cultural image of a fat woman. Most casual observers of plus-size models would not perceive them as "plus-size" or even fat. Indeed, many of these models are of "average" size and weight; retail industry experts estimate that the average American woman weighs approximately one hundred sixty pounds and wears a size fourteen (Vesilind 2009). They are "average" to the ordinary consumer, but, in sharp contrast, they are "plus-size" to the fashion industry. Typically, the industry considers anything over a size eight as "plus-size."

Yes, according to fashion, these plus-size models are fat and they, too, self-identified as fat. These models acknowledged that they work in an industry that has strict and often extreme bodily standards. For example, designer label Ralph Lauren fired model Filippa Hamilton for being too fat (Melago 2009). Hamilton is five feet ten inches tall, weighs 120 pounds, and wears a woman's size four. Both Coco Rocha, whom the industry considers "too big" for high fashion at a size four, and Gemma Ward lost work opportunities because of weight gain (Diluna 2010; Horne 2010).

Generally, plus-size models range from a woman's clothing size ten to size twenty, but most of the models in the top modeling agencies are size ten to size fourteen and must be a minimum height of five feet eight inches, with a usual maximum of six feet tall. In contrast, "straight-size" fashion models (i.e., those we typically see in print advertisements and catalogues), wear a size two through size six, while runway models are smaller and wear between a size zero to size four, depending on each design season's aesthetics. The recent emergence of plus-size models onto the mainstream media landscape provides an opportunity to explore whether their work creates a new "fat aesthetic." Using participant observation and interviews, I document an intensive aesthetic labor process, whereby these models continually develop their bodies according to the demands of their fashion employers. This analysis expands our understanding of aesthetic labor as (1) an ongoing production of the body that involves affective, emotional, and physical labor that (2) depends on preexisting aesthetic ideals that (3) perpetuate women's sense of disembodiment.

Research Method

This personal account of the lived body "under construction" offers new direction in the developing field of carnal sociology, as developed by Loïc Wacquant, and critical insight into the biographical persona of the plus-size model. I took the perspective of the insider, going beyond the traditional ethnographic approach of observation to step into the role of my subject. In this approach, my body became a "tool for inquiry" and a "primary vector of knowledge" as I learned how to walk and pose and transformed from a woman into a model (Wacquant 2004). In the vein of carnal sociology, I drew on the physical experience of the plus-size model as fashion professionals measured, clothed, and posed me. This is a visceral insider account that engaged both the physical and mental nature of modeling. To understand the modeling industry, I learned how to model, for "sociologists who want to understand meaning-making in everyday life have to observe and experience these embodied practices, as they unfold in real time and space, and materialize in real bodies. We, like the people we study, must learn the practices" (Eliasoph 2005, 160). . . .

Data Collection

This study draws on twenty-two months of ethnographic field research conducted at multiple open calls, go-sees, and castings in New York City, recognized as one of the world's leading fashion capitals and home to many leading designers and modeling agencies. Given its overall prominence in fashion, New York City is also home to many top plus-size modeling agencies. During most of my research, I actively pursued modeling work. Combining participant observation and interviews, I met working plus-size models while waiting at castings and jobs and kept field notes on the lived experience of working in the modeling industry. Because of the physical nature of modeling work, I was unable to record observations as they occurred in real time. At the end of a casting session, fitting, or shoot, I retreated to a nearby coffee shop and wrote extensive field notes, relying on my memory to reconstruct events and conversations. While in a casting session or on the job, I was unable to conduct formal interviews with models. Instead, I engaged in informal conversation with them while we waited and then invited them to participate in an open-ended, semi-structured interview either after the casting or at a later scheduled date and time. Conducted in a public place, often a coffee shop, the interviews lasted between one and two hours, with additional followup interviews over the course of the study. In this manner, I gathered a snowball sample of thirty-five plus-size models. To maintain confidentiality, I changed names of people, places, and agencies when requested. . . .

While getting participants for interviews took nominal effort, fitting into a plus-size model crowd posed its own challenges. Often I entered a casting and realized that the other plus-size models grossly outmatched me in terms of experience and amount of curves. Physically, at a size ten, I was at the "small" end of plus-size. At one particular casting, I was, in more blatant descriptive terms, the "token skinny white chick." Coupling my "smaller" stature with the fact that I was racially and ethnically in the minority, my usual role as marginal insider shifted to that of an outsider amid a roomful of glares from the other models. In this case, my token status served as an advantage, given that several models did not perceive me as their competition for the job and agreed to participate in my study.

Participants

. . . The models self-reported their sizes, which ranged from ten to twenty-two with a mode size of fourteen/sixteen. The women ranged in age from eighteen to thirty-four, with an average age of twenty-seven. These plus-size models were older and larger than straight-size fashion models, who model between the ages of fourteen and twenty-four and normally retire from modeling by the time plus-size women start their own modeling careers. It is not uncommon for plus-size models to work into their forties. Of the thirty-five participants, sixteen identified as white, fifteen as African American, and four as Hispanic. Most had some level of college education and worked outside the modeling industry in some capacity. None of the models I met, whether freelance or represented by an agency, listed modeling as their main source of income. Some worked in related artistic fields, such as performance, design, or sales, while others held jobs in the healthcare or legal professions as nurses or paralegals, for example. Others worked as personal assistants or in temporary clerical positions. . . .

Physical Labor

While the participants in this study did not model full-time, they spent a majority of their time finding work and engaging in physical labor to keep their bodies camera-ready. A model must prepare her body for the performance of modeling. Her job is to use her body to strike the right pose and "sell a garment" for a client. In order to effectively do so, a model regulates and disciplines her body. By way of toning and shaping her body through diet and exercise or artificial enhancements, the model prepares her body for the needs of clients.

Contrary to cultural perceptions of fat women, plus-size models are disciplined and engage in constant monitoring and management of their bodily capital. Wacquant utilizes the case of the boxer to explain this concept of bodily capital:

> The successful pursuit of a career [in boxing] . . . presupposes a rigorous management of the body, a meticulous maintenance of each one of its parts, an attention of every moment, in and out of the ring, to its proper functioning and protection. . . . The pugilist's body is at once the *tool* of his work—an offensive weapon and defensive shield—and the *target* of his opponent. (2004, 127)

Here, the boxer's body is a form of commodified physical capital, requiring monitoring and training in order to win a match.

In this way, bodily capital becomes essential to the boxer's habitus, a bodily state of being that is both a medium and outcome of social practice (Bourdieu 1984). Both Wacquant's boxers and the plus-size models in this study convert their bodily capital, that is, the shape and active capacity of a body, into economic capital. For the plus-size model, her body is her career. The condition of her body, the size, shape, and muscle tone, determines her chances for employment.

Training the body increases its utility and capital. In their ethnographic study of aging ballet dancers, Wainwright and Turner (2006) refine Bourdieu's concept of bodily capital. To better describe the athletic nature of the professional dancer, Wainwright and Turner divide the concept of "athletic physical capital" into four criteria: speed, strength, stamina, and suppleness. All four aspects are present in athletes with differing levels of concentrated development. While a dancer may focus on increasing suppleness, a boxer will train to increase strength and speed.

Modeling is similar to other fields, such as sex work, which focus on engendered physical capital, where a worker commodifies her body. For example, both sex workers and fashion models modify their physical appearance to achieve a successful performance of the body. As Wesely (2003) and

Murphy (2003) argue, exotic dancers manipulate their bodies via numerous body technologies to prepare themselves for their public performance as sexualized bodies for male clients. For example, it is not uncommon for an exotic dancer to undergo breast augmentation to achieve the "Barbie doll" body and receive more attention and money from her clients.

Likewise, the models in this study undertook rigorous and meticulous means to manage their bodily capital and trained to increase what I argue is their "model physical capital," measured by body size and shape, runway walk, posing ability, and photogenic features. They cared for their bodies to maintain their buxom figures and participated in ritualistic skin care and grooming regimens. While photographic retouching eliminates the occasional pimple, a model's complexion must be clear and washed thoroughly after a day on set wearing professional-grade makeup. They invested in their smile, straightening and whitening their teeth. Most turned to artificial bodily enhancements to achieve a desired, proportionate figure.

For models with less than ideal proportions, Larissa Laurel explained a trick of the modeling trade:

> Some models, like me, are blessed with big bottoms, but our bust is on the smaller size. So do you know what we do? We stuff our bras with the pillow cups which we lovingly refer to as "chicken cutlets." One model I personally know wears a padded panty to help her rear end look fuller. (Laurel 2008)

Size fourteen fit model Samantha revealed that she worked with models who, under the advisement of their agents, used padding to add inches to their dimensions in order to book work with potentially more profitable clients. In this way, models secured shoulder pads onto their hips in order to add inches to their measurements. For models, body proportions were more important than size, so they used artificial aids, such as "chicken cutlets," body shapers such as the popular Spanx, or shoulder pads in unexpected places.

These plus-size fashion models were aware of their bodies. They knew how to put together an outfit that would flatter the appropriate curves. For each casting, they dressed to impress the casting director. They invested in shapeware (i.e., foundation garments worn underneath clothing that slim, flatten, and enhance different areas of the body including the bust, waist, buttocks, hips, and thighs to create a clean silhouette) and "comfortable" two- to three-inch high heels for runway, tradeshow, and showroom appearances and attended classes to learn how to walk. At castings, clients expected these models to wear shapeware or suitable foundation garments underneath a stylish, figure-flattering outfit, wear heels, and generally "be runway ready" with "a touch of gloss and slick hair."

Controlling Appetites and Battling Eating Disorders

Maintaining their model physical capital required self-monitoring and discipline, yet these models acknowledged the role their insatiable appetites had in creating their voluptuous figures and insisted to me that they eat a balanced diet and routinely exercise. As Nicole, a size sixteen African American commercial print and runway model told me, "Girl, you know I have to exercise because I love to eat!" And eat, they do. At a fashion show rehearsal, a production assistant tantalized us models with the promise of food, and I, surprised by their voracity, followed a pack of hungry plus-size models up the stairs to the feeding area. Much to our chagrin, the food was gone and we headed back downstairs to wait for the fitting. Later, after the show, I followed the same group of plus-size models to the kitchen prep area where they helped themselves to a platter of leftover sandwiches and brownies. While piling a second sandwich onto her plate, size eighteen African American commercial print and runway model Anna appeared conflicted, "I need to watch what I eat." To which Jackie, size sixteen Latina showroom and runway model, quipped, "Yeah, I watch what I eat . . . as it goes in!"

Underneath the levity of this exchange was an earnest call for self-discipline. Anna recognized that she must negotiate her hunger with the physical requirements of modeling. She realized that, at a size eighteen and already at the end of the marketable range for plus-size models, an increase in size would lead to a steep decline in work opportunities.

Complicating this management of model physical capital, several of the models revealed past disordered eating patterns (such as binge eating, compulsive exercising, or yo-yo dieting). Mary, for example, a size fourteen fit model, spent most of her adolescence loathing her body and tried dieting to correct this "defect":

> I even tried this crazy liquid diet and wore little acupressure balls behind my ears. All I ate was a liter of milk and mushy cabbage. After a month, I only lost twelve pounds, and I had to stop because I was too weak to even move.

With such a strained relationship with food and her body, Mary needed to strike a balance between managing her body and controlling it via excessive means. In turn, Mary focused on long-term solutions to body management, such as a portion-controlled diet and a workout regimen of cardiovascular exercise and weight training.

Similarly, Anna and Janice, both recovering binge eaters and compulsive exercisers, made long-term, sustainable adjustments. In order to continue to cultivate her body and remain competitive, Anna made minor shifts in her lifestyle:

> I stopped drinking soda. It was so hard. I was addicted. I drink tons of water, now. I always carry a bottle with me. I heard it helps my skin. But, sometimes I'll sneak in a can of Diet Coke.

After eliminating soda from her diet, Anna noticed positive changes to her body and energy level. On the other hand, Janice found that the natural pace of living in Manhattan facilitated a sufficient level of bodily management:

> I do not go to the gym. Never again. I walk everywhere, take the subway, [and] live in a fifth floor walkup [apartment].

Every day these models managed their physical capital, from minor adjustments in lifestyle to more intensive body projects involving dermatological and orthodontic treatments. Some had to binge and overeat to increase their size. Unlike athletes who have coaches to monitor their progress, they labored on their own to become "permanent overseers of their own bodies" (Mears and Finlay 2005, 333). Their bodies were both subject and object, mindfully managed through self-monitoring and discipline. For these plus-size models, they were their bodies and their bodies were their careers.

Self-Surveillance with a Tape Measure

Models experience an overt, constant pressure to maintain their figures, since there is always someone, whether an agent or client, present with a tape measure. For example, while a group of plus-size models and I waited in the hallway for an open call with an agency, one freelance model, Caroline, anxiously asked the departing models if they had been measured by the agent during the interview. Once Caroline heard that the agent measured the other models "in over a dozen places no one would expect," she turned to me in noticeable panic, explaining that her measurements had changed from the ones listed on her composite card (i.e., a model's business card) since she had gained weight over the holidays. Caroline knew it was common practice for agents to measure models. The act of being measured, itself, did not trouble her. Rather, Caroline feared that the agent would chastise her for her failure to maintain her bodily measurements. Caroline believed that the agent would then perceive her as unprofessional and, thus, refuse to work with her. This level of fear-laden bodily consciousness is not only typical but also necessary for a plus-size model, who is subject to fashion's gaze.

According to Foucault (1995 [1975], 26–28), power relations define the body in economic terms as both a productive body and a subjected body. Here in this Foucauldian view, the bodies of Caroline and other fashion models are subject to an agent's gaze. The fashion industry commodifies a model's body, where each curve determines her economic potential. Consequently, a model tracks her measurements and engages in a number of bodily practices to remain competitive in the field.

A Foucauldian analysis of the body involves mapping the power relations that operate within institutions and ripple down to the individual, affecting daily practices. In this case, the specialization of the modeling industry allows agents to categorize models, subjecting the body to classification. Plus-size models respond to this subjectification by the industry by internalizing the gaze and engaging in new forms of self-discipline. Here, the tape measure is an institutionalized tool of regulation as it measures and evaluates a model's body. No longer confined to the sole possession of an agent or a fashion designer, models also use a tape measure to track their bodies. Working within this web of power relations, models become "docile" bodies to fit the desired image of a plus-size model.

Appearance plays a key role in gendered subjectivity, where "doing looks" is integral to the production of gendered social identity (Frost 2005). Bordo (1993), in Foucauldian fashion, acknowledges the productive role women have in bodily pursuits but ultimately concedes that they become "docile" bodies disciplined to survey and improve their bodies, duped into adhering to idealized constructions of feminine embodiment discursively mediated by the culture through a cosmetic panopticon. An internalized sense of disciplinary power, exercised by self-surveillance and self-policing, maintains a model's gendered subjectivity, resulting in her pursuit of an aesthetic ideal established by fashion. These models internalize a normalizing gaze and, by use of individualized disciplinary practices, reproduce the "subjected and practiced bodies, 'docile' bodies" (Foucault 1995 [1975], 138). Here, these models actively work on their bodies to achieve a look mandated by the cosmetic panopticon. They judge their bodies through fashion's eyes and according to fashion's criteria. When they fail, they experience a sense of shame and insecurity similar to that of Caroline.

As we see from this aesthetic labor process, these women went from "doing looks" to "doing plus-size." Working within an institution that places a high economic value on the physical body, they wage a personal battle to control and discipline their bodies. This pressure intensified for those women who work as fit models.

The Case of Fit Models

Twelve of the plus-size models I encountered primarily worked as fit models. Fashion designers and clothing manufacturers hire fit models to try on garments at various stages of production to determine the fit and appearance of the garment on a live person. Thus, a fit model's job is to comment on the material and the cut of the garment with respect to its fit and feel as the model moves about as the customer would in the future. The model gives this feedback to the designer before the garment is mass produced. As one agent described to me, the fit model is the designer's muse. Fit modeling jobs are billed hourly, with New York City rates ranging from one hundred twenty-five dollars up to three hundred dollars, and designers prefer to use the same model throughout a design season; hence, the hours can add up to profitable work. For example, one fit model in my sample earned on average twenty-seven thousand dollars a year from fit clients alone.

Essential to this process, the model's measurements must remain constant in order to ensure a consistency of sizing and fit in garment production. As a fit model warned:

> If she [the model] is bloated and they [the designers] fit the garment larger, women [in the stores] will think they lost weight.

While based on a form, the true fit and size of a garment is dependent on the fit model used during fittings. Therefore, the model must maintain specific dimensions and proportions, often to within an inch of those she had when she started working for the client. Changes in her dimensions and proportions could mean lost jobs. Clients often fired models whose weight fluctuated. Sarah explained to me that she had a recurring working relationship with one designer until she lost ten pounds. Those ten pounds meant the end of her steady work opportunity. So, throughout the process, clients record and track every inch of a model's body.

For some models, this amplified pressure to maintain one's exact measurements in fit modeling countered the financial benefits. Heather, a size sixteen commercial print and runway model, refused to work fit jobs because of her history with an eating disorder:

> I know I can make some good money but the last thing that I'm gonna do is worry like that. I can keep this [body] in check but I'm not gonna worry about every pound.

Heather successfully disciplined her body so that she maintains her size in order to work in commercial print and runway, but she feared that the added strain of working as a fit model would trigger an eating disorder relapse.

The Shame of Losing Weight

What happens if a model fails to maintain her weight? The case of a fit model, Janice, offers a telling tale of what can happen when a plus-size model loses weight. When I spoke to Janice, she had recently lost weight as an unintended consequence from an attempt at a bodily improvement. She invested (i.e., an out-of-pocket expense since she does not have health insurance) in a retainer to straighten her teeth; however, it was not until after the retainer was made that the doctor instructed her that she would have to wear it for twenty-three hours a day. In order to eat, she would have to remove it and then brush her teeth before she put it back on.

Because of the inconvenience of this orthodontic treatment, Janice lost twenty pounds in a matter of weeks. When she went to her fitting jobs, she noticed a marked difference in the reactions of the clients, who disapproved of her weight loss. A designer client, who hired Janice to fit dresses, sweaters, and shirts for the past three years, stood in horror and exclaimed, "I am going to have to measure you. You lost weight."

To Janice's own amazement, she had lost three inches in her waist and four inches in her bust and hips. The client replaced Janice with some other "big girl." Because of this dramatic weight loss, Janice no longer fit the position as fit model, losing an average of five thousand dollars a year from this one fit client alone. Having lost the weight and a well-regarded job opportunity, Janice experienced a shame equivalent to that one feels after gaining weight, "I hate being told it [the weight loss] is wrong. It is my body."

At another job doing line work for a nationwide retailer, where fit models of various sizes literally line up to model the latest design collection for corporate directors, Janice tried on her usual size eighteen pant, but after buttoning the waist, the pants fell to the floor. She was immediately given a smaller size pant:

> I felt like I was being arrested. The looks I got from these people. I started to give a monologue to the directors, saying I had just had food poisoning and made cracks about eating muffins to gain the weight back.

Conflicted by the demand from her clients that she needed to gain back ten pounds and worry about paying bills, Janice broke down under the pressure and bought weight-gaining powder.

In an industry where the body is a commodified object, a model may sometimes need to engage in deviant behaviors to remain marketable. As in the aforementioned case, when fit clients fired Janice because she lost too much weight, she returned to the binge mentality she learned of years ago while in college, where she would binge on carbohydrates and cheese and then exercise the next day. This time, however, she did not exercise the next day but, instead, "walked slow" and carried a jar of peanut butter in her bag, consuming it by the spoonful. Janice suffered flashbacks from that previous episode in her life and could no longer stomach her daily Ensure shakes mixed with strawberries and ice cream.

As a newly slimmed down plus-size model, Janice experienced resistance from fit clients, who demanded that she return to her larger size. Janice struggled with the issue of having to gain weight in an unhealthy manner, something she never thought she would have to do as a plus-size model. Here, the fit clients demanded a specific body that Janice could not provide. They required this body without thought as to how Janice might go about achieving this sudden weight gain. This push toward fatness and gaining weight is counter to what contemporary American culture dictates about women's bodies. While fashion urges everyday women to lose weight, fashion urges plus-size models, at times, to gain weight. Models push their bodies to extremes. Fashion allowed these women to be fat and occasionally urged them to get fatter in order to build their model physical capital.

Conclusions

This study presents us with a unique example of how labor processes can extend beyond the confines of work, affect the social identity of workers, and aid in the production of fantasy. Other body-centric professionals (i.e., dancers, athletes, exotic dancers, and fitness instructors) adopt techniques of bodily control that affect not only their performance of work but their lived experience. Yet, contrary to a dancer or boxer who trains his or her body toward an established aesthetic (i.e., an athletic, lean, and strong body), plus-size models work within the confines of a cultural field of tastemakers to create aesthetics. As such, they have an active role in molding cultural constructions of fatness.

. . . Because of their size, we assume plus-size models suffer from a "sin by omission"—that is, failure to keep up with necessary engendered bodily devotional practices (Baudrillard 2005, 278). However, as this work demonstrates, they discipline themselves and engage in regimented practices as part of an aesthetic labor process. They utilize their body as capital, embark on a variety of body projects, and, ultimately, reproduce heteronormative imperatives involving female bodies.

Normative values dominate their aesthetic labor process. Even if they are fat, plus-size models emulate a work ethic of self-discipline, strength, and diligence. As women, plus-size models continue to manage and manipulate their bodies in hopes of appealing to fashion's elite. In cultivating themselves as plus-size models, they engage in engendered body projects designed to control their fat. Ultimately, these projects serve to reinforce their sense of disembodiment.

As "docile" bodies, plus-size models engage in a constant battle to control and discipline their bodies. They develop a repertoire of specialized professional techniques to increase their "model physical capital." Technologies of control, such as a tape measure, legitimize and normalize this constant surveillance of the body. As part of the physical strategies employed by plus-size models to remain marketable to clients, models track each measurement and manipulate their bodies by either invasive or noninvasive techniques, ranging from strict dieting and exercise to wearing padding in the appropriate places. . . .

Plus-size models labor over their body landscapes, haunted by a continual sense of imperfection. Whether their bodies are sources of embarrassment and shame or prideful accomplishments, they are treated overwhelmingly as things to control and master. They become objects within the spectacle of fashion. Thus, a plus-sized model's reclamation of embodiment is an illusion. Only ethnographic methods could capture this discrepancy between a staged performance of fat and the backstage aesthetic labor process.

Throughout the course of this study when I was photographed or walked down the runway, I was seduced by a fantasy. As a model pampered and dressed in the latest fashions, I attest to the ease with which a model could get lost in a moment and feel liberated from a stigma. Under the spell of a "cultural goal of becoming photographable," I no longer felt like an ordinary woman (Blum 2003, 101). As a model, I believed that I was special, a standout among the crowd, and no longer burdened by fatness. As models of resistance against a negative cultural discourse surrounding the fat body, these women expose their bodies of curves without shame. For those brief moments, they emerge victorious, reclaim their femininity, and feel empowered. Beyond the performance, however, fashion marginalized these plus-size models within a system of work embedded in a complex web of power relations and practices. The self-surveillance and corporeal discipline required of an aesthetic labor process is antithetical to the task of reclaiming one's embodiment because the body is still an object that the model must control and master. While these plus-size models invest in their bodies, they alienate the self and transform their bodies into manipulated and consumed objects, thereby reproducing prevailing gender ideologies and inequalities. There is no subversion. Preexisting aesthetic ideals direct this process of self-cultivation. Plus-size models try to claim their space in fashion without presenting a counteraesthetic.

After all their aesthetic labor, plus-size models are still fat bodies. Their work is no different from any other model of any size in fashion. All models must control and discipline their bodies. Plus-size models remain disembodied.

References

Bartky, Sandra Lee. 1990. *Femininity and domination: Studies in the phenomenology of oppression*. New York: Routledge.

Baudrillard, Jean. 2005. The finest consumer object. In *The body: A reader*, edited by M. Fraser and M. Greco, 277–82. London: Routledge.

Blum, Virginia L. 2003. *Flesh wounds: The culture of cosmetic surgery*. Berkeley: University of California Press.

Bordo, Susan. 1993. *Unbearable weight: Feminism, Western culture, and the body*. Berkeley: University of California Press.

Bourdieu, Pierre. 1984. *Distinction: A social critique of the judgment of taste*. Cambridge, MA: Harvard University Press.

Diluna, Amy. 2010. Sick world where size 4 is too fat. *Daily News*, February 16.

Eliasoph, Nina. 2005. Theorizing from the neck down: Why social research must understand bodies acting in real space and time (and why it's so hard to spell out what we learn from this). *Qualitative Sociology* 28: 159–69.

Foucault, Michel. 1977. *Discipline and punish: The birth of the prison*. Translated by Alan Sheridan. NewYork: Vintage Books.

Foucault, Michel. 1995 [1975]. *Discipline and punish: The birth of the prison*. New York: Vintage Books.

Frost, Liz. 2005. Theorizing the young woman in the body. *Body & Society* 11: 63–85.

Horne, Sarah. 2010. Gemma Ward, a supermodel betrayed. *Page Six Magazine*, February 11.

Laurel, Larissa. 2008. Physical requirements for plus models. *PLUS Model Magazine*. June 2008. http://www.plusmodelmag.com.

Mears, Ashley, and William Finlay. 2005. Not just a paper doll: How models manage bodily capital and why they perform emotional labor. *Journal of Contemporary Ethnography* 34: 317–43.

Melago, Carrie. 2009. Ralph Lauren model Filippa Hamilton: I was fired because I was too fat! 5–10, 120-lb. beauty gets axed. *Daily News*, October 14.

Murphy, Alexandra G. 2003. The dialectical gaze: Exploring the subject-object tension in the performances of women who strip. *Journal of Contemporary Ethnography* 32: 305–35.

Vesilind, Emili. 2009. Fashion's invisible woman. *Los Angeles Times*, March 1.

Wacquant, Loïc. 2004. *Body & soul: Notebooks of an apprentice boxer*. Oxford: Oxford University Press.

Wainwright, Steven P., and Bryan S. Turner. 2006. "Just crumbling to bits"? An exploration of the body, ageing, injury and career in classical ballet dancers. *Sociology* 40: 237–55.

Wesely, Jennifer K. 2003. Exotic dancing and the negotiation of identity: The multiple uses of body technologies. *Journal of Contemporary Ethnography* 32: 643–69.

Reflective Questions

1. How did the author conduct the research for this study? Why do you think she chose to be a model to do this research? What insights did she derive from her experience as a model? Did this role make it easier or more difficult to study other plus-size models?
2. What is the definition of a plus-size model? Who enforces this definition? Are plus-size models regarded as fat? If so, by whom? How do they view themselves? Why do they try to maintain their size?
3. How do plus-size models train and discipline their bodies? How do they manipulate their bodily appearance to enhance what they see as "appropriate

curves"? How do they regulate their appetites? How do they engage in bodily self-surveillance? How much body work is involved in "doing plus-size"?

4. What does the author mean when claiming that plus-size models have "docile bodies"? How and why do these models feel disembodied and alienated from self? How do they learn to "transform their bodies into manipulated and consumed objects"? How do their appearances and actions reproduce prevailing gender ideologies and inequalities?
5. How is the body a site of social control, especially for women? What are the bodily disciplines practiced by women in everyday life? Why do they engage in these disciplines? How do women suffer from the cultural demands placed upon them to manage their appearances and bodies? For instance, how much time and energy does it take for women to "work on" their faces and bodies in their everyday lives? Why do so many women feel dissatisfied with their bodies? How does this affect their self-images?

15

Corporate Logo Tattoos and the Commodification of the Body

ANGELA OREND AND PATRICIA GAGNÉ

This selection addresses a question that has become central to sociologists who investigate the relationship between culture and the body—that is, do people simply conform to social and cultural pressures when altering or modifying the appearance of their bodies, or do they actively and creatively make choices in this process? In answering this question, Angela Orend and Patricia Gagné examine why individuals elect to get their body tattooed with a corporate logo, such as a Harley Davidson emblem. They also consider whether such an act is a reflection of personal autonomy or an example of the increased commodification of culture and the pervasive power of consumer capitalism.

Drawing on in-depth interviews, Orend and Gagné note that their respondents emphasized the personal freedom and choices they exercised in getting a corporate logo tattoo. When explaining why they chose to mark their bodies in this way, they stressed a variety of personal motivations, each of which suggests that they transformed the symbols presented to them by the culture industry to fit their own goals, such as their desire to communicate brand loyalty, group membership, and a preferred lifestyle. Orend and Gagné found that most of their interviewees believed that getting a corporate logo tattoo was a sign of rebellion, demonstrating their individuality as well as their resistance to the commodification of culture and everyday life. Ironically, however, their interviewees did not see others' tattoos as marks of genuine or effective rebellion. Instead, they thought others used them to fit in or "be cool."

Based on their findings, Orend and Gagné evaluate whether their respondents are more right about themselves or others with respect to corporate tattoos and resistance. In doing so, they consider the ideas of postmodern theorists such as Jean Baudrillard, who asserted that the mass production of signs in postmodern society has resulted in a crisis of identity and a loss of meaning, marked by the lack of connection between signs and their original referents. Like other signs, tattoos have become "commodities on display" that reflect the growing commodification of culture and the body. As Orend and Gagné observe, the increased popularity of corporate logo tattoos reflects this trend. It also illustrates how corporations have extended their effectiveness at branding us as individuals, thereby recruiting us to serve as "walking human billboards."

Orend and Gagné conclude that their respondents are not expressing as much autonomy or resistance as they think when getting a corporate logo tattoo. Despite their best efforts, these individuals cannot effectively invert the meanings associated with their corporate logo tattoos, largely because others interpret these tattoos in light of the discourse of corporate capitalism. That is, others read the corporate logo tattoos as free advertising rather than as expressions of resistance or individuality. Orend and Gagné correspondingly propose that we are not as free or rebellious as we might

Reprinted from: Angela Orend and Patricia Gagné, Corporate Logo Tattoos and the Commodification of the Body. *Journal of Contemporary Ethnography* 38(4): 493–517.

think when engaging in body modifications such as tattooing. Indeed, we may be playing right into the hands of corporate advertisers when getting a tattoo, making ourselves into their servants and promoters even though we are doing so under the guise of expressing resistance and personal agency.

Overall, the authors of this selection offer a perspective that differs somewhat from the viewpoint articulated in most of the previous selections. While acknowledging that we actively construct and negotiate meanings for self, Orend and Gagné contend that these meanings are profoundly influenced by the larger culture industry and the rapidly expanding commodification of culture. In turn, they propose that while we may believe we have the power to define ourselves and resist the culture industry when we engage in practices such as tattooing, the culture industry is the source of that power and thus subverts our resistance. For example, the rebellion that we might seek to express through getting a Harley Davidson tattoo is a commodity produced by the culture industry and corporate capitalism. By purchasing that commodity, we are not expressing real resistance or power. Rather, we are embracing the commodification of our body and reinforcing the cultural and economic systems that promote that process. We are correspondingly buying into the dominant culture rather than resisting it.

Since the late 1960s, Western popular culture has witnessed a resurgence in the practice of body modification, particularly with respect to the popularity of tattoos. An under-recognized but socially salient aspect of this trend has been the growing popularity of permanent corporate logo tattoos. At the turn of the century, for example, Harley was the most widespread corporate logo tattoo in North America (Sheldon, Godward, and DeLongis 2001), with the popularity of logo tattoos expanding to include others, such as Nike, Adidas, Budweiser, Corona, Apple, Ford, Chevy, and Volkswagen, just to name a few (Klein 1999; C. Magill, personal communication). The growing popularity of corporate logo tattoos led one observer to remark that such body art was "the ultimate in chic" (Bradberry 1997, F1).

Little research has examined the rising popularity of corporate logo tattoos, although the literature on tattoos in general provides some insight into this new trend of body modification. This research, together with the sociology of the body and consumption, informs our analysis of the growing popularity of corporate logo tattoos. We situate our data analysis within the literature on the body and consumer culture, which is divided on whether bodily modifications in general are the result of passive actors succumbing to commodification and social pressures to conform (Foucault 1978; Turner 1992, 1996) or whether those who modify their bodies are active agents in an exercise of power (Bakhtin 1968; Featherstone 1991; Frank 1991). Thus, we seek to answer our main research questions: What are the meanings that those who acquire corporate logo tattoos ascribe to them and what motivates some individuals to inscribe themselves with a corporate symbol? Are corporate logo tattoos a form of resistance against the "culture industry" (Adorno and Horkheimer 1976), are they a manifestation of the commodification of the body, or, following the theoretical lead of Patricia Hill Collins (2000), are they "both" the former "and" the latter? This research adds to previous scholarship by situating an analysis of corporate logo tattoos within the literature on the sociology of the body and consumption. . . .

Tattoo Consumers: Rebellious or Commodified Bodies?

Although social scientists generally agree that the body is socially constructed, [they] disagree as to whether those who alter their bodies are passively "duped" into conforming to social and cultural pressures or whether they are active agents in constructing their own bodies (Chapkis 1986; Davis 1995; Douglas 1966; Mulvey 1989). Douglas (1966) maintains that the body is a metaphor for the social system, in which the physical body is an expression of culturally imposed meanings.

By contrast, Frank (1991, 46) argues that social bodies are the result of individual agency. Similarly, Davis (1995) contends that women's use of cosmetic surgery is an act of agency. One way of theoretically making sense of this debate is to draw on the work of Michel Foucault. In some of his work, he argues that the body is "docile" (Foucault 1995), constructed by "a great many distinct regimes" and that it is "the prisoner of culture" (Foucault 1986, 380) that can only be achieved "through a strict regimen of disciplinary action" (Foucault 1995, 136). Foucault argues that the social exercise of power over bodies is carried but through the "panopticon," a metaphor for the way that institutions constantly watch and seek to control people via surveillance methods. Similar to Gramsci's (1971) concept of hegemony, Foucault contends that the power of the panopticon is exercised as people self-regulate. The power of such self-regulation has been empirically demonstrated in the research literature (Chapkis 1986; Davis 1995; Mulvey 1989; Gagné and McGaughey 2002).

One of the difficulties of applying a Foucauldian perspective to an analysis of embodiment is that Foucault (1978, 95) also argued that because power is exercised discursively, "where there is power, there is resistance." Thus, power is not a zero-sum game in which certain agents have it and others do not. Instead, it is diffused in society. Accordingly, people are not passively manipulated into internalizing dominant ideologies, nor do they lose agency as they are pressured by bodily discourse and regimens. For Foucault (1978, 95), because the "body is invested in power relations" it can also express "body power," not as "property, but as strategy" (Foucault 1995, 26).

Applying this Foucauldian perspective, some researchers argue that consumers are not uncritical, passive victims of the capitalist system. Rather, they engage in a discursive exercise of power during consumption (Twitchell 1999). In this vein, advertising and marketing are viewed as reflecting, rather than dictating, the desires of consumers, with consumption offering control over communal meanings ascribed to self and social relations and opportunities to exercise power as shoppers decide which products to buy in the "democracy" of the marketplace (Fiske 1989). Fiske (1989) argues that consumers are engaged in acts of resistance when they alter the intended meanings and uses of commodities.

Thus, we are left with the question whether consumers of corporate logo tattoos have been "duped" into branding their bodies with capitalist insignia, whether they use them as signs of resistance, or if the acquisition of such body art is "both" an expression of a commodity self "and" a form of resistance to the commodification of culture.

Research Method

The data for this article come from qualitative ethnographic observation and fieldwork in tattoo parlors, thirteen in-depth semistructured interviews, and eight conversational interviews. . . .

The first author conducted all of the interviews and ethnographic field-work. By using field observation at local tattoo parlors in addition to semistructured and conversational interviewing methods, she was able to add or delete questions based on the information generated during the interview in addition to gaining a "first hand" look at the context of local tattoo parlors (Lofland and Lofland 1984; Werner and Schoepfle 1987). She conducted thirteen interviews using standard semistructured interview methods with eight interviews face-to-face, three by telephone, and two via an online chat service. She taperecorded all but the online interviews and took notes on the setting and context (Lofland and Lofland 1984; Patton 1990). She conducted most of the eight additional unrecorded conversational interviews in tattoo parlors, recording field notes after the conversations. . . .

In addition to demographic questions and those about the number, type, and bodily location of the subjects' tattoos, our interview guide focused on the history of each tattoo, including the decision-making process before getting each one and what it meant to the subject. We also included questions soliciting opinions about the social acceptability of tattoos, why most people get them, why the subject acquired his or her tattoo(s), whether the subject had any other body modifications, and, if so, what kind. Following those questions, the interviewer focused similar inquiries on the respondent's corporate logo tattoo and what the company and the logo meant to him or her.

Sample

We used a purposive criterion sampling method, designed to select "information-rich cases for in-depth study" (Patton 1990, 168) to recruit and sample research subjects. Toward that end, the first author placed flyers at local tattoo parlors; coffee shops, restaurants, stores, and bars; and two universities in a midsized Midwestern city. In addition, she placed an advertisement in the entertainment section of a free alternative local newspaper and posted a notice about the study on numerous Internet newsgroups, listservers, and chat rooms.

We used the following criteria to determine which tattoos to include and exclude: (1) the logo must be an official trademark (™) or a federally registered (®) symbol of a corporation or a name-brand product and (2) the tattoo must be permanent. We excluded tattoos of band names, album covers, cartoon characters, college or university symbols, sports teams, and other noncorporate logos. Of the twenty-one respondents included in this study, the first author documented the following corporate logo tattoos: Apple (5), Harley Davidson (2), Louisville Slugger (2), Nike (2), and one of each of the following: Churchill Downs (horse racing track), Cat's Meow (New Orleans bar), Crayola, Hershey Kiss, IBM, Ironman (body fitness company), Fender (guitar company), Lego, Pearl (drum company), and a combined tattoo that included Real (dairy corporation) with *Life* (magazine) which read "Real*Life*."[1] We stopped recruiting subjects when we reached a point of theoretical saturation (Lincoln and Guba 1985). . . .

Meaning and Motivations: Corporate Logo Tattoos

Two primary themes emerged from our data regarding the motivations and meanings respondents ascribed to their own corporate logo tattoos. Fifteen respondents said their motivation to get the tattoo was brand loyalty and that, for them, the logo signified personal and group identity as well as adherence to a lifestyle associated with the brand. The second major theme, the simulacrum (Baudrillard 1995), as expressed by six respondents, was the intent to appropriate the logo and to "play" with the meanings the brand represented. In the following section we discuss those motivated by brand loyalty before turning to those who altered the original meaning of the logo.

Brand Loyalty, Identity, Community, and Lifestyle

The key to understanding the most common motivation for getting a corporate logo tattoo is consumers' belief in the meanings behind the symbols. In addition to signifying brand loyalty, our respondents' logo tattoos commonly conveyed individual and group identity, lifestyle, and, for some, membership in a community created by marketers.

Identity

Postmodernists argue that the commodification of culture is made possible, in part, by the fragmentation of society (DeBord 1995; Jameson 1991; Root 1996). Specifically, as individual identities are less rooted in kinship and geographic communities, individuals are influenced by consumer culture to believe that they can purchase individual and group identity through the products they buy. Just as consumers believe that the products they purchase say something about who they are, our brand-loyal respondents reported that their logo tattoos represented something about their social identities. For example, Apple #3 said, "People know me as a Mac guy. There are few things that I'm always gonna be known for, and that's absolutely one of them." . . .

Group Identity and Community

Individual identity was situated within commodified collective identities and communities. Just as our respondents were motivated by brand loyalty and a desire to communicate individual identity to others, they fetishized the logo, buying into the ideology created by the culture industry. This commodification of group identity is similar to "consumer tribes" (Maffesoli 1996). Those with Apple tattoos, for example, believed that users of that computer brand were inherently more creative and "hip" than PC users and that Apple computers were technologically superior to all others. Apple #2, for example, stated as fact that Apple is "the most technologically advanced computer maker" and that the company had "changed the world." He continued, "I am an Apple freak. . . . I live and die by my Mac." Similarly, those with Harley tattoos believed that owners of that brand of motorcycle were more rebellious and free than owners of other brands or non-riders. Lego's tattoo signified his heavy involvement with the "Lego community," groups of people who create robots and other items with Lego blocks, whom he deemed more creative than others. Given that logos and the meanings they represent are created by corporate marketers, such tattoos appear to signify the commodification or "branding" (Klein 1999; Travis 2000) of individual and group identity.

Although not the only source of identity and community among our respondents, corporations appear to have affected their patterns of association. Among our respondents, corporate logo tattoos signified membership in groups that, according to Maffesoli (1996, 9) were "organized around the catchwords, brand names and sound bites of consumer culture." Maffesoli found that membership in consumer tribes was impermanent and fluid. For our respondents, the permanent inscription of signifiers of group membership onto the body connoted relatively permanent membership in the tribe. For most, the inscription of the logo onto their bodies served to reinforce that loyalty, though not in a way that ensured lifelong allegiance. When loyalty diminished or one no longer wished to affiliate with the tribe, such sentiments could be difficult to communicate, particularly when the logo was tattooed on a part of the body difficult to cover.

Lifestyle

In addition to identity, community, and personal history, the logo of a particular corporation signified participation in a lifestyle that included, but frequently moved beyond, one particular brand. The logo was deemed to be the ultimate signifier of the lifestyle in which our participants engaged. For example, Churchill Downs said that horse racing was "the one obsession in my life." He believed that the Churchill Downs race track, home of the Kentucky Derby, hosted the world's ultimate race, but his lifestyle centered on horse racing, in general. Rather than getting a race horse and jockey or another non-logo tattoo to signify his passion for the sport, he chose the track's logo, explaining that it "shows my dedication, not just to Churchill Downs, but to horse racing. . . . It's symbolic of the love I have for the industry." Similarly, Ironman's logo tattoo and the corporation itself represented "people who live an active lifestyle" and were "hard core" dedicated athletes. Rather than a tattoo of himself crossing a finish line, he chose the corporate logo to commemorate the completion of his first triathlon. He explained, "When I got it, I didn't think of it as a corporate symbol. It was more of an accomplishment I made." Similarly, Cat's Meow got the tattoo of a "Hurricane," a pseudonym for the drink for which a particular New Orleans bar was famous. He said that he got "shitfaced" (drunk) and "had a really good time" while on vacation in that city. He explained that the Hurricane tattoo represented "just having a good time," the open-mindedness of the city, and his participation in a lifestyle he described as "people who enjoy being an alcoholic or a drunk," a category in which he included himself.

Among our sample, individuals who harbored greater sentiment for a particular activity than allegiance to a particular company thought of their lifestyles in corporate terms. Although all of our brand-loyal respondents were heavily influenced by a reality constructed by corporations, we believe that those who used the logo to signify their participation in a particular lifestyle most strongly suggest the hegemonic power of corporate symbols. The fact that some respondents do not "think of it as a corporate symbol" suggests the discursive power of marketing. In the next section, we analyze data from six respondents who endeavored to appropriate corporate logos and redefine them to signify something other than the meanings marketed by the corporations.

Appropriating the Logo

Six of our respondents said they used logos to convey meanings other than those intended by the corporations they represented and had expressed no "brand loyalty," per se. Of our formal interviews, those respondents were Real*Life*, IBM, Crayola, Hershey Kiss, and both Louisville Sluggers. Use of logos to signify something other than their intended meaning may be more common among the population of individuals with such tattoos than our sample suggests. According to several tattoo artists we spoke to, many clients request tattoos because they like the artistic style of the logo and not necessarily because of any specified "meaning" of the brand insignia.

Three themes emerged among those who wished to co-opt the logo to signify something other than that intended by the corporation. These included resistance to corporate loyalty, membership in a violent subculture, and the simulacrum.

Corporate Resistance

IBM (a pseudonym) had worked for a company with a strong corporate culture that demanded absolute loyalty from its employees. It was only after securing a job with another company that he acquired a tattoo of the IBM logo. He explained that getting the tattoo was a way of provoking his highly competitive coworkers, each of whom was concerned about demonstrating corporate loyalty. IBM explained that his tattoo "was sort of an in-your-face challenge to the real strutting monkeys in that organization: 'Hey, I like [IBM] so much that I tattooed the logo on my arm. And by the way, I'm outta here.'" He got his tattoo as a form of rebellion against the "corporate types" because he was "frustrated with all the super-egos." For him the tattoo was "more about the appearance of loyalty," a way of telling his coworkers how ridiculous he thought their competitive, paranoid, hyper-loyal actions were. It was a way of creating paranoia in other employees by provoking them to think, "Whoa! Is he really more loyal than I am?" In a personal e-mail to his friends at the corporation, he stated. "I didn't get that tattoo done as an act of loyalty or devotion to [the company]. . . . There is a real in-your-face element in what I've done. . . . The tattoo sort of symbolizes the question. 'Who *really* gives a shit around here?'" In his interview, he explained that he did not hold hard feelings against the company but rather that the intended target of the tattoo was his coworkers, not the corporation itself. For IBM, his corporate tattoo represented "resistance" to corporate America.

Subcultural Membership

Both Louisville Sluggers used their tattoos to express a rebellious identity and a "hard core" lifestyle that entailed involvement in the punk rock and independent music scene. Early in his interview, Louisville Slugger #1 explained that he considered most of his tattoos to be representations of various groups to which he belonged. He said, "I've definitely always had a group mentality, a really tribal like . . . 'I'm a member of this group.'" One of the groups to which he belonged considered the Louisville Slugger corporate logo to be representative of their tribal identity. For them, the logo signified violent imagery, important because of the sometimes rebellious and violent activities in which the group engaged. He explained the "obvious reasons" why the Louisville Slugger was a good symbol for the group. He said,

> Number one, it's a baseball bat. . . . Number two, . . . you know, bludgeoning people with baseball bats is, definitely, you know, is definitely an image. . . . That's a pretty common thing. You know, beating somebody with a baseball bat. It's pretty common imagery. . . . And number three, it's a slugger. A slugger is a person who, you know, a boxer.

He further explained that the tattoo was more about "not being a victim" and a defensive imagery of violence rather than actually behaving violently. He continued, "I have a real tendency to portray myself as a lot more macho than I am."

Both Louisville Slugger respondents indicated that they felt their tattoos were rebellious toward "mainstream" culture and were about being "hard core" within the local punk scene.

The Simulacrum

In contrast to Louisville Slugger and the other respondents in our sample, Crayola, Hershey Kiss, and Real*Life*'s logos were even further distant from the brand logos' intended meaning. For instance, Real*Life* did not adhere to a lifestyle represented by either logo; he was not an avid milk drinker, nor has he had a subscription to *Life* magazine. His personal identity may have been expressed and self-reflexively formed through his tattoos, but if it was, it was based upon meanings he attributed to the logos, not those intended by the corporation or the magazine.

Real*Life* was an Andy Warhol fan and said, "He definitely taught me the power of the symbol." Real*Life* explained that the key to understanding his tattoo was in the meaning of the words *real* and *life* when placed side by side. He said the two words together were "all encompassing" and "can mean just about anything." Real*Life* said he was "playing with the meaning" of signs and symbols and that although he believed that "reality is definitely a constantly shifting perspective," he got the tattoo to remind him to "keep it real." Similar to Ironman, Real*Life* said he never thought about the logos being corporate. Instead, he said, "The symbol now has my meaning. It isn't related to the company."

Similarly, Crayola had a colorful tattoo of the Crayola crayons box because she liked the artistic aspect of the design. She stated that her tattoo was not about "loyalty" to Crayola but about having an "artistic tattoo." In a somewhat similar vein, Hershey Kiss said her tattoo meant something personal to her about being "kissable" and "sexy." For the respondents in this section, the brand logo had entered the simulacrum, where the original significance of the tattoo was altered and transformed into their own personal meanings. These tattoos are representations of the "real" brand logos but their meanings have been intentionally distorted. Baudrillard (1995) argues that the simulacrum is associated with the postmodern era where images are merely representations and "fakes" with no relation to any "real" meaning or reality. Thus, we theorize that the meanings of some corporate logo tattoos have entered the simulacrum. . . .

Discussion: Agents or Dupes?

Regarding corporate logo tattoos, our findings suggest that such body art is acquired primarily to express brand loyalty or to appropriate the logo into a simulated meaning. Beyond Adorno and Horkheimer's (1976) argument that the culture industry appropriates mass culture, re-polishes it, and sells it back to shoppers, our findings suggest that corporate marketers have skillfully constructed a reality that includes individual and group identity, community, and lifestyle. Athletes, for example, no longer think of their accomplishments in terms of mental focus and physical endurance; instead, they are "Ironmen," so steeped in the identity and lifestyle that they fail to think of their accomplishments in terms of crossing a finish line. Musicians and artists are "Mac guys" who "think different." Scholars have long recognized the insidious ways that corporations influence culture. Our research demonstrates the way this corporate construction of reality has seeped its way into public consciousness and, indeed, for some, physical bodies, with identity, community, and lifestyle signified by corporate logos.

All of our respondents used corporate logos to convey meaning about themselves, their communities, or their lifestyles. Although most had reservations about why others get tattoos, all believed they were exercising personal autonomy and agency and that their tattoos represented something intrinsically real about themselves, their communities, and their lifestyles. On the whole, our brand-loyal respondents believed in what the corporations stood for and lived "the advertised life" (Vanderbilt 1997) as represented and marketed by corporations. As much as our brand-loyal respondents believed in the inherent superiority of the products, communities, and lifestyles associated with the logos they had inscribed on their own bodies, most subjects had negative feelings about the corporate logo tattoos of others whose brands differed from their own. Many said they "didn't understand" how corporations could create that much brand loyalty and that people who got them were "silly" and "ridiculous." Harley #2, for example, explained, "I don't see how anything else inspires the brand loyalty that a Harley does." Just as our respondents thought that others got logo tattoos because they had been duped into doing so, most could only understand why someone would get a tattoo of the brand(s) to which they were loyal. Thus, it appears that corporate logo tattoos signify membership in a consumer tribe in much the same way that being heavily tattooed communicates membership in a marginalized subculture. The difference is that the meanings behind logo tattoos were created by corporate marketers rather than representing something personal about the individual.

In contrast to the "advertised lives" of our brand-loyal respondents, those who attempted to appropriate the meaning of their logos were reacting to the commodification of everyday life by taking the signs and symbols presented by the culture industry and altering them to fit their own meanings. We consider that these respondents were engaging in an exercise of personal autonomy, but we believe their exercise of power to be a form of pseudo-rebellion or pseudo-resistance. In essence, their rebellion is futile because they have chosen to resist the commodification of society by exercising power within the symbolic discourse created by the industry itself. To resist the commodification of culture, we believe one must step outside the discourse of consumer capitalism, and while the logos may be simulated versions of the "real" thing, they are still representative of consumer culture.

Significantly, most of our respondents did not see their acquisition of logo tattoos as part of this process, instead seeing themselves outside the process of commodification. Similarly, they believed that others' use of tattoos as expressions of rebellion was, for the most part futile, primarily because their moderate displays had become so popular. In other words, tattoos were a sign of rebellion and deviance before they became an accepted part of mainstream society. Since being commodified, however, their utility as an act of resistance had become limited. Still, our respondents believed that they could signify their rebellion by purchasing more and more tattoos. We see this as another part of the larger culture industry's creation of "rebel consumers," who believe they are mocking the dominant culture while at the same time conforming to emergent norms of self-expression promoted by the tattoo industry.

Our findings on corporate logo tattoos provide strong support for the argument that tattoos are symbolic of the commodification of the body and fail to provide support for the argument that they are effective symbols of resistance. Specifically, the majority of our respondents acquired their corporate logo tattoos as an act of brand loyalty, to signify an identity and identification with the lifestyle associated with the brand, and to symbolize membership in a group affiliated with it. It appears that most of our respondents had moved beyond living "the advertised life" (Vanderbilt 1997) as their bodies became what we conceptualize as "human billboards" for corporations and brand name products.

These findings suggest that the commodification of culture vis-à-vis tattoos has moved beyond the mass marketing of flash body art. It appears that the culture industry has appropriated tattooing as means of "branding" consumers with logos that signify extreme brand loyalty. Those with corporate logo tattoos appear to have internalized the meanings created by corporations, believing that they really have the attributes suggested by the brand and that they live the lifestyle signified by the brand. In this way, corporate logo tattoos signify the commodification of lifestyle and identity, or what we term "pseudo-lifestyle" and "pseudo-identity." Moreover, they serve as visible markers of group affiliation. Unlike tattoos among traditional societies, however, logo tattoos signify membership in consumer tribes (Maffesoli 1996) that have been socially constructed by corporations. Finally, these tattoos have resulted in the commodification of the body in that corporations have appropriated people to serve as "human billboards." These billboards not only provide free advertising but also create a "next level" in brand loyalty, suggesting, for example, that those with logo tattoos have more "mystique," "think more different," or are more serious about the product and its lifestyle. The result is "pseudo-individualism," resulting from the culture industry's ideology, which promotes individualism, non-conformity, and self-expression through the use of name brands (Frank 1997, 232). Even as brand names are inscribed onto the body to affect an individual air, this pseudo-individuality serves to reinforce the ideology of the culture industry, just as Adorno and Horkheimer (1976) warned it would.

In a commodified society, tattoos are purchased to signify identity, group membership, coolness, and rebellion. The fact that signifiers of identities and group membership are for sale gives their purchasers a form of power in that they can choose whether or not to have such insignia inscribed onto their bodies. Yet while tattoo consumers may be expressing their agency in society by purchasing what they like and want, the symbols they consume were created by the culture industry to support the discourse and institution of industrial capitalism. Thus, we believe the power exercised by tattoo consumers is pseudo-power, despite the fact that our respondents truly believed they were exerting real power. Furthermore, when our respondents attempted to appropriate the corporate-created meaning of their logo tattoos, they were, for the most part, unsuccessful, specifically because the insignia—absent a verbal explanation from its bearer—was likely to be interpreted in the discourse of corporate capitalism. As part of the simulacrum, then, symbols need not refer to their original referents, but absent a wide-spread, organized exercise of power, corporate logo tattoos are likely to be interpreted as free advertising, rather than resistance. Foucault (1978) appears to have been correct in asserting that "where there is power, there is resistance," but in this case, it appears that resistance was futile because of the power of corporate capitalism to market tattoos as a form of rebellion and to define the meaning of body art, corporate logos, and the combination of the two. Rebellion against any discursive system, it appears, must come from outside. Individual efforts to appropriate or co-opt corporate symbols are, we believe, doomed to failure.

Conclusion

Theoretically, our data suggest that tattoos have been commodified in mainstream society in that they are consumed as a commodity in what Atkinson (2003) calls the "supermarket era" of tattooing. Furthermore, the increasing popularity of corporate logo tattoos appears to reinforce the process of the commodification of society vis-à-vis lifestyle, identity, group membership, and the body. From a postmodern perspective, the commodification of society is a reaction to social fragmentation. Specifically, as individual identities develop and people are influenced by the commodification of everyday life, they learn that they can purchase cultural products that will give them a certain appearance, lifestyle, and identity and provide them entré into certain consumer tribes. Individuals who acquire corporate logo tattoos to express brand loyalty, adherence to a particular lifestyle, identity, or membership in a particular group may believe they are exercising power. It must be noted, however, that this power is created by the culture industry and supported by corporate capitalism. As such we believe that consumers of corporate logo tattoos use these body modifications as an expression of pseudo-power and pseudo-resistance because the identities, lifestyles, and groups they wish to signify are pseudo-products of an industry that has appropriated human bodies as uncompensated billboards. The extensive power of the culture industry means that even efforts to resist it by appropriating corporate meanings have been, and are likely to continue to be, futile.

Note

1. To protect the confidentiality of two subjects, we changed the names of their corporate logos because we were unable to document at least one other person having one like it. Those were a New Orleans bar we have renamed the Cat's Meow and a technology corporation for which we have substituted the IBM logo. The individual with the Real*Life* tattoo wished to forgo confidentiality, preferring us to use the real tattoo in our presentations and publications.

References

Adorno, Theodor, and Max Horkheimer. 1976. *Dialect of enlightenment.* Trans. John Cumming. New York: Continuum.

Atkinson, Michael. 2003. *Tattooed: The sociogenesis of a body art.* Toronto: University of Toronto Press.

Bakhtin, Mikhail. 1968. *Rabelais and his world.* Boston: MIT Press.

Baudrillard, Jean. 1995. *Simulacrum and simulation.* Trans. Sheila Glaser. London: UMP.

Bradberry, Grace. 1997. Branded for life. *The Times,* November 20. Fl.

Chapkis, Wendy. 1986. *Beauty secrets: Women and the politics of appearance.* Boston: South End.

Collins, Patricia Hill. 2000. *Black feminist thought.* New York: Routledge.

Davis, Kathy. 1995. *Reshaping the female body: The dilemma of cosmetic surgery.* New York: Routledge.

DeBord, Guy. 1995. *The society of the spectacle.* Trans. Donald Nicholson-Smith. New York: Zone Books.

Douglas, Mary. 1966. *Purity and danger.* New York: Praeger.

Featherstone, Mike. 1991. The body in consumer culture. In *The body: Social process and cultural theory,* ed. Mike Featherstone, Mike Hepworth, and Bryan Turner, 170–96. London: Sage.

Fiske, John. 1989. *Reading the popular.* London: Routledge.

Foucault, Michel. 1978. *The history of sexuality: Volume I, an introduction.* New York: Vintage.

Foucault, Michel. 1986. Nietzsche, genealogy, history. In *The Foucault reader,* 76–100. New York: Pantheon.

Foucault, Michel. 1995. *Discipline and punish: The birth of the prison.* Trans. Alan Sheridan. New York: Vintage.

Frank, Arthur. 1991. For a sociology of the body: An analytical resource. In *The body: Social process and cultural theory,* ed. Mike Featherstone, Mike Hepworth, and Bryan Turner, 36–102. London: Sage.

Frank, Thomas. 1997. *Conquest of cool.* Chicago: University of Chicago.

Gagné, Pat, and Deanna McGaughey. 2002. Designing women: Embodiment, elective mammoplasty, and the masculine gaze. *Gender & Society 16*(6): 814–838.

Gramsci, Antonio. 1971. *Selections from the prison notebooks.* London: Lawrence and Wishart.

Jameson, Frederic. 1991. *Postmodernism, or the cultural logic of late capitalism.* Durham, NC: Duke University Press.

Klein, Naomi. 1999. *No logo.* New York: Picador USA.

Lincoln, Yvonne, and Egon Guba. 1985. *Naturalistic inquiry.* Beverly Hills, CA: Sage.

Lofland, John, and Lyn Lofland. 1984. *Analyzing social settings: A guide to qualitative observation and analysis.* 2nd ed. Belmont, CA: Wadsworth.

Maffesoli, Michel. 1996. *The time of the tribes: The decline of individualism in mass society.* London: Sage.

Mulvey, Laura. 1989. *Visual pleasures and narrative cinema.* Bloomington: Indiana University Press.

Patton, Michael Quinn. 1990. *Qualitative evaluation and research methods.* 2nd ed. Newbury Park. CA: Sage.

Root, Deborah. 1996. *Cannibal culture: Art, appropriation, and the commodification of difference.* Boulder, CO: Westview.

Sheldon, Jamie, Cooley Godward, LLP, and Mary DeLongis. 2001. Tattoo you—With a trademark. *International Trademark Association Bulletin Archive,* http://www.inta.org/index.php?option=com_contentandtask=viewandid=216andltemid=l26andgetcontent=l (accessed October 8, 2003).

Travis, Daryl. 2000. *Emotional branding: How successful brands gain the irrational edge.* Los Angeles: Prima.

Turner, Bryan. 1992. *Regulating bodies: Essays in medical sociology.* London: Routledge.

Turner, Byran. 1996. *The Body and Society.* 2nd ed. London: Sage.

Twitchell, James. 1999. *Lead us into temptation: The triumph of American materialism.* New York: Columbia University Press.

Vanderbilt, Tom. 1997. The advertised life. In *Commodify your dissent,* ed. Thomas Frank and Matt Weiland, 127–42. New York: Norton.

Werner, Oswald, and Mark Schoepfle. 1987. *Systematic fieldwork*. Newbury Park. CA: Sage.

Reflective Questions

1. What do the authors mean by consuming culture and commodification of the body? How have corporations seeped their version of reality into public consciousness? Give some examples from your life.
2. What meanings did corporate logo tattoos have for people motivated by brand loyalty? Others co-opted a logo but rejected the meanings advertised by its corporation. (They, in other words, appropriated the tattoo.) What statements were they trying to make with their corporate tattoos?
3. Researchers have previously presented two different interpretations of the relationship between the body and culture. What are they? In the end, which interpretation do Orend and Gagné find the most support for? Are individuals with logo tattoos dupes or agents? What do the authors mean when they say that "consumers of corporate logo tattoos use these body modifications as an expression of pseudo-power and pseudo-resistance"? Why weren't attempts to redefine the meanings underlying a logo more successful?
4. Consumer culture increasingly shapes bodies and our experiences of them in other ways, too. Consider the influence of pornography, now consumed widely by adults. A 2008 study on college students entitled "Generation XXX" found that 87 percent of men and 31 percent of women used pornography. Nearly half of the men reported using pornography at least weekly, and nearly a fifth of them reported using pornography daily or every other day. While the Internet certainly diversifies pornographic content, critics still claim, as Catharine MacKinnon said, pornography "eroticizes hierarchy, it sexualizes inequality. It makes dominance and submission into sex" (Catharine A. MacKinnon, *Feminism Unmodified: Discourses in Life and Law* [Cambridge, MA: Harvard University Press, 1987]). Who creates pornographic portrayals, who is the target audience, and who profits from them? How do these widely consumed portrayals of sexuality influence partners' sexual expectations for each other and themselves? Do they create greater sexual expression, sexual pressure, or something else? Listen to Lena Dunham, creator and star of HBO's *Girls,* describe an awkward sexual experience she had with a partner who wanted to try something sexual he saw on a pornographic website. Jump to 20:20 in her interview on "Fresh Air" at http://www.npr.org/2012/05/07/152183865/lena-dunham-addresses-criticism-aimed-at-girls. Do you agree with Dunham's interpretation of sexuality among Millennials? Have pornography and consumer culture influenced Millennials' views and experiences of sex?

PART

IV

The Social Construction of Self

The experience of self is central to being human. People could not experience a meaningful reality unless they could symbolically convey meanings to themselves as well as to others. In order to do so, they must think of and act toward themselves as if they were someone else. We get angry at, talk to, encourage, and congratulate ourselves much as we do one another. From the perspective of sociological psychology, this is the essence of the human self: to be both the subject and object of one's own thoughts, feelings, and actions. And the self that is the object of our thoughts, feelings, and actions is as much socially constructed as any other object of our experience. Our self becomes real to us as we act toward ourselves as others do. We interpret and define our thoughts, feelings, and actions in terms of shared symbols.

The selections in Part IV examine the social character of the self, the process of its acquisition, and the social influences that continually shape it. In addressing these themes, they offer the following insights:

- *Our sense of selfhood is responsive to and shaped by social processes. We learn who we are through our interactions with others.* It is through these interactions that we come to believe that we have distinct selves and that these selves are meaningful. Thus, the self that we develop is not simply an internal characteristic but rather reflects and emerges out of our social relationships.

As Charles Horton Cooley highlighted in Selection 16, we develop a *looking-glass self* in early childhood. That is, we learn to see ourselves in terms of the "reflection" provided by others. This learning occurs as a result of our ability to take the standpoint of others and imagine how we appear in their eyes. Based on their actions and expressions, we gauge whether they see us in a favorable or unfavorable light. We then internalize the imagined appraisals of others and feel a sense of pride or shame. These feelings serve as a key component of our sense of self-esteem. Yet Cooley emphasized that our sense of selfhood also has elements that do not simply reflect the appraisals of others. We develop and express a feeling of selfhood through active appropriation, or behaviors in which we lay claim to, or strive to possess, things as our own. This behavior is reflected in the assertive and sometimes aggressive acts of young children who exclaim "*my*," "mine," or "give that to *me*," often in resistance to others. Thus, Cooley did not regard the self as something we passively acquire and sustain through our interactions with others. Instead, he saw it as images and feelings we actively appropriate based on how we think others perceive us.

- *Our ability to use language and symbols is crucial to our self-development. Because we can speak and converse with ourselves, we are both the subject and object of our own conduct.* George Herbert Mead, who built upon the ideas of Charles Horton Cooley, was the scholar who most insightfully revealed the social nature and origins of the self. Mead demonstrated the importance of the socialization process in shaping the contents and structure of the self. As Mead illustrates in Selection 17, the self is a social product, emerging through the interactions we have as children and developing in accord with our increasingly sophisticated abilities to internalize the perspectives of others and view the self as a social object. Through our childhood involvements in role-taking activities such as play and organized games, we acquire a self that has a structure—a set of internalized roles and perspectives—that reflects the structure of the communities to which we belong.

- *As we internalize the attitudes of others and become self-reflexive, we acquire the ability to adjust our actions to the expectations of others. This ability makes it possible for us to engage in social life effectively. It does not, however, make us act in ways that mindlessly conform to others' expectations.* We have the capacity to act innovatively, spontaneously, and unpredictably. This is rooted in the dialectical nature of our selves. As Mead points out, we possess selves that include two elements: the "I," or initiating subject, and the "me," or self as social object. These two components of self are intimately connected. Their dialogue provides us with the basis for creating and regulating our conduct. We experience impulses to act and then imagine how others might respond. In turn, we consider alternative actions and eventually choose to engage in behavior that resolves the tension between these impulses and internalized social standards. In some cases, this behavior is conventional but in others it is creative or unexpected. Most importantly, it emerges out of the ongoing internal conversation between the "I" and the "me."

- *In focusing on the self that individuals develop, sociological psychologists also highlight its ethnic, racial, and gendered dimensions. They recognize that in acquiring a self, people develop a conception of self as male or female and as members of particular ethnic or racial groups.* These identities originally develop in early childhood as we interact with significant others and learn to define and respond to ourselves in terms of gender or ethnic categories. We also learn the social meanings and implications of these categories through our interactions with a wider network of others, such as peers, teachers, and schoolmates. Guided by their responses, we build and internalize racial-ethnic and gender identities that shape our ongoing interactions, relationships, and self-presentations.
- *In addition to acquiring gender and racial/ethnic identities, we develop identities linked to particular groups, which are characterized by their own rules, roles, beliefs, and viewpoints.* These groups can have profound implications for the values you embrace and the self you enact. For instance, as Selection 19 reveals, if you become a member of a violent, male-dominated gang, you are required to undergo a major change of identity, which you must validate by displaying your willingness to use a gun to deal with threats to the group or challenges to your toughness.
- *In our postmodern society, we find it increasingly problematic to maintain a stable and unified sense of self.* As Kenneth Gergen notes in Selection 20, the rapid expansion of communication technologies and the accelerating pace of social change has placed the self under siege, exposing it to the diverse and often contradictory perspectives of a broad range of others. In response to the increasingly frayed and fragmented nature of our social environment, we feel more uncertain and disjointed, making us less committed to the notion that we possess a unified and deeply personal self. Instead, we become more likely to regard and experience the self as socially constructed—as something we create and recreate through our relations with others.

16

The Self as Sentiment and Reflection

CHARLES HORTON COOLEY

Charles Horton Cooley was an economist by training who made important contributions to the development of sociological psychology. The influence of Adam Smith's theory of human sentiments is obvious in this selection, which was written around the turn of the twentieth century. In Theory of Moral Sentiments *(1759), Smith maintains that individuals' sympathetic identification with one another's situation provides the moral foundation of human social life. For Cooley, the human self also rests on individuals' emotional responsiveness to one another. He argues that sentiment is the core of the human self and is central to its development. Accordingly, a sense of appropriation is the source of this self-feeling. The individual not only appropriates people and material objects by claiming them as "mine," but he or she also appropriates images of himself or herself reflected in others' treatment of him or her.*

This is what is commonly known as Cooley's theory of "the looking-glass self." Cooley suggests that the individual can only reflect upon and form images of himself or herself through the imaginary adoption of someone else's perspective. The individual imagines how he or she must appear to someone, imagines how that person must be judging his or her appearance and behavior, and consequently feels either pride or shame. Such socially reflected images inform the individual of who and what she or he is, and the consequent feelings of pride and shame provide the grounds for her or his sense of self-worth or esteem.

Cooley's young daughter M. was an important source of inspiration for his theory of the looking-glass self. He closely observed and took meticulous notes on her behavior. Cooley was particularly taken by her use of first-person pronouns like "mine" and "my." As Cooley notes, unlike most other expressions, these pronouns mean something or someone quite different depending on who is speaking. M. could only have learned to use pronouns correctly by reflecting how others used them—by the imaginary adoption of other people's perspectives. Cooley was also amazed at how early in life M. was aware of her influence over others. She recognized the reflections of her own actions in how others responded to her. For us, as for M., others' responses are the looking glass in which we see reflected images of ourselves. It is from these socially reflected images that we construct a self and our feelings about it.

It is well to say at the outset that by the word "self" in this discussion is meant simply that which is designated in common speech by the pronouns of the first person singular, "I," "me," "my," "mine," and "myself." "Self" and "ego" are used by metaphysicians and moralists in many other senses, more or less remote from the "I" of daily speech and thought,

Reprinted from: Charles Norton Cooley, "The Self as Sentiment and Reflection," in *Human Nature and the Social Order*, pp. 168–170, 179–184, 189–194, 196–199.

and with these I wish to have as little to do as possible. What is here discussed is what psychologists call the empirical self, the self that can be apprehended or verified by ordinary observation. I qualify it by the word social not as implying the existence of a self that is not social—for I think that the "I" of common language always has more or less distinct reference to other people as well as the speaker—but because I wish to emphasize and dwell upon the social aspect of it.

The distinctive thing in the idea, for which the pronouns of the first person are names, is apparently a characteristic kind of feeling which may be called the my-feeling or sense of appropriation. Almost any sort of ideas may be associated with this feeling, and that alone, it would seem, is the determining factor in the matter. As Professor James says in his admirable discussion of the self, the words "me" and "self" designate "all the things which have the power to produce in a stream of consciousness excitement of a certain peculiar sort. . . ." The social self is simply any idea, or system of ideas, drawn from the communicative life, that the mind cherishes as its own. Self-feeling has its chief scope within the general life, not outside of it. . . .

That the "I" of common speech has a meaning which includes some sort of reference to other persons is involved in the very fact that the word and the ideas it stands for are phenomena of language and the communicative life. It is doubtful whether it is possible to use language at all without thinking more or less distinctly of someone else, and certainly the things to which we give names, and which have a large place in reflective thought, are almost always those which are impressed upon us by our contact with other people. Where there is no communication there can be no nomenclature and no developed thought. What we call "me," "mine," or "myself" is, then, not something separate from the general life, but the most interesting part of it, a part whose interest arises from the very fact that it is both general and individual. That is, we care for it just because it is that phase of the mind that is living and striving in the common life, trying to impress itself upon the minds of others. "I" is a militant social tendency, working to hold and enlarge its place in the general current of tendencies. So far as it can, it waxes, as all life does. To think of it as apart from society is a palpable absurdity of which no one could be guilty who really *saw* it as a fact of life. . . .

If a thing has no relation to others of which one is conscious, he is unlikely to think of it at all, and if he does think of it, he cannot, it seems to me, regard it as emphatically *his*. The appropriative sense is always the shadow, as it were, of the common life, and when we have it, we have a sense of the latter in connection with it. Thus, if we think of a secluded part of the woods as "ours," it is because we think, also, that others do not go there. . . .

The reference to other persons involved in the sense of self may be distinct and particular, as when a boy is ashamed to have his mother catch him at something she has forbidden; or it may be vague and general, as when one is ashamed to do something which only his conscience, expressing his sense of social responsibility, detects and disapproves; but it is always there. There is no sense of "I," as in pride or shame, without its correlative sense of you, or he, or they. Even the miser gloating over his hidden gold can feel the "mine" only as he is aware of the world of men over whom he has secret power; and the case is very similar with all kinds of hidden treasure. Many painters, sculptors, and writers have loved to withhold their work from the world, fondling it in seclusion until they were quite done with it; but the delight in this, as in all secrets, depends upon a sense of the value of what is concealed.

In a very large and interesting class of cases, the social reference takes the form of a somewhat definite imagination of how one's self—that is, any idea he appropriates—appears in a particular mind; and the kind of self-feeling one has is determined by the attitude toward this attributed to that other mind. A social self of this sort might be called the reflected or looking-glass self:

> "Each to each a looking-glass
> Reflects the other that doth pass."

As we see our face, figure, and dress in the glass, and are interested in them because they are ours, and pleased or otherwise with them according as they do or do not answer to what we should like them to be; so in imagination we perceive in another's mind some thought of our appearance, manners, aims, deeds, character, friends, and so on, and are variously affected by it.

A self-idea of this sort seems to have three principal elements: the imagination of our appearance to the other person; the imagination of his judgment of that appearance; and some sort of self-feeling, such as pride or mortification. The comparison with a looking glass hardly suggests the second element, the imagined judgment, which is quite essential. The thing that moves us to pride or shame is not the mere mechanical reflection of ourselves, but an imputed sentiment, the imagined effect of this reflection upon another's mind. This is evident from the fact that the character and weight of that other, in whose mind we see ourselves, makes all the difference with our feeling. We are ashamed to seem evasive in the presence of a straightforward man, cowardly in the presence of a brave one, gross in the eyes of a refined one, and so on. We always imagine, and in imagining share, the judgments of the other mind. A man will boast to one person of an action—say some sharp transaction in trade—which he would be ashamed to own to another. . . .

[This] view [of] "self" and the pronouns of the first person . . . was impressed on me by observing my child M. at the time when she was learning to use these pronouns. When she was two years and two weeks old, I was surprised to discover that she had a clear notion of the first and second persons when used possessively. When asked, "Where is your nose?" she would put her hand upon it and say "my." She also understood that when someone else said "my" and touched an object, it meant something opposite to what was meant when she touched the same object and used the same word. Now, anyone who will exercise his imagination upon the question of how this matter must appear to a mind having no means of knowing anything about "I" and "my," except what it learns by hearing them used, will see that it should be very puzzling. Unlike other words, the personal pronouns have apparently no uniform meaning, but convey different and even opposite ideas when employed by different persons. It seems remarkable that children should master the problem before they arrive at the considerable power of abstract reasoning. How should a little girl of two, not particularly reflective, have discovered that "my" was not the sign of a definite object like other words, but meant something different with each person who used it? And, still more surprising, how should she have achieved the correct use of it with reference to herself which, it would seem, *could not be copied from anyone else,* simply because no one else used it to describe what belonged to her? The meaning of words is learned by associating them with other phenomena. But how is it possible to learn the meaning of one which, as used by others, is never associated with the same phenomenon as when properly used by one's self? Watching her use of the first person, I was at once struck with the fact that she employed it almost wholly in a possessive sense, and that, too, when in an aggressive, self-assertive mood. It was extremely common to see R. tugging at one end of a plaything and M. at the other, screaming, "My, my." "Me" was sometimes nearly equivalent to "my" and was also employed to call attention to herself when she wanted something done for her. Another common use of "my" was to demand something she did not have at all. Thus, if R. had something the like of which she wanted, say a cart, she would exclaim, "Where's *my* cart?"

It seemed to me that she might have learned the use of these pronouns as follows. The self-feeling had always been there. From the first week she had wanted things and cried and fought for them. She had also become familiar by observation and opposition with similar appropriative activities on the part of R. Thus, she not only had the feeling herself, but by associating it with its visible expression had probably defined it, sympathized with it, resented it, in others. Grasping, tugging, and screaming would be associated with the feeling in her own case and would recall the feeling when observed in others. They would constitute a language, precedent to the use of first-person pronouns, to express the self-idea. All was ready, then, for the word to name this experience. She now observed that R., when contentiously appropriating something, frequently exclaimed, "my," "mine," "give it to *me*," "I want it," and the like. Nothing more natural, then, than that she should adopt these words as names for a frequent and vivid experience with which she was already familiar in her own case and had learned to attribute to others. Accordingly, it appeared to me, as I recorded in my notes at the time, that "'my' and 'mine' are simply names for concrete images of appropriativeness," embracing both the appropriative feeling and its manifestation. If this is true, the child does not at first work out the I-and-you idea in an abstract form. The first-person pronoun is a sign of a concrete thing, after all, but that thing is not primarily the child's body, or his muscular sensations as such, but the phenomenon of aggressive appropriation, practiced by himself, witnessed in others, and incited and interpreted by a hereditary instinct. This seems to get over the difficulty mentioned above, namely, the seeming lack of a common content between the meaning of "my" when used by another and when used by one's self. This common content is found in the appropriative feeling and the visible and audible signs of that feeling. An element of difference and strife comes in, of course, in the opposite actions or purposes which the "my" of another and one's own "my" are likely to stand for. When another person says "mine" regarding something which I claim, I sympathize with him enough to understand what he means, but it is a hostile sympathy, overpowered by another and more vivid "mine" connected with the idea of drawing the object my way.

In other words, the meaning of "I" and "mine" is learned in the same way that the meanings of hope, regret, chagrin, disgust, and thousands of other words of emotion and sentiment are learned: that is, by having the feeling, imputing it to others in connection with some kind of expression, and hearing the word along with it. As to its communication and growth, the self-idea is in no way peculiar that I see, but essentially like other ideas. In its more complex forms, such as are expressed by "I" in conversation and literature, it is a social sentiment, or type of sentiments, defined and developed by intercourse. . . .

I imagine, then, that as a rule the child associates "I" and "me" at first only with those ideas regarding which his appropriative feeling is aroused and defined by opposition. He appropriates his nose, eye, or foot in very much the same way as a plaything—by antithesis to other noses, eyes, and feet, which he cannot control. It is not uncommon to tease little children by proposing to take away one of these organs, and they behave precisely as if the "mine" threatened were a separable object—which it might be for all they know. And, as I have suggested, even in adult life, "I," "me," and "mine" are applied with a strong sense of their meaning only to things distinguished as peculiar to us by some sort of opposition or contrast. They always imply social life and relation to other persons. That which is most distinctively mine is very private, it is true, but it is that part of the private which I am cherishing in antithesis to the rest of the world, not the separate but the special. The aggressive self is essentially a militant phase of the mind, having for its apparent function the energizing of peculiar activities, and, although the militancy may not go on in an obvious, external manner, it always exists as a mental attitude. . . .

The process by which self-feeling of the looking-glass sort develops in children may be followed without much difficulty. Studying the movements of others as closely as they do, they soon see a connection between their own acts and changes in those movements; that is, they perceive their own influence or power over persons. The child appropriates the visible actions of his parent or nurse, over which he finds he has some control, in quite the same way as he appropriates one of his own members or a plaything; and he will try to do things with this new possession, just as he will with his hand or his rattle. A girl six months old will attempt in the most evident and deliberate manner to attract attention to herself, to set going by her actions some of those movements of other persons that she has appropriated. She has tasted the joy of being a cause, of exerting social power, and wishes more of it. She will tug at her mother's skirts, wriggle, gurgle, stretch out her arms, etc., all the time watching for the hoped-for effect. . . .

The young performer soon learns to be different things to different people, showing that he begins to apprehend personality and to foresee its operation. If the mother or nurse is more tender than just, she will almost certainly be "worked" by systematic weeping. It is a matter of common observation that children often behave worse with their mother than with other and less sympathetic people. Of the new persons that a child sees, it is evident that some make a strong impression and awaken a desire to interest and please them, while others are indifferent or repugnant. Sometimes the reason can be perceived or guessed, sometimes not; but the fact of selective interest, admiration, and prestige is obvious before the end of the second year. By that time a child already cares much for the reflection of himself upon one personality and little for that upon another. Moreover, he soon claims intimate and tractable persons as *mine*, classes them among his other possessions, and maintains his ownership against all comers. M., at three years of age, vigorously resented R.'s claim upon their mother. The latter was "*my* mamma," whenever the point was raised.

Strong joy and grief depend upon the treatment this rudimentary social self receives. . . . At about fifteen months old [M.] had become "a perfect little actress," seeming to live largely in imaginations of her effect upon other people. She constantly and obviously laid traps for attention, and looked abashed or wept at any signs of disapproval or indifference. At times it would seem as if she could not get over these repulses, but would cry long in a grieved way, refusing to be comforted. If she hit upon any little trick that made people laugh, she would be sure to repeat it, laughing loudly and affectedly in imitation. She had quite a repertory of these small performances, which she would display to a sympathetic audience, or even try upon strangers. I have seen her at sixteen months, when R. refused to give her the scissors, sit down and make-believe cry, putting up her underlip and sniffling, meanwhile looking up now and then to see what effect she was producing. . . .

Progress from this point is chiefly in the way of a greater definiteness, fullness, and inwardness in the imagination of the other's state of mind. A little child thinks of and tries to elicit certain visible or audible phenomena, and does not go beyond them; but what a grown-up person desires to produce in others is an internal, invisible condition which his own richer experience enables him to imagine, and of which expression is only the sign. Even adults, however, make no separation between what other people think and the visible expression of that thought. They imagine the whole thing at once, and their idea differs from that of a child chiefly in the comparative richness and complexity of the elements that accompany and interpret the visible or audible sign. There is also a progress from the naive to the subtle in socially self-assertive action. A child obviously and simply, at first, does things for effect. Later there is an endeavor to suppress the appearance of doing so; affection, indifference, contempt, etc., are simulated to hide the real wish to affect the self-image. . . .

Reflective Questions

1. What is the social self? Is there a self that exists irrespective of its relationships to others? Explain the looking-glass metaphor. How does the looking-glass translate into an idea of the self? How does it also translate into feelings about the self?
2. How is "my" unique from other pronouns, and why was Cooley so surprised by his toddler's correct use of it? By 16 months, his child play-acted in order to get attention from adults. What relationship between the self and others does her play reflect?
3. A variety of social inputs shape how we imagine others perceive us. Perhaps when you were growing up, other kids gave you a nickname that attested to your athletic or musical ability, or you struggled to distance yourself from the poor academic reputation of an older sibling. Think back to your own childhood. What perceptions of yourself dominated your imagination and energy? Which did you distance yourself from and which did you embrace? How? What social conditions distinguish the two? Who most centrally influenced your self-perceptions and how? Did you become increasingly connected to that identity? Why or why not?

17

The Self as Social Structure

GEORGE HERBERT MEAD

George Herbert Mead is probably the most important figure in the development of sociological psychology. His characterizations of the self and its development are central to distinctively sociological understandings of the human condition. This selection is taken from Mind, Self, and Society, *which is Mead's best-known work, even though he did not actually write it. It was reconstructed from the class notes of students who took a course of that same title from Mead at the University of Chicago in the 1920s. Mead makes a number of important points about the human self in this selection: the self is separate from the body, it arises in social experience, but it is more than a mere product of socially reflected self-images.*

According to Mead, language is crucial to the development of the self. When we speak, we hear ourselves and respond to what we are saying in similar ways, as do those whom we are addressing. In speaking, we are both the subject and an object of our own action. Moreover, because what we say means more or less the same to us as to those being addressed, we can assume their role and anticipate their likely reaction to what we are saying. Mead observes that once children start to acquire language, they literally begin to take on the roles of others in play. They play at being a mother, father, or superhero. In so doing, the child addresses himself or herself in the role of those whom Mead calls significant others and responds accordingly. At this stage, the child develops separate selves that answer to each role he or she plays. That is why, Mead argues, a multiple personality is, in a certain sense, normal. It is when the child starts playing games that he or she begins to tie these multiple selves together into a unified whole.

Games involve the rule-governed coordination of a variety of distinct roles. In order to successfully play a game, the child must simultaneously assume the roles of all the other players. For example, in Mead's favorite example of baseball, a first baseman cannot successfully complete a double play unless she or he takes the role and anticipates the reactions of both the shortstop and the second baseman to a ground ball hit in their direction. By simultaneously assuming such interrelated roles, the individual adopts the perspective of an organized community or generalized other toward himself or herself. Such a generalized perspective provides the individual with a unified view of self. As Mead notes, this implies that the structure of the self will reflect the structure of the various groups of which the individual is a member.

However, in Mead's view, the self consists of more than the "me" that is the object of others' actions. The self is both subject and object. The subject or "I" responds to the object or "me," sometimes questioning and challenging it. The self is not a thing but a process—a continuous interchange between subject and object, "I" and "me."

Mead provides a profoundly social, although not socially deterministic, view of the self. The self is profoundly social not only in the sense that it arises in social experience, but also in the sense that it is a social process—a continuous inner conversation between an "I" and a "me." Social experience may make that conversation possible, but it does not determine what will emerge from it. It can be as lively, creative, and unpredictable as the most entertaining conversation among individuals.

The self has the characteristic that it is an object to itself, and that characteristic distinguishes it from other objects and from the body. It is perfectly true that the eye can see the foot, but it does not see the body as a whole. We cannot see our backs; we can feel certain portions of them, if we are agile, but we cannot get an experience of our whole body. There are, of course, experiences which are somewhat vague and difficult of location, but the bodily experiences are for us organized about a self. The foot and hand belong to the self. We can see our feet, especially if we look at them from the wrong end of an opera glass, as strange things which we have difficulty in recognizing as our own. The parts of the body are quite distinguishable from the self. We can lose parts of the body without any serious invasion of the self. The mere ability to experience different parts of the body is not different from the experience of a table. The table presents a different feel from what the hand does when one hand feels another, but it is an experience of something with which we come definitely into contact. The body does not experience itself as a whole, in the sense in which the self in some way enters into the experience of the self.

It is the characteristic of the self as an object to itself that I want to bring out. This characteristic is represented in the word "self," which is a reflexive, and indicates that which can be both subject and object. This type of object is essentially different from other objects. . . .

The self, as that which can be an object to itself, is essentially a social structure, and it arises in social experience. . . . The individual experiences himself as such, not directly, but only indirectly, from the particular standpoint of other individual members of the same social group, or from the generalized standpoint of the social group as a whole to which he belongs. For he enters his own experience as a self or individual, not directly or immediately, not by becoming a subject to himself, but only insofar as he first becomes an object to himself, just as other individuals are objects to him or in his experience; and he becomes an object to himself only by taking the attitudes of other individuals toward himself within a social environment or context of experience and behavior in which both he and they are involved.

After a self has arisen, it in a certain sense provides for itself its social experiences, and so we can conceive of an absolutely solitary self. But it is impossible to conceive of a self arising outside of social experience. When it has arisen, we can think of a person in solitary confinement for the rest of his life, but who still has himself as a companion, and is able to think and to converse with himself as he had communicated with others. . . . We are continually following up our own address to other persons by an understanding of what we are saying, and using that understanding in the direction of our continued speech. We are finding out what we are going to say, what we are going to do, by trolling the process itself. In the conversation of gestures, what we say calls out a certain response in another and that in turn changes our own action, so that we shift from what we started to do because of the reply the other makes. The conversation of gestures is the beginning of communication. The individual comes to carry on a conversation of gestures with himself. He says something, and that calls out a certain reply in himself which makes him change what he was going to say. One starts to say something, we will presume an unpleasant something, but when he starts to say it, he realizes it is cruel. The effect on himself of what he is saying checks him; there is here a conversation of gestures between the individual and himself. We mean by significant speech that the action is one that affects the individual himself, and that the effect upon the individual himself is part of the intelligent carrying out of the conversation with others. Now we, so to speak, amputate that social phase and dispense with it for the time being, so that one is talking to one's self as one would talk to another person. . . .

We have discussed the social foundations of the self. . . . We may now explicitly raise the question as to the nature of the "I" which is aware of the social "me." . . . The "I" reacts to the self which arises through taking the attitudes of others. Through taking those attitudes, we have introduced the "me" and we react to it as an "I."

The "I" is the response of the individual to the attitude of the community as this appears in his own experience. His response to that organized attitude in turn changes it. . . . [T]his is a change which is not present in his own experience until after it takes place. The "I" appears in our experience in memory. It is only after we have acted that we know what we have done; it is only after we have spoken that we know what we have said. The adjustment to that organized world which is present in our own nature is one that represents the "me" and is constantly there. But if the response to it is a response which is of the nature of the conversation of gestures, if it creates a situation which is in some sense novel, if one puts up his side of the case, asserts himself over against others and insists that they take a different attitude toward himself, then there is something important occurring that is not previously present in experience. . . . Such a novel reply to the social situation . . . constitutes the "I" as over against the "me."

The problem now presents itself as to how, in detail, a self arises. We have to note something of the background of its genesis. . . . We have seen . . . that there are certain gestures that affect the organism as they affect other organisms and may, therefore, arouse in the organism responses of the same character as aroused in the other. Here, then, we have a situation in which the individual may at least arouse responses in himself and reply to these responses, the condition being that the social stimuli have an effect on the individual which is like that which they have on the other. That, for example, is what is implied in language; otherwise, language as significant symbol would disappear, since the individual would not get the meaning of that which he says. . . . It is out of that sort of language that the mind of Helen Keller was built up. As she has recognized, it was not until she could get into communication with other persons through symbols which could arouse in herself the responses they arouse in other people that she could get what we term a mental content, or a self.

Another set of background factors in the genesis of the self is represented in the activities of play and the game.

We find [among] children . . . invisible, imaginary companions. . . . [Children] organize in this way the responses which they call out in other persons and call out also in themselves. Of course, this playing with an imaginary companion is only a peculiarly interesting phase of ordinary play. Play in this sense, especially the stage which precedes the organized games, is a play at something. A child plays at being a mother, at being a teacher, at being a policeman; that is, he is taking different roles, as we say. We have something that suggests this in what we call the play of animals: a cat will play with her kittens, and dogs play with each other. Two dogs playing with each other will attack and defend, in a process which if carried through would amount to an actual fight. There is a combination of responses which checks the depth of the bite. But we do not have in such a situation the dogs taking a definite role in the sense that a child deliberately takes the role of another. This tendency on the part of the children is what we are working with in the kindergarten where the roles which the children assume are made the basis for training. When a child does assume a role he has in himself the stimuli which call out that particular response or group of responses. He may, of course, run away when he is chased, as the dog does, or he may turn around and strike back just as the dog does in his play. But that is not the same as playing at something. Children get together to "play Indian." This means that the child has a certain set of stimuli which call out in itself the responses that they would call out in others, and which answer to an Indian, in the play period the child utilizes his own responses to these stimuli which he makes use of in building a self. The response which he has a tendency to make to these stimuli organizes them. He plays that he is, for instance, offering himself something, and he buys it; he gives a letter to himself and takes it away; he addresses himself as a parent, as a teacher; he arrests himself as a policeman. He has a set of stimuli which call out in himself the sort of responses they call out in others. He takes this group of responses and organizes them into a certain whole. Such is the simplest form of being another to one's self. It involves a temporal situation. The child says something in one character and responds in another character, and then his responding in another character is a stimulus to himself in the first character, and so the conversation goes on. A certain organized structure arises in him and in his other which replies to it, and these carry on the conversation of gestures between themselves.

If we contrast play with the situation in an organized game, we note the essential difference that the child who plays in a game must be ready to take the attitude of everyone else involved in that game, and that these different roles must have a definite relationship to each other. Taking a very simple game such as hide-and-seek, everyone, with the exception of the one who is hiding, is a person who is hunting. A child does not require more than the person who is hunted and the one who is hunting. If a child is playing in the first sense he just goes on playing, but there is no basic organization gained. In that early stage he passes from one role to another just as a whim takes him. But in a game where a number of individuals are involved, then the child taking one role must be ready to take the role of everyone else. If he gets in a "ball nine," he must have the responses of each position involved in his own position. He must know what everyone else is going to do in order to carry out his own play. He has to take all of these roles. They do not all have to be present in consciousness at the same time, but at some moments he has to have three or four individuals present in his own attitude, such as the one who is going to throw the ball, the one who is going to catch it, and so on. These responses must be, in some degree, present in his own make-up. In the game, then, there is a set of responses of such others so organized that the attitude of one calls out the appropriate attitudes of the other.

This organization is put in the form of the rules of the game. Children take a great interest in rules. They make rules on the spot in order to help themselves out of difficulties. Part of the enjoyment of the game is to get these rules. Now, the rules are the set of responses which a particular attitude calls out. You can demand a certain response in others if you take a certain attitude. These responses are all in yourself as well. There you get an organized set of such responses as that to which I have referred, which is something more elaborate than the roles found in play. Here there is just a set of responses that follow on each other indefinitely. At such a stage we speak of a child as not yet having a fully developed self. The child responds in a fairly intelligent fashion to the immediate stimuli that come to him, but they are not organized. He does not organize his life as we would like to have him do, namely, as a whole. There is just a set of responses of the type of play. The child reacts to a certain stimulus, and the reaction is in himself that is called out in others, but he is not a whole self. In his game he has to have an organization of these roles; otherwise, he cannot play the game. The game represents the passage in the life of the child from taking the role of others in play to the organized part that is essential to self-consciousness in the full sense of the term.

The fundamental difference between the game and play is that in the [former] the child must have the attitude of all the others involved in that game. The attitudes of the other players which the participant assumes organize into a sort of unit, and it is that organization which controls the response of the individual. The illustration used was of a person playing baseball. Each one of his own acts is determined by his assumption of the action of the others who are playing the game. What he does is controlled by his being everyone else on that team, at least insofar as those attitudes affect his own particular response. We get then an "other" which is an organization of the attitudes of those involved in the same process.

A multiple personality is in a certain sense normal. . . . There is usually an organization of the whole self with reference to the community to which we belong, and the situation in which we find ourselves. What the society is, whether we are living with people of the present, people of our own imaginations, [or] people of the past, varies, of course, with different individuals. Normally, within the sort of community as a whole to which we belong, there is a unified self, but that may be broken up. To a person who is somewhat unstable and in whom there is a line of cleavage, certain activities become impossible, and that set of activities may separate and evolve into another self. Two separate "me's" and "I's," two different selves, result, and that is the condition under which there is a tendency to break up the personality. There is an account of a professor of education who disappeared, was lost to the community, and later turned up in a logging camp in the West. He freed himself of his occupation and turned to the woods where he felt, if you like, more at home. The pathological side of it was the forgetting, the leaving out of the rest of the self. This result involved getting rid of certain bodily memories which would identify the individual to himself. We often recognize the lines of cleavage that run through us. We would be glad to forget certain things, get rid of things the self is bound up with in past experiences. What we have here is a situation in which there can be different selves, and it is dependent upon the set of social reactions that is involved as to which self we are going to be.

The unity and structure of the complete self reflects the unity and structure of the social process as a whole; and each of the elementary selves of which it is composed reflects the unity and structure of one of the various aspects of that process in which the individual is implicated. In other words, the various elementary selves which constitute, or are organized into, a complete self are the various aspects of the structure of that complete self answering to the various aspects of the structure of the social process as a whole; the structure of the complete self is thus a reflection of the complete social process. The organization and unification of a social group is identical with the organization and unification of any one of the selves arising within the social process in which that group is engaged, or which it is carrying on.

The organized community or social group which gives to the individual his unity of self may be called "the generalized other." The attitude of the generalized other is the attitude of the whole community.

I have emphasized what I have called the structures upon which the self is constructed, the framework of the self, as it were. . . . We cannot be ourselves unless we are also members in whom there is a community of attitudes which control the attitudes of all. We cannot have rights unless we have common attitudes. That which we have acquired as self-conscious persons makes us such members of society and gives us selves. Selves can exist only in definite relationships to other selves. No hard-and-fast line can be drawn between our own selves and the selves of others, because our own selves exist and enter as such into our experience only insofar as the selves of others exist and enter as such into our experience also. The individual possesses a self only in relation to the selves of the other members of his social group; and the structure of his self expresses or reflects the general behaviour pattern of this social group to which he belongs; just as does the structure of the self of every other individual belonging to this social group.

Reflective Questions

1. What does Mead mean when saying that the self is both subject and object? How does the self arise? How is play important in this process?
2. How are games different from play? What do we develop through games? In what sense is a multiple personality normal?
3. Read about the case of Anna, a severely neglected girl who grew up isolated from human contact until age 5, in Kingsley Davis's "Extreme Isolation of a Child" and "Final Note on a Case of Extreme

Isolation." What happens to children who grow up in isolation or without regular interaction with others? What capabilities do they lack? Are those abilities recoverable? How?

4. Watch preschoolers play soccer at http://www.youtube.com/watch?v=9vgov8MyuuA or in person. Then watch middle schoolers play soccer at http://www.youtube.com/watch?v=PxB1W228yOg or another game. What is different about their play? Why don't preschoolers pass to each other? What notions of self do the middle schoolers have that the preschoolers don't have?

18

Young Children's Racial and Ethnic Definitions of Self

DEBRA VAN AUSDALE AND JOE R. FEAGIN

Both Cooley and Mead propose that the individual acquires a self by taking the attitude of others toward himself or herself. What they imply, but do not explicitly address, is that the attitude of others toward the individual, the way they respond to her or him, is guided by social meanings. We define one another in terms of shared systems of social classification and typification. We attribute different identities and different characteristics to one another based on those classifications and respond to one another accordingly. As individuals come to respond to themselves as others do, they define themselves similarly and assume the identities and characteristics others attribute to them. For example, within moments after birth, most newborns are identified as either female or male, and from that moment forward they are responded to as either a girl or a boy. As children come to understand gender classification, they also start to understand the gender-related meanings of names others call them and ways others treat them. Responding to themselves as others do, they adopt the gender identity others attribute to them as their own and take on the characteristics others attribute to them based on that identification. Gender identity thereby becomes an important dimension of the self. By the age of five, if not earlier, most children emphatically identify themselves as either a girl or a boy and insist on dressing, playing with toys, and generally acting in ways that confirm that identity.

Similarly, in a racially and ethnically diverse and conscious society like our own, racial and ethnic identity often is an important dimension of the self. This selection examines young children's use of racial identities in a preschool that promotes racial and ethnic diversity and tolerance. Although many developmental theories argue that very young children cannot understand racial and ethnic distinctions, this study demonstrates otherwise. It illustrates how children use skin color, family background, national origin, and other racial and ethnic "markers" to define themselves and others. More tellingly, it suggests that preschool-age children adopt the racial and ethnic identities others attribute to them as their own.

Although most children eventually do adopt the racial and ethnic identities others attribute to them, they do not passively acquire racial and ethnic identities but actively explore racial and ethnic classification in their interactions with others. Their racial and ethnic classifications often do not correspond to those of adults, but they clearly recognize that such classifications are of some importance. Others', including their peers', responses to their racial and ethnic identifications deepen their understanding of and sharpen their skill in applying the socially prevailing system of racial and ethnic identification. Unfortunately, as this study illustrates, young children consequently learn that different racial and ethnic identities are not equally valued. On the other hand, children's creative uses of racial and ethnic identities reveal just how arbitrary racial and ethnic identification is. The grounds on which they racially and ethnically identify themselves and others are questionable only if the grounds on which adults do so remain unquestioned. Yet, however arbitrary, racial and ethnic identification is an important dimension of self in our own and many other societies. We find ourselves on what might be called, borrowing the language of Zerubavel's earlier selection, racial and ethnic islands of meaning separated by a wide gulf from those on other islands. This separation is not natural but a product of how others have responded to us.

In this [selection] we examine when, where, and how children make use of racial and ethnic understandings and distinctions to define themselves and others in their everyday lives. . . . Our [empirical information] come[s] from extensive observations of fifty-eight preschool age children over nearly a year in a large preschool in an urban setting. The children involved in this study ranged in age from barely three to more than six years of age. . . . The preschool had several racially and ethnically diverse classrooms and employed a popular antibias curriculum. The school's official data on children in the classroom we observed was as follows: white (twenty-four); Asian (nineteen); Black (four); biracial (for example, Black and white, three); Middle Eastern (three); Latino (two); and other (three). . . .

Debra Van Ausdale, who did the classroom observations, made a conscious effort to play down or eliminate the researcher/adult role and to remain nonauthoritarian and supportive in her interactions with the children. While some of the children were initially puzzled by her behavior, they soon accepted that an adult could actually not be in charge of anything or anyone. . . . Debi was able to operate as a non-sanctioning playmate-adult. Debi's activities in the day care center evolved to become a combination of teacher's helper, children's playmate, and official lap for children who needed comforting. Debi was soon accepted by the children as a non-threatening, uninteresting component of the preschool world. . . .

The obvious, physically grounded racial and ethnic markers of skin color, facial features, and hair color and texture were widely used within the children's interactions with each other. A variety of other, more subtle symbols also came into play. . . . Children as young as three invented complex combinations of racial meaning, for themselves and for others, and incorporated social relationships and physical characteristics to produce explanations for how their world was racially constructed and maintained. . . .

[For example, in one] episode in the classroom, skin color . . . takes center stage. It is just after nap, and Mark, a white teacher's aide, is sitting with Lu (3, Chinese), Susan (4, Chinese), Corinne (4, African/white), and Mike (4, Black). The children are listening to a story read by another teacher. The purpose of stories after naptime is to delay the children from racing to the snack tables before their hands are washed. They are required to sit and listen until they are released, and this release is accomplished by allowing only a few children at a time to leave the room. This prevents them from lining up and destroying each other while they wait. A favorite device for delay is to play the "color of the day" game, where children must remain seated unless they are wearing a particular color of clothing. Jeanne, the teacher, finishes her reading and announces, "If you have something brown on, you can get up and wash you[r] hands for snack."

The children look around and seem to collectively decide that this invitation includes brown skin, hair, and eyes. Mike jumps up, yelling, "I have brown skin on!" and rushes to the sink to be the first in line for food. Upon seeing this, Corinne also smiles widely, yells, "Me too!" and dashes away. Mark, regarding Lu with a smile, leans over and tells her, "You have brown skin too." Lu retorts, "I do NOT!" She appears to be very indignant. "I have white skin." Lu looks to Susan to support her. Susan verifies this, telling Mark, "Lu's skin is white, Mark, not brown." Mark seems surprised, then says, "My skin is brown from the sun." Susan nods, remarking, "Lu, you have brown eyes." Lu looks her over and smiles saying, "So do you!" Susan peers deeply into Mark's face, asking him, "Do I have brown eyes?" Mark gazes back, pretending to think deeply. "Why yes, you do have brown eyes!" he finally declares. "So we can both go get snack," Susan declares. All three of them rise and go to the next room.

The desirability of whiteness, of white identity and esteem, is . . . evident in [this] exchange. . . . Lu . . . insists that she . . . is white, not brown, despite the fact that she would probably not be construed by others as white since her skin has an olive tone. She angrily denies having brown skin and draws another child in to support her evaluation. . . . One significant aspect of Lu's denial is her anger at being assumed to have darker skin. She is annoyed that Mark would make such an error and appeals to another child to verify her skin color for him. Her indignation at his mistake is a clear indicator of the importance she is already attaching to her physical appearance and, more importantly, to valuing the category of whiteness. She seems to want to deny that she could possibly be dark or close to the category of Blackness.

Here we see an Asian child trying to find her place in a white-dominated society that implicitly and explicitly accents a racist continuum running from positive whiteness to undesirable Blackness. [C]hildren's actions and understandings in their interactive settings reveal aspects of the larger society and its deep-lying historical roots. As they have entered and increased in number in the United States, each new group of color has usually been placed, principally by the dominant white group, somewhere on a white-to-Black status continuum, the common gauge of social acceptability. . . . This long standing continuum accents physical characteristics and color coding in which European-like features and cultural norms tend to be highly privileged. Not surprisingly, all children in this society learn at an early age that, generally speaking, whiteness is privileged and darkness is not—and thus their choices in this regard are usually not surprising. In particular, Asian and Latino American children, like their parents, may often find themselves placed by whites on the continuum without their active involvement, and thus they may struggle for a better placement, and definition, of themselves on that white-originated continuum. . . .

* * *

Adult definitions and reconstructions of children's activities have a strong influence on . . . children's lived realities. . . . In [the following] episode, . . . we see . . . that the presence of adults radically changes the nature of interaction between children. . . . [C]hildren realize that adults disapprove of some of their activity. Their awareness of adults' opinions prompts them to avoid confrontations or arguments with grown people, choosing instead to merely acquiesce to adult demands.

Debi is sitting with . . . three children on the steps to the deck, playing Simon Says. Brittany (4, white) is Simon. While Debi stays in the background, Rita (3, white/Latina) and Joseph (3, Black) discuss what racial group they belong to. Keep in mind that this conversation is unprompted by adult influence and that the only adult on the scene so far is Debi, who is being thoroughly ignored. Joseph informs Rita, "I'm Black, and you're white." "No," she retorts angrily, "I'm not white, I'm mixed." The two debate back and forth for a few moments, their voices getting louder and angrier. Joseph maintains his definition of Rita, and she as vigorously denies it, reiterating and reinforcing her own conception. Debi listens and watches quietly, ready to intercede if the children get too upset. However, the noise attracts the attention of a teacher who enters the scene from inside the building and approaches as Rita shouts, "I'm mixed, you stupid!" into Joseph's face. He merely rolls his eyes at her, making her even angrier.

Patricia, an African American teacher, enters this scene from inside the classroom . . . [and joins] the children on the playground. She listens to Rita's last declaration, quickly evaluates the situation, and intervenes. "You're not mixed, Rita, you're Spanish. What race am I?" Patricia is making an attempt to change the subject between the two, in hopes of calming the argument. Rita looks up at Patricia and reluctantly replies, "Mixed." "Mixed!?" Patricia responds, laughing. "Mixed with what?" Rita ponders for a moment, looking uncomfortable. "Blue," she says finally. Patricia is wearing an entirely blue outfit today. "Oh," Patricia says, "I'm Black too, like Joseph; I'm not mixed. What an interesting conversation you guys are having." Patricia smiles ineffectively at the children, which prompts them to begin squirming and looking for a way out. Rita says nothing in response, and Joseph has remained silent throughout Patricia's exchange with Rita. The child leading Simon Says (Brittany) finally tells the kids to go to the playground, and Rita and Joseph run off in different directions. Patricia smiles at Debi, shaking her head, but offers no comments. . . .

Here, the teacher seems to allow no mixed category for a child's identity and self-conception. This is suggestive of a common adult tendency to limit children's understandings of the nuances of racial meaning. In Rita's case, her use of the term "mixed" probably referred to her knowledge of her parents' origins. Her mother and father were from different countries in Latin America. While she appeared white to outside observers, with pale skin and curly dark hair, her assessment of herself was that she was mixed. Joseph's insistence that she was white finally provoked her into an angry retort, complete with name-calling. Rita's racial-ethnic group status is very important to her. She reacts to the teacher's inquiry by becoming relatively uncommunicative. Clearly not wishing to engage in the argument with a teacher, Rita and Joseph abandon their interaction and address the more urgent need of responding to an adult. The lesson is not lost on them, however, given their behavior. It is better, in their world, to submit to the adults' definitions of racial matters than to attempt to enter an argument. Young children quickly learn that debates with adults are typically unproductive.

The Children's Views

Both teachers and children regularly seized upon the connections between skin color and other markers of differences between people, although for different reasons. The celebration of ethnic and racially oriented holidays precipitated considerable interaction among the children, and at times this interest incorporated skin color and its salience to ethnic identity. Children were keenly interested in any information about unfamiliar customs and holidays. Non-Jewish children, regardless of race, delighted in activities oriented around Hanukkah, such as the making of challah and storytime books about the Festival of Lights. White children displayed intense interest in explanations of Kwanzaa, asking questions and listening quietly as teachers read books about this holiday. The history of Kwanzaa's origins was covered in the curriculum and was made a point of discussion by the teachers. That different holidays were connected to different racial and ethnic groups was not missed by the children. In the case of Kwanzaa, teachers explicitly connected the holiday to African Americans, as is appropriate. The children, however, refined and extended this meaning on their own. In this next situation, one child uses skin color as a determinant of what kind of ethnic activity another child can do.

Aaron (4, white) taunts Amy (4, Black/white). She is alone, playing quietly near the gazebo. He approaches her and sticks his tongue out, informing her, "You can't celebrate Kwanzaa, you're not Black." Amy retorts, "Oh yes I am. You don't know. You're stupid." "I am not," he replies, sniffing at her and adding, "and you're not Black." "I am too Black!" Amy responds hotly. "My Dad is Black and so is his parents, my granddad and grandma." "Stupid!" he shouts at her. "You're stupid!" she yells right back. "You don't know nothing about me." She rises and faces Aaron with an angry glare on her face. Aaron responds in kind, and they glare at each other until he finally backs down and leaves. Amy resumes her play.

It is immediately apparent that Aaron defined Amy's qualifications to participate in Kwanzaa celebrations according to her skin color. He has named and imposed his comprehension of what Black identity is and how it is to be measured and noted. Amy's skin was pale, and she had curly, dark blond hair. According to Aaron's interpretation, Kwanzaa was for "Black" people as he mentally defined them, and thus Amy was not to be included. She was, to all outward appearances, white. Amy, however, relied on her family history and her knowledge of black and white ancestry and its meaning to define her capacity to be included in Kwanzaa. Each child was basing their interpretation of Amy's status on different criteria, each using a different model of explanation. For the white child, another's skin hue was decisive. For the Black child, skin color was but one gauge. Far more important were her ancestry and knowledge of her family. Her skin color was not a key factor for her. . . .

In yet another situation, skin color provides the opportunity for extensive comparison with the colors of other objects and the color of people. In this scene, Taleshia [3, Black] makes use of color to categorize other things and other people in order to draw a contrast with herself. Her understanding of self, as an abstraction, is evident in this exchange.

Debi sits on the rug, cross-legged, with Taleshia leaning up against her. This is a common position for Debi, and children at times will vie for the use of her as a cushion. They are waiting for a teacher-led activity to begin. Taleshia snuggles up and says, "Your T-shirt is black." Debi agrees and adds, "[I] really like black. It's a pretty color." Taleshia nods, announcing, "Your hair is black." Again Debi agrees. The child continues, "And so is Mike's hair and Steven's hair and Mitchell's hair and Elizabeth's hair." She has named all the Asian and African American children currently in the room. Debi nods, "Black hair is prettier than T-shirt." Taleshia laughs, touches Debi's arm and remarks, smiling, "I'm Black too." Debi says, "Yes, and so is Mike." Taleshia nods again and says, "And Joseph." She holds her hand up, turns it from side to side. "See?" she asks. "I'm Black!" She shouts the last word, delighted; holds up her hands; and sings loudly, "I'm Black, Black, Black." By now she is in Debi's lap. She holds her arm up against Debi's legs. "I'm *real* black," she notes, eyeing the contrast between the two skin tones. "And I'm *real white*," Debi replies, imitating her emphasis. Again Taleshia laughs and sings, "I'm Black, Black, Black!" The two remain in contact, with Taleshia singing and Debi serving as her perch, until the teacher-led activity begins.

The contrast between Debi's pale skin and Taleshia's dark skin is striking. The conversation she started was a device employed to engage Debi, first in a maneuver to gain possession of Debi's lap. Then Taleshia moved her comparisons from clothing to hair color to skin color. She made a game of it, moving with ease from one object to another, all the while proclaiming her awareness and delight in her own color. She also managed to get exclusive control over an adult's attention, quite an achievement for a preschool child. . . .

More mental pictures are created in the next account, with color and skin again incorporating nonhuman objects. There are several rabbits in residence at this school. The two males are gray and white and black and white, and the solitary female is solid white. True to their nature, the rabbits have indulged in procreation, and the result was six bunnies: two solid black in color, three white, and one black and white spotted. Corinne (4, African/white) and Sarah (4, white) are playing with the bunnies, which are temporarily contained in a galvanized bucket while a teacher cleans out their cage. The bunnies are about a week old and are an object of great interest for the children. The two girls count the tiny rabbits and discuss their colors. Corinne announces, "The black ones are girls, and the white ones are boys." Sarah gazes into the bucket, then looks skeptical and asks, "How do you know?" Corinne instructs, "My mommy is Georgine and she is Black and she is a girl, so the black ones are girls. My daddy is David and he is white and he is a boy, so the white ones are boys." Sarah giggles. She picks up the lone black and white spotted bunny and asks Corinne, "Well, what's this one, then?" Corinne gets a huge smile on her face and yells, "That's *me*!" at the top of her lungs. Both girls dissolve into silliness, abandon the bunnies, and run off.

The dual nature of Corinne's origins is very important to her, and she makes great efforts to explain and clarify this to anyone needing educating, whether child or adult. Like all people, she experiments with what she knows to sharpen, deepen, and crystallize her understandings. She makes use of a variety of objects and situations to point out her skin color and its origin. Color matching seems to be one way of drawing out and explaining the relationship of skin color to self. For Corinne, the meaning of skin color and identity is complicated, and she does not try to simplify her explanation. She incorporates gender as well as color and family history to construct an explanation of each to another child. She is exploring the many meanings of racial group, gender, relationships, and color and experimenting with different definitions for each. Clearly, she is developing a strong sense of her multiracial identity and a positive sense of her self, in spite of the constant questioning she must endure from adults . . . about these matters. Faced with the negative imagery that is generally imposed on Black children and biracial children like herself, Corinne presses forward with a very positive interpretation and delineation of her biracial identity.

Drawing on her awareness of her own racial group and her relationship to her parents, she supplies some of those meanings to her friend, extending her awareness of her family's characteristics and her biracial identity to another child. That she is incorrect in her system for assessing the bunnies' gender is inconsequential to the importance of her own self-definition. Her analogies make some experimental sense, to her and another child, affording each with an enhanced idea of the meaning of color differences.

In a separate episode, another child makes use of the center's animals to examine this relationship between color, gender, and self, again expanding and refining the base of personal knowledge. One day, a pregnant cat took up residence near the playground. For weeks, the mother cat evaded capture and cared for her babies, but eventually the animal control staff was successful in capturing her. Her kittens had become habituated to people, and the center's director decided that they would be placed in adoptive homes. Debi volunteered to take the kittens to her veterinarian and have them checked. On her return from this trip, the following exchange with a child took place.

Debi enters the classroom with the carrier full of kittens, and meets Mike (5, Black), who runs up and asks, "Whatcha got?" Debi responds, "These are the kittens that were under the deck." "Oh, I want one!" he replies loudly, snatching at the carrier. "They already have homes, honey," Debi tells him. He ignores her, stating, "I'll have that black one, because I'm Black and me and my mommy are Black." Told again that the kittens already have homes, he says, "Oh. You want to play a game?" He immediately loses interest in the kittens when Debi tells him she must wait for the parents to pick up their new pets and that she cannot play right now. Similar to the way in which Corinne explained her parentage, Mike determines that since one kitten is black it qualifies as a pet for him and his family. In this case, color matching takes on still another meaning. . . .

Racial markers and skin color are also used to point out differences between people. Once again, for Black children and for the children who are of mixed racial-ethnic heritages or from other countries these variables are compelling. One teacher, Jeanne, is reading a storybook to the kids. Afterward, the children respond eagerly to Jeanne's question, drawn from the story, "How are we the same and different at the same time?" The children mention hair, age, and skin color. No prompting or suggestions are needed to get them going. Taleshia sits next to Debi, with her hand on Debi's leg. She studies the contrast once again, then turns and says to Debi, "We're different colors." She continues to study the skin tones, turning her arm over and back several times. Other children make observations about height, hair, and other physical characteristics. Corinne offers, "My mommy and I have the same skin, but my daddy doesn't. But we're one family." For children in families where difference is a part of daily life the nature of racial group, skin color, and other differences may assume particular importance. The more differences are noticed, in any context, the more they become part of dialogue and behavior among the children.

On one occasion talk about racial group and color involved a group of four children. The dialogue begins with a discussion of clothing colors, which moves into a comparison of clothing, hair, and skin colors. Debi is pushing Taleshia (3, Black), Christine (3, Asian), and Amber (3, Asian) on the tire swing. Brittany (4, white) comes over and informs Debi, "You have on white shoes and black socks and then black shorts." "Sure do," Debi replies; "and you have on white socks and blue shorts and a blue shirt." This technique of simply repeating what the children told her has proven to be very effective in carrying on child-centered conversations. Brittany grins, looking down and regarding her clothing with some amusement. The similarity between her clothing and Debi's is apparent. Also apparent is Brittany's ultimate design: she seeks a spot on the tire swing. Taleshia then informs Debi that Debi has black hair. Debi replies, "Yes, but really I have black and white hair. See?" Debi bends toward the children and gestures to the gray streaks in her dark hair. Taleshia looks closely and then nods her head. Debi continues to push the swing, while the three girls chat.

"You," Taleshia says emphatically to Debi, "are white." "Yes," Debi agrees and continues, "and you are Black," once again imitating a child's remarks. Taleshia grins delightedly. "She's white too," Taleshia continues, pointing at Peggy, who has now joined the group. "Yes, she is white too," Debi agrees. Taleshia regards Elizabeth (3.5, Chinese) for a moment and then announces, "She's not white." "She's not white," Taleshia repeats. Debi agrees with the child's assessment and responds, "No, she's not white, she's Chinese." Debi extends Taleshia's remark to include nationality. "She's from China," Taleshia states, verifying Debi's remark and providing evidence that she realizes the connection between "Chinese" and China. "Yes, she is," Debi agrees, while Elizabeth laughs, apparently delighted that another person is bringing her into the conversation. "She's from China too," says Taleshia, pointing at Amber. "Yes, she is from China too," Debi tells her. "She's got black hair like you do," Taleshia continues. "She sure does," Debi notes. "So does Elizabeth. Very pretty black hair," Debi adds, making Elizabeth smile. Taleshia throws her head back and laughs. "Everybody's got black hair," she says. "No," Debi disagrees, "not everybody. Who doesn't have black hair?" Debi asks her. "Robin," she replies. Taleshia thinks for a moment and adds, "Sarah." "Anybody else?" Debi asks. "Peggy!" Taleshia shouts. "Sure enough," Debi says, "but what color is it?" "Brown," Taleshia again shouts, delighted that she is getting the right answers to this game. "Right again. Is that the same as Robin's?" "No!" she shouts again. "What color is Robin's hair?" Debi asks. "Yellow."

Suddenly tired of the talk, Taleshia leans back and begins to sing, "Nanny, nanny, boo, boo, you can't get me!" to Sarah, who is passing by. "I want off now," she demands, and Debi lifts her down from the swing, replacing her with Peggy. Taleshia and Sarah enter a game of chase. Elizabeth and Amber begin to chant, "Ahhhh," starting low and rising up until it ends in screeching laughter as the tire swing moves from low to high.

The details of this scene are complex. Here the children are discussing and playing with various color and cultural issues, sometimes individually, sometimes all at once. They are quite excited by the game. A discussion of clothing quickly dissolved into an activity featuring categorization of different persons into racial and ethnic groups. The children begin their talk with a simple comparison of clothing, but the game soon evolves into a complex dialogue adding racial group, skin color, and national origins. Debi's responses to the children were primarily imitations of those addressed to her. Taleshia demonstrated a sophisticated ability to categorize the other children, recognizing that Elizabeth and Amber are not white. Yet she did not dichotomize color, reducing it to a matter of either black or white. Instead, color, racial group, and nationality are combined. Taleshia extended her evaluation of the Asian girls' color to incorporate their national origin and racial group, noting that while they were not Black, they also certainly were not white. It became necessary to use yet another category: Chinese. This category was not a new one for the children. Taleshia knew immediately that being Chinese meant a person was from China. The complicated nature of difference is not lost on this child, who strives to keep a complex matter intact.

A word here on Debi's involvement in the conversation: All the while she was engaged with the children, it was on her mind that she not lead them to conclusions. When she offered a name for the "not white" category, she was drawing on her knowledge, shared by the children, that Chinese was a category of people. The ideas of nationality and ethnicity were well known to these children. They had been exposed to many different racial, ethnic, and national labels, through their experiences with each other and through structured lessons delivered by the teaching staff. Food, language, dress, and other markers had been widely shared. That Taleshia eagerly concurred with Debi indicates that this view was not novel. Much of what Debi did in this interaction was in imitation of the children, a practice that the children themselves engage in often. . . .

In the next scene the differences between the children become an occasion for mass comparisons. We are at the tire swing again, and Debi is pushing three children, Dao (4, Asian), Rita (3, white/Latina), and Trevor (3, white), and listening to their conversations. Joseph (3, Black) joins them. Rita remarks to Debi, "You know what? I like his hair." She points to Joseph's head. His hair is done in five or six rows of plaits that run from front to back and are gathered in a knot in the back, "it's curly," Rita continues, reaching out and patting Joseph on the head. Joseph smiles at Rita as she touches his head. He says nothing. "I like his hair too," Debi tells Rita. Trevor says to Rita, "That's because he's Black." Rita agrees, adding, "Yeah, and my hair is curly too. And it's getting long and pretty. But I'm not Black, I'm Spanish." Trevor says, "My hair is straight. Debi's hair is straight too, and really, really, really, long. Right?" He looks at Debi for confirmation. "Yup," Debi agrees with him, "my hair is straight and long and dark brown with lots of gray streaks." Trevor adds, "Because you're old." Debi nods. "Old as the hills, right Dao?" Debi addresses another child. Dao nods and says, in a low voice, "My hair is straight and short and dark." This remark is unusual for Dao, who is usually very quiet, rarely saying anything. During this exchange Joseph says nothing, although he has pointed out to Debi in the past that he is Black. . . .

In this case, [the] children feel obliged to point out differences in coloring and hair type and are intrigued by these distinctions. Perhaps they suspect that other children would not notice or comment on differences unless attention is directed toward them. The exchange demonstrates the everyday nature of racial and ethnic comparisons within the center. At least eleven children were involved in the previous two dialogues, a figure that represents a substantial percentage of the center's classroom population. The children sought out differences and remarked on them in detail and at length, often with some sophistication. They are dealing with racial and ethnic identities, as well as racial-ethnic histories and cultural matters. They incorporated into their interactions many aspects of ethnicity and racial group that are not generally believed to be part of preschool children's repertoires of abilities. The extent of this sharing allows them to ask questions, support each other's conclusions, and contribute to the direction of discussion, skills developed to a significant degree outside the teacher-dominated spheres of center life. They are in charge here, acting on their thoughts and considerations. These scenes illustrate how peer relations become a critical aspect in learning about the meaning of racial and ethnic differences. No teacher initiated these conversations. Only one adult was involved and that involvement was limited. The topic of discussion was both salient and spontaneous for the children.

The children here were wrestling with complicated and socially important ideas. These markers of racial and ethnic origin informed them about each other. They named, indicated, and discussed several aspects of racial group and ethnicity. These were frank and curious discussions of social markers useful in understanding the nature of the larger world and relationships within both that world and the more constrained and circumscribed world of the preschool.

Sharing Ideas About Racial Group and Ethnicity

Since the center housed a racially and ethnically diverse population, there was plenty of opportunity for discussion about children's backgrounds. For individual children, skin color was not the only element in the creation of self-identity and self-concept. Nationality and ethnicity also occupied the center of recurring interactions in the classroom and on the playground. Sometimes this discussion arose from an activity or from an adult question to a child. On more than one occasion, however, the children themselves initiated dialogue with each other about their nationality or ethnic background.

In one situation, Kumar (6, Asian), who is visiting the classroom; Corinne (4, African/white); and Susan (4, Chinese) are discussing their origins. Susan says to Kumar, "You're not American. Where are you from?" Kumar replies, "Yes, I am American, I was born here." Susan shakes her head, "You don't look American." Kumar just looks at her, apparently waiting for further remarks, with some irritation on his face. Susan then informs him, "I'm from China. That makes me Chinese." Corinne adds, "Yes, see, she is from Chinese." "No, silly, not Chinese," says Susan, "China. China is the country. Chinese are the people." Corinne volunteers, "I'm from Africa." Susan nods, "Yes, you are from Africa, and now you are here." Corinne nods and smiles. Kumar says, "My brother is from Africa, and my mother and father are from Asia." "How can your brother be from Africa and your mother and father from Asia?" questions Susan. "That's silly. You can't be from different places." "Yes you can!" retorts Kumar. "I am from here and my brother is from Africa and my mommy and daddy are from Asia. We move around a lot," he offers in explanation. "So what *are* you?" Susan asks Kumar. "A person," he replies. He then leaves the group and goes to get a drink from the water fountain.

Kumar offered a detailed and precise explanation of his family's multiple ethnic origins. Not only was he able to describe the complexity of his family, but he offered a reasonable explanation for it. Though originally from Asia, his family had at one time lived in Africa, where a brother was born. He had been born in the United States. Susan questions him in detail, demanding explanations for what appear to her to be contradictions. Kumar was able to provide her with a detailed and accurate accounting of his family's complex national origins. Susan also observes that dark-skinned Kumar doesn't look like an American, a remark that causes him to fluff up in anger. We see that the discussion of nationality and ethnicity among children can arouse strong emotions. Kumar's response indicates that he is aware of what he looks like and that being born in the United States makes him an American. Yet Susan's categorization of what is an "American" does not seem to include dark-skinned, black-haired youngsters. She doesn't explicitly state what "American" looks like, but it is fairly clear that she is confounding a certain light-skinned appearance with American. Clearly, Kumar is uncomfortable with the entire dialogue. His final evaluation of himself is that he is a person, a status with little emotional baggage, but one with great dignity.

This example illustrates key aspects of our arguments about how children use and process ideas, understandings, and language about ethnic, racial, and nationality distinctions. A child has picked up an embedded feature of the surrounding white-dominated society and is experimenting with it in her everyday interactions. One issue here is the general understanding of what an "American" is. In most media reports, in the minds of most white Americans, and in the minds of many other people in the United States and around the globe, "American" is synonymous with native-born white American. . . . In the case above, even a four-year-old Asian child sees another child, whose parents have lived in Africa and southern Asia, as not looking "American." At the same time, she is clearly experimenting with the ideas and is willing to discuss the matter fully.

Experimentation with racial and ethnic concepts was part of most of the children's activities at the center. For the American-born children, trying out new concepts was enhanced by the ready availability of children from other countries. The diversity provided these children with opportunities to juxtapose their developing sense of self with their recognition of others as different, contrasting a sense of self-identity with their growing awareness of others. Racial and ethnic markers became useful tools for the task. The children from other lands often found that their origins became a source of conversation and interaction with others. Their racial, ethnic, and nationality backgrounds afforded them opportunities to engage in personal interaction, thereby gaining attention and increasing their knowledge of how these concepts functioned in social life.

The children of foreign-born parents afforded us with opportunities to watch deep explorations of racial and ethnic meanings and understandings. For example, Corinne, the four-year-old child of a white American parent and a Black African parent, incorporated several social variables in her young life. She was a rich source of information about racial-ethnic understandings among young children. Her biracial, dual-continent origins were questioned on numerous occasions, yet this girl successfully negotiated her biracial identity: not merely Black but also white, not only American but also distinctively African. Her multiple identities confused many adults and other children, yet she easily accounted for and understood her identities and was able to explain them and their meanings to others. She had created an extraordinarily strong sense of her self, one that she defended and explained with great dexterity.

One day, close to parent pickup time, Corinne, Mike (4, Black), and Debi are sitting at a picnic table. The two children are coloring, ignoring Debi and the other children around them. Corinne's father, David, arrives to pick her up, and when she spots him she leaps up and runs to him. They walk back to the table together, holding hands, and sit down again with Mike and Debi. David greets Debi, remarking that he would like to wait and meet his wife here.

"Who's that?" Mike demands, looking at Corinne's father. "That's my daddy," she replies, beaming at her father. Mike regards the man unsmilingly, then sniffs and shakes his head vigorously. "Uh, uh," he declares, indicating his disbelief. Corinne stares at Mike for a moment, then says, "Yes he is!" David looks on in amusement, a smile on his face. "How come he ain't Black?" Mike asks Corinne. "Because he's not," she retorts, glaring at Mike and grabbing her father's hand. "Uh, uh, you can't have a white dad. Black kids have Black dads," Mike states, smiling. "Yes I can. I do. We're from Africa." Corinne's tone has now taken on a quieter quality, but she still frowns at Mike. "Uh, uh," Mike insists, "nope." David sits smiling gently, as though he cannot quite believe what is going on in front of him.

"Stop it!" Corinne is now yelling at Mike, which prompts David to intercede. "Corinne's mommy is Black," he explains to Mike, retaining his smile. Mike does not respond to him, instead staring at the man as though he does not exist. Corinne sticks her tongue out at Mike, who ignores her and continues to stare at David. "When Black people and white people fall in love and get married they have beautiful brown babies," David continues, hugging Corinne and smiling at Mike, who does not reply. At this point, Mike's mother also arrives to pick him up from school, distracting him and ending the episode.

Mike adamantly refused to acknowledge that Corinne's father was white, despite the facts that a white man was sitting right in front of him and that Corinne declared this man to be her father. Mike justified his disbelief by referring to a rule he had garnered from his own experience: Black children could not have white parents. Mike's denial of Corinne's origins, and by implication her multiracial identity, was met with opposition from her and an explanation from her father, but he persisted. As far as he was concerned, Corinne was a Black child, and Corinne's skin color and facial features confirmed his evaluation. Hence she could not have a white parent, since in his experience Black children invariably had Black parents. The contradiction of Corinne's parentage was too much for him to bear.

Mike was not the only person who challenged Corinne's explanation of her origins. Adults, too, questioned whether or not Corinne really knew who, and what, she was. One day, during a sharing circle, Corinne was invited to describe her family and her home. She eagerly launched into a description of her home in Africa, elaborating the story with a tale about riding elephants in the backyard. As Corinne spoke, Debi overheard Cindy and Lynne, two center employees, remarking on her story. "Isn't that cute!" Cindy said, "That little girl thinks she's from Africa." Lynne smiled and said, "Oh, she probably heard her parents say that she was African American and is just confused." Corinne continued with her story, blissfully unaware of the disbelief evident on the adults' faces. . . .

Neither children nor adults had difficulty accepting that several of the children were born in Europe or Asia. Yet, whenever Corinne offered to a newcomer her story that she was from Africa, there was disbelief, especially on the part of adults. The task of explaining her origins became a recurring chore for Corinne. She was forced to continually defend herself, especially to adults, the authority figures in her life. They provided her with the most difficulties. Eventually, she acquiesced and no longer attempted to talk to adults about her origins or correct their mistaken beliefs. One day, when once again instructed by a well-meaning adult that she was African American, Corinne merely rolled her eyes and replied, "Whatever." She had learned a valuable lesson: Adults often do not believe what small children tell them, even if it is true. . . .

The belief held by most white adults that young children have little awareness of their racial-ethnic characteristics and identities acts to exacerbate a child's task of explaining herself to others. Teacher-led activities often did not lend themselves to encouraging children to explain and describe their own racial-ethnic understandings. These teacher-children activities were almost always designed around teacher questions and children's answers to those predetermined questions. This assertion is not an effort to blame teachers, or to suggest that they are somehow scheming to ignore or denigrate youngsters. This is merely the virtually universal nature of the schoolroom. Teachers ask questions; children answer. The nature of the teacher-child interaction in most cases of racial-ethnic sharing did not permit the children to engage in elaborate dialogue or provide detailed stories as they did in interaction with other children or with Debi. The children were usually limited to simple yes/no answers or an occasional explanation of an unusual custom or word. The following episode is illustrative of the pattern present when adults were in charge of self-description.

On a few occasions, especially when a new semester started or new children entered the facility, teachers led activities designed to introduce children to each other. These sharing circles were occasions for reporting all aspects of oneself, including racial group and ethnicity. Shortly after the center reopened from a holiday break, Dean, a teacher from another classroom, arranged to present new students from his room to our classroom. He begins the activity by announcing his name and that he is from the United States. The children then take turns sharing where they are from. "I'm from China," says Susan, predictably. "I'm from Korea," an Asian boy responds. "Where are you from?" Dean asks a boy, whose name tag reads "Emile." Before the child can reply, another teacher in the circle responds, "France." However, Emile vigorously shakes his head no on hearing this and points to the ground. "Are you from here, Emile?" Dean asks. Emile nods and continues to point at the ground, a smile on his face. "Are your parents from France?" Dean continues, smiling at the child. "I don't know," Emile shrugs. Dean turns his attention to the next child in the circle, "I'm from Sweden," a tall blond girl contributes. Most of the children seem to know where they or their parents are from but offer no detail. However, Kumar breaks from this pattern and tells a long, involved story about how he is from the United States, his brother is from Africa, and his parents are from Asia. "My dad is there now," he adds. "Where is your mom?" another boy asks. "She's here," replies Kumar.

Dean interrupts him, moving on to Corinne. She heaves a deep sigh and reports, "I'm from Africa." She waits, looking around her. "Really?" Dean replies, "Are you African American?" The look on Corinne's face is simply priceless. In a display of comical exaggeration, she rolls her eyes, shrugs her shoulders, and flops her hands into her lap in helpless resignation. "Nope, just plain old, stupid African," she sighs, obviously wishing this activity was over. Dean obliges her and moves on without remark. Given the question-and-answer format of these activities, the children learn that adults are not really interested in in-depth discussions with children, or in the racial-ethnic worlds in which they live and interact every day. . . .

Conclusion

In this chapter we showed how white children and children of color use the racial-ethnic concepts widely found in the surrounding societal environment to interact and build and define the meaning of their own selves and the selves of others. We saw how they interact with each other and with adults—finegrained data that are only available from extensive observations. . . . The episodes we observed in children's lives demonstrate how children obtain and organize ethnic and racial information from others and then use this information to construct their social lives. Racial and ethnic attitudes, group preferences, and self-identity are all parts of the same process: building a racial-ethnic reality.

In our study we see that the children are learning from cumulative experiences with racism, color coding, and racial-ethnic identities. Negative and positive experiences accumulate over time and in elaborate interaction, eventually, with a wide variety of different others. This makes such experiences longitudinal and significant as social phenomena. How children come to know themselves in racial-ethnic terms arises in part from their grounding in a racist society and in part from their own daily interaction with other children and with adults. Despite the fact that they might not be aware of the workings of the world in a refined, adult way, they have substantial abilities to employ self, color, and racial concepts by the time they are three. In general, the children we observed were able to use color coding consistently and in detailed comparisons, whether the color was of skin, clothing, hair, eyes, or inanimate objects. They routinely created complex explanations for themselves and each other based on skin color and offered descriptions and verification of physical characteristics in a variety of ways. Some, particularly children of color and those whose parents included someone from another country, were able to construct and maintain very complicated self-identities that incorporated aspects of racial group and ethnicity.

Reflective Questions

1. What is the "racist continuum"? How did kids construct it during their play? How did they challenge it?
2. Did children accept the racial identities that others attribute to them, or did they challenge them or create their own identities? How? What resources did they use? What role did skin color, ethnicity, and nationality play in their constructions? How did teachers and the preschool reinforce or challenge their constructions?
3. Why were racial identities so important to the kids? What emotions and self-conceptions did they have invested in particular identities? What can we learn about how identity formation works from their example?
4. Go to the website https://implicit.harvard.edu/implicit/demo/takeatest.html and take the Race, Asian, Native, Skin-tone, or Arab-Muslim Implicit Association Test. What did your test results show? Do you have an implicit racial bias? Were your test results what you expected or hoped for? Do they match your stated racial beliefs? Around 80% of Americans demonstrate an implicit racial bias. If racial biases become engrained even in the minds of people who espouse egalitarian racial beliefs, what is racism? How do our implicit biases affect our interactions with others? How do they affect our sense of self? How might we combat implicit racial biases?

Gang-Related Gun Violence and the Self

PAUL B. STRETESKY AND MARK R. POGREBIN

Sociologists commonly distinguish between the processes of primary and secondary socialization. Primary socialization refers to the process by which young children learn to become mature and functioning members of society. Secondary socialization refers to the more specific training and interaction individuals experience throughout their lives, such as learning how to be a student, how to drive a car, how to do a job, or how to be a parent.

During the primary socialization process, we learn the culture—or prevailing ways of thinking, feeling, and acting—of our society. We also acquire a sense of self. That is, through interacting with others, we learn who we are, not only as members of our family, community, and society but also as an individual. As we move from childhood into adulthood, we enter a wider array of groups and social worlds. In order to fit into these groups, we must engage in the process of secondary socialization. Through this process we learn the rules, roles, and perspectives that characterize a particular social world, such as a workplace, a college sorority, or a youth gang. As we embrace the rules, roles, and perspectives of this specific world, we are likely to see ourselves in new ways, especially if we are required to engage in new or unconventional behavior.

This selection examines how gangs serve as agents of secondary socialization that shape the conduct and self-conceptions of their members. Drawing on in-depth interviews with 22 gang members, Paul Stretesky and Mark Pogrebin highlight some of the central themes that characterize the process of gang socialization. They note that individuals often become members of a gang at a young and impressionable age, which makes them more susceptible to accepting the gang's perspective, values, and behavioral norms. The authors also reveal how gangs demand a high degree of commitment and, in turn, become the most significant group in their members' lives. Perhaps most crucially, the authors portray how gangs require their members to experience a transformation of self—a transformation that members must demonstrate through their willingness to engage in violence, particularly by using a gun. In a related vein, gangs closely link their members' identities to notions of masculinity, especially as expressed in displays of toughness and the use of violence. For gang members, the ultimate measure of one's manhood is one's willingness to be violent if threatened by someone outside of the group. The biggest peril to one's manhood is posed by those who fail to show proper respect, particularly by calling one's toughness or street reputation into question. Gang members learn that the appropriate way to deal with such expressions of disrespect is to direct serious violence toward the person who engages in them. Thus, according to the code of the gang, the maintenance of respect and a valued "reputation" demands the use of physical force, often in the form of gun violence.

Reprinted from: Mark R. Pogrebin and Paul B. Stretesky, Gang-Related Gun Violence: Socialization, Identity, and Self. *Journal of Contemporary Ethnography* 36(1): 85–114.

On a broader level, the authors of this selection show us that selves are inextricably linked to groups and to the perspectives and practices promoted by those groups. We all learn to develop self-conceptions, or ideas about who we are, through our involvements in groups. We also learn that we can only realize or sustain valued selves within that group by embracing their perspectives and enacting their codes of honor and conduct. Like the members of a gang, we rely on groups to fill us with the "stuff of culture"—values, rules, roles, feelings, meanings, and cherished identities. This "stuff" provides us with the essence of our humanity, especially by enabling us to develop and express a consequential self.

This study considers how gangs promote violence and gun use. We argue that socialization is important because it helps to shape a gang member's identity and sense of self. Moreover, guns often help gang members project their violent identities. As Kubrin (2005, 363) argues, "The gun becomes a symbol of power and a remedy for disputes." We examine the issue of gang socialization, self, and identity formation using data derived from face-to-face qualitative interviews with a sample of gang members who have been incarcerated in Colorado prisons for gun-related violent crimes. Our findings, although unique, emphasize what previous studies have found—that most gangs are organized by norms that support the use of violence to settle disputes, achieve group goals, recruit members, and defend identity. . . .

Methods

The interviews in this study of twenty-two gang members were taken from a larger qualitative study of seventy-five Colorado prison inmates who used a firearm in the commission of their most recent offense. Inmates were asked general questions about their families, schools, peer groups, neighborhoods, prior contact with the criminal justice system, and experiences with firearms. They were also asked a series of questions surrounding the circumstances that lead up to the crime for which they were currently incarcerated. It was from this vantage point that we began to see the importance of gang socialization, self, and identity as important aspects of violence and gun use.

Inmates we interviewed were located in eleven different correctional facilities scattered throughout Colorado and were randomly selected by means of a simple random sample from a list of all inmates incarcerated for a violent crime in which a firearm was involved. The overall sample was composed of 39.1% whites, 40.6% African Americans, 15.6% Hispanics, and 4.7% Asians and Middle Easterners. Eight percent of our subjects were female. The demographics of the inmates in our study correspond closely to the demographics of inmates incarcerated in Colorado prisons (see Colorado Department of Corrections 2005).

We used official inmate case files located at the Colorado Department of Corrections to verify that the twenty-two self-identified gang members were likely to have actually been gang members prior to their incarceration. That validity check substantiated what our subjects said—they did indeed appear to be gang members. Case files were also used to gain information about offenders' past criminal records to determine the validity of each inmate's responses with respect to previous offending patterns as well as characteristics associated with their most current offense.

Gang Socialization, Self, and Identity

Goffman (1959) argues that as individuals we are often "taken in by our own act" and therefore begin to feel like the person we are portraying. Baumeister and Tice (1984) describe this process as one where initial behaviors are internalized so that they become part of a person's self-perception. Once initial behaviors are internalized, the individual continues to behave in ways consistent with his or her self-perception. Related to the current study, the socialization process of becoming a gang member required a change in the subject's self-perception. That is, who did our gang members become as compared with who they once were? Social interaction is highly important in the process of socialization because it helps create one's identity and sense of self, as Holstein and Gubrium (2003, 119 [emphasis added]) point out:

> As personal as they seem, our selves and identities are extremely social. They are hallmarks of our inner lives, *yet they take shape in relation to others. We establish who and what we are through social interaction.* In some respects, selves and identities are two sides of the same coin. Selves are the subjects we take ourselves to be; identities are the shared labels we give to these selves. We come to know ourselves in terms of the categories that are socially available to us.

Most inmates we interviewed indicated that their socialization into the gang began at a relatively young age:

> At about fifteen, I started getting affiliated with the Crips. I knew all these guys, grew up with them and they were there. . . . I mean, it was like an influence at that age. I met this dude named Benzo from Los Angeles at that time. He was a Crip and he showed me a big wad of money. He said, "Hey man, you want some of this?" "Like yeh! Goddamn straight. You know I want some of that." He showed me how to sell crack, and so at fifteen, I went from being scared of the police and respecting them to hustling and selling crack. Now I'm affiliated with the Crips; I mean it was just unbelievable.

Another inmate tells of his orientation in becoming a member of a gang. He points out the glamour he associated with membership at a very impressionable age:

> I started gang banging when I was ten. I got into a gang when I was thirteen. I started just hanging around them, just basically idolizing them. I was basically looking for a role model for my generation and ethnic background; the main focus for us is the popularity that they got. That's who the kids looked up to. They had status, better clothes, better lifestyle. . . .

Consistent with Goffman's (1959) observations, once our subjects became active gang members, their transformation of identity was complete. . . . Violent behavior appeared to play an important role in this transformation. . . . Most gang members noted that they engaged in violent behavior more frequently once they joined the gang.

> At an early age, it was encouraged that I showed my loyalty and do a drive-by . . . anybody they (gangster disciples) deemed to be a rival of the gang. I was going on fourteen. At first, I was scared to and then they sent me out with one person and I seen him do it. I saw him shoot the guy. . . . So, in the middle of a gang fight I get pulled aside and get handed a pistol and he said, "It's your turn to prove yourself." So I turned around and shot and hit one of the guys (rival gang members). After that, it just got more easier, I did more and more. I had no concern for anybody.

A further illustration of [the] transformation of self is related by another inmate, who expresses the person he became through the use of violence and gun possession. Retrospectively, he indicates disbelief in what he had become.

> As a gang banger, you have no remorse. . . . When I first shot my gun for the first time at somebody, I felt bad. It was like, I can't believe I did this. But I looked at my friend and he didn't care at all. Most gang bangers can't have a conscience. You can't have remorse. You can't have any values. Otherwise, you are gonna end up retiring as a gang banger at a young age.

The situations one finds [himself] in, in this case collective gang violence, together with becoming a person who is willing to use violence to maintain membership in the gang, is indicative of a transformed identity. Strauss (1962) claims that when a person's identity is transformed, they are seen by others as being different than they were before. The individual's prior identity is retrospectively reevaluated in comparison with the present definition of a gang member. Such a transformation was part of the processional change in identity that our [interviewees] experienced.

Commitment to the Gang

We found that gang identification and loyalty to the group was a high priority for our subjects.

This loyalty to the gang was extreme. Our subjects reported that they were willing to risk being killed and were committed to taking the life of a rival gang member if the situation called for such action. That is, gang membership helped our subjects nourish their identity and at the same time provided group maintenance (Kanter 1972). As Kanter points out, the group is an extension of the individual and the individual is an extension of the group. This notion of sacrifice for the group by proving one's gang identification is expressed by an inmate who perceives his loyalty in the following terms:

> What I might do for my friends [gang peers] you might not do. You've got people out there taking bullets for their friends and killing people. But I'm sure not one of you would be willing to go to that extreme. These are just the thinking patterns we had growing up where I did.

Another inmate tells us about his high degree of identification with his gang:

> If you're not a gang member, you're not on my level . . . most of my life revolves around gangs and gang violence. I don't know anything else but gang violence. I was born into it, so it's my life.

The notion of the gang as the most important primary group in a member's life was consistently expressed by our study subjects. Our subjects often stated that they were willing to kill or be killed for the gang in order to sustain their self-perception as a loyal gang member. This extreme degree of group affiliation is similar to that of during wartime. The platoon, or in this case, the local gang, is worth dying for. In this sense, the notion of the gang as a protector was an important part of gang life. All members were expected to be committed enough to aid their peers should the need arise. The following gang member points to the important role his gang played for him in providing physical safety as well as an assurance of understanding.

> That's how it is in the hood, selling dope, gang bangin', everybody wants a piece of you. All the rival gang members, all the cops, everybody. The only ones on your side are the gang members you hang with. . . .

[T]here is some debate about whether gang members would be violent without belonging to a gang, or if formal membership in the group provided them with the opportunity to act out this way. However, we find clarity in the inmate accounts that a gang member's identity provided the context necessary to resort to violence when confronted with conflicting events, as the following inmate notes:

> I have hate toward the Crips gang members and have always had hate toward them 'cuz of what they did to my homeboys. . . . I never look back. I do my thing. I always carry a gun no matter what I am a gang member, man! There are a lot of gang members out to get me for what I done. I shot over forty people at least. That's what I do.

This perception of being a person who is comfortable with violence and the perception of himself as an enforcer type characterizes the above inmate's role within his gang. Turner (1978) suggests that roles consistent with an individual's self-concept are played more frequently and with a higher degree of participation than roles that are not in keeping with that individual's self-concept. Our study subject in this situation fits Turner's explanation of role identity nicely. His hatred for rival gangs and his willingness to retaliate most likely led to his incarceration for attempted murder.

Masculinity, Reputation, and Respect

For those gang members we interviewed, socialization into the gang and commitment to the gang appear to be central to the notion of masculinity. That is, all gang members we interviewed spoke of the importance of masculinity and how it was projected (through the creation of a reputation) and protected (through demands for respect). The notion of masculinity was constantly invoked in relation to self and identity. In short, masculinity is used to communicate to others what the gang represents, and it is used to send an important signal to others who may wish to challenge a gang's collective identity. A gang member's masculine reputation precedes him or her, so to speak.

For our gang member study population, the attributes that the gang valued consisted of factors that projected a street image that was necessary to sustain. [This image served as] a survival strategy.

Masculinity

"Every man [in a gang] is treated as a man until proven different. We see you as a man before anything." This comment by a gang member infers that masculinity is a highly valued attribute in his gang. The idea of manhood usually was brought up in the context of physical violence, often describing situations where one had to [show] one's willingness to use physical force when insulted by someone outside of the group.

> Even if you weren't in one [gang], you got people that are going to push the issue. We decide what we want to do; I ain't no punk, I ain't no busta. But it comes down to pride. It's foolish pride, but a man is going to be a man, and a boy knows he's going to come into his manhood by standing his ground.

Establishing a reputation coincides with becoming a man, entering the realm of violence, being a stand-up guy who is willing to prove his courage as a true gang member. This strong association between a willingness to perpetrate violence on a considered rival, or anyone for that matter, was a theme that defined a member's manhood. After eight years in the gang, the following participant was owed money for selling someone dope. After a few weeks of being put off by the debtor, he had to take some action to appease his gang peers who were pressuring him to retaliate.

> I joined the gang when I was eleven years old. So now that I'm in the gang for eight years, people are asking, "What are you going to do? You got to make a name for yourself." So we went over there [victim's residence] and they were all standing outside and just shot him. Everybody was happy for me, like "Yea, you shot him, you're cool," and this and that.

A sense of bravado, when displayed, played a utilitarian role in conflicting situations where a gang member attempts to get others to comply with his demands. . . . Having some prior knowledge of the threatening gang member's reputation is helpful in preventing a physical encounter, which is always risky for both parties involved. Again, the importance of firearms in this situation is critical.

> The intimidation factor with a gun is amazing. Everybody knows what a gun can do. If you have a certain type of personality, that only increases their fear of you. When it came to certain individuals who I felt were a threat, I would lift my shirt up so they would know I had one on me.

In this case, the showing of his firearm served the purpose of avoiding any altercation that could have led to injury or even worse. Carrying a gun and displaying it proved to be an intimidating, preventive factor for this gang member. The opposite behavior is noted in the following example of extreme bravado, where aggressive behavior is desired and a distinction (based on bravery) between drive-by shootings and face-to-face shootings is clear.

> If someone is getting shot in a drive-by and someone else gets hit, it is an accident. You know, I never do drive-bys. I walk up to them and shoot. I ain't trying to get anyone else shot to take care of business. . . .

The image of toughness fits well under masculinity and bravado as an attribute positively perceived by gang members we interviewed. Its importance lies in projecting an image via reputation that conveys [the] physical force they are willing to use when necessary. A clear explanation of this attribute is related by the following subject.

> Everybody wants to fight for the power, for the next man to fear him. It's all about actually killing the mother fuckers and how many mother fuckers you can kill. Drive-by shootings is old school.

The implication here is that having a collective reputation for being powerful motivates this prisoner. He notes that the tough image of shooting someone you are after instead of hiding behind the random shooting characterized by drive-bys projects an image of toughness and power.

There are others who prefer to define their toughness in terms of physical fighting without the use of any weapons—though it was often noted that it was too difficult to maintain a tough reputation under such conditions. For instance, the predicament the following gang member found himself in is one where rival gangs use guns and other lethal instruments, and as a result, his reputation as an effective street fighter proved to be of little value. In short, his toughness and fighting skills were obsolete in life-threatening encounters.

> Like my case, I'm a fighter. I don't like using guns. The only reason I bought a gun was because every time I got out of the car to fight, I'd have my ribs broken, the back of my head almost crushed with a baseball bat. I was tired of getting jumped. I couldn't get a fair fight. Nobody wanted to fight me because I had a bad reputation. Then I decided, why even fight? Everybody else was pulling guns. It's either get out of the car and get killed or kill them.

The fact that this prisoner had good fighting skills ironically forced him to carry a gun. The rules of gang fighting found him outnumbered and unarmed, placing him in a very vulnerable position to defend himself. The proliferation of firearms among urban street gangs is well documented by Blumstein (1995) and others. Lethal weapons, mainly firearms, have drastically changed the defining characteristics of gang warfare. . . .

Reputation

On a collective level, developing and maintaining the gang's reputation of being a dangerous group to deal with, especially from other groups or individuals who posed a threat to their drug operations, was important. The following inmate points out the necessity of communicating the gang's willingness to use violent retaliation against rivals. Guns often played an important role in the development and maintenance of reputation, though they were rarely utilized in situations [of conflict]:

> We had guns to fend off jackers, but we never had to use them, 'cause people knew we were straps. People knew our clique, they are not going to be stupid. We've gotten into a few arguments, but it never came to a gun battle. Even when we were gang bangin' we didn't use guns, we only fought off the Bloods.

Aside from a collective reputation, the group serves the identifying needs of its individual members (Kanter 1972). Our study participants related their need to draw upon the reputation of the gang to help them develop their own reputation, which gave them a sense of fulfillment. People want to present others with cues that will enhance desired [images] of who they are. The following participant discusses the way gang affiliation enhanced his reputation as a dangerous individual, a person not to be tested by others.

> There are people that know me; even ones that are contemplating robbing me know of me from the gang experience. They know if you try and rob me [of drugs and money], more than likely you gonna get killed. I was gonna protect what was mine. I'll die trying.

Another study subject [described how he] attained a reputation through gang activity, and [how] guns clearly played an important role in that process.

> Fear and desire to have a reputation on the streets made me do it. When I got into the streets, I saw the glamour of it. I wanted a reputation there. What better way to get a reputation than to pick up a pistol? I've shot several people.

Although each [of our interviewees] expressed a desire to be known in the community for some particular attribute, there were some gang members who simply wanted to be [widely] known, sort of achieving celebrity status.

> You basically want people to know your name. It's kind of like politicians, like that, you wanna be known. In my generation you want somebody to say, "I know him, he used to hang around with us."

Respect

Strauss (1969) argues that anger and withdrawal occur when a person is confronted with a possible loss of face. For our subjects, this anger was apparent when rivals challenged their self-identity (i.e., when our subjects were disrespected).

According to the gang members we talked to, disrespect, or rejection of self-professed identity claims by others, often was the cause of violence. Violence is even more likely to be the result of disrespect when no retaliatory action may lead to a loss of face. The following inmate relates his view on this subject in general terms.

> Violence starts to escalate once you start to disrespect me. Once you start to second guess my manhood, I'll fuck you up. You start coming at me with threats, then I feel offended. Once I feel offended, I react violently. That's how I was taught to react.

The interface of [violence and] their manhood being threatened seems to be directly associated with Strauss's (1962) concept of identity denial by an accusing other. This threat to one's masculinity by not recognizing another's status claims is an extremely serious breach of gang etiquette.

> When someone disrespects me, they are putting my manhood in jeopardy. They are saying my words are shit, or putting my family in danger. . . . Most of the time, I do it [use violence] to make people feel the pain or hurt that I feel. I don't know no other way to do it, as far as expressing myself any other way.

Hickman and Kuhn (1956) point out that the self anchors people in every situation they are involved in. Unlike other objects, they claim that the self is present in all interactions and serves as the basis from which we all make judgments and plans of reaction toward others that are part of a given situation. When being confronted by gang rivals who have been perceived as insulting an opposing gang member, the definition of street norms calls for an exaggerated response. That is, the disrespectful words must be countered with serious physical force to justify the disrespected individual's maintenance of self (or manhood). A prime example of feeling disrespected is discussed in terms of territory and the unwritten rules of the street by one gang member who told us of an encounter with a rival gang who disrespected him to the point that he felt he was left with no other alternative choice of action but to shoot them. . . .

[He explained that] the gang members in question showed up in [his] neighborhood and shot at him as he was walking with his two small children to a convenience store to get ice cream:

> I was just so mad and angry for somebody to disrespect me like that and shoot. We got a rule on the street. There is rules. You don't shoot at anybody if there is kids. That's one of the main rules of the street. They broke the rules. To me that was telling me that they didn't have no respect for me or my kids. So, that's how I lost it and shot them. I was so disrespected that I didn't know how to handle it.

The notion of disrespect is analogous to an attack [on] the self. Because many of the inmates in our sample reported that masculinity is an important attribute of the self, they believed any disrespect was a direct threat to their masculinity. For those brought up in impoverished high-crime communities, as these study population participants were, there are limited alternatives to such conflicting situations (Anderson 1999). To gang members caught in those confrontational encounters, there is a very limited course of action, that of perpetrating violence toward those who would threaten their self-concept. . . .

Discussion and Conclusion

Gangs not only fulfill specific needs for individuals that other groups in disadvantaged neighborhoods may fail to provide, but as our interviews suggest, they are also important primary groups into which individuals become socialized. It is not surprising, then, that self-concept and identity are closely tied to gang membership. Guns are also important in this regard. We propose that for the gang members in our sample, gang-related gun violence can be understood in terms of self and identity that are created through the process of socialization and are heavily rooted in notions of masculinity. Thus, our analysis provides insight into the way gang socialization can produce violence—especially gun-related violence.

We find that related to the issue of gun violence, the possession and use of guns among gang members is relatively important because, in addition to protecting gang members, guns are tools that aid in identity formation and impression management. As many of our subject narratives suggest, guns were often connected in some way to masculine attributes. Gang members reported to us that they could often use guns to project their reputation or reclaim respect.

It is not clear from our research whether simply eliminating or reducing access to guns can reduce gun-related gang violence. For example, studies like the Youth Firearms Violence Initiative conducted by the U.S. Department of Justice's Office of Community Oriented Policing Services does suggest that gun violence can be reduced by focusing, at least in part, on reducing access to guns (Dunworth 2000). However, that study also indicates that once these projects focusing on access to guns end, gang violence increases to previous levels. Moreover, our interviews suggest that there is little reason to believe that gang members would be any less likely to look to gangs as a source of status and protection and may use other weapons—though arguably less lethal than guns—to aid in transformations of identity and preserve a sense of self. Thus, although reduction strategies may prevent gang-related violence in the short-term, there is little evidence that this intervention strategy will have long-term effects because it does not adequately deal with gang culture and processes of gang socialization.

Appendix

Characteristics of Inmates in Sample

ID	Age	Sex	Race/ Ethnicity	Education (Years)	Offense	Sentence (Years)	Years Served	No. Previous Felonies
1	28	M	Hispanic	11	Attempted first degree murder	16	7	0
2	21	M	Black	7	Second degree kidnapping	16	3	1
3	20	M	Black	11	Attempted first degree murder	21	3	3
4	21	M	Hispanic	11	Second degree assault	3	2	2
5	21	M	Black	12	First degree murder	Life	2	2
6	48	M	White	12	Second degree assault	14	6	7
7	33	M	Black	12	Attempted first degree murder	16	9	2
8	22	M	Black	9	Second degree assault	25	5	4
9	38	M	Black	12	Manslaughter	22	9	1
10	28	M	White	12	Second degree murder	30	8	2
11	25	M	Black	11	First degree murder	Life	4	2
12	23	M	Black	12	First degree assault	14	2	3
13	24	M	White	10	Aggravated robbery	20	5	2
14	32	M	Black	12	First degree murder	40	16	0

ID	Age	Sex	Race/ Ethnicity	Education (Years)	Offense	Sentence (Years)	Years Served	No. Previous Felonies
15	29	M	Hispanic	12	Second degree assault	5	4	1
16	25	M	Black	12	First degree assault	3	1	1
17	32	M	Black	10	Attempted first degree murder	20	3	2
18	20	M	Asian	9	Second degree kidnapping	40	3	0
19	26	F	Black	11	Aggravated robbery	8	4	0
20	43	M	White	12	First degree assault	9	0	2
21	33	M	Black	12	Second degree murder	35	5	0
22	23	M	White	11	First degree assault	45	5	1

References

Anderson, Elijah. 1999. *Code of the street: Decency, violence, and the moral life of the inner city.* New York: W.W. Norton.

Baumeister, Roy, and Dianne Tice. 1984. Role of self-presentation and choice in cognitive dissonance under forced compliance. *Journal of Personality and Social Psychology* 46:5–13.

Blumstein, Alfred. 1995. Violence by young people: Why the deadly nexus? *National Institute of Justice Journal* 229:2–9.

Colorado Department of Corrections. 2005. *Statistical report, fiscal year 2004.* Colorado Springs: Office of Planning and Analysis.

Dunworth, Terence. 2000. *National evaluation of youth firearms violence initiative. Research in brief.* Washington, DC: U.S. Department of Justice Programs, National Institute of Justice.

Goffman, Erving. 1959. *The presentation of self in everyday life.* Garden City, NY: Doubleday.

Hickman, C. Addison, and Manford Kuhn. 1956. *Individuals, groups, and economic behavior.* New York: Dryden.

Holstein, James, and Jaber Gubrium. 2003. *Inner lives and social worlds.* New York: Oxford University Press.

Kanter, Rosabeth. 1972. *Commitment and community: Communes and utopias in sociological perspective.* Cambridge, MA: Harvard University Press.

Kubrin, Charis. 2005. Gangstas, thugs, and hustlas: Identity and the code of the street in rap music. *Social Problems* 52:360–78.

Strauss, Anselm. 1962. Transformations of identity. In *Human behavior and social processes: An interactional approach,* ed. Arnold Rose (63–85). Boston: Houghton Mifflin.

———. 1969. *Mirrors and masks: The search for identity.* New York: Macmillan.

Turner, Ralph. 1978. The role and the person. *American Journal of Sociology* 84:1–23.

Reflective Questions

1. How did joining a gang change people's self-perceptions? What did gang members prioritize after joining the gang?
2. How did gang members maintain a masculine self? How did they protect the reputation of the gang? Why did gang members turn to violence when they were disrespected?
3. What role did guns play in identity formation? Why is reducing access to guns unlikely to eliminate gang violence?
4. Gangs aren't the only ones who disseminate the "stuff" of gang culture. The media do this too, and they do it well beyond the confines of the neighborhood conditions that foster gang membership. If gangs allow members to develop a valued self otherwise difficult to maintain in certain neighborhoods, why do people outside

of those neighborhoods consume gang culture? What identities are they developing? Why? What tools do they use? Does consumption of gang culture have the same effect on identity formation as gang membership? Why or why not?

5. Think back through your teenage years to the group most important to you. What was this group? How did you become socialized into it? What rituals were involved? What effect did they have on your sense of self? Why was this group so important to you as compared to other groups?

The Dissolution of the Self

KENNETH J. GERGEN

Many of the selections in this volume explain and illustrate how the self is formed and shaped by social experience. This most basic principle of sociological psychology clearly implies that the character of the self would change as the character of social life historically changes. That, in turn, suggests that our inner lives and selves are quite different from those of all but our most immediate ancestors. There seems to be little doubt that the character of social life in most human communities has undergone profound changes during the twentieth century. Kenneth Gergen examines some of the psychological consequences of these changes in this selection.

In an earlier selection, George Herbert Mead observed that the individual's adoption of the attitude of an organized community, or generalized other, unifies her or his self. Today, however, such a unification of self is more difficult. Contemporary modes of travel and communication expose us to the often inconsistent attitudes of countless people and communities. They allow us to maintain relationships, despite physical separation, and to participate in communities spread over great distances. Television and movies, not to mention newspapers, magazines, and books, bring us into contact with numerous other actual and fictional people and communities. This is what Gergen calls social saturation, *and it leads to an increasingly dense population of the self. The voices of countless significant and generalized others fill our heads, and those voices are seldom in unison or even in harmony.*

Our adoption of the attitudes of such countless and contentious significant and generalized others does not unify our selves but pulls them apart. Gergen calls this new pattern of self-consciousness multiphrenia, *which literally means "many minds." We are many different things to many different people and to ourselves. We interpret our experiences and define ourselves in many different and often incompatible ways and evaluate ourselves according to many different and incompatible standards. According to Gergen, that is why we often feel overwhelmed, inadequate, and uncertain. Neither our hearts nor our minds speak with a single voice or for a unified self. Consequently, Gergen argues, the belief that we possess a single true or real self begins to erode. We become increasingly aware that it is our connections to others that make us what we are. We no longer ask ourselves, "Who am I?" We ask others, "Who can I be with you?" This is what Gergen calls* postmodern being*—a new kind of human being living a new kind of social life.*

. . . Cultural life in the twentieth century has been dominated by two major vocabularies of the self. Largely from the nineteenth century, we have inherited a romanticist view of the self, one that attributes to each person characteristics of personal depth: passion, soul, creativity, and moral fiber. This vocabulary is essential to the formation of deeply committed relations,

Reprinted from: Kenneth J. Gergen, *The Saturated Self*, pp. 6–7, 61–62, 68–71, 73–80, 146, 170.

dedicated friendships, and life purposes. But since the rise of the modernist world-view beginning in the early twentieth century, the romantic vocabulary has been threatened. For modernists, the chief characteristics of the self reside not in the domain of depth, but rather in our ability to reason—in our beliefs, opinions, and conscious intentions. In the modernist idiom, normal persons are predictable, honest, and sincere. Modernists believe in educational systems, a stable family life, moral training, and rational choice of marriage partners.

Yet, as I shall argue, both the romantic and the modern beliefs about the self are falling into disuse, and the social arrangements that they support are eroding. This is largely a result of the forces of social saturation. Emerging technologies saturate us with the voices of humankind—both harmonious and alien. As we absorb their varied rhymes and reasons, they become part of us and we of them. Social saturation furnishes us with a multiplicity of incoherent and unrelated languages of the self. For everything we "know to be true" about ourselves, other voices within respond with doubt and even derision. This fragmentation of self-conceptions corresponds to a multiplicity of incoherent and disconnected relationships. These relationships pull us in myriad directions, inviting us to play such a variety of roles that the very concept of an "authentic self" with knowable characteristics recedes from view. The fully saturated self becomes no self at all. . . .

I . . . equate the saturating of self with the condition of postmodernism. As we enter the postmodern era, all previous beliefs about the self are placed in jeopardy, and with them the patterns of action they sustain. Postmodernism does not bring with it a new vocabulary for understanding ourselves, new traits or characteristics to be discovered or explored. Its impact is more apocalyptic than that: the very concept of personal essences is thrown into doubt. Selves as possessors of real and identifiable characteristics—such as rationality, emotion, inspiration, and will—are dismantled. . . .

The Process of Social Saturation

A century ago, social relationships were largely confined to the distance of an easy walk. Most were conducted in person, within small communities: family, neighbors, townspeople. Yes, the horse and carriage made longer trips possible, but even a trip of thirty miles could take all day. The railroad could speed one away, but cost and availability limited such travel. If one moved from the community, relationships were likely to end. From birth to death, one could depend on relatively even-textured social surroundings. Words, faces, gestures, and possibilities were relatively consistent, coherent, and slow to change.

For much of the world's population, especially the industrialized West, the small, face-to-face community is vanishing into the pages of history. We go to country inns for weekend outings, we decorate condominium interiors with clapboards and brass beds, and we dream of old age in a rural cottage. But as a result of the technological developments just described, contemporary life is a swirling sea of social relations. Words thunder in by radio, television, newspaper, mail, telephone, fax, wire service, electronic mail, billboards, Federal Express, and more. Waves of new faces are everywhere—in town for a day, visiting for the weekend, at the Rotary lunch, at the church social—and incessantly and incandescently on television. Long weeks in a single community are unusual; a full day within a single neighborhood is becoming rare. We travel casually across town, into the countryside, to neighboring towns, cities, states; one might go thirty miles for coffee and conversation.

Through the technologies of the century, the number and variety of relationships in which we are engaged, potential frequency of contact, expressed intensity of relationship, and endurance through time all are steadily increasing. As this increase becomes extreme, we reach a state of social saturation.

In the face-to-face community, the cast of others remained relatively stable. There were changes by virtue of births and deaths, but moving from one town—much less state or country—to another was difficult. The number of relationships commonly maintained in today's world stands in stark contrast. Counting one's family, the morning television news, the car radio, colleagues on the train, and the local newspaper, the typical commuter may confront as many different persons (in terms of views or images) in the first two hours of a day as the community-based predecessor did in a month. The morning calls in a business office may connect one to a dozen different locales in a given city, often across the continent, and very possibly across national boundaries. A single hour of prime-time melodrama immerses one in the lives of a score of individuals. In an evening of television, hundreds of engaging faces insinuate themselves into our lives. It is not only the immediate community that occupies our thoughts and feelings, but a constantly changing cast of characters spread across the globe. . . .

Populating the Self

Consider the moments:

- Over lunch with friends, you discuss Northern Ireland. Although you have never spoken a word on the subject, you find yourself heatedly defending British policies.
- You work as an executive in the investments department of a bank. In the evenings, you smoke marijuana and listen to the Grateful Dead.
- You sit in a cafe and wonder what it would be like to have an intimate relationship with various strangers walking past.
- You are a lawyer in a prestigious midtown firm. On the weekends, you work on a novel about romance with a terrorist.
- You go to a Moroccan restaurant and afterward take in the latest show at a country-and-western bar.

In each case, individuals harbor a sense of coherent identity or self-sameness, only to find themselves suddenly propelled by alternative impulses. They seem securely to be one sort of person, but yet another comes bursting to the surface—in a suddenly voiced opinion, a fantasy, a turn of interests, or a private activity. Such experiences with variation and self-contradiction may be viewed as preliminary effects of social saturation. They may signal a *populating of the self*, the acquisition of multiple and disparate potentials for being. It is this process of self-population that begins to undermine the traditional commitments to both romanticist and modernist forms of being. It is of pivotal importance in setting the stage for the postmodern turn. Let us explore.

The technologies of social saturation expose us to an enormous range of persons, new forms of relationship, unique circumstances and opportunities, and special intensities of feeling. One can scarcely remain unaffected by such exposure. As child-development specialists now agree, the process of socialization is lifelong. We continue to incorporate information from the environment throughout our lives. When exposed to other persons, we change in two major ways. We increase our capacities for *knowing that* and for *knowing how*. In the first case, through exposure to others, we learn myriad details about their words, actions, dress, mannerisms, and so on. We ingest enormous amounts of information about patterns of interchange. Thus, for example, from an hour on a city street, we are informed of the clothing styles of blacks, whites, upper class, lower class, and more. We may learn the ways of Japanese businessmen, bag ladies, Sikhs, Hare Krishnas, or flute players from Chile. We see how relationships are carried out between mothers and daughters, business executives, teenage friends, and construction workers. An hour in a business office may expose us to the political views of a Texas oilman, a Chicago lawyer, and a gay activist from San Francisco. Radio commentators espouse views on boxing, pollution, and child abuse; pop music may advocate machoism, racial bigotry, and suicide. Paperback books cause hearts to race over the unjustly treated, those who strive against impossible odds, those who are brave or brilliant. And this is to say nothing of television input. Via television, myriad figures are allowed into the home who would never otherwise trespass. Millions watch as talk-show guests—murderers, rapists, women prisoners, child abusers, members of the KKK, mental patients, and others often discredited—attempt to make their lives intelligible. There are few six-year-olds who cannot furnish at least a rudimentary account of life in an African village, the concerns of divorcing parents, or drug-pushing in the ghetto. Hourly, our store-house of social knowledge expands in range and sophistication.

This massive increase in knowledge of the social world lays the ground work for a second kind of learning, a *knowing how.* We learn how to place such knowledge into action, to shape it for social consumption, to act so that social life can proceed effectively. And the possibilities for placing this supply of information into effective action are constantly expanding. The Japanese businessman glimpsed on the street today, and on the television tomorrow, may well be confronted in one's office the following week. On these occasions, the rudiments of appropriate behavior are already in place. If a mate announces that he or she is thinking about divorce, the other's reaction is not likely to be dumb dismay. The drama has so often been played out on television and movie screens that one is already prepared with multiple options. If one wins a wonderful prize, suffers a humiliating loss, faces temptation to cheat, or learns of a sudden death in the family, the reactions are hardly random. One more or less knows how it goes, is more or less ready for action. Having seen it all before, one approaches a state of ennui.

In an important sense, as social saturation proceeds we become pastiches, imitative assemblages of each other. In memory, we carry others' patterns of being with us. If the conditions are favorable, we can place these patterns into action. Each of us becomes the other, a representative, or a replacement. To put it more broadly, as the century has progressed, selves become increasingly populated with the character of others. . . .

Multiphrenia

It is sunny Saturday morning, and he finishes breakfast in high spirits. It is a rare day in which he is free to do as he pleases. With relish, he contemplates his options. The back door needs fixing, which calls for a trip to the hardware store. This would allow a much-needed haircut; and, while in town, he could get a birthday card for his brother, leave off his shoes for repair, and pick up shirts at the cleaners. But, he ponders, he really should get some exercise; is there time for jogging in the afternoon? That reminds him of a championship game he wanted to see at the same time. To be taken more seriously was his ex-wife's repeated request for a luncheon talk. And shouldn't he also settle his vacation plans before all the best locations are taken? Slowly, his optimism gives way to a sense of defeat. The free day has become a chaos of competing opportunities and necessities.

If such a scene is vaguely familiar, it attests only further to the pervasive effects of social saturation and the populating of the self. More important, one detects amid the hurly-burly of contemporary life a new constellation of feelings or sensibilities, a new pattern of self-consciousness. This syndrome may be termed *multiphrenia,* generally referring to the splitting of the individual into a multiplicity of self-investments. This condition is partly an outcome of self-population, but partly a result of the populated self's efforts to exploit the potentials of the technologies of relationship. In this sense, there is a cyclical spiraling toward a state of multiphrenia. As one's potentials are expanded by the technologies, so one increasingly employs the technologies for self-expression; yet, as the technologies are further utilized, so do they add to the repertoire of potentials. It would be a mistake to view this multiphrenic condition as a form of illness, for it is often suffused with a sense of expansiveness and adventure. Someday, there may indeed be nothing to distinguish multiphrenia from simply "normal living."

However, before we pass into this oceanic state, let us pause to consider some prominent features of the condition. Three of these are especially noteworthy.

Vertigo of the Valued

With the technology of social saturation, two of the major factors traditionally impeding relationships—namely time and space—are both removed.

The past can be continuously renewed—via voice, video, and visits, for example—and distance poses no substantial barriers to ongoing interchange. Yet this same freedom ironically leads to a form of enslavement. For each person, passion, or potential incorporated into oneself exacts a penalty—a penalty both of *being* and *of being with.* In the former case, as others are incorporated into the self, their tastes, goals, and values also insinuate themselves into one's being. Through continued interchange, one acquires, for example, a yen for Thai cooking, the desire for retirement security, or an investment in wildlife preservation. Through others, one comes to value whole-grain breads, novels from Chile, or community politics. Yet as Buddhists have long been aware, to desire is simultaneously to become a slave of the desirable. To "want" reduces one's choice to "want not." Thus, as others are incorporated into the self, and their desires become one's own, there is an expansion of goals—of "musts," wants, and needs. Attention is necessitated, effort is exerted, frustrations are encountered. Each new desire places its demands and reduces one's liberties.

There is also the penalty of being with. As relationships develop, their participants acquire local definitions—friend, lover, teacher, supporter, and so on. To sustain the relationship requires an honoring of the definitions—both of self and other. If two persons become close friends, for example, each acquires certain rights, duties, and privileges. Most relationships of any significance carry with them a range of obligations—for communication, joint activities, preparing for the other's pleasure, rendering appropriate congratulations, and so on. Thus, as relations accumulate and expand over time, there is a steadily increasing range of phone calls to make and answer, greeting cards to address, visits or activities to arrange, meals to prepare, preparations to be made, clothes to buy, makeup to apply. . . . And with each new opportunity—for skiing together in the Alps, touring Australia, camping in the Adirondacks, or snorkeling in the Bahamas—there are "opportunity costs." One must unearth information, buy equipment, reserve hotels, arrange travel, work long hours to clear one's desk, locate babysitters, dogsitters, homesitters. . . . Liberation becomes a swirling vertigo of demands.

In the professional world, this expansion of "musts" is strikingly evident. In the university of the 1950s, for example, one's departmental colleagues were often vital to one's work. One could walk but a short distance for advice, information, support, and so on. Departments were often close-knit and highly interdependent; travels to other departments or professional meetings were notable events. Today, however, the energetic academic will be linked by post, long-distance phone, fax, and electronic mail to like-minded scholars around the globe. The number of interactions possible in a day is limited only by the constraints of time. The technologies have also stimulated the development of hundreds of new organizations, international conferences, and professional meetings. A colleague recently informed me that if funds were available, he could spend his entire sabbatical traveling from one professional gathering to another. A similar condition pervades the business world. One's scope of business opportunities is no longer so limited by geography; the technologies of the age enable projects to be pursued around the world. (Colgate Tartar Control toothpaste is now sold in over forty countries.) In effect, the potential for new connection and new opportunities is practically unlimited. Daily life has become a sea of drowning demands, and there is no shore in sight.

The Expansion of Inadequacy

It is not simply the expansion of self through relationships that hounds one with the continued sense of "ought." There is also the seeping of self-doubt into everyday consciousness, a subtle feeling of inadequacy that smothers one's activities with an uneasy sense of impending emptiness. In important respects, this sense of inadequacy is a byproduct of the populating of self and the presence of social ghosts. For as we incorporate others into ourselves, so does the range of proprieties expand—that is, the range of what we feel a "good," "proper," or "exemplary" person should be. Many of us carry with us the "ghost of a father," reminding us of the values of honesty and hard work, or a mother challenging us to be nurturing and understanding. We may also absorb from a friend the values of maintaining a healthy body, from a lover the goal of self-sacrifice, from a teacher the ideal of worldly knowledge, and so on. Normal development leaves most people with a rich sense of personal well-being by fulfilling these goals.

But now consider the effects of social saturation. The range of one's friends and associates expands exponentially; one's past life continues to be vivid; and the mass media expose one to an enormous array of new criteria for self-evaluation. A friend from California reminds one to relax and enjoy life; in Ohio, an associate is getting ahead by working eleven hours a day. A relative from Boston stresses the importance of cultural sophistication, while a Washington colleague belittles one's lack of political savvy. A relative's return from Paris reminds one to pay more attention to personal appearance, while a ruddy companion from Colorado suggests that one grows soft.

Meanwhile, newspapers, magazines, and television provide a barrage of new criteria of self-evaluation. Is one sufficiently adventurous, clean, well traveled, well read, low in cholesterol, slim, skilled in cooking, friendly, odor free, coiffed, frugal, burglar proof, family oriented? The list is unending. More than once, I have heard the lament of a subscriber to the Sunday *New York Times*. Each page of this weighty tome will be read by millions. Thus, each page remaining undevoured by day's end will leave one precariously disadvantaged—a potential idiot in a thousand unpredictable circumstances.

Yet the threat of inadequacy is hardly limited to the immediate confrontation with mates and media. Because many of these criteria for self-evaluation are incorporated into the self—existing within the cadre of social ghosts—they are free to speak at any moment. The problem with values is that they are sufficient unto themselves. To value justice, for example, is to say nothing of the value of love; investing in duty will blind one to the value of spontaneity. No one value in itself recognizes the importance of any alternative value. And so it is with the chorus of social ghosts. Each voice of value stands to discredit all that does not meet its standard. All the voices at odds with one's current conduct thus stand as internal critics, scolding, ridiculing, and robbing action of its potential for fulfillment. One settles in front of the television for enjoyment, and the chorus begins: "twelve-year-old," "couch potato," "lazy," "irresponsible." . . . One sits down with a good book, and again: "sedentary," "antisocial," "inefficient," "fantasist." . . . Join friends for a game of tennis, and "skin cancer," "shirker of household duties," "under exercised," "overly competitive" come up. Work late and it is "workaholic," "heart attack-prone," "overly ambitious," "irresponsible family member." Each moment is enveloped in the guilt born of all that was possible but now foreclosed.

Rationality in Recession

A third dimension of multiphrenia is closely related to the others. The focus here is on the rationality of everyday decision-making instances in which one tries to be a "reasonable person." Why, one asks, is it important for one's children to attend college? The rational reply is that a college education increases one's job opportunities, earnings, and likely sense of personal fulfillment. Why should I stop smoking? one asks, and the answer is clear that smoking causes cancer, so to smoke is simply to invite a short life. Yet these "obvious" lines of reasoning are obvious only so long as one's identity remains fixed within a particular group.

The rationality of these replies depends altogether on the sharing of opinions—of each incorporating the views of others. To achieve identity in other cultural enclaves turns these "good reasons" into "rationalizations," "false consciousness," or "ignorance." Within some subcultures, a college education is a one-way ticket to bourgeois conventionality—a white-collar job, picket fence in the suburbs, and chronic boredom. For many, smoking is an integral part of a risky lifestyle; it furnishes a sense of intensity, offbeatness, rugged individualism. In the same way, saving money for old age is "sensible" in one family, and "oblivious to the erosions of inflation" in another. For most Westerners, marrying for love is the only reasonable (if not conceivable) thing to do. But many Japanese will point to statistics demonstrating greater longevity and happiness in arranged marriages. Rationality is a vital by-product of social participation.

Yet as the range of our relationships is expanded, the validity of each localized rationality is threatened. What is rational in one relationship is questionable or absurd from the standpoint of another. The "obvious choice" while talking with a colleague lapses into absurdity when speaking with a spouse, and into irrelevance when an old friend calls that evening. Further, because each relationship increases one's capacities for discernment, one carries with oneself a multiplicity of competing expectations, values, and beliefs about "the obvious solution." Thus, if the options are carefully evaluated, every decision becomes a leap into gray vapors. Hamlet's bifurcated decision becomes all too simple, for it is no longer being or non-being that is in question, but to which of multifarious beings one can be committed.

Conclusion

So we find a profound sea change taking place in the character of social life during the twentieth century. Through an array of newly emerging technologies, the world of relationships becomes increasingly saturated. We engage in greater numbers of relationships, in a greater variety of forms, and with greater intensities than ever before. With the multiplication of relationships also comes a transformation in the social capacities of the individual—both in knowing how and knowing that. The relatively coherent and unified sense of self inherent in a traditional culture gives way to manifold and competing potentials. A multiphrenic condition emerges in which one swims in ever-shifting, concatenating, and contentious currents of being. One bears the burden of an increasing array of ought, of self-doubts and irrationalities. The possibility for committed romanticism or strong and single-minded modernism recedes, and the way is opened for the postmodern being. . . .

As belief in essential selves erodes, awareness expands of the ways in which personal identity can be created and re-created. . . . This consciousness of construction does not strike as a thunderbolt; rather, it eats slowly and irregularly away at the edge of consciousness. And as it increasingly colors our understanding of self and relationships, the character of this consciousness undergoes a qualitative change. . . . [P]ostmodern consciousness [brings] the erasure of the category of self. No longer can one securely determine what it is to be a specific kind of person . . . or even a person at all. As the category of the individual person fades from view, consciousness of construction becomes focal. We realize increasingly that who and what we are is not so much the result of our "person essence" (real feelings, deep beliefs, and the like), but of how we are constructed in various social groups. . . . [T]he concept of the individual self ceases to be intelligible. . . .

Reflective Questions

1. What are the characteristics of the self of the romantic era? Where does the self reside for modernists?
2. How has technology changed life in the postmodern era? How has it changed relationships? What is social saturation? What is the populating of the self? How does encountering new people increase "knowing that" and "knowing how"?
3. What is multiphrenia? What are its consequences for our experiences of the self?
4. Previous generations grew up without cell phones or nearly constant Internet interconnectivity. How does growing up with these technologies change life for Millennials? How does it shape their relationships? Long-distance relationships? Interactions with others? How do you think these changes affect the identity formation of Millennials and the identities that result?

PART V

The Self and Social Interaction

The self not only arises in social experience, as discussed in Part IV, but is also sustained and changed through social interaction. As individuals, we continually interact with others. Each of these interactions provides us with reflected images of ourselves. How others respond to us conveys their attitude toward us, and, as Cooley and Mead explained, we take each attitude in kind. The self-images reflected in others' responses to us sometimes confirm, occasionally undermine, and gradually alter our sense of self.

We are not, however, passive participants in our interactions. Social interaction is a process of mutual influence. We influence how others define and respond to us as much as they influence us. Through exerting this influence, we can shape the very self-images that others reflect back to us. Moreover, we converse with ourselves, whether interacting with others or alone, and how we talk to ourselves can influence our actions as much as how others respond to us.

The selections in Part V portray how we present, negotiate, and establish selves through social interaction. In doing so, they offer the following insights:

- *We must stage the selves we want to realize in our everyday lives. To have success in these dramaturgical efforts, we must draw upon what Erving Goffman refers to as the arts of impression management.* Like actors on the stage, we must manage elements of our appearance, demeanor, and physical setting to persuade others to see us as a particular kind of person (e.g., an effective teacher, a devoted friend, or a great party host). Since other people cannot directly perceive or evaluate our thoughts, feelings, motives, and character, they must depend on signs and symbols to assess who we "really" are. Above all, they must rely on the information that we communicate to them about ourselves, particularly through our role performances and the management of our appearance, emotions, gestures, and speech.

- *When engaging in impression management, we rely on the collaboration of others. In some cases, these others are part of a team that assists us in pulling off a successful performance,* such as a classroom presentation, a dorm party, or a wedding ceremony. In Selection 22, David Grazian illustrates how college-aged heterosexual men rely on elaborate forms of teamwork when engaging in the often unsuccessful pursuit of sexual partners. Grazian also demonstrates how the dramaturgical displays and impression management efforts of these men differ when they are "front stage" in the presence of the women they are pursuing or "backstage" in a dorm room with friends. In addressing this theme Grazian emulates Goffman, revealing how an important structural element of self-presentation is the manipulation of regions, or places that separate our front-stage performances from our backstage activities.

- *Because of our abilities to think and converse with ourselves, we can inwardly challenge and counter the self-images that others direct toward us, at least for a while. Our inner conversations may temporarily drown out others' external voices, especially if they do not offer a unified response. If others define us in similar ways, however, we will have difficulty preventing their voices from echoing throughout our inward conversations.* In Selection 23, Patti and Peter Adler illustrate this point all too well. They highlight the impact and perils of the "gloried self" conferred upon college basketball players. While the players initially tried to resist the accolades and celebrity selves that fans and media sources attributed to them, they ultimately found these reflected appraisals too seductive to reject. The players thus embraced and enacted the gloried and media-based self that others accorded to them. Unfortunately, while this type of self offers a high level of social value, it also comes with a notable price. That price is the loss of an authentic experience of self and a corresponding sense of self-alienation.

- *In many contemporary societies, computer technologies have provided individuals with access to new and unique "virtual spaces" for the presentation and*

> *realization of selves*. As Simon Gottschalk reveals in Selection 24, interactions in virtual spaces such as Second Life challenge some of Goffman's arguments about the dynamics and boundaries of self-presentation. Virtual worlds offer an array of possibilities for the future, including new, diverse, and unexpected forms of interaction and self-expression. As we become increasingly immersed in these worlds, we can anticipate that our experiences and constructions of self will take on new features. In some cases, these virtual experiences and constructions are likely to promote an enhanced sense of freedom, authenticity, and self-understanding. But, in other cases, these experiences and constructions are likely to have less favorable outcomes, such as fostering a sense of disconnection, hollowness, or fragmentation.

Regardless of where we construct and present selves in the future, we can confidently know that they will continue to depend on the arts of impression management and the realm of interaction for their realization.

21

The Presentation of Self

ERVING GOFFMAN

The name Erving Goffman is virtually synonymous with microsociology. Throughout his life, Goffman argued that social interaction should be studied as a topic in its own right. He maintained that social interaction has its own logic and structure, regardless of the participants' personality characteristics or the social organizational and institutional context in which it occurs. That position is the basis for Goffman's very novel and influential analysis of the self. He was not interested in the individual's subjective self or inner conversations but rather in the social definition and construction of the public self during social interaction.

Goffman's approach to this topic is commonly described as dramaturgical—that is, Goffman views the self, social interaction, and life as dramatic or theatrical productions. Individuals are social actors who play different parts in the varied scenes of social life. Every time individuals interact with one another, they enact a self, influencing others' definition of them and of the situation. They usually arrive at a working consensus concerning the definition of each other's self and of the situation that consequently guides their interaction. Although social actors' performances are sometimes clumsy and unconvincing, they generally cooperate to save each other's individual shows and their collective show as a whole.

Goffman's dramaturgical analysis is more than a creative use of metaphor. We humans cannot peer into one another's hearts and minds, nor can we ever know another's "real" or "true" self. Our knowledge of each other is limited to what we can observe. Our definition of one another's self is necessarily based on appearance, conduct, and the settings in which we interact. In turn, we present a self to one another through how we look and act, and where we go. Regardless of whether these self-presentations are intentional or unintentional, honest or dishonest, they are nonetheless performances. The self is not a material thing that the individual carries around and can show others. It must be dramatically realized on each and every occasion of social interaction.

Goffman wrote this selection in the 1950s, and a few of his illustrative examples trade upon prevailing stereotypes of women at that time. Although contemporary readers may find those dated examples to be sexist, they do not detract from Goffman's insight into the drama of everyday social life.

When an individual enters the presence of others, they commonly seek to acquire information about him or to bring into play information about him already possessed. They will be interested in his general socioeconomic status, his conception of self, his attitude toward them, his competence, his trustworthiness, etc. Although some of this information seems to be sought almost as an end in itself, there are usually quite practical

Reprinted from: Erving Goffman, *The Presentation of Self in Everyday Life*, pp. 1–4, 6–18, 66, 252–253.

reasons for acquiring it. Information about the individual helps to define the situation, enabling others to know in advance what he will expect of them and what they may expect of him. Informed in these ways, the others will know how best to act in order to call forth a desired response from him.

For those present, many sources of information become accessible and many carriers (or "sign-vehicles") become available for conveying this information. If unacquainted with the individual, observers can glean clues from his conduct and appearance which allow them to apply their previous experience with individuals roughly similar to the one before them or, more important, to apply untested stereotypes to him. They can also assume from past experience that only individuals of a particular kind are likely to be found in a given social setting. They can rely on what the individual says about himself or on documentary evidence he provides as to who and what he is. If they know, or know of, the individual by virtue of experience prior to the interaction, they can rely on assumptions as to the persistence and generality of psychological traits as a means of predicting his present and future behavior.

However, during the period in which the individual is in the immediate presence of the others, few events may occur which directly provide the others with the conclusive information they will need, if they are to direct wisely their own activity. Many crucial facts lie beyond the time and place of interaction or lie concealed within it. For example, the "true" or "real" attitudes, beliefs, and emotions of the individual can be ascertained only indirectly, through his avowals or through what appears to be involuntary expressive behavior. Similarly, if the individual offers the others a product or service, they will often find that during the interaction there will be no time and place immediately available for eating the pudding that the proof can be found in. They will be forced to accept some events as conventional or natural signs of something not directly available to the senses. In Ichheiser's terms,[1]

> [T]he individual will have to act so that he intentionally or unintentionally expresses himself, and the others will in turn have to be *impressed* in some way by him.

Taking communication in both its narrow and broad sense, one finds that when the individual is in the immediate presence of others, his activity will have a promissory character. The others are likely to find that they must accept the individual on faith, offering him a just return, while he is present before them, in exchange for something whose true value will not be established until after he has left their presence. (Of course, the others also live by inference in their dealings with the physical world, but it is only in the world of social interaction that the objects about which they make inferences will purposely facilitate and hinder this inferential process.) The security that they justifiably feel in making inferences about the individual will vary, of course, depending on such factors as the amount of information they already possess about him; but no amount of such past evidence can entirely obviate the necessity of acting on the basis of inferences.

Let us now turn from the others to the point of view of the individual who presents himself before them. He may wish them to think highly of him, or to think that he thinks highly of them, or to perceive how in fact he feels toward them, or to obtain no clear-cut impression; he may wish to ensure sufficient harmony, so that the interaction can be sustained, or to defraud, get rid of, confuse, mislead, antagonize, or insult them. Regardless of the particular objective which the individual has in mind and of his motive for having this objective, it will be in his interests to control the conduct of the others, especially their responsive treatment of him. This control is achieved largely by influencing the definition of the situation which the others come to formulate, and he can influence this definition by expressing himself in such a way as to give them the kind of impression that will lead them to act voluntarily in accordance with his own plan. Thus, when an individual appears in the presence of others, there will usually be some reason for him to mobilize his activity, so that it will convey an impression to others, which it is in his interests to convey. Since a girl's dormitory mates will glean evidence of her popularity from the calls she receives on the phone, we can suspect that some girls will arrange for calls to be made, and Willard Waller's finding can be anticipated:

> It has been reported by many observers that a girl who is called to the telephone in the dormitories will often allow herself to be called several times, in order to give all the other girls ample opportunity to hear her paged.[2]

I have said that when an individual appears before others, his actions will influence the definition of the situation which they come to have. Sometimes the individual will act in a thoroughly calculating manner, expressing himself in a given way solely in order to give the kind of impression to others that is likely to evoke from them a specific response he is concerned to obtain. Sometimes the individual will be calculating in his activity but be relatively unaware that this is the case. Sometimes he will intentionally and consciously express himself in a particular way, but chiefly because the tradition of his group or social status require this kind of expression and not because of any particular response (other than vague acceptance or approval) that is likely to be evoked from those impressed by the expression. Sometimes the traditions of an individual's role will lead him to give a well-designed impression of a particular kind, and yet he may be neither consciously nor unconsciously disposed to create such an impression. The others, in their turn, may be suitably impressed by the individual's efforts to convey something, or may misunderstand the situation and come to conclusions that are warranted neither by the individual's intent nor by the facts. In any case, in so far as the others act as *if* the individual had conveyed a particular impression, we may take a functional or pragmatic view and say that the individual has "effectively" projected a given definition of the situation and "effectively" fostered the understanding that a given state of affairs obtains.

There is one aspect of the others' response that bears special comment here. Knowing that the individual is likely to present himself in a light that is favorable to him, the others may divide what they witness into two parts: a part that is relatively easy for the individual to manipulate at will, being chiefly his verbal assertions, and a part in regard to which he seems to have little concern or control, being chiefly derived from the expressions he gives off. The others may then use what are considered to be the ungovernable aspects of his expressive behavior as a check upon the validity of what is conveyed by the governable aspects. In this a fundamental asymmetry is demonstrated in the communication process, the individual presumably being aware of only one stream of his communication, the witnesses of this stream and of one other. For example, in Shetland Isle one crofter's wife, in serving native dishes to a visitor from the mainland of Britain, would listen with a polite smile to his polite claims of liking what he was eating; at the same time, she would take note of the rapidity with which the visitor lifted his fork or spoon to his mouth, the eagerness with which he passed food into his mouth, and the gusto expressed in chewing the food, using these signs as a check on the stated feelings of the eater. The same woman, in order to discover what one acquaintance (A) "actually" thought of another acquaintance (B), would wait until B was in the presence of A but engaged in conversation with still another person (C). She would then covertly examine the facial expressions of A as he regarded B in conversation with C. Not being in conversation with B, and not being directly observed by him, A would sometimes relax usual constraints and tactful deceptions, and freely express what he was "actually" feeling about B. This Shetlander, in short, would observe the unobserved observer.

Now given the fact that others are likely to checkup on the more controllable aspects of behavior by means of the less controllable, one can expect that sometimes the individual will try to exploit this very possibility, guiding the impression he makes through behavior felt to be reliably informing. For example, in gaining admission to a tight social circle, the participant observer may not only wear an accepting look while listening to an informant, but may also be careful to wear the same look when observing the informant talking to others; observers of the observer will then not as easily discover where he actually stands. A specific illustration may be cited from Shetland Isle. When a neighbor dropped in to have a cup of tea, he would ordinarily wear at least a hint of an expectant warm smile as he passed through the door into the cottage. Since lack of physical obstructions outside the cottage and lack of light within it usually made it possible to observe the visitor unobserved as he approached the house, islanders sometimes took pleasure in watching the visitor drop whatever expression he was manifesting and replace it with a sociable one just before reaching the door. However, some visitors, in appreciating that this examination was occurring, would blindly adopt a social face a long distance from the house, thus ensuring the projection of a constant image.

This kind of control upon the part of the individual reinstates the symmetry of the communication process, and sets the stage for a kind of information game—a potentially infinite cycle of concealment, discovery, false revelation, and rediscovery. It should be added that since the others are likely to be relatively unsuspicious of the presumably unguided aspect of the individual's conduct, he can gain much by controlling it. The others, of course, may sense that the individual is manipulating the presumably spontaneous aspects of his behavior, and seek in this very act of manipulation some shading of conduct that the individual has not managed to control. This again provides a check upon the individual's behavior, this time his presumably uncalculated behavior, thus re-establishing the asymmetry of the communication process. Here, I would like only to add the suggestion that the arts of piercing an individual's effort at calculated unintentionally seem better developed than our capacity to manipulate our own behavior; so that, regardless of how many steps have occurred in the information game, the witness is likely to have the advantage over the actor, and the initial asymmetry of the communication process is likely to be retained.

When we allow that the individual projects a definition of the situation when he appears before others, we must also see that the others, however passive their role may seem to be, will themselves effectively project a definition of the situation by virtue of their response to the individual and by virtue of any lines of action they initiate to him. Ordinarily, the definitions of the situation projected by the several different participants are sufficiently attuned to one another so that open contradiction will not occur. I do not mean that there will be the kind of consensus that arises when each individual present candidly expresses what he really feels and honestly agrees with the expressed feelings of the others present. This kind of harmony is an optimistic ideal and in any case not necessary for the smooth working of society. Rather, each participant is expected to suppress his immediate heartfelt feelings, conveying a view of the situation which he feels the others will be able to find at least temporarily acceptable. The maintenance of this surface of agreement, this veneer of consensus, is facilitated by each participant concealing his own wants behind statements which assert values to which everyone present feels obliged to give lip service. Further, there is usually a kind of division of definitional labor. Each participant is allowed to establish the tentative official ruling regarding matters which are vital to him but not immediately important to others, e.g., the rationalizations and justifications by which he accounts for his past activity. In exchange for this courtesy, he remains silent or non-committal on matters important to others but not immediately important to him. We have then a kind of interactional *modus vivendi*. Together, the participants contribute to a single over-all definition of the situation, which involves not so much a real agreement as to what exists, but rather a real agreement as to whose claims concerning what issues will be temporarily honored. Real agreement will also exist concerning the desirability of avoiding an open conflict of definitions of the situation. I will refer to this level of agreement as a "working consensus." It is to be understood that the working consensus established in one interaction setting will be quite different in content from the working consensus established in a different type of setting. Thus, between two friends at lunch, a reciprocal show of affection, respect, and concern for the other is maintained. In service occupations, on the other hand, the specialist often maintains an image of disinterested involvement in the problem of the client; while the client responds with a show of respect for the competence and integrity of the specialist. Regardless of such differences in content, however, the general form of these working arrangements is the same.

In noting the tendency for a participant to accept the definitional claims made by the others present, we can appreciate the crucial importance of the information that the individual *initially* possesses or acquires concerning his fellow participants; for it is on the basis of this initial information that the individual starts to define the situation and starts to build up lines of responsive action. The individual's initial projection commits him to what he is proposing to be and requires him to drop all pretenses of being other things. As the interaction among the participants progresses, additions and modifications in this initial informational state will of course occur, but it is essential that these later developments be related without contradiction to, and even built up from, the initial positions taken by the several participants. It would seem that an individual can more easily make a choice as to what line of treatment to demand from and extend to the others present at the beginning of an encounter than he can alter the line of treatment that is being pursued, once the interaction is under way.

In everyday life, of course, there is a clear understanding that first impressions are important. Thus, the work adjustment of those in service occupations will often hinge upon a capacity to seize and hold the initiative in the service relation, a capacity that will require subtle aggressiveness on the part of the server when he is of lower socioeconomic status than his client. W. F. Whyte suggests the waitress as an example:

> The first point that stands out is that the waitress who bears up under pressure does not simply respond to her customers. She acts with some skill to control their behavior. The first question to ask when we look at the customer relationship is, "Does the waitress get the jump on the customer, or does the customer get the jump on the waitress?" The skilled waitress realizes the crucial nature of this question. . . .
>
> The skilled waitress tackles the customer with confidence and without hesitation. For example, she may find that a new customer has seated himself before she could clear off the dirty dishes and change the cloth. He is now leaning on the table studying the menu. She greets him, says, "May I change the cover, please?" and, without waiting for an answer, takes his menu away from him so that he moves back from the table, and she goes about her work. The relationship is handled politely but firmly, and there is never any question as to who is in charge.[3]

When the interaction that is initiated by "first impressions" is itself merely the initial interaction in an extended series of interactions involving the same participants, we speak of "getting off on the right foot" and feel that it is crucial that we do so. Thus, one learns that some teachers take the following view:

> You can't ever let them get the upper hand on you or you're through. So I start out tough. The first day I get a new class in, I let them know who's boss. . . . You've got to start off tough, then you can ease up as you go along. If you start out easy-going, when you try to get tough, they'll just look at you and laugh.[4]

Similarly, attendants in mental institutions may feel that, if the new patient is sharply put in his place the first day on the ward and made to see who is boss, much future difficulty will be prevented.

Given the fact that the individual effectively projects a definition of the situation when he enters the presence of others, we can assume that events may occur within the interaction which contradict, discredit, or otherwise throw doubt upon this projection. When these disruptive events occur, the interaction itself may come to a confused and embarrassed halt. Some of the assumptions upon which the responses of the participants had been predicated become untenable, and the participants find themselves lodged in an interaction for which the situation has been wrongly defined and is now no longer defined. At such moments the individual whose presentation has been discredited may feel ashamed, while the others present may feel hostile; and all the participants may come to feel ill at ease, nonplussed, out of countenance, embarrassed, experiencing the kind of anomy that is generated when the minute social system of face-to-face interaction breaks down.

In stressing the fact that the initial definition of the situation projected by an individual tends to provide a plan for the co-operative activity that follows—in stressing this action point of view—we must not overlook the crucial fact that any projected definition of the situation also has a distinctive moral character. It is this moral character of projections that will chiefly concern us in this report. Society is organized on the principle that any individual who possesses certain social characteristics has a moral right to expect that others will value and treat him in an appropriate way. Connected with this principle is a second, namely that an individual who implicitly or explicitly signifies that he has certain social characteristics ought in fact to be what he claims he is. In consequence, when an individual projects a definition of the situation and thereby makes an implicit or explicit claim to be a person of a particular kind, he automatically exerts a moral demand upon the others, obliging them to value and treat him in the manner that persons of his kind have a right to expect. He also implicitly forgoes all claims to be things he does not appear to be and, hence, forgoes the treatment that would be appropriate for such individuals. The others find, then, that the individual has informed them as to what is and as to what they *ought* to see as the "is."

One cannot judge the importance of definitional disruptions by the frequency with which they occur, for apparently they would occur more frequently, were not constant precautions taken. We find that preventive practices are constantly employed to avoid these embarrassments and that corrective practices are constantly employed to compensate for discrediting occurrences that have not been successfully avoided. When the individual employs these strategies and tactics to protect his own projections, we may refer to them as "defensive practices"; when a participant employs them to save the definition of the situation projected by another, we speak of "protective practices" or "tact." Together, defensive and protective practices comprise the techniques employed to safeguard the impression fostered by an individual during his presence before others. It should be added that, while we may be ready to see that no fostered impression would survive if defensive practices were not employed, we are less ready perhaps to see that few impressions could survive, if those who received the impression did not exert tact in their reception of it.

In addition to the fact that precautions are taken to prevent disruption of projected definitions, we may also note that an intense interest in these disruptions comes to play a significant role in the social life of the group. Practical jokes and social games are played, in which embarrassments which are to be taken unseriously are purposely engineered. Fantasies are created, in which devastating exposures occur. Anecdotes from the past—real, embroidered, or fictitious—are told and retold, detailing disruptions which occurred, almost occurred, or occurred and were admirably resolved. There seems to be no grouping which does not have a ready supply of these games, reveries, and cautionary tales, to be used as a source of humor, a catharsis for anxieties, and a sanction for inducing individuals to be modest in their claims and reasonable in their projected expectations. The individual may tell himself through dreams of getting into impossible positions. Families tell of the time a guest got his dates mixed and arrived when neither the house nor anyone in it was ready for him. Journalists tell of times when an all too meaningful misprint occurred, and the paper's assumption of objectivity or decorum was humorously discredited. Public servants tell of times a client ridiculously misunderstood form instructions, giving answers which implied an unanticipated and bizarre definition of the situation.[5] Seamen, whose home away from home is rigorously he-man, tell stories of coming back home and inadvertently asking mother to "pass the fucking butter."[6] Diplomats tell of the time a near-sighted queen asked a republican ambassador about the health of his king. . . .[7]

For the purpose of this report, interaction (that is, face-to-face interaction) may be roughly defined as the reciprocal influence of individuals upon one another's actions when in one another's immediate physical presence. An interaction may be defined as all the interaction which occurs throughout any one occasion when a given set of individuals are in one another's continuous presence; the term "an encounter" would do as well. A "performance" may be defined as all the activity of a given participant on a given occasion which serves to influence in any way any of the other participants. Taking a particular participant and his performance as a basic point of reference, we may refer to those who contribute the other performances as the audience, observers, or co-participants. The pre-established pattern of action, which is unfolded during a performance and which may be presented or played through on other occasions, may be called a "part" or "routine." . . .

When an individual plays a part, he implicitly requests his observers to take seriously the impression that is fostered before them. They are asked to believe that the character they see actually possesses the attributes he appears to possess, that the task he performs will have the consequences that are implicitly claimed for it, and that, in general, matters are what they appear to be. In line with this, there is the popular view that the individual offers his performance and puts on his show "for the benefit of other people."

It will be convenient to begin a consideration of performances by turning the question around and looking at the individual's own belief in the impression of reality that he attempts to engender in those among whom he finds himself.

At one extreme, one finds that the performer can be fully taken in by his own act; he can be sincerely convinced that the impression of reality which he stages is the real reality. When his audience is also convinced in this way about the show he puts on—and this seems to be the typical case—then, for the moment at least, only the sociologist or the socially disgruntled will have any doubts about the "realness" of what is presented.

At the other extreme, we find that the performer may not be taken in at all by his own routine. This possibility is understandable, since no one is in quite as good an observational position to see through the act as the person who puts it on. Coupled with this, the performer may be moved to guide the conviction of his audience only as a means to other ends, having no ultimate concern in the conception that they have of him or of the situation. When the individual has no belief in his own act and no ultimate concern with the beliefs of his audience, we may call him cynical, reserving the term "sincere" for individuals who believe in the impression fostered by their own performance. It should be understood that the cynic, with all his professional disinvolvement, may obtain unprofessional pleasures from his masquerade, experiencing a kind of gleeful spiritual aggression from the fact that he can toy at will with something his audience must take seriously.

It is not assumed, of course, that all cynical performers are interested in deluding their audiences for purposes of what is called "self-interest" or private gain. A cynical individual may delude his audience for what he considers to be their own good, or for the good of the community, etc. For illustrations of this we need not appeal to sadly enlightened showmen, such as Marcus Aurelius or Hsun Tzu. We know that in service occupations practitioners who may otherwise be sincere are sometimes forced to delude their customers, because their customers show such a heartfelt demand for it. Doctors who are led into giving placebos, filling-station attendants who resignedly check and recheck tire pressures for anxious women motorists, shoe clerks who sell a shoe that fits but tell the customer it is the size she wants to hear—these are cynical performers whose audiences will not allow them to be sincere. . . .

[W]hile the performance offered by impostors and liars is quite flagrantly false and differs in this respect from ordinary performances, both are similar in the care their performers must exert in order to maintain the impression that is fostered. Whether an honest performer wishes to convey the truth or whether a dishonest performer wishes to convey a falsehood, both must take care to enliven their performances with appropriate expressions, exclude from their performances expressions that might discredit the impression being fostered, and take care lest the audience impute unintended meanings. Because of these shared dramatic contingencies, we can profitably study performances that are quite false in order to learn about ones that are quite honest.

In our society, the character one performs and one's self are somewhat equated, and this self-as-character is usually seen as something housed within the body of its possessor, especially the upper parts thereof, being a nodule, somehow, in the psychobiology of personality. I suggest that this view is an implied part of what we are all trying to present, but provides, just because of this, a bad analysis of the presentation. In this report, the performed self was seen as some kind of image, usually creditable, which the individual on stage and in character effectively attempts to induce others to hold in regard to him. While this image is entertained *concerning* the individual, so that a self is imputed to him, this self itself does not derive from its possessor, but from the whole scene of his action, being generated by that attribute of local events which renders them interpretable by witnesses. A correctly staged and performed scene leads the audience to impute a self to a performed character, but this imputation—this self—is a *product* of a scene that comes off, and is not a *cause* of it. The self, then, as a performed character, is not an organic thing that has a specific location, whose fundamental fate is to be born, to mature, and to die; it is a dramatic effect arising diffusely from a scene that is presented, and the characteristic issue, the crucial concern, is whether it will be credited or discredited.

In analyzing the self, then, we are drawn from its possessor, from the person who will profit or lose most by it; for he and his body merely provide the peg on which something of collaborative manufacture will be hung for a time. And the means for producing and maintaining selves do not reside inside the peg; in fact, these means are often bolted down in social establishments. . . .

The whole machinery of self-production is cumbersome, of course, and sometimes breaks down, exposing its separate components. . . . But well oiled, impressions will flow from it fast enough to put us in the grips of one of our types of reality—the performance will come off, and the firm self accorded each performed character will appear to emanate intrinsically from its performer. . . .

In developing the conceptual framework employed in this report, some language of the stage was used. . . . [However], this report is not concerned with aspects of theater that creep into everyday life. It is concerned with the structure of social encounters—the structure of those entities in social life that come into being whenever persons enter one another's immediate physical presence. The key factor in this structure is the maintenance of a single definition of the situation, this definition having to be expressed, and this expression sustained in the face of a multitude of potential disruptions.

A character staged in a theater is not in some ways real, nor does it have the same kind of real consequences as does the thoroughly contrived character performed by a confidence man; but the *successful* staging of either of these types of false figures involves use of *real* techniques—the same techniques by which everyday persons sustain their real social situations. Those who conduct face-to-face interaction on a theater's stage must meet the key requirement of real situations, they must expressively sustain a definition of the situation, but this they do in circumstances that have facilitated their developing an apt terminology for the interactional tasks that all of us share.

Notes

1. Gustav Ichheiser, "Misunderstandings in Human Relations," supplement to *The American Journal of Sociology,* LV (September 1949), pp. 6–7.
2. Willard Waller, "The Rating and Dating Complex," *American Sociological Review,* II, p. 730.
3. W. F. White, "When Workers and Customers Meet," Chap. VII, *Industry and Society,* ed. W. F. White (New York: McGraw-Hill, 1946), pp. 132–33.
4. Teacher interview quoted by Howard S. Becker, "Social Class Variations in the Teacher-Pupil Relationship," *Journal of Educational Sociology,* XXV, p. 459.
5. Peter Blau, "Dynamics of Bureaucracy" (Ph.D. dissertation, Department of Sociology, Columbia University [1955], University of Chicago Press), pp. 127–29.
6. Walter M. Beattie, Jr., "The Merchant Seamen" (unpublished M.A. Report, Department of Sociology, University of Chicago, 1950), p. 35.
7. Sir Frederick Poison, *Recollections of Three Reigns* (New York: Dutton, 1952), p. 46.

Reflective Questions

1. According to Goffman, what kind of information do people try to acquire about one another or bring into play during their interactions? Why is this information important? How does it shape the nature of their interactions with others?
2. Why do we seek to control the impressions that others have of us? What are the key elements of impression management? How do we manage these elements as we present ourselves to others in various situations? How do we project a "definition of the situation" through the appearances we present to others? How and why are "first impressions" important in this process?
3. How do we "play a part" when presenting ourselves to others? For instance, how do we play a part when going on a job interview, attending a sporting event, listening to a lecture, or hosting a party for friends? Do we often have to "stage" and perform aspects of ourselves as we interact with others? Do we have to give a convincing performance of the self that we claim in order to get it validated by others?
4. What is Goffman's view of the self? Does he regard it as primarily personal or social in nature? For example, does he discuss it as an individual possession or as something others grant to us situationally based on our performances?
5. Visit the Facebook pages of four or five of your friends. How do they present themselves on their Facebook sites? What aspects of themselves do they highlight? What aspects do they conceal? Are they involved in what Goffman describes as impression management? Are we necessarily engaged in the process of impression management when we present ourselves to others?

22

The Girl Hunt

DAVID GRAZIAN

In the previous selection, Erving Goffman articulated a dramaturgical approach to social life. According to this approach, social life mirrors theater, and we are like actors on a stage in our everyday interactions. To realize desired selves, we must be "good actors" who can adeptly engage in the arts of impression management, manipulating props, masks, moods, and settings to persuade others to validate the selves we present. Our selves, then, are dramatic effects—they become established through convincing performances and depend on the responses of others.

Goffman recognized that our efforts to realize desired selves rely on others not only as audiences but also as collaborators. That is, when we engage in the process of presenting and enacting selves, we often depend on a performance "team," or a set of others who cooperate with us in staging a ritual or routine. Moreover, our performances take place in two different kinds of regions. Some of our behavior takes place "front stage" before an audience, in a setting where we try to maintain an appropriate appearance for the part we are playing. Other behavior occurs "backstage," in a region separated from our audience of primary concern. When we are backstage, we can prepare for our front-stage performance or, in some cases, act in ways that knowingly contradict the front-stage appearances we present.

In analyzing the interpersonal ritual known as "the girl hunt," David Grazian demonstrates the elaborate forms of teamwork engaged in by college-aged heterosexual men as they try to display and establish their masculinity, particularly by negotiating sexual liaisons with young, attractive women. Grazian also illustrates how these men engage in backstage behavior, such as "pregaming," that prepares them for the ritual and collaborative activities they will perform when taking part in girl hunts. Most crucially, Grazian reveals why heterosexual college men so frequently participate in these hunts, even though they so rarely result in sexual relations with women. The hunts serve as rituals that allow the men to bond with one another and realize desired selves through dramaturgical displays of masculinity. These displays are designed as much for each other as for the women they pursue.

In addressing these themes, Grazian's article illustrates a larger point highlighted by Goffman. Whether we like it or not or know it or not, our behavior is expressive: it announces and establishes who we are in a given interaction.

Young urbanites identify downtown clusters of nightclubs as direct sexual marketplaces, or markets for singles seeking casual encounters with potential sex partners (Laumann et al. 2004) . . . . In this article I examine girl hunting—a practice whereby adolescent heterosexual men aggres-

Reprinted from: David Grazian, "The Girl Hunt: Nightlife and the Performance of Masculinity as Collective Activity," *Symbolic Interaction* 30(2): 221–243, 2007.

sively seek out female sexual partners in nightclubs, bars, and other public arenas of commercialized entertainment. I emphasize the performative nature of contemporary flirtation rituals by examining how male-initiated games of heterosexual pursuit function as strategies of impression management in which young men sexually objectify women to heighten their own performance of masculinity. While we typically see public sexual behavior as an interaction between individuals, I illustrate how these rituals operate as collective and homosocial group activities conducted in the company of men.

The Performance of Masculinity as Collective Activity

According to the symbolic interactionist perspective, masculinity represents a range of dramaturgical performances individuals exhibit through face-to-face interaction (Goffman 1959, 1977; West and Zimmerman 1987). Like femininity, masculinity is not innate but an accomplishment of human behavior that appears natural because gendered individuals adhere to an institutionalized set of myths they learn through everyday interactions and encounters, and thus accept as social reality (Goffman 1977; West and Zimmerman 1987). Throughout their formative years and beyond, young men are encouraged by their parents, teachers, coaches, and peers to adopt a socially constructed vision of manhood, a set of cultural beliefs that prescribe what men ought to be like: physically strong, powerful, independent, self-confident, efficacious, dominant, active, persistent, responsible, dependable, aggressive, courageous, and sexually potent (Donaldson 1993; Messner 2002; Mishkind et al. 1986). In the fantasies of many boys and men alike, a relentless competitive spirit, distant emotional detachment, and an insatiable heterosexual desire, all commonly (but not exclusively) displayed by the sexual objectification of women (Bird 1996), characterize idealized masculinity. . . .

In contrast to occupational and educational domains in which masculine power can be signaled by professional success and intellectual superiority, sexual prowess is a primary signifier of masculinity in the context of urban nightlife. Indeed, the importance placed on competitive "scoring" (Messner 2002) among men in the highly gendered universe of cocktail lounges and singles bars should not be underestimated. However, a wealth of data suggests that, contrary to representations of urban nightlife in popular culture, such as Candace Bushnell's novel *Sex and the City* ([1996] 2001) and its HBO television spin-off, rumors of the proverbial one-night stand have been greatly exaggerated (Williams 2005). According to the National Health and Social Life Survey, relatively few men (16.7 percent) and even fewer women (5.5 percent) report engaging in sexual activity with a member of the opposite sex within two days of meeting them (Laumann et al. 1994:239). About 90 percent of women aged eighteen to forty-four report that they find having sex with a stranger unappealing (Laumann et al. 1994:163–65). Findings from the Chicago Health and Social Life Survey demonstrate that, across a variety of city neighborhood types, typically less than one-fifth of heterosexual adults aged eighteen to fifty-nine report having met their most recent sexual partner in a bar, nightclub, or dance club (Mahay and Laumann 2004:74).

Moreover, the efficacy of girl hunting is constrained by women's ability to resist unwanted sexual advances in public, as well as to initiate their own searches for desirable sex partners. Whereas the ideological basis of girl hunting stresses vulnerability, weakness, and submissiveness as conventional markers of femininity, young women commonly challenge these stereotypes by articulating their own physical strength, emotional self-reliance, and quick wit during face-to-face encounters with men (Duneier and Molotch 1999; Hollander 2002; Paules 1991; Snow et al. 1991). For all these reasons, girl hunting would not seem to serve as an especially efficacious strategy for locating sexual partners, particularly when compared with other methods (such as meeting through mutual friends, colleagues, classmates, or other trusted third parties; common participation in an educational or recreational activity; or shared membership in a civic or religious organization). In fact, the statistical rareness of the one-night stand may help explain why successful lotharios are granted such glorified status and prestige among their peers in the first place (Connell and Messerschmidt 2005:851). But if this is the case, then why do adolescent men persist in hassling women in public through aggressive sexual advances and pickup attempts (Duneier and Molotch 1999; Snow et al. 1991; Whyte 1988), particularly when their chances of meeting sex partners in this manner are so slim?

I argue that framing the question in this manner misrepresents the actual sociological behavior represented by the girl hunt, particularly since adolescent males do not necessarily engage in girl hunting to generate sexual relationships, even on a drunken short-term basis. Instead, three counterintuitive attributes characterize the girl hunt. First, the girl hunt is as much *ritualistic and performative* as it is utilitarian—it is a social drama through which young men perform their interpretations of manhood. Second, as demonstrated by prior studies (Martin and Hummer 1989; Polk 1994; Sanday 1990; Thorne and Luria 1986), girl hunting is not always a purely heterosexual pursuit but can also take the form of an inherently *homosocial* activity. Here, one's male peers are the intended audience for competitive games of sexual reputation and peer status, public displays of situational dominance and rule transgression, and in-group rituals of solidarity and loyalty. Finally, by the emotional effort and logistical deftness required, rituals of sexual pursuit (and by extension the public performance of masculinity itself) encourage some young men to seek out safety in numbers by participating in the girl hunt as a kind of *collective* activity, in which they enjoy the social and psychological resources generated by group cohesion and dramaturgical teamwork (Goffman 1959). Although tales of sexual adventure traditionally feature a single male hero, such as Casanova, the performance of heterosexual conquest more often resembles the exploits of the dashing Christian de Neuvillette and his better-spoken coconspirator Cyrano de Bergerac (Rostand 1897). By aligning themselves with similarly oriented accomplices, many young men convince themselves of the importance and efficacy of the girl hunt (despite its poor track record), summon the courage to pursue their female targets (however clumsily), and assist one another in "mobilizing masculinity" (Martin 2001) through a collective performance of gender and heterosexuality. . . .

Methods and Data

I draw on firsthand narrative accounts provided by 243 heterosexual male college students attending the University of Pennsylvania, an Ivy League research university situated in Philadelphia. These data represent part of a larger study involving approximately 600 college students (both men and women). The study was conducted at Penn among all students enrolled in one of two semester terms of a sociology course on media and popular culture taught by me during the 2003–4 academic year. Respondents were directed to explore Philadelphia's downtown nightlife by attending at least one nightlife entertainment venue (i.e., restaurant, café, dance club, sports bar, cocktail lounge) located in Philadelphia's Center City district for the duration of a few evening hours' time. They were encouraged to select familiar sites where they would feel both comfortable and safe and were permitted to choose whether to conduct their outing alone or with one or more friends, relatives, intimates, or acquaintances of either gender. . . .

Because young people are likely to self-consciously experiment with styles of public behavior (Arnett 1994, 2000), observing undergraduates can help researchers understand how young heterosexual men socially construct masculinity through gendered interaction rituals in the context of everyday life. But just as there is not one single mode of masculinity but many *masculinities* available to young men, respondents exhibited a variety of socially recognizable masculine roles in their accounts, including the doting boyfriend, dutiful son, responsible escort, and perfect gentleman. In the interests of exploring the girl hunt as *one among many types* of social orientation toward the city at night, the findings discussed here represent only the accounts of those heterosexual young men whose accounts revealed commonalities relevant to the girl hunt, as outlined above.

The Girl Hunt and the Myth of the Pickup

As I argue above, it is statistically uncommon for men to successfully attract and "pick up" female sexual partners in bars and nightclubs. However, as suggested by a wide selection of mass media—from erotic films to hardcore pornography—heterosexual young men nevertheless sustain fantasies of successfully negotiating chance sexual encounters with anonymous strangers in urban public spaces (Bech 1998), especially dance clubs, music venues, singles bars, cocktail lounges, and other nightlife settings. According to Aaron, a twenty-one-year-old mixed-race junior:

> I am currently in a very awkward, sticky, complicated and bizarre relationship with a young lady here at Penn, where things are pretty open right now, hopefully to be sorted out during the summer when we both have more time. So my mentality right now is to go to the club with my best bud and seek out the ladies for a night of great music, adventure and female company off of the grounds of campus.

Young men reproduce these normative expectations of masculine sexual prowess—what I call *the myth of the pickup*—collectively through homosocial group interaction. According to Brian, a nineteen-year-old Cuban sophomore:

> Whether I would get any girl's phone number or not, the main purpose for going out was to try to get with hot girls. That was our goal every night we went out to frat parties on campus, and we all knew it, even though we seldom mention that aspect of going out. *It was implicitly known that tonight, and every night out, was a girl hunt.* Tonight, we were taking that goal to Philadelphia's nightlife. In the meanwhile, we would have fun drinking, dancing, and joking around. (emphasis added)

For Brian and his friends, the "girl hunt" articulates a shared orientation toward public interaction in which the group collectively negotiates the city at night. The heterosexual desire among men for a plurality of women (hot *girls*, as it were) operates at the individual and group level. As in game hunting, young men frequently evaluate their erotic prestige in terms of their raw number of sexual conquests, like so many notches on a belt. Whereas traditional norms of feminine desire privilege the search for a singular and specified romantic interest (Prince Charming, Mr. Right, or his less attractive cousin, Mr. Right Now), heterosexual male fantasies idealize the pleasures of an endless abundance and variety of anonymous yet willing female sex partners (Kimmel and Plante 2005).

Despite convincing evidence to the contrary (Laumann et al. 2004), these sexual fantasies seem deceptively realizable in the context of urban nightlife. To many urban denizens, the city and its never-ending flow of anonymous visitors suggests a sexualized marketplace governed by transactional relations and expectations of personal noncommitment (Bech 1998), particularly in downtown entertainment zones where nightclubs, bars, and cocktail lounges are concentrated. The density of urban nightlife districts and their tightly packed venues only intensifies the pervasive yet improbable male fantasy of successfully attracting an imaginary surplus of amorous single women.

Adolescent men strengthen their belief in this fantasy of the sexual availability of women in the city—the myth of the pickup—through collective reinforcement in their conversations in the hours leading up to the girl hunt. While hyping their sexual prowess to the group, male peers collectively legitimize the myth of the pickup and increase its power as a model for normative masculine behavior. According to Dipak, an eighteen-year-old Indian freshman:

> I finished up laboratory work at 5:00 pm and walked to my dormitory, eagerly waiting to "hit up a club" that night. . . . I went to eat with my three closest friends at [a campus dining hall]. We

> acted like high school freshmen about to go to our first mixer. We kept hyping up the night and saying we were going to meet and dance with many girls. Two of my friends even bet with each other over who can procure the most phone numbers from girls that night. Essentially, the main topic of discussion during dinner was the night yet to come.

Competitive sex talk is common in male homosocial environments (Bird 1996) and often acts as a catalyst for sexual pursuit among groups of adolescent and young adult males. For example, in his ethnographic work on Philadelphia's black inner-city neighborhoods, Anderson (1999) documents how sex codes among youth evolve in a context of peer pressure in which young black males "run their game" by women as a means of pursuing in-group status. Moreover, this type of one-upmanship heightens existing heterosexual fantasies and the myth of the pickup while creating a largely unrealistic set of sexual and gender expectations for young men seeking in-group status among their peers. In doing so, competitive sexual boasting may have the effect of momentarily energizing group participants. However, in the long run it is eventually likely to deflate the confidence of those who inevitably continue to fall short of such exaggerated expectations and who consequently experience the shame of a spoiled masculine identity (Goffman 1963).

Preparing for the Girl Hunt Through Collective Ritual

Armed with their inflated expectations of the nightlife of the city and its opportunities for sexual conquest, young men at Penn prepare for the girl hunt by crafting a specifically gendered and class-conscious nocturnal self (Grazian 2003)—a presentation of masculinity that relies on prevailing fashion cues and upper-class taste emulation. According to Edward, a twenty-year-old white sophomore, these decisions are made strategically:

> I hadn't hooked up with a girl in a couple weeks and I needed to break my slump (the next girl you hook up with is commonly referred to as a "slump-bust" in my social circle). So I was willing to dress in whatever manner would facilitate in hooking up.

Among young college men, especially those living in communal residential settings (i.e., campus dormitories and fraternities), these preparations for public interaction serve as *collective rituals of confidence building*—shared activities that generate group solidarity and cohesion while elevating the personal resolve and self-assuredness of individual participants mobilizing for the girl hunt. Frank, a nineteen-year-old white sophomore, describes the first of these rituals:

> As I began observing both myself and my friends tonight, I noticed that there is a distinct pre-going-out ritual that takes place. I began the night by blasting my collection of rap music as loud as possible, as I tried to overcome the similar sounds resonating from my roommate's room. Martin seemed to play his music in order to build his confidence. It appears that the entire ritual is simply there to build up one's confidence, to make one more adept at picking up the opposite sex.

Frank explains this preparatory ritual in terms of its collective nature, as friends recount tall tales that celebrate character traits commonly associated with traditional conceptions of masculinity, such as boldness and aggression. Against a soundtrack of rap music—a genre known for its misogynistic lyrics and male-specific themes, including heterosexual boasting, emotional detachment, and masculine superiority (McLeod 1999)—these shared ritual moments of homosociality are a means of generating group resolve and bolstering the self-confidence of each participant. Again, according to Frank:

> Everyone erupted into stories explaining their "high-roller status." Martin recounted how he spent nine hundred dollars in Miami one weekend, while Lance brought up his cousins who spent twenty-five hundred dollars with ease one night at a Las Vegas bachelor party. Again, all of these stories acted as a confidence booster for the night ahead.

Perhaps unsurprisingly, this constant competitive jockeying and one-upmanship so common in male-dominated settings (Martin 2001) often extends to the sexual objectification of women. While getting dressed among friends in preparation for a trip to a local strip club, Gregory, a twenty-year-old white sophomore, reports on the banter: "We should all dress rich and stuff, so we can get us some hookers!" Like aggressive locker-room boasting, young male peers bond over competitive sex talk by laughing about real and make-believe sexual exploits and misadventures (Bird 1996). This joking strengthens male group intimacy and collective heterosexual identity and normalizes gender differences by reinforcing dominant myths about the social roles of men and women (Lyman 1987).

After engaging in private talk among roommates and close friends, young men (as well as women) commonly participate in a more public collective ritual known among American college students as "pregaming." As Harry, an eighteen-year-old white freshman, explains,

> Pregaming consists of drinking with your "boys" so that you don't have to purchase as many drinks while you are out to feel the desired buzz. On top of being cost efficient, the actual event of pregaming can get any group ready and excited to go out.

The ritualistic use of alcohol is normative on college campuses, particularly for men (Martin and Hummer 1989), and students largely describe pregaming as an economical and efficient way to get drunk before going out into the city. This is especially the case for underage students who may be denied access to downtown nightspots. However, it also seems clear that pregaming is a bonding ritual that fosters social cohesion and builds confidence among young men in anticipation of the challenges that accompany the girl hunt. According to Joey, an eighteen-year-old white freshman:

> My thoughts turn to this girl, Jessica. . . . I was thinking about whether or not we might hook up tonight. . . . As I turn to face the door to 301, I feel the handle, and it is shaking from the music and dancing going on in the room. I open the door and see all my best friends just dancing together. . . . I quickly rush into the center of the circle and start doing my "J-walk," which I have perfected over the years. My friends love it and begin to chant, "Go Joey—it's your birthday." I'm feeling connected with my friends and just know that we're about to have a great night. . . . Girls keep coming in and out of the door, but no one really pays close attention to them. Just as the "pregame" was getting to its ultimate height, each boy had his arms around each other jumping in unison, to a great hip-hop song by Biggie Smalls. One of the girls went over to the stereo and turned the power off. We yelled at her to turn it back on, but the mood was already lost and we decided it was time to head out.

In this example, Joey's confidence is boosted by the camaraderie he experiences in a male-bonding ritual in which women—supposedly the agreed-upon raison d'être for the evening—are ignored or, when they make their presence known, scolded. As these young men dance arm-in-arm with one another, they generate the collective effervescence and sense of social connectedness necessary to plunge into the nightlife of the city. As such, pregaming fulfills the same function as the last-minute huddle (with all hands in the middle) does for an athletic team (Messner 2002).

It is perhaps ironic that Joey's ritual of "having fun with my boys" prepares him for the girl hunt (or more specifically in his case, an opportunity to "hook up" with Jessica) even as it requires those boys to exclude their female classmates. At the same time, this men-only dance serves the same function as the girl hunt: it allows its participants to expressively perform hegemonic masculinity through an aggressive display of collective identification. . . .

This collective attention to popular cultural texts helps peer groups generate common cultural references, private jokes, and speech norms as well as build in-group cohesion (Eliasoph and Lichterman 2003; Fine 1977; Swidler 2001).

Girl Hunting and the Collective Performance of Masculinity

Finally, once the locus of action moves to a more public venue such as a bar or nightclub, the much-anticipated "girl hunt" itself proceeds as a strategic display of masculinity best performed with a suitable game partner. According to Christopher, a twenty-two-year-old white senior, he and his cousin Darren "go out together a lot. We enjoy each other's company and we seem to work well together when trying to meet women." Reporting on his evening at a local dance club, Lawrence, a twenty-one-year-old white junior, illustrates how the girl hunt itself operates as collective activity:

> We walk around the bar area as we finish [our drinks]. After we are done, we walk down to the regular part of the club. We make the rounds around the dance floor checking out the girls. . . . We walk up to the glassed dance room and go in, but leave shortly because it is really hot and there weren't many prospects.

Lawrence and his friends display their elaborated performance of masculinity by making their rounds together as a pack in search of a suitable feminine target. Perhaps it is not surprising that the collective nature of their pursuit should also continue *after* such a prize has been located:

> This is where the night gets really interesting. We walk back down to the main dance floor and stand on the outside looking at what's going on and I see a really good-looking girl behind us standing on the other side of the wall with three friends. After pointing her out to my friends, I decide that I'm going to make the big move and talk to her. So I turn around and ask her to dance. She accepts and walks over. My friends are loving this, so they go off to the side and watch. . . .
>
> After dancing for a little while she brings me over to her friends and introduces me. They tell me that they are all freshman at [a local college], and we go through the whole small talk thing again. I bring her over to my two boys who are still getting a kick out of the whole situation. . . . My boys tell me about some of the girls they have seen and talked to, and they inform me that they recognized some girls from Penn walking around the club.

Why do Lawrence and his dance partner both introduce each other to their friends? Lawrence seems to gain almost as much pleasure from his *friends'* excitement as from his own exploits, just as they are "loving" the vicarious thrill of watching their comrade succeed in commanding the young woman's attention, as if their own masculinity is validated by his success. In this instance, arousal is not merely individual but represents a collectively shared experience as well (Thorne and Luria 1986:181). For these young men the performance of masculinity does not necessarily require successfully meeting a potential sex partner as long as one enthusiastically participates in the ritual *motions* of the girl hunt in the company of men. When Lawrence brings over his new female friend, he does so to celebrate his victory with his buddies, and in return, they appear gratified by their *own* small victory by association. (And while Lawrence celebrates with them, perhaps he alleviates some of the pressure of actually conversing with her.)

As Christopher remarked above on his relationship with his cousin, the collective aspects of the girl hunt also highlight the efficacy of conspiring with peers to meet women: "We go out together a lot. We enjoy each other's company and we seem to work well together when trying to meet women." In the language of the confidence game, men eagerly serve as each other's shills (Goffman 1959; Grazian 2004; Maurer 1940) and sometimes get roped into the role unwittingly with varying degrees of success. . . .

Among young people, the role of the passive accomplice is commonly referred to in contemporary parlance as a *wingman*. . . . In public rituals of courtship, the wingman serves multiple purposes: he provides validation of a leading man's trustworthiness, eases the interaction between a single male friend and a larger group of women, serves as a source of distraction for the friend or friends of a more desirable target of affection, can be called on to confirm the wild (and frequently misleading) claims of his partner, and, perhaps most important, helps motivate his friends by building up their confidence. Indeed, men describe the role of the wingman in terms of loyalty, personal responsibility, and dependability, traits commonly associated with masculinity (Martin and Hummer 1989; Mishkind et al. 1986). According to Nicholas, an eighteen-year-old white freshman:

> As we were beginning to mobilize ourselves and move towards the dance floor, James noticed Rachel, a girl he knew from Penn who he often told me about as a potential girlfriend. Considering James was seemingly into this girl, Dan and I decided to be good wingmen and entertain Rachel's friend, Sarah.

Hegemonic masculinity is not only expressed by competitiveness but camaraderie as well, and many young men will take their role as a wingman quite seriously and at a personal cost to their relationships with female friends. According to Peter, a twenty-year-old white sophomore:

> "It sounds like a fun evening," I said to Kyle, "but I promised Elizabeth I would go to her date party." I don't like to break commitments. On the other hand, I didn't want to leave Kyle to fend for himself at this club. . . . Kyle is the type of person who likes to pick girls up at clubs. If I were to come see him, I would want to meet other people as well. Having Elizabeth around would not only prevent me from meeting (or even just talking to) other girls, but it would also force Kyle into a situation of having no "wing man."

In the end, Peter takes Elizabeth to a nightclub where, although he *himself* will not be able to meet available women, he will at least be able to assist Kyle in meeting them:

> Behind Kyle, a very attractive girl smiles at me. Yes! Oh, wait. Damn it, Elizabeth's here. . . . "Hey, Kyle," I whisper to him. "That girl behind you just smiled at you. Go talk to her." Perhaps Kyle will have some luck with her. He turns around, takes her by the hand, and begins dancing with her. She looks over at me and smiles again, and I smile back. I don't think Elizabeth noticed. I would have rather been in Kyle's position, but I was happy for him, and I was dancing with Elizabeth, so I was satisfied for the moment.

By the end of the night, as he and Kyle chat in a taxi on the way back to campus, Peter learns that he was instrumental in securing his friend's success in an additional way: "So what ever happened with you and that girl?" I ask. "I hooked up with her. Apparently she's a senior." I ask if she knew he was a freshman. "Oh, yeah. She asked how old you were, though. I said you were a junior. I had to make one of us look older."

Peter's willingness to serve as a wingman demonstrates his complicity in sustaining the ideals of hegemonic masculinity, which therefore allows him to benefit from the resulting "patriarchal dividends"—acceptance as a member of his male homosocial friendship network and its attendant prestige—even when he himself does not personally seek out the sexual rewards of the girl hunt.

In addition, the peer group provides a readily available audience that can provide emotional comfort to all group members, as well as bear witness to any individual successes that might occur. As demonstrated by the preceding examples, young men deeply value the erotic prestige they receive from their conspiratorial peers upon succeeding in the girl hunt. According to Zach, a twenty-year-old white sophomore:

> About ten minutes later, probably around 2:15 am, we split up into cabs again, with the guys in one and the girls in another. . . . This time in the cab, all the guys want to talk about is me hooking up on the dance floor. It turns out that they saw the whole thing. I am not embarrassed; in fact I am proud of myself.

As an audience, the group can collectively validate the experience of any of its members and can also internalize an individual's success as a shared victory. Since, in a certain sense, a successful sexual interaction must be recognized by one's peers to gain status as an in-group "social fact," the group can transform a private moment into a celebrated public event—thereby making it "count" for the male participant and his cohorts.

Of course, as argued above and elsewhere (Laumann et al. 1994) and demonstrated by the sample analyzed here, turning a heterosexual public encounter with a stranger into an immediately consummated sexual episode is a statistical rarity, especially when compared with the overwhelming degree of time, money, effort, and emotion that young men invest in such an enterprise. But if we focus on the *primary* goal of the girl hunt—the performance of normative masculinity—then it becomes clear that the collectivity of the endeavor allows peer group members to successfully enact traditional gender roles even when they ultimately fail at the sexual pursuit itself. Again, the performance of masculinity does not necessarily require *success* at picking up women, just so long as one participates in the endeavor enthusiastically in the company of men.

For instance, Sam, a twenty-two-year-old black senior, observes how one such peer group takes pleasure in one of their members' public rejection at the hands of an unimpressed woman:

> By this time it was around 1:30 am, and the party was almost over. . . . I saw a lot of the guys had their cell phones out while they were talking to the women. I figured the guys were trying to get phone numbers from the girls. So as I walked past one of the guys, I heard him ask a girl for her number. But she just laughed and walked away. That was real funny especially since his friends saw what happened and proceeded to laugh as well.

As young men discover, contrary to popular myths about femininity, it is increasingly uncommon for women to act passively during sexually charged confrontations, even those that may be physically precarious. In such situations, women often resist and challenge the advances of strange men in public through polite refusal or the expression of humor, moral outrage, outright rejection, or physical retaliation (Berk 1977; Hollander 2002; Snow et al. 1991).

Nevertheless, one participant's botched attempt at an ill-conceived pickup can solidify the male group's bonds as much as a successful one. According to Brian, the aforementioned nineteen-year-old Cuban sophomore:

> We had been in the club for a little more than half an hour, when the four of us were standing at the perimeter of the main crowd in the dancing room. It was then when Marvin finished his second Corona and by his body gestures, he let it be known that he was drunk enough and was pumped up to start dancing. He started dancing behind a girl who was dancing in a circle with a few other girls. Then the girl turned around and said "Excuse me!" Henry and I saw what happened. We laughed so hard and made so much fun of him for the rest of the night. I do not think any of us has ever been turned away so directly and harshly as that time.

In this instance, Marvin's abruptly concluded encounter with an unwilling female participant turns into a humorous episode for the rest of his peer group, leaving his performance of masculinity bruised yet intact. Indeed, in his gracelessness Marvin displays an enthusiastic male heterosexuality as emphasized by his drunken attempts to court an unsuspecting target before a complicit audience of his male peers. And as witnesses to his awkward sexual advance, Brian and Henry take pleasure in the incident, as it not only raises *their* relative standing within the group in comparison with Marvin but can also serve as a narrative focus for future "signifying" episodes (or ceremonial exchanges of insults) and other rituals of solidarity characteristic of joking relationships among male adolescents (Lyman 1987:155). Meanwhile, these young men can bask in their collective failure to attract a woman without ever actually challenging the basis of the girl hunt itself: the performance of adolescent masculinity. In the end, young men may enjoy this performance of masculinity—the hunt itself—even more than the potential romantic or sexual rewards they hope to gain by its successful execution. In his reflections on a missed opportunity to procure the phone number of a law student, Christopher, the aforementioned twenty-two-year-old senior, admits as much: "There's something about the chase that I really like. Maybe I subconsciously neglected to get her number. I am tempted to think that I like the idea of being on the look out for her better than the idea of calling her to go out for coffee." While Christopher's excuse may certainly function as a compensatory face-saving strategy employed in the aftermath of another lonely night (Berk 1977), it might also indicate a possible acceptance of the limits of the girl hunt despite its potential opportunities for male bonding and the public display of adolescent masculinity.

References

Anderson, Elijah. 1999. *Code of the Street: Decency, Violence, and the Moral Life of the Inner City.* New York: Norton.

Arnett, Jeffrey Jensen. 1994. "Are College Students Adults? Their Conceptions of the Transition to Adulthood." *Journal of Adult Development* 1(4):213–24.

———. 2000. "Emerging Adulthood: A Theory of Development from the Late Teens through the Twenties." *American Psychologist* 55(5):469–80.

Bech, Henning. 1998. "Citysex: Representing Lust in Public." *Theory, Culture & Society* 15(3–4):215–41.

Berk, Bernard. 1977. "Face-Saving at the Singles Dance." *Social Problems* 24(5):530–44.

Bird, Sharon R. 1996. "Welcome to the Men's Club: Homosociality and the Maintenance of Hegemonic Masculinity." *Gender & Society* 10(2):120–32.

Bushnell, Candace. [1996] 2001. *Sex and the City*. New York: Warner.

Connell, R. W. and James W. Messerschmidt. 2005. "Hegemonic Masculinity: Rethinking the Concept." *Gender & Society* 19(6):829–59.

Donaldson, Mike. 1993. "What Is Hegemonic Masculinity?" *Theory and Society* 22(5):643–57.

Duneier, Mitchell and Harvey Molotch. 1999. "Talking City Trouble: Interactional Vandalism, Social Inequality, and the 'Urban Interaction Problem.'" *American Journal of Sociology* 104(5):1263–95.

Eliasoph, Nina and Paul Lichterman. 2003. "Culture in Interaction." *American Journal of Sociology* 108(4):735–94.

Fine, Gary Alan. 1977. "Popular Culture and Social Interaction: Production, Consumption, and Usage." *Journal of Popular Culture* 11(2):453–56.

Goffman, Erving. 1959. *The Presentation of Self in Everyday Life*. Garden City, NY: Anchor Books.

———. 1963. *Stigma: Notes on the Management of Spoiled Identity*. New York: Simon & Schuster.

———. 1977. "The Arrangement between the Sexes." *Theory and Society* 4(3):301–31.

Grazian, David. 2003. *Blue Chicago: The Search for Authenticity in Urban Blues Clubs*. Chicago: University of Chicago Press.

———. 2004. "The Production of Popular Music as a Confidence Game: The Case of the Chicago Blues." *Qualitative Sociology* 27(2):137–58.

Hollander, Jocelyn A. 2002. "Resisting Vulnerability: The Social Reconstruction of Gender in Interaction." *Social Problems* 49(4):474–96.

Kimmel, Michael S. and Rebecca F. Plante. 2005. "The Gender of Desire: The Sexual Fantasies of Women and Men." In *The Gender of Desire: Essays on Male Sexuality,* edited by M. S. Kimmel. Albany: State University of New York Press.

Laumann, Edward O., John H. Gagnon, Robert T. Michael, and Stuart Michaels. 1994. *The Social Organization of Sexuality: Sexual Practices in the United States.* Chicago: University of Chicago Press.

Laumann, Edward O., Stephen Ellingson, Jenna Mahay, Anthony Paik, and Yoosik Youm, eds. 2004. *The Sexual Organization of the City*. Chicago: University of Chicago Press.

Lyman, Peter. 1987. "The Fraternal Bond as a Joking Relationship: A Case Study of the Role of Sexist Jokes in Male Group Bonding." In *Changing Men: New Directions in Research on Men and Masculinity*, edited by M. S. Kimmel. Newbury Park, CA: Sage.

Mahay, Jenna and Edward O. Laumann. 2004. "Neighborhoods as Sex Markets." In *The Sexual Organization of the City*, edited by E. O. Laumann, S. Ellingson, J. Mahay, A. Paik, and Y. Youm. Chicago: University of Chicago Press.

Martin, Patricia Yancey. 2001. "'Mobilizing Masculinities': Women's Experiences of Men at Work." *Organization* 8(4):587–618.

Martin, Patricia Yancey and Robert A. Hummer. 1989. "Fraternities and Rape on Campus." *Gender & Society* 3(4):457–73.

Maurer, David W. 1940. *The Big Con: The Story of the Confidence Man*. New York: Bobbs-Merrill.

McLeod, Kembrew. 1999. "Authenticity within Hip-Hop and Other Cultures Threatened with Assimilation." *Journal of Communication* 49(4):134–50.

Messner, Michael A. 2002. *Taking the Field: Women, Men, and Sports*. Minneapolis: University of Minnesota Press.

Paules, Greta Foff. 1991. *Dishing It Out: Power and Resistance among Waitresses in a New Jersey Restaurant.* Philadelphia: Temple University Press.

Polk, Kenneth. 1994. "Masculinity, Honor, and Confrontational Homicide." In *Just Boys Doing Business? Men, Masculinities, and Crime,* edited by T. Newburn and E. A. Stanko. London: Routledge.

Rostand, Edmond. 1897. *Cyrano de Bergerac.*

Sanday, Peggy Reeves. 1990. *Fraternity Gang Rape: Sex, Brotherhood, and Privilege on Campus.* New York: New York University Press.

Snow, David A., Cherylon Robinson, and Patricia L. McCall. 1991. "'Cooling Out' Men in Singles Bars and Nightclubs: Observations on the Interpersonal Survival Strategies of Women in Public Places." *Journal of Contemporary Ethnography* 19(4):423–49.

Swidler, Ann. 2001. *Talk of Love: How Culture Matters.* Chicago: University of Chicago Press.

Thorne, Barrie and Zella Luria. 1986. "Sexuality and Gender in Children's Daily Worlds." *Social Problems* 33(3):176–90.

West, Candace and Don H. Zimmerman. 1987. "Doing Gender." *Gender & Society* 1(2):125–51.

Whyte, William H. 1988. *City: Rediscovering the Center.* New York: Doubleday.

Williams, Alex. 2005. "Casual Relationships, Yes. Casual Sex, Not Really." *New York Times,* April 3, pp. 1, 12.

Reflective Questions

1. What is a "girl hunt"? What is the myth of the pickup? Why are young heterosexual men so inclined to go on girl hunts, even though they have a low likelihood of hooking up as a result of these hunts?
2. How do men prepare themselves for girl hunts through collective rituals? What is the key purpose of these rituals? What behaviors are involved in them? How do these behaviors serve as a way for men to present themselves as masculine?
3. What is a "wingman"? What role does he play in the ritual of the girl hunt? How is he involved in dramaturgical teamwork? How does the wingman take part in the display of hegemonic mascu-linity?
4. How do men manage impressions and stage themselves when taking part in girl hunts? What kinds of selves are they allowed to present and realize? How do their self-presentations and collective rituals serve as a way of "managing emotional manhood" (see Selection 9)? How does this emotional identity work reinforce gender inequality?

23

The Gloried Self

PATRICIA ADLER AND PETER ADLER

This selection dramatically illustrates the interrelation between public self-images and individuals' self-concepts or sense of their "true" selves. Patricia and Peter Adler describe how sudden celebrity transformed the self-conceptions of players for a highly successful college basketball program. These players saw themselves reflected not only in others' treatment of them, but also on the television screen and in the pages of newspapers and magazines. The Adlers remind us that others' reactions to an individual are not the only source of self-images today. For celebrities at least, the mass media are also a source of stylized and often exaggerated self-images.

The Adlers also remind us that individuals are not passively molded by socially reflected or media images of themselves. With the encouragement of their coaches, the players attempted to resist the influence of both the hero worship by fans and media hype. Ultimately, however, the glory was too intoxicating and the media portrayals too seductive. What started out as a mere act to give reporters and fans what they expected became a trap. The more effectively the players presented themselves as the media portrayed them, the more the players thought of themselves in those terms.

As the Adlers observe, such celebrity and glory are not without cost. An individual's self-concept is usually multidimensional. It consists of an organized complex of social identities and corresponding self-evaluations. We each may think of ourselves as serious students, good friends, insensitive sons or daughters, relatively unattractive romantic partners, mediocre athletes, and so on. We may consider some of these identities more important than others, but we consider all dimensions of who and what we "really" are. It was just such multidimensionality that the basketball players sacrificed for glory. Their identity as basketball players engulfed other dimensions of their self-concepts. The Adlers describe how the brilliant glory of socially reflected and media self-images can blind an individual to other prior or possible identities. They leave us to ponder the question, what might happen to such an individual's self-concept when his or her glory fades?

In this paper we describe and analyze a previously unarticulated form of self-identity: the "gloried" self, which arises when individuals become the focus of intense interpersonal and media attention, leading to their achieving celebrity. The articulation of the gloried self not only adds a new concept to our self-repertoire but also furthers our insight into self-concept formation in two ways: it illustrates one process whereby dynamic contradictions between internal and external pressures become resolved, and it highlights the ascendance of an unintended self-identity in the face of considerable resistance.

The development of the gloried self is an outgrowth of individuals becoming imbued with celebrity. . . . Development of a gloried self is caused in part by the treatment of individuals' selves as objects by others. A "public person" is created, usually by the media, which differs from individuals' private personas. These public images are rarely as intricate or as complex as individuals' (personal) selves; often, they draw on stereotypes or portray individuals in extreme fashion to accentuate their point. Yet the power of these media portrayals, reinforced by face-to-face encounters with people who hold these images, often causes individuals to objectify their selves to themselves. Individuals thus become initially alienated from themselves through the separation of their self-concept from the conception of their selves held by others. Ultimately, they resolve this disparity and reduce their alienation by changing their self-images to bridge the gap created by others' perceptions of them, even though they may fight this development as it occurs.

Characteristically, the gloried self is a greedy self, seeking to ascend in importance and to cast aside other self-dimensions as it grows. It is an intoxicating and riveting self, which overpowers other aspects of the individual and seeks increasing reinforcement to fuel its growth. Yet at the same time, its surge and display violate societal mores of modesty in both self-conception and self-presentation. Individuals thus become embroiled in inner conflict between their desire for recognition, flattery, and importance and the inclination to keep feeding this self-affirming element, and the socialization that urges them to fight such feelings and behavioral impulses. That the gloried self succeeds in flourishing, in spite of [the] individuals' struggle against it, testifies to its inherent power and its drive to eclipse other self-dimensions.

Drawing on ethnographic data gathered in a college athletics setting, we discuss the creation and the character of the gloried self, showing its effects on the individuals in whom it develops. . . . Over a five-year period (1980–1985), we conducted a participant-observation study of a major college basketball program. . . . The research was conducted at a medium-sized (6,000 students) private university (hereafter referred to as "the University") in the mid-south central portion of the United States, with a predominantly white, suburban, middle-class student body. The basketball program was ranked in the top 40 of Division I NCAA schools throughout our research, and in the top 20 for most of two seasons. The team played in post-season tournaments every year, and in four complete seasons won approximately four times as many games as it lost. Players generally were recruited from the surrounding area; they were predominantly black (70 percent) and ranged from lower to middle class. . . . We analyze [these] athletes' experiences and discuss the aggrandizing effects of celebrity in fostering the gloried self's ascent to prominence. Then we look at the consequent changes and diminishments in the self that occur as the price of this self-aggrandizement. . . .

The Experience of Glory

Experiencing glory was exciting, intoxicating, and riveting. Two self-dimensions were either created or expanded in the athletes we studied: the reflected self and the media self. . . .

The Reflected Self

As a result of the face-to-face interactions between team members and people they encountered through their role as college athletes, the athletes' impressions of themselves were modified and changed. As Cooley (1902) and Mead (1934) were the first to propose, individuals engage in role-taking; their self-conceptions are products of social interaction, affected by the reflected impressions of others. According to Cooley (1902), these "looking-glass" selves are formed through a combination of cognitive and affective forces; although individuals react intellectually to the impressions they perceive others are forming about them, they also develop emotional reactions about these judgments. Together, these reactions are instrumental in shaping their self-images. . . .

The forging and modification of reflected selves began as team members perceived how people *treated* them; subsequently, they formed *reactions* to that treatment. One of the first things they all noticed was that they were sought intensely by strangers. Large numbers of people, individually and in groups, wanted to be near them, to get their autographs, to touch them, and to talk to them. People treated them with awe and respect. One day, for example, the head coach walked out of his office and found a woman waiting for him. As he turned towards her, she threw herself in front of him and began to kiss his feet, all the while telling him what a great man he was. More commonly, fans who were curious about team matters approached players, trying to engage them in conversation. These conversations sometimes made the players feel awkward, because, although they wanted to be polite to their fans, they had little to say to them. Carrying on an interaction was often difficult. As one player said:

> People come walking up to you, and whether they're timid or pushy, they still want to talk. It's like, here's their hero talking face-to-face with them, and they want to say anything just so they can have a conversation with them. It's *hero-worshipping*. But what do you actually say to your hero when you see him?

These interactions, then, often took the form of ritualized pseudo-conversations, in which players and their fans offered each other stylized but empty words.

Many fans [identified the players] socially and expect[ed] them to respond in kind. Players found themselves thrust into a "pseudo-intimacy" (Bensman and Lilienfeld 1979) with these fans, who had seen them so often at games and on television. Yet their relationship with the players was one-sided; fans often expected players to reciprocate their feelings of intimacy. As a result of their celebrity, team members . . . were open to engagement in personal interaction with individuals whom they did not know at all.

Players also found themselves highly prized in interacting with boosters (financial supporters of the team). Boosters showered all players with invitations to their houses for team meetings or dinner. They fought jealously to have players seen with them or gossiped about [them] as having been in their houses. It soon became apparent to players that boosters derived social status from associating with them. . . . This situation caused players to recognize that they were "glory bearers," so filled with glory that they could confer it on anyone by their mere presence. They experienced a sense of the "Midas touch": They had an attribute (fame) that everybody wanted and which could be transmitted. Their ability to cast glory onto others and their desirability to others because of this ability became an important dimension of their new, reflected self-identity.

The Media Self

A second dimension of the self created from the glory experience was influenced largely by media portrayals. . . . Most of the athletes who came to the University had received some media publicity in high school (68 percent); but the national level of the print and video coverage they received after arriving, coupled with the intensity of the constant focus, caused them to develop more compelling and more salient media selves than they had possessed previously.

Radio, television, and newspaper reporters covering the team often sought out athletes for "human interest" stories. These features presented media-framed angles that cast athletes into particular roles and tended to create new dimensions of their selves. Images were created from a combination of individuals' actual behavior and reporters' ideas of what made good copy. Thus, through media coverage, athletes were cast into molds that frequently were distorted or exaggerated reflections of their behavior and self-conceptions.

Team members, for whom the media had created roles, felt as if they had to live up to these portrayals. For instance, two players were depicted as "good students"—shy, quiet, religious, and diligent. Special news features emphasized their outstanding traits, illustrating how they went regularly to class, were humanitarian, and cared about graduating. Yet one of them lamented:

> Other kids our age, they go to the fair and they walk around with a beer in their hand, or a cigarette; but if me and Dan were to do that, then people would talk about that. We can't go over to the clubs, or hang around, without it relaying back to Coach. We can't even do things around our teammates, because they expect us to be a certain way. The media has created this image of us as the "good boys," and now we have to live up to it.

Other players (about 20 percent) were embraced for their charismatic qualities; they had naturally outgoing personalities and the ability to excite a crowd. These players capitalized on the media coverage, exaggerating their antics to gain attention and fame. Yet the more they followed the media portrayal, the more likely it was to turn into a caricature of their selves. One player described how he felt when trapped by his braggart media self:

> I used to like getting in the paper. When reporters came around, I would make those Mohammed Ali type outbursts—I'm gonna do this, I'm gonna do that. And they come around again, stick a microphone in your face, 'cause they figure somewhere Washington will have another outburst. But playing that role died out in me. I think sometimes the paper pulled out a little too much from me that wasn't me. But people seen me as what the paper said, and I had to play that role.

Particular roles notwithstanding, all the players shared the media-conferred sense of self as celebrity. Raised to the status of stars, larger than life, they regularly read their names and statements in the newspaper, saw their faces on television, or heard themselves whispered about on campus. One team member described the consequences of this celebrity:

> We didn't always necessarily agree with the way they wrote about us in the paper, but people who saw us expected us to be like what they read there. A lot of times it made us feel uncomfortable, acting like that, but we had to act like they expected us to, for the team's sake. We had to act like this was what we was really like.

Ironically, however, the more they interacted with people through their dramaturgically induced media selves, the more many of the team members felt familiar and comfortable with those selves ("We know what to do, we don't have to think about it no more"). The media presented the selves and the public believed in them, so the athletes continued to portray them. Even though they attempted to moderate these selves, part of them pressed for their legitimacy and acceptance. Over time, the athletes believed these portrayals increasingly and transformed their behavior into more than mere "impression management" (Goffman 1959). . . . [They] went through a gradual process of . . . becoming more engrossed or more deeply involved in their media selves. The recurrent social situations of their everyday lives served as the foils against which both their public and their private selves developed. The net effect of having these selves placed upon them and of interacting through them with others was that athletes eventually integrated them into their core self.

Self-Aggrandizement

Athletes were affected profoundly by encounters with the self-images reflected onto them by others, both in person and through the media. It was exciting and gratifying to be cast as heroes. Being presented with these images and feeling obligated to interact with people through them, athletes added a new self to their repertoire: a glorified self. This self had a greater degree of aggrandizement than their previous identities. The athletes may have dreamed of glory, but until now they had never formed a structured set of relationships with people who accorded it to them. Yet although they wanted to accept and enjoy this glory, to allow themselves to incorporate it into a full-blown self-identity, they felt hesitant and guilty. They wrestled with the competing forces of their desires for extravagant pleasure and pride and the normative guidelines of society, which inhibited these desires. The athletes' struggle with factors inhibiting and enhancing their self-aggrandizement shows how and why they ultimately developed gloried selves.

Inhibiting Factors

Players knew they had to be careful both about feeling important and about showing these feelings. The norms of our society dictate a more modest, more self-effacing stance. Consequently the players worked hard to suppress their growing feelings of self-aggrandizement in several ways. First, they drew on their own feelings of *fear* and *insecurity.* Although it violated the norms of their peer culture to reveal these feelings, most of the athletes we interviewed (92 percent) had doubts or worries about their playing abilities or futures.

Second, they tried to *discount* the flattery of others as exaggerated or false. . . . Athletes . . . tended to evaluate their behavior less globally than did their audience and to interpret their successes as based less on their own outstanding characteristics than on some complex interaction of circumstances.

Third, the athletes' feelings of importance and superiority were constrained by the actions of the coach and by the norms of their peer subculture. For his part, the coach tried to keep players' self-aggrandizement in check by *puncturing* them whenever he thought they were becoming too "puffed" (conceited). He "dragged" (criticized, mocked) them both in team meetings and in individual sessions, trying to achieve the right balance of confidence and humility.

In addition, players punctured their teammates by ridiculing each other publicly in their informal sessions in the dorms. Each one claimed to be the best player on the team, and had little praise for others. The athletes did not actually think their teammates had no talent; rather, the peer subculture allowed little room for "glory passing." As a result, except for the braggarts (about 20 percent of the group), none of the players expressed in public how good they felt and how much they enjoyed being treated as stars. Instead, they tried largely to suppress the feelings of excitement, intoxication, and aggrandizement, not to let themselves be influenced by the reflected sense of glory. As one player remarked:

> You feel it coming up on you and you know you got to fight it. You can't be letting your head get all out of control.

Fourth, the coach helped to *normalize* the athletes' experiences and reactions by placing them in the occupational perspective. Being adulated was part of the job, he believed, and this job was no more special than any other. . . . He conveyed this sense of occupational duty to his players and assistants. Like him, they had to "get with the program," to play to the public and help support people's sense of involvement with the team. In public, then, players feigned intimacy with total strangers and allowed themselves to be worshiped, meanwhile being told that this was merely a job.

Enhancing Factors

Yet as tired as they were, as repetitive as this behavior became, the athletes knew that this job was unlike any other. The excitement, the centrality, and the secrecy, which did not exist in the everyday world made this arena different. As one assistant coach explained:

> The times were exciting. There was always something going on, something happening, some new event occurring each day. We felt like we were news-makers, we were important. We touched so many more lives, were responsible for so many more people, and so many more people cared, wanted to know something from us. It was very intoxicating. Everyone even close felt the excitement, just from elbow-rubbing.

Athletes also were influenced in their developing feelings of self-importance by the concrete results of their behavior. . . . [T]hey were able to observe the outcomes of their behavior and to use them to form and modify assessments of their selves. Thus, when the team was winning, their feelings of importance, grandeur, talent, and invincibility soared; when they lost, they felt comparatively incompetent, powerless, and small. Because the team's record throughout our research period was overwhelmingly successful, team members reviewed the outcomes of their contests and the season records, and concluded that they were fine athletes and local heroes. . . .

One result of receiving such intense personal interest and media attention was that players developed "big heads." They were admired openly by so many people and their exploits were regarded as so important that they began to feel more notable. Although they tried to remain modest, all of the players found that their celebrity caused them to lose control over their sense of self-importance. As one player observed:

> You try not to let it get away from you. You feel it coming all around you. People building you up. You say to yourself that you're the same guy you always were and that nothing has changed. But what's happening to you is so unbelievable. Even when you were sitting at home in high school imagining what college ball would be like, you could not imagine this. All the media, all the fans, all the pressure. And all so suddenly, with no time to prepare or ease into it. Doc, it got to go to your head. You try to fight it, and you think you do, but you got to be affected by it, you got to get a big head.

Although the players fought to normalize and diminish their feelings of self-aggrandizement, they were swept away in spite of themselves by the allure of glory, to varying degrees. Their sense of glory fed their egos, exciting them beyond their ability to manage or control it. They had never before been such glory-generating figures, had never felt the power that was now invested in them by the crowds or worshipful fans. They developed deep, powerful feelings affirming how important they had become and how good it felt.

All the members of the University's basketball program developed gloried selves, although the degree varied according to several factors. To some extent, their aggrandizement and glorification were affected by the level of attention they received. Individuals with more talent, who held central roles as team stars, were the focus of much media and fan attention. Others, who possessed the social and interpersonal attributes that made them good subjects for reporters, fruitful topics of conversation for boosters, and charismatic crowd pleasers, also received considerable notice. In addition, those who were more deeply invested in the athletic role were more likely to develop stronger gloried selves. They looked to this arena for their greatest rewards and were the most susceptible to its aggrandizing influence. Finally, individuals resisted or yielded to the gloried self depending on personal attributes. Those who were . . . more modest and more self-effacing tried harder to neutralize the effects and had more difficulty in forging grandiose self-conceptions than those who were boastful or pretentious.

The Price of Glory

Athletes' self-aggrandizement, as we have seen, was a clear consequence of the glory experience. Self-diminishment was a corresponding and concomitant effect. Athletes paid a price for becoming gloried in the form of self-narrowing or self-erosion. They sacrificed both the multi-dimensionality of their current selves and the potential breadth of their future selves; various dimensions of their identities were either diminished, detached, or somehow changed as a result of their increasing investment in their gloried selves.

Self-Immediacy

One of the first consequences of the ascent of the gloried self was a loss of future orientation. In all their lives, from the most celebrated player to the least, these individuals had never experienced such a level of excitement, adulation, intensity, and importance. These sensations were immediate and real, flooding all team members' daily lives and overwhelming them. As a result, their focus turned toward their present situation and became fixed on it.

This reaction was caused largely by the absorbing quality of the moment. During the intensity of the season (and to a lesser extent during the off-season), their basketball obligations and involvements were prominent. When they were lying exhausted in their hotel rooms, hundreds of miles from campus, or on their beds after a grueling practice, the responsibilities of school seemed remote and distant. One player described his state of preoccupation:

> I've got two finals tomorrow and one the next day. I should be up in the room studying right now. But how can I get my mind on that when I know I've got to guard Michael Jordan tomorrow night?

Their basketball affairs were so much more pressing, not only in the abstract but also because other people made specific demands on them, that it was easy to relegate all other activities to a position of lesser importance.

Many players who had entered college expecting to prepare themselves for professional or business careers were distracted from those plans and relinquished them (71 percent). The demands of the basketball schedule became the central focus of their lives; the associated physical, social, and professional dimensions took precedence over all other concerns. Despite their knowledge that only two percent of major-college players eventually play in the NBA (Coakley 1986; Leonard and Reyman 1988), they all clung to the hope that they would be the ones to succeed. One of the less outstanding athletes on the team expressed the players' commonly held attitude toward their present and their future:

> You have to have two goals, a realistic and an unrealistic. Not really an unrealistic, but a dream. We all have that dream. I know the odds are against it, but I feel realistically that I can make the NBA. I have to be in the gym every day, lift weights, more or less sacrifice my life to basketball. A lot.

To varying degrees, all players ceased to think about their futures other than as a direct continuation of the present. They were distracted from long-term planning and deferment of gratification in favor of the enormous immediate gratification they received from their fans and from celebrity. What emerged was a self that primarily thought about only one source of gratification—athletic fame—and that imagined and planned for little else.

The players imagined vaguely that if they did not succeed as professional athletes, a rich booster would provide them with a job. Although they could observe older players leaving the program without any clear job opportunities, they were too deeply absorbed in the present to recognize the situation. Ironically, they came to college believing that it would expand their range of opportunities . . . yet they sacrificed the potential breadth of their future selves by narrowing their range of vision to encompass only that which fed their immediate hunger for glory.

Diminished Awareness

Locked into a focus on the present and stuck with a vision of themselves that grew from their celebrity status, all team members, to varying degrees, became desensitized to the concerns of their old selves. They experienced a heightened sensitivity and reflectivity toward the gloried self and a loss of awareness of the self-dimensions unrelated to glory. Nearly everyone they encountered interacted with them, at least in part, through their gloried selves. As this self-identity was fed and expanded, their other selves tended to atrophy. At times the athletes seemed to be so blinded by their glory that they would not look beyond it. . . .

This diminished awareness had several consequences. First, in becoming so deeply absorbed in their gloried selves, athletes relegated non-athletic concerns to secondary, tertiary, or even lesser status. These concerns included commitments to friends, relatives, and school. For example, many athletes (54 percent) began each semester vowing that it would be different this time, but each semester they "forgot" to go to class. Reflecting on this occurrence, one player mused:

> You don't think, it's not like you goin' to be a bad boy today, or you goin' to pull the wool over someone's eyes. You just plain ol' forget. You sleep through it.

For a while the athletes could ignore the facts and the consequences of their behavior, but this denial wore thin as the semester progressed, and they fell behind more noticeably. Then they moved into a stage of neutralization, blaming boring professors, stupid courses, exhaustion, coaches' demands, or injury.

Second, their new personas were expanded, even in their interactions with friends. Players referred to this situation as being "puffed," and each accused the others of it:

> Sometimes I can't even talk to Rich no more. He's so puffed in the head you can't get him to talk sense, he's lost touch with reality. It's like it's full of jello in there and he's talking a bunch of hot air.

What the athletes sensed as filling the heads of these puffed players was the self-image created by the glory experience.

Third, some athletes plunged into various acts because these acts fed their gloried selves (60 percent). They distanced themselves from their old values and took potentially career-ending risks. For example, when a player who filled a substitute role was "red-shirted" (excused from play without losing his scholarship or expending a year of eligibility) for the year because of injury, he was willing to give up this desirable and protective status when asked to do so by the coach. He was convinced easily, despite his secondary position, that the team could not function without him; like others, he blocked off the warnings and the caution that stemmed from an awareness of other needs and interests. The same lack of reflectiveness and self-awareness prevented players with chronic injuries, those who were hobbling and could no longer jump, from admitting to themselves that their playing days were over, that their gloried selves had to retire.

Self-Detachment

For some team members and at times for all, the distinction between their gloried selves and their other selves became more than a separation; the distance and the lack of reflectiveness grew into detachment. In the most extreme cases (18 percent), some athletes developed a barrier between this new, exciting, glamorous self and their old, formerly core selves. They found it increasingly difficult to break through that barrier. They experienced a dualism between these selves, as if occasionally they represented discrete individuals and not multiple facets of the same person; at times, they shifted back and forth between them. Ultimately, the different images became so disparate that they could not be fused, or else individuals became so deeply involved in their gloried selves that they lost control over their efforts to constrain and integrate them. The more these individuals interacted with others through this self, the more it developed a life and a destiny of its own.

For instance, one of the most popular players on the team developed a gloried self that was tied to his self-proclaimed nickname "Apollo." Charismatic and enthusiastic whenever he was in public, he generated enormous amounts of attention and adulation through his outgoing personality. On the court he would work the crowd, raising their emotions, exhorting them to cheer, and talking brashly to opposing players. Reporters thronged to him, because he was colorful, lively, and quotable. In public settings, he was always referred to by his nickname.

Yet, although this player deliberately had created the Apollo identity, eventually it began to control him. It led him to associate at times with people who valued him only for that self; it surfaced in interactions with friends when he had not called it forth. It led him to detach himself from responsibility for things he did while in that persona. As he reported:

> I had a summer job working for some booster at a gas station. I figured he wanted to show off that he had Apollo pumping his gas. I'd go into my act for the customers and the other employees, how fine I was, lotta times show up late or not at all. I figured he wouldn't fire me. But he did. Looking back, I can't see how I just up and blew that job. That ain't like me. That was Apollo done that, not me.

Other team members, who did not go so far as to create separate identities for their gloried selves, still experienced feelings of bifurcation. Their former selves were mundane and commonplace compared to their new, vibrant selves. These contrasting selves called forth different kinds of character and behavior. At times, the team members found it difficult to think of themselves as integrated persons, incorporating these divergent identities into one overall self. Feelings of fragmentation haunted them.

Discussion

As we have shown, high school graduates entered the world of college athletics and underwent a fundamental transformation. Thrust into a whirlwind of adulation and celebrity, they reacted to the situation through a process of simultaneous self-aggrandizement and self-diminishment. The gloried self expanded, overpowering all . . . other . . . self-dimensions; it became the aspect of self in which they lived and invested. They immersed themselves single-mindedly in this portion of their selves, and the feedback and gratification they derived from this identity dwarfed their other identities. They had not anticipated this situation, but gradually, as they were drawn into the arena of glory, they were swept away by stardom and fame. Their commitment to the athletic self grew beyond anything they had ever imagined or intended. Once they had experienced the associated power and centrality, they were reluctant to give them up. They discarded their other aspirations, lost touch with other dimensions of their selves (even to the point of detachment), and plunged themselves into the gloried self.

Athletes' gloried selves arose originally as dramaturgical constructions. Other people, through the media or face to face, conferred these identities on athletes through their expectations of them. Athletes responded by playing the corresponding roles because of organizational loyalty, interactional obligations, and enjoyment. Yet in contrast to other roles, which can be played casually and without consequence, athletes' actions in these roles increased their commitment and their self-involvement in them and made the athletes "more or less unavailable for alternative lines of action" (Kornhauser 1962:321). The gloried self not only influenced athletes' future behavior but also transformed their self-conceptions and identities. . . . [This] entire process . . . illustrates the relationship between dramaturgical roles and real selves, showing how the former comes to impinge upon and influence the latter.

References

Bensman, Joseph and Robert Lilienfeld. 1979. *Between Public and Private.* New York: Free Press.

Coakley, Jay J. 1986. *Sport in Society.* 3d ed. St. Louis: Mosby.

Cooley, Charles H. 1902. *Human Nature and Social Order.* New York: Scribners.

Goffman, Erving. 1959. *The Presentation of Self in Everyday Life.* New York: Doubleday.

Kornhauser, William. 1962. "Social Bases of Political Commitment: A Study of Liberals and Radicals." Pp. 321–339 in *Human Behavior and Social Processes,* ed. A. M. Rose. Boston: Houghton Mifflin.

Leonard, Wilbert and Jonathon Reyman. 1988. "The Odds of Attaining Professional Athlete Status: Refining the Computations." *Sociology of Sports Journal* 5, 162–169.

Mead, George Herbert. 1934. *Mind, Self, and Society.* Chicago: University of Chicago Press.

Reflective Questions

1. What is the gloried self? Why do athletes often strive to have this kind of self? Where does the gloried self come from? What kinds of interactions did the star basketball players have with fans and boosters? What is "pseudo-intimacy"? What role does it play in shaping the reflected self? What was the "media self"? Does it reflect basketball players' images of themselves?
2. Why was the gloried self problematic for players? Why did players fight against it? How did they keep themselves grounded despite being worshipped as heroes? How did winning and losing affect their self-evaluations?
3. What were the demographics of the student body at the University? How did these demographics differ for the basketball players in this study? A popular football player at an ACC school once commented on the contradictions he experienced

as an athlete of color on a predominantly white campus: while white students reached out to touch him when he ran onto the field, the same students crossed the street to avoid him when he walked across campus. How might the backgrounds of the student body and athletes shape the gloried self or the players' response to it? Is it the same for all athletes? For all sports? Why or why not?

4. This study was published in 1989. Since then, the rise of the Internet and reality television has changed the landscape of celebrity. Some celebrities are now famous for nothing more than being famous. How has the gloried self changed as a result? What role does achievement play in the gloried self? How do reality-TV celebrities maintain a gloried self in a fickle market? Why do they try to maintain such a self, especially given its costs?
5. Top Olympic athletes reach the heights of their profession often at a very young age. What happens to their identities and self-evaluations once the Olympic Games are over? What happens to athletes who are predicted to win but fail to perform well during the Games? How do athletes negotiate these challenges to their identities? What other people experience them, or under what circumstances do they experience them? Are these processes unique to athletes and celebrities? Why or why not?

The Presentation of Self in Virtual Spaces

SIMON GOTTSCHALK

Erving Goffman's selection on the presentation of self suggested that in everyday social life we do not simply take the attitude of others toward ourselves but actively influence their attitude toward us. We do so by managing their impressions of us. We thereby elicit social validation for the kind of person or self we want to be and contribute to the social construction of our own selves. Physical characteristics like skin color, secondary sexual characteristics, and bodily markers of age are difficult, although not always impossible, to conceal. The clothes we can afford to buy and places we can afford to frequent constrain our presentations of selves. Moreover, many people whom we encounter in everyday life have prior knowledge of us, either directly or indirectly. The self that we present to them must be at least minimally consistent with that prior knowledge if we hope to avoid being considered a fraud. Although we influence the self that others attribute to us in everyday social life and assume different selves in different situations, our freedom of self-presentation has definite limits.

Contemporary computer technology has expanded our freedom of self-presentation by creating new realms of social interaction and self-construction. Some of these realms, referred to as "social virtual spaces," offer an incredible array of possibilities for interaction and identity building. In this selection, Simon Gottschalk explores how the presentation of self in the realm of Second Life both resembles and differs from the presentation of self in everyday social life. Gottschalk studied Second Life as a participant observer for several months and conducted interviews with a number of people in a variety of Second Life sites. On the basis of the information he gathered, Gottschalk documents how interaction and self-presentation in this virtual world challenge some of Goffman's key arguments.

Gottschalk demonstrates how Second Life serves as a new realm of social being that offers new opportunities for selfhood. Participants in this virtual world are free to construct selves (as avatars) based on their imaginations and their abilities to buy, acquire, or build a variety of bodily resources, including hair, body parts, body shapes, and even different types of skin. The avatars they create may or may not correspond to their "real" physical and social characteristics, although the residents of Second Life typically construct avatars that bear some resemblance to their everyday selves. Most crucially, these residents often revel in the freedom they have to create avatar-selves unconstrained by genetics, aging, habit, or unhappy circumstances. Indeed, because of this freedom, participants in Second Life may feel as if their avatar-selves more genuinely reflect who they "really are" than their everyday roles or identities.

As Gottschalk implies, participants often experience Second Life as a playful and enjoyable social world where they can experience new kinds of

Reprinted From: "The Presentation of Avatars in Second Life: Self and Interaction in Social Virtual Spaces," *Symbolic Interaction* 33(4): 501–525.

relationships and identities. Yet the playful elements of this world do not detract from its seriousness. Many people develop meaningful relationships in Second Life (or other cyberworlds) and become deeply committed to one or another of their cyberselves. For some, this commitment has rewarding and self-fulfilling consequences, but for others, it has tragic results, including broken or severely damaged virtual and nonvirtual relationships.

As people spend greater amounts of time online and technological advances lead to new possibilities for representation and interaction, we can expect them to continue exploring new types of virtual experiences, relationships, and selves. We can also anticipate that their presentations of self will take on new manifestations. What we don't yet know is how people's involvement in emerging virtual communities will affect their understandings and experiences of self. Will their virtual involvements lead to the saturated, "multiphrenic," and fragmented sense of self that Kenneth Gergen discussed in Selection 20? Or, will the emergence of new virtual worlds and possibilities allow people to experience more genuine, meaningful, and coherent selves? While Gottschalk acknowledges the flawed and consumeristic elements of virtual spaces such as Second Life, he also highlights how they can serve as promising arenas for altruism, community, and self-exploration.

Welcome to Second Life
A place to be, be different, be yourself,
Free yourself, free your mind,
Change your mind, change your look,
Be Anyone.
—Promotional messages on the Second Life website, www.SecondLife.com

"I know we're meeting as avatars, but don't forget that there are real people with real emotions on the other side of the screen," writes/says Yael.[1] Or rather her avatar, who goes by the name of Becky. A fiftyish Israeli woman who lives in Arizona, Yael spends about eight hours a day in Second Life. Dahlia, one of her best friends (both in real life and Second Life), once told me she is worried that Yael is getting "increasingly confused" between these two lives. But then, Dahlia also told me that Second Life has allowed her "self to soar." Annette—the avatar of a fortyish French sociologist—confides that about a year ago, she had to completely exile herself from Second Life because of the real emotional pains she endured as a result of a failed virtual romantic relationship there. As I soon discovered, this confusion is not unusual. On the other hand, the very concept of confusion is itself perhaps simplistic . . .

What is Second Life and what am I doing here? Second Life is the Internet's most popular and largest user-created 3-D virtual world community. Produced by UC San Diego graduate Phillip Rosedale in San Francisco's Linden Labs in 2003, Second Life is the virtual home of about 15 million "residents" worldwide who appear to each other (and themselves) as avatars in countless different sites. More than two hundred institutions of higher education have a presence in Second Life, including Yale, Harvard, Stanford, [and] MIT . . . , to name a few. So do the Smithsonian Institution, the Census Bureau, the Center for Disease Control, and NASA. So do the Holocaust Museum, the Vietnam War Memorial, Woodstock, and many other important sites of collective memory. So do multinational corporations such as Nike, Coca-Cola, Manpower, eBay . . . , Dell, and a host of other Fortune 500 companies. Media outlets such as CNN, BBC, NBC, Reuters, and others have virtual buildings in Second Life. The city of Ontario has a welcoming center here, and Sweden is the first country to have established a virtual embassy on this continent. Second Life has classrooms and planetariums, research centers and aquariums, libraries and auditoriums, hospitals and museums, ashrams and atriums . . . .

Second Life also features countless virtual malls where one can purchase absolutely everything. The first quartile of 2009 reported $125 million transacted in Second Life—a great chunk of it in virtual real estate. . . .

Second Life fits Book's (2004:2) definition of a "social virtual world." As she explains, such worlds have six characteristics.

1. Shared Space: the world allows many users to participate at once.
2. Graphical User Interface: the world depicts space visually, ranging in style from 2-D "cartoon" imagery to more immersive 3-D environments.
3. Immediacy: interaction takes place in real time.
4. Interactivity: the world allows users to alter, develop, build, or submit customized content.
5. Persistence: the world's existence continues regardless of whether individual users are logged in.
6. Socialization/Community: the world allows and encourages the formation of in-world social groups like guilds, clubs, cliques, housemates, neighborhoods, and so forth.

The graphical user interface distinguishes social virtual worlds from text-based ones, such as chat rooms, as it enables "residents" of this world to see it, the people who participate in it, and themselves (or rather their avatars), in real time and from every possible angle. They no longer have to write/read about the virtual world and its participants or imagine them (see also Boellstorff 2008). This visual capability is significant, as it enhances the emotional, mental, and physical experience of actually being there. With the recent introduction of a "talk" function, Second Life residents can now also hear and talk to each other using their own voices.

Interactivity and community distinguish social virtual worlds from game-oriented ones. Since residents can alter, develop, build, or submit customized content, the control they have over this world is almost complete. . . . With this capability, residents become creators of this world (and themselves in it) rather than its subjects (see also Lévy 1997:154). As a result, their investments in it are much more significant than in virtual worlds where the landscapes, the residents' range of possible activities, and their appearance are programmed and cannot be significantly altered (Vicdan and Ulusoy 2008).

Since social virtual worlds encourage socializing and community building, residents come here mainly to explore this constantly growing environment and themselves in it, to educate themselves in a mind-boggling diversity of areas, to work, to acquire and create virtual objects, to interact with others, and to build communities, groups, and enduring associations with them. In contrast to virtual worlds designed around games, there is no "mission" to accomplish, no tower to storm, no dragon to slay, no enemy to kill, [and] no winning or losing. Just creativity and interaction. Second Life is thus constantly changing as residents' creativity, imagination, skills, relations, and projects are evolving. Every day witnesses an exponential increase in the number of residents, sites, groups, activities, and communities—from Grateful Dead fans to gay activists, from Palestinian supporters to Parisian artists, from teachers to transsexuals, from philosophers to "furries" [avatars that are hybrids of humans, animals, and machines]. . . .

[T]he unique characteristics of social virtual spaces I discussed above raise new questions about interaction, self-presentation, and self-construction in virtual spaces. Among those, I am chiefly interested in the following: (1) What are the unique characteristics of interaction in social virtual spaces? (2) What do interactions in social virtual spaces suggest about the self and everyday life in the digital age? (3) How do interactions in social virtual spaces shape the self and everyday life in the digital age? . . . [In] a modest attempt to answer those questions, I have conducted participant observation and in-depth interviews in a wide variety of Second Life sites between October 2008 and July 2009. . . .

The Virtual Impulse

> Virtual worlds are simulations. Like a map, they usually start out as reproducing actual worlds, real bodies and situations; but, like simulations . . . they end up taking a life of their own.
>
> —Rob Shields, *The Virtual*

While Second Life is new, the virtual impulse—the desire for the virtual—is quite ancient (see Boellstorff 2008, Ikegami and Hut 2008, and Shields 2003). From the Lascaux cave paintings to virtual reality, it seems that humans have always sought to articulate, (re)create, and manipulate the "real" through a variety of media. Since culture always shapes its expressions and content, the virtual also constitutes a text where participants express their concerns, fears, myths, hopes, and desires. In her work on "portable communities," Mary Chayko (2008) defines virtual worlds as "cognitive entities" and "sociomental spaces." For Book (2004), they are important sites of cultural creativity and (re)production. As liminal spaces, they can be therapeutic and transforming, offering "the opportunity to meet neglected ego needs" and to explore aspects of the self that we hesitate to acknowledge in real life (see Book 2004, Boellstorff 2008, and Daniel 2008).

It is this virtual self that serves as my point of entry into Second Life. How do we construct it, how does it affect us, and what happens to the boundary between "it" and "us"? As contemporary research on computer-mediated communication suggests (Fortunati 2002), it no longer makes sense to distinguish between "online" and "offline" realms. We inevitably manifest our offline self when we interact online, and our online interactions inevitably follow and transform us when we are offline. As Cunningham (2006:16) puts it, "After virtual reality, 'reality' is not the same, but has been altered by the bleeding of both 'worlds' into each other, by their mutual inseparability." . . .

Figure 1 Newbie Avatar.
The clothes are usually dreary and dull, the hair looks like patches of straw pasted on the head. It has poor graphic resolution and looks flat, and the facial features are ill-defined and unattractive in contrast with the looks of more veteran residents (see Fig. 2). Interestingly, however, the more time one spends in Second Life, the more the eyes and mind adjust to those cartoonish features, which can "look" realistic.
Source: http://npirl.blogspot.com/2008/10/openlifes-steve-sima-has-message-for.html

Avatars R Us

To establish our existence in Second Life, we must first create an avatar—a graphic representation of oneself. When logging onto Second Life for the first time, new residents must choose between twelve "default avatars" (six women and six men). These default avatars look rather flat and two-dimensional, and are poorly dressed by Second Life standards. Newbies are typically recognizable by these underdeveloped features, and more veteran residents have learned that they can buy, acquire, or build sophisticated and realistic-looking "skins," hair, body parts, body shapes, a cornucopia of body decorations, and any virtual object they can imagine—from a ring to a private tropical island (see Figs. 1 and 2).

Since the face, body shape, body parts, decorations, and the objects residents wear and display are all (virtual) "sign-vehicles" we use to construct our Second Life self, residents can spend agonizing days and many Lindens sculpting an avatar/self they are satisfied with, regardless of whether it "looks like" their actual physical self. In Second Life, therefore, our digital-physical appearance is no longer determined by genetic baggage or shaped by habit, age, and other natural biological processes. On the contrary, since we can continuously customize every inch or pixel of our avatar, we are now fully responsible for the virtual self we present others. In contrast to Goffman's (1959:29) observations, we no longer possess "a limited range of

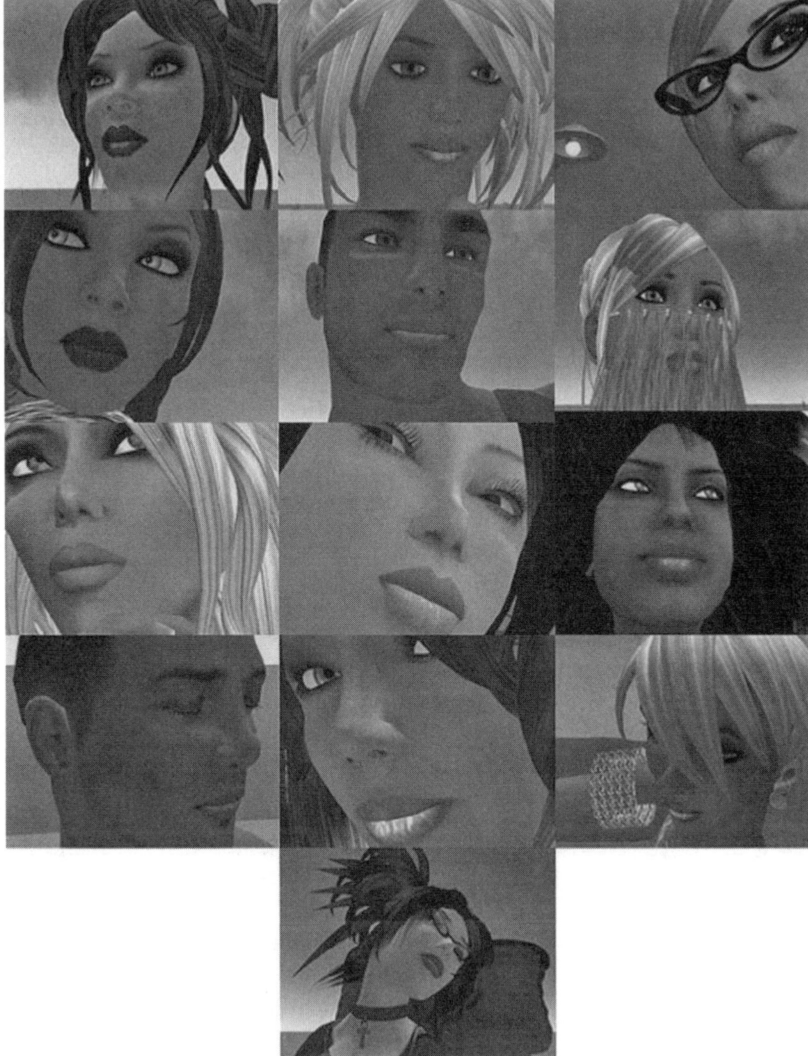

Figure 2 The Avatars Voted Most Beautiful in 2009.
Most avatars who have spent some time in Second Life achieve looks similar to those.
Source: http://www. geeksugar.com/13-Most-Beautiful-Avatars-Second-Life-176164

sign-equipment" and must no longer "make unhappy choices" when (re)presenting ourselves to others. Unsurprisingly, although one can represent oneself in an infinity of ways, most avatars look like their "real" self—only more attractive, more athletic, and typically better endowed (see Fig. 3).

Whether the avatar looks like the person who constructs it has interesting—if unclear—implications. As Book notes (2004:8),

In social world communities there exists a general expectation that avatars should remain at least somewhat faithful to their owners' offline appearances because of the fact that many people are there specifically to initiate friendships or even romantic relationships which may at some point extend to the offline world. Because of this expectation, there is a constant tension . . . between the desire to meet standards of attractiveness versus

Figure 3 Self/Avatar.
With skills, residents can produce avatars who bear an uncanny resemblance to their physical selves. According to research, most residents construct avatars who are idealized versions of themselves. This ability to craft with equal ease an avatar who does or does not resemble the physical self has interesting but yet unexplored consequences.
Source: http://mpop99.com/mypopspace/pages/blog_images/secondlife_main_485.jpg

> accuracy in portraying offline bodies. While everyone recognizes that avatars are likely to be highly idealized, someone who creates an avatar that is a significant variation from his or her offline body (particularly gender) runs the risk of being perceived by others as a "fake" or worse, as someone who is deliberately trying to deceive their friends. . . . This does not mean that performances of radically different identities don't happen in social worlds. They do. The difference is that there is greater risk of confusion and misunderstanding between those who use avatars as vehicles of role play and those who presume the avatars are extensions of real offline selves.

On the other hand, because we can represent ourselves in any way we wish, the factuality of those sociodemographic [characteristics] we display becomes much less important than the perceived consistency between the sign-vehicles we portray and our behaviors. In other words, whether the person behind the young blonde Californian Hippie avatar is "really" young, blonde, Californian, or Hippie matters less than how she performs the persona she claims to be. . . . Paradoxically, however, avatars often change their front and quickly assemble [characteristics] consistent with the persona they wish to portray, the settings in which they find themselves, and those they meet there, in full view of others. In real life, being caught in the backstage of such transformations could lead to embarrassment; here, however, momentary inconsistencies between setting, appearance, and manner are expected and accepted. The potential emotions of shame, embarrassment, "humiliation and sometimes permanent loss of reputation" (Goffman 1959:59) typically suffered in real life do not have the same inhibitory force. Hence one quickly gets used to the fleeting presence of contradictory codes in the ever-changing fronts of many avatars. An overly muscular and aggressive-looking male avatar turns out to be surprisingly shy and gentle, and an oversexed female avatar dressed in a skimpy outfit turns out to be a devoted and modest Muslim. One interesting paradox, therefore, is that while the visual aspects of avatars give them a more compelling degree of "realness" than the typed self-descriptions of chat room participants ("seeing is believing"), residents also share a consensus that we should not believe what we see but pay attention to the alignment between what avatars look/act like and what/how they write.

In this respect, residents' willingness to reveal the "real" self behind the avatar varies widely. While some residents share a great deal of information with me about who they are in real life, often e-mailing photographs, giving me their e-mail addresses, and directing me to (real) websites where I can learn more about them, others are quite adamant about their desire to segregate their real-life self from their Second Life avatar. As Lynn, a French clerk, told me, "I come here to escape from real life, to construct something different. I do not want to discuss it." Most others, it seems, are trying to negotiate the intersections between their real self and their avatar. Dahlia told me that she was once looking for a dress she wanted to wear at a party when she suddenly realized that the dress in question belonged to her avatar's wardrobe. Marla is wondering whether she should feel guilty about the virtual sexual relations she is enjoying in Second Life (she is married). Yael tells me she often implements—in her real-life relations—advice from avatars she met in Second Life, and Vivian had to postpone her plans to launch her (real-life) musician career because her collaboration with another ("soul mate") Second Life musician had reached a dead end.

To elaborate on the famous Thomas theorem, when people define the virtual as real, it becomes real in its consequences, and the reciprocal effects between the self and the avatar extend to more central aspects of one's life as well. As Boellstorff (2008:148) indicates:

> Even residents who were simply shy or withdrawn in the actual world often found that the anonymity and control of a virtual world . . . allowed them to be "more outgoing," a trait that could then transfer back to the actual world. One resident noted how "experimenting with appearance or behavior in Second Life potentially opens up new ways of thinking of things in real life."

In my research, the most interesting case of such blurring must surely be Karen, who had been stuck in an abusive relationship for years and "felt like a prisoner." She went to Second Life and created an avatar (Nina) as a means of escape until one day, as she put it, "Nina took over." Encouraged by the validating encounters and relations Nina/Karen was experiencing in Second Life, Karen decided to model herself after Nina, assuming she would then enjoy the same pleasurable experiences in her real life. She left her abusive relationship and is "a million times happier now."

As Boellstorff (2008:149) aptly remarks, avatars are "not just placeholders for selfhood, but sites of self-making in their own right," and as those stories suggest, this self-making activity informs our "real life." . . .

[S]ince relations in Second Life tend to be democratic, informal, and equalitarian, could spending an increasing amount of time here result in finding the undemocratic, formal, and hierarchical relations that characterize everyday life in most institutions increasingly intolerable? If we can import a newly found outgoingness from Second Life into real life, can similar transitions obtain for more "serious" types of everyday relations? And with what consequences?

The Self-Avatar Paradox

> INTERVIEWER: *Do you find that Dahlia-the-avatar communicates pretty much like the person behind Dahlia?*
>
> DAHLIA: *Dahlia is Dahlia. There is no difference between the two.*

The second tool that residents use to construct a virtual self and . . . to establish "a significant distinction" is through their typed communication style. Thus, if we can modify at will those aspects of one's appearance Goffman identified as permanent (looks, race, gender), those which he identified as dynamic (manner) are reduced almost solely to one's written communication style—a style that we cannot easily change, especially because the pace of Second Life conversations is typically quick. Interestingly, therefore, those aspects of the "front" we use to present our self and assess the selves others present to us have a different weight and importance than Goffman suggested in his analysis of face-to-face interaction. While we can customize every pixel of our avatar's appearance, we cannot invent communication skills we do not actually possess.

The avatar paradox is that while we can create multiple avatars that look different from each other and nothing like ourselves, they essentially always communicate in the same way. Our way. In Second Life as in everyday life, we are what/how we communicate, but since the main medium of communication here is the written word, participation in Second Life may very well "force the self out." In other words, (1) the reduction of many media of communication to just the written one, (2) the disinhibition, hyperpersonal relations, and anonymity characteristic of virtual spaces, and (3) the dynamics of synchronous written conversations all combine to encourage the expression of a self that might be much less rehearsed and performed than in real life. As one of Chayko's (2008) respondents remarked, "We may even be more ourselves when we are not entangled in face-to-face dynamics and pressures." Many of my respondents echo this sentiment and believe that their self becomes paradoxically perhaps most perceptible and "true" when they interact as Second Life avatars.

The Looking-Glass Avatar

> *It is possible that interacting through an avatar might stimulate the "observing ego"—the ability to look at oneself objectively and rationally. (Daniel, 2008)*
>
> *Second Life is a lab where we can work on our problems, a useful learning process for the self. The point is to try to use what we've learnt here and apply it in the world out there.*
>
> —*Marla, interview*

Cooley's concept of the "looking-glass self" nicely synthesizes the idea that the others we interact with reflect us. When we interact with others, we are not solely attending to the particular topic of the interaction but are also assessing how those others respond to us. We accomplish this by attempting to look at ourselves from their viewpoints and using their language, paralanguage, facial gestures, kinesics, proxemics, sounds, touching, and other actions as signs. As Goffman and scholars associated with the Palo Alto school also emphasized, we communicate and perceive such signs both consciously and unconsciously, and we are typically more likely to believe those aspects of others' behaviors that they do not seem to control (the impressions they give off).

On a first level, assessing how others perceive me/my avatar in Second Life is much trickier than in real life, since avatars do not yet possess the full range of facial expressions and kinetic abilities that we take for granted in everyday life. Of course, one can acquire or build "scripts" that will activate the avatar's body and face.... Yet the activation of those scripts requires pressing different keys, which can take time, and the creation of new scripts takes skills, which many avatars do not possess. As a result, unless they click on "pose balls" that activate the avatars in various and context-specific repetitive movements, most avatars' gestures remain relatively constant, except for a few repetitive facial expressions (blinking eyes) and body movements (leaning forward, crossing one's arms and legs, breathing, shifting body weight from one leg to another, etc.).

While this massive reduction in the number of media through which we typically communicate sharply diminishes our ability to self-reflect from the other's points of view, the visual aspect of social virtual worlds allows for more self-reflection than in text-based sites. Here we are no longer just "a product of linguistic manipulation" (Zhao 2005:402) but can self-reflect and represent ourselves and our actions to others visually.

In addition, since I can actually look at my avatar from the perspective of the person I am interacting with (or any perspective, for that matter; see Fig. 4), I can quickly adjust my appearance and proxemics to better attune to or define the virtual "situation." For example, to better frame an encounter as an interview, I would invite respondents to "sit down" and would position my avatar so that we were facing each other or looking in the same direction.

On a second level, the ability to look at and experience one's avatar/self from an external perspective introduces a new and subtler dimension in the experience of self-reflection in social virtual spaces. Mead's notion of the "I-Me" dialogue entails the idea of "mental rehearsals" of various lines of action in response to others' reactions or anticipated reactions to us. Second Life provides the unique opportunity to actually enact those various lines of action and to immediately, visually, and viscerally assess their impact. It provides the now literal (if still virtual) "third party" viewpoint from where I can watch myself/avatar try out different lines of action and see/hear/read how others respond to those. . . . By literally watching others

Figure 4 The Looking-Glass Avatar.
Simon Gottschalk's avatar viewed from his informant's perspective. Thanks to the 360-degree viewing abilities of Second Life, one can virtually observe oneself from every point of view, including the point of view of the avatar one is interacting with.
Source: Snapshot taken by Simon Gottschalk.

respond to me/my avatar, I now have immediate (if still limited) feedback for my self-presentation and communication patterns. Since those others are—just like me—"real people," and since the consequences for initiating the "wrong" lines of action are minimal, it is not difficult to appreciate how this self-reflecting ability might expand the self's repertoire. As research reports, this expanded repertoire does not vanish once we exit Second Life and reenter real life. It continues to inform us offline and online in a (hopefully) self-corrective process.

In Second Life, therefore, not only can one educate oneself about a wide variety of topics, gain new computer skills, explore this expanding virtual continent, meet a constantly changing population, and conduct research, one can also learn about oneself, try out different scripts, and expand one's repertoire of interactional (and hence self) possibilities with others. Because the rules of interaction in Second Life follow different dynamics than in real life, individuals can also experience and explore the self/avatar in unusual and relatively unscripted encounters. Much can be learned about oneself in such interactional conditions.

Conclusions: The Socio-Virtual Imagination

> *People can feel so close to one another, so strongly bonded in portable communities because proximity and presence are perceived by us in ways that transcend the physical.*
>
> —Mary Chayko, *Portable Communities: The Social Dynamics of Online and Mobile Communication*

Social virtual worlds are just emerging, and judging by the substantial financial investments by universities, hospitals, historical societies, research centers, multinational corporations, political parties, and media outlets, they contain the promise for unimaginable future possibilities. In contrast to other historical and anthropological examples of liminal space, which are/were typically separated from everyday life, social virtual worlds such as Second Life are fully embedded in it. They emerge at a historical moment when we are already spending an increasing amount of our time online (e-mailing, Web surfing, blogging, twittering, etc.), interacting with disembodied others, and establishing our presence and existence electronically.

Accordingly, it is not solely the existence of social virtual worlds per se that is interesting, but also their relation to the already virtualized "real" everyday life in the digital age.

Social virtual worlds provide a free "potential space" where real individuals—qua avatars—can and do attempt to create an alternative reality. Here they simultaneously concretize their individualistic fantasies and educate, console, and help each other; fall in love; bare their souls; organize for political causes; share information; develop communities; and enact aspects of their selves they did not know existed, were too embarrassed to admit, or always wanted to master. The disembodied self of e-mails, blogs, websites, and chat rooms is re-embodied as an avatar, who visually interacts with others, is influenced by them, and self-reflects from their perspectives. With their visual and acoustic capacities, promotion of creativity, and emphasis on spontaneous interactivity, social virtual worlds such as Second Life heighten the realism of our participation and the intensity of the emotions we experience there. As a result, the constantly evolving avatar influences the "real" self, who now also orients toward virtual, yet all-too-real others.

By replacing the rigid cultural-structural codes of identity-construction by flexible and recombinant digital ones, we construct and present selves in Second Life that are free to expand, explore, and innovate, and are invited to meet others in radically different ways. That this avatar typically looks like an idealized version of the self should not be interpreted as proof of deception or fakery. After all, we "naturally" present an idealized version of our self in face-to-face interactions. This tendency expresses common psychological impulses, which are—as I have shown—increasingly stimulated by hypermodern cultural norms. Ultimately, avatars are porous graphic shells through which curious minds interact in a boundless space where everything is virtually possible. As this space evolves and avatars mature, these narcissistic needs will eventually subside.

Social virtual worlds are certainly not utopian. Capitalism is still the "commonsense" principle organizing its economy, and there are residents who still reproduce all the regressive "isms." But if social virtual worlds are visibly colonized by capitalist greed, violent libidinal impulses, religious intolerance, and narcissistic pride, they are also energized by communitarian longings, altruistic élans, progressive projects, educational efforts, spiritual yearnings, and interactional desires.

Psychological playground for narcissist turbo-consumers or "cradle of collective intelligence"? Probably both. What seems crucial, however, is that social scientists have never had this kind of access to such an important technology—a technology that invites people to meet, interact, and create alternative forms of association. As socio-mental spaces that an increasing number of people will regularly frequent, social virtual worlds such as Second Life are therefore strategic sites that sociologists should not only investigate but also self-consciously shape in the very process of researching and participating in them. They are promising new are(n)as where we can nurture and promote a sociological imagination for the digital age.

Note

1. I have given all avatars and informants a pseudonym to protect their privacy and uphold confidentiality.

References

Boellstorff, Tom. 2008. *Coming of Age in Second Life: An Anthropologist Explores the Virtually Human*. Princeton, NJ: Princeton University Press.

Book, Betsy. 2004. "Moving Beyond the Game: Social Virtual Worlds." Cultures of Play panel, State of Play 2 conference, October. Retrieved May 16, 2009, from http://www.virtualworldsreview.com/info/contact.shtml.

Chayko, Mary. 2008. *Portable Communities: The Social Dynamics of Online and Mobile Communication*. New York: State University of New York Press.

Cunningham, Kim. 2006. "Virtually Transformed: Second Life's Implications for the Status of the

Body." Paper presented at the meetings of the American Sociological Association.

Daniel, John. 2008. "The Self Set Free." *Therapy Today* 19(9). Retrieved from http://therapytoday.net.

Fortunati, Leopoldina. 2002. "The Mobile Phone: Towards New Categories and Social Relations." *Information, Communication, and Society* 5(4):515.

Goffman, Erving. 1959. *The Presentation of Self in Everyday Life*. New York: Doubleday.

Ikegami, Eiko and Piet Hut. 2008. "Avatars Are for Real: Virtual Communities and Public Spheres." *Journal of Virtual Worlds Research* (1)1. Retrieved from jvwresearch.org.

Shields, Rob. 2003. *The Virtual*. London: Routledge.

Vicdan, Handan and Ebru Ulusoy. 2008. "Symbolic and Experiential Consumption of Body in Virtual Worlds: From (Dis)Embodiment to Symembodiment." *Journal of Virtual Worlds Research* 1(2). Retrieved from jvwresearch.org.

Zhao, Shanyang. 2005. "The Looking-Glass Self: Through the Looking-Glass of Telecopresent Others." *Symbolic Interaction* 3:387–405.

Reflective Questions

1. What is Second Life? How do people experience this virtual space as a "real" world? What distinguishes this social world from game-oriented virtual worlds? What are the unique characteristics of interaction in virtual spaces such as Second Life?
2. How does Second Life serve as an arena for self-presentation? What is an avatar? How do people construct and manage the appearance of their avatars? What is the relationship between an avatar and the self? Do most avatars bear a resemblance to the people who created them? Why? What is the self-avatar paradox?
3. What is the least manageable aspect of the avatars that people present as they interact with others in Second Life? How and why are their communication skills crucial to their self-presentations? Why do some participants in Second Life feel as if the self they present "is most true and perceptible" when they are interacting as avatars?
4. How and why is the experience of "the looking-glass self" more complex in Second Life?
5. How are virtual worlds such as Second Life likely to change our presentations and experiences of self in the future? Will they create new and more fulfilling possibilities for self-expression and social interaction? Or, will they jeopardize and undermine the selves and relationships that characterize our nonvirtual worlds?

PART VI

The Organization of Social Interaction

Social interaction has an organization all its own, apart from the participants' specific characteristics and the larger social environment in which it occurs. Indeed, social interaction is meaningful because it is patterned, organized, and orderly. The individuals participating in an interaction commonly share an implicit understanding of its organization and, therefore, similar expectations of what they and others are likely to do under different circumstances. This shared but implicit understanding turns both action and inaction, the expected and unexpected, into meaningful events. For example, individuals who know one another expect to exchange greetings when they meet. If we walk past others we know without saying hello, they will probably feel snubbed. Our failure to greet them is meaningful, because they expect a greeting. Although we may blatantly ignore expected patterns of interaction, we do so at the risk of sending unintended messages to others, and these messages will have unflattering implications for us.

One of the principal tasks of microsociology is to investigate and describe recurrent patterns of interaction and the principles of their organization. The goal is to understand how individuals achieve mutual understanding and collectively construct meaningful social lives. That is the focus of the selections in this part of the book. They describe the organization of different aspects of social interaction, explain people's commitment to sustaining orderly patterns of interaction, and illustrate how such patterns of interaction provide the glue of social life.

The selections in Part VI also emphasize the following points:

- *Our everyday interactions are grounded in and guided by interpersonal rituals. These rituals help us to claim a socially valued self, or "face," through playing our parts appropriately in a given situation.* As Erving Goffman emphasizes, the two key organizing principles that underlie interaction are (1) if you have certain social characteristics (e.g., you are a Catholic priest), you have the right to expect that others will treat you as that kind of person; and (2) if you signify to others that you possess these characteristics (e.g., you wear a clerical collar), you should actually be the person you claim to be.

- *We typically engage in tacit agreements with others to protect their "face" and corresponding lines of behavior if they do the same for us.* We also engage in two basic types of face-work, which Goffman describes in Selection 25. Both types enable us to sustain an expressive order that facilitates smooth interactions, positive self-feelings, and a sense of social value. When we use these differing face-work strategies, we demonstrate not only that we are savvy social actors, but also that we recognize and abide by prevailing rules of interaction that uphold the sacredness of our own and others' "face."

- *Even in backstage regions of behavior, such as public bathrooms, we abide by and enact interpersonal rituals designed to preserve order and protect our social value.* For instance, as Spencer Cahill illustrates in Selection 26, when we are in public bathrooms we studiously avoid observing or mentioning the toilet-related acts of others, we take steps to ensure that our own bathroom acts are private, we exchange brief greetings with colleagues, we collaborate with others in concealing embarrassing events, we manage our personal fronts, and we prepare for front-stage interactions. What Cahill shows us, above all, is that even in loosely defined situations such as public restrooms, we maneuver within fairly "tight" social expectations and rules of etiquette.

- *Our everyday lives are characterized by an emotional order, and we strive to ensure that intense emotions do not disrupt the harmony of our interactions. To do so, we draw upon a variety of strategies that allow us to manage both our own and others' emotions.* As Cahill and Eggleston demonstrate in Selection 27, some of these strategies include masking our feelings, joking about embarrassing events or comments, ignoring irritating behavior, deflecting the anger of others, suppressing our own feelings of anger or distress, accepting unwanted assistance, and eliciting sympathy from others. Most crucially, the orderliness of everyday life rests heavily on our ongoing involvement in the management of emotions.

- *Social relationships have many forms. They may be more or less distant, or more or less intimate. They may be more or less egalitarian, or more or less hierarchical. Particular social relationships may also assume different forms. They are subject to negotiation and renegotiation every time the involved parties interact. Yet relationships often have enduring features that are grounded in recurrent patterns of interaction. These recurrent patterns are facilitated by group-based codes of conduct.* As illustrated in Selection 28, in some inner-city neighborhoods the guiding code of conduct is known as "the code of the streets." It places a premium on respect and preserving one's reputation for toughness, particularly by displaying a willingness to engage in violence. Guided by this code, inner-city African-American youth strive not only to preserve their "face," but also to navigate interactions in a way that will enhance their long-term survival.

Ultimately, the selections in Part VI demonstrate that social relationships are as flexible and fragile as the interactional rituals and dynamics that sustain them. An unexpected touch, a harsh tone of voice, or a critical comment can radically transform a relationship, threatening cherished self-images and provoking intense feelings that can result in its collapse. Social relationships change along with changing patterns of interaction, and social relationships disappear in the absence of social interaction. They only endure if they are repeatedly constructed through recurring patterns of interaction.

Face-Work and Interaction Rituals

ERVING GOFFMAN

Selection 21 by Erving Goffman examined some of the dramatic or theatrical characteristics of social interaction. It described how individuals enact selves and reach a working consensus concerning the respective parts each will play in the course of their interaction. In this selection, Goffman observes that individuals effectively claim positive social value or "face" through the lines they take or parts they perform during interaction. He also argues that individuals are emotionally invested in claiming and maintaining face. The embarrassment we experience when we stumble, forget our lines, or otherwise bungle a social performance clearly demonstrates his argument.

According to Goffman, the maintenance of face requires that individuals uphold an expressive order. That is, an individual must meet others' expectations of how the type of person that she or he claims to be should act. In turn, others must treat her or him as that type of person. Thus, the maintenance of face depends on an implicit agreement: I will protect your face if you protect mine. We usually honor this agreement because of our common emotional investment in face, resulting in our self-regulated participation in orderly patterns of social interaction.

Goffman describes two basic kinds of face-work that characterize such orderly interaction. The first is self-explanatory: we attempt to avoid places, people, situations, and topics that might threaten our own or others' face and attempt to ignore events that do. However, we do not always succeed, which necessitates the second kind of face-work, or what Goffman calls the corrective process.

Goffman describes the corrective process as a "ritual" for two reasons. First, it consists of a routine interchange of "moves." When a threat to face occurs, we expect the involved parties to engage in a sequence of familiar acts and interpret the absence of any such moves in terms of that expected pattern. If, for example, an individual who has offended someone fails to offer an apology, we are likely to conclude that he or she is cold and uncaring. This example illustrates how socially expected patterns of interaction turn both action and inaction into meaningful events.

Second, the corrective process is like a religious ritual, expressing individuals' mutual reverence for face. The countless times a day that we say "excuse me," "I'm sorry," and "thank you" indicate just how highly we regard both our own and others' face. Thus, Goffman's characterization of face as "sacred" is at most only a slight exaggeration.

Every person lives in a world of social encounters, involving him either in face-to-face or mediated contact with other participants. In each of these contacts, he tends to act out what is sometimes called a line—that is, a pattern of verbal and nonverbal acts by which he expresses his view of the situation and through this his evaluation of the participants, especially himself. Regardless of whether a person intends to take a line, he will find that he has done so in effect. The other participants will assume that he has more or less willfully taken a stand, so that if he is to deal with their response to him he must take into consideration the impression they have possibly formed of him.

The term *face* may be defined as the positive social value a person effectively claims for himself by the line others assume he has taken during a particular contact. Face is an image of self delineated in terms of approved social attributes—albeit an image that others may share, as when a person makes a good showing for his profession or religion by making a good showing for himself.

A person tends to experience an immediate emotional response to the face which a contact with others allows him; he cathects his face; his "feelings" become attached to it. If the encounter sustains an image of him that he has long taken for granted, he probably will have few feelings about the matter. If events establish a face for him that is better than he might have expected, he is likely to "feel good"; if his ordinary expectations are not fulfilled, one expects that he will "feel bad" or "feel hurt." In general, a person's attachment to a particular face, coupled with the ease with which disconfirming information can be conveyed by himself and others, provides one reason why he finds that participation in any contact with others is a commitment. A person will also have feelings about the face sustained for the other participants; and, while these feelings may differ in quantity and direction from those he has for his own face, they constitute an involvement in the face of others that is as immediate and spontaneous as the involvement he has in his own face. One's own face and the face of others are constructs of the same order; it is the rules of the group and the definition of the situation which determine how much feeling one is to have for face and how this feeling is to be distributed among the faces involved.

A person may be said to *have,* or *be in,* or *maintain* face when the line he effectively takes presents an image of him that is internally consistent, that is supported by judgments and evidence conveyed by other participants, and that is confirmed by evidence conveyed through impersonal agencies in the situation. At such times the person's face clearly is something that is not lodged in or on his body, but rather something that is diffusely located in the flow of events in the encounter and becomes manifest only when these events are read and interpreted for the appraisals expressed in them.

The line maintained by and for a person during contact with others tends to be of a legitimate institutionalized kind. During a contact of a particular type, an interactant of known or visible attributes can expect to be sustained in a particular face and can feel that it is morally proper that this should be so. Given his attributes and the conventionalized nature of the encounter, he will find a small choice of lines will be open to him and a small choice of faces will be waiting for him. Further, on the basis of a few known attributes, he is given the responsibility of possessing a vast number of others. His co-participants are not likely to be conscious of the character of many of these attributes until he acts perceptibly in such a way as to discredit his possession of them; then everyone becomes conscious of these attributes and assumes that he willfully gave a false impression of possessing them.

Thus, while concern for face focuses the attention of the person on the current activity, he must, to maintain face in this activity, take into consideration his place in the social world beyond it. A person who can maintain face in the current situation is someone who has abstained from certain actions in the past that would have been difficult to face up to later. In addition, he fears loss of face now partly because the others may take this as a sign that consideration for his feelings need not be shown in the future. There is nevertheless a limitation to this interdependence between the current situation and the wider social world: an encounter with people whom he will not have dealings with again leaves him free to take a high line that the future will discredit, or free to suffer humiliations that would make future dealing with them an embarrassing thing to have to face.

A person may be said to *be in wrong face* when information is brought forth in some way about his social worth which cannot be integrated, even with effort, into the line that is being sustained for him. A person may be said to *be out of face* when he participates in a contact with others without having ready a line of the kind participants in such situations are expected to take. The intent of many pranks is to lead a person into showing a wrong face or no face, but there will also be serious occasions, of course, when he will find himself expressively out of touch with the situation.

When a person senses that he is in face, he typically responds with feelings of confidence and assurance. Firm in the line he is taking, he feels that he can hold his head up and openly present himself to others. He feels some security and some relief—as he also can when the others feel he is in wrong face but successfully hide these feelings from him.

When a person is in wrong face or out of face, expressive events are being contributed to the encounter which cannot be readily woven into the expressive fabric of the occasion. Should he sense that he is in wrong face or out of face, he is likely to feel ashamed and inferior because of what has happened to the activity on his account and because of what may happen to his reputation as a participant. Further, he may feel bad because he had relied upon the encounter to support an image of self to which he has become emotionally attached and which he now finds threatened. Felt lack of judgmental support from the encounter may take him aback, confuse him, and momentarily incapacitate him as an interactant. His manner and bearing may falter, collapse, and crumble. He may become embarrassed and chagrined; he may become shamefaced. The feeling, whether warranted or not, that he is perceived in a flustered state by others, and that he is presenting no usable line, may add further injuries to his feelings, just as his change from being in wrong face or out of face to being shamefaced can add further disorder to the expressive organization of the situation. Following common usage, I shall employ the term *poise* to refer to the capacity to suppress and conceal any tendency to become shame faced during encounters with others.

In our Anglo-American society, as in some others, the phrase "to lose face" seems to mean to be in wrong face, to be out of face, or to be shame-faced. The phrase "to save one's face" appears to refer to the process by which the person sustains an impression for others that he has not lost face. . . .

As an aspect of the social code of any social circle, one may expect to find an understanding as to how far a person should go to save his face. Once he takes on a self-image expressed through face, he will be expected to live up to it. In different ways in different societies, he will be required to show self-respect, abjuring certain actions because they are above or beneath him, while forcing himself to perform others, even though they cost him dearly. By entering a situation in which he is given a face to maintain, a person takes on the responsibility of standing guard over the flow of events as they pass before him. He must ensure that a particular *expressive order* is sustained—an order that regulates the flow of events, large or small, so that anything that appears to be expressed by them will be consistent with his face. When a person manifests these compunctions primarily from duty to himself, one speaks in our society of pride; when he does so because of duty to wider social units, and receives support from these units in doing so, one speaks of honor. When these compunctions have to do with postural things, with expressive events derived from the way in which the person handles his body, his emotions, and the things with which he has physical contact, one speaks of dignity, this being an aspect of expressive control that is always praised and never studied. In any case, while his social face can be his most personal possession and the center of his security and pleasure, it is only on loan to him from society; it will be withdrawn, unless he conducts himself in a way that is worthy of it. Approved attributes and their relation to face make of every man his own jailer; this is a fundamental social constraint, even though each man may like his cell.

Just as the member of any group is expected to have self-respect, so also he is expected to sustain a standard of considerateness; he is expected to go to certain lengths to save the feelings and the face of others present, and he is expected to do this willingly and spontaneously because of emotional identification with the others and with their feelings. In consequence, he is disinclined to witness the defacement of others. The person who can witness another's humiliation and unfeelingly retain a cool countenance himself is said in our society to be "heartless," just as he who can unfeelingly participate in his own defacement is thought to be "shameless."

The combined effect of the rule of self-respect and the rule of considerateness is that the person tends to conduct himself during an encounter so as to maintain both his own face and the face of the other participants. This means that the line taken by each participant is usually allowed to prevail, and each participant is allowed to carry off the role he appears to have chosen for himself. A state where everyone temporarily accepts everyone else's line is established. This kind of mutual acceptance seems to be a basic structural feature of interaction, especially the interaction of face-to-face talk. It is typically a "working" acceptance, not a "real" one, since it tends to be based not on agreement of candidly expressed heart-felt evaluations, but upon a willingness to give temporary lip service to judgments with which the participants do not really agree.

The mutual acceptance of lines has an important conservative effect upon encounters. Once the person initially presents a line, he and the others tend to build their later responses upon it, and in a sense, become stuck with it. Should the person radically alter his line, or should it become discredited, then confusion results, for the participants will have prepared and committed themselves for actions that are now unsuitable. . . .

By *face-work* I mean to designate the actions taken by a person to make whatever he is doing consistent with face. Face-work serves to counteract "incidents"—that is, events whose effective symbolic implications threaten face. Thus, poise is one important type of face-work, for through poise the person controls his embarrassment and hence the embarrassment that he and others might have over his embarrassment. Whether or not the full consequences of face-saving actions are known to the person who employs them, they often become habitual and standardized practices; they are like traditional plays in a game or traditional steps in a dance. Each person, subculture, and society seems to have its own characteristic repertoire of face-saving practices. It is to this repertoire that people partly refer when they ask what a person or culture is "really" like. And yet the particular set of practices stressed by particular persons or groups seems to be drawn from a single logically coherent framework of possible practices. It is as if face, by its very nature, can be saved only in a certain number of ways, and as if each social grouping must make its selections from this single matrix of possibilities.

The members of every social circle may be expected to have some knowledge of face-work and some experience in its use. In our society, this kind of capacity is sometimes called tact, *savoir-faire*, diplomacy, or social skill. Variation in social skill pertains more to the efficacy of face-work than to the frequency of its application, for almost all acts involving others are modified, prescriptively or proscriptively, by considerations of face. If a person is to employ his repertoire of face-saving practices, obviously he must first become aware of the interpretation that others may have placed upon his acts and the interpretation that he ought perhaps to place upon theirs. In other words, he must exercise perceptiveness. But even if he is properly alive to symbolically conveyed judgments and is socially skilled, he must yet be willing to exercise his perceptiveness and his skill; he must, in short, be prideful and considerate. Admittedly, of course, the possession of perceptiveness and social skill so often leads to their application in our society that terms such as politeness or tact fail to distinguish between the inclination to exercise such capacities and the capacities themselves.

I have already said that the person will have two points of view—a defensive orientation toward saving his own face and a protective orientation toward saving the others' face. Some practices will be primarily defensive and others primarily protective, although in general, one may expect these two perspectives to be taken at the same time. In trying to save the face of others, the person must choose a tack that will not lead to loss of his own; in trying to save his own face, he must consider the loss of face that his action may entail for others.

In many societies, there is a tendency to distinguish three levels of responsibility that a person may have for a threat to face that his actions have created. First, he may appear to have acted innocently; his offense seems to be unintended and unwitting, and those who perceive his act can feel that he would have attempted to avoid it had he foreseen its offensive consequences. In our society, one calls such threats to face *faux pas, gaffes, boners,* or *bricks.* Secondly, the offending person may appear to have acted maliciously and spitefully, with the intention of causing open insult. Thirdly, there are incidental offenses; these arise as an unplanned but sometimes anticipated by-product of action—action the offender performs in spite of its offensive consequences, although not out of spite. From the point of view of a particular participant, these three types of threat can be introduced by the participant himself against his own face, by himself against the face of the others, by the others against their own face, or by the others against himself. Thus, the person may find himself in many different relations to a threat to face. If he is to handle himself and others well in all contingencies, he will have to have a repertoire of face-saving practices for each of these possible relations to threat.

The Basic Kinds of Face-Work

The Avoidance Process

The surest way for a person to prevent threats to his face is to avoid contacts in which these threats are likely to occur. In all societies, one can observe this in the avoidance relationship and in the tendency for certain delicate transactions to be conducted by go-betweens. Similarly, in many societies, members know the value of voluntarily making a gracious withdrawal before an anticipated threat to face has had a chance to occur.

Once the person does chance an encounter, other kinds of avoidance practices come into play. As defensive measures, he keeps off topics and away from activities that would lead to the expression of information that is inconsistent with the line he is maintaining. At opportune moments he will change the topic of conversation or the direction of activity. He will often present initially a front of diffidence and composure, suppressing any show of feeling, until he has found out what kind of line the others will be ready to support for him. Any claims regarding self may be made with belittling modesty, with strong qualifications, or with a note of unseriousness; by hedging in these ways, he will have prepared a self for himself that will not be discredited by exposure, personal failure, or the unanticipated acts of others. And if he does not hedge his claims about self, he will at least attempt to be realistic about them, knowing that otherwise events may discredit him and make him lose face.

Certain protective maneuvers are as common as these defensive ones. The person shows respect and politeness, making sure to extend to others any ceremonial treatment that might be their due. He employs discretion; he leaves unstated facts that might implicitly or explicitly contradict and embarrass the positive claims made by others. He employs circumlocutions and deceptions, phrasing his replies with careful ambiguity, so that the others' face is preserved even if their welfare is not. He employs courtesies, making slight modifications of his demands on or appraisals of the others, so that they will be able to define the situation as one in which their self-respect is not threatened. In making a belittling demand upon the others, or in imputing uncomplimentary attributes to them, he may employ a joking manner, allowing them to take the lie that they are good sports, able to relax from their ordinary standards of pride and honor. And before engaging in a potentially offensive act, he may provide explanations as to why the others ought not to be affronted by it. For example, if he knows that it will be necessary to withdraw from the encounter before it has terminated, he may tell the others in advance that it is necessary for him to leave, so that they will have faces that are prepared for it. But neutralizing the potentially offensive act need not be done verbally; he may wait for a propitious moment or natural break—for example, in conversation, a momentary lull when no one speaker can be affronted—and then leave, in this way using the context instead of his words as a guarantee of inoffensiveness.

When a person fails to prevent an incident, he can still attempt to maintain the fiction that no threat to face has occurred. The most blatant example of this is found where the person acts as if an event that contains a threatening expression has not occurred at all. He may apply this studied nonobservance to his own acts—as when he does not by any outward sign admit that his stomach is rumbling—or to the acts of others, as when he does not "see" that another has stumbled. Social life in mental hospitals owes much to this process; patients employ it in regard to their own peculiarities, and visitors employ it, often with tenuous desperation, in regard to patients. In general, tactful blindness of this kind is applied only to events that, if perceived at all, could be perceived and interpreted only as threats to face.

A more important, less spectacular kind of tactful overlooking is practiced when a person openly acknowledges an incident as an event that has occurred, but not as an event that contains a threatening expression. If he is not the one who is responsible for the incident, then his blindness will have to be supported by his forbearance; if he is the doer of the threatening deed, then his blindness will have to be supported by his willingness to seek a way of dealing with the matter, which leaves him dangerously dependent upon the cooperative forbearance of the others.

Another kind of avoidance occurs when a person loses control of his expressions during an encounter. At such times he may try not so much to overlook the incident as to hide or conceal his activity in some way, thus making it possible for the others to avoid some of the difficulties created by a participant who has not maintained face. Correspondingly, when a person is caught out of face because he had not expected to be thrust into interaction, or because strong feelings have disrupted his expressive mask, the others may protectively turn away from him or his activity for a moment, to give him time to assemble himself.

The Corrective Process

When the participants in an undertaking or encounter fail to prevent the occurrence of an event that is expressively incompatible with the judgments of social worth that are being maintained, and when the event is of the kind that is difficult to overlook, then the participants are likely to give it accredited status as an incident—to ratify it as a threat that deserves direct official attention—and to proceed to try to correct for its effects. At this point, one or more participants find themselves in an established state of ritual disequilibrium or disgrace, and an attempt must be made to re-establish a satisfactory ritual state for them. I use the term *ritual* because I am dealing with acts through whose symbolic component the actor shows how worthy he is of respect or how worthy he feels others are of it. The imagery of equilibrium is apt here, because the length and intensity of the corrective effort is nicely adapted to the persistence and intensity of the threat. One's face, then, is a sacred thing, and the expressive order required to sustain it is, therefore, a ritual one.

The sequence of acts set in motion by an acknowledged threat to face, and terminating in the re-establishment of ritual equilibrium, I shall call an *interchange*. Defining a message or move as everything conveyed by an actor during a turn at taking action, one can say that an interchange will involve two or more moves and two or more participants. Obvious examples in our society may be found in the sequence of "Excuse me" and "Certainly" and in the exchange of presents or visits. The interchange seems to be a basic concrete unit of social activity and provides one natural empirical way to study interaction of all kinds. Face-saving practices can be usefully classified according to their position in the natural sequence of moves that comprise this unit. Aside from the event which introduces the need for a corrective interchange, four classic moves seem to be involved.

There is, first, the challenge, by which participants take on the responsibility of calling attention to the misconduct; by implication, they suggest that the threatened claims are to stand firm and that the threatening event itself will have to be brought back into line.

The second move consists of the offering, whereby a participant, typically the offender, is given a chance to correct for the offense and re-establish the expressive order. Some classic ways of making this move are available. On the one hand, an attempt can be made to show that what admittedly appeared to be a threatening expression is really a meaningless event, or an unintentional act, or a joke not meant to be taken seriously, or an unavoidable, "understandable" product of extenuating circumstances. On the other hand, the meaning of the event may be granted and effort concentrated on the creator of it. Information may be provided to show that the creator was under the influence of something and not himself, or that he was under the command of somebody else and not acting for himself. When a person claims that an act was meant in jest, he may go on and claim that the self that seemed to lie behind the act was also projected as a joke. When a person suddenly finds that he has demonstrably failed in capacities that the others assumed him to have and to claim for himself—such as the capacity to spell, to perform minor tasks, to talk without malapropisms, and so on—he may quickly add, in a serious or unserious way, that he claims these incapacities as part of his self. The meaning of the threatening incident thus stands, but it can now be incorporated smoothly into the flow of expressive events.

As a supplement to or substitute for the strategy of redefining the offensive act or himself, the offender can follow two other procedures: he can provide compensations to the injured—when it is not his own face that he has threatened; or he can provide punishment, penance, and expiation for himself. These are important moves or phases in the ritual interchange. Even though the offender may fail to prove his innocence, he can suggest through these means that he is now a renewed person, a person who has paid for his sin against the expressive order and is once more to be trusted in the judgmental scene. Further, he can show that he does not treat the feelings of the others lightly, and that, if their feelings have been injured by him, however innocently, he is prepared to pay a price for his action. Thus, he assures the others that they can accept his explanations without this acceptance constituting a sign of weakness and a lack of pride on their part. Also, by his treatment of himself, by his self-castigation, he shows that he is clearly aware of the kind of crime he would have committed had the incident been what it first appeared to be, and that he knows the kind of punishment that ought to be accorded to one who would commit such a crime. The suspected person thus shows that he is thoroughly capable of taking the role of the others toward his own activity, that he can still be used as a responsible participant in the ritual process, and that the rules of conduct which he appears to have broken are still sacred, real, and unweakened. An offensive act may arouse anxiety about the ritual code; the offender allays this anxiety by showing that both the code and he as an upholder of it are still in working order.

After the challenge and the offering have been made, the third move can occur; the persons to whom the offering is made can accept it as a satisfactory means of re-establishing the expressive order and the faces supported by this order. Only then can the offender cease the major part of his ritual offering.

In the terminal move of the interchange, the forgiven person conveys a sign of gratitude to those who have given him the indulgence of forgiveness.

The phases of the corrective process—challenge, offering, acceptance, and thanks—provide a model for interpersonal ritual behavior, but a model that may be departed from in significant ways. For example, the offended parties may give the offender a chance to initiate the offering on his own before a challenge is made and before they ratify the offense as an incident. This is a common courtesy, extended on the assumption that the recipient will introduce a self-challenge. Further, when the offended persons accept the corrective offering, the offender may suspect that this has been grudgingly done from tact, and so he may volunteer additional corrective offerings, not allowing the matter to rest until he has received a second or third acceptance of his repeated apology. Or the offended persons may tactfully take over the role of the offender and volunteer excuses for him that will, perforce, be acceptable to the offended persons.

An important departure from the standard corrective cycle occurs when a challenged offender patently refuses to heed the warning and continues with his offending behavior, instead of setting the activity to rights. This move shifts the play back to the challengers. If they countenance the refusal to meet their demands, then it will be plain that their challenge was a bluff and that the bluff has been called. This is an untenable position; a face for themselves cannot be derived from it, and they are left to bluster. To avoid this fate, some classic moves are open to them. For instance, they can resort to tactless, violent retaliation, destroying either themselves or the person who had refused to heed their warning. Or they can withdraw from the undertaking in a visible huff—righteously indignant, outraged, but confident of ultimate vindication. Both tacks provide a way of denying the offender his status as an interactant, and hence denying the reality of the offensive judgment he has made. Both strategies are ways of salvaging face, but for all concerned the costs are usually high. It is partly to forestall such scenes that an offender is usually quick to offer apologies; he does not want the affronted persons to trap themselves into the obligation to resort to desperate measures.

It is plain that emotions play a part in these cycles of response, as when anguish is expressed because of what one has done to another's face, or anger because of what has been done to one's own. I want to stress that these emotions function as moves, and fit so precisely into the logic of the ritual game that it would seem difficult to understand them without it. In fact, spontaneously expressed feelings are likely to fit into the formal pattern of the ritual interchange more elegantly than consciously designed ones.

Making Points—The Aggressive Use of Face-Work

Every face-saving practice which is allowed to neutralize a particular threat opens up the possibility that the threat will be willfully introduced for what can be safely gained by it. If a person knows that this modesty will be answered by others' praise of him, he can fish for compliments. If his own appraisal of self will be checked against incidental events, then he can arrange for favorable incidental events to appear. If others are prepared to overlook an affront to them and act forbearingly, or to accept apologies, then he can rely on this as a basis for safely offending them. He can attempt by sudden withdrawal to force the others into a ritually unsatisfactory state, leaving them to flounder in an interchange that cannot readily be completed. Finally, at some expense to himself, he can arrange for the others to hurt his feelings, thus forcing them to feel guilt, remorse, and sustained ritual disequilibrium.

When a person treats face-work not as something he need be prepared to perform, but rather as something that others can be counted on to perform or to accept, then an encounter or an undertaking becomes less a scene of mutual considerateness than an arena in which a contest or match is held. The purpose of the game is to preserve everyone's line from an inexcusable contradiction, while scoring as many points as possible against one's adversaries and making as many gains as possible for oneself. An audience to the struggle is almost a necessity. The general method is for the person to introduce favorable facts about himself and unfavorable facts about the others in such a way that the only reply the others will be able to think up will be one that terminates the interchange in a grumble, a meager excuse, a face-saving I-can-take-a-joke laugh, or an empty stereotyped comeback of the "Oh yeah?" or "That's what you think" variety. The losers in such cases will have to cut their losses, tacitly grant the loss of a point, and attempt to do better in the next interchange. . . .

In aggressive interchanges, the winner not only succeeds in introducing information favorable to himself and unfavorable to the others, but also demonstrates that as interactant he can handle himself better than his adversaries. Evidence of this capacity is often more important than all the other information the person conveys in the interchange, so that the introduction of a "crack" in verbal interaction tends to imply that the initiator is better at footwork than those who must suffer his remarks. However, if they succeed in making a successful parry of the thrust and then a successful riposte, the instigator of the play must not only face the disparagement with which the others have answered him but also accept the fact that his assumption of superiority in footwork has proven false. He is made to look foolish; he loses face. Hence, it is always a gamble to "make a remark." The tables can be turned and the aggressor can lose more than he could have gained had his move won the point. . . .

Cooperation in Face-Work

Since each participant in an undertaking is concerned, albeit for differing reasons, with saving his own face and the face of the others, then tacit cooperation will naturally arise so that the participants together can attain their shared but differently motivated objectives.

One common type of tacit cooperation in face-saving is the tact exerted in regard to face-work itself. The person not only defends his own face and protects the face of the others, but also acts so as to make it possible and even easy for the others to employ face-work for themselves and him. He helps them to help themselves and him. Social etiquette, for example, warns men against asking for New Year's Eve dates too early in the season, lest the girl find it difficult to provide a gentle excuse for refusing. This second-order tact can be further illustrated by the wide-spread practice of negative-attribute etiquette. The person who has an unapparent negatively valued attribute often finds it expedient to begin an encounter with an unobtrusive admission of his failing, especially with persons who are uninformed about him. The others are thus warned in advance against making disparaging remarks about his kind of person and are saved from the contradiction of acting in a friendly fashion to a person toward whom they are unwittingly being hostile. This strategy also prevents the others from automatically making assumptions about him which place him in a false position and saves him from painful forbearance or embarrassing remonstrances.

Tact, in regard to face-work, often relies for its operation on a tacit agreement to do business through the language of hint—the language of innuendo, ambiguities, well-placed pauses, carefully worded jokes, and so on. The rule regarding this unofficial kind of communication is that the sender ought not to act as if he had officially conveyed the message he has hinted at, while the recipients have the right and the obligation to act as if they have not officially received the message contained in the hint. Hinted communication, then, is deniable communication; it need not be faced up to. It provides a means by which the person can be warned that his current line or the current situation is leading to loss of face, without this warning itself becoming an incident.

Another form of tacit cooperation, and one that seems to be much used in many societies, is reciprocal self-denial. Often the person does not have a clear idea of what would be a just or acceptable apportionment of judgments during the occasion, and so he voluntarily deprives or depreciates himself while indulging and complimenting the others, in both cases carrying the judgments safely past what is likely to be just. The favorable judgments about himself he allows to come from others; the unfavorable judgments of himself are his own contributions.

This "after you, Alphonse" technique works, of course, because in depriving himself, he can reliably anticipate that the others will compliment or indulge him. Whatever allocation of favors is eventually established, all participants are first given a chance to show that they are not bound or constrained by their own desires and expectations, that they have a properly modest view of themselves, and that they can be counted upon to support the ritual code. . . .

A person's performance of face-work, extended by his tacit agreement to help others perform theirs, represents his willingness to abide by the ground rules of social interaction. Here is the hallmark of his socialization as an interactant. If he and the others were not socialized in this way, interaction in most societies and most situations would be a much more hazardous thing for feelings and faces. The person would find it impractical to be oriented to symbolically conveyed appraisals of social worth, or to be possessed of feelings—that is, it would be impractical for him to be a ritually delicate object. . . . It is no wonder that trouble is caused by a person who cannot be relied upon to play the face-saving game. . . .

Conclusion

Throughout this paper it has been implied that underneath their differences in culture, people everywhere are the same. If persons have a universal human nature, they themselves are not to be looked to for an explanation of it. One must look rather to the fact that societies everywhere, if they are to be societies, must mobilize their members as self-regulating participants in social encounters. One way of mobilizing the individual for this purpose is through ritual: he is taught to be perceptive; to have feelings attached to self and a self expressed through face; to have pride, honor, and dignity; to have considerateness; to have tact and a certain amount of poise. These are some of the elements of behavior which must be built into the person, if practical use is to be made of him as an interactant, and it is these elements that are referred to in part when one speaks of universal human nature.

Universal human nature is not a very human thing. By acquiring it, the person becomes a kind of construct, built up not from inner psychic propensities but from moral rules that are impressed upon him from without. These rules, when followed, determine the evaluation he will make of himself and of his fellow-participants in the encounter, the distribution of his feelings, and the kinds of practices he will employ to maintain a specified and obligatory kind of ritual equilibrium. The general capacity to be bound by moral rules may well belong to the individual, but the particular set of rules which transforms him into a human being derives from requirements established in the ritual organization of social encounters. . . .

Reflective Questions

1. What is a line? What is face, and where does it come from? What types of encounters produce feelings of goodness? Hurt? What is saving face? Why do we fear losing face? How do we save the face of others?
2. What is face-work? Why do we avoid particular encounters? How else do we avoid threats to face? How do we correct disgracing encounters? Why do we engage in this remedial face-work? What happens when we successfully neutralize a threat?
3. Sometimes we offend people in ways that are minimally threatening to our own face. Why? How do we cooperate in helping others save face?
4. Watch Hamish and Andy "ghost" people at www.youtube.com/watch?v=peAtB_dFUho and www.youtube.com/watch?v=3qWg8h4BNp4. What is ghosting? Does ghosting threaten face? Whose? Why? How do they pick their targets? What are the reactions of passersby? When do Hamish and Andy engage in corrective action? What do they do? What do they say? What mannerisms do they use? Whose face are they protecting? What would happen if they didn't engage in corrective action? Why is ghosting funny? What role do lines, face-work, and rituals play in humor?

The Interaction Order of Public Bathrooms

SPENCER E. CAHILL

This selection illustrates the dramatic and ritual character of everyday social life that Goffman identified with the example of routine behavior in public bathrooms. From Goffman's dramaturgical perspective, bathrooms are backstage regions where individuals can temporarily retire from their front-stage performances. However, public bathrooms do not insulate individuals from potential audiences. When not concealed in toilet stalls, they must be ready to perform and to uphold what Goffman called "the interaction order." Yet, individuals in public bathrooms routinely engage in acts that are inconsistent with their front-stage performances and undermine the "sacred" face they claim through those performances. Thus, public bathrooms are scenes of many socially delicate situations that reveal just how loyal we are to the commonly understood but unspoken rules that govern everyday social interaction.

First, this selection illustrates that much behavior in public bathrooms consists of what Goffman called "interpersonal rituals." Individuals show respect for one another by honoring one another's right to be left alone and the turn order of queues. They show respect for their relationships with others by acknowledging those with whom they are previously acquainted. Other ritual conduct in public bathrooms addresses the socially delicate situations that occur within them. For example, men using adjacent urinals do not glance at one another and then look away as they might under other circumstances but keep their eyes glued to the wall directly in front of them. Other ritual conduct counteracts the profaning implications of the acts for which public bathrooms are explicitly designed.

Second, this selection illustrates the variety of backstage behaviors that routinely occur in public bathrooms. In addition to the acts for which they are explicitly designed, individuals retreat to bathrooms to inspect and repair their front-stage appearance and costumes or "persona fronts." They retreat to bathrooms when overcome by emotion. And, groups who are acting as an ensemble or "performance team" retreat to bathrooms to boost team morale, rehearse lines, and give one another direction.

Both forms of routine behavior in public bathrooms, ritual and backstage, reveal many of the usually unrecognized standards that govern everyday social interaction and our usually unrecognized commitment to them. Backstage behavior reveals, by way of contrast, the behavioral standards that govern our front-stage performances. And, our ritual conduct in public bathrooms demonstrates just how committed we are to upholding the expressive order that sustains the "sacredness" of our own and others' "face." The usually unnoticed but exquisite orderliness of everyday social interaction clearly does not stop at the bathroom door.

Reprinted from: Spencer E. Cahill with William Distler, Cynthia Lachowetz, Andrea Meaney, Robyn Tarallo, and Teena Willard, Meanwhile Backstage: Public Bathrooms and the Interaction Order. *Urban Life* 14: 33–58.

[Some] years ago the anthropologist Horace Miner (1955) suggested, with tongue planted firmly in cheek, that many of the rituals that behaviorally express and sustain the central values of our culture occur in bathrooms. Whether Miner realized it or not . . . there was more to this thesis than his humorous interpretation of bathroom rituals suggests. As Erving Goffman (1959: 112–113) once observed, the vital secrets of our public shows are often visible in those settings that serve as backstage regions relative to our public performances:

> [I]t is here that illusions and impressions are openly constructed. . . . Here the performer can relax; he can drop his front, forgo speaking his lines, and step out of character.

Clearly, bathrooms or, as they are often revealingly called, restrooms, are such backstage regions. By implication, therefore, systematic study of bathroom behavior may yield valuable insights into the character and requirements of our routine public performances. . . .

This study is . . . concerned with routine bathroom behavior. Over a nine-month period, five student research assistants and I spent over one hundred hours observing behavior in the bathrooms of such public establishments as shopping malls, student centers on college campuses, and restaurants and bars at various locations in the Northeastern United States. These observations were recorded in fieldnotes and provide the empirical basis for the following analysis.

The Performance Regions of Public Bathrooms

Needless to say, one of the behaviors for which bathrooms are explicitly designed is defecation. In our society, as Goffman (1959: 121) observed, "defecation involves an individual in activity which is defined as inconsistent with the cleanliness and purity standards" that govern our public performances.

> Such activity also causes the individual to disarrange his clothing and to "go out of play," that is, to drop from his face the expressive mask that he employs in face-to-face interaction. At the same time it becomes difficult for him to reassemble his personal front should the need to enter into interaction occur.

When engaged in the act of defecation, therefore, individuals seek to insulate themselves from potential audiences in order to avoid discrediting the expressive masks that they publicly employ. . . .

In an apparent attempt to provide such privacy, toilets in many public bathrooms are surrounded by partially walled cubicles with doors that can be secured against potential intrusions. Public bathrooms that do not provide individuals this protection from potential audiences are seldom used for the purpose of defecation. In the course of our research, for example, we never observed an individual using an unenclosed toilet for this purpose. If a bathroom contained both enclosed and unenclosed toilets . . . individuals ignored the unenclosed toilets even when queues had formed outside of the enclosed toilets. In a sense, therefore, the cubicles that typically surround toilets in public bathrooms, commonly called stalls, physically divide such bathrooms into two distinct performance regions.

Indeed, Goffman (1971: 32) has used the term "stall" to refer to any "well-bounded space to which individuals lay temporary claim, possession being on an all-or-nothing basis." . . . [A] toilet stall is clearly a member of this sociological family of ecological arrangements. Sociologically speaking, however, it is not physical boundaries, per se, that define a space as a stall but the behavioral regard given such boundaries. For example, individuals who open or attempt to open the door of an occupied toilet stall typically provide a remedy for this act, in most cases a brief apology such as "Whoops" or "Sorry." By offering such a remedy, the offending individual implicitly defines the attempted intrusion as a [violation] and, thereby, affirms his or her belief in a rule that prohibits such intrusions (Goffman 1971: 113). In this sense, toilet stalls provide occupying individuals not only physical protection against potential audiences but normative protection as well.

In order to receive this protection, however, occupying individuals must clearly inform others of their claim to such a stall. Although individuals sometimes lean down and look under doors of toilet stalls for feet, they typically expect occupying individuals to mark their claim to a toilet stall by securely closing the door. On one occasion, a middle-aged woman began to push open the unlocked door of a toilet stall. Upon discovering that the stall was occupied, she immediately said, "I'm sorry," and closed the door. When a young woman emerged from the stall a couple minutes later, the older woman apologized once again but pointed out that "the door was open." The young woman responded, "it's okay," thereby minimizing the offense and perhaps acknowledging a degree of culpability on her part.

As is the case with many physical barriers to perception (Goffman 1963: 152), the walls and doors of toilet stalls are also treated as if they cut off more communication than they actually do. Under most circumstances, the walls and doors of toilet stalls are treated as if they were barriers to conversation. Although acquainted individuals may sometimes carry on a conversation through the walls of a toilet stall if they believe the bathroom is not otherwise occupied, they seldom do so if they are aware that others are present. Moreover, individuals often attempt to ignore offensive sounds and smells that emanate from occupied toilet stalls, even though the exercise of such "tactful blindness" (Goffman 1955: 219) is sometimes a demanding task. In any case, the walls and doors of toilet stalls provide public actors with both physical and normative shields behind which they can perform potentially discrediting acts.

Toilet stalls in public bathrooms are, therefore, publicly accessible yet private backstage regions. Although same-sexed clients of a public establishment may lay claim to any unoccupied toilet stall in the bathroom designated for use by persons of their sex, once such a claim is laid, once the door to the stall is closed, it is transformed into the occupying individual's private, albeit temporary, retreat from the demands of public life. While occupying the stall, that individual can engage in a variety of potentially discrediting acts with impunity.

When not concealed behind the protective cover of a toilet stall, however, occupants of public bathrooms may be observed by others. . . . Same-sexed clients of a public establishment can enter and exit at will the bathroom designated for their use, and it may be simultaneously occupied by as many individuals as its physical dimensions allow. By implication, occupants of public bathrooms must either perform or be ready to perform for an audience. As a result, the behavior that routinely occurs in the "open region" of a public bathroom, that area that is not enclosed by toilet stalls, resembles, in many important respects, the behavior that routinely occurs in other public settings.

The Ritual of Public Bathrooms

As Goffman (1971) convincingly argued, much of this behavior can best be described as "interpersonal rituals." Emile Durkheim (1965), in his [classic] analysis of religion, defined a ritual as a perfunctory, conventionalized act which expresses respect and regard for some object of "ultimate value." . . . Drawing inspiration from Durkheim, Goffman (1971: 63) pointed out that despite the increasing secularization of our society there remain

> brief rituals one individual performs for and to another, attesting to civility and good will on the performer's part and to the recipient's possession of a small patrimony of sacredness.

Still borrowing from Durkheim . . . Goffman (1971: 62) divided these interpersonal rituals into two classes: positive and negative.

According to Durkheim, negative rituals express respect and regard for objects of ultimate value by protecting them from profanation. According to Goffman (1971: 62), negative interpersonal rituals involve the behavioral honoring of the scared individual's right to private "preserves" and "to be let alone." As previously noted, for example, individuals typically refrain from physically, conversationally, or visually intruding on an occupied toilet stall. In doing so, they implicitly honor the occupying individual's right to be let alone and in this respect perform a negative interpersonal ritual.

Similarly, the queues that typically form in public bathrooms when the demand for sinks, urinals, and toilet stalls exceeds the available supply are also products of individuals' mutual performance of negative interpersonal rituals. Individuals typically honor one another's right to the turn claimed by taking up a position in such a queue, even when "creature releases" (Goffman 1963: 69) threaten to break through their self-control. Young children provide an occasional exception, sometimes ignoring the turn-order of such queues. Yet even then the child's caretaker typically requests, on the child's behalf, the permission of those waiting in the queue. Between performances at a music festival, for example, a preschool-age girl and her mother were observed rapidly walking toward the entrance to a women's bathroom out of which a queue extended for several yards down a nearby sidewalk. As they walked past those waiting in the queue, the mother repeatedly asked, "Do you mind? She really has to go."

However, the interpersonal rituals that routinely occur in the open region of public bathrooms are not limited to negative ones. If individuals possess a small patrimony of sacredness, then, as Durkheim (1974: 37) noted, "the greatest good is in communion" with such sacred objects. When previously acquainted individuals come into contact with one another, therefore, they typically perform conventionalized acts, positive interpersonal rituals, that express respect and regard for their previous communion with one another. In a sense, negative and positive interpersonal rituals are two sides of the same expressive coin. Whereas negative interpersonal rituals symbolically protect individuals from profanation by others, positive interpersonal rituals symbolically cleanse communion between individuals of its potentially defiling implications. Although a positive interpersonal ritual may consist of no more than a brief exchange of greetings, failure to at least acknowledge one's previous communion with another is, in effect, to express disregard for the relationship and, by implication, the other individual's small patrimony of sacredness (Goffman 1971:62–94).

Even when previously acquainted individuals come into contact with one another in a public bathroom, therefore, they typically acknowledge their prior relationship. In fact, the performance of such positive interpersonal rituals sometimes interfered with the conduct of our research. On one occasion, for example, a member of the research team was in the open region of an otherwise unoccupied men's bathroom. While he was writing some notes about an incident that had just occurred, an acquaintance entered.

A: Hey! (walks to the urinal and unzips his pants) Nothing like pissin.
O: Yup.
A: Wh'da hell ya doin? (walks over to a sink and washes hands)
O: Writing.
A: Heh, heh, yea. About people pissin . . . That's for you.
O: Yup.
A: Take care.
O: Mmm. Huh.

As this incident illustrates, individuals must be prepared to perform positive interpersonal rituals when in the open region of public bathrooms, especially those in public establishments with a relatively stable clientele. Whereas some of these may consist of no more than a brief exchange of smiles, others may involve lengthy conversations that reaffirm the participants' shared biography.

In contrast, when unacquainted individuals come into contact with one another in the open regions of public bathrooms, they typically perform a brief, negative interpersonal ritual that Goffman (1963: 84) termed "civil inattention." In its canonical form,

> one gives to another enough visual notice to demonstrate that one appreciates that the other is present . . . while at the next moment withdrawing one's

> attention from him so as to express that he does not constitute a target of special curiosity or design.

Through this brief pattern of visual interaction, individuals both acknowledge one another's presence and, immediately thereafter, one another's right to be let alone.

A variation on the canonical form of civil attention is also commonly performed in the open region of public bathrooms, most often by men using adjacent urinals. Although masculine clothing permits males to urinate without noticeably disturbing their clothed appearance, they must still partially expose their external genitalia in order to do so. Clearly, the standards of modesty that govern public behavior prohibit even such limited exposure of the external genitalia. Although the sides of some urinals and the urinating individual's back provide partial barriers to perception, they do not provide protection against the glances of someone occupying an adjacent urinal. In our society, however, "when bodies are naked, glances are clothed" (Goffman 1971: 46). What men typically give one another when using adjacent urinals is not, therefore, civil inattention but "non-person treatment" (Goffman 1963: 83–84): that is, they treat one another as if they were part of the setting's physical equipment, as "objects not worthy of a glance." When circumstances allow, of course, unacquainted males typically avoid occupying adjacent urinals and, thereby, this ritually delicate situation.

It is not uncommon, however, for previously acquainted males to engage in conversation while using adjacent urinals. For example, the following interaction was observed in the bathroom of a restaurant.

> A middle-aged man is standing at one of two urinals. Another middle-aged man enters the bathroom and, as he approaches the available urinal, greets the first man by name. The first man quickly casts a side-long glance at the second and returns the greeting. He then asks the second man about his "new granddaughter," and they continue to talk about grandchildren until one of them zips up his pants and walks over to a sink. Throughout the conversation, neither man turned his head so as to look at the other.

As this example illustrates, urinal conversations are often characterized by a lack of visual interaction between the participants. Instead of looking at one another while listening . . . participants in such conversations typically fix their gaze on the wall immediately in front of them, an intriguing combination of the constituent elements of positive and negative interpersonal rituals. Although ritually celebrating their prior communion with one another, they also visually honor one another's right to privacy.

Due to the particular profanations and threats of profanations that characterize public bathrooms, moreover, a number of variations on these general patterns also commonly occur. In our society, as Goffman (1971: 41) observed, bodily excreta are considered "agencies of defilement." Although supported by germ theory, this view involves somewhat more than a concern for hygiene. Once such substances as urine, fecal matter, menstrual discharge and flatus leave individuals' bodies, they acquire the power to profane even though they may not have the power to infect. In any case, many of the activities in which individuals engage when in bathrooms are considered both self-profaning and potentially profaning to others. As a result, a variety of ritually delicate situations often arise in public bathrooms.

For example, after using urinals and toilets, individuals' hands are considered contaminated and, consequently, a source of contamination to others. In order to demonstrate both self-respect and respect for those with whom they might come into contact, individuals are expected to and often do wash their hands after using urinals and toilets. Sinks for this purpose are typically located in the open region of public bathrooms, allowing others to witness the performance of this restorative ritual. Sometimes, however, public bathrooms are not adequately equipped for this purpose. Most commonly, towel dispensers are empty or broken.

Although individuals sometimes do not discover this situation until after they have already washed their hands, they often glance at towel dispensers as they walk from urinals and toilet stalls to sinks. If they discover that the towel dispensers are empty or broken, there is typically a moment of indecision. Although they sometimes proceed to wash their hands and then dry them on their clothes, many times they hesitate, facially display disgust, and audibly sigh. By performing these gestures-in-the-round, they express a desire to wash their hands; their hands remain contaminated, but their regard for their own and others' sacredness is established.

Because the profaning power of odor operates over a distance and in all directions, moreover, individuals who defecate in public bathrooms not only temporarily profane themselves but also risk profaning the entire setting. If an individual is clearly responsible for the odor of feces or flatus that fills a bathroom, therefore, he or she must rely on others to identify sympathetically with his or her plight and, consequently, exercise tactful blindness. However, this is seldom left to chance. When other occupants of the bathroom are acquaintances, the offending individual may offer a subtle, self-derogatory display as a defensive, face-saving measure (Goffman 1955). Upon emerging from toilet stalls, for example, such persons sometimes look at acquaintances and facially display disgust. Self-effacing humor is also occasionally used in this way. On one occasion, for example, an acquaintance of a member of the research team emerged from a toilet stall after having filled the bathroom with a strong fecal odor. He walked over to a sink, smiled at the observer, and remarked: "Something died in there." Through such subtle self-derogation, offending individuals metaphorically split themselves into two parts: a sacred self that assigns blame and a blame-worthy animal self. Because the offending individual assigns blame, moreover, there is no need for others to do so (Goffman 1971: 113).

If other occupants of the bathroom are unfamiliar to the offending individual, however, a somewhat different defensive strategy is commonly employed. Upon emerging from a toilet stall, individuals who are clearly responsible for an offensive odor seldom engage in visual interaction with unacquainted others. In so doing, they avoid visually acknowledging not only the presence of others but others' acknowledgment of their own presence as well. In a sense, therefore, the offending individual temporarily suspends his or her claim to the status of sacred object, an object worthy of such visual regard. The assumption seems to be that by suspending one's claim to this status, others need not challenge it and are, consequently, more likely to exercise tactful blindness in regard to the offense.

Thus, despite Miner's humorous misidentification and interpretation of bathroom rituals, there is something to recommend the view that many of the rituals that behaviorally express and sustain the central values of our culture occur in bathrooms. Although those "central values do but itch a little," as Goffman (1971: 185) noted, "everyone scratches." And, it must be added, they often scratch in public bathrooms. However, routine bathroom behavior consists of more than the interpersonal rituals that are found in other public settings or variations on their general theme.

Backstage Behavior in Public Bathrooms

Clearly, public establishments differ in the degree to which their clients observe generally accepted standards of behavioral propriety. Moreover, the behavior that routinely occurs within an establishment's bathrooms typically reflects the degree of behavioral "tightness or looseness" (Goffman 1963: 200) that characterizes that establishment. For example, bathrooms in neighborhood bars are characterized by considerably more behavioral looseness than are bathrooms in expensive restaurants. Regardless of the degree of tightness or looseness that characterizes the frontstage region of a public establishment, however, somewhat greater behavioral looseness will be found in the establishment's bathrooms. After all, even the open region of a public bathroom is backstage relative to the setting beyond its doors. As such, public bathrooms offer individuals at least some relief from the behavioral harness that the frontstage audience's eyes impose upon them. . . .

Managing Personal Fronts

When in a public setting, as Goffman (1963: 24) pointed out, individuals are expected to have their "faculties in readiness for any face-to-face interaction that might come" their way. One of the most evident means by which individuals express such readiness is "through the disciplined management of personal appearance or 'personal front,' that is, the complex of clothing, make-up, hairdo, and other surface decorations" that they carry about on their person (Goffman 1963: 25). Of course, keeping one's personal front in a state of good repair requires care and effort. . . . However, individuals who are inspecting or repairing their personal fronts in public encounter difficulties in maintaining the degree of interactional readiness often expected of them; their attention tends to be diverted from the social situations that surround them (Goffman 1963: 66). For the most part, therefore, close [inspection] and major adjustments of personal fronts are confined to backstage regions such as public bathrooms.

Most public bathrooms are equipped for this purpose. Many offer coin-operated dispensers of a variety of "personal care products" . . . and almost all have at least one mirror. The most obvious reason for the presence of mirrors in public bathrooms is that the act of defecation and, for females, urination, requires individuals to literally "drop" their personal fronts. In order to ensure that they have adequately reconstructed their personal front after engaging in such an act, individuals must and typically do perform what Lofland (1972) has termed a "readiness check." For example, the following was observed in the men's bathroom of a neighborhood bar:

> A young man emerges from a toilet stall and, as he passes the mirror, hesitates. He glances side-long at his reflection, gives a nod of approval and then walks out the door.

When such a readiness check reveals flaws in the individual's personal front, he or she typically makes the appropriate repairs: Shirts are often retucked into pants and skirts, skirts are rotated around the waist, and pants are tugged up and down.

Because bodily movement and exposure to the elements can also disturb a disciplined personal front, the post-defecation or urination readiness check sometimes reveals flaws in individuals' personal fronts that are the result of normal wear and tear. Upon emerging from toilet stalls and leaving urinals, therefore, individuals sometimes repair aspects of their personal fronts that are not normally disturbed in the course of defecating or urinating. For example, the following was observed in the women's bathroom of a student center on a college campus.

> A young woman emerges from a toilet stall, approaches a mirror, and inspects her reflection. She then removes a barrette from her hair, places the barrette in her mouth, takes a comb out of her coat pocket, and combs her hair while smoothing it down with her other hand. With the barrette still in her mouth, she stops combing her hair, gazes intently at the mirror and emits an audible "ick." She then places the barrette back in her hair, pinches her cheeks, takes a last look at her reflection and exits.

Interestingly, as both this example and the immediately preceding one illustrate, individuals sometimes offer visible or audible evaluations of their reflections when inspecting and repairing their personal front, a finding that should delight proponents of Meadian sociological psychology. Public bathrooms may protect individuals from the critical reviews of external audiences, but they do not protect them from those of their internal audience.

In any case, public bathrooms are as much "self-service" repair shops for personal fronts as they are socially approved shelters for physiological acts that are inconsistent with the cleanliness and purity standards that govern our public performances.

In fact, individuals often enter public bathrooms with no apparent purpose other than the management of their personal front. For example, it is not uncommon for males to enter public bathrooms, walk directly to the nearest available mirror, comb their hair, rearrange their clothing, and then immediately exit. In our society, of course, females are often expected to present publicly a more extensively managed personal front than are males. Consequently, females often undertake extensive repairs in public bathrooms. For example, the following was observed in the women's bathroom of a student center on a college campus:

> Two young women enter, one goes to a toilet stall and the other immediately approaches a mirror. The second woman takes a brush out of her bookbag, throws her hair forward, brushes it, throws her hair back, and brushes it into place. She returns the brush to her bookbag, smoothes down her eyebrows, and wipes underneath her eyes with her fingers. She then removes a tube of lipstick from her bookbag, applies it to her lips, and uses her finger to remove the lipstick that extends beyond the natural outline of her lips. As her friend emerges from the toilet stall, she puts the lipstick tube back into her bookbag, straightens her collar so that it stands up under her sweater and then exits with her friend.

Even though individuals routinely inspect and repair their personal fronts in the open regions of public bathrooms, they often do so furtively. When others enter the bathroom, individuals sometimes suspend inspecting or repairing their personal fronts until the new arrivals enter toilet stalls or approach urinals. In other cases, they hurriedly complete these activities before they can be witnessed. . . . Despite the furtiveness that sometimes characterizes individuals' inspection and repair of their personal fronts, however, the open region of a public bathroom is often the only available setting in which they can engage in these activities without clearly undermining their frontstage performances. As Lofland (1972: 101) observed in a somewhat different context, "it is apparently preferable to be witnessed by a few . . . in a brief episode of backstage behavior than to be caught . . . with one's presentation down" on the frontstage.

Going Out of Play

While a disciplined personal front may serve to express interactional readiness, public actors must also "exert a kind of discipline or tension" in regard to their bodies in order to actually maintain the degree of interactional readiness that is expected of them (Goffman 1963: 24). After all, a variety of bodily processes can drain individuals' attention away from the social world around them, causing them to turn inward and, interactionally speaking, to go out of play. Of course, the ostensive purpose of public bathrooms and their toilet stalls is to provide public actors with socially approved shelters in which to indulge such bodily processes. . . .

In addition to creature releases that threaten to slip through an individual's self-control, emotional reactions may also cause individuals to go out of play. In such cases, individuals may conclude that precipitant leave taking is preferable to going out of play in full view of their frontstage audience. Under these circumstances, therefore, they may quickly retreat to the protective cover of a toilet stall. Although it is difficult for an observer to ascertain if this has taken place, it was the research team's impression that incidents, such as those described by Margaret Atwood (1969: 71) in her novel, *The Edible Woman*, are not uncommon. The narrator, Marian, was sitting with some friends in a bar when she noticed "a large drop of something wet" on the table near her hand.

> I poked it with my finger and smudged it around a little before I realized with horror that it was a tear. I must be crying then. . . . I was going to break down and make a scene, and I couldn't. I slid out of my chair, trying to be as inconspicuous as possible, walked across the room avoiding the other tables with great care, and went to the Ladies Powder Room. Checking first to make sure no one else was in there—I couldn't have witnesses—I locked myself into one of the plushy-pink cubicles and wept for several minutes.

Depending on how precipitant such leave-taking is, of course, same-sexed members of the individual's frontstage audience may feel justified in conversationally intruding on this private preserve in order to inquire about his or her well-being. It is probably easier, however, to deflect such questions from behind the protective cover of a toilet stall than it would be if the frontstage audience witnessed such a display of emotion.

Parallel to individuals who retire to toilet stalls when they are overcome with emotion, entire "performance teams" (Goffman 1959: 77–105) sometimes retreat into public bathrooms in order to conceal the paralyzing embarrassment that results when a collective performance [collapses]. . . . For example, the following conversation between three young women was recorded in the bathroom of a student center on a college campus. Although the incident that led to this conversation was not observed, it obviously resulted in such paralyzing embarrassment.

A: That was sooo embarrassing! I can't believe that just happened. (general laughter)
B: He must think we are the biggest bunch of losers.
A: I can't believe I just screamed loud enough for everyone to hear.
C: It really wasn't all that loud. I'm sure he didn't hear you.
A: How can you say that? He turned around just as I said it. Why didn't you guys tell me he was standing right there?
B: —, we didn't see him right away, and I did try to tell you but you were so busy talking that I . . .
A: I can't believe that just happened. I feel like such an asshole.
B: Don't worry 'bout it. At least he knows who you are now. Are you ready?
A: I'm so embarrassed. What if he's still out there?
B: You're gonna have to see him at some point.

In addition to concealing a temporary loss of control, these defensive strategies also buy individuals and performance teams time, as this example illustrates, in which to gather themselves together before once again facing the frontstage audience.

However, occupants of public bathrooms and their toilet stalls who use them for purposes other than those for which they were explicitly designed must exercise some caution. Unusual or unusually loud noises and unusually long occupancy, if someone is aware of the duration of the occupancy, may lead others to intrude upon these private preserves. By implication, individuals who use public bathrooms and their toilet stalls in order to conceal autoerotic activities, the usage of illicit drugs, emotional reactions, or other potentially discrediting acts must still exercise a degree of self-control.

Staging Talk

As Goffman (1959: 175) observed, performance teams routinely use backstage regions to gather themselves together [and] discuss . . . problems involved in the staging of their collective performance:

> Here the team can run through its performance, checking for offending expressions when no audience is present to be affronted by them; here poor members of the team . . . can be schooled or dropped from the performance.

In the conversation reproduced above, for example, B and C not only attempt to belittle the discrediting implications of A's earlier actions, but B also schools A in the art of staging collective performances. If, according to B, A had paid more attention to the other team members' directional cues, she could have avoided this embarrassing incident.

In addition to retreating into public bathrooms after the failure of a collective performance, performance teams also retire to public bathrooms in order to take preventive measures against such an occurrence. Here the team may agree upon collusive signals, rehearse their planned performance, and exchange strategic information. In bathrooms in bars, for example, performance teams were sometimes overheard discussing the planned targets of members' erotic overtures, the overtures they had received, the source of such overtures, and their likely responses. By providing other members of a performance team with such strategic information, of course, an individual may prevent them from interfering with his or her personal project and may even enlist their aid in accomplishing it.

Sometimes, moreover, the backstage discussions that occur in public bathrooms are at least partially concerned with a team member's morale or that of the entire team. In the previously discussed conversation between the three young women, for example, B and C attempt to boost A's morale by both belittling the discrediting implications of her earlier actions and encouraging her to "go on with the show." As Goffman (1959: 175) pointed out, backstage derogation of the audience is another strategy that performance teams commonly employ in order to maintain their morale. For example, a young woman was overheard making the following remark to two other young women in the bathroom of a popular nightclub.

> You guys think I'm obnoxious! WELL just take a look at _______, my God!

In any case, both performance teams and individual performers . . . routinely use public bathrooms as staging areas for their public performances. . . .

Conclusion

The behavior that routinely occurs within [public bathrooms] reveals, by way of contrast, some of the requirements that we must meet in order to maintain an unblemished public face. As the preceding analysis indicates, typical bathroom behaviors include the open staging of public performances, the concealment of emotional reactions, the indulgence of creature releases, and the inspection and repair of personal fronts. If, moreover, public bathrooms are backstage regions relative to the public settings beyond their doors, then the behaviors that tend to be confined to public bathrooms are inconsistent with the behavioral standards that govern our public performances. By implication, therefore, these standards would seem to require the presentation of a disciplined personal front, the avoidance of visible concern with its maintenance, the suppression of animal natures, some minimal degree of interactional readiness, and performances that appear "only natural." Without such readily accessible backstage regions as public bathrooms, it becomes increasingly difficult to fulfill these requirements; much of what we do in public bathrooms, then, is what we must not do elsewhere but what we must do somewhere.

In addition to noting such backstage behavior, the preceding analysis indicates that a number of interpersonal rituals found in other public settings are also routinely performed in public bathrooms. Although, at first glance, this finding may seem to contradict the characterization of public bathrooms as backstage regions, even "loosely defined" social situations are, in Goffman's (1963: 241) words, "tight little rooms." In fact, it may be within such loosely defined situations that the central values of our culture itch the most and are, by implication, most in need of scratching. Within public bathrooms, the animal natures behind our expressive masks and the blemishes underneath our disciplined personal fronts are often exposed. When we find ourselves in such ritually delicate situations, we need assurances that we retain our small patrimony of sacredness despite evidence to the contrary. In a sense, interpersonal rituals are routinely performed in public bathrooms because of, rather than in spite of, their backstage character.

In short, systematic study of routine bathroom behavior reveals just how loyal members of this society are to the central values and behavioral standards that hold our collective lives together. Whatever else they may do, users of public bathrooms continue to bear the "cross of personal character" (Goffman 1971: 185), and, as long as they continue to carry this burden, remain self-regulating participants in the "interaction order" (Goffman 1983).

References

Atwood, M. (1969) *The Edible Woman.* Boston: Little, Brown.

Durkheim, E. (1974) *Sociology and Philosophy.* (D. F. Pocock, trans.). New York: Free Press (originally published in 1924).

———. (1965) *The Elementary Forms of the Religious Life.* (J. W. Swain, trans.). New York: Free Press (originally published in 1915).

Goffman, E. (1983) "The interaction order." *Amer. Soc. Rev.* 48 (February): 1–17.

———. (1971) *Relations in Public Microstudies in Public Order.* New York: Basic Books.

———. (1963) *Behavior in Public Places: Notes on the Social Organization of Gatherings.* New York: Free Press.

———. (1959) *The Presentation of Self in Everyday Life.* Garden City, NY: Doubleday.

———. (1955) "On face-work: An analysis of ritual elements of social interaction." *Psychiatry* 18 (August): 213–231.

Lofland, L. (1972) "Self-management in public settings: Part I." *Urban Life* 1 (April): 93–108.

Miner, H. (1955) "Body Ritual Among the Nacirema." *Amer. Anthropologist* 58 (June): 503–507.

Reflective Questions

1. Why are there walls and doors in public bathrooms? What do they protect us from? Why don't we comment on offensive sounds or smells or look at others while they are going to the bathroom? How do stalls mark social spaces and boundaries in public bathrooms? How do our expectations and behaviors change when we move from one space to another?
2. What is a ritual? To what do rituals attest? What common rituals do we engage in when we are in a public restroom? What values are these rituals protecting?
3. Why do we adjust our clothing and hair in public restrooms? Why do we maintain a "disciplined personal front"? Outside of urination, defecation, and adjusting our appearance, what other activities do we do in restrooms? Why there?
4. We enact rituals in other public spaces: consider entering and exiting a building, attending a public talk, or navigating a public bus. What rituals do we practice in each setting, and what values are we protecting? How do our actions rely on the cooperation of others? What role does personal space play in these rituals? Research by Edward Hall found that Westerners have four circles of personal space: an intimacy bubble in which only the closest of contacts interact, a personal bubble reserved for friends and close associates, social distance that characterizes formal encounters, and a public space for performers and audience. How do rituals breach these spaces or reinforce them? Hall also found that Westerners have a smaller social bubble than others. What happens when Westerners interact with others who are accustomed to interacting more closely? What feelings are conjured? Why?

27

Wheelchair Users' Interpersonal Management of Emotions

SPENCER E. CAHILL AND ROBIN EGGLESTON

Everyday interaction is characterized by not only an expressive but also an emotional order. This is nowhere more apparent than in public places where strangers and casual acquaintances routinely meet and sometimes interact. There, calm composure usually prevails and open expressions of intense emotions are rare. Yet, underneath this calm veneer, emotions such as fear, embarrassment, anger, and resentment often boil. This selection illustrates the considerable emotion work required to keep those emotions from boiling over into public interactions with the example of wheelchair users' public experience.

Wheelchair users' public experience is especially emotional. They often find themselves in embarrassing situations. They are treated both rudely and with kindness. They routinely receive needed and unneeded, wanted and unwanted, helpful and harmful assistance from others. All of these circumstances stir their emotions. Yet, as this selection illustrates, wheelchair users usually avoid publicly expressing their embarrassment, anger, and resentment so as to avoid evoking emotions in others. This is only one of the ways that wheelchair users manage both their own and others' emotions in public.

Although unusually demanding, wheelchair users' emotion work in public places illustrates the effort required to sustain the emotional tranquility of everyday public life. Like wheelchair users, we often make humorous remarks to relieve the tension of problematic situations. We suppress our anger so as not to provoke others'. We act graciously toward those who treat us both ungraciously and overgraciously so as not to anger or embarrass them. We manage our own emotions so as to manage others' and thereby sustain the emotional orderliness of everyday social interaction.

Since the 1970s, students of social life have learned many lessons about the social sources and consequences of emotions. Many of us now appreciate that social life is as much an affair of the heart as of the head, but perhaps we do not appreciate this fact deeply enough. We still tend to concentrate on individuals' socially guided management of their own emotions to the neglect of their management of one another's. . . .

Yet, as Goffman (1963a, 1971) demonstrates convincingly, individuals in public places attempt to assure one another of their civility and goodwill so as not to evoke embarrassment, fear, or anger in others or in themselves. Although they often appear emotionally reserved and indifferent, that appearance is a consequence of emotion work rather than its absence. . . . The study of public life has much to teach us about the emotional dynamics of social interaction and life, if only we are willing to learn from those who notice what we usually miss. [And, when it comes to the interpersonal management of

Reprinted from: Spencer E. Cahill and Robin Eggleston, Managing Emotions in Public: The Case of Wheelchair Users. *Social Psychology Quarterly* 57(4): 300–312.

emotions], those whose principal mode of mobility is a wheelchair cannot help noticing what the rest of us can overlook more easily. . . .

Our specific focus is the emotional dilemmas faced by wheelchair users when in public places. We begin by briefly describing the inspiration and empirical basis of our analysis. Then we examine three general types of emotional challenges that wheelchair users confront in public places. Our purpose is not only to provide some insight into wheelchair users' public lives but also to draw from their example more general lessons about the emotional dynamics of contemporary public life and the interpersonal dynamics of emotion management. . . .

The Instruction of Wheelchair Use and Users

Our collective interest in wheelchair users' public experiences grew out of conversations between the first author and second author, who has used an electrically powered wheel chair as her principal mode of public mobility [for some time]. At the urging of the first author, she started to make fieldnotes of her daily participant observation of the social life of a wheelchair user. . . . [T]he first author supplemented these with fieldnotes that he made when using a wheelchair in public places for the specific purpose of participant observation. . . . We also collected and read wheelchair users' autobiographical accounts. . . . In addition, we collectively conducted and recorded interviews with seven women and five men who regularly use a wheelchair in public places. . . .

Although initially we did not intend to focus on the emotional challenges of public wheelchair use, emotional dilemmas loomed large in our own and our informants' accounts and in the published accounts of other wheelchair users' public experiences. Gradually we became convinced that those dilemmas contained a revealing story about the place of wheelchair users in public life, about contemporary public life more generally, and about interpersonal processes of emotion management. The following analysis tells that story.

The Emotional Demands of Public Wheelchair Use

For many wheelchair users, the very decision to venture into public places is emotionally turbulent. The desire for autonomy and for the many pleasures that only public places offer collides with fears—among others, fear of moving past and among much larger vehicles. There is the fear of upsetting others that has kept one of our informants, who recently started using a wheelchair, from using it in restaurants.

> I think it's hard for people to eat food close to people who are ill. There's some thing about the process of eating that makes people even more uptight about disease. . . . My rolling in probably wouldn't affect people in that way, but in the back of my mind I'm afraid it would. I'll have to get over that.

Wheelchair users also fear, with justification, being an embarrassing and embarrassed public spectacle.

Humoring Embarrassment

Like those whom one of our informants calls "stand-up people," wheelchair users face a variety of embarrassing possibilities whenever they venture into public places. For any number of reasons, they may lose control over self or situation (Gross and Stone 1964), falling short of what is generally expected of public actors. Wheelchair users, however, face a number of uniquely embarrassing contingencies because the physical environment, both natural and constructed, is unfriendly to their mode of mobility. Rain and snow can leave them immobile and embarrassingly in need of rescue. Doorway thresholds, uneven sidewalks, and unanticipated depressions at the bottom of curb cuts may cause a wheelchair to tip over, leaving its occupant embarrassingly sprawled on the ground. Crowded and narrow passageways may make it nearly impossible for wheelchair users to avoid knocking merchandise off shelves, rolling into standing strangers, or struggling to maneuver around tight corners in front of anxiously paralyzed bystanders. Although wheelchair users do not welcome such discomfort, many become quite adept at easing the "dis-ease" (Gross and Stone 1964:2) of potentially embarrassing situations because they face them so often.

Humor is the most common and perhaps most effective strategy that wheelchair users employ for this purpose. . . . [L]aughing at or joking about embarrassing events reduces their seriousness and thereby lessens potentially embarrassing concern about them. Laughter and humor are also means of allaying anxiety (Coser 1959:174), which can serve a dual definitional purpose. A wheelchair user's potentially embarrassing situation often provokes anxiety in witnesses to her or his plight. Defining the situation as laughable can ease everyone's particular "dis-ease," as the second author learned when shopping at a clothing store.

> I wheeled up to the entrance to a dressing room while my friend held a number of garments. I forgot to set the brakes on my chair, so when I started to raise myself up with my crutches the chair went rolling backwards while I went falling forward onto the floor. My friend stood there with this look of alarm until I started laughing. The two of us started laughing, and then a saleswoman came rushing over: "My goodness, are you all right?" I answered "Yes, I'm fine" while still laughing. Her facial expression went from alarm to unconcern in a flash, once she realized we were laughing.

Through incidents like this, wheelchair users acquire the experiential wisdom that a sense of humor is "a tremendous asset."

> [I]f you can laugh at yourself, no matter what . . . [a]nd if it's funny to me first, then my feelings aren't hurt. And you don't feel self-conscious because you can laugh with me.

As this 60-year-old woman had learned from countless falls in public places, laughter can both prevent and relieve hurt feelings, anxious self-consciousness, and the contagious "dis-ease" of embarrassment.

On the other hand, humor sometimes has the opposite effect. A woman who had been using a wheelchair in public for only six months told us of her recent experience in a shopping mall bathroom.

> There was a whole line of people waiting to get into these two stalls. It was packed. And I'm trying to back up and not doing a very good job of it and having to start over again, bumping into the washbasin. I finally get myself around, with all these people obviously watching me. There was dead silence. So I finally got myself out, and I looked up at all these people and I went "Now, I would like a big round of applause, please." Nobody did anything. It was like you can't make a joke about this stuff. I thought "Give me a break."

Like hospital patients who joke with the medical staff about death (Emerson 1969), this woman apparently exceeded the topical limits of her audience's sense of humor. At least they blatantly refused her invitation to laugh at her plight and reduce its definitional seriousness (Coser 1959:172). This incident illustrates one of the emotional dilemmas that wheelchair users face when in public places: they must attempt to remain poised and good-humored in frustrating and potentially embarrassing circumstances without thereby increasing others' already considerable discomfort at those circumstances. In public places they often have the double duty of managing their own and others' emotions (Hochschild 1979). . . .

This is clearly the case when wheelchair users are interrogated by curious children, as often happens, about their unusual mode of mobility and physical condition. All but one of our informants report that they gladly answer such young interrogators' questions. One informant, whose left leg had been amputated, had an uncommon sense of humor, but his openness with young children was not unusual.

> Kids go "Where's your leg?" "It's gone. If you find it, I'll give you fifty cents. I've been looking for that damn thing all week." "Can I see it?" "Sure." I take my pants up, show the stump. "Wow, it's gone. You're not sitting on it." "Yep, it's gone." They're frank. They're very candid.

Inquisitive children's accompanying adult caretakers, however, seldom appreciate their young charges' candor. As the man quoted above reported, "The parents turn blue. They turn shades of pink and red. I have to protect the kids from the parents. They want to jerk them away." Other informants reported similar experiences.

> And children, you find that they come up and ask "How come you're in a chair? You mean you can't walk? Really?" But if there's an adult with them, they tend to pull the child back. "Oh now, don't disturb her." And I say "They're not disturbing me."

If our informants are at all representative, most wheelchair users not only graciously endure and satisfy young children's uncivil curiosity when in public places. They also attempt to manage the embarrassment (and sometimes the wrath) of those curious children's adult caretakers in the interest of child protection. Whatever emotion work (Hochschild 1979:561–563) is done is usually done by them.

Fred Davis (1961:127) once observed that "in our society the visibly handicapped are customarily accorded, save by children, the surface acceptance of democratic manners guaranteed to nearly all." He may have been right about children, but many wheelchair users probably would find his attribution of democratic manners to children's elders a bit too generous. In both our own and our informants' experience, most adults indeed accord wheelchair users the surface acceptance of civil inattention in public places (Goffman 1963a:84). Yet there are more than a few exceptions. These include walkers, as they are sometimes called by wheelchair users, who proclaim their admiration of a wheelchair user at the expense of his or her right to be let alone in public (Goffman 1971:62). The older the walker and the younger the wheelchair user, the more common this treatment seems. The second author, for example, who is in her early twenties, is routinely approached by considerably older strangers, who cheerfully inform her that they think she "is wonderful." Although clearly complimentary, such unexpected and seemingly groundless public praise is an embarrassment. Simultaneously flattered, embarrassed, and resentful of the intrusion, the wheelchair user faces the dilemma of formulating an appropriate response, and usually settles for a halfhearted "thank you."

Wheelchair users commonly resolve the emotional dilemmas of their public lives in this way. They expressively mask their own emotions so as to manage others'. They cover their embarrassment with good humor, relieving witnesses' emotional discomfort. They hide resentment behind calm graciousness, saving forward strangers the embarrassment that would be caused by expressing such resentment. Even when wheelchair users feel fully justified in their emotional reactions, their public expression often contrasts sharply with their private feelings. The example of righteous anger suggests some reasons why.

Embarrassing Anger

Like children (Cahill 1990), wheelchair users are alternately treated like "open persons" (Goffman 1963a:126) and subjected to "nonperson" treatment in public places (Goffman 1963a:84). Although both forms of treatment betray others' surface acceptance of wheelchair users, the latter is usually the more maddening. Occupants of various service roles are the culprits mentioned most often. Apparently uncomfortable salesclerks may busy themselves folding merchandise as if a potential customer in a wheelchair were invisible. Restaurant personnel may huddle behind a wheelchair user, close enough to let her overhear their discussion of "where to put her." All kinds of service workers may treat a wheelchair user's walking companions as his or her spokespersons and caretakers. Sometimes they return change to such companions after receiving payment from the wheelchair user, or ask her companions "And what would she like?"

Such nonperson treatment often provokes wheelchair users' anger but seldom the expression of that anger. As one of our informants told us, "I just want to reach out and grab a hold of them and shake them for all they're worth. But I just sit back, and I grit my teeth." Our informants report that they usually try to respond to nonperson treatment not with anger but with calm reminders of their presence and ability to speak for themselves. They also report that this strategy is usually effective in eliciting an embarrassed apology and more civil treatment.

Yet no matter how common and how effective such gentle reminders are, wheelchair users sometimes reveal their anger at nonperson treatment through hostile comments and tone. When a waiter asked the wife of one of our informants whether "he will be getting out of the chair," our informant sarcastically replied, "Yes, he will." Such hostile expressions can be even more effective than calm reminders in eliciting embarrassed apologies, but at the expense of leaving the wheelchair user feeling embarrassed and guilty about his or her lack of emotional poise. In this respect and most others, wheelchair users are as much children of their emotional culture . . . as are most contemporary Americans. To borrow a distinction from Hochschild (1990:122–124), our "feeling rules" sometimes prescribe anger but our "expression rules" proscribe its expression. These contradictions lead to conflicting feelings of justifiable anger and guilt at expressing the anger. Wheelchair users are not alone in experiencing such contradictory feelings in public or elsewhere.

Private guilt and embarrassment are not the only potentially unwelcome consequences of wheelchair users' public expressions of anger. Rather than eliciting embarrassed apologies, their anger may be returned, as one of our informants learned when she protested a robustly walking man's choice of parking places.

> I've had a guy park in a handicapped parking spot and I've gone up and said: "Look, do you realize you're parked in a handicapped parking spot?" And he said "I know it, and I'm sick of you people getting all the good spots. It's reverse discrimination. I'm sick of being discriminated against." "Well," I said, "I'm going to call the police and you can tell your story to them." And he says, "Go ahead. I've had it. It's about time."

Although this man moved his car when our informant wheeled to the nearest public telephone, it was a harder-won moral victory than she had anticipated. . . . [Thus,] wheelchair users who publicly express moral outrage must be prepared to receive what they give. Their angry protest may be met with angry resistance, creating an embarrassing and sometimes alarming public scene that they must then manage or escape.

The angry protests of self-appointed defenders of wheelchair users' public privileges are no less instructive in this regard. One of our informants, who drove a car with hand controls that was otherwise unremarkable, told us of the following public encounter:

> I pull the car into a handicapped place, and this car pulls up alongside me with two young women in it. One of them leans over and says, "You know you're in a handicapped place." And I said, "Yes, I'm disabled." And then she says, "You don't look disabled." And I don't usually do this kind of thing, but I just said, "What does disabled look like?" And they just drove off. Maybe I shouldn't have done that, but it was one of those days.

The informant's hostile retort and the tinge of guilt he apparently felt as a result illustrate both the possible subjective costs and the interpersonal risks of publicly expressing anger. This is one horn of an emotional dilemma that wheelchair users often face in public. Should they suppress their righteous anger and forgo the satisfaction that its expression often brings, or should they assume the costs and risks of expression? As suggested previously, our informants, like the second author, commonly resolve this dilemma in favor of suppression—if not of their anger, then at least of expression.

That decision, however, does not always save wheelchair users from the embarrassing public scenes that angry protests can create. Their walking companions see to that, as a 34-year-old paraplegic woman explains.

> After thirteen and a half years you've heard just about everything, so it's like "Oh, you know." But it's my friends who [say] "Can you imagine the

> nerve? Let's get out of here." They've actually made me leave. My ex-boyfriend, we got up from the table and walked out. . . . [I]t started when they didn't know where to put me, and then the waitress ignored me. And he had just had it. He said "We're out of here." I said "Don't make an issue out of it." "The issue's made." Got my purse, got my coat, and we started to leave. We had the manager on our coattails. I think that's more embarrassing.

As Goffman (1963b:31) observes, "[T]he person with a courtesy stigma can in fact make both the stigmatized and normal uncomfortable" by confronting everyone "with too much morality." Walkers who befriend and accompany wheelchair users in public are apparently no exception. Their easy susceptibility to moral outrage may lead to public scenes that their wheelchair-using companions would just as soon avoid. As if their occasional nonperson treatment were not painful enough, wheelchair users also must sometimes bear the embarrassment of their defenders' self-righteous zeal.

Wheelchair users' experiences with public anger are not unique. Regardless of our mode of mobility, public expressions of anger are risky: they can provoke angry retaliation and create embarrassing scenes. For most of us, much of the time, those potential costs seem to outweigh whatever personal satisfaction we might gain by expressing our righteous rage. Consequently we "surface act" (Hochschild 1979:558) so as to prevent our anger from reaching the surface. Thus, public appearances of emotional indifference are sometimes just that—appearances. Wheelchair users' experiences in public places remind us of how much emotion work may be invested in maintaining those appearances.

Ingratiating Sympathy

Prevailing expression rules, possible retaliation, and potential embarrassment are not the only deterrents to wheelchair users' public expression of righteous anger. They also know that they cannot afford to alienate the walkers who populate the public places they frequent. Experience has taught them that their uncooperative bodies and, more commonly, the unfriendliness of the physical environment to their mode of mobility sometimes leave them hopelessly dependent on others' sympathetic assistance. They may need waiters to move chairs away from a table so that they can wheel their own under it, or to store their wheelchair after transferring to a chair with legs. Often they must rely on strangers to fetch items from shelves that are either too high or too low for them to reach. They may wheel down a curb cut on one side of a street only to find a curb on the other side, over which anonymous passersby must help them if they are to continue along their intended path. Like one of our informants, they may find themselves in a restaurant or bar without "handicap accessible" toilet facilities and themselves without same-sexed companionship, and thus may require the assistance of total strangers to use those much-needed facilities. Or, like another of our informants, they may need to flag down a passing motorist on a city street to help them replace a foot on the footrest of their wheelchair after it has been dislodged by an involuntary spasm. These are only a few of the circumstances in which wheelchair users find themselves requiring the sympathetic assistance of walkers with whom they are unacquainted. . . .

Whatever its form, that assistance qualifies as sympathetic. According to Clark (1987:296), sympathy consists of "empathy plus sentiment, empathy plus display or all three." The assistance that walkers sometimes provide wheelchair users in public places has at least two of those components. It involves empathetic role-taking and is a culturally recognized expression of sympathy, even if not motivated by sincere "fellow-feeling" or sentiment. Regardless of the motivation, its provision stirs emotions.

Although many wheelchair users do not hesitate to ask for assistance when they need it, they are as aware of, and as strongly committed to, prevailing sympathy etiquette (Clark 1987) as other rules of feeling and expression. Therefore they often find themselves torn between concern about making excessive claims on others' sympathy and their immediate need for sympathetic assistance. Guilt is the typical result.

> If I'm in the grocery store, and I need something, and I ask somebody to get it [I say] "Oh, I'm sorry." And I find myself making excuses, saying things like "Oh, it's just not been my day" or "it seems everything I want today is up too high." I feel like I'm putting people out of their way. I feel like I'm imposing on someone to ask for help.

This informant told us that she did not have to apologize or explain herself because "people would bend over backwards to help you," but she seemed implicitly to know better. Even while she laid claim to others' sympathy, her apologies and accounts demonstrated her awareness of sympathy etiquette and its proscription against excessive claims (Clark 1987:305–307). Her guilty penance of remedial work (Goffman 1971:108–118) may have assured her benefactors that she would claim no more sympathy, time, and attention than necessary.

This wheelchair user's sensitivity to the sacrifices of sympathetically helpful strangers is not unusual. Wheelchair users often are forced to request sympathetic assistance from strangers in order to continue on their daily rounds, but still feel a pang of guilt when doing so. Those who have some choice may feel somewhat more than a guilty pang.... For example, one of our informants, who could walk short distances with the aid of a cane, often [felt like a fraud who was exploiting strangers' kindness].

> I've had people do double and triple takes when I get up out of my wheelchair.... Sometimes when I'm using my chair in the grocery store and I can't reach something, I get up; sometimes I ask people to get it for me. I mean, that's where I feel like a fraud, because I can get up. But if I get up, then I feel like a fraud because people can tell that I'm using a wheelchair but I don't need to—I mean I don't *have* to.

Like this woman, many wheelchair users are aware that they must appear strong, independent, and brave so as to avoid "being perceived as self-pitying" and overdemanding of others' sympathy (Clark 1987:307). To avoid such a perception and the resulting guilt, they may take needless risks and expend needless energy rather than requesting even minor aid from strangers. The micropolitical benefits of such dogged self-reliance may also help to compensate for inefficient expenditures of time, energy and personal safety.

Even if wheelchair users defiantly refuse to pay the subjective price of guilt when requesting and accepting sympathetic assistance, they pay an interpersonal price. Whatever the benefits, as Clark (1987:299–300) observes, receiving sympathy obligates the recipient to repay the granter with "emotional commodities such as gratitude, deference and future sympathy." And deferential gratitude is the only emotional currency with which wheelchair users can repay strangers whom they are unlikely to encounter in the future. Using such currency to compensate helpful and sympathetic strangers for their sacrifices is not without micropolitical implications: Wheelchair users thereby elevate their benefactors' interactional standing or "place" at the expense of their own (Clark 1990).

Wheelchair users often pay that price cheerfully when they require and request sympathetic assistance, but those are not the only occasions on which they are expected to pay it. Walkers who are unknown to wheelchair users provide sympathetic assistance not only when it is requested, but also when it is not. The first author learned this in the opening moments of his first public appearance in a wheelchair.

> I got the chair unfolded and assembled and started wheeling down the hallway. As I was approaching the door, a woman walked alongside my chair and asked: "Are you going that way?" Assuming that she meant toward the door, I answered "Yes." She gracefully moved in front of me and opened the first of the double doors. I thanked her. She then just as gracefully opened the outer door once I was through the first, and again I thanked her.

From all reports, this is not an unusual experience for wheelchair users. Walkers often quicken or slow their pace so as to be in a position to open and hold doors for wheelchair users whom they do not know. They offer to push occupied wheelchairs up steep inclines, and sometimes begin to do so without warning. Also, they volunteer to fold and load wheelchairs into users' cars and vans. These are only a few examples of the unsolicited assistance that wheelchair users report receiving from strangers. . . .

[Yet], unsolicited acts of sympathetic assistance place wheelchair users under no less of an obligation than acts that are requested. It is still generally expected that the recipient will repay the granter with "deferential gratitude," and the micropolitical cost of that repayment may be even greater than for requested acts of sympathetic assistance. Simmel offers a theoretical explanation:

> Once we have received something good from another person . . . we no longer can make up for it completely. The reason is that his gift, because it was first, has a voluntary character which no return gift can have (1950:392).

This voluntary character is absent from the provision of sympathetic assistance in response to a request from an apparently "sympathy worthy" (Clark 1987:297–298) wheelchair user. If the provision of the requested assistance is of little moment to the person asked, as is commonly the case, then provision is no less obligatory than repayment. To refuse such a request is to risk being judged hatefully heartless. In contrast, an unsolicited act of sympathetic assistance contains what Simmel (1950:393) calls "the decisive element of . . . freedom," which is absent from the deferential gratitude offered in return. Moreover, as Clark (1990:315) observes, the donor of an emotional gift such as sympathetic assistance "gets to impose his or her definition of what the other wants or needs." To accept such an emotional gift is not only to "contract an irredeemable obligation" (Simmel 1950:393) but also to concede definitional authority over one's own wants and needs to another, thereby doubly diminishing the recipient's interactional standing. Thus the micropolitical implications of the kindness often displayed toward wheelchair users in public places can be quite unkind.

This is not to say that wheelchair users never appreciate unsolicited offers and acts of sympathetic assistance. One of our informants reports that he adjusts the speed of his wheelchair in relation to the reflections of approaching walkers in glass doors so as to ensure that they will reach the door slightly before him and will open and hold it for him voluntarily. At times he is more than willing to absorb the micropolitical losses caused by accepting such a minor expression of sympathetic kindness, and he is not alone.

Yet neither he nor other wheelchair users appreciate all the unsolicited assistance that sympathetic walkers shower on them. Sometimes they resent the costs in definitional authority or in mere time and energy that such acts of kindness impose. In the 1970s, for example, one of our informants was mistaken for a wounded veteran of the Vietnam war by a bouncer at a popular country and western bar. Before our informant could correct the misidentification, the bouncer carried him and his chair past the long queue of people awaiting admittance to the bar, forcibly removed some patrons from a table, and then offered the table to our informant and his companions. When the bouncer left to order "drinks on the house," our informant's wife wisely advised him, "Don't you dare tell him you're not a vet." For the rest of the evening, our informant and his companions were held hostage to the bouncer's definition of the situation, and had to feign knowledge of Vietnamese geography. Another informant reports that bartenders routinely refuse to accept payment for his drinks, insisting that his "money's no good here." A relatively well-paid civil servant, our informant resented the definitional implication that he was unable to pay his own way, but sometimes "let it go because they just wouldn't take my money." At times, too, unsolicited assistance merely makes wheelchair users' lives more difficult, as when walkers insist on helping a wheelchair user disassemble, fold, and load the wheelchair into a car or van, taking twice as long to do so as the user commonly takes and sometimes damaging the wheelchair in the process.

Even more maddening are those occasions on which self-appointed benefactors bear some responsibility for the wheelchair user's plight. One of our informants reported that she called a restaurant to inquire if it was accessible to wheelchair users. After being assured that it was, she made reservations for the following evening.

> [W]e got there to find that they had four or five steps, and there was no way I was going to get up there. So the owner of the restaurant and several of the male kitchen help came out and just picked my chair right up. They made every effort, once I got there, to help, which was really nice, but at the same time I was not happy after what they'd told me. . . . I get embarrassed when people make too much fuss over me.

This embarrassed and unhappy, if not angry, woman never returned to the restaurant in question. Yet on the evening of her first and only visit, she graciously thanked its owner and his employees for helping her over, through, and out of a predicament into which he had lured her. Her apparently insincere expression of seemingly undeserved gratitude is not aberrant among wheelchair users who receive unsolicited and unwelcome acts of sympathetic assistance. Here again, wheelchair users' public expression and their private feelings often contrast sharply.

At least our informants often express gratitude for unsolicited offers and acts of assistance even when they are unneeded, unwelcome, inconvenient, embarrassing, and demeaning. They know all too well the consequences of not doing so: their self-appointed benefactors, as well as those who witness his or her charity, are likely to judge them harshly for any hint of ingratitude. One of our informants learned this on his first trip to a highly recommended barbershop.

> I drove over there and got out of my car and wheeled up to the door. I opened the door and prepared to go in, and one of the two barbers came out and grabbed my handles. Now, as I've said, I like to do and insist on doing things for myself, but this fellow would not let go of the handles. I had my brakes on, preventing him from pushing me, but he insisted that he was going to push me over the threshold. . . . And finally . . . I forget what he said, but I asked for an apology. And he said "Okay, I apologize, but you have a chip on your shoulder, don't you?"

Like recipients of other forms of charity, wheelchair users who refuse or resist unsolicited acts of sympathetic assistance risk being viewed as having . . . "a chip on their shoulders." For many wheelchair users on many occasions, thankful and deferential acceptance of such charitable acts may seem less micropolitically costly than being judged ungrateful, testy, and uncivil.

Even when wheelchair users are willing to pay the price of such harsh judgments rather than cooperating in diminishing their interactional place, another consideration often prevents them from doing so. As Goffman (1963b:113) observes, the treatment of those who bear a stigma conveys to them that their "real group," the one whose interests they must champion, "is the aggregate of persons who are likely to suffer the same deprivations as [they suffer] because of having the same stigma." Wheelchair users are no exception, and many take this lesson to heart. Therefore they feel a sense of responsibility toward other wheelchair users and worry that their example might influence how other wheelchair users are treated in the future.

> I have people falling all over themselves trying to help me. It used to bother me, but, God, the older you get the less it does. But I know a lot of people it does. I've got one friend that's at the point of being rude. This is bad because it sets a bad example. That person in the future may not be quite so willing to help the next person who really needs it.

As in this woman's case but not her friend's, the contradiction between the wheelchair user's immediate micropolitical interests and the presumably greater interests of his or her "real group" often blocks the wheelchair user's expression of his or her subjective emotional reactions to unsolicited and unwelcome offers and acts of assistance. He or she consequently sacrifices interactional place for the presumably greater good of those who share the stigma of moving through public places in a sitting position.

The Wages of Public Acceptance

As late as the early 1970s, persons with visible disabilities were legally banned from public places in a number of American cities. . . . Today wheelchair users are a common presence in public places, attracting only occasional stares and many minor acts of [assistance]. Yet, the surface acceptance and assistance that others commonly grant them are not without a price. . . .

[W]heelchair users still must endure being treated like children in public places. Sometimes they are treated as open persons who can be addressed at will about their condition and the technical means of their mobility. At other times they are discussed and talked past as if absent. Robert Murphy (1987:201) suggests that people with disabilities are treated like children in part because "overdependency and nonreciprocity are considered childish traits," but wheelchair users seldom exhibit such traits in public. Although wheelchair users often depend on others' friendly assistance when the physical features of public places prove difficult to negotiate, most take pains to avoid exhausting the goodwill and sympathy of those who move through public places in a standing position.

The above discussion demonstrates that wheelchair users more than reciprocate . . . the public acceptance and assistance that others grant them with considerable emotion work and micropolitical sacrifices. That work and those sacrifices profit the walkers who they encounter in public. As Goffman (1963b:121) suggests, wheelchair users' public poise, even temper, and good humor ensure that walkers "will not have to admit to themselves how limited their tactfulness and tolerance is." On the contrary, wheelchair users' request for and acceptance of public aid provide walkers an opportunity to demonstrate to themselves, if not others, that they are kind and caring people. The wheelchair users' common expressions of gratitude confirm that self-congratulatory moral identity. . . . [Thus], it is an open question whether walkers help wheelchair users as much in public as wheelchair users help them.

Perhaps wheelchair users who frequent public places are still sometimes treated as children because the attention-attracting assistance they sometimes must request, but more often receive, overshadows all the interactional and identificatory assistance they give others. Yet one can easily discern wheelchair users' efforts and sacrifices on others' behalf by looking beyond the glare of physical feats and into the emotional and micropolitical shadows of public encounters. In those shadows wheelchair users stand tall, supporting the emotional weight of public tranquility and their public benefactors' moral identities.

Public Life and Emotion Management

More general lessons await students of social life in the emotional and micropolitical shadows to which wheelchair users' public experiences lead. Strangers in public places may appear to be acting "almost subliminally, demanding nothing of each other" (Strauss 1961:63–64), but much is demanded of them. . . . Strangers in public places devote considerable energy to preserving their own and one another's privacy, anonymity, and socially valued identities. . . . Wheelchair users' public experiences suggest that [much of that effort is emotional].

Wheelchair users are not the only ones who manage both their own and others' emotions in public places. Walkers who encounter wheelchair users in public undoubtedly sometimes avoid expressing their own private anxieties, aversion, admiration, or sympathetic concern out of concern for the wheelchair users' feelings. It is also doubtful that public encounters between unacquainted walkers and wheelchair users are unusual in this respect. Our public etiquette would seem to proscribe the public expression of emotions that are prescribed by our feeling rules, and public life is often emotionally provocative. Although strangers in public places may take pains to avoid physical contact with one another, nonetheless they touch one another emotionally in a variety of ways. They are touched embarrassingly by one another's presumed judgments as well as by one another's embarrassment. They are caressed reassuringly by others' averted gaze and pinched by fear by others' stares. Others' slights and impositions touch them with anger, and they feel a touch of guilt over their own anger. They touch one another sympathetically when requesting and providing minor acts of public aid, and repay such gifts touchingly in a variety of emotional currencies.

Yet whatever our mode of public mobility, we commonly appear emotionally reserved in public places. We mask our emotions so as not to excite others'. We manage our own expressions and thereby others' feelings. We surface act so as to sustain the tranquil exterior of public life and to avoid being swept away by its emotionally turbulent undercurrents. As suggested by the example of wheelchair users, this is part of the implicit bargain of contemporary public life. It is the price of public acceptance. . . . It is a special characteristic of public anonymity that the very process of producing it socially gives it the appearance of being not only asocial but unemotional as well. Students of social life must look beyond those appearances in order to fully understand public bonds and the bindings of contemporary society. The example of wheelchair users suggests that these bindings include interpersonal processes of emotion management. . . .

References

Cahill, Spencer. 1990. "Childhood and Public Life: Reaffirming Biographical Divisions." *Social Problems* 37: 390–402.

Clark, Candace. 1987. "Sympathy Biography and Sympathy Margin." *American Journal of Sociology* 93: 290–321.

———. 1990. "Emotions and Micropolitics in Everyday Life: Some Patterns and Paradoxes of Place." Pp. 305–333 in *Research Agendas in the Sociology of Emotions,* edited by Theodore Kemper. Albany: SUNY Press.

Coser, Rose. 1959. "Some Social Functions of Laughter: A Study of Humor in a Hospital Setting." *Human Relations* 12: 171–182.

Davis, Fred. 1961. "Deviance Disavowal: The Management of Strained Interaction by the Visibly Handicapped." *Social Problems* 9: 121–132.

Emerson, Joan. 1969. "Negotiating the Serious Import of Humor." *Sociometry* 32: 169–181.

Goffman, Erving. 1963a. *Behavior in Public Places.* New York: Free Press.

———. 1963b. *Stigma.* Englewood Cliffs, NJ: Prentice Hall.

———. 1971. *Relations in Public.* New York: Basic Books.

Gross, Edward and Gregory Stone. 1964. "Embarrassment and the Analysis of Role Requirements." *American Journal of Sociology* 70: 1–15.

Hochschild, Arlie. 1979. "Emotion Work, Feeling Rules, and Social Structure." *American Journal of Sociology* 85: 551–575.

———. 1990. "Ideology and Emotion Management: A Perspective and Path for Future Research." Pp. 117–142 in *Research Agendas in the Sociology of Emotions,* edited by Theodore Kemper. Albany: SUNY Press.

Murphy, Robert. 1987. *The Body Silent.* New York: Holt.

Simmel, Georg. 1950. *The Sociology of Georg Simmel,* edited by Kurt Wolff. Glencoe, IL: Free Press.

Strauss, Anselm. 1961. *Images of the American City.* New York: Free Press.

Reflective Questions

1. Why are public spaces so emotionally turbulent for wheelchair users?
2. How do wheelchair users ease the embarrassing situations they encounter? How do children treat wheelchair users, and how do wheelchair users tend to respond? What about adult walkers, especially elders? How do wheelchair users manage elders' emotions and their own?
3. What is an "open person," and how are they treated? What does nonperson treatment look like? Why don't wheelchair users express the anger they feel at nonperson treatment? What do they risk when expressing anger? What situations elicit sympathy from walkers? What do wheelchair users feel when they ask for help? When they are given help not asked for? Why? What social obligations do wheelchair users have for accepting help?
4. Pay attention as you go about your business in public or semi-public spaces over the next week. Outside of people who use wheelchairs, who else do people in U.S. society treat as open persons or nonpersons? How did people described in this study position others as open or nonpersons? How did the targeted individuals respond? What

strategies of emotion management did they engage in? Why?

5. Walkers may read this piece and think, "I'm damned if I do and damned if I don't." Read the disability etiquette published by the United Spinal Association at http://www.unitedspinal.org/pdf/DisabilityEtiquette.pdf. Pay particular attention to the etiquette for interacting with people with disabilities you know little about. What assumptions should you make when interacting with people with those disabilities? What should you not assume? What changes to your behavior should you make based on these guidelines? If you yourself have a disability, are there any guidelines you disagree with? Which and why?

Working 'the Code' in the Inner City

NIKKI JONES

Individuals' actions are guided by their definitions of the situations in which they act, but those situations are not of their own choosing. Their social structural positions profoundly shape the circumstances under which they must act. Also, their interpretations of those circumstances are not of their own invention but are based on cultural and subcultural meanings borrowed from the social groups to which they belong. Cultural and subcultural understandings historically emerge, in turn, from particular groups' collective attempts to cope with the circumstances they face. Social structures thereby influence individuals' actions both directly and indirectly. They shape the cultural and subcultural meanings individuals use to interpret their current circumstances and largely determine the nature of those circumstances.

This selection highlights the cultural and subcultural meanings that guide the interactions of African-American girls who live in inner-city neighborhoods. The author, Nikki Jones, points out that "survival is an ongoing project" for these girls, particularly because of the violence that surrounds them. To ensure their survival, the girls (like their male counterparts) organize their interactions in terms of "the code of the street." As Elijah Anderson has chronicled, this code consists of informal rules that dictate both how one should comport oneself in public and how one should react if challenged by others. Above all, the code revolves around the issue of respect. To get treated with respect on inner-city streets, young men and women must present a "tough" personal front—a front that conveys their willingness to engage in violence if threatened or challenged.

Jones illustrates how African-American girls interpret the code and use it to guide their actions and interactions. In doing so, Jones portrays how the code of the streets serves as "a system of accountability" and cultural script for these girls. It defines the situation of life on the streets for them, providing a template for how they should present themselves, how they should interact with others, and how they should handle threats to their reputation or well-being. In examining how inner-city African-American girls work the code, Jones also points out the importance of gender, noting how the girls' understandings and actions both overlap and diverge from the understandings and actions of their male counterparts.

The "code of the street" represents the kind of interpretive frames and implicit understandings that people bring to interaction. These frames and understandings organize our perceptions, shape our expectations, and inform the identities we present and negotiate. Once we effectively establish an identity, whether it be "student," "friend," or "bad ass," it suggests what will be expected of us and what we can expect of one another during our interaction. To the extent that we fulfill those expectations, we engage in recurrent patterns of interaction and construct enduring forms of social relationships. Unfortunately, as

Jones demonstrates in this selection, in some cases these recurrent patterns perpetuate structures and outlooks that foster conflict, aggression, and violence.

In mainstream American society, it is commonly assumed that women and girls shy away from conflict, are not physically aggressive, and do not fight like boys and men. Popular representations of 'mean girls', who 'fight with body language and relationships instead of fists and knives' reinforce common understandings about gender-based differences in the use of physical force (Simmons, 2002; Wiseman, 2003). Relying on commonplace dichotomies to explain girls' behavior, however, seriously limits our understanding of those young women who engage in symbolic and physical battles for respect and status.

In this article, I draw on field research among African-American girls in the United States to argue that the circumstances of inner-city life have encouraged the development of uniquely situated femininities that simultaneously encourage and limit inner-city girls' use of physical aggression and violence. First, I begin by arguing that, in the urban environments that I studied, gender—being a girl—does not protect inner-city girls from much of the violence experienced by inner-city boys. In fact, teenaged boys and girls are both preoccupied with 'survival' as an ongoing project. I use my analysis of interviews with young people involved in violent incidents to demonstrate similarities in how young people work 'the code of the street' across perceived gender lines. I conclude this article by describing how gender structures teenaged girls' and boys' use of physical aggression and violence in distinct ways. This in-depth examination of young people's use of physical aggression and violence reveals that while young men and young women fight, survival is still a gendered project.

Race, Gender, and Inner-City Violence

Inner-city life has changed dramatically over the last century and especially over the last 30 years; the country's recent postindustrial shift from a production economy to a service economy has encouraged the growth of white, middle-class suburbs and intensified levels of residential segregation in urban areas (Anderson, 1999; Massey & Denton 1993; Wilson, 1996, 1987, 1980). The concentration of poor, racialised minorities in inner-city neighborhoods in the United States has created a 'harsh and extremely disadvantaged environment' to which inner-city residents, especially poor, Black Americans, must adapt (Anderson, 1999; Massey & Denton, 1993, p. 13; Wilson, 1996, 1987, 1980). Despite declining rates of violent crime over much of the last decade, many inner-city residents remain concerned about the relative prevalence of interpersonal violence in their neighborhoods, which is, according to urban ethnographer Elijah Anderson, governed by the 'code of the street' (Anderson, 1994, 1999).

In his ethnographic account of life in inner-city Philadelphia, Elijah Anderson writes that the code of the street is 'a set of prescriptions and proscriptions, or informal rules, of behavior organised around a desperate search for respect that governs public social relations, especially violence among so many residents, particularly young men and women' (Anderson, 1999, p. 10). Furthermore, the code is 'a system of accountability that promises 'an eye for an eye', or a certain '"payback" for transgressions' (Anderson, 1999, p. 10). . . . According to Anderson, it is this complex relationship between masculinity, respect and violence that, at times, encourages poor, urban young men to risk their lives in order to be recognized and respected by others as a man.

Black feminist scholar Patricia Hill Collins considers Anderson's discussion of masculinity and the 'code of the street' in her recent analysis of the relationship between hegemonic (and racialised) masculinities and femininities, violence and dominance (Collins, 2004, pp. 188–212). . . . Collins (2004) argues that the recent hypercriminalisation of urban spaces is exacerbated by the culture of the code. As young men from distressed urban areas cycle in and out of correctional facilities at historically remarkable rates, she argues, urban public schools, street corners and homes have become a

'... nexus of street, prison and youth cultures', which exerts 'a tremendous amount of pressure on Black men, especially young, working class men, to avoid being classified as "weak"' (Collins, 2005, p. 211). Collins argues that young men's responses to the present-day circumstances of inner-city life reflect elements of hegemonic masculinity, especially the common belief that a 'real man' must demonstrate control 'over all forms of violence', as well as 'contemporary ideas about Black masculinity'....

Criminological Theories on Gender and Violence

Over the last few decades, feminist criminologists and gender and crime scholars have examined women's and girls' experiences with aggression and violence with increasing complexity. . . . Emphasizing how particular material circumstances influence women and girls' relationship to violence shifts the focus from the consideration of dichotomous gender differences to the empirical examination of gender similarities and differences in experiences with violence among young women and men who live in poor, urban areas (Simpson 1991). The analysis presented here follows in this tradition by recognizing the influence of shared life circumstances on young people's use of violence....

The young people from Philadelphia's inner-city neighborhoods that I encountered generally share similar life circumstances, yet how they respond to these structural and cultural circumstances—that is, how they work the code of the street—is also gendered in ways that reflect differences among inner-city girls' and boys' understanding of what you 'got to' do to 'survive'.

Methods

Each of the respondents featured in this study was enrolled in a city hospital-based violence intervention project that targeted youth aged 12 to 24 who presented in the emergency department as a result of an intentional violent incident and were considered to be at either moderate or high risk for involvement in future violent incidents. As a consequence of patterns of racial segregation within the city, almost the entire population of young women and men who voluntarily enrolled in the hospital's violence intervention project were African-American.

My fieldwork for this study took place in three phases over 3 years (2001–2003). During the first phase of the study, which lasted about a year and a half, I conducted 'ride alongs' with intervention counselors who met with young people in their homes shortly after their initial visit to the emergency room. I also conducted a series of interviews with members of the intervention counseling staff. Most of the staff grew up in Philadelphia and were personally familiar with many of the neighborhoods we visited. During this time and throughout the study, I also observed interactions in the spaces and places that were significant in the lives of the young people I met. These spaces included trolley cars and buses (transportation to and from school), a neighborhood high school nicknamed 'the Prison on the Hill', the city's family and criminal court, and various correctional facilities in the area. I also intentionally engaged in extended conversations with grandmothers and mothers, sisters, brothers, cousins and friends of the young people I visited and interviewed (see Anderson, 1999, pp. 10–11; Anderson 2001). I recorded this information in my fieldnotes and used it to complement, supplement, test and, at times, verify the information collected during interviews.

Shared Circumstances, Shared Code

While the problem of inner-city violence is believed to impact boys and men only, my interviews with teenaged inner-city girls revealed that young women are regularly exposed to many of the same forms of violence that men are exposed to in their everyday lives and are deeply influenced by its normative order. In the inner-city neighborhoods I visited, which were often quite isolated from the rest of the city, I encountered young men and young women who could quickly recall a friend, relative or 'associate' who had been shot, robbed or stabbed. In the public high school I visited, I watched adolescent girls and boys begin their school day with the same ritual: they dropped their bags on security belts, stepped through a metal detector, and raised their arms and spread their legs for a police-style 'pat down' before entering the building. Repeatedly, I encountered teenaged girls who, like the young men they share space with in the inner city, had stories to tell about getting 'rolled on', or getting 'jumped', or about the 'fair one' gone bad. It is these shared circumstances of life that engender a shared understanding about how to survive in a setting where your safety is never guaranteed. In the following sections, I provide portraits of four young people involved in violent incidents in order to illustrate what was revealed to me during the course of field research and interviews: an appreciation of 'the code of the street' that cut across gender lines. The first two respondents, Billy and DeLisha, tell stories of recouping from a very public loss in a street fight. The second set of respondents, Danielle and Robert, highlight how even those who are averse to fighting must sometimes put forth a 'tough front' to deter potentially aggressive challenges in the future.

Billy and DeLisha: 'I'm Not Looking Over My Shoulder'

Billy was 'jumped' by a group of young men while in 'their' neighborhood, which is within walking distance of his own. He tells me this story as we sit in the living room of his row home. Billy recently reached his 20s, although he looks older than his age. He is White but shares a class background that is similar to many of the young people I interviewed. His block, like most of the others I visited during this study, is a collection of row homes in various states of disrepair. Billy spends more time here than he would like. He is unemployed and when asked how best the intervention project he enrolled in could help him his request was simple: I need a job. As we talk, I think that Billy is polite—he offers me a drink (a beer, which I decline) before we begin our interview—and even quiet. He recalls two violent battles within the last year, both of which ended with him in the emergency room, without wavering too far from a measured, even tone. The first incident he recalls for me happened in South Philadelphia. He was walking down the block, when he came across a group of guys on the corner, guys who he had 'trouble' with in the past. As he stood talking to an acquaintance, Billy was approached from behind and punched in the back of the head. The force of the punch was multiplied exponentially by brass knuckles, 'split[ting] [his] head open'. Billy was knocked out instantly, fell face-first toward the ground and split his nose on a concrete step. The thin scar from this street-fight remains several months later.

In contrast to Billy's even tone, DeLisha is loud. She is thin with a medium brown complexion. Her retelling of the story of her injury is more like a reenactment as the adrenaline, anxiety and excitement of the day return. She comes across as fiercely independent, especially for a 17-year-old girl. DeLisha, a young mother with a 1-year-old daughter, has been unable to rely on her own drug-addicted mother for much of her life. After years of this independence, she is convinced that she does not need anyone's help to 'make it' in life. While she has been a 'fighter' for as long as she can remember, she was never hurt before. Not in school. Not in her neighborhood, which is one of the most notorious in the city. And not like this. She had agreed to a fight with another neighborhood girl. The younger girl, pressured by her family and peers to win the battle, shielded a box-cutter from DeLisha's sight until the very last minute. When it seemed that she would lose, the girl flashed the box-cutter and slashed DeLisha across the hand, tearing past skin and muscle into a tendon on her arm.

During my interviews with Billy and DeLisha, I asked each of them how these very public losses, which also resulted in serious physical injuries, would influence their mobility within the neighborhood. Would they avoid certain people and places? Would or could they shrug their loss off or would they seek vengeance for their lost battle? Billy's and DeLisha's responses were strikingly similar in tone, nearly identical at some points, and equally revealing of two of the most basic elements of the code of the street: the commitment to maintaining a 'tough front' and 'payback'.

> Billy: I mean, just like I say, I walk around this neighborhood. I'm not looking over my shoulder. . . . I'm not going to walk [and] look around my shoulder because I've got people looking for me. I mean you want me . . . you know where I live. They can call me at any time they want. That's how, that's how I think. . . . I'm not going to sit around my own neighborhood and just say: 'Aww, I got to watch my back'. You want me? You got me.

> DeLisha: I'm not a scared type . . . I walk on the streets anytime I want to. I do anything I want to, anytime I want to do it. It's never been a problem walking on the street 3:00 in the morning. If I want to go home 3:00 in the morning, I'm going to go home. I'm not looking over my shoulder. My grandma never raised me to look over my shoulder. I'm not going to stop because of some little incident [being cut in the hand with a box-cutter].

Billy and DeLisha's strikingly similar responses reveal their commitment to a shared 'system of accountability', the code of the street, which, as Anderson argues, governs much of social life, especially violence, in distressed urban areas (Anderson, 1999). Billy and DeLisha hold themselves accountable to this system ('I'm not going to . . . ') and are also aware that others will hold them accountable for their behaviors and actions. Billy and DeLisha are acutely aware that someone who 'looks over their shoulder' while walking down the street is perceived as weak, a moving target, and both are determined to reject such a fate. Instead, Billy and DeLisha remain committed to managing their 'presentation of self' (Goffman, 1959) in a way that masks any signs of vulnerability.

In addition to their commitment to 'not looking over their shoulder', Billy and DeLisha are also sensitive to the fact that the fights they were in were not 'fair'. These street-level injustices inform Billy and DeLisha's expectations for retaliation. Consistent with the code, both Billy and DeLisha—equally armed with long fight histories—realise the importance of 'payback' and consider future battles with their challengers to be inevitable. When I asked DeLisha if she anticipated another fight with the young woman who cut her, she replied with a strong yes, 'because I'm taking it there with her'. Billy was also equally committed to retaliation, telling me: ' . . . one by one, I will get them'.

Danielle and Robert: 'Sometimes You Got to Fight'

In *Code of the Street* (1999), Anderson demonstrates how important it is for young people to prove publicly that they are not someone to be 'messed with'. One of the ways that young people prove this to others is by engaging in fights in public, when necessary. The following statements from Danielle and Robert, two young people who are adept at avoiding conflicts, illustrate teenaged girls' and boys' shared understanding of the importance of demonstrating that one is willing to fight as a way to deter ongoing challenges to one's well-being:

> Danielle: 'cause sometimes you got to fight, not fight, but get into that type of battle to let them know that I'm not scared of you and you can't keep harassing me thinking that it's okay.

> Robert: . . . you know, if someone keep picking on you like that, you gonna have to do something to prove a point to them: that you not going to be scared of them. . . . So, sometimes you do got to, you do got to fight. Cause you just got to tell them that you not scared of them.

Like DeLisha and Billy, Danielle, a recent high-school graduate, and Robert, who is in the 11th grade, offer nearly identical explanations of the importance of physically protecting one's own boundaries by demonstrating to others that you will fight, if necessary. While neither Danielle nor Robert identify as 'fighters', both are convinced that sometimes you 'got to fight'. Again, this shared language reveals an awareness and commitment to a shared system of accountability, 'the code of the street', which encourages young people—teenaged girls and boys—to present a 'tough front' as a way to discourage on-going challenges to one's personal security. For the young people in this study, the value placed on maintaining a tough front or 'proving a point' cut across perceived gender lines.

In addition to possibly deterring future challenges, Anderson argues that presenting and ultimately proving oneself as someone who is not to be 'messed with' helps to build a young person's confidence and self-esteem: 'particularly for young men and perhaps increasingly among females . . . their identity, their self-respect, and their honor are often intricately tied up with the way they perform on the streets during and after such [violent] encounters' (Anderson, 1999, p. 76). Those young people who are able to perform well during these public encounters acquire a sense of confidence that will facilitate their movement throughout the neighborhood. This boost to one's sense of self is not restricted to young men; young women who can fight and win may also demonstrate a strong sense of pride and confidence in their ability to 'handle' potentially aggressive or violent conflicts, as illustrated by the following interview with Nicole.

Nicole: 'I Feel Like I Can Defend Myself'

My conversation with Nicole typifies the confidence expressed by teenaged girls who can fight and win. Nicole is a smart, articulate young woman who attended some community college courses while still a senior in high school. She planned to attend a state university to study engineering after graduation. While in high school, she tells me, she felt confident in her ability to walk the hallways of her sometimes chaotic public school: 'I feel like I can defend myself'. Unlike some young women who walk the hallways constantly testing others, Nicole's was a quiet confidence: 'I don't, like, I mean, when I'm walking around school or something, I don't walk around talking about "yeah, I beat this girl up"'. Nicole could, in fact, claim that she didn't beat up just one girl but several, at the same time. Nicole explained to me how her most recent fight began:

> We [she and another young woman] had got into two arguments in the hallway and then her friends were holding her back. So I just said, 'Forget it. I'm just going to my class'. So I'm in class, I'm inside the classroom and I hear Nina say, 'Is this that bitch's class?' I came to the door and was like, 'Yes, this is my class'. And she puts her hands up [in fighting position] and she swings. . . . And me and her was fighting, and then I got her on the wall, and then I felt somebody pulling my hair, and it turns out to be Jessica. Right? And then we fighting, and then I see Tasha, and it's me and all these three people and then they broke it all up.

Nicole's only injury in the fight came from the elbow of the school police officer who eventually ended the battle. As Nicole recalls this fight, and her performance in particular, I notice that she is smiling. This smile, together with the tone in which she tells the story of her earlier battle, makes it clear that she is proud of her ability to meet the challenge presented to her by these young women. Impressed at her ability to fight off three teenaged girls at the same time, I ask Nicole: 'How did you manage not to get jumped?' She quickly corrects my definition of the situation: 'No. I managed to beat them up'. After retelling her fight story, Nicole shakes her head from side to side and says: 'I had to end up beating them up. So sad'. I notice her sure smile return. 'You don't really look like you feel bad about that', I say. 'I don't,' she replies.

The level of self-confidence that Nicole displays in this brief exchange contrasts with the passivity and submissiveness that is commonly expected of women and girls, especially white, middle-class women and girls (Collins, 2004). It is young men, not teenaged girls, who are expected to exude such confidence as they construct a 'tough front' to deter would-be challengers (Anderson, 1999). Nicole's confidence is also more than an expressive performance. Nicole knows that she is physically able to fight and win, when necessary, because she has done so in the past. For teenaged girls like Nicole and Sharmaine, whom I discuss below, this confidence is essential to their evaluation of how best to handle potential interpersonal conflicts in their everyday lives.

Sharmaine: '. . . I Have One Hand Left'

Sharmaine, an 8th-grader, displayed a level of self-confidence similar to Nicole's after a fight with a boy in her classroom. Moments before the fight, the boy approached Sharmaine while she was looking out her classroom window, and 'whispered something' in her ear. Sharmaine knew that this boy liked her, but she thought she had made it quite clear that she did not like him. Sharmaine quickly told him to back off and then looked to her teacher for reinforcement. Her teacher, Sharmaine recalls, just laughed at the boy's advances. After he whispered in Sharmaine's ear a second time, she turned around and punched him in the face. Sharmaine later ended up in the emergency room with a jammed finger from the punch. I asked Sharmaine if she was concerned about him getting back at her when she returned to school. She tells me that someone in the emergency room asked her the same question. 'What did you say?' I ask. 'I told them no . . . because I have one hand left'.

For young women like Nicole and Sharmaine, the proven ability to defend themselves translates into a level of self-confidence that is not typically expected in girls and young women. Those girls who are confident in their ability to 'take care of themselves' become more mobile as they come to believe, as DeLisha says, that they can 'do anything [they] want to, anytime [they] want to do it'. Girls who are able to gain and maintain this level of self-confidence are able to challenge the real and imagined gendered boundaries on space and place in the inner city.

Survival: A Gendered Project

Much of the literature on violence and masculinity reveals that for men in general and poor men of colour in particular, 'manhood and survival are often two sides of the same coin' (Anderson, 1999, p. 91; see also Cole & Guy-Sheftall, 2003, pp. 132–141 and Collins, 2004, pp. 185–193). Because the project of accomplishing one's manhood overlaps with the project of survival, it is not enough for a teenaged boy to become an able fighter or to maintain a tough front, as it tends to be for young women. For young men, what is often perceived to be on the line is not only the outcome of the fight but also manhood itself. In contrast to young men's concern with public and potentially life-threatening displays of 'manhood', the young women in this study typically considered the use of physical aggression or violence as a means to an end, rather than a defining characteristic of being a woman. In the remainder of this article, I describe how intersecting survival and gender projects may encourage young men's use of violence and simultaneously encourage and limit inner-city girls' use of physical aggression and violence.

'Boys Got to Go Get Guns'

The need to be 'distinguished as a man'—a benchmark of hegemonic masculinity—often fosters adolescent boys' preoccupation with distinguishing themselves from women (Anderson, 1999; Collins, 2004, p. 210; Connell & Messerschmidt, 2005). This is a gendered preoccupation that was not revealed in urban adolescent girls' accounts of physical aggression and violence. The following statement from Craig, a young man who has deliberately checked his readiness to fight after being shot in the hip, illustrates how the need to 'be a man' influences young men's consideration of violence:

> Yeah, I don't fight no more. I can't fight [because of injury]. So, I really stop and think about stuff because it isn't even worth it . . . unless, I mean, you really want it [a fight] to happen . . . I'm going to turn the other cheek. But, I'm not going to be, like, wearing a skirt. That's the way you got to look at it.

While Craig is prepared to exit his life as a 'fighter', he predicts that his newfound commitment to avoid fights will not stand up to the pressure of proving his manhood to a challenger. Craig is well aware of how another young man can communicate that he 'really want[s] [a fight] to happen'. Once a challenger publicly escalates a battle in this way, young men like Craig have few choices. At this moment, a young man will have to demonstrate to his challenger, and his audience, that he isn't 'wearing a skirt'. Not only must he fight, he must also fight like a man. Craig's admission is revealing of how a young man's concern with not being 'like' a woman influences his consideration of the appropriate use of physical aggression. While a similar type of preoccupation with intergender distinctions was not typically revealed in young women's accounts, I found that teenaged girls were generally aware of at least one significant difference in how young women and men were expected to work the code of the street. As is revealed in my conversation with Shante, a teenaged girl who was hit in the head with a brick by a neighborhood girl, young men are generally expected to use more serious or lethal forms of violence than girls or women. I asked Shante what people in her neighborhood thought about girls fighting.

> 'Today', she asked, 'you mean like people on the street?'
> 'Yeah.'
> 'If [a girl] get beat up, you just get beat up. That's on you.'
> 'Do you think it's different for boys?' I asked.
> 'Umm, boys got to go get guns. They got to blow somebody's head off. They got to shoot. They don't fight these days. They use guns.'

Shante's perception of what boys 'got to' do is informed by years of observation and experience. Shante has grown up in a neighborhood marked by violence. Days before this interview, she saw a young man get shot in the head. She tells me he was dead by the time he hit the sidewalk. When I asked Shante whether or not girls used guns, she could recall just one young woman from the neighborhood—the same young woman who hit Shante over the head with a brick—who had 'pistol whipped' another teenaged girl. While she certainly used the gun as a weapon, she didn't shoot her. These two incidents are actually quite typical of reported gender differences in the use of weapons in violent acts: boys and men are much more likely than girls and women to use guns to shoot and kill. Women and girls, like many of the young women I spoke with during this study, are far more likely to rely on knives and box-cutters, if they use a weapon at all (see also Miller, 1998 & 2001; Pastor, et al., 1996, p. 28). Those young women who did use a weapon, such as a knife or box-cutter, explained that they did so for protection. For example, Shante told me that she carried a razor blade, 'because she doesn't trust people'.

Takeya: 'A Good Girl'

In contrast to the commitment to protecting one's manhood, which Craig alludes to and Elijah Anderson describes in great detail (Anderson, 1999), the young women I spoke to did not suggest that they fought because that's what women do. Furthermore, while young women deeply appreciated the utility of a 'tough front', they were unlikely to use phrases like 'I don't want to be wearing a skirt'. In fact, while young men like Craig work to prove their manhood by distinguishing themselves from women, many of the young women I spoke with—including the 'toughest' among them—embraced popular notions of femininity, 'skirts' and all. For many of the girls I interviewed, an appreciation of some aspects of hegemonic femininity modulated their involvement in violent interactions.

My conversation with Takeya sheds light on how inner-city girls attempt to reconcile the contradictory concerns that emerge from intersecting survival and gender projects. When I asked Takeya, a slim 13-year-old girl with a light brown complexion, about her fighting history, she replied, 'I'm not in no fights. I'm a good girl'. 'You are a good girl?' I asked. 'Yeah, I'm a good girl and I'm-a be a pretty girl at 18'. Takeya's concern with being a 'pretty girl' reflects an appreciation of aspects of hegemonic femininity that place great value on beauty. Her understanding of what it means to be beautiful is also influenced by the locally placed value on skin colour, hair texture and body figure. While brown skin and textured hair may not fit hegemonic (White, middle-class) conceptions of beauty, in this setting, a light brown skinned complexion, 'straight' or 'good' hair, and a slim figure help to make one 'pretty' and 'good' (Banks, 2000). Yet, Takeya also knows that one's ability to stay pretty—to be a pretty girl at age 18—is directly influenced by one's involvement in interpersonal aggression or violence.

In order to be considered a 'pretty girl' by her peers, Takeya knows that she must avoid those types of interpersonal conflicts that tend to result in cuts and scratches to young women's faces, especially the ones that others consider beautiful (in *Code of the Street* [1999], Anderson writes that such visible scars often result in heightened status for the young women who leave their mark on pretty girls). Yet, Takeya is also aware that the culture of the code requires her to become an able fighter and to maintain a reputation as such. After expressing her commitment to being a 'good' girl, Takeya is sure to inform me that not only does she know how to fight, others also recognise her as an able fighter: 'I don't want you to think I don't know how to fight. I mean everybody always come get me [for fights]. [I'm] the number one [person they come to get]'.

Takeya's simultaneous embrace of the culture of code and some aspects of normative femininity, Craig's concern with distinguishing himself from women, and Shante's convincing disclosure regarding what boys 'got to' do highlight how masculinity and femininity projects overlap and intersect with the project of survival for young people in distressed inner-city neighborhoods. Both Craig and Takeya appreciate fundamental elements of 'the code', especially the importance of being known as an able fighter. Yet, Craig's use of physical aggression is likely to be encouraged by his commitment to a distinctive aspect of hegemonic masculinity: being distinguished from a girl. Meanwhile, Takeya's use of physical aggression and violence is tempered—though not extinguished—by seemingly typical 'female' concerns: being a 'good' and 'pretty' girl. In contrast to the project of accomplishing masculinity, which overlaps and, at times, contradicts the project of survival for young men, the project of accomplishing femininity can, at times, facilitate young women's struggle to survive in this setting.

Intersecting Projects: Gender, Survival, and 'the Code'

I have argued that gender does not protect young women from much of the violence young men experience in distressed inner-city neighborhoods, and that given these shared circumstances, it becomes equally important for women and men to work 'the code of the street'. Like many adolescent boys, young women also recognise that reputation, respect and retaliation—the '3 Rs' of the code of the street—organise their social world (Anderson, 1999). Yet, as true as it is that, at times, young men and women work the code of the street in similar ways, it is also true that differences exist. These differences are rooted in the relationships between masculinity, femininity and the use of violence or aggression in distressed urban areas and emerge from overlapping and intersecting survival and gender projects. In order to 'survive' in today's inner city, young women like DeLisha, Danielle, Shante and Takeya are encouraged to embrace some aspects of the 'code of the street', that organises much of inner-city life (Anderson 1999). In doing so, these girls also embrace and accomplish some aspects of hegemonic masculinity that are embedded in the code. My analysis of interviews with teenaged girls and boys injured in intentional violent incidents reveals an appreciation of the importance of maintaining a tough front and demonstrating nerve across perceived gender lines. It is this appreciation of the cultural elements of the code that leads teenaged girls like Danielle to believe strongly that 'sometimes you got to fight'.

My analysis also reveals, however, that teenaged girls do not embrace all elements of hegemonic masculinity that are embedded in the code equally. For example, the inner-city girls I interviewed generally resisted, and at times flatly rejected, the 'coupling' (Collins, 2004) of strength with dominance, which is fundamental to the code of the street. Rather, many of the young women and girls I interviewed believed that escalating the negotiation of conflict to the use of lethal violence was senseless or 'stupid'. Even DeLisha, who easily identifies as a 'fighter' admits: 'I really would beat her up, real bad, and then leave her there. *That would be the end of that*' [emphasis mine]. While boys 'got to go get guns', a belief that highlights the widely perceived connection between masculinity, strength and dominance, the teenaged girls I interviewed typically suggested that 'strong' women 'survive' in the most literal sense.

In many ways, the teenaged girls in this study remain as concerned with survival as 'strong' Black women and girls were in earlier historical periods. However, in today's inner city, where the culture of the code organises much of social life, what a girl has 'got to' do to survive has changed. So, while strength remains a source of power for teenaged girls coming of age in today's inner city it does so with a contradictory twist, since using aggression or violence to demonstrate one's strength can actually increase the likelihood of one's victimisation (Stewart et al., 2006) and seriously undermine the collective wellbeing of a community. That the teenaged girls in this study do not (yet) couple strength with dominance offers some hope that structural and cultural interventions can stem the increasing numbers of girls who enter hospitals or correctional facilities as a result of interpersonal violence. Without such interventions, however, it is possible that a larger number of poor, urban girls may share the experiences of inner-city boys who live and all too often die by the 'code of the street'.

References

Anderson, E. (1994, May). The code of the street. *The Atlantic Monthly*, pp. 80–94.

Anderson, E. (1999). *Code of the street: Decency, violence and the moral life of the inner city*. New York: W.W. Norton.

Anderson, E. (2001). Urban ethnography. In N.J. Smelser & P.B. Baltes (Eds.), *International encyclopedia of the social and behavioral sciences*. Oxford: Pergamon Press.

Banks, I. (2000). *Hair matters: Beauty, power, and Black women's consciousness*. New York: New York University Press.

Cole, J.B., & Guy-Sheftall, B. (2003). *Gender talk: The struggle for women's equality in African American communities*. New York: One World, Ballantine Books.

Collins, P. Hill. (2005). *Black sexual politics: African Americans, gender, and the new racism*. New York: Routledge.

Connell, R.W., & Messerschmidt, J.W. (2005). Hegemonic masculinity: Rethinking the concept. *Gender & Society*, 19(6), 829–859.

Goffman, E. (1959). *The presentation of self in everyday life*. New York: Anchor Books.

Massey, D., & Denton, N. (1993). *American apartheid: Segregation and the making of the underclass*. Cambridge, MA: Harvard University Press.

Miller, J. (1998). Up it up: Gender and the accomplishment of street robbery. *Criminology*, 36(1), 37–66.

Miller, J. (2001). *One of the guys: Girls, gangs, and gender*. Oxford: Oxford University Press.

Pastor, J., McCormick, J., & Fine, M. (1996). Makin' homes: An urban girl thing. In B.J. Ross Leadbeater & N. Way (Eds.), *Urban girls: Resisting stereotypes, creating identities*. New York: New York University Press.

Simmons, R. (2002). *Odd girl out: The hidden culture of aggression in girls*. San Diego, CA: Harcourt.

Simpson, S.S. (1991). Caste, class, and violent crime: Explaining difference in female offending. *Criminology*, 29(1), 115–135.

Stewart, E.A., Schreck, C.J., & Simons, R.L. (2006). 'I ain't gonna let no one disrespect me': Does the code of the street reduce or increase violent victimization among African American adolescents? *Journal of Research in Crime and Delinquency*, 43, 337–351.

Wilson, W.J. (1996). *When work disappears: The world of the new urban poor*. New York: Vintage Books.

Wilson, W.J. (1987). *The truly disadvantaged: The inner city, the underclass, and public policy*. Chicago: The University of Chicago Press.

Wilson, W.J. (1980). *The declining significance of race: Blacks and changing American institutions*. Chicago: The University of Chicago Press.

Wiseman, R. (2003). *Queen bees and wannabes: Helping your daughter survive cliques, gossip, boyfriends, and other realities of adolescence*. New York: Three Rivers Press.

Reflective Questions

1. What is "the code of the street" that informs interaction among inner-city youth? What are the "three R's" that serve as central features of this code? What is the relationship between the code and inner-city violence? How does the code serve as a system of accountability?

2. How does the code of the street organize the interactions of African-American girls in urban neighborhoods? How does the code shape the self-presentations of these girls? For instance, what kind of front do they have to convey in many of their interactions? How does this front help them to earn respect and ward off potential threats?
3. What are the differences between how boys and girls enact the code? How do they vary in the forms of violence they use to issue "payback" and preserve their sense of honor?
4. What code of conduct governs the interaction of students on college campuses? Does this code include some elements of the three R's that characterize the code of the streets? How do students expect one another to respond if their reputations are questioned? What forms of "payback" do they encourage or tolerate? How and why is respect a central feature of this code?

PART

VII

The Construction of Social Boundaries and Structures

The selections in the previous section examined how the "interaction order" profoundly influences people's understandings, experiences, relationships, and actions. Part VII shows how people coordinate their interpretations and actions in ways that lead to broader social patterns. One recurrent pattern involves social boundaries: symbolically dividing people into groups and protecting those boundaries. We make and remake social boundaries when we repeatedly categorize people and attach particular meanings to those groupings. We then act on categorizations so that the divisions between people have social consequences: we interact differently with people based on their classifications, we consider some people to be like us and others to be different from us, we know how to think about ourselves and how to act because we see ourselves as members of one group (e.g., students) and not another (e.g., professors). Social boundaries are the basis for social roles and positions within society. They give us a sense of identity, purpose, and direction.

Another pattern involves our ways of organizing the social world, often referred to as social structures. Social structures allow us to anticipate what others will do and what they expect us to do, often in ways consistent with social roles or positions defined through symbolic boundaries. They provide us with interactional predictability and stability. For this reason, social structures often seem self-perpetuating and permanent, as if they exist in their own right, external to us and outside of our interactions. They may also appear to be independent forces shaping our lives by constraining some actions and enabling others. In these ways, social structures can feel as natural as physical environments. But their power does not come from nature; it comes from human definitions and coordinated actions. Social structures are humanly created and recreated through interaction. The selections in this section examine the interactional establishment, maintenance, and reconstruction of various types of symbolic boundaries and social structures.

Taken together, the readings in Part VII highlight the following themes about collective symbolic interaction:

- *Sociologists use terms such as* institutions, cultures, *and* social structures *as shorthand to refer to individuals engaging in symbolic interaction in repeated and coordinated ways.* While social structures seem as if they exist in their own right, they do not. Ultimately, they rely on human action and interaction. As Herbert Blumer noted, social structures are the product of "joint action." Because joint actions are grounded in social meanings and definitions, they have a contingent nature and are potentially open to challenge and change at any time.

  Guided by Blumer's insights, a sociological psychological approach to social boundaries and structures has profound implications for how we think about and study the social world. It shifts the analytic eye from the *byproduct* of joint action to the *process* of meaning making that produces and sustains it. This framework diminishes the mystique of social structures: they seem much less stable, constraining, and daunting. As Blumer explains, it is "the social process in group life that creates and upholds the rules, not the rules that create and uphold group life."

- *We maintain symbolic boundaries between people, and we use these boundaries to coordinate our actions with others.* Symbolic boundaries allow us to develop meaningful identities as they relate to being part of a group or taking on a particular social role. People often create and reinforce social boundaries in order to make claims about their morality: that they are part of a morally superior and worthy group. Managing emotions is one way of drawing boundaries, and happiness is a particularly appealing emotion to display because of its association with morality. But a particular boundary is neither permanent nor necessary.

- *Other people provide us a model for how to coordinate our interpretations and actions, and they police our actions to be consistent with their expectations.*

This process is called *socialization*. Socialization works by offering us scripts, modeling interpretations, and holding us accountable for our successes and failures at fulfilling expectations. Socialization teaches us what boundaries are important, and how to adapt to various roles and social settings. We learn to behave differently and interpret others' actions differently depending on if we are in a classroom, at home, or at a football game. Likewise, we vary them to be consistent with being a student versus professor, parent versus child, player versus spectator. While socialization begins in childhood when caretakers teach us manners and cultural guidelines, it continues as we age so that peers, media, religious leaders, and other important figures provide us with new ways of doing things. Socialization is key to passing along interpretations and courses of action across generations and through a community. As Selections 29 and 30 reveal, it also teaches us what it means to be a member of a particular group, and what values and symbolic boundaries characterize that group.

- *People often find comfort and direction from routines.* We know what to do in a given situation because we have done it before successfully or because others expect it from people of our position. We know what it means to be a worker or a husband. We feel good about ourselves and the world around us because we know where we fit.

  When the unexpected disrupts our routines, however, we feel unsettled, uncertain, and even threatened. Our sense of stability and moral order gets shaken. People respond to these challenges by protecting established routines and maintaining control of the situation. They use a variety of techniques to keep things going according to plan. These techniques include minimizing disruptions, following rituals, using humor to create emotional distance in the face of traumatic events, or simply keeping going by focusing on one's assigned tasks. Personal crises, chaotic workplaces, and dramatic weather events disrupt everyday routines and thus are ripe places for examining how people strive to sustain social order in the face of profound disruption.

Each of the readings in Part VII reminds us that we organize and structure our own social lives. While some of us may influence those processes more than others, we all participate. And because we participate in the construction of symbolic boundaries and social structures, we can also change them.

Society in Action

HERBERT BLUMER

Herbert Blumer was an important proponent and contributor to the sociological perspective of "symbolic interactionism," a name that he himself gave to it. This approach to the study of social life grew out of George Herbert Mead's ideas about the human self, thought, and interaction. As you may recall, Mead argued that individuals interact with themselves much as they interact with one another. They continually engage in an inner conversation. Rather than blindly responding, they define and interpret their experience. Their action and interaction is symbolic and meaningful.

Blumer argues that the study of social life must start from Mead's basic insights. Human social life is a continual process of individual and collective definition and interpretation. Society, culture, and social structure are not static things but are derived from what people do. And what people do is engage in symbolic interaction, both with one another and with themselves. Through processes of definition and interpretation, humans fit their individual lines of action together and construct joint actions. As Blumer further argues, students of social life cannot afford to ignore the fact that even the action of such human collectivities as societies, nations, and organizations are based on processes of definition, interpretation, and symbolic interaction.

Blumer draws three lessons about the study of social life from this basic insight. First, no matter how stable and orderly, social life is always subject to the "play and fate of meaning." Recurrent patterns of interaction and collective action are based on definitions and interpretations that may change unpredictably. Second, the networks of joint action that are often called "social institutions" are not self-governing and self-sustaining entities, but rather are sustained by human interaction and are governed by human definition and interpretation. Third, the construction of joint action is based on understandings and meanings that emerge from prior interaction. No matter how new they may seem, they have a history. These are the specifications of Blumer's more general lesson: social structures, cultures, institutions, and societies exist only in human action and interaction. Thus, human action and interaction are what students of social life must ultimately study.

Human groups . . . [consist] of human beings who are engaging in action. The action consists of the multitudinous activities that the individuals perform in their lives as they encounter one another and as they deal with the succession of situations confronting them. The individuals may act singly, they may act collectively, and they may act on behalf of, or as representatives of, some organization or group of others. The activities belong to the acting individuals and are carried on by them always with regard to the situations in which they have to act. The import of this simple and essentially redundant characterization is that fundamentally human groups or society *exists in action* and must

Reprinted from: Herbert Blumer, *Symbolic Interactionism: Perspective and Method*, pp. 6–7, 10, 12–13, 15, 16–20.

be seen in terms of action. This picture of human society as action must be the starting point (and the point of return) for any scheme that purports to treat and analyze human society empirically. Conceptual schemes that depict society in some other fashion can only be derivations from the complex of ongoing activity that constitutes group life. This is true of the two dominant conceptions of society in contemporary sociology—that of culture and that of social structure. Culture as a conception, whether defined as custom, tradition, norm, value, rules, or such like, is clearly derived from what people do. Similarly, social structure in any of its aspects, as represented by such terms as social position, status, role, authority, and prestige, refers to relationships derived from how people act toward each other. The life of any human society consists necessarily of an ongoing process of fitting together the activities of its members. It is this complex of ongoing activity that establishes and portrays structure or organization. . . .

The central place and importance of symbolic interaction in human group life and conduct should be apparent. A human society or group consists of people in association. Such association exists necessarily in the form of people acting toward one another and thus engaging in social interaction. Such interaction in human society is characteristically and predominantly on the symbolic level; as individuals acting individually, collectively, or as agents of some organization encounter one another, they are necessarily required to take account of the actions of one another as they form their own action. They do this by a dual process of indicating to others how to act and of interpreting the indications made by others. Human group life is a vast process of such defining to others what to do and of interpreting their definitions; through this process, people come to fit their activities to one another and to form their own individual conduct. Both such joint activity and individual conduct are formed *in* and *through* this ongoing process; they are not mere expressions or products of what people bring to their interaction or of conditions that are antecedent to their interaction. The failure to accommodate to this vital point constitutes the fundamental deficiency of schemes that seek to account for human society in terms of social organization or psychological factors, or of any combination of the two. By virtue of symbolic interaction, human group life is necessarily a formative process and not a mere arena for the expression of preexisting factors.

[H]uman beings must have a makeup that fits the nature of social interaction. The human being is . . . an organism that not only responds to others on the non-symbolic level but as one that makes indications to others and interprets their indications. He can do this, as Mead has shown so emphatically, only by virtue of possessing a "self." Nothing esoteric is meant by this expression. It means merely that a human being can be an object of his own action. Thus, he can recognize himself, for instance, as being a man, young in age, a student, in debt, trying to become a doctor, coming from an undistinguished family, and so forth. In all such instances, he is an object to himself; and he acts toward himself and guides himself in his actions toward others on the basis of the kind of object he is to himself. . . .

[T]he fact that the human being has a self . . . enables him to interact with himself. This interaction is not in the form of interaction between two or more parts of a psychological system, as between needs, or between emotions, or between ideas, or between the id and the ego in the Freudian scheme. Instead, the interaction is social—a form of communication, with the person addressing himself as a person and responding thereto. We can clearly recognize such interaction in ourselves, as each of us notes that he is angry with himself, or that he has to spur himself on in his tasks, or that he reminds himself to do this or that, or that he is talking to himself in working out some plan of action. As such instances suggest, self-interaction exists fundamentally as a process of making indications to oneself. . . .

The capacity of the human being to make indications to himself gives a distinctive character to human action. It means that the human individual confronts a world that he must interpret in order to act instead of an environment to which he responds because of his organization. He has to cope with the situations in which he is called on to act, ascertaining the meaning of the actions of others and mapping out his own line of action in the light of such interpretation. He has to construct and guide his action instead of merely releasing it in response to factors playing on him or operating through him. He may do a miserable job in constructing his action, but he has to construct it. . . .

This view of human action applies equally well to joint or collective action, in which numbers of individuals are implicated. Joint or collective action constitutes the domain of sociological concern, as exemplified in the behavior of groups, institutions, organizations, and social classes. Such instances of societal behavior, whatever they may be, consist of individuals fitting their lines of action to one another. It is both proper and possible to view and study such behavior in its joint or collective character instead of in its individual components. Such joint behavior does not lose its character of being constructed through an interpretive process in meeting the situations in which the collectivity is called on to act. Whether the collectivity be an army engaged in a campaign, a corporation seeking to expand its operations, or a nation trying to correct an unfavorable balance of trade, it needs to construct its action through an interpretation of what is happening in its area of operation. The interpretive process takes place by participants making indications to one another, not merely each to himself. Joint or collective action is an outcome of such a process of interpretative interaction.

As stated earlier, human group life consists of, and exists in, the fitting of lines of action to each other by the members of the group. Such articulation of lines of action gives rise to and constitutes "joint action"—a societal organization of conduct of different acts of diverse participants. A joint action, while made up of diverse component acts that enter into its formation, is different from any one of them and from their mere aggregation. The joint action has a distinctive character in its own right, a character that lies in the articulation or linkage as apart from what may be articulated or linked. Thus, the joint action may be identified as such and may be spoken of and handled without having to break it down into the separate acts that comprise it. This is what we do when we speak of such things as marriage, a trading transaction, war, a parliamentary discussion, or a church service. Similarly, we can speak of the collectivity that engages in joint action without having to identify the individual members of that collectivity, as we do in speaking of a family, a business corporation, a church, a university, or a nation. . . .

In dealing with collectivities and with joint action, one can easily be trapped in an erroneous position by failing to recognize that the joint action of the collectivity is an inter-linkage of the separate acts of the participants. This failure leads one to overlook the fact that a joint action always has to undergo a process of formation; even though it may be a well-established and repetitive form of social action, each instance of it has to be formed anew. Further, this career of formation through which it comes into being necessarily takes place through the dual process of designation and interpretation that was discussed above. The participants still have to guide their respective acts by forming and using meanings.

With these remarks as a background, I wish to make three observations on the implications of the interlinkage that constitutes joint action. I wish to consider first those instances of joint action that are repetitive and stable. The preponderant portion of social action in a human society, particularly in a settled society, exists in the form of recurrent patterns of joint action. In most situations in which people act toward one another, they have in advance a firm understanding of how to act and of how other people will act. They share common and pre-established meanings of what is expected in the action of the participants, and accordingly each participant is able to guide his own behavior by such meanings. Instances of repetitive and pre-established forms of joint action are so frequent and common that it is easy to understand why scholars have viewed them as the essence or natural form of human group life. Such a view is especially apparent in the concepts of "culture" and "social order" that are so dominant in social-science literature. Most sociological schemes rest on the belief that a human society exists in the form of an established order of living, with that order resolvable into adherence to sets of rules, norms, values, and sanctions that specify to people how they are to act in their different situations.

Several comments are in order with regard to this neat scheme. First, it is just not true that the full expanse of life in a human society, any human society, is but an expression of pre-established forms of joint action. New situations are constantly arising within the scope of group life that are problematic and for which existing rules are inadequate. I have never heard of any society that was free of problems nor any society in which members did not have to engage in discussion to work out ways of action. Such areas of unprescribed conduct are just as natural, indigenous, and recurrent in human group life as are those areas covered by pre-established and faithfully followed prescriptions of joint action. Second, we have to recognize that even in the case of pre-established and repetitive joint action, each instance of such joint action has to be formed anew. The participants still have to build up their lines of action and fit them to one another through the dual process of designation and interpretation. They do this in the case of repetitive joint action, of course, by using the same recurrent and constant meanings. If we recognize this, we are forced to realize that the play and fate of meanings are what is important, not the joint action in its established form.

Repetitive and stable joint action is just as much a result of an interpretative process as is a new form of joint action that is being developed for the first time. This is not an idle or pedantic point; the meanings that underlie established and recurrent joint action are themselves subject to pressure as well as to reinforcement, to incipient dissatisfaction as well as to indifference; they may be challenged as well as affirmed, allowed to slip along without concern as well as subjected to infusions of new vigor. Behind the facade of the objectively perceived joint action, the set of meanings that sustains that joint action has a life that the social scientists can ill afford to ignore. A gratuitous acceptance of the concepts of norms, values, social rules, and the like should not blind [us] to the fact that any one of them is subtended by a process of social interaction—a process that is necessary not only for their change but equally well for their retention in a fixed form. It is the social process in group life that creates and upholds the rules, not the rules that create and uphold group life.

The second observation on the interlinkage that constitutes joint action refers to the extended connection of actions that make up so much of human group life. We are familiar with these large complex networks of action involving an interlinkage and interdependency of diverse actions of diverse people—as in the division of labor extending from the growing of grain by the farmer to an eventual sale of bread in a store, or in the elaborate chain extending from the arrest of a suspect to his eventual release from a penitentiary. These networks with their regularized participation of diverse people by diverse action at diverse points yields a picture of institutions that have been appropriately a major concern of sociologists. They also give substance to the idea that human group life has the character of a system. In seeing such a large complex of diversified activities, all hanging together in a regularized operation, and in seeing the complementary organization of participants in well-knit interdependent relationships, it is easy to understand why so many scholars view such networks or institutions as self-operating entities, following their own dynamics and not requiring that attention be given to the participants within the network. Most of the sociological analyses of institutions and social organization adhere to this view. Such adherence, in my judgment, is a serious mistake. One should recognize what is true, namely, that the diverse array of participants, occupying different points in the network, engage in their actions at those points on the basis of using given sets of meanings. A network or an institution does not function automatically because of some inner dynamics or system requirements; it functions because people at different points do something, and what they do is a result of how they define the situation in which they are called on to act. A limited appreciation of this point is reflected today in some of the work on decision-making, but on the whole the point is grossly ignored. It is necessary to recognize that the sets of meanings that lead participants to act as they do at their stationed points in the network have their own setting in a localized process of social interaction—and that these meanings are formed, sustained, weakened, strengthened, or transformed, as the case may be, through a socially defining process. Both the functioning and the fate of institutions are set by this process of interpretation as it takes place among the diverse sets of participants.

A third important observation needs to be made, namely, that any instance of joint action, whether newly formed or long established, has necessarily arisen out of a background of previous actions of the participants. A new kind of joint action never comes into existence apart from such a background. The participants involved in the formation of the new joint action always bring to that formation the world of objects, the sets of meanings, and the schemes of interpretation that they already possess. Thus, the new form of joint action always emerges out of and is connected with a context of previous joint action. . . .

[H]uman society [is] people engaged in living. Such living is a process of ongoing activity in which participants are developing lines of action in the multitudinous situations they encounter. They are caught up in a vast process of interaction in which they have to fit their developing actions to one another. This process of interaction consists in making indications to others of what to do and in interpreting the indications as made by others. . . . This general process should be seen, of course, in the differentiated character which it necessarily has by virtue of the fact that people cluster in different groups, belong to different associations, and occupy different positions. They accordingly approach each other differently, live in different worlds, and guide themselves by different sets of meanings. Nevertheless, whether one is dealing with a family, a boy's gang, an industrial corporation, or a political party, one must see the activities of the collectivity as being formed through a process of designation and interpretation.

Reflective Questions

1. What is Blumer's definition of "self"? What is the purview of sociologists?
2. What does Blumer mean in saying that society "exists in action"? What is a social institution then? What is "joint action"? How does it work?
3. Blumer argues that it is "the social process in group life that creates and upholds the rules, not the rules that create and uphold group life." What does he mean by this? Blumer is in part problematizing reification. Reification is the failure to recognize the process of formation behind joint action, to treat the byproduct of joint action, such as an institution, as if it exists in its own right and acts as a force independent of actors. Why is this problematic for sociological psychologists?
4. The incarceration rate in the United States has skyrocketed in the past thirty years. The focus in the criminal justice system has shifted from rehabilitating offenders to punishing them. The war on drugs, mandatory sentences, privatization of prisons, and three-strikes rules are all manifestations of the shift. According to the Bureau of Justice Statistics, by the end of 2010, 2.3 million people were incarcerated, and 1 in 33 U.S. adults were under the supervision of the adult correctional system. Incarceration and supervision are not evenly distributed across the population. Young black men with little education have especially high incarceration rates: according to *Punishment and Inequality in America* by Bruce Western, 32.4% of black male high school dropouts between the ages of 20 and 40 were incarcerated in 2000, compared to 6.7% of non-Hispanic whites in the same group and 6.0% of Hispanics. What is your reaction to these data? Is this level of incarceration problematic to you? Why or why

not? How do you think young black males feel after hearing those statistics? If you are/were a part of this group, how do/would you view the police? The criminal justice system in general? How do people's interpretations of crime translate into punitive social policies and mass incarceration of black men? How does an understanding of joint action shape our personal responsibility for mass incarceration? What actions can individuals take to remedy the situation?

Collective Emotions and Boundary Work Among Evangelical Christians

AMY C. WILKINS

Social relationships have many forms. They may be more or less distant, or more or less intimate. They may be more or less egalitarian, or more or less hierarchical. Particular social relationships may also assume different social forms. They are subject to negotiation and reformulation every time the involved parties interact. We often outline the form our relationships will assume on a given occasion through our management and expression of emotions. We obviously initiate relationships by exchanging displays of emotion, as in the case of flirting between future romantic partners. Additionally, when we have an ongoing relationship with another person we feel that they owe us and we owe them the exchange of certain emotions, such as love, caring, or sympathy. If either partner in the relationship fails to meet these often implicit emotional obligations, they can alter and perhaps even destroy the relationship. That is just one of the ways we can change the form of a relationship through the social exchange of emotions. For example, displays of heartfelt concern can enhance the intimacy of a formally distant relationship while guilt-evoking displays of hurt or anger can alter the distribution of power in a relationship. In these and various other ways, the flow of emotions between ourselves and others ties us into complex relational networks with them.

This selection examines how and why evangelical Christians learn to emphasize and exchange the emotion of happiness as they interact with others and talk about the meaning of their faith. Amy Wilkins highlights how students who join a university-based Christian organization (University Unity) become part of an emotional culture that instructs them in how they are supposed to feel as evangelical Christians. Through their socialization into this culture, students learn to identify and express the positive feelings that result from "accepting Jesus into their hearts" and developing a close relationship with God. They also learn to manage and suppress negative emotions (anxiety or sadness) by redirecting their focus from "bad thoughts" to "good thoughts," such as the blessings they receive from God and the happiness they derive from their involvement in University Unity. Above all, Unity Christians learn that they have a moral duty to be happy. Within the emotional culture of their group, happiness is the marker of moral goodness and the authenticity of their faith. In turn, Unity Christians quickly recognize that they should transmit and exchange feelings of happiness in their interactions with other group members. Their failure to do so threatens to undermine the moral and social order of the group.

Wilkins also reveals how happiness serves not only as the central emotional and moral requirement for Unity members, but also as a symbolic boundary that confirms their Christian identity and distinguishes them from others. For Unity Christians, it is the experience of "authentic happiness" that separates them from non-Christians. Moreover, it is happiness

Reprinted from: Amy C. Wilkins. Happier than Non-Christians: Collective Emotions and Symbolic Boundaries among Evangelical Christians. *Social Psychology Quarterly* 71(3): 281–301.

that enables them to separate good feelings from bad feelings, prevents them from engaging in acts that might lead to bad feelings, and bonds them to other Unity members. Through exchanging and talking about happiness, Unity Christians announce and realize desired moral selves. That is, they present themselves as good people who can genuinely feel good about themselves, particularly because they relate to others in ways that allow them to exchange the emotions of warmth and happiness.

Ironically, although Unity Christians stress the emotional differences that exist between themselves and non-Christians, their emphasis on happiness clearly reflects the dominant discourse of middle-class culture in the United States. Indeed, as Wilkins notes, most members of the U.S. middle class strive to be happy and regard happiness as a sign of their moral virtue. Moreover, they often use their feelings of happiness to distinguish themselves from others, such as members of more disadvantaged social groups. They also engage in happiness talk to justify their social position and daily practices. Thus, the happiness-based emotional culture of Unity Christians may not be as distinct as they assume. Instead, it may reflect their acceptance and promotion of the values of middle-class culture, at least in some respects.

In this article, I examine talk about happiness in a university-based evangelical Christian organization that I call University Unity (the name of the organization, and all names herein, are pseudonyms). Unity Christians claim that Jesus has brought them unprecedented happiness and that they are therefore happier than non-Christians. The preponderance of happiness talk within this organization is not, on the surface, surprising. Religious participation is a widespread coping mechanism associated with positive affect and lower rates of depression. Unity (and other) Christians say they are happy because they have found Jesus, but social scientists find that a number of other features of religion lead to the association between religion and emotional well-being, including community support, strong social ties, and a sense of meaning (Koenig and Larson 2001).

Unity Christianity shares these features with other religions, but I view their happiness from a different vantage point. Instead of treating happiness as a mental health outcome of specific features of religious communities, I look at it as a group culture that is created, sustained, and made meaningful through community participation. In becoming Unity Christians, Unity staff and student leaders teach participants to talk about themselves as happy. They also coach participants in methods of emotional control, and teach them to think of their controlled emotions as happiness. In interactions with each other and outsiders, Unity Christians shape their emotional culture by crafting appropriate ways to feel and to think and talk about those feelings.

Unity Christians attribute their happiness to "Jesus' work in their hearts," but Unity happiness follows particular feeling and display rules that are consistent with other dimensions of contemporary emotional expectations (Hochschild 1979, 1983; Stearns 1994). Unity's emotional culture also draws on the meanings and expectations of the umbrella evangelical Christian organization of which it is a chapter and of the emotional lessons of the local Christian churches participants attend. Insomuch as their lessons correspond with Unity's emotional culture, these sites provide "usable culture" (Fine 1979).

In this paper, I am concerned both with how Unity Christians learn to think and talk about themselves as *happy,* and what this emotion language—and its feeling rules—do for them. By viewing Unity happiness as a collective achievement, I argue that while Unity's emotional culture brings the benefit of good feelings, it is also a means of social control. Furthermore, Unity participants use their happiness as a symbolic boundary with which they make claims about moral position. . . .

Data for this paper come from multiple qualitative methods. I gained initial access to Unity through a student who knew a Unity member. I conducted twelve months of participant-observation at University Unity meetings, social events, and the home church of most of my participants. I also examined local and national organizational materials. I supplemented the fieldwork with formal interviews with sixteen self-identified Unity Christians (7 men and 9 women). Interview participants included almost all of the Unity student leadership and a range of "rank-and-file" members. I recruited participants at Unity meetings, at tables set up in the campus center, and through Unity networks. I conducted the interviews, which typically lasted a little over an hour, in the campus center. Interviews were structured around the question, "What does it mean to be a Christian?" I probed participants about their lives before and after becoming a Christian, but the questions were deliberately open-ended, allowing flexibility to follow up on emergent themes. . . .

"The Next Day I Remember Feeling So Much Different": Stories of Emotional Transformation

For Unity Christians, conversion is characterized by emotional change. Before they became Christians, Unity Christians describe feeling bad. They were "angry," "depressed," "lonely" or "dissatisfied," "looking for it," and "looking for intimacy." Nothing they did brought them meaning. Becoming Christians, by their own accounts, transformed their emotions, dissolving the bad feelings and replacing them with "happiness," "joy," "peace," "hope," and "relief"—good feelings that came from "Jesus' work in their hearts." Their accounts of transformation are consistent despite differences in their experiences before becoming Christians.

It is not surprising that conversion is accompanied by emotional relief. As participants take on the Unity identity, they are folded into a new community, promised God's unwavering and unconditional love, provided with a sense of meaning, and assured that their behavior and interests are morally superior (as long as one is "really" a Christian). Moreover, one can imagine the elation that likely comes when one is told that she is among the "chosen." But to take these emotional transformations at face value misses the ways in which conversion stories become organized around characteristics that take on meaning after the conversion, rather than before.

In her study of women who have become racists, Blee (1996) finds that conversion stories do not provide "reliable accounts of actual political recruitment or ideological conversion" but rather "accord intent, calculation, and meaning to radically changing self-identities" (689, 692). Unity conversion stories similarly elide the processes by which the storytellers became Christians. Some Unity Christians were raised in Christian homes and socialized into Christian expectations from a young age, while others were introduced to Christianity as young adults, but each participant was recruited through Christian social networks, and attended a series of Christian-sponsored activities and spiritual counseling before coming to identify as a Christian. Yet, despite the incremental adoption of Christian identities, Unity participants all tell stories that identify conversion as a moment identifiable by accompanying emotional change.

Like participants in other institutions, Unity participants tell stories that integrate personal details into a common narrative structure, and rely on a common emotional vocabulary (Irvine 2000). Cain (1991:215) argues that "the personal story is a cultural vehicle for identity acquisition" (see also Irvine 2000; Mason-Schrock 1996). In Cain's study, participants in Alcoholics Anonymous acquire the "alcoholic" identity by learning and then telling the AA story. Because the story has limited parameters, members learn to fit their own stories into the AA template. Their storytelling, in turn, restructures their autobiographies, so that they come to think of their lives in terms of the AA story.

Unity participants similarly create Christian identities by telling and retelling the Unity story. This story is central to Unity evangelist techniques and, as I explained in the last section, part of everyday Unity talk. It is told in Bible studies and during individual mentoring. A seasoned participant always tells her or his conversion story in the weekly meetings. Similar stories pepper the organizational material (both weekly handouts and web materials). This repetition teaches new participants to use emotional change to think and talk about their own identities as Unity Christians.

Moreover, although Unity participants all tell stories of profound emotional transformation, it is difficult to assess these emotional changes. Unity conversion narratives are both retroactive and formulaic accounts. Just as participants learn to talk about good emotions, they also learn to refer to their pre-Christian lives in terms of bad emotions. Emotions take on meaning through the process of storytelling. In many accounts, what they describe as bad emotions seems to be the absence of the kind of emotional control they develop as Unity Christians. For example, we have heard Hannah explain that she was "cold" and that she "was not an emotional person" before becoming a Christian. Descriptions like hers indicate that, at least for some participants, Unity does not so much replace bad emotions with good ones, but increases emotional self-consciousness, which participants interpret, in turn, in terms of good feelings. Happiness, like other emotions, is not a universal category with unambiguous content. Here, happiness takes on meaning and social value in as much as it corresponds with other emotional expectations, including a cultural emphasis on emotional self-awareness and emotional control.

Unity stories of emotional change create and mark the boundary between their pre-Christian and their Christian selves. Emotion stories help them fashion identities as Unity Christians; at the same time, feelings that seem like happiness help participants experience their stories as real (Wolkomir 2001). In the next section, I show how Unity practices teach new participants to create, recognize, and value Unity emotions.

"Stepping from Feelings of Unworthiness to Forgiveness": Learning to Be Happy

In "Becoming a Marihuana User," Becker (1953) argues that the "high" that comes from smoking marihuana is not just pharmacological but learned. People become marihuana users through social interactions in which mentors teach them to get high by showing them how to use the drug properly, and to look for and appreciate particular effects of the drug. In the absence of successful learning, a person will not enjoy smoking marihuana and will not become a user.

Like Becker's marihuana users, Unity participants must learn to recognize and appreciate the good feelings—the "high"—that comes from the relationship with God. They must learn to enjoy Unity Christianity. Initially, the expectations of Unity participation may seem boring or meaningless, and may distract them from the things they used to do to have fun. For example, instead of partying, Unity participants go to Thursday night meetings. They hang out with Unity friends, playing board games or eating ice cream. They talk about God instead of sex or dating or who got drunk and did what. They read the Bible, write in journals, and pray instead of engaging in more raucous behavior with dorm friends. Unity Christians may describe becoming a Christian in terms of instantaneous emotional transformation, but many do not initially enjoy Christianity. They come to understand themselves as Christians, and to commit themselves to participation, as they learn to associate Unity participation with good emotions and learn to think of the emotional experiences associated with Unity as pleasant and desirable—as "'happiness.'"

In University Unity, ongoing lessons in Christian emotions accompany lessons in doctrine. In Unity, participants learn 1) that Christians have a "personal relationship with God"; 2) that this relationship needs "to be fed" and thus requires ongoing work, which includes daily introspection; 3) that such work will be rewarded with good feelings, including peace, joy, a feeling of being loved, and a sense of meaning, through "God's work in their hearts"; and 4) that said good feelings are a sign of authentic Christianity and of one's true self. Unity emotion work is imagined as the work of building a relationship with God.

Unity comes together regularly for Thursday night meetings, in which participants gather together in the campus center for two hours of "fellowship." For new participants, these meetings provide initial entrée into the Unity community, while seasoned participants attend meetings regularly and identify meetings (but not church) as essential to their Christian lives. Meetings provide both early and ongoing emotional learning for Unity members, molding their emotions by creating a feeling of happy community, modeling expected emotional performances, shaping the community's emotional vocabulary and linking it to the Christian identity, and, as discussed in the previous section, teaching newcomers to look for emotional transformation as the principal sign of authentic Christianity.

Weekly meetings are public and open: the meeting room and time is posted, like all other university-sponsored meetings, on a board just inside the campus center, as well as on the group's web site. Participants, dressed in casual college wear (jeans and sweatshirts) trickle into the room before, and just after, the meeting is scheduled to start, finding seats in the rows of fold-up chairs arranged to face the front of the room. Meetings follow a set format, which includes prayer, live music, and two kinds of talks: one in which a seasoned participant tells his or her conversion story and another in which the group leader, Chuck, who was hired by the national organization and is in his late twenties, gives a lesson. Chuck's lesson, like a sermon, connects Biblical interpretation to "real" life scenarios that engage the concerns of college students. Unity meetings are upbeat, combining what Aaron calls "happy music" with rituals of cheerful camaraderie and energetic, positive talks. Meeting rituals create "communitas"—a powerful feeling of social connection and belonging that transcends formal social boundaries (Turner 1974; see also Schwalbe 1996; Moon 2004), ties the shared mood to the Christian identity, and models the vocabulary and patterns of Unity emotion talk. Here I focus on singing and prayer, which are central, though not unique, to Thursday night meetings.

Meetings open and close with live music, typically acoustic guitars and singing, performed by Unity members—always the same two to three men. The lyrics are projected onto a large screen in the dimmed room, and participants sing along, standing and swaying in time to the music, often clapping with the rhythm, sometimes lifting one or both hands upward, as if toward God in heaven. The songs are familiar to most returning participants; even when the song is new, the tempo and lyrics are familiar. Tempos are upbeat, energizing, and fun. Song lyrics frame Unity emotional culture by attributing emotions like "love" and "joy" to the Christian identity. For example:

> Every song I sing brings me back to you and the joys of knowing you / It's all I need to get me through just one more day / Loving you, all I need, just loving you / It's all I want, it's all I really need, it's all I have, it's all I am / It's so good to be here / I do love to be here.

Songs such as this one reveal the continuity between secular romantic schemas and the ways in which Unity Christians imagine their relationships with God. This song is typical in its framing of Christian emotions. It attributes good feelings—e.g., "joys"—to the relationship with God ("loving God"), and ties these feelings to selfhood: e.g., "it's all I am."

Prayer provides another opportunity for both emotional framing and modeling. In the weekly meetings, the group leader, Chuck, prays after the opening music and announcements, and again after the closing songs. Chuck marks the beginning of the prayer by saying "Let us pray," and marks the ending with "In Jesus' name we pray" (at which point participants collectively say "amen"). During the prayer, participants are silent and bow their heads. Protestant prayer is often conceived of as extemporaneous ("talking to God"), and thus less constrained than the formalized prayers in traditions such as Catholicism. But Unity prayers adhere to their own ritualized format—one shared with many other Protestants. The supplicant, in this case, Chuck, thanks Jesus for the group, for bringing each person to the group, and for the feelings of peace, love, or joy the group has when they are together and when they are "in the presence of Jesus Christ." He makes specific prayer requests (most often that people in trying circumstances will feel emotions such as strength or a "tender heart"), and then he thanks Jesus for "his work in [our] hearts," and asks him to keep participants safe and "open to god's word." These prayers model both structure and content. When Unity participants pray at the meetings or at other events, such as Bible studies or meals, their prayers follow the formula Chuck uses. The familiarity of the prayer—its common language and sentiments, collective silence and shared amen, and specific reference to the group—further builds communitas among participants, serving as a ritualized reminder of a shared, and special, identity. By attributing good feelings to Christ, Unity prayers propose that the "relationship" with God alone brings enduring good feelings. As I discuss further below, prayers also model Unity emotion work.

Moon (2004:44) argues that communitas is a matter of "individuals' perceptions rather than . . . [an] actual collective experience." Accordingly, meeting participants may not initially experience the good feeling of communitas. Some participants recall finding meetings "weird" or "hokey" at first. Nonetheless, the singing and sense of camaraderie and purpose create a climate of emotional possibility—the expectation that meetings, and thus Christianity itself, will bring the promised good feelings.

It is not enough, however, for Unity Christians to feel good once a week in the company of other Christians. "Real Christians" must learn to transport the good mood generated in meeting into private space. Accordingly, Unity personnel and seasoned participants encourage members to "build their relationship with God" through daily prayer and journal writing, reading and contemplating the Bible, and talking to each other about God, the Bible, and their feelings. Christians cultivate good feelings in their private lives by practicing and mastering emotional control through these introspective techniques. Specifically, Unity methods teach participants to eradicate negative feelings by focusing on good thoughts, to attribute the resultant emotional control to Christ, and to think of emotional control as happiness.

Most participants recall that they had to be pushed to engage in introspection, suggesting that introspection does not yield good feelings as quickly as meetings do. Jillian, for example, explains that that she didn't "grow as a Christian" until Cara, one of the Unity paid staff, instructed her "to set time a part everyday to spend time with God or to study the Bible." Most Unity Christians were initially reluctant to devote time to introspection, but committed participants learned to not just appreciate but to need such practices. Indeed, as I show later, participants identify their successful mastery of introspective techniques with their acquisition of an authentically Christian self. Unity participants come to value the sensations achieved by slowing down and by refocusing their attention away from daily irritants and onto a loving God. For example, Hannah says, "God is a daily, constant presence. I try to take an hour each day to read the Bible and pray and write in a journal. If I don't take the time the day would get all frazzled when I interact with people." Much like yoga or breathing slowly, daily introspection forces Unity Christians to slow down, facilitating feelings like calmness and peace, and reducing unwanted emotions like anger and anxiety. Unity is just one among many middle-class subcultures that actively encourages emotional restraint via introspection, and describes such practices as the path to emotional well-being (e.g., yoga and meditation are part of "wellness" programs; Codependents Anonymous encourages similar emotion work and calls the resultant emotional control "serenity" (Irvine 1999)).

Unity Christians achieve emotional control by transferring attention from personal irritants, anxieties, or sadness, onto the blessings they believe have been bestowed by a loving God. Tom exemplified this practice when he described to me how there had been a time when he felt he "needed to explode," and how he had altered his emotions by refocusing his thoughts on God through reading and prayer. He says, "I was able to come back and think, why am I here, why am I with God?" Now, he forestalls bad feelings by sleeping with worship music on so that he can "wake up praising him."

As in Tom's story, Unity participants create the feelings they want by managing the ones they don't want. In contrast to the ventilation model of emotional management, which presumes that expressing negative emotions will lead to good feelings by dissipating bad ones, Unity emotion work generates desirable feelings by refocusing attention away from bad thoughts onto good thoughts. This approach is like the method of emotion management used in cognitive behavioral therapy, which advocates changing one's feelings by changing one's thoughts. The following guidelines for prayer, part of a longer set of written instructions for daily introspection distributed and discussed at a weekly meeting, elucidate this method:

> Pray: Spend time in prayer. The ACTS strategy for prayer is a good model to begin with. Adoration: Spend time praising the Lord by praying the Psalms back to Him (Psalm 28:7 and 100:4). Sing hymns, listening to a praise tape or praise Him for his attributes. Confession: Ask God to search your heart (Psalm 139:23,24). Confess any sins the Holy Spirit reveals to you (Psalm 66:18, I John 1:9). Make certain that you're filled with the Spirit (Ephesians 5: 15–20). Thanksgiving: Thank God for all that He's done and is doing in your life and the lives of others. Write a list of what you're thankful for. Supplication: Pray for specific things such as personal concerns, family, upcoming events, friends, missionaries, etc. Write down your requests so you'll have a record of God's guidance and faithfulness.

The ACTS method of prayer helps Christians generate positive feelings by encouraging them to imagine a loving (not a vengeful) God, recall the good things in their lives, and anticipate more good things. Although the method invites participants to ask God for help with specific concerns, it does not encourage the pouring out of personal sorrow. Because Unity Christians see God as loving and generous, the directive to "be filled with the Spirit" requires that they also adopt an attitude of well-being that we've heard participants describe as a feeling of being loved and having one's "yoke lightened."

Because they are small and personal, Bible studies—typically (but not always) same-gender groups that meet once a week to read and discuss the Bible according to nationally distributed lesson plans—are an ideal site for teaching the methods that lead to good emotions. Bible studies provide opportunities for more seasoned participants to guide new participants' emotion work. Although I was unable to observe this unit of Bible study, I include it here because its theme—"stepping from feelings of unworthiness to forgiveness"—demonstrates both the deliberateness of Unity's emotional agenda and the ways it is connected to a broader evangelical Christian emotional culture. The directions for the unit told the leader to use her own story to model the ways in which her relationship with God allowed her to transform her feelings of "unworthiness" into feelings of "forgiveness," and to redirect participants' talk about (bad) behavior by asking about feelings, and emphasizing God's role in changing (bad) feelings.

Church services provide opportunities to practice. For example, at one service, the organizers played a video in which a middle-aged white woman, whose young son had drowned in the family pool, spoke about her experience and its aftermath. As the woman spoke of her son's death, I found myself struggling to control my tears. Twice, the video stopped, and a band played a ballad about God's love. In between these interludes, the woman spoke of the grief, despair, and anger she felt before becoming a Christian. After the second musical interlude, she said, "I didn't have God to fall back on because I didn't have a relationship with him at the time. So I just got angry." Becoming a Christian brought her happiness; now, she said, she realizes that her son's death was God's way of bringing her to Christ. I was stunned by this claim, but I seemed to be the only one who was. When I asked others afterward about their reactions, they described her story as a powerful "testimony of God's love," a claim that confirmed their mastery of the Unity emotional repertoire.

This event taught participants the Christian way to interpret tragedy, but it also provided a concrete lesson in emotion management. During the presentation, I was not the only one on the verge of tears. The musical interludes provided an opportunity to transfer attention from sadness to the music, which gently reminded the audience of God's love, while the presentation's framing reminded the audience that love, peace, and happiness are Christian emotions.

In sum, then, Unity teaches participants to be happy by framing Unity emotions, by modeling Unity emotional techniques, and by providing direct instruction in introspective methods and collective opportunities to practice emotional control. These practices simultaneously teach participants techniques of emotional control, and teach them to attribute their good feelings to God and to their identities as Christians. Unity Christians learn not just to create emotional control but to think of emotional control as desirable by associating it with happiness, joy, forgiveness, and so forth. Just as learning to use marihuana correctly and interpret its effects as "getting high" makes one a marijuana user, so too does learning Unity emotional work and thinking of its effects as happiness make one a Unity Christian. In the next section, I will show how collective and individual emotional monitoring facilitates a cohesive Unity emotional culture.

"The Biggest Change Is in Getting to Know Who I Am": Accountability and Authenticity

In Unity, rituals of emotional sharing are built into Bible studies, mentoring relationships, and friendships. *Accountability*—the expectation that participants will tell each other when they are failing to live up to the Unity model—is a valued aspect of Unity relationships, at least among women. Catherine was raised Catholic but likes Unity's Protestant orientation better. She explains that in Unity, "there's a lot more to be happy and grateful about," and describes the importance of feedback from her Christian friends. Unity friends, she explains, will tell her what she really needs to hear instead of pacifying her. She views this monitoring as a sign that her Christian friends really "care about [her] as a person," unlike her non-Christians friends, who, she complains, will say anything just "to keep [her] friendship." Gretchen also appreciatively describes how monitoring by her Christian friends helped her shape her own emotions:

> I really learned how to love God everyday. Accountability is a really big thing. Having people tell you if you're doing something wrong or if you're hurting them. If you're lucky, they'll just tell you. This summer I was complaining a lot about my job and my roommate said, "you need to not complain so much," and I thought about it. She was right. It was a good summer.

By identifying her emotional display as inappropriate, Gretchen's roommate prompted Gretchen to adjust her emotions. For Gretchen, accountability pushes her to "love God everyday," to fulfill Unity emotional expectations, so she feels like a real Christian. Just as seasoned Christians encourage newer Unity participants to engage more frequently in introspection, so too does collective monitoring of their emotional expressions encourage them to more diligently manage their own emotions.

Sharing rituals may be deeply meaningful to participants, yet they are also a mandatory part of active participation in Unity Christianity. Expectations of sharing facilitate the transmission and enforcement of Unity emotional norms. Foucault (1978) argues that the confession is a form of contemporary discipline. Talk seems freeing, but by opening our inner lives to public scrutiny, it allows others to define, label, and control our experiences. Harris (2004) contends that the "incitement to talk," premised on feminist notions of giving "voice" to women, has become an especially powerful means of controlling contemporary women, young and old. In Unity, gendered rituals of sharing provide opportunities both to prove that one has successfully mastered the Unity emotional repertoire and for other Christians to assess and shape Unity participants', especially women's, emotional responses.

Participants value accountability because it pushes them to change their internal responses. It is not enough to perform Christian emotions: Unity Christians must also experience them as authentic. They engage in what Hochschild (1983: 36) describes as "deep acting"—they learn to "creat[e] the inner shape of a feeling." Perhaps more importantly, then, Unity participants hold themselves accountable for the right emotions, engaging in what Irvine (2000:24) describes as "impression management *directed at oneself*." For example, Hannah told me a powerful story about a car accident that reveals both the way Unity Christians use Unity emotional practices in their daily lives and the importance of relentless emotional management to participants' self-perceptions. She recalls:

> I was in a car accident. I'm alone in a bad situation. I remember my dad saying, "If you're ever in a bad situation, just call on Jesus." I thought, what do I have to lose? Jesus was there immediately, offering words of comfort, keeping me warm. My eyes were shut from blood. It was one of the sweetest days of my life. It should have been traumatic but it was just Him.

By applying the Unity techniques described in the previous section, which Hannah describes as "calling on Jesus," she engendered an unusual degree of emotional control in a situation in which most people would be afraid or angry. Hannah's ability to control her more difficult emotions and to generate more desirable feelings helped her get through a bad situation, but it also made her feel good about herself, as it confirmed her Christian identity. Hannah told me this story to illustrate both her own—and Christians' more generally—distinctive emotional control, but it was also important to *her* that she was able to achieve good feelings. To Hannah, this story is evidence of her authentic Christianity. Outsiders who read this story, however, often find her feelings disturbing; in a context in which we continue to value some vestiges of the "unmanaged heart" (Hochschild 1983), to many people, Hannah's response is a sign of emotional inauthenticity, not emotional authenticity. Even if we bracket the question of emotional authenticity, Hannah's story reveals the relentlessness of Unity emotional expectations and the central role of self-monitoring in their production.

As they become more practiced in introspection, Unity Christians are able to produce emotional control, to "call on Jesus" across settings, as Hannah's story shows. The ideal Unity Christian is one who is continuously introspective, as in Jillian's admiring description of her friend: "I saw how everything she did was for God and about God. She was looking to God in every situation." Hannah also explains that for Christians, prayer should be "like breathing"—constant and life-giving.

Continuous introspection shapes Unity feelings both because it manages their emotions and because engaging in it helps them see themselves as real Christians. In many ways, these processes are inseparable to the Christian herself. In Unity, self-monitoring is essential to the construction of an authentic Christian self because the right emotions are a sign that one is both authentically Christian and an authentic person. Good feelings thus measure Unity participants' successful acquisition of a Unity Christian identity. Accordingly, Unity participants describe themselves as *real* Christians only after they feel the right emotions. Gretchen explains that when she first began to explore Christianity, she was still having a "lousy time. . . . I had a hard time staying in the Scripture. I hadn't made God a priority. I read the Scripture about once a week, if things were going wrong." Once she engaged in regular introspection, she was able to think about herself as *really* Christian. She reports, "I liked my life a lot more. I thank God because God was showing me that my life had meaning."

Unity stories portray the quest for Christianity as a quest for self. Carolyn explains that she came to University intent on "figur[ing] out who [she] was" and that she "[found] herself" in Unity. Describing Unity as a "really calming presence," she adds: "I'm a lot more focused now." Like other Unity Christians, Aaron ties emotion talk to self talk. After describing his changed emotions (discussed earlier), he summarizes: "I'm a lot more self-aware now. The biggest change is in getting to know who I am, who I was, and about who God wants me to be." The connections Unity participants draw between emotions, Christian identities, and authenticity are similar to those in other groups in which people learn to change their emotions and then identify their new, properly adjusted emotions with their "real" selves (Irvine 1999; Wolkomir 2001). For Unity Christians, as for many of their contemporaries, "good" emotions are a sign that they have found their real selves. At the same time, because Unity members see "good" emotions as coming from Jesus—as "Jesus' work in their hearts"—, such feelings prove one's authentic Christianity.

If a Christian is happy because Jesus has worked in her heart and given her access to her true self, then the absence of happiness indicates either that she has not sufficiently put her faith in Christ *or* that her true self is not really Christian. Thus, the admission of bad emotions threatens the authenticity of one's identity—not just to others but to oneself too. In other words, one cannot be a real Christian and *not* be happy. Moreover, because of the link between Christianity and one's real self, one's own sense of authenticity is also potentially threatened by a failure to maintain the requisite emotions. For Unity Christians, then, good feelings are not just an outcome of being in a supportive community but a prerequisite for ongoing community participation. But one's self-perception as a real Christian is also contingent on feeling happy. Because Unity Christians believe that a person is authentically Christian if she is happy, and that a person is happy if he is authentically Christian, for the Unity Christian, happiness is compulsory.

"I Have a Reason for Everything I Do": Unity Happiness, Moral Selves, and Symbolic Boundaries

Unity's emotion culture creates boundaries around Christian identities, around appropriate emotions, and between Christians and non-Christians. For Unity Christians, happiness is an index of both authentic Christianity and moral goodness. First, in Unity transformation stories, happiness divides pre-Christian selves from Christian selves. Second, Unity emotion work excludes negative emotions, including anger and anxiety. Third, the rules of Unity happiness talk create social boundaries between Unity participants and outsiders, with whom participants come to feel they cannot share their excitement about Jesus, and whose failure to engage in Unity rituals of accountability leads them to be seen as inauthentic friends.

Participants claim that their happiness makes them different from other people. For example, when I asked Kevin to tell me what it means to be a Christian, he said succinctly, "A lot of the Christians I know seem happier than a lot of the non-Christians I know." Later, I specifically asked him if he thinks Christians are different from non-Christians, and he talked about emotions again: "I think it depends. I think there's a lot of non-Christians who I see myself as being like. But I know people who get really depressed, really upset if something little happens. That's not what I'm like really." The video presentation, discussed earlier, about the experiences of the woman whose son had drowned drew a similar boundary by identifying despair and anger as the emotions of non-Christians. Hannah's proud story about her cool response to her car accident further shows the ways in which Unity Christians employ these distinctions to think and talk about themselves.

I witnessed another, powerful example of the ways in which Unity Christians use emotions to draw lines around Protestant evangelicals at a Unity meeting in which student leaders presented a short video clip, prepared by the national organization, on a spring break trip to Mexico. Such trips, which are sponsored by the national organization and bring together evangelical college students from across the nation to go to popular spring break destinations with the purpose of evangelizing to the locals, are popular among Unity Christians. The clip juxtaposed images of desperately poor and homeless Mexicans with shots of (middle-class) Unity Christians. The commentary, surprisingly to me, did not mention living conditions but instead emphasized the "sadness" and "despair" of the Mexicans, who were presumably Catholic and thus not "Christian" according to Unity definitions. This example again shows the importance of emotions to Unity constructions of symbolic boundaries.

Unity talk distinguishes authentic happiness from inauthentic happiness. For example, an organizational webpage designed for potential and new Christians features a list of "frequently asked questions," including: "Why do I need God to be happy?" The site explains:

> You're right, you can find happiness in life without having need of God in your life. Many people enjoy financial wealth, a loving family, and few problems in life. However, no matter how much happiness you have right now, your life would be more fulfilling with God in it. Knowing God makes a HUGE difference. Think of it like this. Riding a tricycle seems fun to a child, but later if that child grows up and drives a Porsche, the tricycle seems pretty boring. You might think you've got all you'd ever want in life, but know that you might be saying that from the perspective of someone riding a tricycle.

Other things may provide what seems like happiness, the site claims, but the happiness that comes from being a Christian is *real*. By describing Christianity as bringing them "true happiness," Unity Christians also employ this distinction. In a sermon at one of the churches participants attend, the pastor's high-octane sermon, intended for a primarily young adult audience, similarly reminded congregants: "I'll tell you when you believed. When God shined his light in your heart. You can't shine the light yourself. You need God to do it." In this model, God is the only source of the truly good feelings that come with having "light in one's heart"; only authentic Christians can feel truly good.

It is not just that Unity Christians are happier, however. It is also that their good feelings confirm their good selves. Here, the conventional link between feelings and conceptions of a true self is again useful. If feelings are a sign of the self, then good feelings are a sign of a good self. Just as guilt and shame alert people to their violation of cultural rules (Turner and Stets 2006), so does happiness tell people that they are complying with cultural expectations, and that they are therefore "good people." As Irvine (1999:122) notes, "A person who believes that he or she possesses a naturally good, 'inner' self would also believe that such a self would tend toward happiness and stability, or serenity."

For Unity Christians, emotional display also verifies others' goodness. For example, when I first met Carolyn, who sees herself as a less-committed Christian than other Unity participants, she told me she wished I could meet Susan, Molly, and Jillian, who she describes as the kind of Christian she hopes to someday be. She explains, "[They have a] warm aura. My friend [Molly] has such a respect for the world. The way I see them they have a lot of things going for them and they're not cocky about it. They're just good people.... They're not spiteful." The notion that someone is a "good person," rather than an ordinary person who does good things, implies an essential moral self that shapes outward behavior. Katz (1975:1370) argues that "persons conceive of essences as personal qualities which exist independently of, and cannot be verified in, observed conduct.... [P]ersons give moral significance to the essences they impute." For Carolyn, "warm auras"—displays of good feelings—express the goodness of her Christian friends. Lucas' comment ... that Christians "shine," similarly suggests an inner goodness that radiates out and impacts other people (Wilkins 2008).

Thus, emotional display signals a person's inner goodness, but in the Unity model, good emotions also lead to desirable socioemotional styles, especially for women (Ridgeway and Johnson 1990; Rudman and Glick 2001). Happy people, they imply, are nice, warm, and generous to others. For example, Hannah links warmth to morality—or more precisely, links coldness to immorality. She says, "Before I was a Christian, I used to look at people how I could use them, a really cold way to be. I really didn't want to be that kind of person. I wanted to love them the way [Jesus] did." Hannah's claim that becoming a "warm" person made her a better person by helping her treat people better is like those made by other Unity Christians. Susan explains, "I have a responsibility to live my life in the way that represents Christ: to love people.... "

Unity members use these links between good feelings, "nice" sociorelational styles, and caring behavior to think of themselves as "good people," but Unity participants also credit their emotions with creating other kinds of moral behavior. For example, in answer to the same question I had posed to Kevin (about how Christians might be different from non-Christians), Jillian replied:

> That's a hard question. I think it [Christianity] gives a definite sense of meaning to why you're here. I think that's something people struggle with but I don't feel it so much. I think the big thing is like whereas everyone has like morals that they abide by, with Christians there's this strong sense of connection to God that keeps them from like lying.... I know for me, my conscience works over time and I think that's why.

When I asked Susan what it means to her to be a Christian, she gave a similar explanation:

> It means, I have a center—kinda—I have a reason for everything I do. I realized that was the It. God was definitely the It. [I'm not] just flailing around looking for the combination of things that will make me happy. It's given me the strength to make decisions that I'll wish I made—because I never had any idea that a relationship with God was possible before—or the depth of peace and love.

In these and other accounts, the good feelings that come from their relationships with God affect their behavior, prompting them to make the "right" choices.

Good choices about behavior also lead to good feelings. For example, Unity Christians explain that they are abstinent because non-marital sex might lead to bad feelings. Aaron says: "Sex isn't wrong but God designed it for something. It's so intimate that to do it without that strong commitment that marriage brings could just be hurtful for both people." Just as nonmarital sex can lead to bad feelings, waiting until marriage to have sex, they expect, will bring more joy and passion. Gretchen uses the same logic to explain why she no longer drinks; drinking, she explains, makes people feel bad about themselves. Importantly, Unity claims assume that bad feelings are a universal outcome of the behaviors from which they abstain. In this logic, the desire for good feelings motivate, explain, and naturalize other moral choices. These choices, in turn, allow Unity Christians to think of themselves as strong, grounded, purposeful, and self-controlled (see also Wilkins 2008).

It is important to Unity Christians that they forgo behaviors that are common for other college students (such as drinking and sex), yet they avoid condemning other students for their behavior as they do not want to appear intolerant of non-Christians. Emotion talk provides a way to talk about the morality of Unity behavior that does not seem either intolerant or political. In her study of two Protestant congregations, Moon (2004:204) found that, "Languages of emotions appealed to members precisely at the moments when they wished to stay out of political-seeming debates and controversies." Paired with claims of tolerance, Unity happiness works similarly, allowing Unity Christians to think of themselves as different without invoking the charged cultural politics associated with the Christian Right.

In sum, Unity Christians think of themselves as different because they are happy, and they think of their happiness as different from other claims to happiness. Happiness signifies their authentic relationship with God and their moral goodness. Happiness leads them to engage in more morally desirable behaviors—to treat others with warmth and love, and to be purposeful and responsible about their choices. Their relentless exclusion of bad emotions leads them to avoid behaviors common among their peers because they fear such behaviors will make them feel bad. Although Unity's emotional culture creates inclusion among participants, then, it also depends on multiple exclusions: the exclusion of emotions like anger and anxiety, the exclusion of people who do not share their emotional repertoire, the exclusion of behaviors that might create bad feelings, and so forth.

Unity Christians use happiness to create symbolic boundaries in two ways: first, for them, happiness itself distinguishes them from other people. Second, through its links to morality, happiness talk provides materials for the crafting of more complex boundaries. Together, these boundaries bolster the rightness of Unity Christianity, in as much as it is the only path to authentic happiness. Unity Christianity is a desirable choice; and because happiness leads Unity Christians to be good people, it is also a desirable choice.

Conclusions

Despite increasing sociological attention to the social construction of emotions, happiness is often treated as if it is a real emotion that can be measured, as in Diener's life-satisfaction scale. In this paper, I have used the case of Unity Christians to demonstrate the ways in which happiness is constructed and given meaning through social interactions. The association between religion and mental health found in other studies may arise from the emotional expectations of religious subcultures, as much as from the other social effects of religious participation. The example of Unity Christians also urges caution in our quest for happiness.

Unity participants describe Unity's emotional culture as desirable (and, remember, it is those participants who learn to find it desirable that become committed), but its benefits come with a price. First, it is compulsory. Because one's identity as a Unity Christian is predicated on being happy, one cannot sustain committed membership without the requisite emotions. Second, Unity happiness is attained through intense emotional control in which participants work relentlessly to manage their emotions into happiness. Unity emotional expectations shut off outlets for the exploration of alternative emotions. This applies even, as we saw with Hannah's car accident, in situations that many would consider traumatic. Third, because Unity emotions signify their moral selves, "happiness" casts a wide emotional net; participants are expected to love and care for others, to exercise self-control, and to make specific choices about behaviors. These expectations create an all-or-nothing emotional culture in which participants who cannot meet group expectations all the time may question both their authenticity and their "goodness," and reap fewer of the social rewards of Unity Christianity. Finally, although the culture of happiness applies to both men and women, there is some evidence that the expectations for women are more stringent and all-encompassing. . . .

As I have shown, Unity expectations teach participants to be content with what they have, and to shut down outlets for questioning the conditions of one's life and for discussing feelings or experiences that don't correspond with Unity social values. Part of what Unity participants learn to do is to apply the label "happiness" to the existing conditions of their lives, as with Gretchen's emotional adjustment about her summer job. . . . [H]appiness talk is a way to counter cultural discourses about the oppression or difficulties associated with traditional feminine roles. In other words, in as much as happiness proves the desirability of a lifestyle, it may be used defensively against charges that a lifestyle is unenlightened or bad for women. In these ways, the uncritical acceptance of happiness as a social good—in combination with its naturalization—may lead people to exclude or diminish social ideals like gender equality, and probably other values as well.

. . . [T]he notion that happiness itself is more desirable than other emotional states accentuates its use as a symbolic boundary. As I have argued, Unity participants use happiness itself to construct a boundary—Unity participants see themselves as happier (and more authentically so) than others—but also use it as material in the crafting of more complex moral boundaries in which happiness is both sign and cause of other kinds of "goodness." Happiness is an effective boundary not just because Unity Christians themselves want to be happy, but because most members of the middle class want to be happy, and because it builds on broader associations between happiness and morality. . . .

References

Becker, Howard. 1953. "Becoming a Marihuana User." *American Journal of Sociology* 59(5):235–42.

Blee, Kathleen. 1996. "Becoming a Racist: Women in Contemporary Ku Klux Klan and Neo-Nazi Groups." *Gender and Society* 10(6):680–702.

Cain, Carole. 1991. "Personal Stories: Identity Acquisition and Self-Understanding in Alcoholics Anonymous." *Ethos* 19(2):210–53.

Fine, Gary Alan. 1979. "Small Groups and Culture Creation: The Idioculture of Little League Baseball Teams." *American Sociological Review* 44(5): 733–45.

Foucault, Michel. 1978. *The History of Sexuality, Volume 1: An Introduction.* New York: Pantheon Books.

Harris, Anita. 2004. *Future Girl: Young Women in the Twenty-first Century.* New York: Routledge.

Hochschild, Arlie Russell. 1979. "Emotion Work, Feeling Rules, and Social Structure." *American Journal of Sociology* 85:551–75.

———. 1983.*The Managed Heart: Commercialization of Human Feeling.* Berkeley, CA: University of California Press.

Irvine, Leslie. 1999. *Codependent Forevermore: The Invention of Self in a Twelve Step Group.* Chicago, IL: University of Chicago Press.

———. 2000. "Even Better Than the Real Thing: Narratives of the Self in Codependency." *Qualitative Sociology* 23(1):9–28.

Katz, Jack. 1975. "Essences as Moral Identities: Verifiability and Responsibility in Imputations of Deviance and Charisma." *The American Journal of Sociology* 80(6):1369–1390.

Koenig, Harold G. and David B. Larson. 2001. "Religion and Mental Health: Evidence for an Association." *International Review of Psychiatry* 13:67–78._

Mason-Schrock, Doug. 1996. "Transsexuals' Narrative Construction of the 'True Self.'" *Social Psychology Quarterly* 59(3): 176–92.

Moon, Dawne. 2004. *God, Sex, and Politics: Homosexuality and Everyday Theologies.* Chicago, IL: University of Chicago Press.

Ridgeway, Cecilia and Cathryn Johnson. 1990. "What Is the Relationship Between Socioemotional Behavior and Status in Task Groups?" *American Journal of Sociology* 95(5): 1189–1212.

Rudman, Laurie A. and Peter Glick. 2001. "Prescriptive Gender Stereotypes and Backlash Toward Agentic Women." *Journal of Social Issues* 57(4):743–62.

Schwalbe, Michael. 1996. *Unlocking the Iron Cage: The Men's Movement, Gender Politics, and American Culture.* New York: Oxford University Press.

Stearns, Peter. 1994. *American Cool: Constructing a Twentieth-Century Emotional Style.* New York: New York University Press.

Turner, Jonathon H. and Jan E. Stets. 2006. "Moral Emotions" in *Handbook of the Sociology of Emotions*, edited by Jan E. Stets and Jonathan H. Turner. New York: Springer: 544–66.

Turner, Victor. 1974. *Dramas, Fields, and Metaphors: Symbolic Action in Human Society.* Ithaca, NY: Cornell University Press.

Wilkins, Amy C. 2008. *Wannabes, Goths, and Christians: The Boundaries of Sex, Style, and Status.* Chicago, IL: University of Chicago Press.

Wolkomir, Michelle. 2001. "Emotion Work, Commitment, and the Authentication of the Self: The Case of Gay and Ex-Gay Support Groups." *Journal of Contemporary Ethnography* 30(3):305–34.

Reflective Questions

1. What separates Christians from non-Christians at the university? What is emotion work within Unity Christianity like? How do other Unity Christianity members enforce emotion work? How is an "authentic Christian" supposed to feel?
2. If conversion stories are not actual historical accountings of people's transformation into a Christian, what are they? How do conversions shape their understanding of their own past? Where do they learn the formulaic narratives for conversion stories?
3. Where do Unity Christians learn to be happy from? How do they foster happiness? How do they interpret tragedy? What role does morality play in the students' claims to happiness?
4. Wilkins argues that Unity Christianity practices creating an emotional culture of happiness. What other groups foster an emotional culture? What emotions? How do they do it? Consider, for example, addiction recovery groups, white supremacist groups, or pro-anorexia groups. If participating in a culture of happiness allows middle-class Americans to claim moral superiority, what sort of identity or morality claims can people in these other groups make using these other emotions?
5. Watch Frontline's "A Class Divided" at http://www.pbs.org/wgbh/pages/frontline/shows/divided/. How did the teacher get children to divide into blue eyes and brown eyes? What social resources

did she use to reinforce the boundary? That is, what advantages did the children in the privileged group get? How did the teacher use her authority to reinforce the boundary? Did children participate in making the boundaries themselves? How so? Why? Did children resist the eye-color divide? What did they do? How did others try to overcome their resistance? What socially valued characteristics became associated with the dominant group?

31

Managing Emotions in an Animal Shelter

ARNOLD ARLUKE

Social structures endure because one generation transmits to the next the symbols, classification systems, meanings, and rules that structure action, interaction, and social life. Each subsequent generation consequently engages in recurrent patterns of action and interaction that reproduce those social structures. They seldom perfectly replicate social structures, but alter them in various ways that sometimes lead to profound restructuring over time. Even such imperfect replication of social structures is not guaranteed but subject to what Herbert Blumer called "the play and fate of meaning." Yet, social structures are more or less enduring thanks to processes of socialization.

This selection examines how emotional socialization promotes the reproduction of social structure, in this case a specific social institution. It concerns a Humane Society shelter where euthanasia of animals was and is routine. As Arluke observes, people in Western societies have inconsistent and often conflicting attitudes toward animals. On the one hand, we believe that at least some sentient creatures deserve affection and care. On the other hand, we regard others, even of the same species, as utilitarian objects to be used as we see fit. Arluke shows how such conflicting meanings caused new workers at the shelter emotional difficulties. The kinds of animals they had previously learned to love, care for, and protect were being routinely killed, often with their involvement. In turn, the workers learned emotion management and interpretive strategies that relieved their emotional discomfort and convinced them of the nobility of their gruesome tasks. This socialization process produced a new generation of workers who would reproduce the social institution of the animal "kill shelter."

We may be more similar to these kill shelter workers than we might first recognize. Our work often requires us to do things that we find morally troubling and emotionally disturbing. However, we usually learn ways of excusing what we do that calm our emotions. Like the "kill shelter" workers, we learn how to live with all the little murders that we commit as part of our jobs, convincing ourselves that they are necessary and perhaps even noble. The reproduction of social structures requires sacrifices, and most of us learn to make them with hardly a thought and only a twinge of emotion.

From the sociologist's perspective, what is most interesting in the study of conflicts in the contemporary treatment of animals is not to point out that such conflicts exist or to debate the assumptions that underlie them—a task more ably served by philosophers—but to better understand what it is about modern society that makes it possible to shower animals with affection as sentient creatures while simultaneously maltreating or killing them as

Reprinted from: Arnold Arluke, "Managing Emotions in an Animal Shelter," in Aubrey Manning and James Serpell (eds.), *Animals and Human Society*, pp. 145–165.

utilitarian objects. How is it that a conflict that should require a very difficult balancing of significant values has become something that many people live with comfortably? Indeed, they may not even be aware that others may perceive their actions as inconsistent. How is it that instead of questioning the propriety of their conflicts, many don ethical blindfolds?

As with any cultural contradiction, these attitudes are built into the normative order, itself perpetuated by institutions that provide ways out of contradictions by supplying myths to bridge them and techniques to assuage troubled feelings. . . .

Humane and scientific institutions, for example, must teach newcomers in shelters and laboratories to suspend their prior, ordinary or commonsense thinking about the use and meaning of animals and adopt a different set of assumptions that may be inconsistent with these prior views. The assumptions are not themselves proved but rather structure and form the field upon which the activity plays out its life. Typically, these assumptions are transmitted to nascent practitioners of a discipline, along with relevant empirical facts and skills, as indisputable truths, not as debatable assumptions. They must come to accept the premise of the institution—often that it is necessary to kill animals—and get on with the business of the institution. But exactly how do they get on with this business?

In addition to learning to think differently about the proper fate of animals in institutions, workers must also learn to feel differently about them in that situation. Uncomfortable feelings may be experienced by newcomers even if the premise of the institution is accepted at an intellectual level. Although institutions will, no doubt, equip newcomers with rules and resources for managing unwanted emotions, researchers have not examined how such emotion management strategies actually work and the extent to which they eliminate uncomfortable feelings. In the absence of such research, it is generally assumed that newcomers learn ways to distance themselves from their acts and lessen their guilt. These devices are thought to prevent any attachment to and empathy for animals (Schleifer 1985) and to make killing "a reflex, virtually devoid of emotional content" (Serpell 1986:152).

To examine these assumptions, I conducted ethnographic research over a seven-month period in a "kill-shelter" serving a major metropolitan area. Such a case study seemed warranted, given the sensitivity of the topic under study. I became immersed in this site, spending approximately 75 hours in direct observation of all facets of shelter work and life, including euthanasia of animals and the training of workers to do it. Also, interviews were conducted with the entire staff of sixteen people, many formally and at length on tape, about euthanasia and related aspects of shelter work. . . .

The Newcomer's Problem

Euthanasia posed a substantial emotional challenge to most novice shelter workers. People seeking work at the shelter typically regarded themselves as "animal people" or "animal lovers" and recounted lifelong histories of keeping pets, collecting animals, nursing strays, and working in zoos, pet stores, veterinarian practices, and even animal research laboratories. They came wanting to "work with animals" and expecting to spend much of their time having hands-on contact with animals in a setting where others shared the same high priority they placed on human-animal interaction. The prospect of having to kill animals seemed incompatible with this self-conception.

When first applying for their jobs, some shelter workers did not even know that euthanasia was carried out at the shelter. To address this possible misconception, applicants were asked how they would feel when it was their turn to euthanize. Most reported that they did not really think through this question at this time, simply replying that they thought it was "Okay" in order to get the job. One worker, for instance, said she "just put this thought out of [her] mind," while another worker said that she had hoped to "sleaze out" of (or avoid) doing it. Many said that having to do euthanasia did not fully sink in until they "looked the animal in its eyes." Clearly, newcomers were emotionally unprepared to actually kill animals.

Once on the job, newcomers quickly formed strong attachments to particular animals. In fact, it was customary to caution newcomers against adopting animals right away. Several factors encouraged these attachments. At first, workers found themselves relating to shelter animals as though they were their own pets because many of the animals were healthy and appealing to workers, and since most of the animals had been pets, they sometimes initiated interaction with the workers. Newcomers also saw more senior people interacting with animals in a pet-like fashion. Shelter animals, for example, were all named, and everyone used these names when referring to the animals. While newcomers followed suit, they did not realize that more experienced workers could interact in this way with animals and not become attached to them. Moreover, newcomers found that their work required them to know the individual personalities of shelter animals in order to make the best decisions regarding euthanasia and adoption, but this knowledge easily fostered attachments. Not surprisingly, the prospect of having to kill animals with whom they had become attached was a major concern for newcomers. This anticipated relationship with shelter animals made newcomers agonize when they imagined selecting animals for euthanasia and seeing "trusting looks" in the faces of those killed. They also worried about having to cope with the "losses" they expected to feel from killing these animals.

Further aggravating the novices' trepidation was the fact that they had to kill animals for no higher purpose. Many felt grieved and frustrated by what they saw as the "senseless" killing of healthy animals. Several newcomers flinched at the shelter's willingness to kill animals if suitable homes were not found instead of "fostering out" the animals. In their opinion, putting animals in less than "ideal" homes for a few years was better than death.

The clash between the feelings of newcomers for shelter animals and the institution's practice of euthanasia led newcomers to experience a caring-killing "paradox." On the one hand, they tried to understand and embrace the institutional rationale for euthanasia, but on the other hand, they wanted to nurture and tend to shelter animals. Doing both seemed impossible to many newcomers. Acceptance of the need to euthanize did not remove the apprehension that workers felt about having to kill animals themselves or to be part of this process. Their everyday selves were still paramount and made them feel for shelter animals as they might toward their own pets—the thought of killing them was troubling. They even feared getting to the point where they would no longer be upset killing animals, commonly asking those more senior, "Do you still care?" or "Doesn't it still bother you?" Experienced shelter workers acknowledged the "paradox" of newcomers, telling and reassuring them that:

> There is a terrible paradox in what you will have to do—you want to care for animals, but will have to kill some of them. It is a painful process of killing animals when you don't want to. It seems so bad, but we'll make it good in your head. You will find yourself in a complex emotional state. Euthanizing is not just technical skills. You have to believe it is right to make it matter of fact.

Emotion Management Strategies

How did shelter workers manage their uncomfortable feelings? Workers learned different emotion management strategies to distance themselves enough to kill, but not so much as to abandon a sense of themselves as animal people. These strategies enabled workers at least to hold in abeyance their prior, everyday sensibilities regarding animals and to apply a different emotional perspective while in the shelter.

Transforming Shelter Animals into Virtual Pets

New workers often had trouble distinguishing between shelter animals and their own pets. Failure to make this distinction could result in emotionally jarring situations, especially when animals were euthanized. However, they soon came to see shelter animals as virtual pets—liminal animals lying somewhere between the two categories of pet and object. In such a liminal status workers could maintain a safe distance from animals while not entirely detaching themselves from them.

One way they accomplished this transformation was to lessen the intensity of their emotional attachments to individual animals. Almost as a rite of passage, newcomers were emotionally scarred by the euthanasia of a favorite animal, leaving them distraught over the loss. They also heard cautionary tales about workers who were very upset by the loss of animals with whom they had grown "too close" as well as workers whose "excessive" or "crazy" attachments resulted in harm to animals—such as the person who was fired after she released all the dogs from the shelter because she could no longer stand to see them caged or put to death. Newcomers soon began consciously to restrict the depth of their attachments. As one worker observed: "I don't let myself get that attached to them."

On the other hand, certain mottoes or ideals were part of the shelter culture, and these underscored the importance of not becoming detached from their charges or becoming desensitized to euthanasia. One worker, for instance, told me that you "learn to turn your feelings off when you do this work, but you can't completely. They say if you can, you shouldn't be on the job." Another worker noted: "If you get to the point where killing doesn't bother you, then you shouldn't be working here."

While they stopped themselves from "loving" individual shelter animals, because of their likely fate, workers learned that they could become more safely attached by maintaining a generalized caring feeling for shelter animals as a group. As workers became more seasoned, individual bonding became less frequent, interest in adopting subsided, and a sense emerged of corporate attachment to shelter animals as a population of refugees rather than as individual pets.

Workers also came to see shelter animals differently from everyday pets by assuming professional roles with their charges. One role was that of "caretaker" rather than pet owner. As a worker noted: "You don't set yourself up by seeing them as pets. You'd kill yourself; I'd cut my wrists. I'm a caretaker, so I make them feel better while they are here. They won't be forgotten so quickly. I feel I get to know them. I'm their last hope." Comparing her own pet to shelter animals, another worker noted: "No bell goes off in your head with your own pet as it would with a shelter animal, where the bell says you can't love this animal because you have to euthanize it." If not caretakers, they could become social workers trying to place these animals in homes of other people.

New workers came to view their charges as having a type of market value within the larger population of shelter animals. Their value was not to be personal and individual from the worker's perspective. Rather, they were to be assessed in the light of their competitive attractiveness to potential adopters. This view was nowhere more apparent than in the selection of healthy and well behaved animals to be euthanized in order to make room for incoming animals. An experienced shelter worker described these "tough choices" and the difficulty newcomers had in viewing animals this way:

> When you go through and pull [i.e., remove an animal for euthanasia]—that's when you have to make some real tough choices. If they've all been here an equal amount of time, then if you've got eighteen cages and six are filled with black cats, and you have a variety in here waiting for cages, you're going to pull the black ones so you can have more of a variety. It's hard for a new employee to understand that I'm going to pull a black cat to make room for a white one. After they've been here through a cat season, they know exactly what I'm doing, and you don't have to say anything when you have old staff around you.

In addition, newcomers learned to think differently when spending money for the medical care of shelter animals than they would when spending on their own pets. Although an occasional animal might receive some medical attention, many animals were killed because it was not considered economically feasible to treat them even though they had reversible problems and the cost might be insubstantial. For example, while two newcomers observed the euthanizing of several kittens, an experienced worker pointed to a viral infection in their mouths as the reason behind their deaths. One newcomer asked why the kittens could not be treated medically so they could be put up for adoption. The reply was that the virus could be treated, but "given the volume, it is not economical to treat them."

Keeping shelter mascots further helped workers separate everyday pets from their charges, with mascots serving as surrogate pets in contrast to the rest of the shelter's animals. Cats and dogs were occasionally singled out to become the group mascots, the former because workers took a special interest in them, the latter because workers hoped to increase their adoptability. Unlike other shelter animals, mascots were permitted to run free in areas reserved for workers, such as their private office and front desk, where they were played with and talked about by workers. Importantly, they were never euthanized, either remaining indefinitely in the shelter or going home as someone's pet. Although most shelter workers interacted with the mascots as though they were pets, one shelter worker, akin to an owner, often took a special interest in the animal and let it be known that she would eventually adopt the animal if a good home could not be found. Some of their actions toward these mascots were in clear contrast to the way they would have acted toward regular shelter animals. In one case, for example, a cat mascot was found to have a stomach ailment requiring expensive surgery. In normal circumstances this animal would have been killed, but one of the workers used her own money to pay for the operation.

Using the Animal

By taking the feelings of animals into account, workers distracted themselves from their own discomfort when euthanizing. Workers tried to make this experience as "good" as possible for the animals and, in so doing, felt better themselves. Some workers, in fact, openly admitted that "it makes me feel better making it [euthanasia] better for the animal." Even more seasoned workers were more at ease with euthanasia if they focused on making animals feel secure and calm as they were killed. A worker with twenty years' experience remarked that "it still bothers you after you're here for a long time, but not as much. Compassion and tenderness are there when I euthanize, so it doesn't eat away at me."

One way workers did this was to empathize with animals in order to figure out how to reduce each animal's stress during euthanasia. By seeing things from the animals' perspective, workers sought to make the process of dying "peaceful and easy." As a worker pointed out: "You make the animal comfortable and happy and secure, so when the time to euthanize comes, it will not be under stress and scared—the dog will lick your face, the cats will purr." In the words of another worker: "They get more love in the last few seconds than they ever did." Workers were encouraged to "think of all the little things that might stress the animal—if you sense that some are afraid of men, then keep men away." For example, one worker said that she decided not to have cats and dogs in the euthanasia room at the same time. Observation of euthanasia confirmed that workers considered animals' states of mind. In one instance, where a cat and her kittens had to be euthanized, the mother was killed first because the worker thought she would become very upset if she sensed her kittens were dying. And in another case a worker refused to be interviewed during euthanasia because she felt that our talking made the animals more anxious.

Another way that taking animals into consideration helped workers distract themselves from their own concerns was to concentrate on the methodology of killing and to become technically proficient at it. By focusing on the technique of killing—and not on why it needed to be done or how they felt about doing it—workers could reassure themselves that they were making death quick and painless for animals. Workers, called "shooters," who injected the euthanasia drug were told to "focus not on the euthanasia, but on the needle. Concentrate on technical skills if you are the shooter." Even those people, known as "holders," who merely held animals steady during the injection, were taught to view their participation as a technical act as opposed to a demonstration of affection. In the words of a worker:

> The holder is the one who controls the dog. You have your arm around her. You're the one who has got a hold of that vein. When they get the blood in the syringe, you let go. But you have to hold that dog and try and keep him steady and not let him pull away. That's my job.

Bad killing technique, whether shooting or holding, was bemoaned by senior workers. As one noted: "I get really pissed off if someone blows a vein if it is due to an improper hold."

Since euthanasia was regarded more as a technical than as a moral or emotional issue, it was not surprising that workers could acquire reputations within the shelter for being "good shots," and animals came to be seen as either easy or hard "putdowns"—a division reflecting technical difficulty and increased physical discomfort for animals. If the animal was a "hard putdown," workers became all the more absorbed in the mechanics of euthanasia, knowing that the sharpness of their technical skills would affect the extent of an animal's distress. . . .

Workers could also take animals into consideration, rather than focus on their own feelings, by seeing their death as the alleviation of suffering. This was easy to do with animals who were very sick and old—known as "automatic kills"—but it was much harder to see suffering in "healthy and happy" animals that were killed. They too had to be seen as having lives not worth living. Workers were aware that the breadth of their definition of suffering made euthanasia easier for them. One worker acknowledged that: "Sometimes you want to find any reason, like it has a runny nose." Newcomers often flinched at what was deemed sufficient medical or psychological reason to euthanize an animal, as did veterinary technicians working in the adjoining animal hospital who sometimes sarcastically said to shelter workers and their animals: "If you cough, they will kill you. If you sneeze, they will kill you."

Workers learned to see euthanasia as a way to prevent suffering. For example, it was thought that it was better to euthanize healthy strays than to let them "suffer" on the streets. One senior worker told newcomers:

> I'd rather kill than see suffering. I've seen dogs hung in alleys, cats with firecrackers in their mouths or caught in fan belts. This helps me to cope with euthanizing—to prevent this suffering through euthanasia. Am I sick if I can do this for fifteen years? No. I still cry when I see a sick pigeon on the streets, but I believe in what I am doing.

Once in a shelter, healthy strays, along with abandoned and surrendered animals, were also thought better dead than "fostered out." A worker noted: "I'd rather kill it now than let it live three years and die a horrible death. No life is better than a temporary life." Even having a potential adopter was not enough; the animal's future home, if deemed "inappropriate," would only cause the animal more "suffering." One worker elaborated:

> Finding an appropriate home for the animal is the only way the animal is going to get out of here alive. The inappropriate home prolongs the suffering, prolongs the agony, prolongs the neglect, prolongs the abuse of an animal. The animal was abused or neglected in the first place or it wouldn't be here.

This thinking was a problem for newcomers who believed that almost any home, even if temporary, was better than killing animals. Particularly troubling were those people denied an animal for adoption even though their resources and attitudes seemed acceptable to workers. Some potential adopters were rejected because it was thought that they were not home often enough, even though by all other standards they seemed likely to become good owners. In one case, a veterinary hospital technician wanted to adopt a four-month-old puppy, but was rejected because she had full-time employment. Although she retorted that she had a roommate who was at home most of the time, her request was still denied.

But newcomers soon learned to scrutinize potential adopters carefully by screening them for certain warning flags, such as not wanting to spay or neuter, not wanting to fence in or leash animals, not being home enough with animals, and so on, in addition to such basics as not having a landlord's approval or adopting the pet as a gift for someone else. Most workers came to see certain groups of people as risky adopters requiring even greater scrutiny before approval. For some workers, this meant welfare recipients because they were unwilling to spay or neuter, or policemen because they might be too rough with animals.

Although workers accepted the applications of most potential owners, they did reject some. But even in their acceptances, they reaffirmed their concern for suffering and their desire to find perfect homes; they certainly did so with their rejections, admonishing those turned down for whatever their presumed problems were toward animals. Occasionally, rejected applicants became irate and made angry comments such as "You'd rather kill it than give it to me!" These moments were uncomfortable for newcomers to watch since, to some extent, they shared the rejected applicant's sentiment—any home was better than death. More experienced workers would try to cool down the applicant but also remind newcomers that some homes were worse than death. In one such case, the shelter manager said to the rejected applicant, but for all to hear, "it is my intention to find a good home where the animal's needs can be met."

Resisting and Avoiding Euthanasia

New workers, in particular, sometimes managed their discomfort with euthanasia by trying to prevent or delay the death of animals. Although there were generally understood euthanasia guidelines, they were rather vague, and workers could exert mild pressure to make exceptions to the rules. Certainly, not all animals scheduled or "pink-slipped" to be killed were "automatic kills." As a worker noted: "If a 12-year-old stray with hip dysplasia comes in, yes, you know as soon as it walks in the door that at the end of the stray holding period it's going to be euthanized, but not all of them are like this." A worker described such an instance:

> Four weeks is really young. Five weeks, you're really pushing it. Six weeks, we can take it, but it depends on its overall health and condition. But sometimes we'll keep one or two younger ones, depending on the animal itself. We just had an animal last week—it was a dachshund. She is a really nice and friendly dog. In this case, we just decided to keep her.

Sometimes a worker took a special liking to a particular animal, but it was to be euthanized because the cage was needed for new animals, or it was too young, too old, somewhat sick, or had a behavior problem. The worker might let it be known among colleagues that they were very attached to the animal, or they might go directly to the person making the euthanasia selection with a plea for the animal's date of death to be delayed in the hopes of adoption. One worker had a favorite cat that was to be euthanized, but succeeded in blocking its euthanasia, at least for a while, by personally taking financial responsibility for its shelter costs.

However, opposing euthanasia had to be done in a way that did not make such decisions too difficult for those making them. Workers could not object repeatedly to euthanasia or oppose it too aggressively without making the selector feel uncomfortable. One worker felt "guilty" when this happened to her:

> There was one technician—Marie—who used to make me feel guilty. I have to make room for new animals because we have so few cages. I must decide which old ones to kill to make room for

> new ones. Marie would get upset when I would choose certain cats to be killed. She would come to me with her runny, snotty nose, complaining that certain cats were picked to be killed. This made me feel guilty.

If opposing euthanasia failed, workers were able to avoid the discomfort of doing it. One worker said that he would not "be around" if his favorite cat was killed, and noted:

> There's not an animal I'm not attached to here, but there's a cat here now that I like a lot. There's a good chance that she'll be euthanized. She's got a heart murmur. I guess. It's a mild one, but . . . any type of heart murmur with a cat is bad. She's also got a lump right here. They've already tested her for leukemia and it's negative, so they are testing her for something else. But she's just got an adorable face and everything else with her is fine. I like her personality. But I have two cats at home. I can't have a third, I won't be around when they euthanize her. I'll let somebody else do it. I would rather it be done when I'm not here.

Although workers could be exempted from killing animals with whom they had closely bonded, there was a strong feeling that such persons should be there for the animal's sake. Yet if present, they could indicate to others that they did not want to be the "shooter" and instead be the "holder," allowing them to feel more removed from the actual killing. A worker said:

> Especially if it's one I like a lot, I would rather be the one holding instead of injecting. If you don't want to inject, you just back up and somebody else does it. Everybody here does that. I just look at it, I don't want to be the one to do it. Even though people say that holding is the harder of the two, I would look at it as, well, I am the one who is doing this. And sometimes, I don't want to be the one to do it.

Customizing the division of labor of euthanasia to fit their own emotional limits, other workers preferred not to do the holding. One worker observed:

> One of the ways that I detach myself from euthanasia is that I do the shooting rather than the holding so that I don't feel the animal dying. I'm concentrating on the technical skill behind the actual injection. And with a dog, you literally feel the animal's life go out of it in your arms, instead of giving the injection and letting it drop.

Using the Owner

Shelter workers could also displace some of their own discomfort with euthanasia into anger and frustration with pet owners. Rather than questioning the morality of their own acts and feeling guilty about euthanasia, workers came to regard owners, and not themselves, as behaving wrongly toward animals. As workers transferred the blame for killing animals to the public, they concentrated their energies on educating and changing public attitudes to pets and making successful adoptions through the shelter.

The public was seen as treating animals as "property to be thrown away like trash" rather than as something having intrinsic value. One worker bemoaned:

> A lot of people who want to leave their pets have bullshit reasons for this—like they just bought new furniture for their living room and their cat shed all over it.

This lack of commitment resulted in many of the surrendered animals being euthanized because they were not adoptable and/or space was needed. Speaking about these owners, one worker candidly acknowledged:

> I would love to be rude once to some of these people who come in. I'd like to say to these people, "Cut this bullshit out!"

Another worker concluded: "You do want to strangle these people."

Even if pet owners did not surrender their animals to the shelter, they became tainted as a group in the eyes of workers, who saw many of them as negligent or irresponsible. A common charge against owners was that their pets were allowed to run free and be hurt, lost or stolen. One senior worker admitted: "A bias does get built in. We're called if a cat gets caught in a fan belt. We're the ones that have to scrape cats off the streets." Owners were also seen as selfish and misguided when it came to their pets, thoughtlessly allowing them to breed, instead of spaying or neutering them. Workers often repeated the shelter's pithy wish: "Parents will let their pets have puppies or kittens so they can show their children the miracle of birth—well, maybe they should come in here to see the miracle of death!" Workers could be heard among themselves admonishing the public's "irresponsibility" toward breeding and the deaths that such an attitude caused. A worker explained: "The only reason why it has been killed is that no one took the time to be a responsible pet owner. They felt the cat deserved to run free or they didn't want to pay the money to have it spayed or neutered, or that she should have one litter. Well great, what are you to do with her six offspring?" Even owners who declared great love and affection for their pets sometimes came across in the shelter environment as cruel to their animals. These were owners who let their animals suffer because they could not bear to kill them. A worker noted:

> I'll get a 22-year-old cat. And the owner is crying out there. I tell her, "You know, twenty-two years is great. You have nothing to be ashamed of. Nothing." But you get some others that come in and they [the animals] look absolutely like shit. You feel like taking hold of them and saying "What in the hell are you doing? He should have been put to sleep two years ago."

According to shelter workers, owners should have to suffer pangs of conscience about their treatment of animals, but did not. Some owners seemed not to want their pets, and this shocked workers, as one noted: "You'd be surprised at how many people come right out and say they don't want it any more. They are usually the ones who call us to pick it up, otherwise they'll dump it on the street. And of course, we're going to come and get it. I feel like saying 'It's your conscience, not mine, go ahead, do it.' Of course, I don't do that." Many surrenderers, in the eyes of shelter workers, just did not care whether their animals lived or died. At the same time that surrenderers were seen as lacking a conscience, shelter workers were afforded the opportunity to reaffirm their own dedication to and feelings for animals. A worker commented:

> Some surrenderers take them back after we tell them we can't guarantee placement. Most say, "Well that's fine." Like the owner of this cat, he called this morning and said, "I've got to get rid of it, I'm allergic to it." Of course, he didn't seem at all bothered. He goes, "That's fine." Or somebody is going to surrender a pet because they're moving, well, if it was me, and I'm sure quite a few other people here feel the same way, I'd look for a place where pets were allowed. People are just looking out for themselves and not anything else.

In the opinion of the workers, it was important for newcomers to learn not to bear the "guilt" that owners should have felt. To do this, they had to see owners as the real killers of shelter animals. As one worker put it, "People think we are murderers, but they are the ones that have put us in this position. We are morally offended by the fact that we have to carry out an execution that we didn't necessarily order." A senior shelter worker recounted how she came to terms with guilt:

> Every night I had a recurring dream that I had died, and I was standing in line to go to heaven. And St. Peter says to me, "I know you, you're the one that killed all those little animals." And I'd sit up in the bed in a cold sweat. Finally, I realized it wasn't my fault, my dreams changed. After St. Peter said, "I know you, you're the one that killed all those little animals," I turned to the 999,000 people behind me and said, "I know you, you made me kill all these animals." You grow into the fact that you are the executioner, but you weren't the judge and jury.

Shelter workers redirected their emotions and resources into changing public attitudes about pets in order to curtail the never-ending flow of animals—often called a "flood"—that always far exceeded what was possible to adopt out. Overwhelmed by this problem, workers wanted to do something about it other than killing animals. By putting effort into adoption or public education, they felt they were making a dent in the overpopulation problem instead of feeling hopeless about it. For many, combating pet overpopulation became addictive and missionary. Rather than chew over the morality of their own participation in euthanasia, they felt part of a serious campaign—often described as a "battle"—against the formidable foe of the pet owner and in defense of helpless animals.

Owners were used in ways other than as objects of blame. Successful adoptions helped to accentuate the positive in a setting where there were few opportunities to feel good about what workers were doing. Finding homes for animals came close to the original motivation that brought many workers to the shelter seeking employment. One worker commented: "For every one euthanized, you have to think about the one placed, or the one case where you placed in a perfect family." Another worker said that "you get a good feeling when you see an empty cage." She explained that she did not think that it was empty because an animal had just been killed, but because an animal had just been adopted. Indeed, out of self-protection, when the cage of someone's "favorite" was empty, workers did not ask what happened to the animals so they could assume that it was adopted rather than killed. They talked about how all of their animals were "either PWP or PWG—placed with people or placed with God." Shelter workers felt particularly satisfied when they heard from people who had satisfactorily adopted animals. Sometimes these owners came into the shelter and talked informally with workers; at other times, they wrote letters of thanks for their animals. Besides taping this mail on the walls for all to see, workers mounted snapshots of adopters and their animals in the shelter's lobby.

Dealing with Others

For workers to manage their emotions successfully, they had to learn to suspend asking hard ethical questions. While this was easy to do within the confines of the shelter, it was more difficult outside. Many reported feeling badly when outsiders learned they killed animals and challenged them about the morality of euthanasia. Workers dealt with these unwanted feelings in two ways.

Outside work, they could try to avoid the kinds of contact that give rise to unwanted emotions and difficult questions. Workers claimed that roommates, spouses, family members, and strangers sometimes made them feel "guilty" because they were seen as "villains" or "murderers." As one worker said, "You expect your spouse, your parents, your sister, your brother, or your significant other to understand. And they don't. And your friends don't. People make stupid remarks like, 'Gee, I would never do your job because I love animals too much.'" Workers claimed that they had become "paranoid" about being asked if they killed animals, waiting for questions such as, "How can you kill them if you care about animals so much?" Sometimes people would simply tell workers: "I love animals, I couldn't do that." One worker claimed that these questions and comments "make me feel like I've done something wrong." Another said, "So what does it mean—I don't love animals?" If workers were not explicitly criticized or misunderstood, they still encountered people who made them feel reluctant to talk about their work. One worker noted that "I'm proud that I'm a 90 percent shot, and that I'm not putting the animals through stress, but people don't want to hear this."

In anticipation of these negative reactions, many workers hesitated to divulge what they did. One worker said that she had learned to tell people that she "drives an animal ambulance." If workers revealed that they carried out euthanasia, they often presented arguments to support their caring for animals and the need for euthanasia. As one worker noted, "I throw numbers at them, like the fact that we get 12,000 animals a year but can only place 2,000." While concealing their work and educating others about it were by far the most common strategies used with outsiders, some workers would occasionally take a blunter approach and use sarcasm or black humor. The following worker talked about all these approaches:

> People give me a lot of grief. You know, you tell them where you work, and you tell them it's an animal shelter. And they say, "Well, you don't put them to sleep, do you?" And I always love to say, "Well actually I give classes on how to do that," just for the shock value of it. Or it's the old, "I could never do what you do, I love animals too much." "Oh, I don't love them at all. That's why I work here. I kill them. I enjoy it." But sometimes you don't even mention where you work because you don't want to deal with that. It depends on the social situation I am in as to whether I want to go in to it or not, and it also depends on how I feel at a given time. Some people are interested, and then I talk about spaying and neutering their pets.

Another way workers dealt with outsiders was to neutralize their criticism of euthanasia. The only credible opinions about euthanasia were seen as coming from those people who actually did such killing as part of the shelter community. Humor was one device that helped workers feel part of this community. It gave them a special language to talk about death and their concerns about it. As with gallows humor in other settings, it was not particularly funny out of context, and workers knew this, but learning to use it and find it humorous became a rite of passage. For instance, people telephoning the shelter might be greeted with the salutation, "Heaven." Referring to the euthanasia room and the euthanasia drug also took on a light, funny side with the room being called "downtown" or the "lavender lounge" (its walls were this color) and the drug being called "sleepaway" or "go-go juice" (its brand name was "Fatal Plus").

But no ritual practice gave more of a sense of "we-ness" then actually killing animals. No single act admitted them more into the shelter institution or more clearly demarcated the transition of shelter workers out of the novice role. As they gained increasing experience with euthanasia, workers developed a firmer sense of being in the same boat with peers who also did what they did. They shared an unarticulated belief that others could not understand what it was like to kill unless they had also done so. Even within the shelter, kennel workers often felt misunderstood by the front-desk people. As one worker reflected, "It does feel like you can't understand what I do if you can't understand that I don't like to kill, but that I have to kill. You'd have to see what I see. Maybe then." Since outsiders did not share this experience, workers tended to give them little credibility and to discount their opinions. By curtailing the possibility of understanding what they did and communicating with others about it, workers furthered their solidarity and created boundaries between themselves and outsiders that served to shield them from external criticism and diminish any uncomfortable feelings easily raised by the "uninformed" or "naive."

The Imperfection of Emotion Management

Certainly, the killing of animals by shelter workers was facilitated by the kinds of emotion management strategies that have been discussed. Yet it would be wrong to characterize these people, including those with many years' experience, as completely detached. These strategies were far from perfect. It would be more accurate to say that their institutional socialization was incomplete. All workers, including those with many years of experience, felt uneasy about euthanasia at certain times.

For the few who continued to experience sharp and disturbing feelings, quitting became a way to manage emotions. For example, one worker felt "plagued" by a conflict between her own feelings for the animals which made killing hard to accept and the shelter's euthanasia policy with which she intellectually agreed. She said it was "like having two people in my head, one good and the other evil, that argue about me destroying these animals." This conflict left her feeling "guilty" about deaths she found "hard to justify." After nine months on the job, she quit.

For most workers this conflict was neither intense nor constant, but instead manifested itself as episodic uneasiness. From time to time euthanasia provoked modest but clearly discernible levels of emotional distress. There was no consensus, however, on what kind of euthanasia would rattle people and make them feel uncomfortable, but everyone had at least one type that roused their feelings.

The most obvious discomfort with euthanasia occurred when workers had to kill animals to which they were attached or that they could easily see as pets. While newcomers were more likely to have formed these attachments, seasoned workers could still be troubled by euthanasia when animals reminded them of other attachments. As one veteran worker reflected:

> I haven't been emotionally attached to a dog, except for one, for quite a while. I know my limit. But there are times when I'll look at a dog when I'm euthanizing it and go, "You've got Rex's eyes." Or it's an Irish setter—I have a natural attachment to Irish setters. Or black cats—I hate to euthanize black cats. It's real hard for me to euthanize a black cat.

Even without attachments, many workers found it "heartbreaking" to euthanize young, healthy and well-behaved animals merely for space because they could have become pets. Without a medical or psychological reason, euthanasia seemed a "waste."

For many, euthanasia became unsettling if it appeared that animals suffered physically or psychologically. This happened, for example, when injections of the euthanasia drug caused animals to "scream," "cry," or become very disoriented and move about frantically. But it also happened when animals seemed to "know" they were about to be killed or sensed that "death was in the air." "Cats aren't dumb. They know what's going on. Whenever you take them to the room, they always get this stance where their head goes up, and they know," observed one worker. Another said that many animals could "smell" death. These workers became uneasy because they assumed that the animals were "scared." "What is hard for me," said one worker, "is when they are crying and they are very, very scared." Another said that she could "feel their tension and anxiety" in the euthanasia room. "They seem to know what's happening—that something is going to happen," she added to explain her discomfort.

Ironically, for some workers the opposite situation left them feeling unsettled. They found it eerie when animals were not scared and instead behaved "as though they were cooperating." According to one worker, certain breeds were likely to act this way as they were being killed: "Greyhounds and Dobermans will either give you their paw or willingly give you their leg, and look right past you. It's as though they are cooperating. The other dogs will look right at you."

Killing large numbers of animals in a single day was disconcerting for nearly everyone. This happened to one worker when the number of animals killed was so great she could not conceptualize the quantity until she picked up a thick pile of "yellow slips" (surrender forms), or when she looked at the drug log and saw how many animals had been given euthanasia injections. The flow of animals into the shelter was seasonal, and workers grew to loathe those months when many animals were brought in and euthanized. The summer was a particularly bad time, because so many cats came in and were killed. As one worker said, "They are constantly coming in. On a bad day, you might have to do it [euthanasia] fifty times. There are straight months of killing." Another observed, "After three hours of killing, you come out a mess. It drains me completely. I'll turn around and see all these dead animals on the floor around me—and it's "What have I done?" And yet another worker noted:

> It's very difficult when we are inundated from spring until fall. Every single person who walks through the door has either a pillow case, a box, a laundry basket or whatever—one more litter of kittens. And you only have X number of cages in your facility and they are already full. So the animal may come in the front door and go out the back door in a barrel. It's very difficult if that animal never had a chance at life, or has had a very short life.

Even seasoned workers said that it did "not feel right" to spend so much time killing, particularly when so many of the animals they killed were young and never had a chance to become a pet.

All workers, then, experienced at least some uneasiness when facing certain types of euthanasia, despite their socialization into the shelter's culture. The emotions generated by these situations overruled attempts by the shelter to help them manage their emotions and objectify their charges. When emotion management and objectification failed, workers felt some degree of connection and identification with the animals which in turn elicited feelings of sadness, worry, and even remorse.

Conclusion

The initial conflict faced by newcomers to an animal shelter was extreme—because of their prior, everyday perspective toward animals, killing them generated emotions that caused workers to balk at carrying out euthanasia. However, on closer inspection, this tension was replaced by a more moderate and manageable version of the same conflict. The conflict was repackaged and softened, but it was there, nonetheless. Shelter workers could more easily live with this version, and their emotion management strategies got them to this point. These strategies embodied an underlying inconsistency or dilemma between the simultaneous pulls toward objectifying the animals and seeing the animals in pet-related terms—a conflict between rational necessity and sentimentality, between head and heart, between everyday perspective and that of the institution. . . .

A final look at these strategies reveals this underlying tension. By transforming shelter animals into virtual pets, the workers could objectify the animals to some degree, while also categorizing them as something like, yet different from, everyday pets. When it came to actually killing them, workers could play the role of highly skilled technicians efficiently dispatching animal lives seen as not worth living, simultaneously trying to take the emotional and physical feelings of animals into account. Being able to avoid or postpone killing was itself viewed as a struggle between emotion and rationality; importantly, this was allowed, thereby acknowledging some degree of emotion but within limits that reaffirmed a more rational approach. When it came to their view of owners (perhaps a collective projection of a sort), it was the public, and not themselves, that objectified animals; whatever they did, including the killing, paled by comparison and was done out of sentiment and caring. Indeed, outsiders came to be suspected, one-dimensionally, as a distant and alien group, while workers increasingly cultivated a strong sense of we-ness among themselves—humans, too, seem to have two fundamentally different kinds of relations with each other. . . .

It is . . . not surprising that these strategies were sometimes imperfect, failing to prevent penetration of the everyday perspective toward animals into the shelter. Even the most effective programs of organizational socialization are likely to be fallible when workers face situations that trigger their prior feelings and concerns. Many shelter workers may have felt uneasy because at certain times their personal, everyday thinking and feeling about animals in general may have taken precedence over the institutional "rules" for thinking and feeling about animals. . . .

Yet, in the end, by relying on these strategies workers reproduced the institution (e.g., Smith and Kleinman 1989), thereby creating a new generation of workers who would support the humane society model and the kind of human-animal relationship in which people could believe they were killing with a conscience. Far from being a unique situation, the shelter worker's relationship with animals is but our general culture's response to animals writ small. It is not likely that we ourselves are altogether exempt from this inconsistency, as our individual ways of managing our thought and feelings may similarly dull the conflict just enough for it to become a familiar uneasiness. For shelter workers, the conflict is merely heightened and their struggle to make peace with their acts is more deliberate and collective.

References

Schleifer, H. (1985) "Images of death and life: Food animal production and the vegetarian option," in P. Singer (ed.), *In Defense of Animals*. New York: Harper & Row, pp. 63–74.

Serpell, J. (1986) *In the Company of Animals*. Oxford: Basil Blackwell.

Smith, A., and Kleinman, S. (1989) "Managing emotions in medical school: Students' contacts with the living and the dead." *Social Psychology Quarterly* 52: 56–68.

Reflective Questions

1. Workers at the kill shelter felt a confusing array of emotions. What emotions did they feel? Why? What competing identities did workers try to protect by managing their emotions?
2. How did workers emotionally distance themselves from the killing they performed? How did they avoid participating in euthanizing animals they were especially attached to? How did they deal with negative judgments made by others? How did other workers socialize them into these techniques?
3. Some emotion work in the shelter eased workers' discomfort with killing animals. What interpretations of their work did so? Emotion management did not always relieve workers' guilt over killing animals. What happened then?
4. Does emotional detachment take away from people's humanity in some situations? Is emotional detachment necessary in some lines of work? Why or why not? Does emotional attachment carry greater risks than detachment? Take the case of a medical resident who was rotating through the ER the night a pregnant woman—the same age and stage of pregnancy as his own partner—arrived by ambulance and died during a code. What are the consequences of feeling closely attached to patients or clients? Do some workplaces socialize workers to closely attach? How? Why? Is close attachment better in some moral sense? Why or why not?
5. Workers often have emotional or moral qualms about some of the tasks they perform at work. Their duties may require them to fire a single father because of his poor performance, even though his children depend on his income and health insurance. Workers may tie down a violent patient in a hospital, or chain a pregnant inmate to a gurney while she gives birth because state law requires it. Recall a time when you carried out a work duty even though you had moral misgivings about doing so. Why do workers carry out these tasks? How do they interpret their work in order to make themselves feel better? What role do other workers and authority figures play in helping us ease our discomfort? Why don't workers simply find other work when faced with a morally questionable task, or work to change the requirements of the job?

Protecting the Routine from Chaos

DANIEL CHAMBLISS

Many contemporary social organizations are considered bureaucratic. They are characterized by various units and positions with specific duties, clearly defined lines of authority, formal rules and procedures, and mountains of forms and records. Although such bureaucratic organizations seem to have a life of their own, they do not. Individuals give them life by engaging in recurrent patterns of interaction. This life does not result from people merely following the formal rules and procedures of the organization or its specific units. People must interactionally accomplish the order that those rules and procedures imply. They rely on more implicit and informal procedures for that purpose.

This selection by Daniel Chambliss examines the implicit and informal procedures that nurses follow to accomplish order in a hospital setting, particularly when unexpected or traumatic events threaten to disrupt their orderly routines. Based on a 10-year participant observation study, Chambliss chronicles the traumas and threats that have the potential to create chaos for nurses as they go through their daily rounds. These threats present themselves in two forms. The first is external to the nurse and usually involves intrusion by an outsider, such as the entrance of a panicked family member during a resuscitation effort. The second arises within the nurse and consists of disruptive emotions, such as panic or grief, which he or she may experience when dealing with a severe trauma. These emotional reactions are problematic for the nurse because they can prevent him or her from staying composed and performing essential tasks.

To address these challenges and protect their social world from chaos, nurses rely on a variety of strategies, including following established routines, preventing outsiders from knowing what is happening, and using humor to distance themselves from the events at hand. But, when these strategies fail and chaos threatens to overwhelm the order of the hospital, nurses typically respond by "keeping going." That is, they continue to work and remain calm, employing techniques that allow them to handle disruptions in ways that make them seem routine and manageable. As Chambliss points out, by routinizing the chaos that emerges around them, nurses "modify what counts as normal" and transform the moral world of everyday life. In the process, they not only redefine the reality of trauma and emergency but also create and sustain a sense of order in the social world of the hospital.

While Chambliss focuses on how order is constructed in the sometimes chaotic context of a hospital, his findings demonstrate the crucial insight that social order is a negotiated process. As Herbert Blumer implied in Selection 29, social order emerges out of, and becomes altered through or sustained by, our ongoing interactions with others. When we look at any organization, whether it is a hospital, a business, or a university, we find that it depends on individuals engaging in behavioral routines and interacting with one another in particular ways. However, it is not simply these routines and interactions that create the structure of that organization, but rather their sedimentation

Reprinted from: Daniel Chambliss, "Protecting the Routine from Chaos." *Beyond Caring*, pp. 42–55, 58–60.

into a system of action that individuals view as appropriate. In this sense, we are all like the nurses that Chambliss describes—we carve out and preserve a sense of order, albeit somewhat fragile, through our ongoing interactions and behavioral routines.

Every unit in the hospital, then, has its own normality, its own typical patients, number of deaths, and crises to be faced. But just as predictably, every unit has its emergencies that threaten the routine and challenge the staff's ability to maintain workaday attitudes and practices. Emergencies threaten the staff's ability to carry on as usual, to maintain their own distance from the patient's suffering, and to hold at bay their awe at the enormity of events. Occasionally breakdowns occur in unit discipline or the ability to do the required work.

Staff follow several strategies when trying to manage the threat of breakdowns; they will keep outsiders outside, follow routinization rituals, or use humor to distance themselves. Finally, even when all efforts fail, they will keep going, no matter what. Consider in turn each of these implicit maxims:

1. Keep Outsiders Outside. Every hospital has policies about visiting hours, designed not only to "let patients rest" but also to protect staff from outsiders' interference in their work. Visitors are limited to certain hours, perhaps two to a patient room for fifteen-minute visits; they may have to be announced before entering the unit or may be kept waiting in a room down the hall. No doubt many such policies are good for the patient. No doubt, too, they keep visitors out of the nurse's way, prevent too many obtrusive questions or requests for small services, and prevent curious laypersons from seeing the messier, less presentable sides of nursing care.

When visitors cannot be physically excluded, they can still be cognitively controlled, that is, prevented from knowing that something untoward is happening. Typically, the staff behave in such episodes as if everything were OK, even when it is not. This is similar to what Erving Goffman observed in conversations: when the shared flow of interaction is threatened by an accidental insult or a body failure such as a sneeze or flatulence, people simply try to ignore the break in reality and carry on as if nothing has happened. Such "reality maintenance" is often well-orchestrated, requiring cooperation on the part of several parties. For Goffman, normal people in normal interactions accept at face value each other's presentation of who they are:

> A state where everyone temporarily accepts everyone else's line is established. This kind of mutual acceptance seems to be a basic structural feature of interaction, especially the interaction of face-to-face talk. It is typically a "working" acceptance, not a "real" one. (Goffman 1967:11)

And when this routine breaks down, the immediate strategy is simple denial:

> When a person fails to prevent an incident, he can still attempt to maintain the fiction that no threat to face has occurred. The most blatant example of this is found where the person acts as if an event that contains a threatening expression has not occurred at all (Goffman 1967:17–18).

In the hospital, the unexpected entrance of outsiders into a delicate situation can disrupt the staff's routine activities and create unmanageable chaos. To avoid this, the staff may pretend to outsiders that nothing special is happening; this pretense itself can be part of the routine. During a code (resuscitation) effort I witnessed, there were three such potential disruptions by outsiders: another patient calling for help, a new incoming patient being wheeled in, and the new patient's family members entering the unit. All three challenges were handled by the staff diverting the outsiders from the code with a show, as if nothing were happening:

> Code in CCU [Cardiac Care Unit] . . . woman patient, asystole [abnormal ventricle contractions]. Doc (res[ident]) pumping chest—*deep* pumps, I'm struck by how far down they push. Serious stuff. Matter of factness of process is striking. This was a surprise code, not expected. Patient was in Vtak [ventricular fibrillation], pulse started slowing,

> then asystole. N[urse]s pumping for a while, RT [Respiratory Therapist] ambu-bagging [pumping air into lungs]. Maybe 7–8 people in patient's room working. Calm, but busy. Occasionally a laugh.
>
> Pt in next room (no more than 10 feet away) called for nurse—a doc went in, real loose and casual, strolled in, pt said something; doc said, "There's something going on next door that's taking people's time; we'll get to you"—real easy, like nothing at all happening. Then strolls back to code room. Very calm. . . .
>
> Two N[urse]s came into unit wheeling a new patient. One said, "Uh, oh, bad time," very quietly as she realized, going in the door, that a code was on. Somebody said, "Close the door"—the outside door to the unit, which the Ns with the new pt were holding open. . . .
>
> When the new pt was brought in and rolled into his room, the family with him was stopped at unit door, told to stay in waiting room and "we'll call you" with a casual wave of hand, as if this is routine. [No one said a code was on. Patient lying on gurney was wheeled in, went right by the code room and never knew a thing.] [Field Notes]

This is a simple example of protecting the routine from the chaos of a panicking patient or a horrified family; the outsiders never knew that a resuscitation was occurring fifteen feet away. The staff's work was, in their own eyes, routine; their challenge was protecting that routine from outside disruption.

2. *Follow Routinization Rituals.* The staff's sense of routine is maintained by the protective rituals of hospital life. Under stress, one may use them more and more compulsively, falling back on the old forms to reconvince oneself that order is still present. Frantic prayers in the foxhole are the prototype cases.

Most prominent of such rituals in hospitals are "rounds," the standard ritual for the routine handling of patient disasters in the hospital. "Rounds" is the generic term for almost any organized staff group discussion of patients' conditions. "Walking rounds" refers to a physician walking through the hospital, usually trailed by various residents and interns, going from patient to patient and reviewing their condition. "Grand rounds" are large meetings of the medical staff featuring the presentation of an interesting case, with elaborate discussion and questions, for the purpose of education and review of standard practices. Nursing rounds usually consist of a meeting between the staff for one (outgoing) shift reporting to the staff of the next (incoming) shift on the condition of all patients on the floor. Here the staff collectively explains what has happened and why, bringing every case into the staff's framework of thinking, and systematically enforcing the system's capability for handling medical problems without falling to pieces. In rounds, the staff confirm to each other that things are under control. Once a week, for instance, the Burn Unit at one hospital holds rounds in their conference room with a group of residents, one or two attendings, several nurses, the social workers, dieticians, and physical therapists. The patients here are in terrible shape; one can sometimes hear moans in the hallway outside as patients are taken for walks by the nurses. But rounds continue:

> Macho style of the docs very evident. . . . Resident will present a case, then the attendings take rapid-fire shots at what he [the resident] had done: wrong dressing, wrong feeding schedule, failure to note some abnormality in the lab results. Much of the talk was a flurry of physiological jargon, many numbers and abbreviations. The intensity of the presentation, the mercilessness of the grilling, is surprising. . . . Focus is on no errors made in situation of extreme pressure—i.e., both in patient treatment and then here in rounds presenting the case. Goal here is to be predictable, controlled, nothing left out. [Field Notes]

3. *Use Humor to Distance Yourself.* Keeping outsiders away and following the standard rituals for maintaining normality can help, but sometimes the pathos of hospital life becomes psychologically threatening to staff members. One response is to break down, cry, and run out, but this is what they are trying to avoid; the more common reaction is the sort of black humor that notoriously characterizes hospitals and armies everywhere. Humor provides an outlet; when physical space is not available, humor is a way to separate oneself psychologically from what is happening. It says both that I am not involved and that this really isn't so important. (In brain surgery, when parts of that organ are, essentially, vacuumed away, one may hear comments like "There goes 2d grade, there go the piano lessons," etc.) With laughter, things seem less consequential, less of a burden. What has been ghastly can perhaps be made funny:

> Today they got a 600-gram baby in the Newborn Unit. When Ns heard [the baby] was in Delivery, they were praying, "Please God let it be under 500 grams"—because that's the definite cutoff under which they won't try to save it—but the doc said admit it anyway. Ns unhappy.
>
> I came in the unit tonight; N came up to me and said brightly, with a big smile, "Have you seen our Fetus?" Ns on the Newborn Unit have nicknames for some. There's "Fetus," the 600-gram one; "Munchkin"; and "Thrasher," in the corner, the one with constant seizures. Grim humor, but common. ["Fetus" was born at 24 weeks, "Munchkin" at 28.] [Field Notes]

The functions of such humor for medical workers have been described in a number of classic works of medical sociology. Renée Fox, writing in her book *Experiment Perilous* about physicians on a metabolic research unit, says, "The members of the group were especially inclined to make jokes about events that disturbed them a good deal," and she summarizes that

> by freeing them from some of the tension to which they were subject, enabling them to achieve greater detachment and equipoise, and strengthening their resolve to do something about the problems with which they were faced, the grim medical humor of the Metabolic Group helped them to come to terms with their situation in a useful and professionally acceptable way. (Fox 1974:80–82)

Fox and other students of hospital culture (notably Rose Coser [1980]) have emphasized that humor fills a functional purpose of "tension release," allowing medical workers to get on with the job in the face of trauma; their analyses usually focus on jokes explicitly told in medical settings. This analysis is correct as far as it goes, but in a sense I think it almost "explains away" hospital humor—as if to say that "these people are under a lot of strain, so it's understandable that they tell these gruesome jokes." It suggests, in a functionalist fallacy, that jokes are made because of the strain and that things somehow aren't "really" funny.

But they are. An appreciation of hospital life must recognize that funny things—genuinely funny, even if sometimes simultaneously horrible—do happen. Hospitals are scenes of irony, where good and bad are inseparably blended, where funny things happen, where to analytically excuse laughter as a defense mechanism is simultaneously to deny the human reality, the experience, that even to a nonstressed outsider *this is funny*. The humor isn't found only in contrived jokes but in the scenes one witnesses; laughter can be spontaneous, and it's not always nervous. True, one must usually have a fairly normalized sense of the hospital to laugh here, but laugh one does.

Certainly, the staff make jokes:

> In the OR:
> "This is his [pt's] 6th time [for a hernia repair]."
> "After two, I hear you're officially disabled."
> "Oh good, does that mean he gets a special parking place?" [Field Notes]
> In the ICU, two Ns—one male, one female—working on pt.
> Nurse 1 (male): "This guy has bowel sounds in his scrotum."
> Nurse 2 (female): "In his scrotum?"
> Nurse 1: "Yeah, didn't you pick that up?"
> Nurse 2: "I didn't put my stethoscope there!" (Big laughs.) [Field Notes]

Sometimes jokes are more elaborate and are obviously derived from the tragedy of the situation:

> In another ICU, staff member taped a stick to the door of the unit, symbolizing (for them) "The

Stake," a sign of some form of euthanasia [perhaps the expression sometimes used, "to stake" a patient, derives from the myth that vampires can only be killed by driving a stake through the heart]. Periodically word went around that a resident had just won the "Green Stake Award," meaning that he or she had, for the first time, allowed or helped a patient to die. [Field Notes]

> Some colorful balloons with "Get Well Soon" were delivered to a patient's room. The patient died the following night. Someone on the staff moved the balloons to the door of another patient's room; that patient died! Now the staff has put the balloons at the door of the patient they believe is "most likely to die next." [Field Notes]

But jokes have to be contrived; they are deliberate efforts at humor and so make a good example of efforts to distance oneself, or to make the tragic funny. But the inherent irony of the hospital is better seen in situations that spontaneously provoke laughter. These things are funny in themselves; even an outsider can laugh at them:

> Nurse preparing to wheel a patient into the OR tells him, "Take out your false teeth, take off your glasses . . . ," and continuing, trying to make a joke, "Take off your leg, take out your eyes." The patient said, "Oh, I almost forgot—" and pulled out his [false] eye! [Interview]

Or:

> Lady patient [Geriatric floor] is upset because she called home, there's no answer; she's afraid her husband has died. Sylvia [a nurse] told her he probably just went somewhere for lunch, but patient said he would have called. She's afraid.
>
> [Later] Sylvia went back in lady's room—she's crying. Husband called! Sylvia happy, smiling, "You should be happy!" "But," says the old lady, "he called to say he was out burying the dog!"
>
> Sylvia had to leave the room because she was starting to laugh; she and Janie laughing at this at the N's station, saying it's really sad but funny at the same time. [Field Notes]

Or:

> In looking at X-rays of a patient's colon, the resident explains to the team a shadow on the film: "Radiology says it could be a tumor, or it might just be stool." Jokes all around about how "helpful" Rays [Radiology] is. [Field Notes]

One needn't be under pressure to find such things funny. People do laugh to ease pressure or to distance oneself. But sometimes the distance comes first: laughter is made possible by the routinization that has gone before.

4. *When Things Fall Apart, Keep Going.* Sometimes routinization fails: outsiders come into the room and, seeing their dead mother, break down, screaming and wailing; or a longtime, cared-for patient begins irretrievably to "decompensate" and lose blood pressure, sliding quickly to death; or emergency surgery goes bad, the trauma shakes the staff, and there are other patients coming in from the ambulances. Any of these can destroy the staff's sense of "work as usual." In such cases, the typical practice seems to be, remarkably: just keep going. Trauma teams specialize in the psychological strength (or coldbloodedness, perhaps) to continue working when the world seems to be falling apart. Finally, nurses and physicians are notable for continuing to work even, in the final case, after the patient is for almost all purposes dead, or will be soon.

> A resident said to the attending on one floor, discussing a terminal patient: "If we transfuse him, he might get hepatitis."
>
> Another resident: "By the time he gets hepatitis he'll be dead."
>
> Attending: "OK, so let's transfuse." [Field Notes]

Perseverance is a habit; it's also a moral imperative, a way of managing disaster as if it were routine.

In every unit there are nurses known for being good under pressure. These are people who, whatever their other skills (and, typically, their other skills are quite good), are able to maintain their presence of mind in any crisis. Whereas "being organized" is a key quality for nurses in routine situations, staying calm is crucial in emergency situations. Compare two nurses known for remaining calm (Mavis and Anna) to two others who are prone to alarm (Linda and Julie):

> Mavis [in Neonatal IGU] is cited as a good nurse (great starting IVs, e.g.) who doesn't get shook, even in a code, even if her pt is dying, she still keeps doing what you're supposed to do. Linda, by contrast, is real smart, very good technically, but can freak out, start yelling, etc., if things are going badly. [Field Notes]

> Julie [in Medical ICU], hurrying around, looks just one step ahead of disaster, can't keep up, etc. Doc says something about the patient in room 1. Julie says, walking past, "He's not mine," keeps going. But Anna, calm, walks in pt's room—pt with oxygen mask, wants something. Anna goes out, calmly, comes back in a minute w/cup of crushed ice, gives pt a spoonful to ease thirst. She *always* seems to be doing that little thing that others "don't have time for"—never flustered and yet seems to get more done than anyone else. [Field Notes, Interview]

But to "keep going" depends not so much on the individual fortitude of nurses such as Mavis and Anna, but on the professional and institutional habits of the nursing staff and the hospital. The continuance of care even in the face of obvious failure of efforts is itself a norm. Whatever one's personal disposition, one keeps working; the staff keep working, often when the patient is all but dead, or "dead" but not officially recognized as such:

> Dr. K., walking rounds with four residents, discussing a 30-year-old male patient, HIV-positive, gone totally septic [has bloodstream infection, a deadly problem], no hope at all of recovery—Dr. K. says this is a "100 percent mortality" case; so they decide how to proceed with minimal treatment, at the end of which Dr. K. says brightly, "And if he codes—code him!" [Field Notes]

Coding such a patient is an exercise in technique; there is no hope entailed, no optimism, no idea that he might be saved. There is only the institutional habit which substitutes for hope, which in many cases obviates the staff's pessimism or lack of interest. When standard procedure is followed, courage is unnecessary. It is one thing to be routinely busy, caring for vegetative patients; it happens every day. It is quite another to handle emergency surgery with no time and a life at stake. Sometimes such a case will challenge all the staff's resources—their personal fortitude, their habitualization of procedures, the self-protection offered by an indefatigable sense of humor. To maintain one's composure while under tremendous pressures of time and fatefulness requires all the courage a staff can muster.

One such case was that of emergency surgery on a thirty-five-year-old woman who came to Southwestern Regional hospital in severe abdominal pain; she was diagnosed with a ruptured ectopic pregnancy estimated at sixteen weeks. The case provides us with a dramatic example of the pressure placed on the staff to retain their composure in the face of disaster.

The long description which follows is graphic. The scene was more than bloody; it was grotesque. More than one staff member—including one member of the surgical team itself—left the room during the operation, sickened. Other nurses, even very experienced ones, told me they have never witnessed such a scene and hope never to witness one. I include it here, in some detail, to exemplify both what health professionals face in their work and how, incredibly, some of them can carry on. The description is reconstructed from Field Notes (some written at the time on the inside of a surgical mask, some on sheets of paper carried in a pocket), and from interviews afterward with participants:

> Saturday night OR suite; hasn't been busy. Only one case so far, a guy who got beat up with a tire iron (drug deal), finished about 8:30 P.M. It's about 10:00. 2 Ns—the Saturday night staff—sitting around in the conference room, just chatting and waiting for anything that happens.

> Call comes over intercom: ruptured tubal (pregnancy) just came in OR, bringing to the crash room. 35-year-old black woman, very heavy—250

pounds maybe—apparently pregnant for 16 weeks, which means she's been in pain for 10 weeks or more without coming in. Friends brought her to ER screaming in pain. Blood pressure is at "60 over palpable," i.e., the diastolic doesn't even register on the manometer. She's obviously bleeding bad internally, will die fast if not opened up. Ns run to OR and set up fast. I've never seen people work so quickly here, no wasted motion at all. This is full speed *emergency*.

When patient is rolled in, fully conscious, there are more than a dozen staff people in the room, including three gynecological surgery residents, who will operate; all three are women. The surgeons are scrubbed and gowned and stand in a line, back from the table, watching without moving, the one in charge periodically giving orders to the nurses who are setting up. At one point there are twelve separate people working on the patient—IVs going into both arms, anesthesiologist putting mask on pt to gas, nurse inserting a Foley [bladder] catheter, others tying pt's arms to the straightout arms of the table, others scrubbing the huge belly, an incredible scene. The patient is shaking terribly, in pain and fear. Her eyes are bugging out, looking around terribly fast. She's whimpering, groaning as needles go in, crying out softly. No one has time even to speak to her; one nurse briefly leans over and speaks into her ear something like "try not to worry, we're going to take care of you," but there is no time for this. I've never seen anyone so afraid, sweating and crying and the violent shaking.

As soon as they have prepped her—the belly cleansed and covered with Opsite, in a matter of minutes, very, very fast, the anesthesiologist says, "All set?" And someone says "yes," and they gas her. I'm standing right by her head, looking to the head side of the drape which separates her head from her body; the instant that her eyes close, I look to the other side—and the surgeon has already slit her belly open. No hesitation at all, maybe before the patient was out.

What happened next, more extraordinary than the very fast prep, was the opening. Usually in surgery the scalpel makes the skin cut, then slowly scissors are used, snipping piece by piece at muscle, the Bovie cauterizing each blood vessel on the way, very methodical and painstaking. This was nothing like that. It was an entirely different style. They cut fast and deep, sliced her open deep, just chopped through everything, in a—not a panic, but something like a "blitzkrieg," maybe—to get down into the Fallopian tube that had burst and was shooting blood into the abdomen.

When they first got into the abdominal cavity, usually there would be some oozing blood; here as they opened blood splattered out all over the draping on the belly. It was a godawful mess, blood everywhere. They had one surgeon mopping up with gauze sponges, another using a suction pump, a little plastic hose, trying to clean the way. Unbelievable. They got down to the tubes, reaching down and digging around with their hands. And then they found it—suddenly out of this bloody mess down in the abdomen, with the surgeons groping around trying to feel where things were, out of this popped up, right out of the patient and, literally, onto the sheet covering her, the 16-week fetus itself. Immediately one surgeon said mock-cheerfully, "It's a boy!" "God, don't do that," said the scrub tech, turning her head away.

The scrub tech then began to lose it, tears running down her cheeks. Two other people on the team—there were maybe six around the table—said about the same time, nearly together, "Damien!" and "Alien!" recalling recent horror movies, "children of the devil" themes. The fetus lay on the sheet just below the open abdomen for a few moments. The head surgery resident, working, just kept working. The scrub tech should have put the fetus into a specimen tray, but she was falling to pieces fast, crying, and starting to have trouble handing the proper tools to the surgeon, who said something like, "What are you doing?" At this point the circulating nurse, a man, said, "If nobody else will do it," picked up the fetus and put it in a specimen tray, which he then covered with a towel and put aside. He then told another nurse to help him into a gown—he wasn't scrubbed. This violates sterile

> technique badly, for him to start handling tools, but the scrub tech was becoming a problem. The circulating nurse then quickly gowned and gloved, gently pulled the scrub tech aside and said, "I'll do it." The scrub tech ran out of the room in tears. And the circulating nurse began passing tools to the surgeons himself. It is the circulating nurse's responsibility to handle problems this way, and he did. Another nurse had gone out to scrub properly, and when she came back, maybe ten minutes later, she gowned and gloved and relieved him; so he (the circulating nurse) went back to his regular job of charting the procedure, answering the phone, etc.
>
> By this time, things were under control; the bleeding was stopped, the tube tied off. The other tube was OK and left alone so the pt can get pregnant again. The blood in the abdomen was cleaned up—over 1500 cc's were lost, that's just under a half-gallon of blood. The pt would have died fast if they hadn't gotten in there.
>
> Within two hours after the patient had first rolled in, the room was quiet, only three staff members left, two surgeons and the scrub nurse closing up and talking quietly. Most of the mess—the bloody sponges, the used tools, and all—was gone, cleared away, and all the other staff people, including the chief surgeon, had left. Very calm. The patient, who two hours ago was on the end of a fast terrible death, will be out of the hospital in two days with no permanent damage beyond the loss of one Fallopian tube. [Field Notes, Interviews]

In this situation, we can see two somewhat distinct problems in maintaining the routine order of things: first, the challenge simply in getting the work done; and second, the challenge of upholding the moral order of the hospital. The first issue was resolved by replacing the scrub tech so the operation could continue. The second issue is trickier. The scrub tech's response appeared to be set off not by the horror of what she saw—the bloody fetus—but by the reaction of the assisting surgeon—"It's a boy!" I can only guess that the joke was too much for her. In continuing to work without her, and continuing without noticeable change of demeanor, the surgical team was asserting not only the imperative to protect the operational routine but also, I think, to protect the moral order of emergency surgery as well. That order includes:

1. The job comes first, before personal reactions of fear or disgust.
2. Cynicism is an acceptable form of expression if it helps to maintain composure and distance.
3. The medical team is rightfully in charge and above what may be happening in the OR.
4. Preserving life is the central value; others (such as niceties of language or etiquette) fall far behind.

There is clearly a morality here. Just as clearly, it is not the morality of everyday life.

Conclusion: The Transformation of the Moral World

. . . In concluding, I would like to make two final points: first, that every nurse does set limits to what she can tolerate; and second, that routinization entails a transformation of the moral world. Routinization entails an implicit decision to modify what counts as normal. In the hospital, what was sacred (handling and inspection of bodies) becomes ordinary; what was unique (the human being with a disease) becomes just another case; what was serious (the death of a pet, the resuscitation of a dying old man) becomes funny; what was grotesque or disgusting (facial fungi, necrotic stumps) becomes a tale to tell over lunch. Instead of tying old people to bed rails, nurses "restrain" them; instead of doping up a crazy lady, they "sedate a confused patient." In becoming a nurse, then, one transforms important elements of one's moral world. The transformation is based on specific learning, as we have seen, but there is more to it than that. Routinization is more than the sum of many specific concrete activities (although it is that); it really does seem, finally, to happen "one day," as the nurses put it. Their "frame" has shifted, to use Erving Goffman's 1974 term. What in daily life would be outrageous—a body sliced by a knife, a throat invaded with a metal tube—in the medical context becomes normal, a relatively routine procedure.

This is why so much of conventional debate about medical and nursing ethics is inadequate: the frame shift of routinization has bracketed out a vast array of moral difficulties. Everyday hospital practice does not present itself as the typical "ethics dilemma" discussed by hospital committees of lawyers and doctors and chaplains; it is not typically discussed in philosophy books, or covered in *Time* magazine articles about young women, victims of car accidents, who have been vegetative for six years. Those cases are dramatic, notable. Many times during my research nurses have asked me if I was meeting with ethics committees, going to official "ethics rounds," or talking with Dr. So-and-So, the renowned "ethics guy" in the hospital. "If you want to know about ethics, you should . . . ," they would say. But behind them, just over their shoulders, would be a young man dying of AIDS whose parents refused to visit him; or an old woman, who when not lost in a drugged stupor would beg to die; or a hopelessly deformed infant who hadn't breathed on her own for four months. Committees only hear of such cases if they become problems, and committees are themselves unusual groups. Hence ethics committees and ethics rounds are a poor site for discovering what typically occurs. This is not to say that nurses aren't aware of the problems under their own noses, but often they don't see them as "ethics problems," and neither do the powers that be, nor the media, nor the academics who talk about such things. The great ethical danger, I think, is not that when faced with an important decision one makes the wrong choice, but rather that one never realizes that one is facing a decision at all.

To an outsider the ordinary work of the hospital is itself morally problematic. The bureaucracy of the hospital poses a problem; the "professionalization" of staff has moral implications; the objectification of patients' bodies matters far more than the official "ethics dilemma" which occasionally pops its head above the surrounding routine. In the normal course of "getting used to" the hospital, nurses and other health care workers become in some measure inured to the profound differences between the hospital and the world beyond it. And if this routine is itself morally problematic, this fact is far more important than whether to continue tube feedings to a patient who for half a decade has been comatose.

Routinization—the acceptance of the hospital as a normal place—happens in the course of things, and often the transition itself is unnoticed ("I can't say exactly when it happened"). Readers of this chapter may have undergone a kind of routinization experience during their reading, becoming used to the examples, starting to learn a little of the jargon, seeing one or two of the same faces in these pages, beginning to be less shocked by later hospital scenes than by those in the beginning of the chapter. The readers may have, in a sense, forgotten that hospitals are unusual; it really isn't normal for people to do what is being done in the operating room, or to say what people there say. As the shock value of these stories wears off, the change is not in the stories but in readers' attitudes toward them. And it happened somewhere in the reading.

References

Coser, Rose L. 1980. "Some Social Functions of Laughter," pp. 81–97 in Lewis Coser (ed.), *The Pleasures of Sociology* (New York: New America Library).

Fox, Renee C. 1974. *Experiment Perilous* (Philadelphia: University of Pennsylvania Press).

Goffman, Erving. 1967. "On Face-Work," in *Interaction Ritual: Essays on Face-to-Face Behavior* (New York: Pantheon Books).

———. 1974. *Frame Analysis*. (New York: Harper and Row).

Reflective Questions

1. What is reality maintenance? How and why do we engage in it?
2. Chambliss argues that hospitals often are sites of humor, even at the same time as something horrible is happening. What different types of humor took place? What was your reaction to the

humor? Why? Would the jokes have been funny in front of family members of the patients? Why or why not? Other sociologists have found people making dark jokes at work in funeral homes and at the diagnosis of a disability. What role does humor play in these settings? Have you participated in dark humor? Where? Under what circumstances?

3. What does Chambliss mean by "When things fall apart, keep going"? Why do doctors code a patient they know is going to die? If perseverance isn't the byproduct of one's personality or individual fortitude, what is it?
4. Perhaps you attend one of the many universities or colleges where tuition has risen substantially over the last decade. Or perhaps you pay an increasing share of the cost of your education through tuition, while previous generations enjoyed more generous support of taxpayers. If you are like many students, you may find this unfair, and you may question whether specific courses you take are worth the money or years of debt. In such instances, you may find yourself concluding that a given course has not been worth it to you. Fair enough. Demand your money back and refuse to pay your next tuition bill until you get it. What would happen? What if you went to the departmental, business, or registrar's office and pleaded your case? What would happen? What would happen if you refused to leave until you got your money back? If you ask any individual business office worker, registrar, professor, or campus police officer, he or she likely will tell you that the cost of higher education is exorbitant. Why then is he or she unlikely to help you? What would you have to do to get your money back?

PART

VIII

Reproducing and Resisting Inequalities

We often speak of social relationships as if they were things that existed apart from social interaction. We imply this, for example, when we say that we have a certain kind of relationship with someone, such as a friendship. Yet social relationships are not so much something we have as something we do. Social interaction is the source and sustenance of social relationships. Their only existence apart from interaction is in memory and imagination. And even there, they tend to wither away without the nourishment of social interaction.

Our understanding of different kinds of relationships clearly influences how we interact with one another. For example, most of us do not tell checkout clerks in supermarkets intimate details about our private lives. However, it is because we do not do so that our relationship with checkout clerks is fleeting and relatively anonymous. If we did share our intimate secrets with a checkout clerk, and she or he reciprocated, then our relationship would be intimate.

Relationships are ways individuals relate to one another, which is just another way of referring to patterns of social interaction. These patterns serve as the bedrock of social institutions. Indeed, as Herbert Blumer observed in Selection 29, social institutions exist only in and through human interactions and relationships.

Social relationships provide the immediate context of our social lives and experience. They support and challenge our sense of self. They tie us emotionally to others in bonds of mutual obligation. Our positions in networks of relationships determine our social standing in the neighborhood, at school, at work, and even in our families. And, how others relate to us shapes our most personal experiences.

The selections included in Part VIII focus attention on the interactional dynamics of unequal relationships and how they shape our lives and experiences. The selections examine how our daily interactions and the meanings we give to our bodies, selves, and routine practices reproduce and resist unequal relationships. When unequal relationships accumulate over time and space, they result in social structural patterns we call inequalities. Racism and patriarchy are common examples.

Inequalities are the unearned advantages enjoyed by certain groups of people at the expense of others. Inequalities do not result from differences in natural abilities or hard work. Nor are they inevitable or somehow naturally occurring, even though they often seem that way. Rather, we *create* them, and they cannot exist without us continuing to do so. Sociological psychologists study inequalities to understand what we each do to reproduce (and challenge) inequalities: how our thinking, acting, and interacting with others provides unearned resources to some but not others. The creation of inequalities can be—and historically often has been—the result of overt bigotry and cruel intentions. But it need not be. And here is where sociological psychology has the most to offer: it allows us to see how perfectly thoughtful and well-meaning people contribute to inequalities *unintentionally* through everyday actions that have hidden consequences.

The selections in Part VIII highlight the following themes about reproducing and resisting inequalities:

- *Inequalities depend on our enforcing symbolic boundaries that position some people as more valuable than others.* Parts I and VII laid the groundwork for understanding how boundary making can transform into inequalities. Distinguishing people from each other and categorizing them according to particular characteristics help us to make sense of the world and coordinate our activities with others. Social categories and identities serve as shortcuts that allow us effectively to navigate ambiguous, complex, and speed-driven social environments.

  Differentiation leads to inequality when we pair it with social evaluations about people's competence, value, or morality. We come to associate a particular characteristic, often accompanied by physical markers, with these cultural assessments. We then enter interactions with implicit attitudes and judgments unknowingly at the ready. Once these judgments are activated, they cloud our interpretations of ourselves and others, as well as our courses of action. We may, in turn, opt to choose one job candidate over another even if they both have similar qualifications. Or we may attribute a negative motive to someone's harmless behavior, like wearing baggy pants. Or we may shape social policy to benefit people we view as "good like us" rather than as "bad" like members of a less powerful group. These routine, everyday judgments and interactions accumulate into widespread differences in opportunities and resources, such as wealth increasingly concentrating in the hands of a few, wage disparities persisting between men and women, and men of color being incarcerated at disproportionate rates. These disadvantages cannot be sustained without the continued reinforcement of symbolic boundaries.

- *We need not intend for our thoughts and actions to result in inequalities in order for them to do so.* Unequal relationships are what they are because we interactionally make them that way, not because we intend them to be that way. The way we relate to particular others is often guided by unquestioned cultural understandings of what different kinds of relationships and identities should look like. Moreover, we are often invested in unequal relationships. For example, if we are subordinates we may identify with disadvantaged groups, even if others look down on our associations. Powerful others may also give us attention or rewards for acting out stereotypes. Or our financial, cultural, or emotional well-being may depend on keeping these powerful people happy. Protecting our investments then prevents us from questioning resource imbalances, and it encourages us to recreate them. Inequalities are especially difficult to challenge when the actions that create them are hidden behind good will or admirable goals. But being sociologically mindful means understanding the consequences of our actions rather than only our intentions.

- *People who are unfairly disadvantaged challenge their own oppression.* Inequalities have an assortment of negative consequences for subordinated people. They lead to resource deprivation, resentment at bad treatment, and damaged self-images. As a result, marginalized people use whatever social, psychological, and material resources they can to challenge their subordination. They resist the negative assessments associated with their identities, for example, and create new positive meanings for being who they are. They also coordinate with other oppressed individuals to challenge gatekeepers who exclude them from opportunities, and they craft their own social agendas and use political maneuvering to advance them. Even though others may disparage them and cast them off as rejects, the oppressed develop ideologies, identities, and subcultural practices that offer them a sense of orientation and value. They also effect widespread change, as evidenced in the civil rights, feminist, and social welfare movements.

- *Oppressed individuals can contribute to their own and others' marginalization.* Inequalities are most importantly reproduced by the people who benefit from them. Nonetheless, sociological psychologists understand that people often act against their broad group interests. The working class, for example, has mobilized itself in voting campaigns to support candidates and policies that undermine unionizing and redistribute tax benefits to the wealthy. Sociological psychologists ask how and why this happens. While being on the receiving end of social devaluation and restricted resources can produce social cohesion and coordinated resistance, it does not always. Many on the bottom are so busy with the everyday concerns of survival—feeding their families, finding some social meaning—that they have little time and energy for anything else. They also may develop emotional investments that align their interests with the dominant group. Or they may experience more immediate or greater social return from policing symbolic boundaries that position them above some unlucky others. Such was the case with white working-class voters who were not voting against their class interests so much as voting in favor of their racial interests.

- *Oppressed individuals can contribute to their own and others' marginalization.* Inequalities are most importantly reproduced by the people who benefit from them. Nonetheless, sociological psychologists understand that people often act against their broad group interests. The working class, for example, has mobilized itself in voting campaigns to support candidates and policies that undermine unionizing and redistribute tax benefits to the wealthy. Sociological psychologists ask how and why this happens. While being on the receiving end of social devaluation and restricted resources can produce social cohesion and coordinated resistance, it does not always. Many on the bottom are so busy with the everyday concerns of survival—feeding their families, finding some social meaning—that they have little time and energy for anything else. They also may develop emotional investments that align their interests with the dominant group. Or they may experience more immediate or greater social return from policing symbolic boundaries that position them above some unlucky others. Such was the case with white working-class voters who were not voting against their class interests so much as voting in favor of their racial interests.

Through addressing these themes, the selections in Part VIII illustrate how sociological psychology provides us with a valuable perspective for understanding how power and inequality get enacted, negotiated, and resisted in our relationships and identity work. Each of the selections demonstrates how we "do" relationships and identities whether we fully realize what we are doing or not.

33

Borderwork Among Girls and Boys

BARRIE THORNE

Gender is one of the most fundamental dimensions of the social structure of all known human societies. Yet gender is as much a human creation as any other dimension of social structure. Anatomical sex may be a natural fact of human life, but its meanings are not. It is these meanings, rather than reproductive biology, that constitute gender. Femininity and masculinity are as much products of human definition, interpretation, and interaction as any other human meanings. In this selection, Barrie Thorne examines the construction and reproduction of gender among elementary-school children. She concentrates on a recurrent pattern of interaction that she calls "borderwork."

Most children define themselves as either a boy or girl during the preschool-age years. Once they do, they tend to prefer the company of "their own kind." The result is a kind of self-imposed segregation between girls and boys. Boys tend to play with other boys and girls tend to play with other girls. Although girls and boys do continue to interact with one another, much of that interaction serves to erect, rather than break down, the invisible symbolic barrier between them. This kind of interaction is what constitutes the borderwork pattern.

Thorne examines three varieties of borderwork: chasing games, such as "chase-and-kiss"; rituals of pollution, such as "cooties"; and invasions, usually of girls' activities and territories by boys. As she demonstrates, these familiar and memorable forms of interaction create gender divisions and perpetuate prevailing gender stereotypes. When engaged in borderwork, girls and boys treat each other as members of opposing, if not antagonistic, teams. Their gender identities take priority over their personal identities. For example, a boy who is being chased by a girl is much more likely to exclaim, "Help, a girl's chasing me!" than "Help, Susie's chasing me!" They also tend to lump all boys and all girls together. "Boys are mean." "Girls have cooties." They thereby exaggerate gender difference and perpetuate gender stereotypes.

Thorne suggests that interaction between men and women often resembles the borderwork of school-age children, in that adults also enact gender stereotypes and exaggerate gender difference. Like boys and girls, men and women interactionally produce and reproduce their gender and the often rocky relations between the sexes. And what is interactionally produced can be interactionally changed. Gender—the meanings of anatomical sex—is not imposed on us by nature or social structure. To borrow from Blumer, our femininity and masculinity are derived from what we do, not from what we are.

My husband, Peter, and I became parents several years after I had . . . started to teach and do research on gender. . . . Parenting returned me to the sites of childhood—the Lilliputian worlds of sandboxes, neighborhood hideouts, playgrounds, elementary-school lunchrooms. I found that these sites, that the sheer presence of groups of children,

Reprinted from: Barrie Thorne, *Gender Play: Girls and Boys in School*, pp. 2–3, 6–7, 64–66, 68–70, 73–77, 84–88.

evoked memories of my own childhood. . . . Those memories, and my experiences as a parent, whetted my interest in learning, more systematically, about girls' and boys' daily experiences of gender. I decided to hang out in an elementary school, keeping regular notes on my observations, especially of boys' and girls' relationships with one another. . . .

During the 1976–77 school year, I observed for eight months in a public elementary school in a small city on the coast of California. I gained initial access to this school, which I will call Oceanside (all names of places and people have been changed), through the teacher of a combined fourth-fifth-grade class. I regularly observed in Miss Bailey's classroom and accompanied the students into the lunchroom and onto the playground, where I roamed freely and got to know other kids as well.

In 1980, when I was living in Michigan, I did another stint of fieldwork, observing for three months in Ashton School, my pseudonym for a public elementary school on the outskirts of a large city. . . . In addition to observing in an Ashton kindergarten and a second-grade classroom, I roamed around the lunchroom, hallways, and playground. This experience helped me broaden and gain perspective on the more focused and in-depth observations from the California school. . . .

Borderwork

Walking across a school playground from the paved areas where kids play jump rope and hopscotch to the grassy playing field and games of soccer and baseball, one moves from groups of girls to groups of boys. The spatial separation of boys and girls constitutes a kind of boundary, perhaps felt most strongly by individuals who want to join an activity controlled by the other gender. When girls and boys are together in a relaxed and integrated way, playing a game of handball or eating and talking together at a table in the lunchroom, the sense of gender as boundary often dissolves. But sometimes girls and boys come together in ways that emphasize their opposition; boundaries may be created through contact as well as avoidance.

The term "borderwork" helps conceptualize interaction across—yet, interaction based on and even strengthening—gender boundaries. This notion comes from Fredrik Barth's [1969] analysis of social relations that are maintained across ethnic boundaries (e.g., between the Saami, or Lapps, and Norwegians) without diminishing the participants' sense of cultural difference and of dichotomized ethnic status. Barth focuses on more macro, ecological arrangements, whereas I emphasize face-to-face behavior. But the insight is similar: *although contact sometimes undermines and reduces an active sense of difference, groups may also interact with one another in ways that strengthen their borders.* One can gain insight into the maintenance of ethnic (and gender) groups by examining the boundary that defines them rather than by looking at what Barth calls "the cultural stuff that it encloses" [Barth 1969, p. 15].

When gender boundaries are activated, the loose aggregation "boys and girls" consolidates into "the boys" and "the girls" as separate and reified groups. In the process, categories of identity, that on other occasions have minimal relevance for interaction, become the basis of separate collectivities. Other social definitions get squeezed out by heightened awareness of gender as a dichotomy and of "the girls" and "the boys" as opposite and even antagonistic sides. Several times I watched this process of transformation, which felt like a heating up of the encounter because of the heightened sense of opposition and conflict.

On a paved area of the Oceanside playground, a game of team handball took shape (team handball resembles doubles tennis, with clenched fists used to serve and return a rubber ball). Kevin arrived with the ball, and, seeing potential action, Tony walked over with interest on his face. Rita and Neera already stood on the other side of the yellow painted line that designated the center of a playing court. Neera called out, "Okay, me and Rita against you two," as Kevin and Tony moved into position. The game began in earnest with serves and returns punctuated by game-related talk—challenges between the opposing teams ("You're out!" "No, exactly on the line") and supportive comments between team members ("Sorry, Kevin," Tony said, when he missed a shot. "That's okay," Kevin replied). The game proceeded for about five minutes, and then the ball went out of bounds. Neera ran after it, and Tony ran after her, as if to begin a chase. As he ran, Rita shouted with annoyance, "C'mon, let's play." Tony and Neera returned to their positions, and the game continued.

Then Tony slammed the ball, hard, at Rita's feet. She became angry at the shift from the ongoing, more cooperative mode of play, and she flashed her middle finger at the other team, calling to Sheila to join their side. The game continued in a serious vein until John ran over and joined Kevin and Tony, who cheered; then Bill arrived, and there was more cheering. Kevin called out, "C'mon Ben," to draw in another passing boy; then Kevin added up the numbers on each side, looked across the yellow line, and triumphantly announced, "We got five and you got three." The game continued, more noisy than before, with the boys yelling "wee haw" each time they made a shot. The girls—and that's how they now seemed, since the sides were increasingly defined in terms of gender—called out, "Bratty boys! Sissy boys!" When the ball flew out of bounds, the game dissolved, as Tony and Kevin began to chase after Sheila. Annoyed by all these changes, Rita had already stomped off.

In this sequence, an earnest game, with no commentary on the fact that boys and girls happened to be on different sides, gradually transformed into a charged sense of girls-against-boys/boys-against-the-girls. Initially, one definition of the situation prevailed: a game of team handball, with each side trying to best the other. Rita, who wanted to play a serious game, objected to the first hint of other possibilities, which emerged when Tony chased Neera. The frame of a team handball game continued but was altered and eventually overwhelmed when the kids began to evoke gender boundaries. These boundaries brought in other possibilities—piling on players to outnumber the other gender, yelling gender-based insults, shifting from handball to cross-gender chasing—which finally broke up the game.

Gender boundaries have a shifting presence, but when evoked, they are accompanied by stylized forms of action, a sense of performance, mixed and ambiguous meanings . . . and by an array of intense emotions—excitement, playful elation, anger, desire, shame, and fear. . . . These stylized moments evoke recurring themes that are deeply rooted in our cultural conceptions of gender, and they suppress awareness of patterns that contradict and qualify them. . . .

Chasing

Cross-gender chasing dramatically affirms boundaries between boys and girls. The basic elements of chase and elude, capture and rescue are found in various kinds of tag with formal rules, as well as in more casual episodes of chasing that punctuate life on playgrounds. These episodes begin with a provocation, such as taunts ("You creep!" "You can't get me!"), bodily pokes, or the grabbing of a hat or other possession. A provocation may be ignored, protested ("Leave me alone!"), or responded to by chasing. Chaser and chased may then alternate roles. Christine Finnan (1982), who also observed schoolyard chasing sequences, notes that chases vary in the ratio of chasers to chased (e.g., one chasing one, or five chasing two); the form of provocation (a taunt or a poke); the outcome (an episode may end when the chased outdistances the chaser, with a brief touch, wrestling to the ground, or the recapturing of a hat or a ball); and in use of space (there may or may not be safety zones). Kids sometimes weave chasing with elaborate shared fantasies, as when a group of Ashton first- and second-grade boys played "jail," with "cops" chasing after "robbers," or when several third-grade girls designated a "kissing dungeon" beneath the playground slide and chased after boys to try to throw them in. When they captured a boy and put him in the dungeon under the slide, two girls would guard him while other boys pushed through the guards to help the captured boy escape.

Chasing has a gendered structure. Boys frequently chase one another, an activity that often ends in wrestling and mock fights. When girls chase girls, they are usually less physically aggressive; for example, they less often wrestle one another to the ground or try to bodily overpower the person being chased. Unless organized as a formal game like "freeze tag," same-gender chasing goes unnamed and usually undiscussed. But children set apart cross-gender chasing with special names. Students at both Oceanside and Ashton most often talked about "girls-chase-the-boys" and "boys-chase-the-girls"; the names are largely interchangeable, although boys tend to use the former and girls the latter, each claiming a kind of innocence. At Oceanside, I also heard both boys and girls refer to "catch-and-kiss"; and, at Ashton, older boys talked about "kiss-or-kill," younger girls invited one another to "catch boys," and younger girls and boys described the game of "kissin'." In addition to these terms, I have heard reports from other U.S. schools of "the chase," "chasers," "chase-and-kiss," "kiss-chase," and "kissers-and-chasers." The names vary by region and school but always contain both gender and sexual meanings.

Most informal within-gender chasing does not live on in talk unless something unusual happens, like an injury. But cross-gender chasing, especially when it takes the form of extended sequences with more than a few participants, is often surrounded by lively discussion. Several parents have told me about their kindergarten or first-grade children coming home from school to excitedly, or sometimes disgustedly, describe "girls-chase-the-boys" (my children also did this when they entered elementary school). Verbal retellings and assessments take place not only at home but also on the playground. For example, three Ashton fourth-grade girls who claimed time-out from boys-chase-the-girls by running to a declared safety zone, excitedly talked about the ongoing game: "That guy is mean, he hits everybody." "I kicked him in the butt."

In girls-chase-the-boys, girls and boys become, by definition, separate teams. Gender terms blatantly override individual identities, especially in references to the other team ("Help, a girl's chasin' me!" "C'mon Sarah, let's get that boy!" "Tony, help save me from the girls!"). Individuals may call for help from, or offer help to, others of their gender. And in acts of treason, they may grab someone from their team and turn them over to the other side. For example, in an elaborate chasing scene among a group of Ashton third-graders, Ryan grabbed Billy from behind, wrestling him to the ground. "Hey girls, get 'im," Ryan called.

Boys more often mix episodes of cross-gender with same-gender chasing, a pattern strikingly evident in the large chasing scenes or melees that recurred on the segment of the Ashton playground designated for third- and fourth-graders. Of the three age-divided playground areas, this was the most bereft of fixed equipment; it had only a handball court and, as a boy angrily observed to me, "two stinkin' monkey bars." Movable play equipment was also in scarce supply; the balls were often lodged on the school roof, and, for a time, the playground aides refused to hand out jump ropes because they said the kids just wanted to use them to "strangle and give ropeburns." With little to do, many of the students spent recesses and the lunch hour milling and chasing around on the grassy field. Boys ran after, tackled, and wrestled one another on the ground, sometimes so fiercely that injuries occurred. Girls also chased girls, although less frequently and with far less bodily engagement than among boys. Cross-gender chases, in every sort of numeric combination, were also less physically rough than chasing among boys; girls were quick to complain, and the adult aides intervened more quickly when a boy and a girl wrestled on the ground. Cross-gender chasing was full of verbal hostility, from both sides, and it was marked by stalking postures and girls' screams and retreats to spots of safety and talk.

In cross-gender and same-gender chasing, girls often create safety zones, a designated space that they can enter to become exempt from the fray. After a period of respite, often spent discussing what has just happened, they return to the game. The safety zone is sometimes a moving area around an adult; more than once, as I stood watching, my bubble of personal space housed several girls. Or the zone may be more fixed, like the pretend steel house that the first- and second-grade Ashton girls designated next to the school building. In the Oceanside layout, the door to the girls' restroom faced one end of the playground, and girls often ran into it for safety. I could hear squeals from within as boys tried to open the door and peek in. During one of these scenarios, eight girls emerged from the restroom with dripping clumps of wet paper towels, which they threw at the three boys who had been peeking in, and then another burst of chasing ensued. . . .

"Cooties" and Other Pollution Rituals

Episodes of chasing sometimes entwine with rituals of pollution, as in "cooties" or "cootie tag" where specific individuals or groups are treated as contaminating or carrying "germs." Cooties, of course, are invisible; they make their initial appearance through announcements like "Rochelle has cooties!" Kids have rituals for transferring cooties (usually touching someone else, often after a chase, and shouting "You've got cooties!"), for immunization (writing "CV"—for "cootie vaccination"—on their arms, or shaping their fingers to push out a pretend-immunizing "cootie spray"), and for eliminating cooties (saying "no gives" or using "cootie catchers" made of folded paper). While girls and boys may transfer cooties to one another, and girls may give cooties to girls, boys do not generally give cooties to other boys. Girls, in short, are central to the game.

Either girls or boys may be defined as having cooties, but girls give cooties to boys more often than vice versa. In Michigan, one version of cooties was called "girl stain." . . . And in a further shift from acts to imputing the moral character of actors, individuals may be designated as "cootie queens" or "cootie girls." Cootie queens or cootie girls (I have never heard or read about "cootie kings" or "cootie boys") are female pariahs, the ultimate school untouchables, seen as contaminating not only by virtue of gender, but also through some added stigma such as being overweight or poor. And according to one report, in a racially mixed playground in Fresno, California, "Mexican" (Chicano/Latino) but not Anglo children give cooties; thus, inequalities of race, as well as gender and social class, may be expressed through pollution games. In situations like this, different sources of oppression may compound one another.

I did not learn of any cootie queens at Ashton or Oceanside, but in the daily life of schools, *individual* boys and girls may be stigmatized and treated as contaminating. For example, a third-grade Ashton girl refused to sit by a particular boy, whom other boys routinely pushed away from the thick of all-male seating, because he was "stinky" and "peed in his bed." A teacher in another school told me that her fifth-grade students said to newcomers, "Don't touch Phillip's desk; he picks his nose and makes booger balls." Phillip had problems with motor coordination, which, the teacher thought, contributed to his marginalization.

But there is also a notable gender asymmetry, evident in the skewed patterning of cooties; *girls as a group are treated as an ultimate source of contamination,* while boys *as* boys—although maybe not, as Chicanos or individuals with a physical disability—are exempt. Boys sometimes mark hierarchies among themselves by using "girl' as a label for low-status boys and by pushing subordinated boys next to the contaminating space of girls. In Miss Bailey's fourth-fifth-grade class, other boys routinely forced or maneuvered the lowest-status boys (Miguel and Alejandro, the recent immigrants from Mexico, and Joel, who was overweight and afraid of sports) into sitting "by the girls," a space treated as contaminating. In this context, boys drew on gender meanings to convey racial subordination. In contrast, when there was gender-divided seating in the classroom, lunchroom, music room, or auditorium, which girls sat at the boundary between groups of girls and groups of boys had no apparent relationship to social status.

Boys sometimes treat objects associated with girls as polluting; once again, the reverse does not occur. Bradley, a college student, told me about a classroom incident he remembered from third grade. Some girls gave Valentine's Day cards with pictures of Strawberry Shortcake, a feminine-stereotyped image, to everyone in the class, including boys. Erik dumped all his Strawberry Shortcake valentines into Bradley's box; Bradley one-upped the insult by adding his own Strawberry Shortcake valentines to the pile and sneaking them back into Erik's box.

Recoiling from physical proximity with another person and their belongings because they are perceived as contaminating is a powerful statement of social distance and claimed superiority. Pollution beliefs and practices draw on the emotion-laden feeling of repugnance that accompanies unwanted touch or smell. Kids often act out pollution beliefs in a spirit of playful teasing, but the whimsical frame of "play" slides in and out of the serious, and some games of cooties clearly cause emotional pain. When pollution rituals appear, even in play, they frequently express and enact larger patterns of inequality, by gender, by social class and race, and by bodily characteristics like weight and motor coordination. When several of these characteristics are found in the same person, the result may be extreme rituals of shaming, as in the case of cootie queens. Aware of the cruelty and pain bound up in games of pollution, teachers and aides often try to intervene, especially when a given individual becomes the repeated target. . . .

Invasion

. . . [I]n chasing, groups of girls and groups of boys confront one another as separate "sides," which makes for a kind of symmetry, as does the alternation of chasing and being chased. But rituals of pollution tip the symmetry, defining girls as more contaminating. Invasions, a final type of borderwork, also take asymmetric form; boys invade girls' groups and activities much more often than the reverse. When asked about what they do on the playground, boys list "teasing the girls" as a named activity, but girls do not talk so routinely about "teasing boys." As in other kinds of borderwork, gendered language ("Let's spy on the girls" "Those boys are messing up our jump-rope game") accompanies invasions, as do stylized interactions that highlight a sense of gender as an antagonistic social division.

On the playgrounds of both schools, I repeatedly saw boys, individually or in groups, deliberately disrupt the activities of groups of girls. Boys ruin ongoing games of jump rope by dashing under the twirling rope and disrupting the flow of the jumpers or by sticking a foot into the rope and stopping its momentum. On the Ashton playground, seven fourth-grade girls engaged in an intense game of four-square; it was a warm October day, and the girls had piled their coats on the cement next to the painted court. Two boys, mischief enlivening their faces, came to the edge of the court. One swung his arm into the game's bouncing space; in annoyed response, one of the female players pushed back at him. He ran off for a few feet, while the other boy circled in to take a swipe, trying to knock the ball out of play. Meanwhile, the first boy kneeled behind the pile of coats and leaned around to watch the girls. One of the girls yelled angrily, "Get out. My glasses are in one of those, and I don't want 'em busted." A playground aide called the boys over and told them to "leave the girls alone," and the boys ran off.

Some boys more or less specialize in invading girls, coming back again and again to disrupt; the majority of boys are not drawn to the activity. Even if only a few boys do most of the invading, disruptions are so frequent that girls develop ritualized responses. Girls verbally protest ("Leave us alone!" "Stop it, Keith!"), and they chase boys away. The disruption of a girls' game may provoke a cross-gender chasing sequence, but if girls are annoyed, they chase in order to drive the boy out of the space, a purpose far removed from playful shifting between the roles of chaser and chased. Girls may guard their play with informal lookouts who try to head off trouble; they are often wary about letting boys into their activities. . . .

Why Is Borderwork So Memorable?

The imagery of "border" may wrongly suggest an unyielding fence that divides social relations into two parts. The image should rather be one of many short fences that are quickly built and as quickly dismantled. . . . [Earlier] I described a team handball game in which gender meanings heated up. Heated events also cool down. After the team handball game transmuted into a brief scene of chasing, the recess bell rang and the participants went back to their shared classroom. Ten minutes later the same girls and boys interacted in reading groups where gender was of minimal significance. . . . [W]hy [then] are the occasions of gender borderwork so compelling? Why do episodes of girls-chase-the-boys and boys-against-the-girls *seem* like the heart of what "gender" is all about? Why do kids regard those situations as especially newsworthy and turn them into stories that they tell afterward and bring home from school? And why do adults, when invited to muse back upon gender relations in their elementary school years, so often spontaneously recall "girls-chase-the-boys," "teasing girls," and "cooties," but less often mention occasions when boys and girls were together in less gender-marked ways? (The latter kinds of occasions may be recalled under other rubrics, like "when we did classroom projects.")

The occasions of borderwork may carry extra-perceptual weight because they are marked by conflict, intense emotions, and the expression of forbidden desires. These group activities may also rivet attention because they are created by kids themselves, and because they are ritualized, not as high ceremony, but by virtue of being stylized, repeated, and enacted with a sense of performance. . . . [For example,] cross-gender chasing has a name ("chase and kiss"), a scripted format (the repertoire of provocations and forms of response), and takes shape through stylized motions and talk. The ritual form focuses attention and evokes dominant beliefs about the "nature" of boys and girls and relationships between them.

Erving Goffman [1977, p. 321] coined the term "genderism" to refer to moments in social life, such as borderwork situations, that evoke stereotypic beliefs. During these ritually foregrounded encounters, men and women "play out the differential human nature claimed for them." Many social environments don't lend themselves to this bifurcated and stylized display, and they may even undermine the stereotypes. But when men engage in horseplay (pushing, shoving) and mock contests like Indian wrestling, they dramatize themes of physical strength and violence that are central to [prevailing] constructions of masculinity. And, in various kinds of cross-gender play, as when a man chases after and pins down a woman, he pretends to throw her off a cliff, or threatens her with a snake, the man again claims physical dominance and encourages the woman to "provide a full-voiced rendition [shrinking back, hiding her eyes, screaming] of the plight to which her sex is presumably prone" [Goffman 1977, p. 323]. In short, men and women—and girls and boys—sometimes become caricatures of themselves, enacting and perpetuating stereotypes.

Games of girls-against-the-boys [and] scenes of cross-gender chasing and invasion . . . evoke stereotyped images of gender relations. Deeply rooted in the dominant culture . . . of our society, these images infuse the ways adults talk about girls and boys and relations between them; the content of movies, television, advertising, and children's books; and even the wisdom of experts. . . . This [prevailing] view of gender—acted out, reinforced, and evoked through the various forms of borderwork—has two key components:

1. *Emphasis on gender as an oppositional dualism.* Terms like "the opposite sex" and "the war between the sexes" come readily to mind when one watches a group of boys invade a jump-rope game and the girls angrily respond, or a group of girls and a group of boys hurling insults at one another across a lunchroom. In all forms of borderwork, boys and girls are defined as rival teams with a socially distant, wary, and even hostile relationship; heterosexual meanings add to the sense of polarization. Hierarchy tilts the theme of opposition, with boys asserting spatial, physical, and evaluative dominance over girls.
2. *Exaggeration of gender difference and disregard for the presence of crosscutting variation and sources of commonality.* Social psychologists have identified a continuum that ranges

> from what Henri Tajfel [1982] calls the "interpersonal extreme," when interaction is largely determined by *individual* characteristics, to the "intergroup extreme," when interaction is largely determined by the *group membership* or social categories of participants. Borderwork lies at the intergroup extreme. When girls and boys are defined as opposite sides caught up in rivalry and competition, group stereotyping and antagonism flourish. Members of "the other side" become "that boy" or "that girl." Individual identities get submerged, and participants hurl gender insults ("sissy boys," "dumb girls"), talk about the other gender as "yuck," and make stereotyped assertions ("girls are cry-babies," "boys are frogs; I don't like boys").

Extensive gender separation and organizing mixed-gender encounters as girls-against-the-boys set off contrastive thinking and feed an assumption of gender as dichotomous and antagonistic difference. These social practices seem to express core truths: that boys and girls are separate and fundamentally different, as individuals and as groups. Other social practices that challenge this portrayal—drawing boys and girls together in relaxed and extended ways, emphasizing individual identities or social categories that cut across gender, acknowledging variation in the activities and interests of girls and boys—carry less perceptual weight. . . .

The frames of "play" and "ritual" set the various forms of borderwork a bit apart from ongoing "ordinary" life. As previously argued, this may enhance the perceptual weight of borderwork situations in the eyes of both participants and observers, highlighting a gender-as-antagonistic-dualism portrayal of social relations. But the framing of ritualized play may also give leeway for participants to gain perspective on dominant cultural images. Play and ritual can comment on and challenge, as well as sustain, a given ordering of reality. . . . I [once] watched and later heard an aide describe a game the Oceanside students played on the school lunchroom floor. The floor was made up of large alternating squares of white and green linoleum, rather like a checkerboard. One day during the chaotic transition from lunch to noontime recess, [a boy named] Don . . . jumped, with much gestural and verbal fanfare, from one green square to another. Pointing to a white square, Don loudly announced, "That's girls' territory. Stay on the green square, or you'll change into a girl. Yuck!"

It occurred to me that Don was playing with gender dualisms, with a basic structure of two oppositely arranged parts whose boundaries are charged with risk. From one vantage point, the square-jumping game, as a kind of magical borderwork, may express and dramatically reaffirm structures basic to . . . the gender relations of the school. In the dichotomous world of either green or white, boy or girl, one misstep could spell transformative disaster. But from another vantage point, Don called up that structure to detached view, playing with, commenting on, and even, perhaps, mocking its assumptions.

References

Barth, Fredrik. 1969. "Introduction." Pp. 9–38 in *Ethnic Groups and Boundaries*, edited by F. Barth. Boston: Little, Brown.

Finnan, Christine. 1982. "The Ethnography of Children's Spontaneous Play." Pp. 358–380 in *Doing the Ethnography of Schooling*, edited by George Spindler. New York: Holt, Rinehart, and Winston.

Goffman, Erving. 1977. "The Arrangement Between the Sexes." *Theory and Society* 4:301–336.

Tajfel, Henri. 1982. "Social Psychology of Intergroup Relations." *Annual Review of Psychology* 33: 1–39.

Reflective Questions

1. What is borderwork and what are its unintended consequences for girls and boys? What boundaries are kids reinforcing when they chase each other? Who is polluting and why? What happens when boys and girls invade each others' spaces?
2. Thorne collected her data in the 1970s. Think back to your own days on the playground. Did you engage in chasing, pollution rituals, and invasion? How was your borderwork similar to that observed by Thorne? How was it different? Where did you

learn these games from? How did your teachers, siblings, friends, and parents reinforce or challenge borderwork? Did kids maintain boundaries around social characteristics other than gender, such as social class or body size? To what consequence? How does borderwork transform from establishing differences between groups into inequalities between them?

3. Perhaps you read this and thought, "Come on, they are just trying to have fun. Sociologists read too much into child's play." Why do sociologists think we should analyze play? How do these games shape our development of the self? Relationships? Expectations for others?
4. Draw a line down a sheet of paper to create two columns. In one column, write down all of the slang terms you can think of for men. Then, in the other, write down all of the slang terms you can think of for women. Look for patterns within each list by placing words into categories based on their meanings or references. What meanings do we use to praise men? Disparage them? How do we praise and disparage women? Now compare the lists. How do we use slang to engage in borderwork?
5. Borderwork is isolated neither to kids nor to gender. How do adults create gender boundaries in college, workplaces, and relationships? What consequences do they have for women's and men's access to resources (e.g., pay, promotion, status)? What other social boundaries do we most vigorously create and defend as adults?

Salvaging Decency

MARGARETHE KUSENBACH

We saw in the previous section that borderwork creates boundaries between social groups through self-imposed segregation and exaggerated group differences. A second important form of boundary making occurs when one group stigmatizes another in order to define itself as superior. Sociological psychologists call this social process "othering," which references the creation of a social other. When othering, individuals compare themselves to another group and transform them into a social foil. The dominating group positions the other to be inferior morally, culturally, or in some other socially important way and consequently less deserving of power and status. They then police the symbolic boundary between the in-group—"us"—and the out-group—"them." People engage in othering to secure their membership in the dominating group and to legitimize the group's exclusive access to particular resources. Othering creates winners and losers.

History offers countless examples of how othering works. In the 19th century, European immigrants claimed their whiteness by socially distancing themselves from blacks, who they claimed to be morally and intellectually inferior. By framing themselves as whites, immigrants ensured their right to vote and political influence. More recently, politicians used the othering of poor black women to pass welfare reform, the changes instituted in the Personal Responsibility and Work Opportunity Act of 1996. Aid to Dependent Children was a cash entitlement program originally created in 1935 to support single women so they could care for their children. After numerous legal challenges opened up access to benefits across the next decades, welfare reform in the 1990s added layers of stipulations for receiving cash assistance, including career caps and work requirements. Politicians and middle-class Americans used the image of a "welfare queen"—an unemployed single woman of color having children simply to game the system—to distinguish between who should be deserving of anti-poverty assistance and who should not.

In the following selection, Kusenbach examines how mobile home residents deal with one consequence of being othered: social stigma. Our identities are linked to where we live. Middle-class and working-class Americans position themselves more favorably by denigrating trailer living and especially "trailer trash." The ubiquity of negative images of mobile homes challenges residents' senses of self-worth and moral decency. As Kusenbach shows, mobile home residents deal with stigma of being othered by socially distancing themselves from the images of trailer trash. Kusenbach identifies two ways: bordering and fencing. When bordering, residents reject the trash associations altogether by distinguishing between where they live—and thus the kind of people they are—and stereotypical trailer parks. They frame their own places as resorts, highly regulated communities, and family-friendly oases. They point to these differences as evidence that they are nothing like trailer trash. Fencing involves making distinctions within the same locale, thus offer-

Reprinted from: Kusenbach, Margarethe. "Salvaging Decency: Mobile Home Residents' Strategies of Managing Stigma of 'Trailer' Living." *Qualitative Sociology* 32:399–428. Copyright 2009. Reprinted by permission of publisher.

ing some recognition of trailer trash. Residents who engage in fencing see trashy residents as threats to them from the inside, and they distance themselves from them by claiming to not act or look indecent like they do. They engage in othering against their own group. Which strategy subordinates use depends upon their own social resources and how easily they can claim other socially valued identities.

Kusenbach's findings offer two additional sociological psychological lessons. First, our frame of reference—whether we compare up, down, or sideways—is important in determining how we think about ourselves and the people around us. A classic example of this is married women's levels of satisfaction with an unequal division of household labor. Married women with partners who do little housework evaluate their situation very differently depending against whom they routinely compare their circumstances. A woman who grows up with a miserable mother and a father who did no housework may be satisfied with her husband's small contribution, while the same woman may be dissatisfied if she compares her own arrangement to that of her more progressive friends. She will also be less satisfied if she compares herself directly to her partner, or if her husband's contribution declined once they had children. Subordinates evaluate their circumstances differently depending on their frame of reference. Those who differentiate downward feel better about themselves. Also, stigmatized individuals do not necessarily develop empathy and compassion for other stigmatized groups. Rather, they often find themselves fighting with each other for resources, as demonstrated by the mobile home residents discussed in this selection. They even employ the same stereotypes used against them to belittle others, thereby reinforcing those very stereotypes. When individuals are left to fight at the bottom, they have less to invest in challenging the othering that denigrates them in the first place.

According to current (2005–2007) estimates by the American Community Survey, approximately 17.9 million people live in 8.7 million mobile homes in the United States. Mobile homes and mobile home residents can be found in every state and region of the country, yet they are most concentrated in the Sunbelt. A record 880,000—or fully 10%—of the nation's mobile homes are located in Florida, where the research for this paper was conducted. Approximately 1.5 million Florida residents, roughly one in twelve, permanently live in mobile homes . . . .

Contemporary popular culture is rife with negative images of people living in mobile homes and provides derogatory names that are utilized by many without quotation marks. Everyone knows that the designation "trailer trash" is not meant as a compliment. The low social prestige of "trailer" living presents a challenge that mobile home residents in Florida and elsewhere routinely encounter in their daily lives. The question of how recipients of these labels manage and deflect their negative, stigmatizing associations provides the thematic focus for this paper. Its larger goal is to contribute to our understanding of the experience of stigmatization, folk conception of decency, symbolic and social differentiation, as well as race and class dynamics . . . .

Stigma and Mobile Homes in Previous Research

As a subform of identity work, stigma management is generally aimed at avoiding or reducing the impact of a negative image on one's public or private self. According to Goffman (1963, 3ff.), a stigma is a "deeply discrediting attribute" that makes its carriers less desirable and respectable than so-called regular people. Goffman emphasizes that no single characteristic is discreditable in itself yet comes to be viewed as suspicious within the context of historically and culturally specific beliefs. Mobile home residents are prone to experiencing two kinds of stigma described by Goffman: "blemishes of individual character" and "tribal stigma." These two kinds of stigma vary in the perceived origin of the discrediting attribute and, accordingly, in the emotions stigmatized individuals might experience, such as shame for blemishes of individual character, or anger in the case of tribal stigma. A stigma's perceived source and embodied meaning are very consequential for how it is managed in interactions with others. The stigma of living in a mobile home is different from some other compromising features in that it allows for passing (Goffman 1963, pp. 73–91). Unlike many bodily and some tribal stigmas, the discrediting attribute—living in a "trailer"—is neither always immediately apparent nor can it be hidden permanently from everyone. Given its hideable, changeable and disembodied aspects, how then can mobile home living become such a serious and hurtful source of indignity? May I suggest three possible explanations.

First, the sharp punch of the trailer stigma lies in the extent to which people consider homes to be symbolic expressions of their identities and social statuses in contemporary society. . . . [H]omes are much more than physical shelters: they are powerful symbols of individual and collective identities and relationships. Denigrations of one's home may thus be felt as a direct assault on one's identity and community, as a symbolic challenge of one's place in society.

Second, the trailer stigma hits hard because of its racial implications. The label "trailer trash" is predominantly aimed at low-income Whites, as frequent combinations with the historic insult "White trash" indicate. . . . [T]his term is most often used by Whites in order to distance themselves from other Whites who are feared and despised because of their economic and physical proximity to minorities. According to Neewitz and Wray (1997), the conception of some people as "trash" not only justifies the marginalization of others who are clinging to the lower rungs of the economic ladder, it also fundamentally challenges the privileges of recipients' White racial identity. . . .

And third, labels such as "trailer" and "trailer trash" undermine one's personal integrity: they are viewed as a broad attack on one's self worth and moral decency. . . . [D]ecency is a central principle guiding the lives of virtually all members of non-middle-class groups—even though the details of how this value is practiced in daily life are fiercely contested. Regardless of content, members of low-status groups often claim to have a clear sense of what "indecency" looks like among their peers. It seems that physical and symbolic proximity to others who are perceived as "indecent" increase attempts at differentiation (Lamont and Molnár 2002), thereby aiding the construction and maintenance of boundaries within marginalized groups. . . .

Research and Data

Research was conducted between summer 2005 and spring 2008 in four adjacent Florida counties in a total of 21 communities. . . . Nearly 340,000 mobile home residents—almost 2% of the nation's total—are estimated to permanently live in this four-county area. Having been a major destination for trailer travel in the 1920s and 1930s, this region is considered to be the birth place of mobile home communities in the United States.

Eighteen of the selected sites are mobile home parks, and three are mobile home neighborhoods in which houses are placed on individually owned parcels of land. Of the mobile home parks, one is a so-called migrant worker "camp" in which homes are rented by migrant farm workers. Eight parks are age-restricted senior communities (55 years and over), and nine are so-called family parks where no such restrictions exist. One of the senior parks is a resident-owned facility, meaning each resident owns a share of the park cooperative. With the exception of the resident-owned park and the migrant worker camp, all selected parks are of the land lease variety where residents are required to own their home yet pay rent to a park owner for the land on which it is placed. Virtually all research sites, whether urban, suburban or rural, were physically separated from other types of housing by streets, fences and/or natural features. Not unlike traditional subdivisions, most mobile home parks provide one or two access points from the outside and a maze of internal roads; many are gated and shielded from view.

In 2007, monthly lot rents of mobile home owners ranged from the mid $100s to the high $400s, depending on a park's location, size, and amenities. The estimated value of our informants' homes ranged from $2,000 for a deteriorating single-wide model from the 1960s to nearly $100,000 for a new double-wide unit with vaulted ceilings. . . .

Ten undergraduate research assistants and I conducted interviews with members of 45 households, between one and ten at each research site. Four couples were interviewed together, resulting in a total of 49 study participants. . . .

Mobile Home Residents' Strategies of Managing Stigma

Mobile home residents have developed a number of proactive and reactive strategies to cope with the negative views of their lifestyle expressed in public opinion and, occasionally, personal encounters. . . . The most common technique mentioned and displayed by residents was distancing, meaning instances of separating oneself and one's community from others who better fit the existing stereotypes. . . .

Distancing

We observed that the majority of informants distanced themselves and their associates from other mobile home residents and communities whom they considered fundamentally less worthy. This skillful strategy reflects Goffman's (1963, pp. 107–108) insight that members of stigmatized groups have adopted and internalized "the norms of wider society."

> Whether closely allied with his own kind or not, the stigmatized individual may exhibit identity ambivalence when he obtains a close sight of his own kind behaving in a stereotyped way, flamboyantly or pitifully acting out the negative attributes imputed to them. The sight may repel him, since after all he supports the norms of the wider society, but his social and psychological identification with these offenders holds him to what repels him, transforming repulsion into shame, and then transforming ashamedness itself into something of which he is ashamed.

Goffman here suggests that members of disparaged groups experience "identity ambivalence." They can be repulsed and even shamed by appearances and behaviors of their peers which lowers their self esteem and further increases their distance from dominant groups. Interestingly, signs of self-disparaging identity ambivalence were practically absent among mobile home residents interviewed for this study. It appeared that such feelings were preempted through cognitive and practical operations of distancing or, as it is sometimes called, othering.

Schwalbe et al. (2000) speak of "defensive othering among subordinates" in describing the efforts of disparaged individuals to deflect the stigma they are subjected to by others. . . . Schwalbe et al. (2000, p. 425) state that

> [t]he process, in each case, involves accepting the legitimacy of a devalued identity imposed by the dominant group, but then saying, in effect, "There are indeed Others to whom this applies, but it does not apply to me."

This seems to be the exact thought process behind the many instances of distancing or othering among mobile home residents who carefully erect symbolic boundaries between themselves and certain others whom they stigmatize in turn. To foreshadow one major result of the research, while a few informants were okay with calling their own home a "trailer" and their community a "trailer park," none of the interviewees embraced the term "trailer trash" as a positive identity; it was only used as a negative marker. All these terms however were applied by participants in reference to other mobile home dwellers, including other interviewees who fit the given descriptions. The strategy of passing the stigma down the social pecking order to even more subordinate people serves to redraw the symbolic boundary between "good" and "bad." It elevates the moral decency of one's self and social group vis-à-vis others who, to outsiders, might look similar yet are fundamentally less worthy.

Upon close inspection, our data suggested a difference between two forms of distancing which could be described as "bordering" and "fencing." "Bordering" shall refer to accounts and actions aimed at erecting boundaries between one's own community and geographically, culturally, and/or structurally distant others. This type of disassociation is relatively easy for residents of parks that have positive characteristics such as upscale-sounding names, age restrictions, or preferred locations. In contrast, I shall call "fencing" those accounts and actions that emphasize differences within someone's community. This version of othering requires a more nuanced thought process and was often observed among residents of mobile home parks that lack valued status characteristics. Both strategies were rooted in social differences between groups as well as in purely symbolic differences.

Bordering

This strategy deflects the stigma of trailer living to other types of people and communities that are located somewhere else; for instance, on the proverbial other side of the tracks. Mobile home residents construct a difference between communities that conform to the label and views of a "trailer park" and their own communities which do not fall into this category and thus do not deserve the name and its associations.

Hank, a divorced White man in his late 60s, is a retired coal miner who lives in a rural senior park. His newer double-wide home looked inviting and clean, and family photographs decorated many of the walls. He explains the difference between his community and a "stereotypical" mobile home park in the following way:

> A lot of people stereotype mobile home people. They create creatures, trailer trash, things like that. And when I tell people that I live in a mobile home park, I try to stress it's not a stereotypical mobile home park, it's more like a resort, an adult community. (. . .) It's more than a community, it's like a big family. (. . .) For the most part, I've met some real fine people in here and it's not people all from your same place. You got so much diversity of people; some bankers that get along with coal miners—it don't seem to make any difference. We're all in the same boat, so to speak.

Hank first sets up a contrast between his own "resort," "adult" type of community and a "stereotypical mobile home park" that may be associated with the "trailer trash" creatures people often have in mind. In a second step, Hank then downplays class and cultural differences within his own park to stress the sense of equality and shared identity that is prevalent here. He even calls it a "big family" and conjures up the image of the same boat.

The careful attention Hank pays to labels and names was shared by many other informants. A number of seniors told us that they would never move into a community that calls itself a "trailer park." Instead, they sought out, and now take pride in inhabiting, communities that carry more prestigious sounding names, such as "Meadowbrook Village," "Winward Lakes," "Shady Acres Estates," or "Country Aire" (these are real names of mobile home communities in the larger area that resemble the names of communities inhabited by some senior research participants). Generally speaking, MHP—standing for "Mobile Home Park," is a common ingredient of community names and viewed as acceptable by a majority of participants, even though many prefer community names that do not reference anything less than regular homes.

Aside from names, another major difference between a mobile home park and a "trailer park," in the eyes of many informants, lies in the existence of rules and regulations. Consider the following excerpt from the interview with Bella, a widowed White woman in her late 60s, who lives by herself in a well maintained suburban family park that used to be a senior community. Management has recently converted a tennis court to a fenced skate park, a rare amenity that is greatly appreciated by parents and youth.

> BELLA: You know the only thing that I hate? You people have both used the word "community," "mobile home community." When people come in and refer to it as a "trailer park"! This is not a trailer park! I know what they mean by "trailer park," but other people

> cannot make the distinction, okay? This has rules and regulations, this has restrictions, okay? You must keep your property looking so and so. In a trailer park, you know, they. . . .
>
> LISA [interviewer]: Yeah, do whatever. . . .
>
> BELLA: Yeah, do whatever you want. Junk cars—and that's another thing, you know, your tags have to all be current, otherwise she tickets them and it's an eviction if you don't follow through on the rules and regs.

Given its tight rules and regulations, Bella considers "trailer park" to be an incorrect description of her community. While she vehemently opposes the label with respect to her own park, Bella implies that the term can be applied correctly to other places where residents are less regulated. The view that strict park rules regarding appearance coincide with a higher quality of residents that defy the common stereotypes was very common. Ironically, it was even held by people who despise their park's rules as unfair and ridiculous in other contexts.

Another example of this view was given by Lee, a White man in his mid-60s who recently retired from a middle management position and currently lives in an upscale suburban senior park with his wife. Being the park's representative of the mobile home owner's association, Lee uses the politically correct term "manufactured homes" even when speaking of less desirable places.

> There's manufactured homes and parks I wouldn't want to live in! They're trashy, they look junky. You might have a nice place and keep it up but your neighbors have got . . . they're working on an old junk car outside. They've got, you know . . . they aren't . . . we can't do that! We've got an RV park [a fenced section in one corner of the park] and if somebody has an RV or a 5th wheeler, that's where it's got to go. You can park on the street for a limited time, maybe about a half a day, 3, 4, 5 hours, but not overnight.

Lee here pictures "trashy" parks in which residents might work on "old junk cars," a widely used image symbolizing indecency that is borrowed from public stereotypes. In contrast, his community does not even allow residents to park vehicles on the street for more than a few hours. Lee would not make the mistake of moving into one of these "trashy" parks, even though he admits that they might include nice homes as well.

Thus far, according to many participants, park names and rules are important indicators of two very different kinds of mobile home communities and people: clean and respectable ones versus trashy and morally suspect others. . . .

The following example again illustrates geographical distancing yet also introduces a new feature separating "good" and "bad" parks. Rick is a currently unemployed construction worker, a White man in his 40s who lives with his second wife and their young daughter in an urban family park located in an economically depressed part of town. The family does not have a telephone and their older single-wide home is in dire need of repair.

Unlike many others, Rick does not object to calling his community a "trailer park" yet he maintains that there are still important differences.

> I've seen a lot, over there in Zephyrhills, there's a lot of trailer parks in a lot worse shape than what this trailer park is, and a lot older trailers than what this park is! And this park is basically a more family atmosphere park than most of them around, I imagine.

Rick suggests that the "family atmosphere" of his park separates it from other, less desirable communities. He also draws on the more refined appearance and the lower age of homes in his park to support his, noticeably careful, claim . . . .

Consider a last example. Frankie, a single Hispanic man in his 50s, is a former construction worker who is now disabled. He lives with his mother, who is in very poor health, and a dog in an old single-wide unit in the same family community as Rick. Frankie owns an older model pickup truck and sometimes helps out neighbors who do not have transportation.

AUTHOR: So, you figure you'd like to remain in the park! You think it was a good place to go?

FRANKIE: Yeah, it's okay. It's a nice place. I've seen trailer parks, oh, they're nasty!

AUTHOR: Where?

FRANKIE: It's around here. There's was one. . . . Rosie took me one time to pick up a dog. And that trailer park was so bad, people were moving out. You'd see trailers halfway hanging around back. And I've been to other trailer parks, I mean, they're nasty! They don't have grass, everything is sand, you know, the road's all messed up and, I mean, it ain't worth living in those things! And they pay more rent than I do. They pay about 400 to 500 a month. And they don't own the trailer!

AUTHOR: So you think this is one of the nicer parks?

FRANKIE: Yeah, it's a really nice park.

Frankie's view of his park as "really nice" in contrast to some other parks that are "nasty" is interesting. He grounds his description of his own community on appearance rather than location, noting that bad looking parks can be found "around here." Frankie further emphasizes that residents of these other parks do not own their trailers, whereas he does, thereby highlighting the difference between owner-occupied and renter-occupied parks.

To sum up this section, bordering, as a form of distancing, invokes critical boundaries between the following categories: places that are called "trailer parks" versus more prestigious sounding names (with "mobile home park" being an acceptable neutral term), senior versus family parks, parks that have strict rules and regulations versus those that do not, parks that charge high rents versus those that charge low rents, differences between certain neighborhoods and towns, family-oriented parks versus others that are not, owner-occupied versus renter-occupied parks, and simply nice-looking versus nasty-looking parks. The general implication is that one's own park, and, by extension, one's self, are more respectable than other, distant communities and people. Interestingly, the social and economic diversity that might exist in one's own park is viewed as something positive because, by definition, it does not cross the decency divide.

Fencing

In his autobiographical essay, Berube (1997) highlights the importance of social differentiation within the mobile home parks he grew up in. His family's sense of respectability was built on its perceived difference from less decent neighbors. . . . I found a very comparable process in our data which I here call "fencing." Fencing is more subtle and complex than bordering because it requires the construction of internal differences within a given location or community. Residents cannot simply rely on broad social or geographic differences; they need to construct more nuanced, localized boundaries to justify their own placement on the good side of the decency divide.

At the time of our interview Liz, a White former nurse in her 60s who now works part-time at a convenience store, was the district president of the mobile home owners association. She shared a single-wide waterfront home with her third husband and a small dog, living right next door to her adult son, a sufferer from bipolar disorder. In the following excerpt, Liz claims that certain people in her urban family park are far from perfect.

LIZ: There's just so many things that are not right about the park! But it is a wonderful place to live, if we ever get it cleaned up and get the riff-raff out. And that's what the present administration is trying to do. They're really trying to get rid of the people that are drug addicts. I won't say "alcoholics" because we got a lot of alcoholics and that's all over the world. You know, so I won't say that they're targeting them. But they're certainly targeting drug dealers.

AUTHOR: Well, that makes sense.

> Liz: Oh yeah. We used to be an all White park. And now we have Blacks, we have Hispanics, Latinos, whatever . . . .
>
> Author: Does it cause conflict when there is turnover of who is living in the park?
>
> Liz: They're having some problems. We have the police in here quite frequently.
>
> Author: Is there drugs?
>
> Liz: Drugs and domestic violence and kids stealing.

Liz here associates the ongoing decline of her community with the presence of "riff-raff." She includes drug addicts and drug dealers in the category of "bad" people yet she excludes alcoholics because she considers alcoholism to be a more universal and benign problem. Liz thus draws a clear distinction between two types of problems: one forgivable and not reflective of a person's character, and the other unforgivable and indicative of a person's compromised moral values, echoing popular constructions of the "deserving" and "undeserving" poor (Katz 1989). Later, she adds "domestic violence" and deviant children to the latter kinds of problems currently rampant in her park. Liz also seems to suggest that non-White people are responsible for most of the serious problems. Her use of the pronouns "we" and "they" aids her construction of two basic categories of people. There is no doubt that Liz, as an old-time resident who did not witness any major issues in the past, considers herself to be a member of the respectable group.

Another interesting example of fencing is seen in the following passage from my interview with Ruby, a White woman in her mid-30s who works part-time as a gas station attendant and lives in a suburban family park. Ruby shares a large double-wide home with her husband and her mother (who was severely intoxicated when she returned to the house from a shopping trip during the interview), as well as 22 indoor/outdoor cats.

> When Home Town [the park's new management company] took over, there were a couple of things that needed to be done. And one of them that they did do was they got a lot of the drug dealers out. Which was a good thing. The other thing is that they got a lot of the old and rundown trailers out of here! And I say "trailers" because that's what they were! You won't ever hear anybody who lives in a mobile home park refer to their home as a "trailer." I mean, that's just one thing we don't do. As far as anything else that they've done, we had a Homeowner's Association, and they had a part in abolishing it.

Ruby here calls some of the former homes in her park "trailers." She applies this term to homes that "needed" to disappear, just like the "drug dealers." However, in the very next sentence she denies that "anybody" living in a mobile home would ever call his or her home a "trailer." She then qualifies that this is something "we" would never do. Clearly, Ruby does not consider drug dealers and trailer residents to be part of her community. She draws a symbolic boundary between people like herself, who should remain in the park, and drug dealers and trailer residents on the other side who are not part of the community and thus deserve to be removed. In the excerpt, Ruby credits the new management company for this achievement, even though she despises it otherwise because they have "abolished" the Homeowner's Association she and her mother were actively involved in, and because they recently impounded her broken-down car that had been sitting in the driveway for quite some time, as she tells me later. Based on her "junk car," her mother's alcoholism, the many cats, as well as some other characteristics, Ruby and her family fit some of the "trailer trash" stereotypes invoked by other informants. Yet Ruby vehemently claims her family's decency and community membership by differentiating herself from other residents who live in less attractive homes and are involved in illegal activities.

Distancing is especially difficult for people who have children because they fall into the category of people who potentially have, and cause, serious problems. The next excerpt from the interview with Rick, who was introduced above, illustrates this. . . . Rick and his wife live together with their young daughter in an urban family park, and . . . both are currently unemployed.

> You gotta watch your kids here, because you got a lot a young people with the boom boxes and running faster than what they should be through here. I've called on a couple of them myself, and the old man over here next door has too. Basically, anywhere you go in this country you're gonna run into kids like that, you know. I haven't forgotten that I was a teenager one time myself, but you've got. . . . The younger generation has got to have a little bit of respect for the children out here playing! That's the biggest thing. It's not a bad place it's just. . . . you got a few people, especially the young breed. . . . the old breed, they don't mess with nobody, they pretty well keep to theirselves, but the younger people. . . . boy, I've heard them come in here [at] late hours of the night before. I don't know, most the time I've seen guys like that run during late-at-night time, they're either in here messing with stuff or dealing drugs. And which you're gonna have that, no matter where you are, those kind of things. But, you know, as far as a family neighborhood, it's not off too bad. (. . .) Some of the older Hispanics here, you can tell that they well maintain their property. And the younger breed, a lot of them, they'll put up junk cars! I mean, you can tell a difference. A lot of people judges a whole neighborhood by what they see when they walk [around]. It's just like judging a book by its cover, and that's basically what happened here. Everybody says, you know, well, that's a trailer park, and they assume the worst about a lot of trailer parks.

Rick isolates the problems in his park as a matter of out-of-control teenagers which he views as something the entire country has to deal with, not only his park. It is the "young breed" you cannot trust, whereas the "old breed" and the families with smaller children, such as his own, are okay. Rick also invokes the wisdom that looks can be deceiving. It would be wrong to "assume the worst" about everyone living in his park just because a few teens run wild. Even though the conduct and dealings of the few indecent people are very visible, Rick insists that he can "tell a difference" because of his greater experience.

Telling the difference between "decent" and "bad" people thus involves local knowledge, a skill that resembles the type of "street wisdom" Anderson (1999) found to be at work in inner cities. Rick also invokes another, historic difference, the one between his own and the current teenage generation who appears to have "less respect" for children. Lastly, Rick emphasized that the "older Hispanics" are part of the respectable people, meaning he does not view the decency divide as a racial boundary. To sum up Rick's view, decency is primarily a matter of age.

The following last example of fencing also deals with deceptive appearances, yet in a different manner. Heather is an unemployed White woman in her mid-30s who lives with her four children and one grandchild, as well as several dogs, in an older single-wide home in a small rural family park.

> HEATHER: And when I saw it, you know, it looked nice. And it looked clean, so I thought it wouldn't be like living in a trailer park, you know, I thought it'd be a better place. It's not! It's just like any other trailer park. . . .
>
> AUTHOR: Like a mobile park. . . .
>
> HEATHER: It's full of trailer trash!

Heather originally relied on the "nice" and "clean" look of the community to make sure that she and her family ended up living in a good place. However, she learned that the initially decent appearance of the park was misleading. It turned out to be "just like any other trailer park," meaning it is occupied by people with questionable moral values (she later cites drug dealing as an example). Heather refuses my awkward offer to soften her term "trailer park" and even goes one step further by calling other residents "trailer trash."

Interestingly, Heather's classification of her neighbors as "trailer trash" appears to be rooted in their behavior as opposed to the appearance of their homes—a view that is consistent with her personal situation. Heather's place was, by far, the most untidy looking home in her park: two damaged cars, one completely disabled, were sitting in her driveway, and the overgrown lawn area around her house was littered with children's toys, broken bicycles, and indoor furniture. I also noticed that none of Heather's school-age children attended school on the morning of our interview, and that her teenage son was playing music very loudly. Given these and a number of other circumstances, there is no doubt that the majority of our participants would consider Heather's home and personal situation to be a fitting example of the "trailer" lifestyle they are trying to disassociate from. Heather however refuses this view and, in turn, distances herself from her neighbors who managed to deceive her by falsely appearing decent. As could be expected, Heather, whom I met through her oldest daughter, was not willing to refer me to other residents of her community—in fact, she frequently spoke of her wish of moving out.

Generally speaking, distancing was thus aimed at nearby others who might be of different racial and ethnic backgrounds, who might be more recent arrivals, people perceived to be "drug addicts," "drug dealers" and thieves, teenagers, people with family problems, and generally people living in dilapidated "trailers." Many residents did not consider these others to be part of the local community and insisted that they be removed. Reversely, a few informants considered themselves to be different from the majority of people in their park and isolated themselves as a result (see also Edwards 2004). . . .

Conclusion

. . . Our study revealed a range of techniques participants use in response to media or personal denigrations of their homes and communities. Their strategies serve to downplay, dissolve, deny, and deflect the negative image of living in a "trailer." . . . My analysis newly differentiates between two subforms of the widely used technique of distancing which is a strategy meant to deflect stigma, here called "bordering" and "fencing." The above discussion illuminates structural and situational variations in the use of distancing which might be useful to consider in future research on stigma.

Interestingly, one otherwise common strategy of stigma management is conspicuously rare in our data. Historically, members of many stigmatized groups have managed to deconstruct disparaging views and terms by embracing them in their fight for equality. . . . It could be argued that such cognitive and semantic shifts helped to deflate attacks on the respectability of historically oppressed groups. There is no doubt that most people we encountered in our research are proud of their homes and communities. Some explicitly pointed out the advantages of their lifestyle, and a few even tolerated the terms "trailer" and "trailer park" in reference to their living situation. While these findings indicate some degree of embracing the mobile home life style and its negative views, nobody in our sample accepted the terms "trailer trash" or "White trash" in reference to themselves. These epithets were only used in negative, distancing statements even though examples of adopting the "trash" label can occasionally be found in public discourse. . . .

Second, the struggle for acceptance into the moral mainstream displayed by mobile home residents is another sign that the desire to be "decent" transcends the middle class and is, arguably, universal in our society. . . . It is actually more than a desire: decency was portrayed as a character trait that is already possessed by people like oneself yet lacking in certain others. . . .

And third, the above analysis contributes to our knowledge of social and symbolic differentiation within the bottom half of American society. . . . The personal experience of stigmatization does not automatically result in deeper, empathetic insight into the mechanics of victimization, and it certainly does not lead to a rejection of stigmatization per se. Ironically, most mobile home residents seem to draw on the same stereotypes in their own construction of boundaries which they despised when they were applied to themselves. Our research further indicates that the "trailer" stigma is of particular concern to heterosexual Whites who largely embrace traditional family values, thus presenting an interesting form of social exclusion within a category of people that considers itself to be dominant in other contexts. There are clear racial subtexts to White-on-White struggles over decency. . . .

Finally, my analysis indicates that the trailer stigma is most frequently applied to people who lack material resources and/or possess compromising conditions prohibiting them from moving into "better" communities elsewhere, thus obtaining the privilege of decency via geography. It appears that the greater one's own chance of victimization, the more vehemently the stigma is passed to people down below which, in some cases, means next door. The fight over decency seems toughest at the bottom of the economic ladder. Under such high pressure, bets on the unity of one's neighborhood community are called off quickly, giving rise to constructions of "outsiders within." It is not entirely surprising that poverty and a lack of respect nurture tensions within local community contexts. Future research on mobile home residents and other morally disparaged groups, especially those with ambivalent status characteristics, will hopefully facilitate deeper insights into the aggregated social-level—in addition to individual-level—costs of stigmatization, and into self-perpetuating cycles of moral abuse.

References

Anderson, E. (1999). *Code of the street: Decency, violence, and the moral life of the inner city*. New York: Norton.

Berube, A. (1997). Sunset trailer park. In M. Wray & A. Newitz (Eds.), *White trash: Race and class in America* (pp. 15–39). New York: Routledge.

Edwards, M. L. K. (2004). We're decent people: Constructing and managing family identity in rural working-class communities. *Journal of Marriage and Family*, 66, 515–529.

Goffman, E. (1963). *Stigma: Notes on the management of spoiled identity*. Englewood Cliffs: Prentice Hall.

Katz, M. B. (1989). *The undeserving poor: From the war on poverty to the war on welfare*. New York: Pantheon.

Lamont, M., & Molnár, V. (2002). The study of boundaries in the social sciences. *Annual Review of Sociology*, 28, 167–195.

Neewitz, A., & Wray, M. (1997). What is "white trash"? Stereotypes and economic conditions of poor whites in the United States. In M. Hill (Ed.), *Whiteness: A critical reader* (pp. 168–184). New York: New York University Press.

Schwalbe, M., Godwin, S., Holden, D., Schrock, D., Thompson, S., & Wolkomir, M. (2000). Generic processes in the reproduction of inequality: An interactionist analysis. *Social Forces*, 79, 419–452.

Reflective Questions

1. What is stigma? How is stigma related to social inequalities? Why is trailer living so stigmatizing?
2. What is distancing, and how does it work? How does bordering serve as a distancing strategy? In the residents' eyes, how are mobile communities different from a trailer park? What distinguishes "respectable" mobile home residents from "indecent" ones?
3. How is fencing different from bordering? How does fencing relieve stigma?
4. Mobile home residents are not the only stigmatized people who establish their decency by distancing themselves from others. Why do they do this rather than approaching others with empathy? Who else does this? How?
5. If people with few material resources use distancing to establish their respectability, how do you make sense of redneck and blue collar humor? Go to YouTube and watch a few sessions of Bill Engvall,

Larry the Cable Guy, Ron White, and Jeff Foxworthy. What aspects of redneck life do the comedians praise? What do they poke fun at? Do they engage in distancing? Why or why not? Does redneck humor have negative consequences for those who fit redneck stereotypes? Several redneck comedians have become famous and established lucrative careers. Does their personal situation change the meaning of their redneck humor? Why or why not?

"For the Betterment of Kids Who Look Like Me"

CARISSA FROYUM

For many Americans, "racism" conjures two mental images: eras gone by in which whites ruled blacks through brutal systems of slavery and Jim Crow segregation, or personal animus for people of a different color. Racism, many suggest, used to be expressed openly through nasty language and violence but is no longer socially acceptable. Inequality scholars certainly agree that discriminatory social policies and individuals' hatred have been foundational to racism, the hierarchical system that elevates whiteness and secures a variety of resources, from mortgages to votes, for whites. They argue that they still are. But sociologists increasingly are interested in the subtle ways everyday interactions produce racial stratification, particularly when actors do not express dislike for others who look different from them.

In Froyum's study of a youth agency, we encounter well-intentioned whites who have dedicated their careers and volunteerism to helping low-income black youth better their lives. They care deeply for the kids at Kidworks. They desperately want them to be successful in life and especially to go to college. They could easily invest their time, money, and talents in other causes. At the same time, Kidworks is characterized by dramatic racial hierarchy. An elite group of whites control policy making and cultivate a consciously crafted image of Kidworks to the public, one that depends on othering blacks. They use Kidworks to foster social networks exclusive to other upper-middle-class and upper-class whites. They promote whites into highly paid administrative positions. The questions then become: How does this happen? How do we have both good intentions and racial stratification?

Sociologists define power as the ability to get others to do what you want, even when it is not in their best interest to do so. Racism is a system of stratified power. Historically, whites have exercised power in two general ways. First, they have dominated through force and coercion. They created police units to capture runaway slaves. They passed laws that excluded everyone but whites, who were defined differently depending on the place and time, from owning property. Exerting power through the instruments of law and violence continue today: through the mass incarceration of men of color, for example. Second, whites rule by gaining the consent of whites and non-whites alike. That is, whites essentially convince others that they are better and deserve more or that being subordinate is in everyone's best interest. Rule by consent is insidious and difficult to challenge because it camouflages inequality and disguises its wrongfulness.

Kidworks shows us how this second process works on the ground level, and the role that emotions play in ruling by consent. At Kidworks, whites expected what other people in superordinate positions expect: emotional experiences that make them feel good and superior. White administrators required unreciprocated emotional deference from blacks. They demanded what

Reprinted from: Carissa Froyum, "For the Betterment of Kids Who Look Like Me": Professional Emotional Labour as a Racial Project." *Ethnic and Racial Studies,* 2012. Copyright 2012 by Taylor and Francis Group. Reprinted by permission of publisher and author. DOI: 10.1080/01419870.2011.644309.

they wanted from black workers, when they wanted it, and however they wanted with little or no regard for the workers' feelings. White volunteers remained committed to Kidworks as long as their experiences paid off emotionally and they felt essential to a triumphant success storyline. Both emotional relationships existed along racial lines: with whites getting emotional benefits through blacks' subordination. Moreover, whites often characterized black kids and families in racist ways—as culturally dysfunctional or as entertainment—to position themselves to receive emotional benefits.

Why didn't black workers protest or quit? And why would they help cultivate success stories by recruiting and training kids to give public testimonials that framed blacks as destitute? As Froyum shows, black workers were often uncomfortable with the racial dynamics at Kidworks, and they did protest at times. But mostly they consented to these racial dynamics because they believed in Kidworks' cause and the professionalism standard that whites used to enforce blacks' emotional deference. Professionalism dictated that they put the kids' needs before their own and suppress negative emotions to do so. Everything else became a means to the end of saving kids. When workers did challenge racism, they risked failing the kids and being unprofessional. Whites and even other blacks quickly reprioritized for them. In essence, black emotional deference under the guise of professionalism became a tool of white racial rule by consent.

The larger sociological psychological lessons are clear. Emotions—what we expect from others, how we manage them—are tools for securing power. They are also central to blinding us to power imbalances that exist. Finally, we need not be hateful or intend bad things in order for our actions to create them. If we take the latter seriously, this piece calls us to look closely at the consequences of our own emotional expectations.

Work often includes emotional labor, or conjuring emotional states in others and managing one's own emotions for pay (Hochschild 1983, p. 7). Research has demonstrated how stratification systems shape emotional labor and criticized the consequences for workers. Workers with high status enjoy a range of emotional expressions and control "feeling rules," the scripts to evoke particular emotional states (Hochschild 1983; Pierce 1995; Sloan 2004). They more often expect emotional deference than give it, producing positive emotional experiences. Organizations prescribe deferential feeling rules for lower-status workers, alternatively, creating negative or conflicted emotions (Hochschild 1983; Leidner 1999). Managers suppress criticism of inequality by conditioning workers' emotional subjectivities (Kunda and Maanen 1999; Schwalbe et al. 2000; Jocoy 2003). Despite their connecting emotions to inequalities, studies have rarely examined emotional labor processes in relation to race, leaving a misimpression of race neutrality or inconsequentiality.

. . . This study examines an emotion-based racial project in a workplace where whites prescribed deferential emotional labor but black youth workers internalized it. It uses Schwalbe et al.'s (2000) concept of regulating discourse to analyze how administrators used professionalism to define and police deferential emotion work in ways that reinforced racial structuring. It asks: Why did black workers engage in deferential emotional work? How did workers resolve conflicts stemming from racializing feeling rules? How did emotional labor stabilize racial organizing? In answering these questions, this study illustrates how emotional labor elicited the participation of black workers in their own racial subordination.

Kidworks

Kidworks (KW) was a non-profit youth agency with a mission of cultural change: to help disadvantaged children become productive adults. It provided life-skills and recreational programs at six locations in a mid-sized US city with moderate levels of racial residential segregation. My analysis focuses on two sites in a neighborhood disproportionately black and poor. . . . These sites served mostly low- and middle-income black girls and boys, ages six to twelve, in gender-segregated facilities I call Girlworks and Boyworks.

KW's workplace was racially stratified. The direct-care workers who carried out the mission of the organization primarily identified as black. Between both sites, the direct-care workforce consisted of a couple dozen black workers. Two or three usually black full-time salaried "professionals," most with college degrees, worked at either site at any time. They earned between $28,500 and $47,000 yearly and had little chance for promotion. Boyworks employed men and women, while Girlworks only employed women. A dozen part-time college students worked at both sites; black and some white women worked with girls, while women and men worked with boys. Most made about seven dollars an hour. A young black woman was the volunteer coordinator. She also handled "accountability" to benefactors and hosted fundraisers; she earned $32,000 yearly.

Yet, those with high status and policy-making authority were nearly universally upper-middle-class and upper-class whites. The director, a well-connected white man, earned $103,000. The assistant director, a white man, earned $75,000. White women served as resource developer, government relations officer, and personal assistant. Thirty-four whites (twenty-six men) and one black man constituted the board of directors. Its members were established white businessmen with social networks in real estate, finance, and banking. The board made policy, networked, and fundraised to secure KW's $4.5 million annual revenues. In 2006, the top board fundraiser solicited over $33,000. Younger white lawyers and financial officers created another group that planned and hosted fundraisers. At KW, then, whites nearly exclusively dictated policy and standards of behavior for black workers who carried out KW's mission.

Data

I volunteered and conducted participant observation at KW between October 2004 and June 2006. Around 300 hours at life-skills groups, art classes, volunteer events, fundraising events and interviews produced 2,000 pages of field notes and transcripts....

I also conducted semi-structured in-depth interviews with forty workers, administrators, volunteers, fundraisers, board members, and kids. The relevant interviewees included ten self-identified white volunteers and administrators, fifteen self-identified black workers or volunteers, and one self-identified Latino worker. Interviews focused on work and volunteer experiences, relationships between kids and adults, and actors' interpretations....

Findings

Emotional Experiences to Overcome Cultural Dysfunction

Kidworks created an informal code of conduct around professionalism. Professionalism attests to workers' skill and expertise (Harris 2002), and workers feel compelled to act professionally in order to demonstrate competence (Erickson 2004; Lewis 2005). At KW, administrators appropriated professionalism as a regulating discourse (Schwalbe et al. 2000) that promoted deferential forms of emotional labor which conjured feelings of "belonging" among children, emotional release among white volunteers, and devotion among black workers. KW administrators, board members, and official documents labeled full-time workers "trained, professional staff." The label was so ubiquitous and valued that professionalism standards applied to both full-time and part-time direct-care workers, who routinely called themselves "professionals," even though their positions did not rise to professional status. Workers learned professionalism at regional and local trainings, and through interactions with administrators.

Professionalism prescribed emotional labor among black workers in order to overcome what whites perceived as poor black kids' social disadvantage. White administrators and volunteers at Kidworks drew on long-standing racist stereotypes about black cultural dysfunction (Collins 2004) when describing the challenges that KW children faced. A primary problem, from their perspective, was neighborhood and home instability: environments marred by drugs, violence, parental instability, and neglect. Wanda, a white fundraiser, characterized KW kids' backgrounds as "socially weaker" and "economically weaker." She explained further: " . . . there's shootings, the police cars . . . even those things that those kids have to go through whether it's verbal abuse, maybe other kinds of changes, being in foster homes or God knows what." Whites believed these circumstances undercut kids' life chances by divesting them from achieving. Kidworks' challenge, in turn, was to help children overcome the cultural dysfunction around them. A white board member explained: she wanted kids to "know that the world is larger than what they experience every day, and they don't have to let their family circumstances hold them back."

Creating an Emotional Refuge

Whites thought kids needed to connect with adults in order to motivate them to change their lives. KW materials explained that the agency provided "a safe place to learn and grow," "ongoing relationships with caring, adult professionals," and "life-enhancing programs and character development experiences." Administrators tasked direct-care workers, largely black, with creating an emotional refuge through professionalism. Wanda espoused this perspective when she juxtaposed the security that KW "professionals" created to the "majority" of homes of the children, which "probably don't have that": KW provided "a safe place," where children "get a relationship with a KW professional [knowing] that when they go there [to Kidworks], [they're] being heard, they have a sense of belonging. . . . " According to KW discourse, feelings of comfort and connectedness made personal development possible by fostering emotional stakes among children. Then kids felt obligated to act as adults, who presumably had their best interests at heart, directed. Belonging also offered a sense of purpose and meaning. Edward, a white administrator, described emotional connection as an agent of change:

> Nowadays to get [kids] to respond to you, they have to have . . . that connection with you individually . . . so that they don't want to disappoint you. . . . [Otherwise] they don't have a stake in Kidworks. . . . And so you try to build that feeling of "I'm part of something."

Administrators similarly touted emotional connection between children and workers as the foundation for long-term influence: "When kids come back years later, they always tell us that they forget the programming, but they remember the people" (Richard, white administrator, during a presentation to white donors).

Professionalism generally allows workers emotional autonomy and control over their feeling scripts, but at KW professionalism dictated deferential emotional labor that set the "right" priorities—the kids and KW's brand, as a place of change, over self. Tasha, a black worker, explained that KW's code of conduct was "about protecting the brand, protecting kids, and protecting yourself. So kids come first, brand comes second, you come last." The code established connecting emotionally with children as a primary requirement of direct-care work, one that further involved employees devoting themselves to their jobs and integrating their personal identities with their worker role. Relating this way involved transforming KW into a home-like atmosphere filled with familiarity, comfort, and emotional availability. In a report's description of KW's "highest priority," a board member explained: "We believe that Kidworks provides a 'home away from home' for many children, where young people receive the guidance and support to overcome the most daunting obstacles, and where children learn to live honorably." Workers created a "home" or "family" at work by integrating children into their emotional lives and making themselves readily available. Libby, a black worker, stated:

> [Kids] can call me anytime they need to talk . . . they're not always able to talk to their parents about everything. "So you can call me if need be. Or give me your number and I'll call you." . . . sometimes on the weekend, I'll just go get [two specific girls] and they stay at my house all day and Miss Casey [another worker] comes over . . . we'll just sit there, laugh and talk. . . . I try to get them as much as I can, so they feel some type of love and some type of

> support in things they do because they don't get the attention they need at home.

By giving out their cell numbers and bringing girls home with them, Libby and Casey extended themselves emotionally so that girls' problems became their own. They positioned themselves as the girls' confidants, and they tried to fill their emotional needs by making them feel loved. Other workers acted like family by meeting with kids' teachers and intervening when their relationships or lives took a wrong turn. Ben, a black employee, "kept tabs" on Eric, whose mother was seriously ill. Ben worried that Eric "wouldn't know what to do" if his mother died because "nobody from his family would take [him and his brother] in. . . . Pretty much Eric is taking care of himself." Ben fretted about "his sad situation." Because Eric's family did not help him, Ben made a point to: "I will do anything for the guy, like I donate clothes and shoes to him. . . . I do things so they can stay positive so they won't have to go out here and do the wrong thing." Consistent with KW's dictate of professionalism, Ben took his work home with him.

Professionalism also encouraged workers to find fulfillment through emotionally investing in children. A mailing described KW professionals as "men and women who use their education, training and energies to help young people. They enjoy being with kids, they understand them and get satisfaction from seeing them become responsible citizens and leaders." Employees internalized this call; they routinely described loving the children. Libby, for instance, described the rewards of her job as worth the frustration she felt with some of the girls: "I get joy just being around them every day. . . . I love them all like if they were mine. I really do. It's a few bad ones that get on my nerves. But you know what? I love them all." According to professionalism, love and making a difference were their own rewards.

But integrating work and family was one-sided: while professionalism prescribed emotional labor that integrated children into workers' lives, it proscribed letting employees' emotional lives intrude on their jobs. This was part of what Tasha meant by putting the needs of kids first. Here, professionalism discourse treated the workers' personal lives as potential pollutants to be contained and controlled. To prevent workers' own emotions from becoming overbearing or their own needs from interfering, workers were to separate the personal from the professional: "If you're having a bad day at home, you gotta leave that outside that door," Ben learned from his training. "Because once you come in here, you gotta go to work. . . . You gotta come in with a positive attitude." Maintaining a "positive attitude" entailed compartmentalizing in order to prioritize the children. Ben explained: "Working here at Kidworks and [having a] family, you have to keep those separated because here you have to have your full attention on the kids in this building." For Sharice, a black worker, professionalism encouraged workers to give kids their due attention rather than "bad attitude":

> You can't come into Kidworks with your head held down acting like you know the weight of the world is on your shoulders. Like I tell [workers] every day, "We all go through personal stuff, but [kids] have not done anything to us. So when you come through those doors, whatever problems you have brought with you to work, you need to leave them beside those doors."

Not taking one's personal frustration out on the kids, furthermore, entailed suppressing negative emotions. Edward, a white administrator, looked to employees to temper these emotions, demonstrating what he called "temperament" and "aptitude," especially during "mad moments" when kids acted out or staff became frustrated. After Warner, a black worker, lost his temper during a confrontation with a kid, a white administrator challenged him to control himself: "Warner, you just, you've got to learn to humble yourself. And when you learn to do that, [kids] will do the same thing."

Fostering Whites' Investment

Additionally, prioritizing the kids and brand meant fostering whites' commitment to KW through emotional labor. The professional code of conduct existed in part to maintain a funding stream to KW, which primarily depended on individuals, corporations, and foundations. This is what Tasha termed prioritizing KW's brand, as a nonprofit that truly influenced lives. Changes in resource allocation have led nonprofits to adopt capitalist business models where donors are clients and fundraisers are marketers (Dees and Battle Anderson 2003). Because of their dependence upon public patronage, nonprofits cultivate emotional experiences that invest donors in organizations. The most effective strategies (Merchant, Ford and Sargeant 2009) situate donating as a release from negative emotions and [a] source of positive ones. KW fit these patterns. Fundraising and volunteer recruitment were major enterprises at KW, which tapped into elite white real estate and finance networks to garner personal and financial support. Nearly all Kidworks' donors and the vast majority of volunteers, especially those who fundraised, were middle-class to upper-class whites. Emotional experiences made Kidworks their "charity of choice" (June, a white volunteer fundraiser, who worked in sales and marketing). Whites became attached to KW when they felt a "warm glow" (Andreoni 1990) by altering the life course of children—when they felt generous, important, and socially conscious.

In experiencing these emotions, however, whites othered the kids as needy, in turn framing themselves as redemptive. Like administrators, white donors and volunteers attributed poor and black kids' vulnerability to culturally dysfunctional backgrounds. Miranda, a white volunteer fundraiser who worked in finance, stated: "I can't imagine what it's like for kids who not only don't have someone pushing them to achieve in life but . . . they don't even have the basics to learn how to be a good person." In contrast to black workers below, white donors and volunteers distinguished their "lucky," "privileged" childhoods full of love, encouragement, and opportunity from what they understood as the deprivation experienced by "underprivileged" kids. June juxtaposed her experiences to the kids' using a framework of cultural function versus dysfunction: " . . . I had such a happy family life. I can't understand how people grow up without a happy family life. . . . KW sorta piles all types of people from all types of different, challenging backgrounds into one pot." After I asked her what made her volunteer work meaningful, she stated:

> The kids, the "thank-you's," the hugs, the "I love you," how much they need attention, how it tugs on your heart strings that they might not get the attention at home and how much Kidworks is a source for them to get the attention and the guidance and the affirmation, to me is tops. . . . it does your heart good and breaks your heart a little bit to be there at the same time.

For whites who "can't imagine" or "understand" what they perceived as neglectful backgrounds, KW elicited pity through othering, and giving made them feel important and influential.

Essential to these emotions was observing results personally but without losing control over the emotional experience. KW did not expect or require volunteers or donors to expose themselves emotionally by creating a home, becoming like family, or overlooking their own emotional needs. Rather, it employed its direct-care staff to create an emotional experience that cultivated emotional release for whites by facilitating seeing kids change, interacting with grateful children, and viewing programs and facilities in use and well cared for. These results made giving time and money feel worthwhile. As Miranda put it: "It really brings it home if I can feel what I'm working for." Professionalism at KW, thus, also tasked creating an emotional experience for potential volunteers and funders so they could feel what they were working for.

One strategy was to charge professional employees with preparing triumphant stories (Merchant, Ford and Sargeant 2009) for public consumption at fundraising events and scholarship contests. These stories gave whites a feel of their influence by eliciting pity about kids' backgrounds and attesting to the potential for change with their resources. They followed this narrative: Marlesa came from a broken background that led her down the wrong path,

KW gave her the support she needed, now she is headed the right way, you can help girls like her. Administrators invited workers to share their own stories, and they assigned them with finding and telling kids' stories. An annual report featuring Jeremiah, a black boy around ten, modeled for black workers how to, in the terms of a white fundraiser, "tell a success story" and personalize. The report described him as struggling in school and delinquent. Staff, it read, worked until closing for a year until Mark improved academically and behaviourally. "Proof again," it concluded, "that KW changes, enhances—even saves—the lives of young people." Employees became skilled in describing the work of KW as saving so that potential donors *felt* influential without actually knowing the kids. Ben grew up in the neighborhood and attended KW. Of his close friends, a handful graduated from high school:

> Everybody else was just caught up in the streets. . . . I believe that Kidworks was a good, positive way for me to learn the right things and . . . to teach you how to be a responsible young man. Kidworks was really influential in my life.

More impressive, however, were children testifying themselves. Workers recruited kids to testify and coached them how under the rubric of practicing public speaking or getting recognition or scholarship money. Samuel, a white volunteer fundraiser, learned the story of Marcesha at a KW event. He juxtaposed her success to the troubles of her brother due to her involvement in KW: "He really wasn't as active as she was and didn't really participate in everything like she did. And she felt like if it wasn't for KW, she'd be down that same road." For a scholarship contest, employees nominated kids and helped them prepare extensive applications which testified about their background, KW involvement, and influence of KW. They coached kids how to dress and present themselves, and they drove kids to the contest where a group of 26 mostly upper-middle class whites acted as judges who questioned the kids about their deservedness through several rounds of interviews. Among the criteria KW supplied to judges were "obstacles overcome," which elicited the triumphant storylines that contestants then relayed at fundraising events. June, who served as a judge, described learning about a boy whose:

> mom was single, pregnant, been through four husbands. . . . Certainly there was nobody waiting for him at home. But if he didn't have anywhere else to go, then he probably would have ended up a little bit misguided. And he'll probably look back one day and know how much Kidworks has done for him.

One scholarship winner, Carl, a teenage black boy, especially made lasting impressions on white volunteers. He told the judges: "When I was seven, I was adopted. I think my biggest obstacle in life was trying to put my past behind me. I witnessed a lot of alcohol and drugs, physical abuse. And I feel like I never want to be that way." Miranda was so moved by this testimonial that she recalled it a year later: "I think he has every opportunity to come from that unhealthy lower-class-struggling-to-get-by-type-of-existence into the American dream." Carl's story was known throughout the organization because, as Warner, a black employee, explained, workers enlisted him "to speak at just about every big event we have." Staffers had invested considerable resources into his success by securing tutors, jobs, and scholarships for college. As Warner stated: "We're really working on him and putting a lot of time in him."

Darin invited another "respectful" boy, Martin, with "positive attitude" to represent KW "every time we have a speaking engagement." One event was a major fundraiser featuring a jewelry auction at an upscale department store. Workers prepared several kids by renting tuxedoes and coaching them to greet whites by opening the door, hanging their jackets, and ushering them onto a red carpet. While other kids represented KW's importance in speeches, Martin, dressed in his tuxedo, mingled with white donors who gathered around him, saying: "You're so handsome! Look at you. What a cutie!" For much of the night, he danced for his admirers, evoking Jim Crow era caricatures of blacks as entertaining exotic others. These strategies had their desired emotional effect, as Miranda shows:

> To see the kids and know these are some of the kids that we are helping by being here and having a good time, bidding up the auction to support, I think it makes a big impact. . . . I see the kids at the door and I hear the little boy talk about what Kidworks means to him and all of a sudden I'm thinking I need to buy more.

Finally, administrators charged black workers with creating a personal experience for whites who came to visit or volunteer. Administrators instructed them to use the term "we" rather than "I" whenever discussing KW so that they felt vital to KW's functioning. A white administrator mentored a black worker to make volunteers feel special by learning their names and showering praise and thanks at elaborate "volunteer celebrations." She routinely sent cards with personalized messages. When potential donors entered the buildings, administrators had workers immediately accommodate them: greet them with a smile, invite them in, provide tours, and describe the programs that made KW successful.

In sum, professionalism at KW prescribed deferential emotional labor for blacks working directly with kids and white donors and volunteers. Based on the racist assumptions that black kids were culturally dysfunctional, white administrators employed a professionalism discourse that framed workers as family members who loved the children and devoted themselves to them. Not letting their personal lives impede on the work added additional layers of deferential emotion work. Administrators, furthermore, required black workers to facilitate cross-race interactions, which left whites feeling a warm glow. These personalization strategies were unidirectional and unreciprocated (Lewis 2005) across race lines. They reinforced stereotypes of blacks as exotic others.

Effects of Professionalism on Workers

Black workers often internalized KW's standards of professionalism. Workers adopted the discourses administrators professed in public, routinely word-for-word as Darin did. He adopted the "remember the people" language from above: "That's where the impact comes in. That's what we hope when the kids leave here," he explained. "They won't remember every tournament they were in, but they will remember Ben or Warner . . . and the positive impact they had on their lives." Professional emotional labor made the work feel important.

Loving the children and creating a home, then, were no longer what administrators wanted from workers; they were what workers wanted for themselves. Workers' devotion to children aligned their interests with the organization's. Through professional emotional labor, workers identified closely with children. Compare the workers' descriptions of "giving back" to the othering accounts of white volunteers above. Workers wanted children to experience the same benefits they experienced at KW. Darin stated:

> I grew up here in southwest Sherburne where the kids are served. So the same streets and community and houses that they live in, I lived in. . . . [Working here] was an opportunity to give back to kids like I was given back to.

Others wanted to make life easier than they had it. Yolanda, a black volunteer, struggled after her mother died: "I try to help children to get what I didn't get." No whites related to kids this way.

But loving the kids facilitated overlooking racial meanings and the degrading emotion work employees performed. They understood humbling themselves to be part of the job and necessary, and they were willing to sacrifice to help children they related to so closely. Two examples illustrate the processes.

Even though each KW facility had custodians, administrators ordered direct-care workers to clean floors and take garbage around the outside of the building rather than through the administration area. Workers and kids picked up garbage in the ditches along KW's property, a task I found dangerous. These beautification strategies were part of KW's efforts to make volunteers feel comfortable and their resources well invested. When Casey, a black worker, did not maintain the gym to white administrator Richard's satisfaction, he sent her an email holding her accountable, using professionalism:

> Casie [sic], I walked in the gym this morning in preparation for a site visit with a new Board Member and was appalled by its condition . . . it still looks like a trash dump. . . . There are many people who have given of their resources to ensure that these children have a facility in which they can take pride. . . . As a Kidworks professional you have the responsibility to ensure the safety and cleanliness of your program areas. You have until I come to work at 7:30 AM Friday morning to make the gym the cleanest, most orderly, and safest facility in Sherburne.

Casey was "really offended" and confused. Had she really done something wrong? Was she not a professional? Casey tried to meet with Richard to seek some clarity, but he did "not have time." She crafted an email that expressed concern over "a lack of communication between employees and the administration" and requested he address future concerns in person. But Casey's superiors policed her into interpreting the situation less critically. Her black supervisor told her: "You have to take stuff with a grain of salt. You have to let it roll off. You've got to not show your emotions on your face and that type of stuff." A white administrator instructed her to not take it personally because being rebuked happens to everyone. He explained the reprimand would have been worse in person. While she did not regret sending the email, these conversations led Casey to conclude: "I need to work on being submissive. I do." The next day, Richard reinforced Casey's new interpretation after a brief meeting: "He said I'm doing a good job. The gym looks good now. The request to meet with him in person was a part-time person's complaint. . . . I can see his point."

This exchange taught Casey the importance of deferential emotional labor as part of her job. When she challenged administrators' interpretation of her work and their methods for conveying criticism, supervisors quickly reinforced that others' emotional experiences mattered more than hers. They framed her reaction as overreacting and insisted that being a professional required emotional restraint and muted criticism of superiors. Professionalism regulated Casey into reinforcing a racist structure she wanted to challenge by fostering self-doubt and challenging her interpretation of mistreatment. Richard did the same above with Warner when he told him to "humble" himself. In practice, then, professionalism policed workers into *wanting* to submit to white authority.

Tamera's experiences with a white volunteer who claimed racial discrimination illustrate a second process. In a form of symbolic boundary maintenance (Schwalbe et al. 2000), black workers contrasted their commitment to kids to "wrong priorities": self-interestedness and self-promotion. Warner criticized: "There are people who come here for pay checks. . . .They're here just to get that check and go home. They're not here for the kids." To "come for a pay check" was to be "fake." Personal gain did not matter, conversely, to "genuine" people "with a heart" who were "here for the kids." Staff, in turn, measured their own importance as workers through their self-sacrifice and child-centeredness. This practice led to colorblindness and muted criticism, particularly during conflicts. Tamera relayed:

> [White volunteers] felt like they were being picked on because they were the minority in the group now. . . . Lisa was white and she felt like she didn't get any respect from the black staff. Or no one tried to really help her.

According to Tamera's account, volunteer Lisa was "really, really concerned with the kids, and they weren't accepting her." She wanted the staff to help her connect better with them, but when they did not, she charged racism. Tamera tried to broker a meeting with the relevant workers because "we don't want people unhappy." But Lisa refused and instead emailed administrators, saying "she would never step foot back in KW again and that she would continue to support the organization but that we should look at how we treat minority [white] people."

Professionalism guided Tamera's response to this and other problematic whites. Lisa provoked frustration, skepticism, and an interpretation of racism. Tamera stated: "I really doubted that that was the situation [Lisa was mistreated as a white] because we have great employees and that doesn't really make a lot of sense." Instead, she thought Lisa had unrealistic expectations that disrespected the staff: "She wanted to be patted on the back *constantly*" and "You can't come in here and expect that someone's going to baby you." She thought Lisa was like other volunteers, whose expectations were racially offensive—"I think they want to feel like I saved this poor little black kid"—and who espoused stereotypes that black kids "be like needy, can't function, semi-brain-dead, [disheartened] kids that they can hold and rock and tell them that everything is going to be okay." Other workers shared her frustration: "[An administrator] wants us to raise all this money. That's *their* job. . . . Don't ask me to go to these events. Don't make me parade kids around for all these rich people. I don't want to do it" (Darin). Tamera wanted to challenge Lisa directly. But despite her claims that "volunteers are not VIPs" and workers "don't want to" or "have time to kiss their butts," she did not. She instead fostered Lisa's commitment so that Lisa worked events where "she can be thoroughly recognized" and "around other white people."

In this example, what Tamera wanted to do, based on her feelings of frustration due to her interpretation of racism, conflicted with what she was supposed to as a professional employee. Tamera transformed her negative feelings into positive ones based in self-sacrifice:

> I deal with a lot of non-minorities [whites] on a daily basis that I wouldn't ever deal with in my regular life. But it's for the betterment of kids who look like me. . . . If I have to smile in somebody's face that I know may not really like me and would never hang in the same circles as I or speak to me in the street . . . I'm going to smile 'cause . . . it's about creating opportunities for these kids.

When Sharice hit her breaking point, she similarly stated: "I'll go on record: the only reason that I'm still here is for my girls." After discussing Lisa's situation with her bosses, Tamera altogether abandoned the racism interpretation of the volunteer deemed "really important to the organization" in favor of a new, colorblind interpretation. She attributed Lisa's complaints to a personality flaw: "We understood that it's important to maintain that relationship with her but we knew some people are just happy to be unhappy." Professionalism, thus, conditioned workers to self-regulate and overlook race.

Discussion and Conclusion

Previous research too often treats emotional labor as racially neutral, neglecting its racial foundations and implications. This study demonstrates how emotional labor functioned as a racial project that contributed to racial hegemony through its appropriation of professionalism. I identify three social processes that fostered the consent of racial subordinates to degrading racial meanings and structuring.

First, appropriated professionalism aligned black workers' interests with white administrators' goals. Like many others, Kidworks' organizational hierarchy itself was racialized: white administrators dictated feeling rules for black, direct-care workers, even though administrators considered employees professionals. Accordingly, workers signified their competence by fulfilling the emotional labor prescribed to them rather than through freedom of expression. Opposite its "professional" designation, this emotion work was deferential in nature. Creating a refuge for kids and fostering whites' emotional investment required prioritizing others' needs, even when it created conflict. Thus, although professionalism generally provides emotional freedom, it had the opposite effect here: it legitimized the subordination of black employees by framing their emotional deference as necessary to the work. Staff who invested themselves in their work, thusly, believed in the importance of acting deferentially—for the children's sake. They *wanted* to be devoted and loyal to KW because self-sacrifice signified their worth as workers. Emotional labor reinforced racial subordination by investing black workers in submitting to whites.

Second, professionalism diffused negative emotions, which cultivate discontent with racial structuring. Emotional labor itself drew on long-standing racist stereotypes about black cultural dysfunction and white superiority and paternalism, creating resentment and frustration among black workers. These emotions fuel disruptions to stratification systems, while satisfaction, complacency, and resignation stabilize them (Jocoy 2003). But feeling scripts often deny blacks the expression of "negative" emotions (Wingfield 2010). At KW, workers learned to consider them contagions. When negative emotions did surface, supervisors used professionalism to police them. Employees repressed them, emphasizing the children's needs instead. Even though emotionally relating is often unevaluated and uncompensated, devotion made the work *feel* meaningful and important. Black employees, moreover, felt morally superior when they juxtaposed their self-sacrifice to the superficial priorities of whites, even though emotional labor subordinated them structurally. Professionalism, consequently, mediated workers' negative emotions, thereby stabilizing the racial structure.

Third, professionalism muted racial critiques and fostered colorblindness. Under the guise of acting professionally, workers transformed their racially-laden interpretations into racially neutral ones while repressing frustration. Testimonials were no longer stereotypical but an opportunity for kids to speak publicly. Accommodating whites was not racially insulting but a fundraising necessity. Even racial interpretations of whites' belittling actions were labelled overreactions.

Thus, professionalism served as a racial project that not only drew on and reinforced racist meanings but also conditioned the emotional subjectivities of black workers so that they consented to race-based organizing. This finding has implications beyond KW to other workplaces that are racially stratified or have racialized emotional content. In the globalized capitalist economy, workplace stratification often coincides with race, and workers of color, especially women, routinely perform devalued carework.... Under these circumstances, emotional labor can have insidious racial consequences....

References

Andreoni, James 1990 'Impure altruism and donations to public goods: A theory of warm-glow giving', *The Economic Journal*, vol. 100, pp. 464–77.

Collins, Patricia Hill 2004 *Black sexual politics: African Americans, gender, and the new racism*, New York: Routledge.

Dees, J. Gregory & Battle Anderson, Beth 2003 'Sector-bending: Blurring lines between nonprofit and for-profit', *Society*, vol. 40, no. 4, pp. 16–27.

Erickson, Karla 2004 'To invest or detach? Coping strategies and workplace culture in service work', *Symbolic Interaction*, vol. 27, no. 4, pp. 549–72.

Harris, Lloyd C. 2002 'The emotional labour of barristers: An exploration of emotional labour by status professionals', *Journal of Management Studies*, vol. 39, no. 4, pp. 553–84.

Hochschild, Arlie Russell 1983 *The managed heart: Commercialization of human feeling*, Berkeley: University of California Press.

Jocoy, Christine L. 2003 'Vying for hearts and minds: Emotional labour as management control', *Labor & Industry*, vol. 13, no. 3, pp. 51–72.

Kunda, Gideon & Maanen, John Van 1999 'Changing scripts at work: Managers and professionals', *The Annals of the American Academy of Political and Social Science*, vol. 561, pp. 64–80.

Leidner, Robin 1999 'Emotional labor in service work', *The Annals of the American Academy of Political and Social Science*, vol. 561, pp. 81–95.

Lewis, Patricia 2005 'Suppression or expression: An exploration of emotion management in a special care baby unit', *Work, Employment and Society*, vol. 19, no. 3, pp. 565–81.

Merchant, Altaf, Ford, John B. & Sargeant, Adrian 2009 'Charitable organizations' storytelling influence on donors' emotions and intentions', *Journal of Business Research*, vol. 62, no. 7, pp. 754–62.

Pierce, Jennifer L. 1995 *Gender trials: Emotional lives in contemporary law firms*, Berkeley, CA: University of Berkeley Press.

Schwalbe, Michael, *et al.* 2000 'Generic processes in the reproduction of inequality: An interactionist analysis', *Social Forces*, vol. 79, no. 2, pp. 419–52.

Sloan, Melissa M. 2004 'The effects of occupational characteristics on the experience and expression of anger in the workplace', *Work and Occupations*, vol. 31, no. 1, pp. 38–72.

Wingfield, Adia Harvey 2010 'Are some emotions marked 'whites only'? Racialized feeling rules in professional workplaces', *Social Problems*, vol. 57, no. 2, pp. 251–68.

Reflective Questions

1. What did the workplace hierarchy at Kidworks look like? Who held power, and who was paid the best?
2. What did professionalism mean at Kidworks? What emotional experiences did white administrators and volunteers expect black workers to foster? How did they create these experiences?
3. How did black workers resist what they viewed as racist and classist expectations from whites? Were they successful in resisting? Why or why not? Why didn't the workers reject professionalism? What were the consequences of professionalism for the racial hierarchy at Kidworks?
4. Movies conjure a variety of common emotional experiences among viewers. Suspenseful movies evoke terror and excitement. Romantic comedies produce anticipation and comfort. Rags-to-riches movies inspire us and foster hope for a better future. Watch *The Blind Side*, the dramatization of football player Michael Oher's success, which earned over $255 million at the box office and earned Sandra Bullock an Oscar for Best Leading Actress. What emotions did you feel most prominently while you watched? What other emotions did you feel and at what points in the movie? What strategies did the director and actors use to conjure those different feelings? Now consider the racial undertones of the movie or read some racial critiques. (You can do a web search or see one at: http://www.dallasobserver.com/2009-11-19/film/the-blind-side-what-would-black-people-do-without-nice-white-folks/). How do you think most whites feel when watching this movie? What about blacks? What feelings do you think dominate for them? What images of blacks and whites set up your emotional responses? To what extent are these portrayals conscientious on the part of the movie makers? Does thinking about the racial content change your emotional experience? Why or why not? Where else do we see racial portrayals that are designed to evoke particular emotional responses? See the National Association of Black Social Workers' position paper that addresses transracial adoption here: http://www.nabsw.org/mserver/PreservingFamilies.aspx. What is their position? Why?

Escaping Symbolic Entrapment, Maintaining Social Identities

SHANE SHARP

As we saw in Parts IV and V, identities make us feel valued and important. They provide a way for us to develop a sense of competence, and they give the world order by helping us organize our thoughts and interactions with others. For these reasons, we develop what Michael Schwalbe[*] calls "identity stakes": investment in protecting widely valued identities that offer us important social, personal, and psychological benefits.

Critical events can damage people's core identities and their associated images of worthiness and order. Returning from war, injured soldiers who find themselves dependent upon others' care for the first time in adulthood may question their value. Who am I if I'm not self-sufficient? What do I have to contribute to my family and society? When an elderly spouse or partner dies after a prolonged illness, the surviving partner may wonder, who am I if not my partner's caretaker? When our identity stakes are challenged, we struggle to find new ways to make sense of the world and ourselves in it. We feel confused, overwhelmed, and lonely—until we find new identities to reorder our world or reconcile our experiences with new ways of thinking about our established identities. The soldier may come to think of herself as a hero who is owed a debt of gratitude, or the surviving partner may redirect his caretaking to his grandchildren.

As Shane Sharp shows us in this study of conservative Christian women abused by their partners, social identities come with a unique set of identity stakes. Not only are women's conceptions of self and worthiness related to their Christian identity but so are their friendships, communities, and moral understanding. Being abused puts all of these benefits at risk for the women, and they feel trapped between enduring the damaging effects of abuse and engaging in what they see as an immoral action—divorce. Their husbands, family, friends, and religious leaders further encase women in what Sharp calls "symbolic entrapment": they overtly discourage them from divorcing, even when they are aware of the horrors of their abuse.

But the women in Sharp's study, like all humans, are exceedingly resourceful. They draw on the cultural resources in their social world to alleviate their conundrum. Rather than rejecting their conservative Christian values or continuing to risk their emotional and physical safety, the women develop narratives of motive that allow them to divorce while keeping their conservative Christian identities intact. They take their knowledge of religious scripture, reshape their understanding of it to apply to their situation, and then use these teachings to convince themselves and others that divorcing is not only okay but the right and Godly thing to do. They protect their identity stakes.

In Sharp's study, narratives of motive allow women to challenge their abuse, an abuse rooted in a

[*] Michael Schwalbe, *Rigging the Game: How Inequality Is Reproduced in Everyday Life*. New York: Oxford University Press, 2008.

religious dictate that men should be heads of household and women should be submissive to them under nearly all circumstances. Their resistance not only has personal consequences but challenges a broader gender order that subordinates women to men.

Our identity stakes can also reproduce inequalities—and without us even realizing it. We may laugh when our teammates degrade someone as "retarded," for example, because we don't want to risk our association with the team. Or we may advocate for social policies that gut resources to the poor because we want them to go to more "worthy" people, like ourselves and associates. Or people may violently enforce symbolic boundaries between groups when others attack their identity stakes. Such is the case with many school shooters, who are typically young males whose peers have relentlessly teased them.[†] *They reestablish their "manhood" by engaging in extreme acts of violence. Identity stakes invest us in drawing symbolic boundaries, finding value and connectedness through those boundaries, and protecting the resources associated with them.*

Sharp's piece draws our attention to another important sociological psychological issue that has consequences for our understanding of inequalities: the relationship between motives and action. Inequality scholars are interested in how people make sense of the inequalities they encounter. With each generation, Americans are increasingly egalitarian in their ideologies. They largely believe that everyone, regardless of their background, should have a chance to get an education, have meaningful work, and otherwise lead a fulfilling life. For many, these beliefs define the United States uniquely as a place of opportunity, hope, and personal freedom. Despite these beliefs, inequalities stubbornly persist, and inequality scholars are quick to point out that Americans often seem more interested in getting past inequalities than addressing them. That is, what they say about inequalities does not match how they act about them. In fact, inequality scholars often think of ideologies as justifications for acting in ways that maintain a status quo that advantages a few at a cost to many. Sharp raises the prospect, though, that cultural narratives about equality and fairness need not inhibit action. Rather, they can motivate people to challenge inequalities directly—and convince others of the justness in doing so.

After experiencing almost a year of abuse from her husband, Tori—a conservative Church of Christ member in her early 30s—decides to leave her husband and seek a divorce in order to maintain her physical and emotional well-being. When Tori tells her husband of her intentions, he begins to shake violently and falls to the kitchen floor. He lies in a fetal position, crying and screaming that this is all because of his parents and that he is going to kill them. Afraid for her safety, Tori gets in her car and starts to drive. While behind the wheel, Tori calls her in-laws to tell them about what has occurred, fearing that her husband might follow through on his threats. With her mother-in-law on the other end of the line, Tori recounts all the details of the incident and the threats her husband made. Rather than thank her for the warning, Tori's mother-in-law asks, "Why are you leaving him?" Tori tells her mother-in-law that she can no longer stand the abuse and that she has to leave for her own physical and psychological welfare. This is an insufficient reason for her mother-in-law—a fellow member of the Church of Christ—who tells Tori that "the sin of divorce" is going to be "on her head" because spousal abuse is not a biblical justification for divorce. Days after the incident, Tori's husband calls to tell her that he has "been reading the Bible" and has concluded that she had no right to leave him because he had not committed adultery. He ends the call by telling Tori that she will have to answer to God on judgment day for leaving him for "nonbiblical reasons."

Marianne—a Southern Baptist in her early 50s—decides that she has experienced enough abuse in her 10-year marriage and decides to leave her husband. While her husband is at work and her children are at school, Marianne packs suitcases for

† Michael S. Kimmel and Matthew Mahler. 2003. "Adolescent Masculinity, Homophobia, and Violence: Random School Shootings, 1982–2001." *American Behavioral Scientist* 46(10):1439–1458.

herself and her children in preparation for several nights of sleeping in hotels as they make their way to her mother's. As she packs, Marianne thinks to herself that she should seek the counsel of the pastor at her Southern Baptist congregation to make sure that leaving is the right thing to do. So, she takes a break from packing and drives to her church. She meets with her pastor and tells him about all of the violence she has suffered and how she has tried "EV-ER-Y-THING" she can to make her husband happy. Marianne tells the pastor that she feels justified in leaving her husband because of his abusive behavior. The pastor does not agree. He asks her if she is not to blame for the violence and tells her that if she goes home and submits to her husband everything will be fine. After the meeting, Marianne drives home and unpacks the suitcases. She "tries and tries and tries" to be a better wife, but the violence continues. Marianne remains in the abusive marriage for another 15 years.

As these two vignettes demonstrate, conservative Christian victims of spousal abuse often experience what I call "symbolic entrapment." Symbolic entrapment occurs when a person is prevented from taking courses of action because these actions threaten symbolic boundaries that crucially define important and salient social identities. . . .

Symbolic Boundaries and Social Identities

Social psychologists make a distinction between personal and social identities (Owens 2003). Personal identities are conceptualizations of the self that differentiate an individual from others within a particular social context. Social identities, on the other hand, are "categorizations of the self into more inclusive social units that depersonalize the self-concept" (Brewer 1991:477). "Conservative Christian" is a social identity because it involves categorizations of the self as part of larger social units, which in this case would be denominational affiliation (Southern Baptist, Church of Christ, Assembly of God, etc.).

Social identities, as a number of scholars have pointed out, are defined by symbolic boundaries. Symbolic boundaries are the subjective boundaries that individuals draw using beliefs, symbols, values, and other cultural materials in order to make distinctions between themselves and others. Symbolic boundaries often define social identities relationally; that is, by defining who one is by defining who one is not. . . .

Because symbolic boundaries often refer to specific behavioral markers, they often prevent people from performing certain actions that may damage these boundaries in an effort to avoid a "spoiled" (Goffman 1963) social identity. In such cases, individuals experience symbolic entrapment. For instance, symbolic boundaries related to cultural consumption practices prevent people of high status groups from consuming culture related to the underclasses (NASCAR, professional wrestling, etc.). In addition, Mormons cannot drink caffeinated beverages because the consumption of caffeine is a behavioral symbolic boundary used to differentiate Mormons from non-Mormons.

While the above are somewhat trivial examples of symbolic entrapment, there are situations in which symbolic entrapment can be psychological and/or physically detrimental for individuals. One of these situations occurs when biblical prohibitions against divorce keep conservative Christian wives in abusive marriages.

Conservative Christianity, Negative Attitudes toward Divorce, and Symbolic Entrapment

Various scholars document the importance of traditional family values in symbolically defining conservative Christian identities. For example, one of the most salient beliefs of conservative Christianity is the belief that the husband is the "head of the household" and that a wife should be subordinate or "submissive" to her husband (Ammerman 1987; Bartkowski 2001; Denton 2004; Gallagher 2003; Gallagher and Smith 1999; Smith 2000).

Conservative Christians also use the belief that divorce is a sin as a symbolic boundary marker that sets them apart from what they see as the individualistic and selfish "culture of divorce" current in American society. . . .

Although viewing divorce as a sin is an important symbolic boundary marker for conservative Christians, this boundary can be detrimental if it symbolically entraps conservative Christians in bad and "unhealthy" marriages. . . .

Responding to Symbolic Entrapment

Although not couched in the same terms, previous scholars have documented two main responses by social actors to experiences of symbolic entrapment. The first response is for social actors to remain symbolically entrapped in order to maintain their social identities. . . .

The second response to symbolic entrapment is to disavow a social identity by leaving the group to which one belongs and/or by categorizing oneself no longer as a member of the group. . . .

While the above two responses are common, there is nevertheless a third response to symbolic entrapment that previous researchers have neglected that I discovered in the course of my research on how religious beliefs and institutions affect the experiences and behaviors of intimate partner violence victims. This response consists of escaping symbolic entrapment while also maintaining one's social identity by using and creating various types of motives that make taking ordinarily boundary damaging courses of action seem appropriate in terms of a particular social group's culture.

The Varieties of Vocabularies of Motives and Escaping from Symbolic Entrapment

C. Wright Mills (1940:907) defines motives as statements that serve as "unquestioned answers to questions concerning social and lingual conduct" to the various actors in a given social situation. In other words, motives are the reasons, explanations, excuses, and justifications for chosen courses of action that actors use to satisfy themselves and others. According to Mills, various groups, organizations, and societies have their own established "vocabularies of motive." For example, in American society an acceptable motive for marriage is "love." An unacceptable motive for marriage, however, is wealth, which explains the negative views of people seen as "gold-diggers" and "gigolos."

I show in this article that individuals escape symbolic entrapment while maintaining their social identities by using three distinct types of vocabularies of motive. The first type of motive is what I call normative motives. Mills (1940) argues that particular groups, institutions, and societies have shared normative vocabularies of motive for certain acts. These common or "typal" responses to or explanations for questionable behavior are well known and socially expected. . . .

The second type of motive used to escape symbolic entrapment is transforming motives. These motives convert motives ordinarily used by other groups into motives that conform to the culture of the particular social group in which the threatened social identity is based. . . .

The third type of motive used to escape symbolic entrapment while maintaining social identities is neutralizing motives. These are motives in which people admit that a course of action is wrong, but argue that they are justified, or free of blame, in taking it because of their actual or promised performance of culturally-appropriate "acts of contrition" that neutralize untoward actions. . . .

The motives I document in this analysis are not merely *ex post facto* justifications for actions; rather, I argue that they enable action—and thus allow a person to escape symbolic entrapment—by allowing individuals to take boundary damaging courses of action by mitigating the risks of these actions to their social identities. . . .

Methods and Analysis

This article is part of a larger in-depth interview project investigating the role religion plays in the lives and experiences of intimate partner abuse victims. . . . I recruited participants for this study from the middle Tennessee and southern Wisconsin areas. . . .

I focus mainly on the experiences of 15 conservative Christian victims of spousal abuse who were previously or are currently married to their abusive partners. I focus on conservative Christians who were married to their abusive partners in the present analysis because participants of more moderate and liberal religiosities in my sample did not express experiencing any conflict between seeking a divorce from their abusive partners and the biblical prohibitions against divorce. . . .

All 15 participants who are the focus of this paper are religiously active; most attended church at least once a week, prayed more than once a day, read the Bible on a regular basis, participated in other religious activities such as Bible study, and consumed various forms of religious media such as Christian radio and popular Christian books. All participants claimed that religion was an integral and important aspect of their lives. The participants come from a variety of occupations, education levels (average number of years of education: 14.6 years), and age groups (average age: 43.5 years). Most participants are white, with one African-American and one non-native Hispanic.

I conducted semi-structured in-depth interviews with all 15 participants who are the focus of this study. The interviews consisted of a variety of questions that assessed the participants' demographic and religious characteristics, childhood history, abuse history, and the various ways that religion and popular culture influenced their perceptions, experiences, and decisions regarding their abusive situations. The interview also consisted of questions about their experiences with religious and secular domestic violence agencies, as well as questions that solicited advice for individuals currently experiencing intimate partner violence and for domestic violence agencies.

Experiencing Symbolic Entrapment

The conservative Christian victims in this study experienced strong feelings of symbolic entrapment. They wanted to divorce their abusive husbands, but at the same time they were aware that the Bible defines divorce as a sin. This experience kept many conservative Christian victims in abusive marriages much longer than they avowed they would have otherwise and caused them to feel high levels of guilt and shame for considering divorce. For example, Janine, a Church of Christ member, said that her faith's prohibitions against divorce kept her from leaving her abusive husband:

> I didn't want my marriage to end in divorce like my parents' because of my religious background and upbringing in the Church of Christ. And, uh, the Church of Christ really don't believe in divorce unless it's, uh, uh, adultery. . . . That kept me from leaving. And I really thought, you know, I wasn't supposed to get a divorce.

Feelings of symbolic entrapment became explicit and were exacerbated in instances in which significant others reminded victims that the Bible prohibits divorce. For example, when Christine—a Southern Baptist—would tell her husband that she wanted a divorce, he would respond by telling her that she couldn't leave him because of her faith's prohibitions against divorce. He would also tell Christine that she would lose her Christian friends if she did divorce him:

> He [my husband] would say you can't get divorced. You're a Christian and all of your Christian friends are going to frown upon and, and you won't have any friends left. . . . I think that if, you know, did anybody ever deter me or try to deter me or say anything, he [my husband] did more so than anybody ever did about me not divorcing him, [saying] God will be disappointed with you. He did it far more than anybody ever did it. . . .

Escaping Symbolic Entrapment and Maintaining Identity Through Motives

Although they experienced symbolic entrapment, the conservative Christian spousal abuse victims I interviewed found ways to escape while maintaining their religious identities. They did so by using three distinct and nonmutually exclusive types of motives: (1) normative motives, (2) transforming motives, and (3) neutralizing motives.

Normative Religious Motives for Divorce

A couple of victims used normative religious motives for divorce. In both of these cases, the normative religious motive for divorce was because of sexual adultery. For example, consider Marjorie, a black Pentecostal married to an abusive husband for almost 30 years. Marjorie's husband, along with being physically and emotionally abusive, also was shamelessly sexually unfaithful. Speaking on the subject of her divorce from her husband, Marjorie told me, "Well, I sure had a reason for it [divorce] when it came to adultery (laughs)." When I asked Marjorie what she would have done if her husband had not committed sexual adultery, she claimed that she "would still be married to him." Although a response to a hypothetical situation, Marjorie's reply demonstrates the perceived importance of adequate religious motives for conservative Christian abused wives who do seek a divorce.

Marianne, the Southern Baptist in the second opening vignette, also used this motive to justify divorcing her abusive husband. Toward the end of the 25-year marriage, Marianne's husband started to have sexual affairs with prostitutes and women he met in online chat rooms. For Marianne, this was an adequate motive for divorce: "Well, he was unfaithful, and Jesus is quoted as saying that it's, well, I'm paraphrasing it, that it is acceptable to divorce your spouse for adultery."

On the individual level, normative motives easily prevent any conflict between actions and belief. Since the denominations that Marjorie and Marianne belonged to allow divorce in cases of sexual adultery, seeking a divorce did not threaten their religious identities. These motives also work on the interpersonal level because they easily convince fellow conservative Christians of the appropriateness of their actions.

Many victims, however, did not have the "brutal luxury" of having an available normative religious motive for divorce. This is because their husbands neither had extramarital sexual affairs nor deserted them. However, they still escaped symbolic entrapment while maintaining their Christian identities by using transforming and neutralizing motives.

Transforming Motives for Divorce

As stated above, transforming motives are motives that transform ordinary and pre-existing nongroup motives into motives that conform to the culture of the social group in which the threatened social identity is based. In the present case, these motives transform the secular motive for divorce (i.e., spousal abuse) into a religious one through the strategic manipulation of cultural elements of conservative Christianity. . . .

Strategic Interpretation of Scripture

One type of transforming motive that several victims used consisted of strategically interpreting scripture. With these motives, victims took advantage of the ambiguities, interpretive gaps, and contexts of various verses in the Bible in ingenious and creative ways to develop religious justifications for divorce in cases of spousal abuse.

One way in which victims strategically interpreted scripture to justify divorce in cases of spousal abuse was by contextualizing Malachi 2:16, a verse in the Bible conservative Christians often cite as proof that divorce is a sin. Several victims argued that, when read in context, this verse allows spouses to divorce because of violence. For example, consider Sara—a Church of Christ member in her early 50s. Sara remained in her abusive marriage for several years before deciding to leave. Sara recounted to me how she struggled over her decision to leave her husband because of the biblical prohibitions against divorce. Sara resolved this struggle, however, by coming to an understanding of Malachi 2:16 as justifying divorce in cases of spousal abuse:

> After it says, "God hates divorce," it says, "and God hates a man that covers himself in anger." So, that's very clear to me, that He hates divorce, but He hates that, too. . . . I believe the Bible teaches that if the marriage covenant is broken by one of the people, and being abusive to someone is breaking

> the marriage covenant, then your husband's already broken it by treating you this way.

Sara acknowledges that the Bible does define divorce as a sin, but she is also quick to point out that following this prohibition is a prohibition against violence. Sara ingeniously exploits this fact to assert a conditional relationship between divorce and violence: "being abusive to someone is breaking the marriage covenant." That is, she takes advantage of an interpretive gap inherent within the verse to transform the secular abuse motive for divorce into one that adheres to scripture. . . .

Marital Unfaithfulness

Another transforming motive several abused wives used consisted of a generalization of the notion of "marital unfaithfulness." That is, victims reinterpreted the biblical verses that many conservative Christians believe allow divorce in cases of sexual adultery to develop a motive for divorce in cases where sexual adultery did not occur or was not an issue. With this motive, victims took advantage of the unfixed meaning of the term "marital unfaithfulness," going beyond the common conservative Christian understanding of the term to justify divorce in their specific cases. Using this broader definition, several victims argued that they had the biblical right to divorce because their abusive husbands committed acts of "marital unfaithfulness."

For instance, consider Christine, the Southern Baptist introduced earlier. Christine remained with her abusive husband for several years because she did not feel that she had biblical justification for leaving him. Christine finally decided to divorce her husband, however, after generalizing the notion of "marital unfaithfulness" beyond just sexual adultery. Specifically, Christine came to understand unfaithfulness as referring not only to sexual unfaithfulness, but also to "emotional unfaithfulness." She defines emotional unfaithfulness as a spouse wanting to have extramarital sexual relations, whether or not these wants are actually carried out. According to Christine, her husband committed acts of emotional unfaithfulness by constantly telling her that he wanted to have sex with other women, including her friends. By adhering to this broader definition, then, Christine came to interpret her husband's actions as evidence of marital unfaithfulness. By doing so, she was able to develop a religious motive for divorce. . . .

Wish of God

Another transforming motive that several victims used to escape symbolic entrapment is the "wish of God" motive. This motive consisted of the argument that God does not want anyone to be in an abusive marriage because of the love that He has for them. For instance, Rose—a Church of Christ member—justified her divorce from her abusive husband by arguing that "God would not want me to be injured or hurt in some manner, or dead, . . . because I am a child of God."

Rose strategically draws upon specific cultural resources inherent in conservative Christian cultures to transform a secular motive for divorce into a religious one. Two cultural resources that Rose uses in particular stand out. First, Rose employs the God-concept of a protective and loving paternal God, which is common among conservative Christian denominations and congregations. This is revealed by Rose's use of the pronoun "He" to refer to God throughout the interview and her claim that she is "a child of God." Simply put, Rose justifies her divorce by asserting that just as a loving human father would not want his daughter to be in an abusive situation, neither does the Heavenly Father want one of his children in a situation of violence.

The second cultural resource that Rose draws upon in developing her motive is the belief that a "good" Christian has a personal relationship with God. One of the most distinctive aspects of conservative evangelical belief is the notion that a Christian should have an intimate relationship with God and Jesus Christ (Smith 2000). Rose asserts a close and personal relationship with God by claiming that she has correct knowledge of what God wants: "God would not want me to be injured or hurt in some manner, or dead." By avowing this relationship, Rose creates a religious motive, at least in part, by arguing that her intimacy with God trumps biblical authority. Thus, she exploits the various and contradictory strands of authority (textual, experiential, relational, etc.) found in conservative Christianity (Smith 2000; Woodberry and Smith 1998) to develop a motive that would allow her to divorce her abusive husband while sustaining her religious identity. Like normative motives, transforming motives work on both the intrapersonal and interpersonal levels. On the intrapersonal level, transforming motives relieve cognitive dissonance by making the spousal abuse motive congruent with the victims' conservative Christian beliefs. Transforming motives also work on the interpersonal level because they provide victims with biblical and theological arguments they can use to convince fellow conservative Christians of the appropriateness of their actions.

Neutralizing Motives for Divorce

. . . Neutralizing motives are those in which people admit that a course of action is wrong, but argue that they are justified or free of blame in taking it because of their performance of culturally appropriate "acts of contrition" that neutralize symbolic boundary damaging courses of action. For conservative Christian abused wives, this motive consisted of (1) an admission of having sinned for divorce and (2) claiming that one has asked God for forgiveness.

For example, consider Jane, a conservative Christian who was married to her abusive husband for a decade. Jane acknowledged that seeking a divorce from her abusive husband was a "sin" and thus damaged the symbolic boundaries that define her religious identity. She claims, however, that she has asked God for forgiveness and that the performance of this act maintains the integrity of her religious identity:

> Not to say that any of it's right. Uh, whenever everybody goes through a divorce, there's sin involved on both sides. And, um, I think that, you know, I've asked for forgiveness for that and, uh, believe I have been forgiven. . . .

Like the other motives, neutralizing motives work on both the intrapersonal and interpersonal levels. On the intrapersonal level, they relieve feelings of cognitive dissonance by counteracting the perceived sin of divorce with the belief that God forgives sins. On the interpersonal level, neutralizing motives work by providing victims with a statement that will satisfy fellow conservative Christians who might question the validity of victims' conservative Christian identities. This statement demonstrates remorse on the part of the victim for getting a divorce and the victim's active efforts at rectification of the "sinful" act.

Of course, neutralizing motives do not easily fall into the oft-used motive categories of "justifications" and "excuses" (Scott and Lyman 1968). Motives, however, are more than this. As Mills (1940) states, "a motive tends to be one which is to the actor and the other members of a situation an unquestioned answer to questions concerning social and lingual conduct" (p. 907). In other words, motives are the statements social actors tell themselves and others that will satisfy the questioners of an act. To see the "satisfying" nature of neutralizing motives, one only needs to think of what would occur if Jane or Rachel said to a "questioning" conservative Christian (which includes themselves) that they do not believe that divorce is a sin or that they did not ask God for forgiveness if they do believe it is a sin. Such a response would not satisfy a conservative Christian who questions these victims' decisions to seek a divorce or the validity of their conservative Christian identities.

Motives as Enablers of Action

Mills (1940) argues that motives are not only *ex post facto* justifications for behavior, although they also function in this way and thus resemble Scott and Lyman's (1968) notion of accounts. Rather, motives "are accepted justifications for present, *future*, and past programs or acts" and that the availability of acceptable motives "for different situations are significant determinants of conduct" (Mills 1940:908, emphasis added). Sociologists, however, have focused almost exclusively on *ex post facto* rationalizations of deviant and questionable conduct. This is unfortunate, since Mills (1940) contends that empirical researchers can investigate the effects of available motives for future social action: "It is a hypothesis worthy and capable of test that typal vocabularies of motives for different situations are significant determinants of conduct" (p. 908).

Narrative data from victims who eventually divorced their husbands and "negative cases" (Glaser and Strauss 1967) in which victims either (a) did not have religious motives before they sought divorce or (b) where the motives used were not seen as appropriate by fellow conservative Christians provide evidence that Mills (1940) is right in asserting that motives are important causal factors in future social actions. Having acceptable motives enables action, I argue, by relieving the cognitive dissonance associated with taking certain courses of action and by providing individuals with arguments to convince fellow group members of the appropriateness of their actions. In other words, the availability of acceptable motives has a significant impact on whether a person successfully escapes symbolic entrapment.

Narrative data provide evidence for needing motives beforehand to relieve cognitive dissonance. As seen throughout this article, many victims recounted their internal turmoil between wanting to leave their abusive husbands and their religious beliefs. They also told of how they solved this turmoil through developing appropriate religious motives. For example, Marjorie claims that if her husband had not been sexually unfaithful to her, she "would still be married to him." In addition, Janine said that she found "the courage to leave" once she developed a transforming motive for divorce. Also, . . . Christine . . . recounted how [she] did not feel comfortable seeking [a] divorce from [her] husband until [she] reinterpreted "martial unfaithfulness."

A "negative case" in my sample also provides evidence that motives enable action by relieving cognitive dissonance. One conservative Christian in my sample—Tori—did not have a religious motive for divorce before she actually divorced her husband. According to Tori, she divorced her abusive husband after almost a year of marriage because she did not want to be a victim and because she felt that she did not deserve to suffer from abuse. Tori experienced a tremendous amount of guilt, however, because she did not have a religious motive for divorcing. These feelings influenced Tori's behavior in several ways. First, they caused her to return to her husband after the first time she left, which occurred around the sixth month of marriage. When I asked Tori why she went back, she said because she "didn't want to be a failure in the church." The guilt that Tori felt for leaving her abusive husband was especially salient when she left her abusive husband for good. Her comments indicate that the main source of this guilt came from her perceived violation of biblical teachings:

> Because, you know, biblically we were taught that you should stick it out, and you should be married for life. You know, it doesn't matter how much society is getting divorced, it's still is in your head. It's still a shame and guilt and you feel like you're used after you get divorced. . . . In the eyes of God and everybody else you married this person. And now you're telling the world that, "Oh, well, I didn't mean what I meant. I'm out of here." You know, "Oh, well the going gets tough I'm just going to go."

When I asked Tori if she still felt guilty five years after her divorce became final, she said no. She no longer felt guilty because she now had a transforming motive (here, the "wish of God") that helped her relieve the cognitive dissonance caused by the discrepancy between her actions and her religious identity: "Jesus was a lover of women and a protector of women when He walked on Earth. . . . God would not feel bad that I did what I had to do."

There also is evidence from narratives that motives enable action by offering explanations that convince fellow group members of the appropriateness of actions. The opening vignette with Marianne demonstrates that not having motives accepted by fellow conservative Christians prevents people from taking certain courses of action. More positively, many victims recounted to me how they felt justified in getting divorced because their family, friends, and other significant others accepted their motives.

A negative case in my sample also provides evidence for the claim that having accepted motives influences whether or not a person takes a particular course of action. I interviewed Carol—a Church of Christ member—several times over the course of two years. Carol was living in a transitional housing program for domestic violence victims when I first met her. At that time, Carol was seriously considering divorcing her abusive husband. She had the appropriate legal documents filled out and sitting on the dresser in her apartment. When I asked Carol why she felt justified in seeking a divorce, she said because her husband's abusive behavior was not reflective of how "Christ loved the church." However, Carol's best friend and fellow Church of Christ member, Molly, told her that the only biblically appropriate reason for getting a divorce is when the spouse commits adultery: "[My friend said,] well, you know the only scriptural reason for divorce in the Bible is adultery." Carol admitted that this conflict between her motive for divorce and her friend's claim that divorce is only allowed in cases of adultery made her hesitant to file the divorce papers: "I'm stuck sort of in the middle, and I guess that's why I haven't gotten my divorce, because I'm still trying to make up my mind."

I interviewed Carol six months later, and she had since made up her mind. She was trying to "work things out" with her husband, and she wanted to make her marriage "work." When I asked her what caused this change in attitude, Carol told me about an incident in which a Church of Christ preacher told her that if she divorced, she would have to remain unmarried and celibate for the rest of her life. He said this even though he was fully aware of her husband's abusive behavior:

> He [the Church of Christ preacher] says to me, "I want to look at you and I want to be honest with you, because if you divorce him [your husband], or he divorces you, you have to live a life of celibacy. Are you ready to think about that?"

In short, Carol decided not to divorce her abusive husband because she did not have a motive that satisfied her preacher.

I talked with Carol again six months later. She was once again living with her husband. When I asked Carol why she made the decision not to divorce her husband, she said because she didn't "want to go to Hell." When I probed into what she meant by this, Carol told me that it says in the Bible that she cannot get a divorce unless adultery is involved. Since she had no proof that her husband committed sexual adultery, Carol said that she had to forgive him and try to make her marriage work. When I asked her how she came to this decision, she cited her encounter with the Church of Christ preacher above. Although Carol admitted to me that she was still afraid that her husband might abuse her again, she was determined to make her marriage "work."

Discussion and Conclusion

Symbolic entrapment is a ubiquitous part of social life. People often do not perform certain actions because they threaten the symbolic boundaries that define important and salient social identities. This may even be the case in situations in which these actions might be in the best interests of the individual, as when symbolic boundaries related to conservative Christian identities keep individuals in abusive marriages. By using the case of conservative Christian victims of spousal abuse, I theorize that individuals are able to escape symbolic entrapment while also maintaining their identities by using normative, transforming, and neutralizing motives that make these courses of action seem appropriate within the cultural context of social groups. These motives help individuals escape symbolic entrapment by relieving cognitive dissonance and by providing them with culturally-resonant arguments and statements that convince fellow group members of the appropriateness of their actions.

References

Ammerman, Nancy T. 1987. *Bible Believers: Fundamentalists in the Modern World.* New Brunswick, NJ: Rutgers University Press.

Bartkowski, John P. 2001. *Remaking the Godly Marriage: Gender Negotiation in Evangelical Families*. New Brunswick, NJ: Rutgers University Press.

Brewer, Marilyn B. 1991. "The Social Self: On Being the Same and Different at the Same Time." *Personality and Social Psychology Bulletin* 17:475–82.

Denton, Melinda L. 2004. "Gender and Marital Decision Making: Negotiating Religious Ideology and Practice." *Social Forces* 82:1151–80.

Gallagher, Sally K. 2003. *Evangelical Identity and Gendered Social Life*. New Brunswick, NJ: Rutgers University Press.

Gallagher, Sally K. and Christian Smith. 1999. "Symbolic Traditionalism and Pragmatic Egalitarianism: Contemporary Evangelicals, Families, and Gender." *Gender and Society* 13:211–33.

Glaser, Barney G. and Anselm L. Strauss. 1967. *The Discovery of Grounded Theory: Strategies for Qualitative Research*. Chicago: Aldine.

Goffman, Erving. 1963. *Stigma: Notes on the Management of Spoiled Identity*. New York: Touchstone.

Mills, C. Wright. 1940. "Situated Actions and Vocabularies of Motive." *American Sociological Review* 5:904–13.

Owens, Timothy J. 2003. "Self and Identity." Pp. 205–32 in *The Handbook of Social Psychology*, edited by J. Delamater. New York: Kluwer Academic/Plenum Publishers.

Scott, Marvin B. and Stanford M. Lyman. 1968. "Accounts." *American Sociological Review* 33:46–62.

Smith, Christian. 2000. *Christian American? What Evangelicals Really Want*. Berkeley: University of California Press.

Woodberry, Robert D. and Christian Smith. 1998. "Fundamentalism et al.: Conservative Protestants in America." *Annual Review of Sociology* 24:25–56.

Reflective Questions:

1. What is symbolic entrapment? What does it feel like to be symbolically entrapped? How do individuals typically escape symbolic entrapment, according to previous research? Why don't the women in this study use the same strategies? How did other people contribute to the symbolic entrapment experienced by the women here?
2. What vocabularies of motive helped women to leave their abusers but maintain their Christian identities? How do they help women to satisfy themselves that they are acting appropriately? How do they help women satisfy others?
3. Sharp argues that motives do not simply justify actions to others but also enable future action. How do they serve this function?
4. Draw a circle on a sheet of paper to create a pie. Generate a list of the *social* identities most important to you. Then divide the pie chart according to their salience to you and label each section of the chart. Looking at the chart, which social identity is most important to you? What kinds of benefits do you get from this identity? If you suddenly could no longer claim this identity, how would you feel? What relationships and resources would you lose? Would you lose other social benefits? Think of a behavior or two that is repugnant to people within that group. What social conditions could compel you to act that way? Do you know people who have engaged in that behavior? How did they reconcile the conflict between their identity and their actions? What sort of vocabularies of motive did they—or could you—use to convince themselves and others to act in that way?

37

Doing Gender as Resistance

CHAUNTELLE ANNE TIBBALS

People in social structural positions of power can impose systems of meaning and action on others. Administrators, executives, and managers of varied organizations impose systems of meaning and action on their employees, clients, and, often, customers. For example, executives and managers of restaurants commonly mandate how tasks will be divided and performed in minute detail, what employees can and cannot wear to work, and how they should interact with customers. Yet such social structural power has its limits. Those who are subject to it seldom passively accept its dictates and definitions of situations. Rather, they subtly, and sometimes not so subtly, resist the efforts of those in more structurally powerful positions to shape their conduct and thinking. They draw upon local and cultural sources of power in those efforts and protect their sense of self from organizational definitions of who they should be, including who they should be as men or women.

In this selection, Chauntelle Anne Tibbals illustrates the gender-based resistance engaged in by servers who work at family and corporate restaurants. In doing so, she reveals how and why this resistance took on different forms in these differing types of restaurants. At both the family and corporate restaurants, owners or managers established rules for the servers' appearance and conduct. For instance, they told waitresses how to restrain their hair style and required them to wear work uniforms with standardized shirts, shoes, skirts, or pants. In the case of the corporate restaurant, management also required waitresses to abide by an androgynous form of service and self-presentation in an effort to remove gender-related expectations or performances from their role. More generally, the policies implemented by both restaurants promoted an image of food service work as a form of servitude.

Tibbals found that waitresses at both the family and corporate restaurants actively resisted the restrictions imposed on them and the symbolism of service these restrictions promoted, especially by drawing upon normative versions of gender when presenting themselves to others. At the family restaurant, waitresses drew upon stereotypical gender performances, such as the "nurturing" caretaker or "sexy party girl," in their table serving acts. In doing so, they tailored their performances in ways that enabled them to realize desired goals, including enhancing their tips, building a collection of loyal regulars, and minimizing or subverting the status differential between themselves and their customers. Because of corporate restrictions and service standards, the waitresses at the corporate restaurant did not have the option to engage in the same kinds of gender performances as their counterparts at the family restaurant. Nor could they derive the same benefits from "doing gender" in stereotypical ways. Nevertheless, Tibbals found that these waitresses still chose to engage in some normative and seemingly conformist gender performances because this enabled

Reprinted from: Chauntelle Anne Tibbals, Doing Gender as Resistance: Waitresses and Servers in Contemporary Table Service. *Journal of Contemporary Ethnography* 36(6): 731–751. Copyright © 2007 Sage Publications. Reprinted by permission of the publisher.

them to resist corporate standardization. For instance, the waitresses wore stylish or decorative belts, left some of their shirt buttons open, and exchanged gender stereotypical comments (e.g., "you look so good") that mocked the androgynous selves they presented in their standardized uniforms. Ironically, the waitresses used these expressions of gender conformity as strategies for exercising power and self-protection, particularly by engaging in "role distance." That is, the Concept Restaurant waitresses used conventional gender strategies to express their detachment from the androgynous server role imposed upon them, thereby showing others that their sense of self was not invested in this role.

The examples of the waitresses at the family and corporate restaurants illustrate both the power of social structure to shape our everyday social lives and its limits. Like these waitresses, we often find ourselves in situations where those in social structural positions of greater power pressure us to think, feel, and act as they see fit. They often determine the circumstances under which we must act. However, we seldom passively accept their dictates or our circumstances. Rather, we respond to them, sometimes reluctantly bending to them, sometimes actively challenging or reshaping them, and sometimes resisting them in subtle ways, such as by engaging in role distance. Often we engage in all of these strategies, even at the same time. Thus, while social structural arrangements clearly shape our everyday lives, they do not determine them because they are, at least in part, of our own making.

"Doing gender" refers to a complex array of socially guided behaviors that render particular pursuits and activities as evidentiary expressions of masculinity and femininity (West and Zimmerman 1987). Moreover, doing gender produces, reproduces, and legitimates normatively acceptable versions of masculine and feminine expression (West and Zimmerman 1987). Doing a successful version of gender—successful in that it is accepted as appropriate and understandable by other persons—can thus be conceptualized as a practice of social conformity. Previous work suggests refraining from doing normative gender can be used as a form of resistance. The question then arises: can normatively acceptable versions of gender be done as resistance?

To explore this question, I studied women table servers doing gender in two restaurant settings: "waitresses" in a traditional family-owned establishment and "servers" in a standardized corporate chain restaurant. A considerable amount of work has been done on the topic of doing gender as a waitress; however, there has been no analysis of doing gender as a server in a routinized corporate restaurant setting. This article comparatively examines experiences of doing gender as a waitress in a traditional restaurant setting and doing gender as a server in a routinized restaurant setting to explore the possibility of persons doing normative gender as resistance. . . .

Method

The data used in this article were obtained through ethnographic research conducted over the course of twenty-two months (February 2001 to November 2002) in two restaurant settings. I performed the duties of a table server in a traditional family-owned pizza and pasta restaurant, which I refer to as the Family Restaurant, from February to September 2001 and in an outlet of a steadily expanding, standardized chain restaurant, which I refer to as the Concept Restaurant, from October 2001 to November 2002. My table-serving duties in both venues included taking customers' food and drink orders, attempting to ensure patrons received and were satisfied with their meals, and presenting bills and collecting payments. At the Family Restaurant, there were no additional logistical or sales requirements guiding the table-serving labor. The work could be completed in whatever manner the table server saw fit, as long as it was completed. At the Concept Restaurant, however, I was also required to "suggestive sell" (attempt to augment a table's bill by suggesting additional, more expensive food and drink items to patrons), orchestrate each table in conjunction with a corporate-prescribed "service timeline," and perform "running side work" duties.

These restaurants represent extremes of the contemporary table-serving experience—"waitressing" at the nonstandardized Family Restaurant versus "serving" at the routinized Concept Restaurant. Waitresses work in noncorporate restaurants with a predominantly female wait staff. Each waitress independently manages her own workload and balances the tasks she must perform to satisfy the particular dining needs of her patrons. "Serving" refers to a contemporary and increasingly prevalent concept of table service. Servers are found in chain restaurants and can be men or women and are presented in as androgynous a manner as possible. This may be a consequence to such establishments' desire for predictability and replicability (Ritzer 2000). Servers are members of a restaurant table service "team" wherein each member of the wait staff is responsible for the needs of each restaurant patron. The Concept Restaurant provides servers with a "Service Time Line" (The Concept Restaurant *Server Training Manual*), an outline of the schedule each server must abide by to satisfy the dining needs of each restaurant patron. The nature of these two distinct types of restaurant establishments generates standardized and nonstandardized iterations of what superficially appears to be the exact same labor position.

My time as an employee and participant observer totaled approximately 1,900 hours (550 at the Family Restaurant and 1,350 at the Concept Restaurant). In each setting, I made my role as a researcher known to the managerial staff. I took notes in each setting as I worked, usually on the backs of tickets (forms used to record a table's order) or on register tape that fit easily in my restaurant-issued server notebook(s). These notes were elaborated at the end of each shift, and grounded theory was used to inform their subsequent analysis (Strauss and Corbin 1998).

The Restaurants

The Family Restaurant, established in 1968, is a casual family-oriented establishment located in an upper middle-class Los Angeles area suburb that serves lunch and dinner seven days a week. The dining area consisted of booths covered in burgundy vinyl and tables of birch-colored wood (forty-eight total booths or tables, approximately 150 seats). Leafy green plants were distributed throughout the restaurant, and watercolor prints of nature scenes decorated the walls. The Family Restaurant had a very simple Italian menu, serving pizzas and simple pasta dishes ranging in price from four to eighteen dollars. The beverage selection consisted of "the basics" (soda, coffee, milk, and tea), two draft beers, and three selections of wine.

Twenty-two waitresses and one waiter were employed at the Family Restaurant during the course of this study. Ages ranged from early twenties to midsixties, with the approximate average age being mid- to late thirties. Each waitress had worked for the Family Restaurant for at least two years at the beginning of this study, but most had worked there much longer. There was no employee turnover during the time I worked at the Family Restaurant. Fifteen of the waitresses had at least one child; of these fifteen women, ten were single (never married) or divorced. Each waitress was apparently white and heterosexual.

The original Concept Restaurant was opened in 1979, a subsidiary venture of a nationwide breakfast restaurant chain. At the time of this study, there were twenty-three existing Concept Restaurants and four planned openings. The outlet of the Concept Restaurant where I was employed opened in October 2001 and was located a few miles from the Family Restaurant. It was a large restaurant with forty-six indoor booths and tables, thirty stools surrounding a large circular bar, and eight tables located in an outdoor dining area (approximately two hundred seats). The Concept Restaurant was decorated with a safari/jungle-animal motif (standard for all Concept Restaurants), complete with tiki torches lining the entryway and "Larger than Life" giraffe and elephant statues positioned throughout the dining area. "Larger than Life" is how the Concept Restaurant describes the type of service presentation it intends to "WOW!" patrons with (The Concept Restaurant *Server Training Manual*). The Concept Restaurant had a varied menu consisting of steak, seafood, burgers, stir-fry dishes, salads, pasta dishes, sandwiches, and desserts, ranging in price from five to fifteen dollars. The beverage selection included "the basics," a full bar, several draft and bottled beer options complete with two home-brewed specialty selections, a wine list, and a myriad of specialty alcoholic and nonalcoholic beverages.

At the time I began working at the Concept Restaurant, there were approximately seventy servers hired and trained for the store's opening. There were forty-eight women and men servers and eight women cocktail servers employed at the completion of this study fourteen months later. The turnover of employees was quite rapid; only seventeen of the final forty-eight servers had been waiting tables for the Concept Restaurant over the entire time I worked there. The final ratio of women to men servers was thirty-four to fourteen; this roughly two-to-one ratio was reflective of the wait staff's gender composition throughout the course of this study. Wait staff ages ranged from the late teens to the early twenties, with the main concentration of servers in their early twenties. At the completion of this study, there were two mothers and no fathers working in the wait staff; both mothers were single. Previous employees with children, who had since turned over, were always an anomalous few. The servers employed throughout the course of this study were overwhelmingly white and heterosexual, although there were a few black, Hispanic, and GLBT individuals.

Doing Gender in the Family and Concept Restaurants

Presentation as a Waitress and Presentation as a Server: The Work Uniform

At the Family Restaurant, each waitress was required to wear a long- or short-sleeved white shirt with a collar, black pants or skirt, black shoes, a plain full burgundy or green apron, and a color-coordinated bowtie. The bowtie was the only purely decorative item a Family Restaurant waitress was required to wear and, as will be discussed later, was strongly disliked by the younger waitresses. Both a burgundy and a green apron/bowtie set were provided by the restaurant. Name tags were not required, although some employees did wear them. Waitresses were given five table-serving books, each of which could be decorated as the waitress saw fit, with which they were to stow their money and tickets and present checks to customers. Hair needed to be restrained enough to keep it from contacting food. A waitress was not required to wear any items with "Family Restaurant" logos while working.

Shirts could be as tight or loose as the waitress desired; pants could range from standard, functional work-uniform-store fare to cotton-polyester blends of Lycra stretch. Articles of clothing could be taken directly from one's everyday wardrobe and incorporated into one's work "uniform" if necessary or desired. A Family Restaurant waitress did not necessarily have to spend money constructing a work uniform, and each woman was permitted to tailor her work attire to her own personal preference and, thus, to her own particular gender presentation.

At the Concept Restaurant, the corporation aspired for an androgynous, interchangeable wait staff. Every server was required to wear a work uniform consisting of a "safari shirt," a tan, short-sleeved, buttoned-up men's shirt sold exclusively by the Concept Restaurant for twenty dollars each. These shirts were cut for a man's frame, and they required precisely ironed sleeve and back creases. Servers were also required to wear black pants with no externally showing pockets. Women servers were instructed to refrain from wearing pants that fit too tightly. "We don't wanna be able to see that [you are] not wearing underwear," said Mark, one of the managers, during employee training. Two particular brands of pants, each costing over forty dollars, were suggested in the *Server Training Manual.* Servers were required to wear black "Shoes for Crews," nonslip work shoes ranging in price from twenty to forty-five dollars. The catalog through which a server could purchase these shoes was provided by the Concept Restaurant. Servers were also required to wear plain black socks, a plain black belt, a black half apron, and a Concept Restaurant logo-embossed name tag. Half aprons were sold by the restaurant for seven dollars each. A server's initial name tag was provided by the restaurant; any additional were two dollars each. Servers were given one "Concept Restaurant" server book, which was not to be decorated (bills were presented to customers on plastic trays). The Concept Restaurant's *Server Workbook* states, "Your uniform should be clean and pressed and free of defect such as holes, tears, and obvious stains." It then enthusiastically states, "Always invest in your appearance!! It PAYS off!!"

Servers had strict requirements for restraining their hair. Common hairstyles for women, such as ponytails for longer hair, were considered too loose. Braids or buns were preferred. Visible jewelry, with the exception of one stud earring per ear and one ring per hand; tattoos; and "unnaturally colored hair" were not permitted. Outlandish and/or ostentatious makeup was also not permitted. Thus, according to store policy, a server could do virtually nothing to tailor her work uniform to her own personal preference and, thus, to her own particular gender presentation.

These rules and regulations were not consistently enforced, however. Cultivating an amiable relationship with managers facilitated many exceptions. For example, Joselyn's red and black quarter-sized star tattoos, located very obviously behind each of her earlobes when her hair was pulled back into a bun, were never mentioned. These standards were also not enforced for the cocktail servers, members of the wait staff who worked in the bar only. They were technically to be held to the same uniform standards as women servers with the exception of replacing the men's safari shirt with a more fitted women's leopard-printed v-neck shirt. Cocktail servers, all of whom were women throughout the course of this study, were regularly permitted to incorporate elements of (heterosexually normative) sexualized femininity into their presentation. According to management, uniform differences and allowances were made in light of the cocktail servers' role in the bar and thus their role in generating more revenue for the restaurant.

Servers and cocktail servers were given reference materials, which outlined some of the Concept Restaurant's policies and operating procedures, upon their hire. A "Service Time Line," guidelines for suggestive selling, uniform standards, and supplementary server duties were outlined by the Concept Restaurant's *Server Training Manual* and *Server Workbook,* two 50-plus-page spiral bound folios. These "service standards" were monitored by management and by secret shoppers. "Shoppers" were contracted by the Concept Restaurant's corporate office to conduct surveillance missions, usually twice per month. Shoppers would pose as customers and dine in the restaurant, unbeknownst to the servers, managers, or other restaurant employees, and score the quality of the entire restaurant experience. The restaurant was evaluated on many points, including restaurant cleanliness, the performance of the "hostess(es)," the quality of the food, and the performance of the server. The server's performance was evaluated by her adherence to a dining timeline, requisite questions and suggestions, and physical motions specified in the *Server Training Manual.* A perfect composite score of 100 percent resulted in a two hundred dollar cash reward for the server only, and a score of less than 80 percent resulted in the termination of all employees involved with the shopper report (server, busser, hostess, and so on where applicable). Like most rules at the Concept Restaurant, however, the cash reward and punitive termination(s) were selectively enforced. During the time I worked at the Concept Restaurant, no individual received the cash award, several but not all servers scoring below 80 percent were terminated, and many bussers and hostesses mentioned in "shopper reports" were suspended for one to three shifts.

Waitress Characterizations: Nurturing or (Heterosexually) Sexualized

Each table server employed at the Family Restaurant had the ability to incorporate different degrees of waitress character typifications into her presentation.

The malleable dress code, the broad age demographic of the waitresses, and the fact that each woman could develop her own methods for completing work tasks all contributed to variations in gender presentation. Two common presentations were observed, which I refer to as the "nurturing waitress" and the "sexualized waitress." Although only some waitresses epitomized one of these characterizations, each waitress incorporated some degree of one of these presentations into her act of table serving. Each characterization seemed to involve an incorporation of stereotypically feminine qualities into a crafted presentation of (waitress) self.

The nurturing waitresses tended to wear loose-fitting and functional work "costumes" and sturdy work shoes and incorporated subtle feminine touches into their presentation. Loosely tied back hair with strategically curled tendrils, jewelry such as earrings and necklaces, or pictures of children affixed to the outside of (table server) books were common. The nurturing waitress incorporated stereotypically feminine characteristics, such as kindness and patience, into the table-serving act. This characterization also included the waitress's exhibition of personal consideration and care for her "regular" customers. For example,

> Rachel, who had worked at the Family Restaurant since the early 1970s, came rushing back from the front lobby. There were no tables working in the restaurant, but an elderly couple—the very frail-looking woman using a walker—was being seated at that moment in her section. "It's my 'Little Old Couple,'" she said. "They come in every week or so, but less now because she's been real sick. They're hard to wait on, really picky." I must have made a quizzical face because she went on, "I don't mind (the extra work). They always get so happy when I have their wine ready and their lunch going by the time they sit down. They order the same thing every single time. I don't think she has much time left anyway."

In this example, Rachel makes a point of having her customers' needs met before they have the opportunity to articulate them. The degree to which Rachel customizes her routine for her "Little Old Couple" goes beyond simply bringing a provision to the table without being asked. The thought, concern, and motivation with which the nurturing waitress serves her customers characterizes her entire work presentation, even in the case of non-regulars. In another example,

> The restaurant was packed with people due to an early dinner rush. Only Ashley and I were working, each of us with half the restaurant's tables, and we were both very busy. At one point I glanced across the room just in time to see her standing next to a table serving pizza slices onto the plates of each person. I later asked her about it, and she explained: "I always [serve the pizza like that]. . . . [P]eople just seem to like the attention more."

Ashley's behavior in this example exemplifies nurturing and care. In spite of the fact that the restaurant was busy, she paid specific attention to the table's needs. In fact, she claimed to pay this specific type of caring attention to every customer simply because people seemed to prefer it. This example shows Ashley as both a nurturing waitress and a pragmatic table server.

Another example of waitress gender typification is what I refer to as the (heterosexually normative) "sexualized waitress." A sexualized waitress presented herself in a manner coincident with various heterosexually normative concepts of "sexy." This general iteration of the Family Restaurant "costume" involved tight form-fitting pants and top paired with more fashionable and less functional shoes. This iteration of the uniform was background to the personal touches the sexualized waitress would adorn herself with to tailor her particular "sexy" presentation. For example, some waitresses opted for a relatively glamorous and vamp-like, aggressive presentation. These waitresses, such as Rhonda, wore elaborate heavy makeup, had long brightly colored acrylic fingernails, and wore boots with heels. The mainstay of the "vamp-sexualized" waitress performance, however, was the forward and familiar manner in which she interacted with her tables. In one such case,

> Rhonda was chatting with two local civil service men in for lunch, leaning against one side of the booth with her knee propped up on the seat. "Why don't we go out this weekend?" one of them suggested. Rhonda responded suggestively, "If you go out with me this weekend baby, it'll be the best weekend of your life." They all laughed heartily. I later heard them speculating as to whether or not Rhonda was a "party girl."

Immediately following her response, each man appeared flushed and overjoyed at the prospect of taking a forward-acting blonde "party girl" out for "the best weekend of [their] life." Over the course of these observations, however, Rhonda, a mother of three in the middle of a divorce, never indicated she socialized with customers outside of work. Her forward comment piqued the interests of the civil servants, however. They consistently requested "Raunchy Rhonda" as their waitress for the duration of my observations.

Other waitresses opted for a more little-girl type presentation. These waitresses, such as Sunny, are more cheerful, flirtatious, and deferent in their table-serving performance. Body and face glitter, little-girl jewelry (plastic items with butterflies and hearts in pastel colors) and hair accessories, clip-on hair extension pieces configured into elaborate coifs, or server book decorations with the owner's name emblazoned in flowers are some examples of extra uniform elements. As was the case with the nurturing and the vamp-sexualized waitress, the mainstay of the "girly-sexualized" waitress's presentation was the distinctive manner in which she served tables. For example,

> Sunny sashayed up to the table, flipping her hair all the while. After a minute or so of her giggling and pointing out words that rhymed with "Sunny," the table of men patrons appeared awestruck. "Remember," I heard her call as they left the restaurant after finishing their meal, "whenever you come to the Family Restaurant, ask for Sunny. It rhymes with Honey."

Not only did Sunny make an impression on her new table with her self-presentation and serving skills, she made sure they remembered her name; thus, she immediately began cultivating an additional "regular" customer.

Some degree of gender typification, from nurturing to sexualized, was commonly incorporated into a waitress's self-presentation at her table to augment her tips, which account for seventy to eighty percent of a table server's income. Waitresses assessed each of their tables and incorporated particular service characteristics that they determined would facilitate their goal of maximizing tips. Table evaluations were shared among waitresses via the running commentary they engaged in while, for example, passing each other in the aisles or fetching drinks throughout the duration of a shift. When a table was evaluated as incompatible or financially undesirable, waitresses would often attempt to pass on or swap the table with a coworker who had determined the same table to be more compatible or less financially undesirable. For example, less "nurturing" waitresses often attempted to pass tables that included elder individuals and children. When a table was evaluated as compatible or financially desirable, waitresses would often attempt to obtain the opportunity to serve it, sometimes by trading multiple neutrally evaluated tables for one desirable prospect. In example, waitresses would often trade multiple tables to obtain the perceived financial opportunity to wait on one table of men. Waitresses would then "waitress" tables in the gender-typified manner they determined appropriate.

The financial payoff for an accurately matched customer-to-waitress presentation was often great. Based on my observations, Sunny would not have considered passing or trading the table described in the following example. Had it not been assigned to her initially, she probably would have traded multiple tables to obtain the opportunity to wait on it.

> Sunny stood at a table of men fidgeting with her acrylic nails. "Tskuh," she said "My nails are so thrashed. Look at this one." She held up her hand.

> No man seemed to notice those nails, but they did seem to notice her hand's line of sight position to her breasts, augmented double-Ds straining out the top and sides of her apron. "Wanna pay for my manicure?" She giggled and flipped her hair, enhanced with a flamboyant clip-on ponytail piece, while walking away. Twenty dollars cash later appeared in her book in addition to the charged tab and tip.

This type of gendered presentation would be tailored to the table's needs, expectations, and level of tolerance, as not all tables were the same. The exchange involving Sunny and her manicure might not have been as well received from another group of customers. It is important to note that even sexually characterized waitresses would deliver nurturing and deferent performances for tables of women and children. They would, however, present sexualized performances for tables of men and children. It was up to the waitress to make an appropriate presentation-determining evaluation before interacting with a table, or at least in a nascent stage of serving them. This skill took time to develop and cultivate, but the reward for successful patron assessment was cash in hand at the end of a shift.

In addition to augmenting her tip return, the sexualized waitress used her presentation to regain control of or recast the character of a table-serving exchange. Customers expect "good service," yet sometimes they do not receive overt friendliness or deference. It was observed that flirtatiousness through sexual allusions and sexualized illusion was capable of re-characterizing a table-serving exchange or compensating for a performance that might otherwise be considered an exhibition of "poor service." In example, an allusion to sexiness overshadowed an impertinent attitude from a waitress displaying poor service:

> They had been sitting for a few minutes when I finally got to their table. They looked unhappy. "You're all sparkly!" said the man, commenting on the glitter make-up on my eyes, arms, and neck. "Leftover from work last night?"
>
> "Yeah," I stated sarcastically. "At my other job I'm a third-grader." This statement and a wink induced a red face in the man and a grudging laugh from the woman, who had said "Jesus Jim, she probably borrowed [the glitter] from her little sister," under her breath in response to his insinuation.

In this example, Jim's inappropriate comment regarding what a decorative presentation might mean indicates both displeasure with the service and awareness of a prestige differential existing between him and the waitress. His attempt to augment this differential by implying that, in addition to engaging in a sexualized performance of low-prestige labor, I may also engage in sex work itself might have been directly linked to the affront he felt at not receiving "good service." My response played on his sexualized allusion. This brief exchange seemed to recharacterize the interaction, and the patrons' thereafter friendly demeanors indicated that they were willing to disregard my nondeferent attitude and initial delivery of substandard table service. This implies that, if occurring in the presence of the appropriate type of table/customers, a measure of "poor service" can be compensated for with a sexualized performance.

In each of the previously discussed examples, gender and "waitress" are done successfully. Waitresses used appropriate and understandable gendered presentations to augment their tips, bolster their cache of "regulars," and manage the prestige differential present between themselves and their customers. Normatively expressed gender is a tool used by Family Restaurant waitresses to accomplish their work-related goals and, simultaneously, is a practice of social conformity.

Server Characterization: Interchangeable and "Androgynous"

The degree to which waitresses were permitted to cultivate their various self-presentations and table server characterizations at the Family Restaurant was, in contrast, virtually absent in Concept Restaurant servers. Considering the stringent nature of the requisite uniform, the age demographic of the Concept Restaurant's women and men servers, and the fact that each server was required to work within corporate written scripted "service standards," each server at the Concept Restaurant was considered an interchangeable member of a "team." Consequently, stereotypical feminine gender presentation was difficult to incorporate into a server's uniform or work tasks. For example,

> I was being followed around the bar by Tony (the restaurant manager), who intercepted me by the bar well. "What daya think this is, Studio 54? What's all over your neck?" "Glitter," I answered. "People like glitter. '100% guest satisfaction,' right?" I quoted from the *Server Training Manual*. "Wrong, we don't do glitter here," he said. "Go wash it off."

Similar exchanges between managers and servers occurred in instances of using "too much makeup," wearing earrings that were considered "too big," having "too much stuff in [the server's] hair" in the form of hair clips or barrettes, and leaving the safari shirt's second button undone. "Button up," Tony chastised once while he fastened the second button of my safari shirt. Unlike the Family Restaurant waitresses, women servers in the Concept Restaurant did not have license to use appropriate and understandable gendered presentations in the workplace. However, repressing gender expression did not emerge as the Concept Restaurant's predominant goal. Preventing servers from distinguishing themselves through self-presentation to support the Concept Restaurant's larger goal of "team service" did.

The Concept Restaurant's advocacy of "team service," wherein each server is trained to provide table service in a replicable and interchangeable step-wise manner, often resulted in multiple, virtually indistinguishable members of the wait staff serving one table. Although the server taking the initial food order is technically responsible for the table, a different server may bring the food to the table, another the cocktails; one server may clear plates, another may deliver the dessert. Because of "team service" and standardized server presentation, it is often difficult for patrons to identify "their" server. For example,

> A woman from a table neighboring one of mine called out to me as I walked by: "I asked you for some honey!?" "Oh, sorry, I'll be right back," I said not slowing my pace. As I was walking back to the table with the honey I passed Alexis, another blonde woman, who said "I totally forgot that woman's honey! Thanks [for getting it]!"

In this example, it is difficult to determine if the customer (incorrectly) recognized me as her server. Regardless, I knew exactly what was expected of me as a "team service" employee. This example illustrates restaurant employee acceptance of interchangeable team service facilitated by the routinization and standardization of labor and self-presentation.

An interesting artifact of interchangeable team service was observed in customer tipping practices. Concept Restaurant patrons consistently tipped servers around 15 percent of their total bill, the contemporary standard tip amount. This was done in spite of the quality of service provided or the patron's apparent enjoyment—or even recognition—of their server. Occasional "stiffs" (no tip left at all) and extremely rare "overtips" (more than 15 percent of the bill) occurred, but standard compensation could usually be expected. Such regulated tipping practices illustrate that customers are themselves routinized into accepting and eventually compensating routinized, interchangeable table service. Tipping practices were not similar at the Family Restaurant, where standard compensation and the occasional "stiff" could also be expected, but extravagant tips were often left by regulars.

The server's lack of ability to tailor her work uniform to suit her appropriated table server character in conjunction with the scripted service standards leaves her with a small window of opportunity in which to do gender. Attempts to deviate too far outside the scripted standard service advocated by the restaurant could result in the loss of one's job, especially if a service standard monitoring "shopper" reported too many discrepancies. As a result, the server would eventually find herself repeating the same lines and suggestions over and over, incorporating very little sincerity and very few elements of individual personality into the scripted task that cycled again and again.

Resistance Through Normative Gender? Physical Presentation and Attitude

Family Restaurant waitresses often resist servility by presenting a version of their gendered selves at work that is very different from their presentation off-the-clock. For example,

> One Wednesday afternoon, a bright yellow sundress- and sandal-clad woman strolled casually into the restaurant, flipping her long wavy red hair over her shoulders. She leaned on the counter like she owned the place, took off her sunglasses, and proceeded to stick her head into the kitchen and shout: "Hey Dan, can you get me my check, ah-kaaay?" I did a double take on hearing the familiar sounding "ah-kaaay." I turned to Paige sitting on the bench beside me. "Is that *Grace?*" I asked. It was.

With her tightly coiffed bun to practical work costume, Grace epitomized the no-nonsense austere waitress who strode around the Family Restaurant with an air of extreme competence and purpose when working. Grace's strolling, casual off-the-clock presentation was extremely different from the waitress-self she presented to the customers. Grace distanced herself from the servility of her low-prestige labor position by presenting a different version of "Grace" to her customers.

Some waitresses would shed or alter one integral component of their work attire whenever they felt they would not be reprimanded: the bowtie. Immediately after the kitchen manager left for the evening, the relatively younger Family Restaurant waitresses (Sunny, Mya, Tiffany, Kelly, and myself) would immediately remove their decorative bowties. It is interesting to note that, when unsupervised, the younger waitresses would immediately remove their bowties, whereas the older waitresses would not. Because not all—or even most—of the women removed the tie, it is not likely that the younger waitresses removed it out of physical discomfort. This phenomenon indicates instead that the bowtie held some significance for the younger women waitresses, conscious or not. I would speculate that the subservience and low prestige indicated by an artifact such as a bowtie was managed differently by younger and older waitresses. Management of such labor and gender prestige differentials may be due in part to individuals' ages and eras of gender and labor socialization.

Waitresses also distanced themselves from their low-prestige labor positions through their attitudinal presentations. Consider, for example, the previous discussion wherein a man customer alluded to what my version of appropriate and acceptable gender display might mean ("You're all sparkly! Leftover from work last night?"). My impertinent response helped me to regain control of the waitress-patron interaction, while simultaneously preventing him from lumping my low-prestige table-service position in with other, lower prestige service occupations.

While Family Restaurant waitresses were able to use normative gender presentations to accomplish their work goals (conformity) and had license to alter their presentation to distance themselves from servility, Concept Restaurant servers would do normative gender to resist standardization. Oftentimes, decorative printed socks in a color other than black would become visible as the server knelt down to perform some task. Servers attempted to wear more stylish belts of embossed leather or decorated with silver metal studs, which were very quickly identified as a wardrobe violation. Many women Concept Restaurant servers would attempt to leave the second button of their safari shirt undone while working; this was one button more than the restaurant permitted. Candace attempted to tailor her safari shirt to fit her own petite frame because she was "swimming in [an] extra-small" and was promptly forced to purchase a new one. Upon clocking out, practically every woman server would immediately free her hair and remove her safari shirt, revealing some form of undershirt beneath. The presence of the undershirt allowed the server to loiter in the restaurant, be seen by patrons and coworkers, and leave the restaurant out of an androgynous server presentation. Each of these instances, regardless of their recalcitrance, is a small yet significant attempt to convey the message that there is a gendered person beneath the work ensemble.

In another example, an interesting sort of ritual phenomenon began occurring at the Concept Restaurant. Servers would often enter the restroom at the beginning of a shift to adjust their work uniform or hair. If at least two servers were present, there would inevitably be a sarcastic discussion about how nice they looked, punctuated with compliments such as "You look so good tonight!" Servers also discussed how flattering their safari shirts were with sarcastic expressions, such as "That's the cutest shirt! Where did you get it?" and how attractive the safari shirt made them feel with "I think I'm gonna wear this out [after work] tonight." This mocking of their presented selves in Concept Restaurant attire seemed to be a reaction to the lack of ability they had to alter their physically unflattering server presentations. Through a description of that which rendered them "androgynous" entities—a *man's* safari shirt—as feminine or sexy, these repetitious restroom exchanges imply that the Concept Restaurant employees desired some form of distance from their standardized "server" selves.

I observed one very unique and interesting example of resistance through conformity during my observations at the Concept Restaurant. Dominique wore the name tag "Sam" for several shifts at the Concept Restaurant before being told by management to wear only her correct attribution. During Dominique's foray into "Sam," there were six total employees actually named Sam, or an iteration of Sam, such as Sammy, Samuel, or Samantha, working at the Concept Restaurant. Two were women and four were men. Dominique attempted to veil her easily identifiable name with what had (inadvertently) become the Concept Restaurant's standardized employee attribution. In this example, attempting to standardize oneself even further was done as a form of resistance. Not only was Dominique presented in as androgynous a physical manner as possible via her uniform, she attempted to blend further into the standardized landscape of the Concept Restaurant by becoming just another androgynously attributed "Sam." Regardless of this one ironic exception, successful, normative gender is done by women servers in the standardized Concept Restaurant as a form of resistance and thus without conformity.

Conclusion: Doing Gender as Resistance

As was previously discussed, gender can be done in the workplace as long as it is done in a manner that reflects the ideologies and conceptualizations commonly affiliated with the workplace itself (Leidner 1993). Based on Leidner's findings, presentation of a feminized version of gender is to be expected of persons working in notoriously feminized jobs, such as table service. Prior work has suggested that persons do gender under the guiding praxes of emphasized femininities and hegemonic masculinities. With these versions of gender as guides, employers and labor institutions permit varying amounts of opportunity for employees to do normatively appropriate and acceptable gender in the workplace. The data from the Family Restaurant exemplify yet another illustration of this social phenomenon.

Because of the rationalization and standardization of venues such as the Concept Restaurant, a very different version of gender is expected in some workplaces, and the ideological compulsion to do an androgynous, degendered version of gender presents an interesting situation wherein a new use for doing normatively appropriate and acceptable gender performance is revealed. As my observations have shown, a degendered version of gender is expected from standardized and routinized Concept Restaurant women servers (the man's safari shirt notwithstanding). In venues such as the Concept Restaurant, normatively appropriate and acceptable versions of gender become recalcitrant, and engaging them becomes a method of resistance and nonconformity. By juxtaposing the Family and Concept Restaurants' allowances and regulations of gender performativity, the possibility for any gendered performance tactic—such as wearing body glitter—to become an act of conformity or an act of resistance depending on the workplace environment is vividly illustrated.

Doing normative versions of gender in a standardized and routinized workplace such as the Concept Restaurant relates to Lorraine de Volvo's (2003) conceptualization of "microresistance." According to de Volvo (2003), acts of microresistance are virtually imperceptible acts of workplace recalcitrance done in opposition to customer and workplace devaluation of one's self and one's labor. This work has shown doing gender as a form of resistance and also as an iteration of microresistance. Although doing gender at the microresistance level may be a useful tactic for individual persons to resist conformity, standardization, and routinization, it is unclear if doing gendered microresistance may aid society in the resistance of conformity, standardization, and routinization. Although the answer to that puzzle is beyond the scope of this project, as routinization and standardization become increasingly prevalent in society, it will be interesting to consider the possibility of doing gender as a wider reaching tactic of nonconformity and resistance.

Considering the spread of standardization, routinization, and McDonaldization into all aspects of culture (Leidner 1993; Ritzer 2000), the relevance of gender as a mode of nonconformity becomes clear. This work reveals a presentation tactic that may initially be overlooked or read as social conformity to be a subversive method of asserting individual identity and personhood. Moreover, although only women workers doing normative gender as resistance were discussed here, this work opens the door for future exploration of other persons, classes, races, ages, and identity orientations doing normative gender as a method of resistance.

References

de Volvo, Lorraine B. 2003. Service and surveillance: Infrapolitics and work among casino cocktail waitresses. *Social Politics* 10(3): 346–76.

Leidner, Robin. 1993. *Fast food, fast talk: Service work and the routinization of everyday life.* Los Angeles: University of California Press.

Ritzer, George. 2000. *The McDonaldization of society* (New Century Edition). Thousand Oaks, CA: Pine Forge Press.

Strauss, A., and J. Corbin 1998. *Basics of qualitative research: Techniques and procedures for developing grounded theory.* Thousand Oaks, CA: Sage.

West, Candace, and Don H. Zimmerman. 1987. Doing gender. *Gender and Society* 1: 125–51.

Reflective Questions

1. What is the difference between waitressing and serving? What were the expectations for workers at the family restaurant and the corporate restaurant?
2. What gendered presentations of self did waitresses make at the family restaurant? How did waitresses decide on a particular performance? What benefits did they receive for a performance well done and well matched to the clientele? What were waitresses distancing themselves from?
3. Why didn't servers at the corporate restaurant enact the same gendered performances? What is team service, and how did it shape the service experience at the corporate restaurant? Why did customers usually tip 15% regardless of the quality of service?
4. In this study, workers are doing gender in order to resist being degraded through their service work. What is the relationship of gender to social class? Does doing gender in these ways recreate gendered expectations that women may find degrading or a system of gender that disadvantages women as a group? How so or why not?
5. What is the worst job at which you have worked? What made it so bad? Have you worked in a service industry? What did you do? Besides uniforms, what do service employers such as airlines, grocery stores, fast food restaurants, and retail chains standardize for their workers? Why? How do they do it? For example, how do they teach workers scripts and enforce them? What do machines now do that employees used to do? Does standardization lead to a deskilling of the work? A loss of creativity? Freedom from trivial tasks? Something else? What effect does standardization have on workers?

Customers? Are white collar service workers or professionals immune from routinization and standardization? What microresistances do workers engage in to save face in service interactions? Watch David Letterman work the drive-thru at a fast food restaurant here: http://www.youtube.com/watch?v=AtPGdOs7zOM. What happens when routinized interactions break down?

The Politics of Social Reality

One of the central themes of this volume is that people inhabit socially constructed realities. Through interaction with one another, we endow the world of brute, physical facts with meaning and create symbolic universes that transcend that world. We interpret and structure our subjective experience in terms of social symbols and meanings. Thus, our reality is socially shaped and decided.

However, people's definitions of their subjective or bodily experiences, themselves, others, social situations, their society and its past, and their surrounding environment do not always coincide. When such definitional contests occur, power usually decides whose definitions will prevail. In our society, for example, the medical profession's authoritative definitions of illness commonly prevail over the Christian Scientists' definitions, and psychiatrists' definitions of subjective experience prevail over their patients'. The politics of reality decide who will participate in the social construction of reality, how they will participate, and how much they can contribute.

The more familiar form of politics also involves contested definitions of reality. The social problems that policymakers are urged to address are particular constructions of reality. Individuals and groups make different claims about what social conditions are problems, what kind of problems they are, and how they should be addressed. The politics of reality decide what conditions get defined as problems, how they get defined, and what actions are taken to address them. History, too, is a product of the politics of reality. The past that is transmitted to us is never an unfiltered report of events but involves selection and interpretation. Different views of the past vie to decide what events and historical figures will be remembered and how they will be remembered. Which view of the past prevails depends on the power and influence of their proponents at the time—upon the politics of reality. *These politics of reality are the most fundamental politics of human social life that decide what reality everyone in a given social circle will inhabit and, in some cases, whether they will live at all.* The selections in this section examine various aspects of the politics of social reality and their consequences.

The Moral Career of the Mental Patient

ERVING GOFFMAN

The politics of reality are perhaps most obvious in mental hospitals. Yet students of social life paid little attention to the political struggles of reality construction in mental hospitals before the publication of Goffman's widely read study Asylums. *They simply assumed the perspective of mental health professionals and did not take seriously their patients' often clashing views of reality. Goffman took a different tack. He attempted to learn about the social life of a mental hospital from the perspective of its patients. This selection, taken from* Asylums, *reveals the politics of reality at that hospital and how they shaped patients' moral careers.*

What is at stake in the politics of reality that brings individuals to a mental hospital and keeps them there is their very definition of self. In this selection, Goffman reports that family members, friends, and mental health professionals commonly form a political coalition against patients even before they get to the mental hospital. Once there, the patients' past lives and current circumstances are interpreted so as to justify admittance. From that point forward, patients' definitions of self are hostages to the definitional power of the institution and its staff.

Like those outside the walls of the mental hospital, patients attempt to maintain "face" or effective claims to positive social value. Yet their very presence in the institution indicates that they have fallen from social grace. As Goffman observes, the mental hospital is a mirror that continually reflects unflattering self-images to patients. Although patients attempt to counter these mortifying definitions of self with what Goffman calls "sad tales," they are challenged by everything around them and by everyone in the hospital. Their misdeeds are recorded in case records, reported at staff meetings, and discussed informally. Patients' own presentations of self cannot counter the weight of information that the hospital's staff possesses about them. They consequently have little influence over how others define and treat them. In the politics of reality of the mental institution, patients are virtually powerless.

The goal of the mental institution and its staff is to convince patients to internalize the psychiatric view of reality and themselves. Yet, as Goffman observes, the constant assaults upon patients' definitions of self may have a quite different effect, at least temporarily. Unable to claim or maintain face, patients may conclude that they have nothing to lose by acting shamelessly and do so. Thus, the very institution that is supposed to entice deviant individuals back to the official social reality may sometimes drive them further away. Therein lies a more general sociological lesson. Those who have no power to wield over the politics of reality may simply choose not to participate.

In 1955–56, I did a year's field work at St. Elizabeth's Hospital, Washington, D.C., a federal institution of somewhat over 7000 inmates that draws three quarters of its patients from the District of Columbia.... My immediate object in doing field work at St. Elizabeth's was to try to learn about the social world of the hospital inmate, as this world is subjectively experienced by him....

It was then and still is my belief that any group of persons—prisoners, primitives, pilots, or patients—develop a life of their own that becomes meaningful, reasonable, and normal once you get close to it, and that a good way to learn about any of these worlds is to submit oneself in the company of the members to the daily round of petty contingencies to which they are subject....

The world view of a group functions to sustain its members and expectedly provides them with a self-justifying definition of their own situation and a prejudiced view of non-members, in this case, doctors, nurses, attendants, and relatives. To describe the patient's situation faithfully is necessarily to present a partisan view. (For this last bias, I partly excuse myself by arguing that the imbalance is at least on the right side of the scale, since almost all professional literature on mental patients is written from the point of view of the psychiatrist, and he, socially speaking, is on the other side)....

Traditionally the term *career* has been reserved for those who expect to enjoy the rises laid out within a respectable profession. The term is coming to be used, however, in a broadened sense to refer to any social strand of any person's course through life. The perspective of natural history is taken: unique outcomes are neglected in favor of such changes over time as are basic and common to the members of a social category, although occurring independently to each of them. Such a career is not a thing that can be brilliant or disappointing; it can no more be a success than a failure. In this light, I want to consider the mental patient....

The category "mental patient" itself will be understood in one strictly sociological sense. In this perspective, the psychiatric view of a person becomes significant only in so far as this view itself alters his social fate—an alteration which seems to become fundamental in our society when, and only when, the person is put through the process of hospitalization. I, therefore, exclude certain neighboring categories: the undiscovered candidates who would be judged "sick" by psychiatric standards but who never come to be viewed as such by themselves or others, although they may cause everyone a great deal of trouble; the office patient whom a psychiatrist feels he can handle with drugs or shock on the outside; the mental client who engages in psychotherapeutic relationships. And I include anyone, however robust in temperament, who somehow gets caught up in the heavy machinery of mental-hospital servicing. In this way, the effects of being treated as a mental patient can be kept quite distant from the effects upon a person's life of traits a clinician would view as psychopathological....

The career of the mental patient falls popularly and naturalistically into three main phases: the period prior to entering the hospital, which I shall call the prepatient phase; the period in the hospital, the inpatient phase; the period after discharge from the hospital, should this occur, namely, the ex-patient phase. This paper will deal only with the first two phases....

The Prepatient Phase

The prepatient's career may be seen in terms of an extrusory model; he starts out with relationships and rights, and ends up, at the beginning of his hospital stay, with hardly any of either. The moral aspects of this career, then, typically begin with the experience of abandonment, disloyalty, and embitterment. This is the case even though to others it may be obvious that he was in need of treatment, and even though in the hospital he may soon come to agree....

In the prepatient's progress from home to the hospital, he may participate as a third person in what he may come to experience as a kind of alienative coalition. His next-of-relation presses him into coming to "talk things over" with a medical practitioner, an office psychiatrist, or some other counselor. Disinclination on his part may be met by threatening him with desertion, disownment, or other legal action, or by stressing the joint and exploratory nature of the interview. But typically the next-of-relation will have set the interview up, in the sense of selecting the professional, arranging for time, telling the professional something about the case, and so on. This move effectively tends to establish the next-of-relation as the responsible person to whom pertinent findings can be divulged, while effectively establishing the other as the patient. The prepatient often goes to the interview with the understanding that he is going as an equal of someone who is so bound together with him that a third person could not come between them in fundamental matters; this, after all, is one way in which close relationships are defined in our society. Upon arrival at the office, the prepatient suddenly finds that he and his next-of-relation have not been accorded the same roles, and apparently that a prior understanding between the professional and the next-of-relation has been put in operation against him. In the extreme but common case, the professional first sees the prepatient alone, in the role of examiner and diagnostician, and then sees the next-of-relation alone, in the role of adviser, while carefully avoiding talking things over seriously with them both together. And even in those non-consultative cases where public officials must forcibly extract a person from a family that wants to tolerate him, the next-of-relation is likely to be induced to "go along" with the official action, so that even here the prepatient may feel that an alienative coalition has been formed against him. . . .

The final point I want to consider about the prepatient's moral career is its peculiarly retroactive character. Until a person actually arrives at the hospital, there usually seems no way of knowing for sure that he is destined to do so, given the determinative role of career contingencies. And, until the point of hospitalization is reached, he or others may not conceive of him as a person who is becoming a mental patient. However, since he will be held against his will in the hospital, his next-of-relation and the hospital staff will be in great need of a rationale for the hardships they are sponsoring. The medical elements of the staff will also need evidence that they are still in the trade they were trained for. These problems are eased, no doubt unintentionally, by the case-history construction that is placed on the patient's past life, this having the effect of demonstrating that all along he had been becoming sick, that he finally became very sick, and that if he had not been hospitalized much worse things would have happened to him—all of which, of course, may be true. Incidentally, if the patient wants to make sense out of his stay in the hospital, and, as already suggested, keep alive the possibility of once again conceiving of his next-of-relation as a decent, well-meaning person, then he, too, will have reason to believe some of this psychiatric work-up of his past. . . .

The Inpatient Phase

The last step in the prepatient's career can involve his realization—justified or not—that he has been deserted by society and turned out of relationships by those closest to him. Interestingly enough, the patient, especially a first admission, may manage to keep himself from coming to the end of this trail, even though, in fact, he is now in a locked mental-hospital ward. On entering the hospital, he may very strongly feel the desire not to be known to anyone as a person who could possibly be reduced to these present circumstances, or as a person who conducted himself in the way he did prior to commitment. Consequently, he may avoid talking to anyone, may stay by himself when possible, and may even be "out of contact" or "manic" so as to avoid ratifying any interaction that presses a politely reciprocal role upon him and opens him up to what he has become in the eyes of others. When the next-of-relation makes an effort to visit, he may be rejected by mutism, or by the patient's refusal to enter the visiting room, these strategies sometimes suggesting that the patient still clings to a remnant of relatedness to those who made up his past, and is protecting this remnant from the final destructiveness of dealing with the new people that they have become. . . .

Once the prepatient begins to settle down, the main outlines of his fate tend to follow those of a whole class of segregated establishments—jails, concentration camps, monasteries, work camps, and so on—in which the inmate spends the whole round of life on the grounds, and marches through his regimented day in the immediate company of a group of persons of his own institutional status.

Like the neophyte in many of these total institutions, the new inpatient finds himself cleanly stripped of many of his accustomed affirmations, satisfactions, and defenses, and is subjected to a rather full set of mortifying experiences: restriction of free movement, communal living, diffuse authority of a whole echelon of people, and so on. Here one begins to learn about the limited extent to which a conception of oneself can be sustained when the usual setting of supports for it are suddenly removed. . . .

Once lodged on a given ward, the patient is firmly instructed that the restrictions and deprivations he encounters are not due to such blind forces as tradition or economy—and hence dissociable from self—but are intentional parts of his treatment, part of his need at the time, and, therefore, an expression of the state that his self has fallen to. Having every reason to initiate requests for better conditions, he is told that when the staff feel he is "able to manage" or will be "comfortable with" a higher ward level, then appropriate action will be taken. In short, assignment to a given ward is presented not as a reward or punishment, but as an expression of his general level of social functioning, his status as a person. Given the fact that the worst ward levels provide a round of life that inpatients with organic brain damage can easily manage, and that these quite limited human beings are present to prove it, one can appreciate some of the mirroring effects of the hospital.

The ward system, then, is an extreme instance of how the physical facts of an establishment can be explicitly employed to frame the conception a person takes of himself. In addition, the official psychiatric mandate of mental hospitals gives rise to even more direct, even more blatant, attacks upon the inmate's view of himself. The more "medical" and the more progressive a mental hospital is—the more it attempts to be therapeutic and not merely custodial—the more he may be confronted by high-ranking staff arguing that his past has been a failure, that the cause of this has been within himself, that his attitude to life is wrong, and that if he wants to be a person he will have to change his way of dealing with people and his conceptions of himself. Often the moral value of these verbal assaults will be brought home to him by requiring him to practice taking this psychiatric view of himself in arranged confessional periods, whether in private sessions or group psychotherapy.

Now a general point may be made about the moral career of inpatients which has bearing on many moral careers. Given the stage that any person has reached in a career, one typically finds that he constructs an image of his life course—past, present, and future—which selects, abstracts, and distorts in such a way as to provide him with a view of himself that he can usefully expound in current situations. Quite generally, the person's line concerning self defensively brings him into appropriate alignment with the basic values of his society, and so may be called an apologia. If the person can manage to present a view of his current situation which shows the operation of favorable personal qualities in the past and a favorable destiny awaiting him, it may be called a success story. If the facts of a person's past and present are extremely dismal, then about the best he can do is to show that he is not responsible for what has become of him, and the term "sad tale" is appropriate. Interestingly enough, the more the person's past forces him out of apparent alignment with central moral values, the more often he seems compelled to tell his sad tale in any company in which he finds himself. Perhaps the party responds to the need he feels in others of not having their sense of proper life courses affronted. In any case, it is among convicts, "winos," and prostitutes that one seems to obtain sad tales the most readily. It is the vicissitudes of the mental patient's sad tale that I want to consider now.

In the mental hospital, the setting and the house rules press home to the patient that he is, after all, a mental case who has suffered some kind of social collapse on the outside, having failed in some overall way, and that here he is of little social weight, being hardly capable of acting like a full-fledged person at all. These humiliations are likely to be most keenly felt by middle-class patients, since their previous condition of life little immunizes them against such affronts, but all patients feel some downgrading. Just as any normal member of his outside subculture would do, the patient often responds to this situation by attempting to assert a sad tale proving that he is not "sick," that the "little trouble" he did get into was really somebody else's fault, that his past life course had some honor and rectitude, and that the hospital is, therefore, unjust in forcing the status of mental patient upon him. This self-respecting tendency is heavily institutionalized within the patient society where opening social contacts typically involve the participants' volunteering information about their current ward location and length of stay so far, but not the reasons for their stay—such interaction being conducted in the manner of small talk on the outside. With greater familiarity, each patient usually volunteers relatively acceptable reasons for his hospitalization, at the same time accepting without open, immediate question the lines offered by other patients. Such stories as the following are given and overtly accepted:

> I was going to night school to get a M.A. degree, and holding down a job in addition, and the load got too much for me.
>
> The others here are sick mentally, but I'm suffering from a bad nervous system and that is what is giving me these phobias.
>
> I got here by mistake because of a diabetes diagnosis, and I'll leave in a couple of days. [The patient had been in seven weeks.]
>
> I failed as a child, and later with my wife I reached out for dependency.
>
> My trouble is that I can't work. That's what I'm in for. I had two jobs with a good home and all the money I wanted.

The patient sometimes reinforces these stories by an optimistic definition of his occupational status. A man who managed to obtain an audition as a radio announcer styles himself a radio announcer; another who worked for some months as a copy boy and was then given a job as a reporter on a large trade journal, but fired after three weeks, defines himself as a reporter.

A whole social role in the patient community may be constructed on the basis of these reciprocally sustained fictions. For these face-to-face niceties tend to be qualified by behind-the-back gossip that comes only a degree closer to the "objective" facts. Here, of course, one can see a classic social function of informal networks of equals: they serve as one another's audience for self-supporting tales—tales that are somewhat more solid than pure fantasy and somewhat thinner than the facts.

But the patient's apologia is called forth in a unique setting, for few settings could be so destructive of self-stories except, of course, those stories already constructed along psychiatric lines. And this destructiveness rests on more than the official sheet of paper which attests that the patient is of unsound mind, a danger to himself and others—an attestation, incidentally, which seems to cut deeply into the patient's pride, and into the possibility of his having any.

Certainly, the degrading conditions of the hospital setting belie many of the self-stories that are presented by patients, and the very fact of being in the mental hospital is evidence against these tales. And, of course, there is not always sufficient patient solidarity to prevent patient discrediting patient, just as there is not always a sufficient number of "professionalized" attendants to prevent attendant discrediting patient. As one patient informant repeatedly suggested to a fellow patient:

> If you're so smart, how come you got your ass in here?

The mental-hospital setting, however, is more treacherous still. Staff have much to gain through discreditings of the patient's story—whatever the felt reason for such discreditings. If the custodial faction in the hospital is to succeed in managing his daily round without complaint or trouble from him, then it will prove useful to be able to point out to him that the claims about himself upon which he rationalizes his demands are false, that he is not what he is claiming to be, and that in fact he is a failure as a person. If the psychiatric faction is to impress upon him its views about his personal make-up, then they must be able to show in detail how their version of his past and their version of his character hold up much better than his own. If both the custodial and psychiatric factions are to get him to co-operate in the various psychiatric treatments, then it will prove useful to disabuse him of his view of their purposes, and cause him to appreciate that they know what they are doing, and are doing what is best for him. In brief, the difficulties caused by a patient are closely tied to his version of what has been happening to him, and if co-operation is to be secured, it helps if this version is discredited. The patient must "insightfully" come to take, or affect to take, the hospital's view of himself.

The staff also have ideal means—in addition to the mirroring effect of the setting—for denying the inmate's rationalizations. Current psychiatric doctrine defines mental disorder as something that can have its roots in the patient's earliest years, show its signs throughout the course of his life, and invade almost every sector of his current activity. No segment of his past or present need be defined, then, as beyond the jurisdiction and mandate of psychiatric assessment. Mental hospitals bureaucratically institutionalize this extremely wide mandate by formally basing their treatment of the patient upon his diagnosis and hence upon the psychiatric view of his past.

The case record is an important expression of this mandate. This dossier is apparently not regularly used, however, to record occasions when the patient showed capacity to cope honorably and effectively with difficult life situations. Nor is the case record typically used to provide a rough average or sampling of his past conduct. One of its purposes is to show the ways in which the patient is "sick" and the reasons why it was right to commit him and is right currently to keep him committed; and this is done by extracting from his whole life course a list of those incidents that have or might have had "symptomatic" significance. The misadventures of his parents or siblings that might suggest a "taint" may be cited. Early acts in which the patient appeared to have shown bad judgment or emotional disturbance will be recorded. Occasions when he acted in a way which the layman would consider immoral, sexually perverted, weak-willed, childish, ill-considered, impulsive, and crazy may be described. Misbehaviors which someone saw as the last straw, as cause for immediate action, are likely to be reported in detail. In addition, the record will describe his state on arrival at the hospital—and this is not likely to be a time of tranquility and ease for him. The record may also report the false line taken by the patient in answering embarrassing questions, showing him as someone who makes claims that are obviously contrary to the facts:

> Claims she lives with oldest daughter or with sisters only when sick and in need of care; otherwise with husband, he himself says not for twelve years.
>
> Contrary to the reports from the personnel, he says he no longer bangs on the floor or cries in the morning.
>
> . . . conceals fact that she had her organs removed, claims she is still menstruating.
>
> At first, she denied having had premarital sexual experience; but when asked about Jim, she said she had forgotten about it 'cause it had been unpleasant.

Where contrary facts are not known by the recorder, their presence is often left scrupulously an open question:

> The patient denied any heterosexual experiences, nor could one trick her into admitting that she had ever been pregnant or into any kind of sexual indulgence, denying masturbation as well.
>
> Even with considerable pressure, she was unwilling to engage in any projection of paranoid mechanisms.
>
> No psychotic content could be elicited at this time.

And, if in no more factual way, discrediting statements often appear in descriptions given of the patient's general social manner in the hospital:

> When interviewed, he was bland, apparently self-assured, and sprinkles high-sounding generalizations freely throughout his verbal productions.
>
> Armed with a rather neat appearance and natty little Hitlerian mustache, this 45-year-old man, who has spent the last five or more years of his life in the hospital, is making a very successful adjustment living within the role of a rather gay liver and jim-dandy type of fellow who is not only quite superior to his fellow patients in intellectual respects, but who is also quite a man with women. His speech is sprayed with many multi-syllabled words which he generally uses in good context, but if he talks long enough on any subject it soon becomes apparent that he is so completely lost in this verbal diarrhea as to make what he says almost completely worthless.

The events recorded in the case history are, then, just the sort that a layman would consider scandalous, defamatory, and discrediting. I think it is fair to say that all levels of mental-hospital staff fail, in general, to deal with this material with the moral neutrality claimed for medical statements and psychiatric diagnosis, but instead participate, by intonation and gesture, if by no other means, in the lay reaction to these acts. This will occur in staff-patient encounters as well as in staff encounters at which no patient is present.

In some mental hospitals, access to the case record is technically restricted to medical and higher nursing levels, but even here, informal access or relayed information is often available to lower-staff levels. In addition, ward personnel are felt to have a right to know those aspects of the patient's past conduct which, embedded in the reputation he develops, purportedly make it possible to manage him with greater benefit to himself and less risk to others. Further, all staff levels typically have access to the nursing notes kept on the ward, which chart the daily course of each patient's disease, and hence his conduct, providing for the near present the sort of information the case record supplies for his past. . . .

The formal and informal patterns of communication linking staff members tend to amplify the disclosive work done by the case record. A discreditable act that the patient performs during one part of the day's routine in one part of the hospital community is likely to be reported back to those who supervise other areas of his life where he implicitly takes that stand that he is not the sort of person who could act that way.

Of significance here, as in some other social establishments, is the increasingly common practice of all-level staff conferences, where staff air their views of patients and develop collective agreement concerning the line that the patient is trying to take and the line that should be taken to him. A patient who develops a "personal" relation with an attendant, or manages to make an attendant anxious by eloquent and persistent accusations of malpractice, can be put back into his place by means of the staff meeting, where the attendant is given warning or assurance that the patient is "sick." Since the differential image of himself that a person usually meets from those of various levels around him comes here to be unified behind the scenes into a common approach, the patient may find himself faced with a kind of collusion against him—albeit one sincerely thought to be for his own ultimate welfare.

In addition, the formal transfer of the patient from one ward or service to another is likely to be accompanied by an informal description of his characteristics, this being felt to facilitate the work of the employee who is newly responsible for him.

Finally, at the most informal of levels, the lunch-time and coffee-break small talk of staff often turns upon the latest doings of the patient, the gossip level of any social establishment being here intensified by the assumption that everything about him is in some way the proper business of the hospital employee. Theoretically, there seems to be no reason why such gossip should not build up the subject instead of tear him down, unless one claims that talk about those not present will always tend to be critical in order to maintain the integrity and prestige of the circle in which the talking occurs. And so, even when the impulse of the speakers seems kindly and generous, the implication of their talk is typically that the patient is not a complete person. For example, a conscientious group therapist, sympathetic with patients, once admitted to his coffee companions:

> I've had about three group disrupters, one man in particular—a lawyer [*sotto voce*] James Wilson—very bright—who just made things miserable for me, but I would always tell him to get on the stage and do something. Well, I was getting desperate and then I bumped into his therapist, who said that right now behind the man's bluff and front he needed the group very much and that it probably meant more to him than anything else he was getting out of the hospital—he just needed the support. Well, that made me feel altogether different about him. He's out now.

In general, then, mental hospitals systematically provide for circulation about each patient the kind of information that the patient is likely to try to hide. And, in various degrees of detail, this information is used daily to puncture his claims. At the admission and diagnostic conferences, he will be asked questions to which he must give wrong answers in order to maintain his self-respect, and then the true answer may be shot back at him. An attendant whom he tells a version of his past and his reason for being in the hospital may smile disbelievingly, or say, "That's not the way I heard it," in line with the practical psychiatry of bringing the patient down to reality. When he accosts a physician or nurse on the ward and presents his claims for more privileges or for discharge, this may be countered by a question which he cannot answer truthfully, without calling up a time in his past when he acted disgracefully. When he gives his view of his situation during group psychotherapy, the therapist, taking the role of interrogator, may attempt to disabuse him of his face-saving interpretations and encourage an interpretation suggesting that it is he himself who is to blame and who must change. When he claims to staff or fellow patients that he is well and has never been really sick, someone may give him graphic details of how, only one month ago, he was prancing around like a girl, or claiming that he was God, or declining to talk or eat, or putting gum in his hair.

Each time the staff deflates that patient's claims, his sense of what a person ought to be and the rules of peer-group social intercourse press him to reconstruct his stories; and each time he does this, the custodial and psychiatric interests of the staff may lead them to discredit these tales again. . . .

Learning to live under conditions of imminent exposure and wide fluctuation in regard, with little control over the granting or withholding of this regard, is an important step in the socialization of the patient, a step that tells something important about what it is like to be an inmate in a mental hospital. Having one's past mistakes and present progress under constant moral review seems to make for a special adaptation consisting of a less than moral attitude to ego ideals. One's shortcomings and successes become too central and fluctuating an issue in life to allow the usual commitment of concern for other persons' views of them. It is not very practicable to try to sustain solid claims about oneself. The inmate tends to learn that degradations and reconstructions of the self need not be given too much weight, at the same time learning that staff and inmates are ready to view an inflation or deflation of a self with some indifference. He learns that a defensible picture of self can be seen as something outside oneself that can be constructed, lost, and rebuilt, all with great speed and some equanimity. He learns about the viability of taking up a standpoint—and hence a self—that is outside the one which the hospital can give and take away from him.

The setting, then, seems to engender a kind of cosmopolitan sophistication, a kind of civic apathy. In this unserious yet oddly exaggerated moral context, building up a self or having it destroyed becomes something of a shameless game, and learning to view this process as a game seems to make for some demoralization, the game being such a fundamental one. In the hospital, then, the inmate can learn that the self is not a fortress, but rather a small open city; he can become weary of having to show pleasure when held by troops of his own, and weary of having to show displeasure when held by the enemy. Once he learns what it is like to be defined by society as not having a viable self, this threatening definition—the threat that helps attach people to the self society accords them—is weakened. . . .

In the usual cycle of adult socialization, one expects to find alienation and mortification followed by a new set of beliefs about the world and a new way of conceiving of selves. In the case of the mental-hospital patient, this rebirth does sometimes occur, taking the form of a strong belief in the psychiatric perspective, or, briefly at least, a devotion to the social cause of better treatment for mental patients. The moral career of the mental patient has unique interest, however; it can illustrate the possibility that, in casting off the raiments of the old self—or in having this cover torn away—the person need not seek a new robe and a new audience before which to cower. Instead he can learn, at least for a time, to practice before all groups the amoral arts of shamelessness.

Reflective Questions

1. What does the category "mental patient" mean in a sociological sense? What are the stages of the patient's career? Why do patients experience a "downgrading" upon entering a mental hospital?
2. What various "self-stories" do patients tell? What are "sad tales" and how do patients end up telling them? How do patients use different stories to paint particular versions of themselves? What role does the hospital setting play in breaking down particular self-stories?
3. Do hospital staff depict patients' behavior neutrally? How do staff meetings help staffers to discredit patients? How else do they organize hospitals to facilitate discrediting patients?
4. Review the qualifications of the members of the task force, study groups, and working groups that are developing the DSM-V (the *Diagnostic and Statistical Manual of Mental Disorders* discussed in question 4 of Selection 4). What qualifications are necessary to be part of these decision-making bodies? Do the groups include individuals labeled with the disorder? What are the benefits of including individuals who would be affected by the diagnoses in the groups that define them? What are the unforeseen consequences? What are the consequences of having only medical professionals make these decisions?
5. Watch an episode of A&E's *Intervention* at http://www.aetv.com/intervention/index.jsp and compare the prepatient phase here to the one described by Goffman. Who set up the intervention, and how do family and friends construct the history of the target to the interventionists and television audience? Closely examine the interactions of all the players during the intervention itself and consider how they negotiate the politics of definition. How do different players (family, friends, interventionists, target) define reality and what tools do they use to convince each other (and you) that their version is more legitimate than that of the other players? How do family and friends try to convince the target that he or she has "fallen" and needs to change his/her attitude, interactions with others, and conception of the self? Do they discredit and break down the target so that he or she eventually accepts their version of reality? How? What role does the setting of the intervention play? What social and personal resources do targets use to resist? What are the bases of power in these interactions? What happens when targets are powerless?
6. We organize institutions in ways that delegitimate the claims, identities, and behaviors of particular people. What tools do people in positions of power use to discredit others within universities? Prisons? Churches? The military?

The Dynamics of Family Trouble: Middle-Class Parents Whose Children Have Problems

ARA A. FRANCIS

Sociologists point out that relationships rest on linked categorical identities, such as mother and daughter, friend and friend, and husband and wife. This implies that the activation of a social relationship reflects self-images of the relevant categorical identity back to the involved individuals. As earlier selections suggested when discussing the self, individuals consequently come to define themselves in terms of the categorical identities that link them to others in social relationships. Social relationships thereby shape and sustain individuals' self-concepts, serving as significant sources of self-validation and "reality maintenance." Close relationships are particularly important in this regard. Closely related individuals frequently and often extensively interact, mutually influencing each other's images of self and interpretations of experience. In this sense, they collectively construct their own distinct reality.

Ideally at least, family relationships are viewed as the closest connections we can experience in our society. We often hail families as the bedrock of community and society. We also regard them as the group within which we can experience our most intimate and harmonious bonds. Yet we know that families are often less than ideal, and they can serve as a source of discord and personal pain. They can also serve as the group within which we experience and grapple with troubles. When these troubles arise, families must figure out what they mean and how to respond to them. In this process, they often feel compelled to turn to "third parties"—professionals or experts who provide them with understandings and labels that allow them to define the "reality" of their situation. While these labels reduce uncertainty and offer some answers, they also come with some costs. These costs can include disrupted relationships, dismantled identities, and the loss of private subworlds.

In this selection Ara Francis describes how middle-class families experience and come to terms with troubles. She highlights how parents make sense of and respond to a child's experience of significant medical, emotional, or developmental problems. In their efforts to determine the causes and implications of those problems, parents typically engage in social comparisons and rely heavily on interpretations offered by doctors, psychologists, or support groups. The definitions provided by these third parties shape parents' understandings of whether a "real problem" exists, where it is ultimately rooted, and how it should be addressed.

In addition to demonstrating how children's difficulties become defined as serious troubles, Francis chronicles the far-reaching consequences that these troubles have for family life, particularly in absorbing parents' time and attention, altering their relationships, and disrupting cherished roles and identities. Above all, Francis reveals how the reality of a family trouble does not speak for itself. Instead, it is defined and negotiated through ongoing interaction. Moreover, the meaning and significance of the trouble is

Reprinted from: Ara Francis, "The Dynamics of Family Trouble: Middle-Class Parents Whose Children Have Problems," *Journal of Contemporary Ethnography* 41: 371–401, August 2012.

shaped largely by the extent to which family members' self-images are invested in particular routines and relationships.

Family Trouble

Research in the sociology of the family suggests that parenthood has emerged in the last several decades as a master status, or a position that strongly influences and takes precedence over individuals' other statuses, roles, and identities (Hughes 1945). Feminist scholars argue that today's parenting culture is characterized by an ideology of intensive mothering that constructs motherhood as an all-consuming project (see Douglas and Michaels 2004; Hays 1996; Thurer 1994). Fatherhood has become more intensive as well; in contrast to the image of the distant breadwinner, today's ideal father participates in the routine care of infants (Pleck 1987, 93; also see Coltrane 1997). Women remain disproportionately responsible for routine parenting, but fathers have increased their participation in child rearing over the last three decades (Bianchi 2000). In fact, both mothers and fathers devote more time to childcare than their counterparts did forty years ago (Gauthier, Smeedeng, and Furstenberg 2004; Sayer, Bianchi, and Robinson 2004).

As this scholarship suggests, for some men and women parenting is a demanding undertaking that encourages heavy self-investment. In this cultural context, children's problems are highly disruptive. Among the parents in this study, children's deviance and disabilities unsettled—and, in some cases, upended—large swaths of everyday life. Participants' experiences of disruption were characterized by five elements. First, parents defined their situations as troublesome. Second, they experienced a breakdown in their daily routines. Third, parents' relationships to one another, family members, and friends became distant, uneasy, and in some cases confrontational. Fourth, parents found it challenging to maintain cherished role performances and salient identities. Finally, they experienced inner turmoil in the form of anxiety, sadness, loneliness, anger, or guilt. . . .

These five aspects of parents' experiences were linked together in such a way that disruption tended to gain momentum and cause further disruption. Inner turmoil, for example, commonly led to further relationship disruption. Relationship strain further challenged cherished identities, and the growing departure from daily routine contributed further to a definition of the situation as troublesome. Rather than unfolding in a particular sequence, disruption emerged from, and flowed between, multiple arenas of parents' microsocial worlds.

Given its history in sociology, "trouble" is a fitting term for this dynamic process of disruption. . . . [T]rouble is . . . a property of interactions, relationships, groups, and institutions. [It] manifests *between* people, not just within them. . . . I refine the concept of trouble to capture the relationship between inner turmoil and microsocial order. Focusing on disruption as it unfolds in the context of families, I define "family trouble" as an upheaval in interaction between family members that involves a threat to some salient aspect of the self and results in inner turmoil. . . .

Methods and Participants

I designed this research project to explore how middle-class mothers and fathers make sense of misfortune and how parents play a role in the construction of childhood deviance and disability. I intentionally focused on middle-class parents. . . . The recruitment parameters were broad; any middle-class parent who identified his or her child as having a "significant problem" was eligible to participate. . . . I sought participants through support and advocacy groups, nonprofit organizations, and schools for children with special needs. I recruited others through the use of snowball sampling (see Lofland et al. 2006, 43). These strategies yielded thirty-four mothers and twenty-one fathers from thirty-six different families. The group included sixteen married couples, one separated couple, two divorced couples, and seventeen individuals (fifteen women and two men) who did not participate with a partner. . . .

Participants' annual household incomes ranged from $30,000 to $250,000, and the median for household incomes was $90,000 per year. All parents in the sample had completed high school. Of the thirty-four mothers in the study, twenty-seven had college educations, and eleven of these held master's or postgraduate degrees. Among the twenty-one fathers, all but two had bachelor's degrees, and eight had completed graduate or postgraduate programs of study. All but five families owned their own homes, and all but three participants were white.

Children varied widely in terms of problem type and age. . . . Children often had multiple problems, and Table 1 (see below) reflects their primary labels and diagnoses. Five of the families in this study had adopted their children, and their accounts of disruption were surprisingly similar to those of the biological parents I interviewed. Also, although the majority of children were between the ages of six and eighteen at the time of the interview, the sample does include twelve "adult children." A single participant accounted for five of these, and her sons and daughters, who ranged from twenty-four to forty-four years old, were much older, on average, than the others. The remaining adult children ranged in age from nineteen to twenty-five years old. Three of the seven still lived at home, and two others relied on their parents for financial assistance. . . .

Table 1: Summary of Children's Problems

Types of Problems	*n*
Learning disabilities (attention deficit/hyperactivity disorder, dyslexia, and auditory processing disorder)	7
Developmental disabilities (pervasive developmental disorder, autism, Asperger's syndrome, Down syndrome, cerebral palsy, and fetal alcohol syndrome)	16
Mental health problems (depression, anxiety, attachment disorder, obsessive compulsive disorder, trichotillomania, bipolar disorder, oppositional defiance disorder)	8
Drug or alcohol addiction	8
Medical problems without developmental disabilities	1
Total	40[a]

[a]Some participating families had more than one child with problems. This is why the total number of children in the sample is forty, even though there are only thirty-six participating families.

Parents in Trouble

Defining the Situation as Troublesome

From a symbolic interactionist perspective, objects and experiences do not have inherent meanings. As Emerson and Messinger (1977) illustrate in their seminal piece on the micropolitics of trouble, it is only through social interaction and interpretation that situations emerge as "problematic." As indicated by children's eventual labels and diagnoses, parents deemed a wide range of conditions and behaviors to be troublesome. Initial "signs" and "symptoms" that something was amiss included underachievement in school or sports, disobedience, inability to participate in commonplace interactions, emotional outbursts, not acting one's age, and physical ailments. While some cases involved less interpretive work than others, children's conditions and behaviors did not automatically lead parents to define the situation as problematic. Such definitions grew out of an indeterminate, contentious process facilitated by social comparison and others' corroboration that something was seriously wrong.

Family trouble took shape over the course of weeks, months, and even years as parents . . . compared their sons and daughters to siblings, friends, and the nonspecific, "normal" children they read about in child rearing manuals. Lauren,[1] who adopted her twin daughters when they were just infants, recalled,

> I went and bought all kind of baby development books, and "Oh, they should be doing this at this age, and this at that age." . . . at two [years old], [my daughters] didn't talk a lot. They had maybe a vocabulary of five to ten words, which is not very much. So I questioned the pediatrician.

Participants also used other parents' experiences as a measure of their own. Mike, whose son was later diagnosed with Attention Deficit/Hyperactivity Disorder, said that he became sharply aware of his son's problematic behaviors when he spent time with other families. He said, "Seeing our situation and getting together with other families, it [was] like, 'God, they're not having to work this damn hard!'"

Emerson and Messinger (1977) point out that third-party interpretation and intervention play a key role in determining whether or not trouble "exists" and, if it does, what kind of trouble it is. . . . For many parents, concerns that were once nebulous or transitory began to solidify when children garnered negative attention from school officials. Phil and his spouse did not think their son had "real" problems until he started getting into trouble in high school.

> [My wife and I] were always, I think, a little concerned. [But] I put it off more to—as I told you earlier—[a] boy being a boy. . . . It wasn't until really his freshman year . . . that we really started to get some inkling of, "There's some real deep issues here." . . . [at] the start of the sophomore year . . . he [got into three] fights and was expelled right around Thanksgiving.

Although corroboration was key to the emergence of family trouble, people commonly disagreed about the nature [and meaning] of children's conditions or behaviors. As Emerson and Messinger's work (1977) illustrates, vested interests in the construction of trouble lead people to vie for particular definitions of the situation. As primary caregivers and potential targets of judgment and blame, it was often mothers who first defined the situation as requiring remediation. Fathers, who were less often subject to people's assessments, were more likely to view their children's conditions and behaviors as normal, temporary, or insignificant (see also Singh 2003). Martha became convinced that her daughter had a learning disability, but her husband was skeptical. Martha said,

> One of the hardest things was my husband's denial . . . kind of the guy macho-thing, "There's nothing wrong with my kid . . . we can remedy this. We just have to work harder. She doesn't have a problem. What's this dyslexia thing? That's crazy, that's ridiculous. No, no," simply, "No."

Perhaps in an effort to manage mother-blame, women often advocated for biological or psychological definitions of the situation that located the problem within the child, rather than between the child and parent.

Although the timing was variable, all of the parents in this study eventually sought professional medical advice. In most cases, experts did not initiate the labeling process but served to confirm or contradict parents' growing suspicion that something was wrong. It was not uncommon for mothers to visit doctors or psychologists with specific labels or diagnoses in mind. When I asked Jen how her adopted daughter came to be diagnosed with an attachment disorder, she replied,

> Actually, I found it on the Internet, is what happened. I, like, typed in the symptoms. 'Cause it was so frustrating not to know what was going on! And it was clear that that's what it was.

Jen then sought the help of an attachment specialist and received professional support for her definition of the situation. Support groups sometimes provided parents with a language for naming children's problems. Judy came to view her son, then in the sixth grade, as having Attention Deficit/Hyperactivity Disorder (ADHD) after she attended a support group meeting for parents whose children have ADHD.

> I went to [the meeting] . . . to see if [my son] really might be [ADHD], or maybe not, or whatever . . . that's when I thought, "This is what's going on here with this child!"

Not all experts were amenable to mothers' definitions of the situation. A number of parents reported that doctors and psychologists dismissed their concerns, could not definitively say what the problem was, or could not offer remedial advice. When they were dissatisfied with one expert's assessment, parents sought out other doctors or psychologists whose definition of the situation more closely aligned with their own.

It is tempting to view family trouble as beginning with a given problem—a learning disability, an addiction, or a seizure disorder, for example—that goes on to upset interactions between family members. However, few interviews evinced such a linear trajectory. In most cases, parents were coming to view their children as having significant problems *at the same time* that other aspects of their lives were coming undone. In fact, disrupted routines, relationships, roles, identities, and emotions further contributed to parents' definition of the situation as troublesome.

The Disruption of Routine

Patterns of time are constitutive elements of the social order (Zerubavel 1981). Our sense of reality depends on some events occurring before or after others. We expect activities to begin and end at certain times and to reoccur at regular intervals. The temporal structure of action and interaction "[helps] us to attain some peace of mind regarding our environment" (Zerubavel 1981, 14). Children's problems commonly upended the temporal organization of parents' lives. By requiring mothers and fathers to spend more time parenting, they disrupted daily routines, squeezed out other activities, and led to further disruption.

Parents' efforts to name or fix the problem, or to determine whether or not a problem existed, were particularly disruptive in this respect. Sergio, who later learned that his son was at risk for developing schizophrenia, recalled what it was like when he and his spouse first sought medical advice for their son's symptoms.

> He was complaining a lot about stomach aches and headaches and throwing up at school. He'd call us up and we'd come get him from school. This was an *every other day thing*... [and] we just kept going to doctors.... I mean, we got to the point where we were going to doctors *on a weekly basis*.... (emphasis added)

Attending to children's problems meant that parents had less time for other activities. To varying degrees, men and women compromised time in the paid labor force and with friends, time with one another, and time for themselves. Jessica, whose four-year-old son was so disobedient and aggressive that other parents wanted him expelled from their local preschool, explained,

> [You have] to just take care of yourself. I mean, that's something I'm struggling and working with.... [I'm not] exercising.... I wish I could have at least a weekend away with my husband.... I wish I had time to take a class.

Bill echoed Jessica's comments when he said,

> It's overwhelming . . . you're not taking care of yourself. You're not eating right, you're not exercising, you're not sleeping.... My health deteriorated, was going downhill very fast....

The degree of temporal disruption depended on the perceived nature and severity of children's problems. Learning problems involved extra visits to children's schools and additional time spent overseeing homework, for example, but these changes did not constitute a wholesale upending of parents' daily rounds. Nonetheless, even parents in these situations noted a shift. Martha, for example, recalled how much time she used to spend working with her dyslexic daughter:

> I would read to her... 'cause she couldn't read!... She'd get home from school, we'd curl up on the couch and the bed. I mean, from a family point of view, *there were lots of dinners that weren't made*... [because] we had been reading for hours. (emphasis added)

[P]arents also emphasized the inordinate amount of time they spent *thinking* about children's problems. Judy, whose twenty-five-year-old son was diagnosed with Attention Deficit Disorder when he was in the sixth grade, commented,

> I felt like it was with me *all the time*. I felt like this kid and his situation was at the forefront of my life *almost all the time*.... It kind of takes the joy out of life in general. (emphasis added)

Thus, even when problems did not require much concrete action (such as frequent doctor visits or round-the-clock supervision), they displaced parents' patterns of thought. Whether mothers and fathers were frantically searching for a remedy or simply worrying about children's fates, children's problems upended parents' everyday lives by consuming their time.

The Disruption of Relationships

Like the organization of time, relationships anchor us in social interaction and bring order to our daily lives (McCall and Simmons 1966). Our connections to lovers, friends, family members, coworkers, neighbors, and acquaintances indicate the statuses that we occupy. They enable and constrain our role performances and shape our identities. Just as they upended parents' routines, children's problems disrupted men's and women's relationships. Time constraints, the stigma of having a "problem child," and others' discomfort with misfortune had the cumulative effect of isolating the parents in this study.

Because parents' relationships were embedded in the patterns of time described above, the disruption of routine was one means by which children's problems affected their connections to other people. Sam, who said that his daughter's Attention Deficit Disorder had become "the biggest, most consistent concern or issue in the whole household for all of us," explained,

> I see [my daughter's problems] as probably having limited me from expressing myself in other ways, [from] doing some things that I *don't have time for now* . . . socializing with people, friends. . . . I think *it has shortened our social circle.* (emphasis added)

As Sam's comments illustrate, the disruption and reorganization of parents' routines often left them with less time for building and maintaining relationships. This included their relationships with one another. When I asked Peter, Jessica's spouse, whether or not his son's problems changed their marriage, he replied,

> In terms of it taking energy away from it, yeah. There were plenty of days and nights when we were just kind of at the end of our rope dealing with this situation. And it didn't leave a lotta extra energy for having fun, you know? For just having light times or humor or romance . . . so, yeah, it had an effect.

The disruption of relationships was more than just a matter of time constraints. Parents reported that children's problems made others feel uncomfortable. As previous research indicates, the courtesy stigma of having a problem child is a source of isolation (e.g., Birenbaum 1970; Gray 2002). Tim, whose son has developmental disabilities, said

> People are often uncomfortable with someone who is different from them . . . so you see this kid making all these weird noises, these weird facial expressions, things like this. And people were just uncomfortable with it. [Our friends'] kids wanted to hang out with other "normal" kids . . . and those parents were taking their kids to soccer games and to little league games and associating with other parents who were taking their kids to the same soccer games and little league games. So as the time went on . . . our world became more and more insulated.

As Tim's comments suggest, courtesy stigma was a source of isolation in at least two respects. First, friends had withdrawn because they were uncomfortable with his son's condition. Second, "normal" children connect parents to others through shared activities. Because their son did not play soccer or participate in little league games, Tim and his spouse could not use those activities as venues for making or maintaining friendships. In some cases, blame was a central feature of stigma. As noted above, this was more common among the women I interviewed. Maria, whose son was frequently in trouble for fighting with other children in elementary school, felt as if other parents avoided her because they held her responsible for her son's bad behavior.

> (People) always saw my son as the problem child in class. And I think their tendency is to blame the parent. . . . I haven't really formed any relationships with my son's peers. . . .

The judgment and isolation that women experienced further encouraged them to define the situation as troublesome and in need of remediation.

The disagreements that men and women had about the nature of their children's problems caused marital tension. Mothers frequently expressed frustration at what they saw as their spouses' denial.

For example, until his son was suspended from school for facilitating a drug deal, Matt was reluctant to view him as having a "problem." Sarah, his spouse, believed there was a problem early on. When I asked them whether or not this affected their marriage, she explained,

> We [usually] talk at length about stuff and we can come together and be connected and united. But the issues with [our son] have been harder than anything else, at least for me. . . . You know, I've been more suspicious. I've seen evidence. I'm more detail-oriented anyway, but I notice and I say to him, "Oh, he seemed high," or . . . whatever.

In cases like these, mothers usually convinced fathers to adopt their definitions of the situation. However, a few parents reported that disagreements about children's problems contributed to the dissolution of marriages that were not strong to begin with.

Finally, the mere presence of misfortune sometimes distanced parents from family members and friends. Some participants worried that the anxiety, guilt, and grief stemming from children's problems were burdensome to others. Lauren's family members told her quite directly that she was talking too much about her twin daughter's developmental delays.

> I have worn out relatives, specifically my mother and my sister . . . sometimes they're as blatant as, "I don't want to talk about it anymore." So then I'll say, "Fine, if you don't let me vent in any way I can, and as much as I can, I'm just not gonna tell you anything." And that's when I say I feel kind of alone. . . .

The Disruption of Role Performances and Salient Identities

Roles serve as a bridge between person and structure, self and society. In Sheldon Stryker's words (2002), they "build 'up' to larger and more complex social units," while also "build[ing] 'down' to the social person" (225). Parents' interviews demonstrate that, in the course of disrupting their routines and relationships, children's problems hindered the performance of key roles and challenged the identities associated with those performances. It is here that the connection between the disruption of microsocial order and the disruption of selves emerged quite clearly.

First and foremost, children's problems disrupted men's and women's role performances as mothers and fathers. As Spencer Cahill (1987) illustrates in his research on children in public settings, adults assume moral responsibility for children's deviance, and children's bad behavior is face-threatening for caretakers. Parents had entered into child rearing with a host of ideas about the activities that parenthood would involve and what kind of mothers or fathers they would be. Many of these notions were predicated on having "normal" children, which meant that children's problems posed serious obstacles to the enactments of parenthood that men and women had envisioned for themselves. Tim said that it was still painful to imagine what fatherhood would have been like, had his son not had developmental disabilities.

> I still miss all the things I'd be doing with [my son] if he were a "normal" seventeen-and-a-half-year-old kid. . . . I just kind of thought that as he grew up we might find some things in common. Like, whether it was watching football or going on bike rides or playing softball or going on nature walks, watching him play in a high school basketball game, whatever. All those things you just kind of *assume* are gonna happen in life. . . . (emphasis added)

While some fathers echoed Tim's comments, children's problems had a more salient effect on women's expectations of motherhood and their identities as mothers. More specifically, women often reported that children's problems challenged their ability to perform and see themselves as "good" mothers. Here, Andrea explains how her daughter's truancy, drug abuse, and fighting challenged her maternal identity:

> Here you're trying to be the perfect parent, to do as well as you can. And no matter what you do, it's not turning out that way. I mean, I tried to be perfect. But you know, that doesn't mean anybody else is gonna want to be!

Many women shared Andrea's sentiments. As Jessica commented, "I sometimes imagine the more perfect mother I'd be if I'd been given a child a little less challenging." Motherhood is often a central feature of women's identities, and the public holds women especially accountable for children's conditions and behaviors (Collett 2005; Thurer 1994). Consequently, children's ailments posed serious challenges to women's maternal performances and personal identities as "good mothers."

As noted above, parenthood tended to operate for these participants as a master status, organizing other role performances and identities. In some cases, the smooth performance of spousal roles depended on the "normal" performance of fatherhood and motherhood, and children's problems prevented participants from being the wives or husbands they had been or wanted to be. Joan, who had developed fibromyalgia, said that her tireless efforts to find a treatment for her son's condition hindered her role performance as a wife.

> I did all of that, but I did it, unknowingly, at a cost to my own health. And a cost to a strained marriage, and a continued strained marriage. . . . now [my husband] has a wife that has fibromyalgia and she's not the woman that she was.

. . . Children's problems disrupted parents' job performances and work-related identities in a similar way. For example, many women either cut down on their employment hours or withdrew from the paid labor force altogether when children first developed problems. Andrea explained,

> I did stop working full-time and only worked part-time. I made that change because I felt when she was in junior high and went through the depressed period that I just need to be around more. . . . I only worked three days a week.

Whether they led parents to leave the workforce, change jobs, remain in jobs they didn't like or work fewer hours, children's problems often altered women's and men's career performances [and prompted] them to experience identity shifts. . . .

Inner Turmoil

Parents' interviews were shot through with accounts of sorrow and angst. When describing the emotional ramifications of children's problems, they used words such as "devastating" and "traumatic." Two mothers, one whose twin daughters suffered from developmental disabilities and the other whose adult son was an alcoholic, said they felt as if they were "dying." Parents' emotional lives reflected the turmoil described above. Seth, whose daughter had run away and was living on the streets, said it was the most painful experience he had ever had.

> I would rather have lost a limb, you know? I don't know why. When [your kids] are born, they weasel their way so deeply into your heart, they're a part of you. . . . *you make so many accommodations in your life to take care of that.* . . . it's your life . . . nothing else matters. (emphasis added)

Parents' inner turmoil highlights the connection between the place of children in middle-class families and the inner workings of the self. Parents' lives and selves were structured to reflect the central and cherished place of children; as Seth explained, his children *are* his life. Because participants' inner worlds had been sustained by now-disrupted social patterns, the family trouble stemming from children's problems not only rippled outward into multiple spheres of their lives but also deepened inward, churning their cognitive and emotional worlds. . . .

Family Trouble as a Sensitizing Concept

The sense of anomie that stems from a disruption of social patterns on which important parts of the self rely is a defining feature of troubling family experiences. . . . In his discussion of manic patients who live at home, for example, Erving Goffman (1971) describes how the ill person's frenetic activity threatens families' patterns of authority, work, leisure, and the distribution of resources. As Goffman explains, this jeopardizes family members' perceptions of self and reality.

> In ceasing to know the sick person, [family members] cease to be sure of themselves. In ceasing to be sure of [the patient] and themselves, they can even cease to be sure of their way of knowing. A deep bewilderment results. Confirmations that everything is predictable and as it should be cease to flow from [the patient's] presentations. The question as to what it is that is going on is not

> redundantly answered at every turn but must be constantly ferreted out anew (367). . . .

[Yet, as they make sense of disruptions and the feelings they evoke, families do not necessarily define them as troublesome.] Some parents refuse to construct their children's poor school performances as indicative of serious problems (Harry 1992), and some people experience relief following separation, divorce, or the death of a family member (Riessman 1990; Umberson and Chen 1994; Vaughan 1986). Illness is not always disruptive and can even serve to bolster family-related identities (Wilson 2007). The concept of family trouble illuminates only those circumstances that social actors themselves identify and experience as problematic.

What constitutes family trouble depends, in part, on the degree to which people's selves are anchored to particular patterns of family interaction. Vaughan (1986) finds that uncoupling is easier for couples in long-distance relationships because each partner maintains a separate identity prior to parting ways. Umberson and Terling (1997) demonstrate that, among adults, the intensity of grief following the loss of a parent varies according to what the relationship meant to the bereaved person. As these examples illustrate, the events and circumstances that constitute family trouble are as diverse as people's interpretations and self-constructions.

Instead of referring to particular situations, then, family trouble captures a dynamic process of disruption. As noted above, it refers broadly to any upheaval in interaction between family members that threatens some salient aspect of the self and results in emotional turmoil. The degree to which a particular case of family trouble involves the features that characterized parents' troubles—the upsetting of routines, relationships, roles, and identities—is an empirical question. Family trouble is necessarily a "sensitizing concept" that directs our attention to certain empirical possibilities without offering prescription for what we will find (Blumer 1969).

Nonetheless, routines, relationships, roles, and identities are basic elements of taken-for-granted reality. Since people's embeddedness in social life relies on the relative stability of these microsocial patterns, one can reasonably expect that at least some of these elements are implicated in every case of family trouble.

Note

1. In order to preserve participants' confidentiality, I use pseudonyms throughout this article.

References

Bianchi, Suzanne M. 2000. Maternal Employment and Time with Children: Dramatic Change or Surprising Continuity? *Demography* 37: 401–14.

Birenbaum, Arnold. 1970. On Managing Courtesy Stigma. *Journal of Health and Social Behavior* 11: 196–206.

Blumer, Herbert. 1969. *Symbolic Interaction: Perspective and Method*. Berkeley: University of California Press.

Cahill, Spencer E. 1987. Children and Civility: Ceremonial Deviance and the Acquisition of Ritual Competence. *Social Psychology Quarterly* 50: 312–21.

Collett, Jessica. 2005. What Kind of Mother Am I? *Symbolic Interaction* 28: 327–47.

Coltrane, Scott. 1997. *Family Man*. New York: Oxford University Press.

Douglas, Susan, and Meredith Michaels. 2004. *The Mommy Myth*. New York: Free Press.

Emerson, Robert M., and Sheldon L. Messinger. 1977. The Micro-Politics of Trouble. *Social Problems* 25: 121–35.

Gauthier, Anne H., Timothy M. Smeedeng, and Frank F. Furstenberg. 2004. Are Parents Investing Less Time in Children? Trends in Selected Industrialized Countries. *Population and Development Review* 30: 647–71.

Goffman, Erving. 1971. The Insanity of Place. In *Relations in Public: Micro Studies of the Public Order*, 335–90. New York: Basic Books.

Gray, David. 2002. "Everybody Just Freezes. Everybody Is Just Embarrassed": Felt and Enacted Stigma among Parents of Children with High Functioning Autism. *Sociology of Health and Illness* 24: 734–49.

Harry, Beth. 1992. Making Sense of Disability: Low-Income, Puerto Rican Parents' Theories of the Problem. *Exceptional Children* 59: 27–40.

Hays, Sharon. 1996. *Cultural Contradictions of Motherhood*. New Haven, CT: Yale University Press.

Hughes, Everett C. 1945. Dilemmas and Contradictions of Status. *American Journal of Sociology* 50: 353–59.

Lofland, John, David Snow, Leon Anderson, and Lyn H. Lofland. 2006. *Analyzing Social Settings: A Guide to Qualitative Observation and Analysis*. Thousand Oaks, CA: SAGE.

McCall, George J., and J. L. Simmons. 1966. *Identities and Interactions*. New York: Free Press.

Pleck, Joseph 1987. American Fathering in Historical Perspective. In *Changing Men: New Directions in Research on Men and Masculinity*, edited by Michael S. Kimmell. Thousand Oaks, CA: SAGE.

Riessman, Catherine Kohler. 1990. *Divorce Talk: Women and Men Make Sense of Personal Relationships*. Piscataway, NJ: Rutgers University Press.

Sayer, Liana C., Suzanne M. Bianchi, and John P. Robinson. 2004. Are Parents Investing Less in Children? Trends in Mothers' and Fathers' Time with Children. *American Journal of Sociology* 110: 1–43.

Singh, Ilina. 2003. Boys Will Be Boys: Fathers' Perspectives on ADHD Symptoms, Diagnosis and Drug Treatment. *Harvard Review of Psychiatry* 11(6): 308–16.

Stryker, Sheldon. 2002. Traditional Symbolic Interactionism, Role Theory, and Structural Symbolic Interactionism: The Road to Identity Theory. In *Handbook of Sociological Theory*, edited by Jonathan H. Turner, 211–33. New York: Springer.

Thurer, Shari L. 1994. *The Myths of Motherhood: How Culture Reinvents the Good Mother*. Boston: Houghton Mifflin.

Umberson, Debra, and Meichu D. Chen. 1994. Effects of a Parent's Death on Adult Children: Relationship Salience and Reaction to Loss. *American Sociological Review* 59: 152–68.

Umberson, Debra, and Toni Terling. 1997. The Symbolic Meaning of Relationships: Implications for Psychological Distress Following Relationship Loss. *Journal of Social and Personal Relationships* 14: 723–44.

Vaughan, Diane. 1986. *Uncoupling*. New York: Oxford University Press.

Wilson, Sarah. 2007. "When You Have Children, You're Obliged to Live": Motherhood, Chronic Illness, and Biographical Disruption. *Sociology of Health and Illness* 29: 610–26.

Zerubavel, Eviatar. 1981. *Hidden Rhythms: Schedules and Calendars in Social Life*. Chicago: University of Chicago Press.

Reflective Questions

1. What is a master status? How and why has parenthood emerged as a master status in recent decades? How do family troubles alter the status of parents?
2. According to Francis, what is a "trouble"? What does she mean when she asserts that a trouble is a property of interactions and relationships that "manifests between people, not just within them"?
3. How do children's physical, developmental, or behavioral issues become defined as family troubles? How do parents make sense of these issues? How do third-party (or professional) interpretations and interventions become crucial in determining whether or not a trouble is "real"? Do parents always accept the interpretations of third parties? How do they work out disagreements between themselves about the reality of a trouble?
4. What disruptions in family routines, relationships, and role performances make parents more likely to define a child's situation as troublesome? How do troubles involving a child jeopardize parents' perceptions of self and reality? What emotional consequences does this have for parents?
5. Think of conflicts or issues that have emerged in your own family. What kinds of disruptions did they cause? How did they affect your self-image and emotional life? Did these conflicts or issues get defined as family troubles? Why or why not? Did third parties (e.g., therapists or medical specialists) get involved in interpreting them? If so, how did they define the situation? Did they focus on individuals or interactions? Were their definitions accepted or challenged by your family members?

Being Middle Eastern American in the Context of the War on Terror

AMIR MARVASTI

In Selection 38, Erving Goffman describes how life in a mental hospital was designed to break down patients' existing views of themselves and to encourage their internalization of a psychiatric view of reality and themselves. It also highlights how mental patients are relatively powerless to protect themselves from the constant assaults that are directed toward their definitions of self. In turn, they may choose to act shamelessly and to stop defending their cherished self-images. Outside of institutions such as a mental hospital, however, individuals typically have more power to shield themselves against critical or unflattering social appraisals. Thus, they are likely to draw upon a variety of defensive interactional strategies that can enable them to avoid stigma and preserve a valued sense of self.

In the aftermath of the attacks that took place in the United States on September 11, 2001, Middle Eastern Americans suddenly found themselves in a new and profoundly different social context. Within this context, they became targets of hostility, suspicion, and social stigma and, as a result, were subjected to insults, harassment, and demeaning or unequal treatment. Unfortunately, for many Middle Eastern Americans, this experience of ethnically based stigmatization and discrimination has persisted in the landscape of post-9/11 America. In turn, they have had to find ways to address the challenging politics of reality that surround their ethnic status.

In this selection, Amir Marvasti explores how Americans of Middle Eastern descent respond to the negative reactions and unflattering self-images directed toward them by others. In doing so, he highlights how they effectively negotiate the politics of identity, especially by actively engaging in attempts to avoid, neutralize, or challenge stigmatizing images of self. Middle Eastern Americans primarily rely on artful strategies of impression management and information control, marked by the use of different types of accounts, for this purpose. These strategies include using humor to divert attention away from stereotypes that would stigmatize them, proactively educating others about Middle Eastern cultures and thereby correcting their inaccurate perceptions, and directly challenging others' stigmatizing attitudes and requiring them to explain those attitudes. In some cases, Middle Eastern Americans also choose to avoid stigma by passing, which involves the careful management of their appearance to conceal their ethnic identity and thereby avoid negative social reactions.

As Marvasti illustrates, through employing these creative interactional strategies Middle Eastern Americans find ways to preserve valued identities and a sense of self-worth. Their success in his regard is a tribute to the human spirit and to our ability as individuals to defend our self-conceptions from social evaluations. However, what Marvasti implies, but never explicitly addresses, is that we, as individuals, need some degree of social support for our self-protective identity work. It is an open question just how long we

Reprinted from: Amir Marvasti, Being Middle Eastern American: Identity Negotiation in the Context of the War on Terror. *Symbolic Interaction* 28(4): 525–547, ISSN 0195–6086, electronic ISSN 1533–8665.

can resist the influence of social appraisals, especially demeaning ones, without a little help from our friends. Many of the selections in this volume suggest the answer: not very long.

About a year after September 11, 2001, I was in a shopping mall in a northeastern city. For the last thirty minutes, I had been acutely aware of a security guard who had been following me around the mall. I was not completely surprised to see him follow me into the restroom. I was, however, taken aback when he moved closer to me near the urinal and looked over my shoulder as I was urinating. I was not sure what to say or do. I thought, "Is he worried that I am going to contaminate the city's water supply with my toxic urine?" I felt violated but did not want to cause a scene. So I started singing, "Chances are, 'cause I wear a silly grin the moment you come into view. . . ." I had learned the lyrics from a Taco Bell toy that played the song when you squeezed it. I did not really know the rest of the song, but it did not matter, crowing in English seemed to have done the job. The security guard backed off and left me alone for the rest of my time at the mall.

As this story from my own life shows, September 11th and the ensuing period that has been named "the War on Terror" have significantly changed the daily lives of Middle Eastern Americans. For members of this ethnic group, it was indeed "the day that changed everything." In the days following September 11th, anything seemed possible, even mass detentions on a scale similar to what Japanese Americans were subjected to after Pearl Harbor. Such fears were so real that on the night of September 11th, I actually packed some of my belongings and essential documents in a small suitcase in preparation for mass detentions. I was, after all, born in Iran and physically resembled the terrorists, whose images were relentlessly displayed in all the mass media.

The extreme measures I feared did not materialize in the aftermath of the terrorist attacks; however, our lives have, in many ways, changed for the worse. In particular, Middle Eastern Americans experience more stereotyping more frequently than before. We are asked to explain our intentions, politics, and personal beliefs, even in the course of the mundane routines of everyday life, such as shopping at a mall. Although prejudice and discrimination against this ethnic group existed for decades before September 11th, the recent intensity and regularity of these demands are unprecedented. As one of my respondents put it, it happened before, "but not with this magnitude, and not with the accusatory tone. . . . Before it was just out of curiosity, and it was incidental, but this is an even more demanding tone of 'Who are you? And why did your people do this?'"

In this article, I investigate how Middle Eastern Americans respond to these disruptions of their daily routines. My original intention was to use interview data as well as my personal experiences as an Iranian immigrant to show how Middle Eastern Americans manage the stigma of their "spoiled identities" (Goffman 1963), especially in the aftermath of September 11th. While working on the first draft, I told my Iranian friend Ahmad, with whom I was having lunch, that I was working on a paper titled "Stigma Management Strategies of Middle Eastern Americans." He nodded with his head down as he swallowed his food. After a short pause, he asked: "Why 'stigma?' What is the stigma?"

I was a little surprised that he failed to see the obvious. I explained, "After September 11th, people from the Middle East, especially Muslims, are treated with suspicion and subjected to ethnic profiling. That's why we are stigmatized."

He replied in a matter-of-fact tone. "Not always. Sitting here with you, talking in this school cafeteria, I don't feel stigmatized."

I began to wonder if this was a case of what Marx would call "false consciousness." I tried harder to convince him of the gravity of the situation of Middle Eastern Americans in a post-9/11 world. Ahmad did not disagree with the entire argument, he just refused to see himself as someone with a chronic stigma, or a permanent and enduring negative identity.

My friend convinced me that in some situations the stigma of being Middle Eastern goes unnoticed or is altogether nonexistent for all practical purposes. How do we then empirically study stigma or even know if it actually exists? One way to answer this question is to explore differences or similarities between audience and self-perceptions. In other words, we can compare Ahmad's self-image with his audience's perceptions of him and then go on to make certain conclusions about the relation between the two perspectives. For example, we may find that many people do in fact have negative perceptions of Ahmad, but he is fortunate to enjoy a high self-esteem that shields him from any emotional damage. This line of thinking could tell us a good deal about the mental state of both sides, but it offers less insight into everyday practice, or what people actually do when they interact with one another.

Self or audience perception are not fixed; they change in the course of practice. Similarly, the meaning of "stigma" varies situationally. A friend in graduate school jokingly referred to me as "the swarthy Iranian" (I did not find that funny). My same brown complexion apparently evoked a different audience response when a waitress at a Denny's told me, "You have such a nice tan!" (To which I smugly replied, "I was born with it.")

How do I really feel about having a brown complexion? Well, it depends on how it is used. I cannot really discuss it without referring to specific interactions and the social context that made my skin tone relevant. In the same vein, the empirical reality of being Middle Eastern is not just a mental property of the self or audience, but is enacted under the concrete conditions of everyday life. Audience or self perceptions about stigma become experientially meaningful and accessible when articulated in a specific setting and for a particular purpose.

Thus, to appreciate the complexity of Ahmad's experiences as a Middle Eastern American, it seemed that I needed to attend to situational variations surrounding how individuals define, enact, and cope with stigma in everyday encounters. This article first offers brief discussions of how I conceptualized stigma and everyday practice for the purpose of this study, and then presents my analysis of how Middle Eastern Americans manage their identities in the aftermath of September 11th.

Stigma and the Management of Spoiled Identity

Numerous studies have highlighted how stigmatized individuals employ various resistance and management strategies in response to negative labels (Cahill and Eggleston 1994; Davis 1961; Evans, Forsyth, and Foreman 2003; Feagin and McKinney 2003; Fothergill 2003; Herman 1993; Karp 1992; Riessman 2000; Roschelle and Kaufman 2004; Snow and Anderson 1987). This body of research treats normal–deviant interactions as an ongoing drama in which the stigmatized try to create positive identities. As they reveal, individuals use various techniques, such as humor and selective disclosure, to either avoid being stigmatized or soften the impact of the stigma on their "spoiled identity."

Much of the scholarship cited above is inspired by Goffman's seminal work *Stigma* (1963), in which he states:

> [When a stranger] is present before us, evidence can arise of his possessing an attribute that makes him different from others. . . . He is thus reduced in our minds from a whole and usual person to a tainted, discounted one. Such an attribute is a stigma. (Pp. 2–3)

For Goffman, stigma is a variable social construct and not a fixed characteristic of the person. Stigma is bound by social roles and expectations and derives its meaning from particular social contexts. An ascribed status or attribute, such as one's race or ethnicity, is not inherently stigmatizing, but becomes so under a specific set of social rules and social conditions. For example, a number of studies have suggested that recent demographic and sociopolitical trends in North America may gradually lower the rank of whiteness from a preferred racial status to a social stigma (Killian 1985; Kusow 2004; Storrs 1999).

Furthermore, as Link and Phelan's work (2001) notes, stigma is a multifaceted concept. Accordingly, studies of stigma can be classified on the basis of which aspect of the stigmatization process they emphasize. In this article, I am most interested in the "obtrusiveness" of stigma (Goffman 1963:129) and its "disruption" of daily routines (Harvey 2001). Specifically, I focus on encounters that become "incidents" or "scenes" (Goffman 1959:210–12). In such situations, as the norms of "audience tact" and "disattention" are suspended, the stigmatized individuals find themselves caught in the interactional spotlight, forced to explain themselves to others. From the perspective of the stigmatized, these disruptions are especially significant for their "moral careers"—or how they judge themselves and others over time (Goffman 1962:128). As one respondent put it, in such moments "the thin veneer of civility" is stripped away and negative labels are openly applied and contested.

We can view these instances of identity dispute as occasions for eliciting and producing "accounts." I borrow this term from Lyman and Scott (1989) to refer to encounters in which a person is called to "explain unanticipated or untoward behavior—whether that behavior is his or her own or that of others, and whether the approximate cause of the statement arises from the actor himself or someone else" (p. 112). Thus, we give accounts when confronting an unusual situation or individual. In their discussion of stigma, Evans, Forsyth, and Foreman (2003) note that "understanding the way individuals use accounts to construct positive self-identities, in the face of occupying a stigmatized . . . position, is indeed important turf for social science" (p.373).

This article examines stigma-related accounts as performances that involve both the substance of everyday experience (i.e., *what* is being contested or questioned and under *what* conditions) and the social construction of reality (i.e., *how* it is presented). This view of stigma is consistent with the symbolic interactionist premise that objects are not inherently meaningful; rather, individuals assign meanings in general, and identities in particular, through interaction. Stigma is realized in the reflexive interplay between social conditions and self-presentation. The meaning and practical significance of stigma is interactionally achieved in everyday encounters. To better highlight this reflexive approach to accounts and stigma, the next section discusses interpretive practice as an analytic framework that attends to both the substance of stigma and its dramaturgical management.

Interpretive Practice and Accounting

"Interpretive practice," as developed by Gubrium and Holstein (2000), provides a view of lived experience that is faithful to both individual agency and structural conditions. On the one hand, its emphasis on artful practice echoes the interactionist dictum of "if [people] define situations as real, they are real in their consequences" (Thomas and Thomas 1928:572). That is to say, reality is socially constructed through symbolic interaction. On the other hand, an interpretive practice approach has affinities with the Marxist notion that people "make their own history, but they do not make it just as they please; they do not make it under circumstances chosen by themselves, but under circumstances directly encountered, given, and transmitted from the past" (McLellan 2000:329). Approaching social interaction as interpretive practice implies that actors are neither completely passive nor autonomous. Instead, interpretive practice focuses on social life as it is empirically manifested in the interplay between artful construction and concrete circumstance. Indeed, Gubrium and Holstein caution against placing too much emphasis on either the conditions or artfulness of everyday practice. In their words, "Being the two sides of interpretive practice, conditions and artfulness are reflexively intertwined so that the reification of one in service to the analysis of the other is virtually impossible" (1997:121).

Following this approach, stigmatizing encounters involve both concrete realities and fluid practices in which actors use language to settle identity disputes. In this sense, stigma becomes a locally-circumscribed achievement. Applying these insights to Middle Eastern Americans' encounters with those who question their identities, specific cultural resources (i.e., racist stereotypes and fear of terrorism perpetuated by the media) provide the social context for inquiries about Middle Eastern people. However, the outcomes of these encounters are never predetermined; each is an occasion for negotiating the practical meaning of Middle Eastern American identity. Each is replete with its own nuances and artful practices.

Social Context and History

Accounts are conditioned by structural factors. As Lyman and Scott point out (1989), there are patterned differences between those actors who request accounts and those who have to account for themselves. In their words,

> The point with respect to accounts is their right to be requested, their establishment of social identity, and their efficacy to change in accordance with the changing status of the group involved. . . . Situations of account confusion are especially acute when a group in transition from one status position to another is undergoing a collective identity crisis. Racial groups provide numerous examples. Before the 1920s some Japanese in America insisted on their identity as "free white persons" in order to circumvent naturalization and franchise barriers, but found few others would accept this definition of their racial status. (P. 151)

In many ways, the case of Middle Eastern Americans is similar to that of Japanese Americans in the first half of the twentieth century. Political turmoil in the Middle East and terrorism have created an identity crisis for those with ancestral ties to that part of the world. The negative stereotypes of Middle Eastern Americans ("Arabs" in particular) predate the September 11th tragedies. For example,

> An ABC News poll, conducted during the Persian Gulf crisis in February 1991, found 43% of Americans had a high opinion of Arabs while 41% said they had a low opinion. In that poll, majorities of Americans said the following terms applied to Arabs: "religious" (81%), "terrorists" (81%), "violent" (58%) and "religious fanatics" (56%). (Jones 2001:1)

In fact, negative opinions toward Middle Eastern Americans date back at least to the hostage crisis of 1972 in which Palestinian militants took eleven Israeli athletes hostage during the Olympic Games in Munich. The German authorities' attempt to rescue the hostages ended in a massacre that claimed the lives of all eleven hostages and five of the eight terrorists. Shortly after this event, the Federal Bureau of Investigation launched one of its first national campaigns to interview and deport Arab Americans (Marvasti and McKinney 2004:56). Later, the Iranian hostage crisis in 1979, the first Gulf War in 1991, and the 1993 bombing of the World Trade Center all reinforced negative stereotypes of Middle Eastern Americans. Each conflict was followed by a wave of hate crimes and discrimination. Mosques were vandalized, and people were fired from jobs and assaulted on the streets (Feagin and Feagin 2003:327–30; Marvasti and McKinney 2004:53–60; Schaefer 2006:299–302; U.S. Congress 1986).

These backlashes were relatively isolated and episodic until September 11, 2001, when systematic discrimination against Middle Eastern Americans received considerable public support. A *Newsweek* poll conducted shortly after the terrorist attacks, on September 14–15, 2001, indicated that "32% of Americans think Arabs living in this country should be put under special surveillance as Japanese Americans were" (Jones 2001:3–4). Similarly, in June 2002 a Gallup survey of 1,360 American adults showed that "of the five immigrant groups tested [Arabs, Hispanics, Asians, Africans, and Europeans], the public is least accepting of Arab immigrants, as 54% say there are too many entering the United States" (Jones 2002:3).

Since September 11, 2001, accountability has become an everyday reality for Middle Eastern Americans in light of official policies that systematically demand that they explain their every action. Former Attorney General John Ashcroft articulated this state of heightened awareness quite clearly in public addresses by suggesting that if suspected terrorists as much as spit on the sidewalk, they would be arrested (Gorman 2002). The term "suspected terrorists" has become so broadly defined as to include thousands of Middle Eastern men who have been interviewed, arrested, or deported for minor immigration violations.

Interestingly, under U.S. immigration laws, Middle Eastern Americans (officially defined as those with ancestral ties to a region stretching from Turkey to North Africa) are classified as "white." Indeed, most affirmative action forms specifically instruct people of Middle Eastern descent to identify themselves as "white." However, the phrase "Middle Eastern–looking," almost always used in connection with a terrorist threat, has come to connote the same meaning as the words "black suspect." Their official classification as "white" seems to have no practical relevance in everyday life as Middle Eastern Americans are singled out for antiterrorism measures.

In the post-9/11 era, "Middle Eastern–looking" people, men in particular, have been verbally harassed, physically attacked, and sometimes killed, regardless of their actual nationality or association with Islam or the Middle East. In Mesa, Arizona, an Indian Sikh was shot and killed for being dark-skinned, bearded, and wearing a turban (Delves 2001). The man responsible for this crime also fired shots at a Lebanese gas station worker and an Afghan family. In addition to the rash of indiscriminate violence, in several incidents across the country "Middle Eastern–looking" men were removed from flights after completing all security checks and being seated (Brown 2001). The reason offered in most cases was as vague as the crew not feeling safe flying with them.

Furthermore, the current terror warning system, which is intended to alert the public about potential terrorist attacks, acts as an accounting catalyst. As the level of terror is "elevated," for example, from yellow to orange, public fears and suspicions are equally increased, and subsequently more Middle Eastern people are forced into the position of account-givers. At the same time, terror warnings call on ordinary citizens to be "alert" and report anything "suspicious"—in a sense, deputizing them as semiofficial account-takers. In essence, the terror alert system encourages the suspension of tact and disattention, especially to the detriment of "Middle Eastern-looking" people. To borrow from Goffman (1963), Middle Eastern Americans are suffering "ill-fame" perpetuated by the mass media. In his words, their "public image . . . seems to be constituted from a small selection of facts which . . . are inflated into dramatic news-worthy appearance, and then used as a full picture [of their identity]" (p. 71). Under these circumstances, aspects of one's life that would ordinarily be considered private are routinely subjected to public and official scrutiny in everyday encounters.

However, the outcomes of such encounters are not uniform or predetermined. As Goffman states (1963), and Gubrium and Holstein develop in relation to interpretive practice (2000), stigma is not the property of a person, but of relationships that always unfold through symbolic interaction. Building on these insights, the stigma of being Middle Eastern American is not external to interactions but is constructed or rejected *through* interaction, accounts, and self-presentational strategies.

Methods and Data

From May 2002 to May 2004, my wife (a white woman from the southern United States) and I conducted twenty in-depth interviews with twelve male and eight female respondents, whose age ranged from eighteen to fifty-five years. All were either enrolled in college or had earned a four-year degree (at minimum), and lived in three different states (Florida, Pennsylvania, and Virginia). Eighteen were naturalized citizens and two were long-time immigrants who had lived and worked in the United States for over ten years and planned to become citizens. In our interviews, we asked respondents how they managed being Middle Eastern, particularly when facing discrimination. We began our interviews with demographic questions about age, country of origin, and education. We then followed with questions about whether respondents had experienced any form of ethnic discrimination at work, in school, or in their communities because of their religion, names, accents, appearance, or style of dress. We used probes like "What did you do then?" to encourage respondents to elaborate on their narratives. . . .

The interview data was supplemented with autoethnographic data from my experience as an Iranian immigrant who has lived in the United States since 1983. For the purpose of this study, autoethnography refers to an orientation that allows the researcher to use her or his experiences as data in the form of a cultural insider's personal narratives (Ellis and Bochner 2000; Hayano 1979; Ronai 1992).

I represent my own and my respondents' accounting for stigma in narrative form to highlight the contextual and existential quality of these experiences. Because the stories I analyze here are reconstructions of normal deviant encounters, they are subject to retrospective distortions. Having said that, retrospective accounts of accounts have been the primary source of data in many studies of stigma management. Encounter narratives are the norm in the sociology of stigma for both practical and theoretical reasons. Practically, it is difficult to position oneself as a researcher to observe stigma management firsthand. Researchers would have to shadow the stigmatized through their daily routines to isolate specific stigma-related encounters. Theoretically, a person defines stigmatization experiences largely in retrospect. It is after reflecting on an encounter that a person might say, "I am/was stigmatized" or "I resist/resisted stigma in this way." Additionally, similarities between my respondents' accounts suggest that their narratives are not random fictions but reflections of a patterned experience.

Middle Eastern individuals presented or accounted for their selves in disrupted social encounters or "incidents" (Goffman 1959:212). Accounting practices took mainly five forms: humorous accounting, educational accounting, defiant accounting, cowering, and passing. Analyzing these accounting strategies enables us to vividly grasp the interplay between artful self-presentations and obdurate social conditions. Each constitutes a different interpretive practice individuals use to establish a situationally practical and useful Middle-Eastern self.

Humorous Accounting

When questioned about their ethnic identity, respondents sometimes use humor as a way of shifting attention away from the stereotypes that threaten their identities. In this way, they use humor as a diversion technique (Taub, McLorg, and Fanflik 2004). Consider, for example, how Ali accounted for his Middle Eastern–sounding name.

> AM: Do you get any reactions about your name? Like people asking you what kind of name is that?
>
> ALI: Sometimes they do; sometimes they don't. Sometimes, if they haven't met me or if they are sending me correspondence, they think it's a lady's name and a lot of correspondence comes in Ms. Ali [last name]. They think I'm either Alison or something like that. Nowadays, when my name comes up [in face-to-face contacts with clients], I use my sense of humor. For example, when they can't spell my name or ask questions about it, I say, "I'm the brother of Muhammad Ali, the boxer."

Ali's deliberate use of associations with the famed boxer places his name in a cultural context his account-takers are familiar with. In this type of accounting, individuals use humor to establish a common ground or "facilitating normalized role-taking" (Davis 1961:128).

Another respondent, whose first name, Ladan (the name of a flower in Persian), brings up unwelcome and troubling associations with the notorious terrorist Osama Bin Laden, tells this story about how she used humor with an inquisitive customer.

> AM: With the name Ladan, do you run into any problems?
>
> LADAN: Where I work [at a department store] we all wear nametags, with the name Ladan very clearly spelled out L A D A N. And this old couple, they approached me and I was very friendly with them—I usually chitchat with my customers. And he started asking me all these questions like, "You're so pretty, where're you from?" [I respond,] "I'm from Iran." [He says,] "What?" [I repeat,] "I'm

from Iran." So he asks, "What's your name?" And I say, "Ladan." So he bent down to read my nametag and he just looked at me with a funny face and asked, "Are you related to Bin Laden?"

AM: Was he joking?

LADAN: No, he was not. But I did joke back to him and I said, "Yes, he's my cousin and actually he's coming over for dinner tonight." [She chuckles.]

AM: So, when this sort of thing happens, you use humor to deal with it?

LADAN: Yeah, I do, because otherwise, if I don't turn it into a joke or a laughing mood, I get upset. I get really, really offended.

AM: So what was this guy's reaction? Did he laugh with you?

LADAN: When this guy realized my name is Ladan and I'm from Iran, he changed his attitude. He became reserved and he even went one step backward. When I noticed he was uncomfortable, I completed the transaction with his wife and let them leave as soon as they wanted.

In this case, Ladan's use of humor does not necessarily result in the proverbial "happy ending," or a clearly discernible resolution. The customer turned away and ended the interaction. Whether Ladan remained stigmatized by this encounter or whether the customer walked away feeling that he successfully applied the stigma is unknown, perhaps even for the participants involved in the interaction. What is clearer is that Ladan's account allowed her to highlight the ludicrousness of the account-taker's assumptions and his right to solicit an account. Here, the way of speaking shapes the substance of the identity. Ladan is not giving a specific and accurate account of who she "really" is, but is using humor to construct an encounter-specific account that implicitly questions the account-taker's right to ask her questions about her identity.

I also use humor to account for my name. The following encounter took place on election day (November 14, 2002) at a voting precinct in a small town in Pennsylvania where I went to cast my vote in the midterm elections. The encounter begins with the examination of my photo identification.

ELECTION SUPERVISOR: Okay . . . this is a hard one! [squinting at my driver's license] You're ready? [alerting her coworker] It says Amar. . . . It's A . . .

I wait, silent and motionless, as the three old women probe my ID. I fear that any sudden movement might send people running out of the building screaming for help. "Speak!" I scream in my head. The words finally roll out of my mouth:

AM: You know, my dad gave me a long name, hoping that it would guarantee my success in life. [They laugh.]

ELECTION SUPERVISOR: Well, you must be a doctor because you sure sign your name like one.

AM: [I cannot resist] Actually, I am a doctor. . . . So maybe my dad had the right idea after all.

In this case, I use humor as a method of introduction, a way of constructing an identity for the occasion that gives more weight to *how* one speaks rather than *what* one speaks. It was not clear to me what they thought about me, but I sensed that they were still puzzled—I had to account for who I am. The immediate substance of my identity was not in question—they had my photo identification in front of them and most likely could tell from my swarthy appearance that I was not a native Pennsylvanian. Instead, humorous accounting allowed me to shape the broad contours of my identity for the occasion. Namely, I was able to communicate that I come from a "normal" family that aspires to the universal notion of "success in life," that I am aware that there are concerns about my identity, and am capable of responding to them in a sensible way.

In humorous accounting, the substance of the account is incidental and is deliberately trivialized. The account-giver acknowledges the demands of the encounter while simultaneously undermining the legitimacy and the urgency of the request for an account. How the account-giver handles the substance of the matter shapes the identity in question.

Educational Accounting

Sometimes accounting takes on a deliberate pedagogical form. In such cases, the account-giver assumes the role of an educator, informing and instructing the account-taker about relevant topics. This strategy of "normalization" (Goffman 1963) combats stigma by correcting stereotypes. Unlike humorous accounting, educational accounting centers on the informational substance of the account.

In response to suspicions and antagonism from his neighbors, a Pakistani Muslim, Hassan, conducted a sort of door-to-door educational accounting:

> After September 11th, I walked the street the whole week and talked to every single one of my neighbors. . . . And one of my neighbors—his brother was in Tower Two and he got out, and his mother was there and she was *furious* with Muslims and me. And we were there for three hours, my wife, my kids, her [the neighbor], her son and her other son that came out of the World Trade Center—he had come down by the time the buildings came down. And I was like, "Look, that's not Islam. That's not who Muslims are. Ask your son, what type of person am I? What type of person is my wife? Do I oppress my wife? Do I beat my wife? Have you ever heard me say anything extreme before?" . . . They all know I don't drink, they all know that I pray five times a day, they all know I fast during the month of Ramadan. At the end of Ramadan, we have a big party and invite everyone over to help celebrate the end of fast. This year, they'll all probably fast one day with me so they can feel what it's like.

Hassan's approach is proactive; it addresses potential questions before they are explicitly asked. In some ways, this form of educational accounting is similar to what Hewitt and Stokes (1975:1–3) call "disclaimers" or a "prospective construction of meaning" that individuals use in an attempt to avoid being categorized in an undesirable way. In this example, Hassan tries to transform the relationship between him, as an account-giver, and the account-takers who suspect him of being an "evildoer." Unlike humorous accounting, where account-givers deliberately trivialize cultural stereotypes, educational accounting explicitly and diligently addresses them in order to debunk them.

Account-givers have to give considerable attention to deciding which inquiries are worthy of an educational account. For example, an Iranian respondent, Mitra, indicates that she filters inquiries about her culture and identity before answering them:

> If they ask about the government or the senate over there [Iran], I don't know anything about it. I know who the president is, but they ask me about the senate or the name of the senator over there, I don't know. Since I don't know I'm not going to get involved. I'll say I don't know or I'm not interested. If they say, "Oh, you are from *that* country!" or "You are from the Middle East and you are a terrorist," those kinds of comments I'm not going to get into. I'll just say, "*No*, I'm not." But if they ask me about the culture I'll tell them, "Alright," and inform them about it—as much as I know.

Although inclined to assume the role of an educator, Mitra is unwilling or unprepared to respond to every question. Part of her educational accounting strategy involves evaluating the degree of her expertise on the subject and the tone of the questions. As she says, if the account-taker begins with accusations, such as "you are a terrorist," the only reasonable reply might be to deny the accusation and end the interaction.

Educational accounting was a common strategy for Middle Eastern Muslim women in my sample, especially those who wear the *hijab*. Many of them were approached by strangers who asked questions such as "Isn't it hot under there?" "Does that come in many colors?" "Why do you wear that?" "Are you going to make *them* [referring to the ten- and twelve-year-old girls who were standing in a grocery store line with their mother] wear it too?" These women were literally stopped on the street by strangers who asked questions about the *hijab*, sometimes so directly as to constitute rudeness. My respondents reported that whenever time and circumstances allowed, they provide accounts of their religious practices and beliefs. Some of these answers include "I wear it because it is my culture," "I wear it so that you won't stare at my body when you are talking to me," or a more flippant response such as, "It's cooler under my scarf than you think." . . .

Defiant Accounting

When prompted to provide an account, Middle Eastern Americans sometimes express righteous indignation. I call this defiant accounting. Similar to humorous accounting, the account-giver exerts agency by challenging the other's right and the rationale to request it. However, whereas humorous accounting entails indirect and fairly conciliatory objections to stigma, in defiant accounting the stigmatized make explicit demands for counter explanations from the "normals." For example, consider how Alham, a young Iranian woman, describes her experiences with a coworker.

> She [the coworker] would tell me, "I don't know which country you come from but in America we do it like this or that." I let it go because I was older than her and we had to work together. . . . But one day I pulled her aside and I told her, "For your information where I come from has a much older culture. And what I know, you can't even imagine. So why don't you go get some more education. And if you mention this thing again—'my country is *this*, your country is *that*'—, I'm going to take it to management and they're going to fire you or they're going to fire me." And that was it.

Alham does not provide an account to repair the interaction or to restore it to a state of equilibrium. On the contrary, she explicitly seeks to challenge the conventional format of the encounter. Instead of aiming for consensus, defiant accounting foregrounds conflicting viewpoints and signals the account-giver's objection to the entire affair. The interaction is explicitly focused on the fairness of the exchange between the account-giver and the account-taker.

Account-givers are especially likely to use defiant strategies when they find the request for an account unfair. Specifically, ethnic minorities who are subjected to profiling may become defiant in response to the practice. For example, when I learned that, unlike myself, my white colleagues were not asked to show ID cards upon entering the campus gym, I felt justified in becoming defiant. In one instance, while pulling out my ID card from my wallet, I asked the woman at the front counter why my white faculty friend, who had just walked in ahead of me, was not asked to present an ID. She explained that she had not noticed the other person entering or she would have asked him to do the same.

This encounter highlights the unpredictability of defiant accounting for both parties involved in the interaction. At its core, this strategy counters an account request with another: they ask for my ID and I ask why I should be the only one subjected to this rule. In turn, the other side presents its account and so on. This chain of accounts and counter-accounts could result in a formal dispute. Though it is possible that in some cases, when confronted, the account-takers simply back down and cease their efforts, it is just as likely that they intensify their demands, especially when they are backed by policies or other public mandates.

Defiant accounting is a risky approach that can either shield the account-giver from a potentially humiliating process or generate additional requests and demands. In some cases, defiant accounting can become a type of mass resistance, as with African Americans and the passive resistance component of the civil rights movement of the 1960s. . . .

Passing

The goal of passing (Goffman 1963) is information control and the concealment of stigmatizing attributes from "normals." As an accounting strategy, passing means eliminating the need for an account (see Lyman and Scott 1989:126–27). How individuals present their identity can potentially eliminate the need for accounting altogether. My respondents accomplished passing by manipulating their appearance. The stereotypical image of a Middle Eastern person roughly translates into someone with dark hair, large facial features, swarthy skin, non-European foreign accent, facial hair on men, and veils and scarves on women. Faced with these stereotypes, some respondents consciously altered their looks to avoid any outside marker that might associate them with these stereotypes. Self-presentation (Goffman 1959), especially attention to clothes and grooming, is an equally important consideration for successful passing. For example, wearing jeans and being clean-shaven draws less attention and leads to fewer occasions for accounting.

Some Middle Eastern Americans try to pass by trading their own ethnic identity for a less controversial one. The simplest way to do this is to move to an ethnically diverse region. The respondents who live in South Florida stated that one reason they did not experience negative episodes of ethnic accounting is because they are perceived as Hispanic. For example, an Iranian woman was asked what kind of Spanish she was speaking when she was having a conversation with her teenage daughter in Farsi at the mall. Another Iranian man tried to pass as Italian by placing an Italian flag vanity license plate on his car. As a general rule, my respondents displayed Western or patriotic symbols (e.g., an American flag) at work, in front of their homes, or on their cars to avoid ethnic accounting. After September 11th, my neighbors gave me an American flag to place outside my apartment. As he put it, "This is for your own safety." In a sense, patriotic symbols are accounting statements in their own right and act as "disidentifiers" (Goffman 1963:93) that help separate "loyal Americans" from suspected terrorists.

Another strategy for passing is to give an ambiguous account in response to ethnic identity questions. For example, asked about his country of origin, an Egyptian man stated that he was Coptic (a pre-Islamic Egyptian culture). He noted that uninformed account-takers typically find it too embarrassing to ask follow-up questions, pretend to know what "Coptic" means, and drop the subject altogether. Iranians create this kind of ambiguity by stating that they are Persians (the designation of ancient Iran). Another way to circumvent accounts is to name one's city of birth instead of country of birth. I once told a college classmate that I was from Tehran. To my astonishment, he asked,"Is that near Paris?"

Changing one's name is another way to pass. Some respondents change their Muslim names (e.g., Akbar) to typical American names (e.g., Michael). When asked why he changed his name, Ahmad explained that he was tired of people slamming down the phone when he made inquiries about jobs. Some change from widely known ethnic-sounding names to lesser known ones as in the change from Hossein to Sina.

Passing strategies pose their own risks for the stigmatized. In particular, the media have constructed passing among Middle Eastern Americans as an extension of the "evil terrorist plot." After September 11th, it was widely reported that the hijackers were specifically instructed to wear jeans and shave their faces to pass as native born ethnics. Therefore, rather than being viewed as a sign of cultural assimilation, Middle Eastern Americans' conspicuous attempts at passing can be cast as a diabolical plan to form a "sleeper cell" or to disguise "the wolves among us." These days, when I go to an airport, I am very conscious of how much passing would be considered legitimate. Trying to conceal too much information about oneself can arouse suspicion. In fact, I sometimes wear my gold medallion with its Allah (Arabic for "God") inscription conspicuously on the outside of my shirt to indicate that I am not attempting to "misrepresent" myself or deceive anyone.

Conclusions: Interpretive Practice and Stigma Management

The interpretive practice model used in this study combines the interactionist concepts of accounts and stigma management with the structural emphasis on concrete social conditions. This analysis focuses on accounting as an interpretive process for establishing situationally specific ethnic identities. Rather than treating stigma as an objective reality, I examine the interpretive practices individuals use to establish or dispute stigma and stigmatized identities.

I reject a more objective conceptualization of stigma in part because, as noted by Riessman

(2000), such an approach exaggerates the influence of the dominant culture. Instead of considering the myriad ways would-be targets challenge or altogether dismiss stigma, the objective view takes for granted the reality of stigma and proceeds to analyze its management, concealment, or consequences for the stigmatized. As a result, Goffman's original stipulation on the situationally variable and interactionally embedded nature of stigma is lost. Lost also is the understanding that, at least according to Goffman (1963), stigma is a tentative reality project. As he states, "The normal and the stigmatized are not persons but rather perspectives. These are generated in social situations during mixed contacts" (p. 138). Therefore, stigma, the stigmatized, and stigmatizers become meaningful within specific social interactions. The assumption that stigmas are obdurate qualities of particular groups of people might contradict empirical evidence, or the actors' own experiences.

The case of Middle Eastern Americans' spoiled identities suggests that two sets of empirical observations have to be incorporated into the analysis. On the one hand, there is the reality of the so-called War on Terror and pervasive fear of terrorism, both of which have made Middle Eastern Americans "legitimate" targets of scrutiny in everyday life. Similarly, the political turmoil in the Middle East directly affects their lives in the United States, so much so that there is almost a direct correspondence between the volatility of the region and the instability of Middle Eastern identities in the United States. Every terrorist attack, every hostage taking, and every virulent speech issued from the Middle East triggers a corresponding wave of public scrutiny in the United States. These are the conditions, but how do we get at everyday practices? How do Middle Eastern Americans cope in real life situations? Answering these questions requires wearing a different analytic hat, so to speak.

One way my respondents and I cope with these conditions is by being adaptable and fluid with our self presentations. We do not enter daily interaction as members of a stigmatized group. Many of us are devout Muslims who practice our religion proudly despite stereotypes and the negative press. To suggest that we are narrowly defined by the stigma of being Middle Eastern is an empirically unfounded claim. It is equally problematic to imply that the majority of Americans are engaged in a mass stigmatization campaign. On a general level, my analysis is informed by the idea that ethnic difference is variable and interactionally achieved (Garfinkel 1967), and suggests that Middle Eastern Americans use a range of interpretive practices to define their ethnic-national identities in the context of everyday life during the War on the Terror.

My respondents and I experience being forced into positions where we have to account for our ethnic identities. What triggers these accounting encounters (e.g., genuine interest, fear, or malice) is of secondary relevance. As C. Wright Mills (1939) suggests, the motives for these encounters are themselves situated and discerned in the course, and in the language, of the interaction. In these encounters, account-givers and account-takers monitor each other at every turn and respond accordingly. I have labeled this type of interaction *accounting encounters*, and have underlined some of the self-presentation strategies Middle Eastern Americans use as they account for their identity (humorous, educational, and defiant accounting, and passing)....

What these accounting strategies share is that they are all attempts at salvaging spoiled identities in disrupted routine interactions. My respondents indicated that they measure the quality of their lives by the number of disruptions they face (i.e., a good day means not receiving unwanted attention). It is true that most people experience some type of "incident" or "scene" in their daily lives, but it is also true that most find "their predicament . . . much less charged and more easily set to rights" (Davis 1961:132).

In addition to its economic effects, stigma also forces its targets to become excessively and constantly conscious about themselves, others, and social interactions in general (Goffman 1967). A poignant example of this heightened state of consciousness is illustrated in my encounter with another shopper at a Wal-Mart store in Florida.

> We were both waiting in a checkout line. The woman, who was momentarily distracted by a tabloid cover, looked up at me abruptly and asked, "Where did you come from?" I hesitated for a second, wondering if I should try to pass as "an average Floridian," but ethnic pride took a hold of me. So I stuck out my chest and blurted, "I am Iranian." She responded with a perplexed look, "I mean, how'd you get in front of me in this line?" I did not know what to say after that. I just kept my head down, paid for my items, and left the store. I did not look back out of embarrassment.

Although laughable, such encounters could have the unfortunate effect of further alienating and weakening the account-givers' bonds with "normal" society. Ultimately, no accounting strategy is a suitable substitute for social interaction unencumbered by stereotypes and the acts of discrimination they engender.

At a different level, this article also hints at the onerous emotional labor (Hochschild 1983) unwilling account-givers have to perform in order to cope with stigma. I believe that examining stigma as interpretive practice has clear political implications. As Gubrium and Holstein put it, interpretive practice "presents the recognition that we could enact alternate possibilities or alternative directions. . . . If we make visible the constructive fluidity and malleability of social forms, we also reveal a potential for change" (2000:503). Like most studies of deviance and stigma, my work is intended to humanize myself and my respondents, but beyond that, I hope for social change. By voicing my own and my respondents' perspectives, I want to inspire my readers to initiate new interpretive practices. Ultimately, this article is a purposeful account in its own right that aims to change negative perceptions and hurtful practices.

References

Brown, Anthony. 2001. "Nervous Pilots Order Off 'Arab' Passengers." *The Observer,* September 23, p.2.

Cahill, Spencer and Robin Eggleston. 1994. "Managing Emotions in Public: The Case of Wheelchair Users." *Social Psychology Quarterly* 57:300–12.

Davis, Fred. 1961. "Deviance Disavowal: The Management of Strained Interaction by the Visibly Handicapped." *Social Problems* 9:121–32.

Delves, Philip. 2001. "New Prejudices Emerge in an Embittered City: New York's Arab Community Is Living in Fear of Attack." *The Daily Telegraph,* September 20, p. 7.

Ellis, Carolyn and Arthur P. Bochner. 2000. "Autoethnography, Personal Narrative, Reflexivity: Researcher as Subject." Pp. 733–68 in *Handbook of Qualitative Research,* 2nd ed., edited by N. Denzin and Y. S. Lincoln. Thousand Oaks, CA: Sage.

Evans, Rhonda D., Craig J. Forsyth, and Rachel A. Foreman. 2003. "Psychic Accounts: Self-Legitimation and the Management of a Spoiled Identity." *Sociological Forum* 23:359–75.

Feagin, Joe and Clairece Feagin. 2003. *Racial and Ethnic Relations,* 7th ed. Upper Saddle River, NJ: Prentice Hall.

Feagin, Joe and Karyn McKinney. 2003. *The Many Costs of Racism.* Lanham, MD: Rowman and Littlefield.

Fothergill, Alice. 2003. "The Stigma of Charity: Gender, Class, and Disaster Assistance." *Sociological Quarterly* 44:659–80.

Garfinkel, Harold. 1967. *Studies in Ethnomethodology.* Englewood Cliffs, NJ: Prentice Hall.

Goffman, Erving. 1959. *The Presentation of Self in Everyday Life.* Garden City, NY: Doubleday Anchor Books.

———. 1962. *Asylums: Essays on the Social Situation of Mental Patients and Other Inmates.* Garden City, NY: Doubleday Anchor Books.

———. 1963. *Stigma: Notes on the Management of Spoiled Identity.* Englewood Cliffs, NJ: Prentice Hall.

———. 1967. "The Nature of Deference and Demeanor, " in *Interaction Ritual.* Garden City, NY: Doubleday.

Gorman, Siobhan. 2002. "National Security: The Ashcroft Doctrine." *National Journal* 34:3712–19.

Gubrium, Jaber and James Holstein. 1997. *The New Language of Qualitative Method.* Thousand Oaks, CA: Sage.

———. 2000. "Analyzing Interpretive Practice." Pp. 487–508 in *Handbook of Qualitative Research,* 2nd ed., edited by N. Denzin and Y. S. Lincoln. Thousand Oaks, CA: Sage.

Harvey, Richard D. 2001. "Individual Differences in the Phenomenological Impact of Social Stigma." *The Journal of Social Psychology* 14:174–89.

Hayano, David M. 1979. "Auto-ethnography: Paradigms, Problems, and Prospects." *Human Organizations* 38:113–20.

Herman, Nancy J. 1993. "Return to Sender: Reintegrative Stigma-Management Strategies of Ex-Psychiatric Patients." *Journal of Contemporary Ethnography* 22:295–330.

Hewitt, John P. and Randall Stokes. 1975. "Disclaimers." *American Sociological Review* 40:1–11.

Hochschild, Arlie, 1983. *The Managed Heart: Commercialization of Human Feeling*. Berkeley: University of California Press.

Jones, Jeffrey M. 2001. "Americans Felt Uneasy toward Arabs Even before September 11th," *The Gallup Organization* (www.gallup.com).

———. 2002. "Effects of September 11th on Immigration Attitudes Fading but Still Evident," *The Gallup Organization* (www.gallup.com).

Karp, David A. 1992. "Illness Ambiguity and the Search for Meaning: A Case Study of a Self-Help Group for Affective Disorders." *Journal of Contemporary Ethnography* 21:130–70.

Killian, Lewis M. 1985. "The Stigma of Race: Who Now Bears the Mark of Cain?" *Symbolic Interaction* 8:1–14.

Kusow, Abdi M. 2004. "Contesting Stigma: On Goffman's Assumptions of Normative Order." *Symbolic Interaction* 27:179–97.

Link, Bruce and Jo Phelan. 2001. "Conceptualizing Stigma." *Annual Review of Sociology* 27:363–85.

Lyman, Stanford and Marvin Scott. 1989. *A Sociology of the Absurd*. Dix Hills, NY: General Hall.

Marvasti, Amir and Karyn McKinney. 2004. *Middle Eastern Lives in America*. New York: Rowman and Littlefield.

McLellan, David. 2000. *Karl Marx: Selected Writings*. New York: Oxford University Press.

Mills, C. Wright. 1939. "Situated Actions and Vocabularies of Motive." *American Sociological Review* 5:904–13.

Riessman, Catherine K. 2000. "Stigma and Everyday Resistance Practices: Childless Women in South India." *Gender & Society* 14:111–35.

Ronai, Carol R. 1992. "The Reflexive Self through Narrative." Pp. 102–24 in *Investigating Subjectivity*, edited by C. Ellis and M. Flaherty. Newbury Park, CA: Sage.

Roschelle, Anne R. and Peter Kaufman. 2004. "Fitting In and Fighting Back: Stigma Strategies Among Homeless Kids." *Symbolic Interaction* 27: 23–46.

Schaefer, Richard T. 2006. *Racial and Ethnic Groups*, 10th ed. Upper Saddle River, NJ: Prentice Hall.

Snow, David and Leon Anderson. 1987. "Identity Work among the Homeless: The Verbal Construction and Avowal of Personal Identities." *American Journal of Sociology* 92:1336–71.

Storrs, Debbie. 1999. "Whiteness as Stigma: Essentialist Identity Work by Mixed Race Women." *Symbolic Interaction* 22:187–212.

Taub, Diane E., Penelope A. McLorg, and Patricia L. Fanflik. 2004. "Stigma Management Strategies among Women with Physical Disabilities: Contrasting Approaches of Downplaying or Claiming Disability Status." *Deviant Behavior* 25:169–90.

Thomas, William I. and Dorothy S. Thomas. 1928. *The Child in America: Behavior Problems and Programs*. New York: Knopf.

U.S. Congress. House of Representatives. Subcommittee on Criminal Justice of the House Judiciary Committee. July 16, 1986. *Ethnically Motivated Violence against Arab Americans*. 99th Cong., 2nd sess. Serial no. 135. Washington, DC: U.S. Government Printing Office.

Reflective Questions

1. What is a "spoiled identity"? Why don't people with those identities always feel stigmatized? How is stigma the byproduct of social expectations and contexts?
2. What do "scenes" look like and why do they produce "accounts"?
3. What forms of accounting do Middle Eastern Americans engage in and to what effect? How are their accounts influenced by their social contexts?
4. Perhaps you or someone close to you has experienced negative social appraisals related to appearance, ability, or some other characteristic in certain contexts. What circumstances make these appraisals the most likely to occur? Which make them difficult to contest? How do you/they elicit support from family and friends? What kinds? What sort of support most helps you maintain a sense of self-worth? What toll does it take on family and friends?
5. The Internet provides a new venue for individuals to gather resources, craft alternative selves, and

gather support after being stigmatized. Go to dailystrength.org, the experienceproject.com, or an online support group of your choice. Pick a few stigmatized experiences, and then read several exchanges. What interactional strategies do online communities use to foster valued identities and meaningful senses of self in the face of stigmatization? How are they different from the ones described by Marvasti? What sorts of "incidents" do communities most aggressively try to counteract? What happens when no one responds, or they respond in a way that other posters view as unsupportive?

Nazi Doctors at Auschwitz

ROBERT JAY LIFTON

Although humans socially construct reality, they seldom experience it as their construction. We usually take the socially constructed reality that we inhabit for granted as the reality rather than a reality. We dismiss alternative constructions of reality as symptoms of demonic possession or mental illness or as products of ignorance or depravity. People's faith in the inevitability of their particular reality provides them with security and meaning in a sometimes senseless world. However, it has also led to such horrors as war and oppression throughout human history.

There is probably no better example of the power and potential horrors of socially constructed reality than Nazi Germany. The Nazis constructed a reality in which Jews and other so-called "undesirables" were the cause of all Germany's problems, and National Socialism was its savior. Those who embraced this construction of reality or were merely caught up in it either participated in or ignored all manner of human atrocities. This selection examines how Nazi ideology or interpretations of reality and the reality of the infamous Auschwitz concentration camp led physicians to participate in mass murder. Robert Jay Lifton describes these Nazi doctors' socialization to killing and to the horrific reality of Auschwitz based on interviews with surviving doctors and camp prisoners. He focuses on the doctors' participation in "selections" of Jewish prisoners for immediate execution in Auschwitz's infamous gas chamber or for, usually temporary, survival as camp workers. Although many doctors were initially reluctant to participate in such "selections," their reluctance was overpowered by the reality of Auschwitz and their own Nazi ideology. They came to view the largely hidden and efficient extermination of Jews as less disturbing than the living horrors of Auschwitz. Over time, most came to accept the mass murder of Jews and their participation in it as inevitable, necessary, and routine. They even considered the killing necessary to protect the health of inmates who were spared that fate. Although not all doctors approved of the mass execution of Jews by gassing, all were convinced that the "Jewish problem" needed to be solved and that this "Final Solution" would finally solve it.

Lifton argues that these doctors' acceptance of the horrific reality of Auschwitz involved the psychological process he calls "doubling." Faced with that horrific reality, Nazi doctors developed an Auschwitz self alongside their existing "normal" self. The Auschwitz self was the dutiful and efficient medical supervisor of mass killing. Their other, humane self was nurtured by occasional acts of kindness and medical concern toward still living inmates and regular visits with family and friends away from the camp. However, the doctors kept their lives at the camp and away from it quite separate, supporting the psychological schism between their two selves. According to Lifton, it is this psychological doubling that allowed doctors to participate in killings without thinking of themselves as murderers. Rather,

Reprinted from: Robert Jay Lifton, *The Nazi Doctors: Medical Killing and the Psychology of Genocide*, pp. 1, 2, 6, 7, 147–148, 193, 195–200, 202–206, 210–213, 419, 422, 425, 493, 503.

they could think of themselves as normal people who had to do a dirty but necessary job.

Lifton suggests that Auschwitz illustrates the power of a social situation to command the psychological doubling that enables individuals to commit atrocities. It was the reality of Auschwitz and Nazi ideology, not some psychological disposition toward cruelty, that led doctors who had taken the Hippocratic oath to participate in the routine taking of human life. That is a sobering lesson. It suggests that, under certain social conditions, just about anyone can become a killer or tormentor in the cause of some construction of reality. The example of Nazi doctors at Auschwitz alerts us to the kind of social situations and realities that can transform us into such monsters.

I gained an important perspective on Auschwitz from an Israeli dentist who had spent three years in the camp. We were completing a long interview, during which he had told me about many things, including details of SS dentists' supervision of prisoners' removal of gold fillings from the teeth of fellow Jews killed in the gas chambers. He looked about the comfortable room in his house with its beautiful view of Haifa, sighed deeply, and said, "This world is not this world." What I think he meant was that, after Auschwitz, the ordinary rhythms and appearances of life, however innocuous or pleasant, were far from the truth of human existence. Underneath those rhythms and appearance lay darkness and menace.

The comment also raises questions of our capacity to approach Auschwitz. From the beginning there has been enormous resistance on the part of virtually everyone to knowledge of what the Nazis were doing and have done there. That resistance has hardly abated, whatever the current interest in what we call "the Holocaust." Nor have more recent episodes of mass slaughter done much to overcome it. For to permit one's imagination to enter into the Nazi killing machine—to begin to experience that killing machine—is to alter one's relationship to the entire human project. One does not want to learn about such things.

Psychologically speaking, nothing is darker or more menacing, or harder to accept, than the participation of physicians in mass murder. However technicized or commercial the modern physician may have become, he or she is still a healer—and one responsible to a tradition of healing, which all cultures revere and depend upon. Knowledge that the doctor has joined the killers adds a grotesque dimension to the perception that "this world is not this world." During my work I gained the impression that, among Germans and many others, this involvement of physicians was viewed as the most shameful behavior.

When we think of the crimes of Nazi doctors, what come to mind are their cruel and sometimes fatal human experiments. Those experiments, in their precise and absolute violation of the Hippocratic oath, mock and subvert the very idea of the ethical physician, of the physician dedicated to the well-being of patients. . . .

Yet when we turn to the Nazi doctor's role in Auschwitz, it was not the experiments that were most significant. Rather it was his participation in the killing process—indeed his supervision of Auschwitz mass murder from the beginning to end. This aspect of Nazi medical behavior has escaped full recognition—even though we are familiar with photographs of Nazi doctors standing at the ramp and performing their notorious "selections" of arriving Jews, determining which were to go directly to the gas chamber and which were to live, at least temporarily, and work in the camp. . . .

My assumption from the beginning, in keeping with my twenty-five years of research, was that the best way to learn about Nazi doctors was to talk to them; interviews became the pragmatic core of the study. But I knew that, even more than in earlier work, I would have to supplement the interviews with extensive reading in and probing of all related issues—having to do not only with observations by others on Nazi medical behavior but with the Nazi era in general, as well as with German culture and history and with overall patterns of victimization in general and anti-Jewishness in particular. . . .

I interviewed three groups of people. The central group consisted of twenty-nine men who had been significantly involved at high levels with Nazi medicine, twenty-eight of them physicians and one pharmacist. . . . I interviewed a second group of twelve former Nazi nonmedical professionals of some prominence: as lawyers, judges, economists, teachers, architects, administrators, and Party officials. . . . Very different was the third group I interviewed: eighty former Auschwitz prisoners who had worked on medical blocks, more than half of them doctors. . . .

While Auschwitz genocide came to encompass Gypsies, Poles, and Russians, only Jews underwent systematic selections. For the primary function of Auschwitz . . . was the murder of every single Jew the Nazis could (in Himmler's words) lay their hands on anywhere.

The SS doctor did no direct medical work. His primary function was to carry out Auschwitz's institutional program of medicalized genocide. Consider the SS doctor's activities in Auschwitz. He performed initial large-scale selections of arriving Jewish prisoners at the Birkenau camp. . . . These selections were usually conducted according to formula: old and debilitated people, children, and women with children all selected for gas chamber; while relatively young adults were permitted to survive, at least temporarily. . . .

After the selection, the presiding doctor was driven in an SS vehicle usually marked with a red cross, together with a medical technician (one of a special group of "disinfectors" . . .) and the gas pellets, to a gas chamber adjoining one of the crematoria. As *Führer,* or "leader," of the team, the doctor had supervisory responsibility for the correct carrying out of the killing process, though the medical technician actually inserted the gas pellets, and the entire sequence became so routine that little intervention was required. The doctor also had the task of declaring those inside the gas chamber dead and sometimes looked through a peephole to observe them. This, too, became routine, a matter of permitting twenty minutes or so to pass before the doors of the gas chamber could be opened and the bodies removed.

SS doctors also carried out two additional forms of selections. . . . Jewish inmates were lined up on very short notice at various places in the camp and their ranks thinned in order to allow room for presumably healthier replacements from new transports. The other type of selections took place directly in the medical blocks in a caricature of triage. Rather than simply permitting those closest to death to die—in order to use limited medical resources to treat those who might be saved—as in traditional medical triage (the meaning given the term as originally used by the French military), the Nazis combined triage with murder by sending to the gas chamber those judged to be significantly ill or debilitated, or who required more than two or three weeks for recovery. . . .

Socialization to Killing

Virtually all Nazi doctors in Auschwitz complied in conducting selections, although they varied in how they did so and in their attitudes toward what they were doing. . . . [A]ll SS doctors were greatly influenced by . . . practical . . . issues: their shared relationship to an institution and to its selections demands, as regulated by higher medical and command authorities. And as greater numbers of transports arrived, selections were going on much of the time: as Dr. B. put it, "There was no way of avoiding [viewing] them if one had work to do in camp."

Under increasing pressure to select, most SS doctors underwent what he viewed as an extraordinary individual-psychological shift from revulsion to acceptance: "*In the beginning it was almost impossible. Afterward it became routine.*"

This shift involved a *socialization* to Auschwitz, including the important transition from outsider to insider.

Alcohol was crucial to this transition. Drinking together, often quite heavily, evenings in the officers' club, doctors "spoke very freely" and "expressed the most intimate objections." Some would "condemn the whole thing" and insist that "this is a filthy business . . . !" Dr. B. described these outbursts as so insistent as to be "like a mania . . . a sickness . . . over Auschwitz and . . . the gassings."

Such inebriated protest brought about no repercussions—indeed, it may even have been encouraged—and was unrelated to commitment or action. Consequently, "whether one condemned it or not was not really so much the issue." The issue, as Ernst B. defined it, was that "Auschwitz was an existing fact. One couldn't . . . really be against it, you see, one had to go along with it whether it was good or bad." That is, mass killing was the unyielding *fact of life* to which everyone was expected to adapt.

Whenever an SS doctor arrived at Auschwitz, the process was repeated as questions raised by the newcomer were answered by his more experienced drinking companions:

> He would ask, "How can these things be done there?" Then there was something like a general answer . . . which clarified everything. What is better for him [the prisoner]—whether he croaks . . . in shit or goes to heaven in [a cloud of] gas? And that settled the whole matter for the initiates. . . .

This ostensibly humane argument, Dr. B. was saying, was itself an assertion of Auschwitz reality as the baseline for all else. His language of initiation is appropriate in that selections were the specific "ordeal" the initiate had to undergo in order to emerge as a functioning Auschwitz "adult." And by exposing and combating doubts, the drinking sessions helped suppress moral aspects of the prior self in favor of a new Auschwitz self. . . .

At the same time there was constant pressure from above toward maximum involvement in selections, particularly from the spring of 1944 when dentists and pharmacists were also ordered to take their turns on the ramp. One of those dentists later testified that his plea to [Eduard] Wirths that he did not feel capable of performing selections, and wished to leave the camp, was met with a cool declaration that "according to a 'Führer order,' service in a concentration camp was considered front-line duty, and that any refusal was considered a desertion." . . .

Pressure and mentorship could combine, as in the case of Franz Lucas who, known to have a certain reluctance to select, was taken to the ramp by Wirths and [Joseph] Mengele and more or less shown how to go about things. Lucas apparently tried several ploys, including feigned illness, to avoid selecting; and even after complying, his kindness and medical help to prisoners led to a dressing down and an eventual transfer. . . .

The socialization of SS doctors to Auschwitz killing was enhanced by the camp's isolation from the world outside. The connecting medical figure with outside authority was Enno Lolling, who came frequently to the camp from his Berlin office and was essentially incompetent and a heavy drinker. Ernst B. had the impression that Lolling's superiors preferred not to know too many details about the camps, and that there was a general policy of "screening them off" from regular SS units. Camp doctors perpetuated this isolation by their reluctance, in Dr. B's phrase, to let others "see their cards." The result was, as he put it with only partial exaggeration, that "a concentration camp [became] a totally self-contained entity, absolutely isolated from everything—especially Auschwitz."

Doctors assigned there, then, had limited contact with anything but Auschwitz reality. They became preoccupied with adapting themselves to that reality, and moral revulsion could be converted into feelings of discomfort, unhappiness, anxiety, and despair. Subjective struggles could replace moral questions. They became concerned not with the evil of the environment but with how to come to some terms with the place.

They then became creatures of what Dr. B. described as the all-important Auschwitz milieu or atmosphere: "In that atmosphere everything is seen differently from the way it would be viewed now." On the basis of all the pressures and adaptive inclinations I have described, "after a few weeks in that milieu, one thinks: 'Yes.'" . . . Participation in selections was also enhanced by a sense that they did not come first in the hierarchy of horrors. Dr. B., for instance, stressed that "other things were much worse"—such as scenes of starving children in the Gypsy camp, where 80 percent of the inmates in general were starving to death while a few could be "living very well." He stressed the difficulty of "having this in front of you every day, continuously," and how "it took a long time to be able to live with that."

There, as in other situations, what mattered was what one could see, what confronted one's senses: "The killing was mostly excluded [from conversation], . . . [since] it was not what was directly visible. But very visible were the so-called *Muselmanner* [or living corpses]. [Also] visible were the ones who were starving . . . to death. . . . That was a bigger problem. . . . One was more oppressed by that."

By not quite seeing it, doctors could distance themselves from the very killing they were actively supervising. The same purpose was served by drawing upon their having witnessed what they claimed were worse horrors—in camps for Russian prisoners of war and in other concentration camps—which enabled them to conclude that "they've got it a lot better here." . . .

Doctors were further enabled to do selections by the shared sense that Auschwitz was morally separate from the rest of the world, that it was, as Dr. B. put it, "extraterritorial." He referred not to Auschwitz's geographical isolation, but to its existence as a special enclave of bizarre evil, which rendered it exempt from ordinary rules of behavior. . . .

[L]egitimaters . . . of medicalized Auschwitz killing were aided in their function by their sense that all Jews were already condemned. What Dr. Magda V. said of Mengele applies more generally to SS doctors: "It didn't matter to him [whether he selected someone or not] because he thought that sooner or later they're going [to the gas chamber]. . . . For him I think we . . . were just dead anyhow." Another survivor similarly called the whole process "only a play": that is, a staged drama in which "we were all there to be killed. The question was only who was to be first."

For the SS doctor, efficiency in selections became equated with quarantine arrangements and the improvement of actual medical units, all in the service of keeping enough inmates able to work and the camp free of epidemics. Within that context, the SS doctor inevitably came to perceive his professional function to be in neither the killing nor the healing alone, but in achieving the necessary balance. That *healing-killing balance,* according to the SS doctor Ernst B., was "the problem" for Auschwitz doctors. From that standpoint, as he further explained, the principle of "clearing out" a block when there was extensive diarrhea—sending everyone on it to the gas chambers—could be viewed as "pseudo ethical" and "pseudo idealistic." Dr. B. meant that such a policy in that environment could be perceived by the doctors themselves as ethical and idealistic in that they carried out their task to perfection on behalf of the higher goal of camp balance. . . .

Ideology and the "Jewish Problem"

Crucial to the capacity to perform selections was a doctor's relationship to Nazi ideology. Important here was the basic early attraction on the part of most of these doctors to the Nazi promise of German resurgence—a tie that could sustain them through reservations and discomfort: "We looked at it [Auschwitz] as a totally messed-up thing. [But] you could not change it, you see. That's like in a democracy, where you may find many things wanting, but you cannot change it. Or rather, you stick with it nonetheless. Because [you] think democracy is better." The strong implication is that Nazism *even with Auschwitz* was the best of all possible worlds.

However ironic, these medical participants in mass murder were held to the regime behind the murder by the principles of what Dr. B. called "coherent community" . . . and "common effort" . . . in discussing his and others' sense of the Nazi movement's commitment to overcoming staggering national problems. Hence he could speak of "a faith" . . . and, more than that, of a "practiced faith" joined to a community; in all this, "the bridge . . . is the ideology," and that "bridge" could connect the Nazi doctors to an immediate sense of community and communal purpose in their Auschwitz work.

Anti-Jewishness was an active ingredient in that ideology. While there was individual variation, Dr. B. claimed that all physicians were absolutely convinced that the Jews were our misfortune. . . . When

I mentioned the phrase "gangrenous appendix" an SS doctor had applied to Jews, . . . Dr. B. quickly answered that the Nazi doctors' overall feeling was: "Whether you want to call it an appendix or [not], it must be extirpated." He went so far as to say that even the policy of killing all Jews was readily justified by this "theoretical and ideological" stance, so that "of course they supported it." . . .

Doctors could call forth an absolutized Nazi version of good and evil as both justification for what they were seeing and doing and further avoidance of its psychological actuality (as Ernst B. explained):

> Precisely because they were convinced of the justness . . . or of the . . . National Socialist "world blessing" . . . and that the Jews were the root evil . . . of the world—precisely because they were so convinced of it did they believe, or were strengthened—[in that belief], that the Jews, even existentially, had to be absolutely exterminated. . . .

And although "not everybody approved of the gassing" and "many theories were discussed," one had to admit that gassing was an improvement over the inefficiency of previous methods:

> The main argument for the gassing was that when one tried to create ghettos . . . they never lasted longer than one or two generations. And then the ghetto—let us say—would become porous. . . . That was the main argument for the gassing. Against the gassing there were a number of different kinds of the most nonsensical speculations . . . forced sterilization and so on. . . . Lots of theorizing went on.

Now there was a more successful approach to the "Jewish problem" and, as Dr. B. added, "a means of confirmation" of the success.

In talking about these matters, he never directly answered one question I repeatedly asked him: whether doctors disagreed with one another about the necessity to kill Jews, or agreed about that and disagreed only about the means. I believe that the ambiguity has psychological significance beyond his evasion. From what Dr. B. and other observers have conveyed, it is probably accurate to say that most Nazi doctors in Auschwitz believed that something they perceived as "Jewishness" had to be eliminated, whether that meant sending Jews to Madagascar, forcing Jews to leave Germany while permitting a small well-established minority to remain and undergo complete assimilation, or murdering every last one of them. By clinging to this ambiguity, Nazi doctors had an additional means of avoiding the psychological reality of the decision for mass murder and its implementation. And by viewing the whole matter as a problem that needed to be "solved," by whatever means, that pragmatic goal could become the only focus. The very term "Final Solution" served both psychological purposes: it stood for mass murder without sounding or feeling like it, and it kept the focus primarily on problem solving. So given a minimum agreement on the necessity of solving the "Jewish problem," doctors and other Nazis could come to accept, even to prefer, the mass-murder project, because it alone promised a *genuine* solution, a clearing up of the matter once and for all, and a *final* solution. . . .

The Schizophrenic Situation: Doubling

The SS doctor was deeply involved in the stark contradictions of the "schizophrenic situation" that Ernst B. considered to be the key to understanding Auschwitz; I see it as a further expression of "extraterritoriality"—of the sense that what happened there did not count. The heart of that schizophrenia for doctors lay in the idea of doing constructive medical work within a "slaughterhouse." A related dimension of the schizophrenia, as B explained, was the "split situation" between the idealism of a world-bettering great German state along with the specific Nazi "world blessing"—and what he called (still reluctant to speak directly of mass murder) "the other situation, the one working with those . . . methods there." . . .

[One] way Nazi doctors coped with Auschwitz was to lead a double life that both reflected and enhanced their psychological doubling. Thus, they spent most of their time in the camp (except for occasional professional or pleasure trips to nearby areas) but went on leave for a few days every other month or so to spend time, usually in Germany, with their wives and children. They remained extremely aware of the separateness of the two worlds. One's wife, children, and parents came to stand for purity, as opposed to an inner sense of Auschwitz filth. Ernst B., for instance, managed to get home every two or three months for about a week's time but spoke strongly against the idea of his wife ever visiting him at Auschwitz: "I could never have subjected my wife to a closer look at things. . . . I can't even express myself properly, [but] the thought of her coming there would have caused [me] great [inner] resistance. One simply gave it no consideration whatsoever."

Dr. B. observed that each SS doctor could call forth two radically different psychological constellations within the self: one based on "values, generally accepted" and the education and background of a "normal person"; the other based on "this [Nazi-Auschwitz] ideology with values quite different from those generally accepted." The first tendency might be present one day, the second on the next, and it was hard to know which to expect on a given occasion or whether there would be a mixture of both.

Only a form of schism or doubling can explain the polarities of cruelty and decency in the same SS doctor. Klein is perhaps the best illustration here. This cruel and fanatical racist was seen by Dr. Magda V. as profoundly hypocritical and simply a "bad man," and by another prisoner physician, Olga Lengyel, as "one of the fervent zealots" who ran the Nazi annihilation project. Yet this latter doctor also spoke of him as a person capable of kindness, as when he brought her medicine for her patients and protected her from cruel SS personnel . . . ; he was, Lengyel said, "the only German in Auschwitz who never shouted." Another prisoner also had a surprisingly positive experience with Klein: when walking in the camp, this man took the highly unusual and dangerous step of approaching the SS doctor directly in order to ask him to have his (the prisoner's) wife, a nurse, transferred from an attic working place, where a great deal of sawdust caused her to cough incessantly, back to a medical block where she had worked in the past. Instead of saying, "Away with this fellow!" as everyone thought he would, Klein complied. This survivor commented, "These things are so intermingled—murdering and extermination on the one hand, and the very small details where something could work out quite the other way." He further reflected:

> When I tell this . . . after thirty-five years, I think, How could it be possible? . . . That one could influence this god and make a man who . . . exterminated thousands of people . . . to have interest in one prisoner girl, and save her. . . . There are things that happen in human nature . . . that an experienced analyst even cannot understand. . . . This split, . . . it can be very delicate. Maybe with these small [positive] things—with Klein, there [was] something of . . . medical tradition in them. But, in general, I believe they were no longer doctors. They were SS officers. In these things, the group spirit is one thousand times mightier than the individual spirit.

This survivor was saying that Klein functioned primarily in relation to the collective SS ethos, or what I call the "Auschwitz self"; but that he had available a humane dimension of self that could emerge at certain times.

The existence of that humane element of self may, in fact, have contributed to Klein's and other Nazi doctors' cruelties. For instance, when SS doctors asked pregnant women to step forward so that they could receive a double food ration—only to send those who did to the gas chamber the following day—it is possible that a brief sense of potential "medical activity" (improving the diet of pregnant women) contributed to the doctors' psychological capacity to carry out this hideous hoax.

In my interviews with Dr. Lottie M., she raised several questions she asked me to explore with Nazi doctors: How far did they look upon all of Auschwitz as "an experiment [on] how much a person can stand"? How much were they able to recognize "the irrationalism of . . . the racial theory"? At what point had "they started to be afraid of the end"? But what she was most curious about was "this question of split loyalty"—of conflicting oaths, contradictions between murderous cruelty and momentary kindness which SS doctors seemed to manifest continuously during their time at Auschwitz.

For the schism tended not to be resolved. Its persistence was part of the overall psychological equilibrium that enabled the SS doctor to do his deadly work. He became integrated into a large, brutal, highly functional system. Thus Dr. Henri Q. could wisely urge me to concentrate upon Nazi doctors' relation to this system rather than upon a single, infamous individual such as Mengele: "What impressed us was the fact that Auschwitz was a collective effort. It was not just a single person, but many. And the disturbing thing was that it was not something passionate [irrational]. It was something calm—there was nothing emotional about Auschwitz." . . .

The key to understanding how Nazi doctors came to do the work of Auschwitz is the psychological principle I call "doubling." . . . Doubling is an active psychological process, a means of *adaptation to extremity.* That is why I use the verb form, as opposed to the more usual noun form, "the double." The adaptation requires a dissolving of "psychological glue" as an alternative to a radical breakdown of the self. In Auschwitz, [the Nazi doctor] needed a functional Auschwitz self . . . [a]nd that Auschwitz self had to assume hegemony on an everyday basis, reducing expressions of the prior self to odd moments and to contacts with family and friends outside of camp. Nor did most Nazi doctors resist that usurpation as long as they remained in the camp. Rather they welcomed it as the only means of psychological function. If an environment is sufficiently extreme, and one chooses to remain in it, one may be able to do so *only* by means of doubling. . . .

Indeed, Auschwitz as an *institution*—as an atrocity-producing situation—ran on doubling. An atrocity-producing situation is one so structured externally (in this case, institutionally) that the average person entering it (in this case, as part of the German authority) will commit or become associated with atrocities. Always important to an atrocity-producing situation is its capacity to motivate individuals psychologically toward engaging in atrocity.

In an institution as powerful as Auschwitz, the external environment could set the tone for much of an individual doctor's "inner environment." The demand for doubling was part of the environmental message immediately perceived, by Nazi doctors, the implicit command to bring forth a self that could adapt to killing without one's feeling oneself a murderer. Doubling became not just an individual enterprise but a shared psychological process, the group norm, part of the Auschwitz "weather." And that group process was intensified by the general awareness that, whatever went on in other camps, Auschwitz was the great technical center of the Final Solution. One had to double in order that one's life and work there not be interfered with either by the corpses one helped to produce or by those "living dead" (the *Muselmanner*) all around one. . . .

No individual self is inherently evil, murderous, genocidal. Yet under certain circumstances virtually any self is capable of becoming all of these. A self is not a thing or a person but an inclusive representation or symbolization of an individual organism—as experienced by a particular person and . . . by other people. To emphasize activity, shift, and change, we may speak of "self-process." . . .

The self's capacity for [mass killing] is always influenced by ideological currents in the environment. . . . [I]n terms of self-process, the sequence from ordinary doctor to Nazi doctor to ordinary doctor suggests the extraordinary power of an environment to issue a "call" to genocide. Everything said here about the self's response to that call depends importantly upon idea structures of a collective nature, upon shared mentality rather than any isolated self. . . .

Nazi doctors doubled in murderous ways; so can others. Doubling provides a connecting principle between the murderous behavior of Nazi doctors and the universal potential for just such behavior. The same is true of the capacity to murder endlessly in the name of national-racial cure. Under certain conditions, just about anyone can join a collective call to eliminate every last one of the alleged group of carriers of the "germ of death."

Yet my conclusion is by no means that "we are all Nazis." We are *not* all Nazis. That accusation eliminates precisely the kind of moral distinction we need to make. One of these distinctions concerns how, with our universal potential for murder and genocide, we for the most part hold back from evil. A sensitive healer aghast at discovering her own impulses to slap a patient who had become unruly wrote to me of this "problem of our daily humanity." But we learn from the Nazis not only the crucial distinction between impulse and act, but the critical importance of larger ideological currents in connecting the two in ways that result in mass evil. . . .

Reflective Questions

1. Why do many consider Nazi doctors' primary role in the mass murder of Jews to be especially shameful? How were doctors involved in selection processes?
2. Killing Jews fundamentally contradicts the Hippocratic oath, in which doctors pledge to practice medicine ethically and do no harm to those in their charge. At times, Nazi doctors engaged in acts of kindness and loving family relationships. Nonetheless, they coordinated mass murders and viewed their role in killing as routine and practical. How did doctors maintain this contradiction? How did doctors come to accept that mass killing—and their participation in it—was a "fact of life" to adapt to? What interpretations of reality, cultural characteristics, and ideologies facilitated doctors' involvement? When some doctors resisted selecting, how did other doctors ensure their participation? What were the bases of authority and legitimacy at Auschwitz?
3. Lifton's piece raises questions about the ethnographic approach to research. One of the core tenets of ethnographic research is to understand how the social world is experienced from the vantage point of research participants. That requires researchers to some degree to put themselves in their participants' shoes and to give voice to their perspective. What are the benefits of an ethnographic approach to research? What moral dilemmas might it raise for researchers studying people or behaviors they find objectionable? Is an ethnographic approach appropriate for studying child rapists? "Terrorists"? Why or why not? What insights can sociological psychologists learn from studying them, and are the scientific merits worth the risks of giving murderers a platform for recruiting others to their ideologies? Should ethnographers take an active role in helping the U.S. government to understand them in order to facilitate punishing them? Why or why not?
4. The result of an ethnographic approach here is a complex picture that contextualizes Nazis' behavior in ways that readers may find uncomfortable. How is explaining behavior different from excusing it? This contextualizing leads Lifton to conclude "no individual self is inherently evil, murderous, genocidal. Yet under certain circumstances virtually any self is capable of becoming all of these." Perhaps you prefer to think Nazis or terrorists or other mass murderers are insane or evil individuals who are fundamentally different from you. Or perhaps it's more comforting to think that selecting Jews to be murdered is an extreme case of personal moral failure. Why might we gravitate toward those conclusions versus a sociological psychological one? What fundamental beliefs about human nature, humanity, and yourself does Lifton challenge?
5. Groups of people routinely engage in morally objectionable acts. Consider witnesses who watch a rape in progress in an apartment hallway rather than call the police, community leaders who help pedophiles gain access to kids or cover up abuse, or students who drive a classmate to suicide through bullying them as "gay" or "retarded." How might sociological psychologists explain the behavior of individuals in these circumstances? Think of something you have done, failed to do, or thought in the past that you find morally objectionable. What sociological psychological factors facilitated your actions? If we take Lifton's conclusions seriously, we find ourselves asking not why do people do bad things but rather how do we safeguard each other from doing bad things? We find ourselves questioning how to arrange our social lives in order to protect life, dignity, and opportunity for all. What cultural characteristics and ideologies facilitate regard for human rights and social justice? What social circumstances, cultural expectations, and ideologies ensure people protect others who are vulnerable? What facilitates bystanders disrupting abusive behavior they witness? How can we institutionalize these lessons?

Collective Forgetting and the Symbolic Power of Oneness

BARRY SCHWARTZ

In one way or another, all of the selections in this book are guided by the belief that if social scientists want to understand human behavior, they must understand how people construct and define reality. More specifically, they must consider how people define the things—objects, events, individuals, groups—they encounter in their environment. These things do not have a fixed or intrinsic meaning. Rather, their meanings differ depending on how people interpret and respond to them. Even seemingly fixed realities such as "the past" have uncertain and varying meanings. Indeed, as George Herbert Mead observed, the past is as uncertain as the future. Like other meanings, the meaning of the past is constructed and negotiated by human beings and, thus, is open to new and shifting interpretations. If we want to understand the past, we need to consider how people define, remember, and make use of it.

In recent years, sociologists have focused increased attention on "collective memory," or how groups remember historical events or figures and transmit those memories to others. In examining the dynamics of collective memory, sociologists ask questions such as: How do we understand the reality of the past? What do we see as the key events that constitute this past? Who do we see as the crucial historical figures or groups who shaped these events? How do we remember these individuals or groups? Why do we remember them this way? For example, how do our memories of the past get shaped by our social relationships as well as by larger cultural and political forces?

As Gary Alan Fine has noted, our collective memories are staked in and shaped by the social construction of reputations. In many respects, we link our memories of the past to particular individuals and their reputations. For instance, Abraham Lincoln has come to stand for the Civil War and the emancipation of African American slaves. By contrast, Adolf Hitler has come to represent the entire Nazi government of Germany and its genocidal slaughter of millions of European Jews. As these examples illustrate, particular individuals become symbolic stand-ins for a historical period and the events that characterized it. We come to know the events of this period in terms of the reputations of the leaders who shaped them. But, we have to remember that these leaders' reputations do not emerge simply from their actions or from the events that surrounded them. Instead, they are socially constructed realities that reflect a variety of forces, including the efforts of specific groups to construct them in ways that promote or protect their own political interests. This selection examines how and why Rosa Parks acquired the reputation of being the "mother of the bus boycott" and eventually the "mother of the Civil Rights Movement," despite the fact that she was only one of many African Americans who actively resisted segregated busing during the 1950s. The author of the selection, Barry Schwartz, highlights three key themes in explaining this

Reprinted from: Barry Schwartz, Collective Forgetting and the Symbolic Power of Oneness: The Strange Apotheosis of Rosa Parks. *Social Psychology Quarterly Snaps* 72(2): 123–142.

phenomenon. First, nature imposes certain cognitive limits on human memory that push us to condense and organize information in ways that make it easier for us to retrieve it when needed. Second, the natural limits of memory are reinforced and exaggerated by "oneness," or the human tendency to recognize one exceptional person while simultaneously forgetting or disregarding others. This tendency is promoted by social and cognitive processes, such as the Matthew Effect, that we use to fit reality into schemas, particularly by turning a prominent person into a "summarizing symbol." Third, as illustrated by the case of Rosa Parks, this transformation of an individual into a summarizing symbol allows us to remember the story of a historical event, such as the Montgomery bus boycott, while also recalling the guiding ideals of the people and groups who participated in that event.

In the end, Schwartz reveals how the construction of the reputation of Rosa Parks was marked by the "politics of reality." Parks earned the reputation of being the mother of the Civil Rights Movement not so much for what she did but because of what she represented. As a soft-spoken, virtuous, and churchgoing woman, Parks served as a compelling representative of civil rights activists in the eyes of the black community and the larger nation. She also symbolized the quiet but fierce determination of African Americans to overcome the injustice of racial segregation in the South. Leaders such as Martin Luther King Jr. and Ralph Abernathy astutely used these images of Parks to raise money and promote the goals of the Montgomery bus boycott and the larger Civil Rights Movement. In more recent years, these images have been used in U.S. society to commemorate the history of the Civil Rights Movement in a way that makes it more memorable. The transformation of Rosa Parks into a prominent civil rights leader thus clearly illustrates Charles Horton Cooley's observation that "fame may or may not represent what men [or women] were, but it always represents what humanity needs for them to have been."

Collective forgetting refers to what is unregistered in the imagination of the individual, unchronicled in research monographs and textbooks, and/or uncommemorated by monuments, relics, statues, and ritual observances. A metaphor for failure to transmit information about the past, collective forgetting refers not only to people's forgetting events they once knew but also to having never known them in the first place. One example of this phenomenon involves America's most prominent civil rights heroine: Rosa Parks. Why have so many men and women whose conduct was more consequential than Mrs. Parks's been forgotten? What does society gain from their oblivion?

William Goode (1978) observed many years ago that "winners in various kinds of competition, even when they are marked off from the losers by minute differences in performance, or, (as in science) by narrow differences in the time of discovery or achievement, seem to be given far greater amounts of prestige than those differences would appear to justify" (p. 66). Because it usually costs less (in terms of attention) to admire a field's best (a single task) than to admire its first *and* second best (a multiple task), Goode's explanation of why the magnitude of reward is often out of proportion to achievement is persuasive, but it skirts the related questions of (1) whether people are *unwilling* or *unable* to admire slightly less adept performers, and (2) why these performers not only fail to receive due credit but are often forgotten altogether.

Cognition and Memory: Capacity Limits

Two premises frame our present understanding of forgetting. First, the central nervous system's capacity to organize, store, and retrieve information is severely limited. Although human long-term memory is almost infinite (during an average lifetime it will have accumulated more than five times the information contained in all the printed material in the world [Marois 2005:30]), much of this material fades from disuse, is "overwritten" by more recently acquired knowledge, or is coded to make it irretrievable by working memory (Vockell 2006).

Direct demonstration provides the most accurate measure of cognitive limits. The parietal cortex, according to recent magnetic resonance image (MRI) studies, becomes more active as more objects (visual images, concepts, plans, people, and other chunks of information) are held in working memory, but once its limit of four objects (on average) is reached, the adding of more objects causes no further increase in cortex activity (Marois 2005; see also Ricoeur 2004).

The second premise is that individuals adapt to the limits of their long- and short-term memory by "heuristic" strategies enabling them to ignore most of the information to which they are exposed. History buffs, therefore, can name all American presidents but few vice-presidents. The typical baseball fan can identify last year's division winners in both American and National leagues but probably knows few if any of the respective second-place winners. Olympic (first place) Gold Medal recipients are far more likely to be remembered than (second and third place) recipients of Silver and Bronze Medals. In science, literature, and artistic award ceremonies, all nominees are known but winners alone are remembered. However, this tendency toward "oneness" cannot result exclusively from cognitive limits.

Oneness

Oneness is a confusing term beset by contradictory definitions: in the popular realm it concerns singularity and uniqueness; in many religious belief systems, it is the condition of being at one with fellow believers and transcendent powers. In this essay, *oneness refers to the recognizing of one exceptional individual and ignoring of others, many of whom may have performed as well as or better than the one acclaimed.*

Oneness, as an adaptation to cognition's limits, is always "realm-specific." In baseball, for example, separate awards are given for the "Most Valuable Player," for the highest batting average, most home runs, most strikeouts, most wins, lowest earned run average, and other offensive and defensive achievements. Beauty pageants produce a general winner (Miss America) and winners in various sub-competitions (talent, bathing suit, evening gown, congeniality). In the academic world, awards are given in different disciplines and sub-disciplines for the most distinguished careers, books, and articles. The Pulitzer Prizes, Academy Awards, Tony Awards, and Nobel Prizes are also examples of single awards given within different realms of achievement. These awards not only reflect organizations' need for exemplars to articulate their ideals but also the convention of exemplifying each ideal by one person.

Contingencies

The relationship between nature and convention, between cognitive capacity limits and the practice of limiting recognition to single recipients, must be qualified.

1. Because working memory's limit, according to most investigators, is four bits of information (Cowan 2005), nature alone cannot account for the phenomenon of oneness.
2. Cognitive limits can be transcended at will. Baseball experts, for example, possess vast knowledge of many categories of offensive and defensive performance. This is possible because their working memory encodes every relevant chunk of new information, transfers it to long-term memory, where it is aligned *meaningfully* through typing, classification, and schema, then stored, with relevant existing information. The constant interplay between efficient encoding and organizing of information in working and long-term memory distinguishes "experts" from "novices" (Ericsson and Kinch 1995, pp. 239–240).

That many individuals are motivated to acquire vast knowledge in one or more realms of activity (usually occupational) means that oneness is the default option, not the sole option, for human cognition. But individuals mastering one or more bodies of knowledge cannot master all there is to know. Even they are "cognitive misers" because they oversimplify reality by ignoring its "details," but they are also "motivated tacticians" because deliberate ignoring of information allows them to attend to the most relevant and complex tasks. Short cuts, no less than prolonged attention to complex problems, are tactically motivated (Fiske and Taylor 1991, p. 13).

3. The more knowledge one has of the achievement realm within which a person is recognized, the more likely he or she will know of others who have accomplished at least as much or more. Singular recognition is most likely to promote resentment among insiders.
4. The singling out of winners reinforces or undermines social structures. Among individualistic communities, "winner take all" situations are most common, while egalitarian communities believe singling out winners undermines group solidarity and individual esteem. Differentiation of a field also affects the feasibility of single awards. Between 1902 and 1949, for example, 85 percent of Nobel Prizes in physics were given to single recipients; 2 percent, to three recipients. Between 1950 and 1999, single recipients received only 26 percent of the awards; three recipients received 38 percent. In six of the first seven years of the twenty-first century, three recipients shared the prize. Physics produces more winners as it becomes more complex and innovative. It should be noted, however, that the Nobel Committee has never awarded its prize to *more* than three physicists in any one year—a number that happens to be within working memory's limits.
5. The media through which information is transmitted restricts the amount any individual can possess. A history text can devote only a limited number of pages to a given event; a newspaper or magazine, only so many columns; television and radio stations, only so many minutes (Hilgartner and Bosk 1988). Media limits add to the effect of cognitive limits.
6. When no single representative can be selected to symbolize a field of activity, the pool of "contestants" can be condensed into a single unit and identified by their number. The Little Rock Nine, namely, the three boys and six girls chosen by the NAACP to integrate the Little Rock Central High School in 1957, is a relevant example. Nine individuals are easy to forget, but when condensed into one name are readily remembered.
7. Not all events in the collective memory are symbolized by a single person or collectivity. In the sport of baseball, for example, pairs and trios often represent something special about a team or an achievement. The Boston Braves of the late 1940s depended heavily on two pitchers, Warren Spahn and Johnny Sain—hence the cautious war-cry: "Spahn and Sain, and pray for rain." Likewise, early twentieth-century baseball fans represented the difficult double-play by its supposed virtuosi, "Tinker to Evers to Chance." In other fields, including entertainment, duos (Sonny and Cher) and trios (Peter, Paul, and Mary) are recognized individually. Future work will determine whether duos and trios are exceptions to, or different forms of, oneness, but raising the question must not prevent us from exploring the phenomenon of oneness itself.

The concept of oneness describes a *non-universal* but powerful *tendency* for individuals and groups to simplify complex comparisons by choosing one prominent performer. This tendency is reinforced by memory's limits, but such a hindrance does not make single awards imperative. Why, then, does a conventional limit—the recognition of one person—exaggerate a natural (cognitive) limit which, although obdurate, permits the recognition of several people? Why is human convention so stingy, why does it cause us to remember so few and forget so many, what social realities does it reinforce, and how does the answer to these questions bear on our general understanding of collective forgetting? Rosa Parks, as noted, is the case in point.

The Rise of Rosa Parks

Forgotten Events and Protesters

Throughout the Jim Crow era, many African Americans rebelled against segregated seating in public transportation, but their number vastly increased after World War II. By the mid-1950s, defiance of bus segregation had become common. A host of unrecognized men and women ("invisible leaders," as Bernice Barnett [1993] calls them [see also Hendrickson 2005]) preceded Rosa Parks. "Invisible leaders" are in fact quite visible to scholars whose business is to search for them, but to the general public they are unknown. The following chronology includes a sample of the unknown persons and events that helped end bus segregation in Montgomery.

May 21, 1954. Jo Ann Robinson, president of Montgomery, Alabama's Women's Political Council, complained in a letter to Mayor W. A. "Tacky" Gayle about humiliations endured by black bus passengers (including herself) and warned of a boycott against Montgomery's bus company.

March 2, 1955. In Montgomery, Alabama, Claudette Colvin refused to move to the back of a segregated bus; she was arrested, convicted, and fined.

April 19, 1955. Aurelia Browder of Montgomery refused to take her legal bus seat; she, too, was arrested, convicted, and fined.

October 21, 1955. Mary Louise Smith of Montgomery was arrested, convicted, and fined for violating the city's bus segregation code. Several days later, Suzi McDonald was arrested and fined for the same offense.

December 1, 1955. Rosa Parks was arrested, then convicted and fined for refusing to surrender her seat to a white passenger. Next day, the Montgomery bus boycott, planned for a single day, went into effect.

December 3, 1955. Active leaders of Montgomery's black community formed a new entity, The Montgomery Improvement Association (MIA), in order to distance themselves from conservative ministers and avoid legal entanglements with the local NAACP branch. The Association appointed Martin Luther King, Jr. its president.

December 5, 1955. Several hours after Rosa Parks was fined, thousands gathered for a meeting at a local church under the black community's new (MIA) leadership. King's speech electrified the audience, which voted to extend the boycott indefinitely.

February 1, 1956. Realizing that the boycott had failed to achieve its modest goals of improving courtesy and convenience within a segregated transportation system, attorney Fred Gray convinced his MIA colleagues to bring legal suit against the city. He named Browder, Colvin, Smith, McDonald, and one other woman, Jeanetta Reese, as plaintiffs against Montgomery's mayor, claiming bus segregation violated their 14th Amendment (equal protection) rights. Jeanetta Reese had also been ejected from a Montgomery bus for refusing to give up her seat, but she removed her name from the suit after receiving threats on her life.

February 21, 1956. Rosa Parks, among eighty-nine other black resisters, was arrested and fingerprinted for violating the city's anti-boycott law.

June 5, 1956. Six months after the filing of the *Browder v. Gayle* suit, the three-judge Fifth Federal Circuit Court ruled against the city of Montgomery and its mayor. The city immediately appealed to the Supreme Court.

November 13, 1956. The U.S. Supreme Court upheld the district court ruling. Five weeks later (December 20) federal marshals served the enforcement order.

December 21, 1956. The NAACP marked the desegregation order by asking Rosa Parks to pose for a photograph on a city bus.

Because pictorial information is more readily remembered than verbal (MacInnis and Price

1987), this photograph reinforced the public's belief in Rosa Parks as the symbol of the civil rights movement. It also takes us to the nub of the problem. Why did the NAACP choose Rosa Parks to represent a boycott in which so many played equally important roles?

Singling Out Rosa Parks

When two or more investigators make an identical discovery within a short time span, Robert Merton (1957) observes, credit is assigned to the person who makes the discovery first. If this priority rule is generalized to social movements, then one must recognize that Rosa Parks was last, not first, to challenge Montgomery's bus segregation practice. After Claudette Colvin was arrested in March 1955, Jo Ann Robinson, president of the Women's Political Council, E. D. Nixon, director of the Montgomery NAACP, and attorney Fred Gray thought the youngster would be a good plaintiff in a lawsuit to end bus segregation and a good symbol to mobilize Montgomery's heretofore compliant (King 1958, pp. 34–37) black community. But the plan fell through. Although a member of the NAACP youth organization, Miss Colvin was pregnant with a married man's child. In October 1955 eighteen-year-old Mary Louise Smith refused to give up her bus seat, but her father's alcoholism ruled her out as a plaintiff and symbol. To the extent that Colvin and Smith deviated from what Barnett calls "The cult of black women's respectability and womanhood," their arrests, according to E. D. Nixon, would be less likely to impress a court and arouse the indignation of Montgomery's African Americans (Raines 1977, pp. 43–44). Little personal information on Suzie McDonald, 78 at the time of her protest and arrest, is available; however, the Montgomery police had also arrested Aurelia Browder, an NAACP member and activist. Browder worked for years as a seamstress, then finished high school, entered college, and graduated with honors with majors in mathematics and science. Not until Rosa Parks was arrested, however, did Robinson, Nixon, and Gray believe they had found the plaintiff and symbol they sought. Two attributes made Rosa Parks the most effective plaintiff and symbol: (1) she had no skeletons in her closet and (2) as NAACP secretary, she was better known throughout the black community than any of the other arrested women, including Browder (King 1958, p. 44; Williams 1987, pp. 63, 67; Parks 1992, pp. 124–125). Her arrest, however, plays a minor part in the boycott's history.

The full story of the Montgomery bus boycott is the story about black representatives confronting Montgomery municipal officials, even as their homes are bombed and their families threatened; about black attorneys countering city and state legal maneuvers; about weekly meetings in churches (also bombing targets) to reinforce the motivation of the protesters; about ordinary people struggling to maintain their livelihood by pooling resources and supporting one another. In these stories Rosa Parks plays no visible role. Reverend Robert Graetz, white minister of Montgomery's black Lutheran congregation and boycott participant, reports: "Sadly, Mrs. Parks had very little to do with the boycott. Once it was past the beginning, she faded into the background" ([*Montgomery*] *Advertiser Company* 2005, p. 113). Between her February arrest and the November Supreme Court decision, Rosa Parks traveled the country on speaking engagements, but she had no part in the front line of battle, as did Graetz. Besides making his own fund-raising trips, Graetz served as secretary of the Montgomery Improvement Association, was particularly hated by white segregationists, lived under continual surveillance, suffered nightly telephone threats on his children's lives, and endured an attempted murder and two bombings (Graetz 1991).

Fred Gray, Montgomery Improvement Association attorney, was also exposed to a wide range of harassment. While threatened with disbarment and summoned for review of his draft status by Montgomery's Selective Service Board, Gray designed and executed the *Browder vs. Gayle* action. His role in the Supreme Court's bus desegregation decision was indispensable (Gray 1995; Burns 1997, pp. 147–152).

Nevertheless, Rosa Parks emerged as the symbol of the struggle and the victory.

When Rosa Parks Became a *National* Celebrity

Rosa Parks refused to pay the $14 fine imposed for her December 1, 1955 violation, and on February 22, 1956 was sentenced to fourteen days in jail. Appealing to the State Supreme Court, she was released on bond. She was also arrested on February 26, 1956 on an anti-boycott charge, fingerprinted under the eyes and cameras of the press, and indicted. At this time, when the state's mass prosecutions dominated national attention, Rosa Parks's name appeared most frequently in the national media.

Apotheosis

In early 1956, no one knew or could have known how brilliantly the light of the mass media would soon shine on Rosa Parks and how much more intensely it would shine as decades passed. Indeed, when Rosa Parks died in her Detroit home in October 2005, fifty years after the boycott, state and local establishments reacted with extraordinary reverence. Following the pattern of a "royal progress," the ceremonial form by which kings and queens take possession of their realm (Geertz 1983), the NAACP moved her body to Montgomery's St. Paul A.M.E. church, where she had been a member. Many officials, including the U.S. Secretary of State, participated in the service. Throughout the city, the first row of seats on all buses remained empty in her memory. From Montgomery, her body was flown to the Baltimore-Washington International Airport, named after Thurgood Marshall, with whom Fred Gray consulted during the legal battle. The motorcade, accompanied by a symbolic 1955-era bus, carried her remains to the U.S. Capitol Rotunda, where they were placed in state. Emergency legislation, initiated by the Michigan House delegation led by John Conyers and signed by the president, provided for this honor, previously reserved for presidents, statesmen, and military heroes. After signing a bill authorizing a statue of Rosa Parks to be erected in the U.S. Capitol Building, the President of the United States ordered all flags to be flown at half-staff; he and other federal officials visited the Rotunda privately to pay their respects. Then the great Rotunda doors were opened and tens of thousands wound their way around the military guard and coffin.

Mrs. Parks's remains were next moved to Detroit's Greater Grace Temple for a seven-hour service. Entertainers, including Aretha Franklin, civil rights leaders, and political and business leaders attended, as did Michigan's two senators and many House members, black politicians from many states, and prominent white figures including Bill Clinton, Hillary Clinton, John Kerry, Nancy Pelosi, and Bill Ford, CEO of Ford Motor Company. Her body was finally placed on a gold-trimmed horse-drawn carriage for the seven-mile procession to the cemetery. The release of scores of doves coincided with her arrival and entombment.

Commemoration: Primary Vehicle of Oneness

History records events over time; commemoration lifts from the historical record events that best symbolize the ideals of the society. History informs; commemoration inspires and motivates (Schwartz 2001). For most people, commemoration alone tells who is worth remembering and why.

That commemoration, not history, preserves Rosa Parks's *oneness* was never more evident than when she lay in state in the U.S. Capitol Rotunda. She was honored so spectacularly, according to CNN's announcer Gary Nurenberg, because the remarkable gains of the civil rights movement resulted from the will of "one woman on one bus in Montgomery fifty years ago." Joseph Lowery agreed: Yes, "she sat down so we could stand up. . . . She was the one woman whom God chose to do extraordinary things." To list all comments would be tedious, but it is important to note they are profuse, attribute the boycott's success to her alone, and originate from the widest array of people conceivable; black and white, liberal and conservative, Southern and non-Southern.

Because commemoration could not perform its function if it were not selective, the outpouring of attention on Rosa Parks would have been impossible if she had to share the spotlight with other women, including those who risked as much, enjoyed less protection, and displayed as much courage. What if the federal government had to organize spectacular funerals for the entire cast of resisters? CNN announcer Carol Lin, present at the Capitol Rotunda when Mrs. Parks laid in state, raised this question simply and clearly: "Really, I think people are grasping *what it must have been like* for this woman back in 1955 to be so brave" (italics added). Many women back in 1955 were brave, but if all these women received their due, grasping "what it must have been like" would be difficult. Multiple commemoration rites—the making of the calendar into something resembling a sequence of funeral and award announcements—would make incoherent the very ideal these rites affirm.

Determinants of Oneness

Condensation

The figure of a single black woman who refused to give up her seat to a white passenger is more easily representable than all the Montgomery women who worked on behalf of civil rights. Foreshadowing a fundamental premise of cognitive psychology, Emile Durkheim ([1915] 1965) declared: "we are unable to consider an abstract entity, which we can represent only laboriously and confusedly, the source of the strong sentiments which we feel. We cannot explain them to ourselves except by connecting them to some concrete object of whose reality we are vividly aware" (p. 251). This "concrete [singular] object," Rosa Parks, helps represent morally and emotionally what the civil rights movement meant to its beneficiaries. Promoting attachment rather than enlightenment, Rosa Parks's image encouraged commitment to the civil rights movement as an undifferentiated whole. She was, as Sherry Ortner (1973) would define her, the civil rights movement's "summarizing symbol."

Matthew Effect

In the first phase of her public career, the figure of Rosa Parks condensed a local resistance campaign, but as her renown grew she became dissociated from local protest and situated on the national scene. The mother of a bus boycott became the "mother of the civil rights movement." As the media broadcast the image of Rosa Parks, it grew, as Edward Sapir (1930) would have said, "deeper and deeper roots in the unconscious and diffused its emotional quality to types of behavior or situations apparently far removed from [its] original meaning" (p. 493).

Robert Merton's (1968) "Matthew Effect" describes further this diffusion process. The Gospel of Matthew is Merton's source: "For unto every one that hath shall be given, and he shall have abundance, but from him that hath not shall be taken away even that which he hath." The Matthew Effect is actually a variant of what general systems scholars call "positive feedback," a process that creates new meanings by converting initial responses into virtuous cycles (Buckley 1967). Observers, thus, react toward the beneficiaries of recognition in ways that exaggerate their initial prestige and cause competitors to be forgotten. The beneficiary is invited to events, seated next to leaders, asked to judge the merit of others' traits and achievements. The Matthew Effect thus vindicates earlier reward decisions, regardless of whether or not they were the wisest.

Rosa Parks's fate exemplifies the power of the Matthew Effect. Her initial recognition set off a virtuous cycle: she accompanied Martin Luther King, Ralph Abernathy, E. D. Nixon, and other leaders on trips around the country to raise funds for the Montgomery Improvement Association. Invited to national NAACP meetings, she met for the first time such celebrities as A. Philip Randolph, Roy Wilkins, and Eleanor Roosevelt. Highlander School in Tennessee, where she once studied non-violent resistance, recruited her to teach a course on reform tactics, as if she were the boycott's tactician. She was invited to appear around the country and the world, met with heads of state, including Pope John Paul, and she received the Presidential Medal of Freedom and Congressional Gold Medal. She found places named for her: twenty-one streets in fourteen states; thirty-two public and commercial establishments in thirteen states. Not one comparable site is named for the other bus segregation resisters.

Functions of Oneness

Rosa Parks's renown reflects mainly on the illusions of achievement. That she was the Mother of the Civil Rights Movement is false. That she was first to challenge bus segregation in Alabama is false. That she spearheaded the struggle against Montgomery's white establishment is false. That hers was a "test case" against segregation is false. Martin Luther King, Jr., E. D. Nixon, and Ralph Abernathy, not Rosa Parks, mobilized the black community to resist bus segregation. Fred Gray devised the law suit that ended bus segregation, and it was Aurelia Browder whom Gray chose for his test case.

Given the limits of human cognition, however, complete information confuses. If we saw all there is to be seen of the 13-month boycott, if we experienced the long walk to work by all those unable to find a ride, if we heard and read what every participant said about the boycott and how it affected him, if we could grasp every aspect of it, the result would be not understanding but perplexity. The action of a single individual, on the other hand, is easy to grasp and remember. Nothing makes this clearer than the way human nature and society protect us from remembering too much.

Oneness: Font of Idealism

Nature limits the power of cognition, but society alone can press these limits to the service of oneness. "Singling out" and "setting examples" do more than reward individuals; they provide the community with concrete exemplars of its moral values, standards, virtues, and powers.

The underlying structure of the ideal is its singularity. According to the *Standard College Dictionary*, an ideal is an "ultimate object of attainment" or "standard of perfection," which can only be conceived as a single thing and represented as such. As an adjective, the ideal "conforms to an absolute standard of excellence . . . representing the best of its kind." In these representative statements the ideal is never plural; it is a unique model to which people orient their aspirations and conduct. It may be said, without twisting the term too much, that there is something "sacred" about ideals and their symbols. In modern societies, the sacred, according to Emile Durkheim, surrounds every individual, and modern societies are sustained by what he calls the "cult of the individual" (1974, pp. 58–59; Goffman 1967, pp. 47–48). But if "objects become sacred and judgments attribute value when they reflect a social ideal" (Durkheim 1974, p. xxv), then this ideal must dramatize the gap between ordinary and extraordinary events and beings. Society cannot sustain itself without creating standards in its various spheres (Durkheim 1974, p. 93). This is why, "in the present day as in the past, we see society constantly creating sacred things out of ordinary ones" (Durkheim [1915] 1965, p. 245). Sacred things cannot be adored, however, if their aura is blurred by competitors. The greater the number of *beau ideals* within any realm of activity, the more ambiguous their referent becomes. The natural limits of cognition, therefore, reinforce the ideals which express culture's most valued traits and achievements.

Oneness, Schema, and Reality

What is owed to the principle of oneness can be known by imagining the result of our doing without it. Remove Rosa Parks, and the average person will have a much vaguer notion of both the origins of the civil rights movement and the ideals that drove it. Remove Rosa Parks, and the story of a wronged innocent is replaced by tedious details about carpools, pickup points, fundraising, weekly MIA meetings, petty internal disputes—details which conceal the schema of the larger struggle.

Rosa Parks's story is "schematic" (Fiske and Taylor 1991; Bartlett [1932] 1995) because it simplifies the Montgomery protests and aligns them with classical stories of oppressed people's struggle for justice. A humble seamstress finishes a day of hard work, boards a bus, pays her fare, takes a seat, is ordered to move to the back of the bus when a white passenger appears, refuses because she is tired of a lifetime of humiliation. She is arrested, tried, and fined. Montgomery's long-suffering black community, angered by her arrest, boycotts the city's buses for a year, forcing the white government to relent and desegregate. Such is the schema abstracted from Rosa Parks's conduct. People who cannot remember the bus boycott as a whole can retrieve the schema in which its elements are stored: a mild woman's run-in with an angry bus-driver in a Jim Crow city sums it up.

The story presents a self-flattering as well as concise account: segregation is conquered by the iron will of a tyrannized community, exemplified by a black seamstress, not by a white court and its judges. Indeed, the narrative presumes that federal courts would have ruled against integration if not pressured by black resistance. "So when you ask why the courts had to come in," JoAnn Robinson, President of the Women's Political Council, explains, "they *had* to come in. You get 52,000 people in the streets and nobody's showing any fear, something had to give. So the Supreme Court had to rule that segregation was not the way of life" (Williams 1987, pp. 71, 89). Robinson's statement has two implications: (1) the boycott broke the back of the segregationists by putting unbearable pressure on the bus company and downtown merchants, and (2) the boycott forced the courts to rule against the city. Both implications underestimate the autonomy of the courts and overestimate the power of public demonstrations.

Long before Montgomery's boycott began, the Supreme Court had handed down a series of liberal decisions on jury selection, housing, public education, voting rights, professional school integration, and equal access to publicly funded resources, including golf courses, swimming pools, beach houses, and public parks. By the time of the (1954) *Brown* decision, not made under the pressure of public protest, little was left of the Plessy-Ferguson principle. Furthermore, the Fifth Circuit Court's unpressured integration of Columbia, South Carolina's bus system in *January* 1956 makes implausible the claim that a boycott forced the Fifth Circuit Court to integrate Montgomery's bus system in *November* 1956.

Martin Luther King believed the *Browder* decision was significant because it broke the deadlock between resisters and the city (Williams 1987, p. 89). In fact, there was no deadlock. After eleven months, the black community was far worse off than the white, and the city had no incentive to give in. When an Alabama circuit court was about to prohibit the use of car pools, the boycott was, in fact, on the verge of collapse (Glennon 1991, p. 83), and it would have collapsed had not the federal district court issued its *Browder* ruling. No direct cause and effect relationship, observes legal scholar Robert J. Glennon, exists "between the boycott and the end of segregated buses in Montgomery." The Browder case "could have proceeded without the attendant boycott and the Court result would have been identical" (p. 93). Put differently, Montgomery's buses would have been integrated whether or not Rosa Parks had given up her seat.

The memory of the Gray/Browder litigation has been replaced by the more resonant story of Rosa Parks's defiance and an oppressed black community's arising on its own to overcome white oppression. But if the Rosa Parks story distorts history, its appeal does not reside in its distortion. Rosa Parks's occupying the fateful bus seat, her arrest and subsequent apotheosis are real episodes in a historic movement. Her renown, whatever the NAACP's role in creating it, keeps alive the memory of 381 days of authentic courage, perseverance, and sacrifice.

The boycott's consequence, then, was real, but not in the way we usually think about it. As a cause of bus segregation's demise its effect was questionable; its true function was to (1) enhance the dignity and solidarity of the black community by demonstrating its members' willingness to go to jail for their beliefs (Valien 1989, pp. 90), which whites were unprepared to do when the courts ruled against them; (2) impress the legitimacy of black grievances on fair-minded whites; (3) draw national attention to the cause of racial justice; and (4) inspire protests in other places.

To represent every protester as dramatically as Rosa Parks and every leader as clearly as Martin Luther King—and this point cannot be overemphasized—would blur the two realms of protest, leadership and following, and would confound, not clarify, the meaning and consequence of their struggle. In 1955, it would have made no difference if one of Mrs. Parks's peers had been chosen to be Mother of the Civil Rights Movement, but once a unique presence is established it becomes indispensable. In fact, Rosa Parks symbolizes a revolution of such significance as to make her selection over others a trivial matter. Her aura resides in the social realities she marks.

Conclusion

Man's limited memory is understood better now than ever before, but the question remains as to why a humanly instituted deficit should be added to a natural one. If working memory's capacity were independent of culture, then this essay would be about the symbolic power of fourness, not oneness, for human working memory readily manages several chunks of information. The most natural path, then, would be to recognize the several women who defied Montgomery's bus laws.

However, social conventions are limited by, not hostage to, nature. Condensation (a cognitive heuristic) and the Matthew Effect (a social process) work together, transforming fourness into oneness by deliberately simplifying complexity, distinguishing one contributor to a project—in this case, Rosa Parks—and forgetting others, thus symbolizing the ideals all participants in the project pursue. The power of oneness is in this sense overdetermined: however weak the condensation effect in promoting any one reputation, human memory limits recognition—sometimes *to* one person or event, always *toward* one. Even if man's working and long-term memory capacities were greater, the Matthew Effect's positive feedback process would limit recognition—sometimes *to* one person or event, always *toward* one. Cognitive deficit, thus, reinforces rather than creates the symbolic power of oneness.

References

Barnett, Bernice McNair. 1993. "Invisible Southern Black Women Leaders in the Civil Rights Movement: The Triple Constraints of Gender, Race, and Class." *Gender and Society* 7: 162–182.

Bartlett, F. C. [1932] 1995. *Remembering: A Study in Experimental and Social Psychology.* Cambridge, UK: Cambridge University Press.

Buckley, Walter. 1967. *Sociology and Modern System Theory.* Englewood Cliffs, NJ: Prentice-Hall.

Burns, Stewart. Ed. 1997. *Daybreak of Freedom: The Montgomery Bus Boycott.* Chapel Hill, NC: University of North Carolina Press.

Cowan, Nelson. 2005. *Working Memory Capacity.* New York: Psychology Press.

Durkheim, Emile. [1911] 1974. "Value Judgments and Judgments of Reality." Pp. 80–97 in *Emile Durkheim: Sociology and Philosophy.* Edited by G. G. Peristiany. New York: FreePress.

———. [1915] 1965. *The Elementary Forms of the Religious Life.* New York: Free Press.

Ericsson, K. A. and W. Kinch. 1995. "Long-Term Memory." *Psychological Review* 102: 211–245.

Fiske, Susan T. and Shelley E. Taylor. 1991. *Social Cognition* (Second Edition). New York: McGraw-Hill.

Geertz, Clifford. 1983. "Centers, Kings, and Charisma: Reflections on the Symbolics of Power." Pp. 121–146 in *Local Knowledge.* New York: Basic Books.

Glennon, Robert Jerome. 1991. "The Role of Law in the Civil Rights Movement: The Montgomery Bus Boycott, 1955–1957." *Law and History Review* 9: 59–112.

Goffman, Erving. 1967. "The Nature of Deference and Demeanor" in *Interaction Ritual.* Garden City, NY: Doubleday.

Goode, William J. 1978. *The Celebration of Heroes: Prestige as a Control System.* Berkeley: University of California Press.

Gray, Fred. 1995. *Bus Ride to Justice: Changing the System by the System.* Montgomery, AL: Black Belt Press.

Graetz, Robert S. 1991. *Montgomery: A White Preacher's Memoir.* Minneapolis, MN: Fortress Press.

Hendrickson, Paul. 2005. "The Ladies Before Rosa: Let Us Now Praise Unfamous Women." *Rhetoric and Public Affairs* 8.2: 287–298.

Hilgartner, Stephen and Charles L. Bosk. 1988. "The Rise and Fall of Social Problems: A Public

Arenas Model." *American Journal of Sociology* 94: 53–78.

King, Martin Luther, Jr. 1958. *Stride Toward Freedom: The Montgomery Story*. New York, NY: Harper & Row.

MacInnis, Deborah J. and Linda L. Price. 1987. "Imagery in Information Processing: Review and Extensions." *Journal of Consumer Research* 13: 473–491.

Marois, Rene. 2005. "Capacity Limits of Information Processing in the Brain." *Phi Kappa Phi Forum* 85: 30–33.

Merton, Robert K. 1957. "Priorities in Scientific Discovery: A Chapter in the Sociology of Science." *American Sociological Review* 22: 635–659.

———. 1968. "The Matthew Effect in Science." *Science* 159:56–63.

Parks, Rosa. 1992. *My Story*. New York: Dial Books.

Ortner, Sherry. 1973. "On Key Symbols." *American Anthropologist* 75: 1338–1346.

Raines, Howell. 1977. *My Soul Is Rested: Movement Days in the Deep South Remembered*. New York: G.P. Putnam's Sons.

Robinson, JoAnn Gibson. 1987. *The Montgomery Bus Boycott and the Women Who Started It*. Knoxville, TN: University of Tennessee Press.

Ricoeur, Paul. 2004. *Memory, History, Forgetting*. Chicago, IL: University of Chicago Press.

Sapir, Edward. 1930. "Symbolism." Pp. 492–495 in *Encyclopedia of the Social Sciences*. New York: Macmillan.

Schwartz, Barry. 2001. "Commemorative Objects." Pp. 2267–2272 in *International Encyclopedia of the Social and Behavioral Sciences*. Edited by Neil Smelser and Paul D. Bates. Oxford, UK: Elsevier.

Valien, Preston. 1989. "The Montgomery Bus Protest as a Social Movement." Pp. 83–98 in *The Walking City: The Montgomery Bus Boycott, 1955–1956*. Edited by David J. Garrow. Brooklyn, NY: Carlson Publishing Inc.

Vockell, Edward. 2006. "Memory and Information Processing" in *Educational Psychology: A Practical Approach*. http://education.calument.purdue.edu/vockell/EdpsyBook.

Williams, Juan. 1987. *Eyes on the Prize: America's Civil Rights Years, 1954–1965*. New York: Viking.

Reflective Questions

1. What is collective forgetting? Why do we forget who finishes in second place in competitive contests? Under what conditions do we recognize more than one winner?
2. What actions preceded Rosa Parks's refusal to change bus seats? If Rosa Parks wasn't the first to challenge bus segregation and her situation wasn't the "test case," how did she end up being recognized as the key challenger of this form of segregation?
3. Memories are crafted collectively. How does the education system and media shape and reinforce our tendency toward oneness?
4. We often transform historical figures into symbols of what we need them to be. When you think of Rosa Parks, what images, words, and qualities come to mind? What about the 1980 Miracle on Ice? Flight 93? What do these events symbolize to us and why? Have their meanings changed over time or for different generations? Why or why not?
5. While redemption and heroism are popular American variations of oneness, so is evil. After each mass shooting, for example, we cull the histories of the shooters in order to craft an understandable story about what went wrong with them. What storylines have we developed about mass shooters and their motives? Do we craft their evilness as unique? What do mass shooters symbolize in our collective memory? What do we think and feel when someone we've constructed as "good" engages in "evil"?